1001 RECIPES FROM YOUR FAVORITE HOMETOWN NEWSPAPER

D1400614

1001 RECIPES FROM YOUR FAVORITE HOMETOWN NEWSPAPER

by Aileen Claire
Food Editor, Newspaper Enterprise Association

GRAMERCY PUBLISHING COMPANY
NEW YORK

Copyright © 1984 by Newspaper Enterprise Association
All rights reserved.

This 1984 edition is published by Gramercy Publishing
Company, distributed by Crown Publishers, Inc., by
arrangement with Newspaper Enterprise Association.

Manufactured in the United States of America

Library of Congress Cataloging in Publication Data
  Main entry under title:

1001 recipes from your favorite hometown newspaper.

  Includes index.
  1. Cookery.   I. Claire, Aileen.
TX651.A15 1984   641.5 83-15304
ISBN: 0-517-427028

h g f e d c b a

Contents

Introduction

Like so many food writers, I come from a family that likes to eat. So, a few years ago when my Uncle Wendell told me he had tried armadillo while visiting a friend in Florida, I merely looked at him sideways. To that, he said, "I'll try anything once." "How was it?" I asked. "Not bad. Not bad at all," he replied. He was in his early sixties at the time.

Not everyone has to try armadillo to prove to me that he or she has an open-minded approach toward food. But the incident did remind me of how locked in we often get in our food attitudes. For example, I never was able to persuade a writer colleague to taste kiwi fruit, clams, or goat cheese. Or Chinese food. Forget it. He was strictly a cheeseburger-and-Coke man.

However, for those of us who enjoy food in all its guises, this is a wonderful era, as travel and transportation have dramatically changed the types of food we eat and their availability. Variety is the key, despite the flourishing fast-food eateries.

Even with the new popularity of cuisines such as Vietnamese, Thai, Indian, Brazilian, and others, we are rediscovering *American* cooking—those good hometown favorites that we grew up with—and are adapting them to modern tastes and life-styles.

Added to these basic recipes are the fruits and vegetables available to us from other lands, foods such as plantain, *bok choy*, and *chayote*—a Latin American vegetable resembling a green potato. Today there is a whole new world of learning experiences in the kitchen and at the table.

And, that is what food is all about. It is more than nutritional statistics and sustenance. Food is fun. If you are dieting but do not enjoy the foods you are allowed to eat, you will be a dieting flop.

I have discovered in planning recipes for youngsters that you can sneak nutrition into their systems via soups, sandwiches, or desserts they like to eat. Through the years I also have been most concerned about the haphazard eating habits of singles—widowed, divorced, never married—and the elderly, and I have offered them recipes and suggestions of menus easy for them to prepare, as economically as possible, in portions to share with others or freeze for another quick meal.

With all the goodies available to us in today's cornucopia it is wrenching for most of us to be told by our doctors to change our eating habits. Nutritionists are pointing out that we eat an unnecessary and excessive amount of protein, especially animal protein. And, we do not eat a proper amount of fresh fruits and vegetables. Government and private studies show that most of us consume too many calories, eat too much salt and sugar and too much fat, especially saturated fat.

If you are a parent and concerned about your children's future health, help them build better eating habits and follow your own advice, too. You might start with the young athlete in the family; he or she is usually more open to eating foods that will contribute to physical well-being.

Join your family in eating more fruits, vegetables, and whole grains, more poultry and fish, and less fatty meats. To help all of us improve our daily diets the Department of Health and Human Services and the Department of Agriculture have issued seven dietary guidelines. They are:

- Eat a variety of foods.
- Maintain an ideal weight.
- Avoid too much fat, saturated fat, and cholesterol.
- Eat food with adequate starch and fiber.
- Avoid too much sugar.
- Avoid too much sodium.
- If you drink alcohol, do so in moderation.

Following these basic recommendations does *not* mean you'll be eating dishes that are less flavorful.

Keep in mind that vegetable oils are alternatives to butter and, in most instances, salt may be eliminated when called for in a recipe. Lemon juice and spices and herbs may be used instead to enhance flavors for those on low-sodium diets. Keep in mind that most fresh-produce items are low or relatively low in sodium and generally low in calories. Many produce items also have good amounts of potassium, a nutrient often found to be low in sodium-restricted diets. You will find scores of fresh fruits and vegetables to choose from in the produce department of your supermarket. What an assortment to add to your recipes, even if you are in some way restricted in your diet.

Spices and herbs are recommended in preparing foods, and are especially helpful for special diets. Colonial cooks valued knowing their spices and herbs and this cooking sleight of hand is being revived. It is easy to grow your own herbs—they're pretty, fragrant, and add zest to soups, salads, meats, fish, poultry, and desserts you will not soon forget.

Some recipes in this book call for monosodium glutamate (MSG)—especially Oriental-style dishes. MSG is a flavor enhancer. Some individuals report allergic reactions to MSG in their food. Those on a sodium-restricted diet also prefer not to use it in recipes because of its higher sodium content. You do not need to use MSG in cooking. Eliminate it from a recipe when called for in this book. Use an appropriate herb, if desired, or no substitute. There will be little loss of flavor.

Here are some suggested uses of spices and herbs for the various food groups (courtesy of the American Spice Trade Association).

BEEF, PORK, LAMB
Bay leaf
Caraway seed
Chili powder
Cloves
Curry powder
Dill seed
Italian seasoning
Marjoram
Mustard
Nutmeg
Oregano
Rosemary
Tarragon
Thyme

POULTRY
Chili powder
Curry powder
Dill weed
Ginger
Italian seasoning
Marjoram
Nutmeg
Oregano
Paprika
Poultry seasoning
Rosemary
Sage
Tarragon
Thyme

GREEN VEGETABLES
Basil
Dill weed
Italian seasoning
Marjoram
Mint
Nutmeg
Oregano
Poppy seed
Rosemary
Tarragon
Thyme

YELLOW VEGETABLES
Allspice
Anise
Chives (freeze-dried)
Cinnamon
Cloves
Dill weed
Marjoram
Mint
Tarragon
Thyme

POTATOES, RICE, PASTA
Basil
Caraway seed
Chili powder
Chives
Curry powder
Dill weed

FISH, SEAFOOD
Basil
Bay leaf
Celery seed
Curry powder
Dill weed
Italian seasoning

Italian seasoning
Marjoram
Oregano
Paprika
Tarragon
Thyme

Marjoram
Oregano
Paprika
Rosemary
Thyme

SALADS AND DRESSINGS
Basil
Caraway seed
Celery seed
Chili powder (low-sodium)
Cinnamon
Curry powder
Dill weed
Italian seasoning
Mint
Oregano
Poppy seed

FRUITS
Allspice
Anise
Apple pie spice
Cinnamon
Cloves
Ginger
Mace
Mint
Nutmeg
Pumpkin pie spice
Sesame seed

Black pepper, onion powder, and garlic powder are particularly useful in low-sodium diets and are used in all categories except fruit.

Again, food is fun and its preparation in many families has become a group activity—no longer thought of as a daily chore for only the woman of the house.

This book contains a wide variety of recipes, a number of them adapted from home cooking of other countries. There are American regional favorites and recipes of the new cuisine reflecting our changing tastes.

Enjoy sampling them. I did!

AILEEN CLAIRE

New York
1984

Hors d'Oeuvres & Appetizers

Have you noticed that next to the weather as a favored topic, when two people get together the talk quickly shifts to diets? Often, such chatter takes place while the two are noshing at a party.

Despite the guilt-driven urge of guests to at least acknowledge dieting, few hors d'oeuvres or appetizers are left over when dining out.

But, back to dieting. Have you noticed the shift to more lower-calorie noshes at parties? You're more likely to see more guests gathering around a bowl of cut vegetables or fruit than at the meatball or egg-roll platter.

Finger foods and dips especially lend themselves to even the noncook's kitchen efforts. When preparing hors d'oeuvres, make sure there's always a selection, something for everyone's mood.

DILL TOMATO TAKE-ALONGS

4	Italian plum tomatoes (about 3 ounces each)
6	tablespoons grated Cheddar cheese
2	tablespoons chopped dill pickle
16	slices dill pickle (½ cup)

Slice tomatoes in half lengthwise. Scoop-out tomato leaving tomato shells. Chop pulp. Combine chopped tomato, cheese and chopped pickle. Line inside of each tomato shell with pickle slices. Fill with tomato-cheese mixture.   *Makes 2 servings.*

EMPANADILLAS DE CHORIZO

2	cups all-purpose flour
1	teaspoon salt
10	tablespoons butter
6	tablespoons water
1	beaten egg yolk
	or
	Use 1 package (10 ounces) prepared frozen puff pastry
½	pound chorizo sausage, pepperoni, or other long spicy sausage, cut into 36 slices

Sift flour, add salt and cut in the butter with a pastry blender or 2 knives. Mix into a dough with the water and knead until smooth. Roll out evenly, dust with flour and fold the dough into thirds. Refrigerate for 15 minutes. Repeat this procedure 3 times, then refrigerate for 1 hour. Divide the dough in half.

Roll each half into a 12-inch square. Place the sausages on one section of the dough, cover with the other square and press down lightly. Cut between the rows of sausages into squares. Seal the edges of the dough together and prick the tops with a fork.

Or: Thaw the prepared puff pastry, in its wrapping, overnight in the refrigerator and roll out on floured surface to ½-inch thickness to a 12 × 24-inch oblong. Arrange sausages on one-half of the pastry, fold the other half on top and press down lightly, then cut as in previous directions. Seal down the edges of the dough and prick tops with a fork.

Bake empanadillas in a preheated 400-degree oven for 15 to 20 minutes or until brown.
Makes 36 empanadillas.

PICKLE-EGG "SANDWICHES"

4	hard-cooked eggs, sliced lengthwise
1	tablespoon sweet fresh cucumber pickle liquid
¼	cup sweet fresh cucumber pickle slices

Drizzle egg yolks with pickle liquid. Top 2 egg halves with pickles. Close with remaining egg, re-forming egg shape. Skewer with toothpick.
Makes 2 servings.

PICKLE-STUFFED CELERY

1	package (3 ounces) cream cheese, softened
¼	cup grated Cheddar cheese
2	ribs celery (about 10 inches long)
6	small whole sweet gherkin pickles

Blend cheeses. Fill celery with cheese. Arrange pickles over cheese. To serve, cut between each pickle.   *Makes 2 servings.*

SPICY STUFFED MUSHROOMS

18	medium-size mushrooms
2	tablespoons butter or margarine
2	shallots, chopped
1	package (3 ounces) cream cheese
1	package (8 ounces) cream cheese with herbs and garlic
⅓	cup dry bread crumbs
¼	cup coarsely chopped pecans
2	tablespoons Fino sherry
	Salt
	Additional pecan halves

Remove stems from mushrooms. Wash caps and dry thoroughly. In a small skillet, heat butter and saute shallots until golden. Cool. Mash cream cheese in a bowl until fluffy. Stir in sauteed shallots and their drippings. Stir in cream cheese with herbs and garlic, bread crumbs, pecans and sherry. Season to taste with salt. Use mixture to stuff mushroom caps. Decorate with pecan halves. These mushrooms can be eaten cold or can be heated in a 400-degree oven for 10 to 15 minutes until golden brown. They also can be broiled for 5 minutes or until cheese is melty. If broiled, garnish with pecan halves after broiling.   *Makes 18 stuffed mushrooms.*

VEGETABLE RELISHES WITH GARLIC-HERB DIP

1	cup low-fat cottage cheese
¼	cup low-fat plain yogurt
1	garlic clove, sliced
1	teaspoon prepared spiced mustard
2	teaspoons lemon juice or vinegar
½	teaspoon salt
¼	teaspoon tarragon, crumbled
4–6	drops hot red pepper sauce
1½	teaspoons chopped parsley
	Cucumber and carrot slices, cauliflowerets, celery sticks and radish roses

In electric blender container, combine cottage cheese and the next seven ingredients. Cover and blend on low speed 30 seconds or until smooth. Add parsley; whirl just to blend. Turn mixture into serving dish; cover. Chill several hours or overnight to blend flavors. Serve with choice of vegetable relishes such as cucumber slices.

Makes 1¼ cups dip.

DILL-CAPPED MUSHROOMS

1	can (3½ ounces) tuna, drained and flaked
1½	tablespoons mayonnaise
1	tablespoon sweet pickle relish
8	large mushrooms (about ½ pound), stems removed
8	dill pickle slices

Combine tuna, mayonnaise and pickle relish. Fill mushroom caps with tuna-relish mixture. Top with dill pickle slices. *Makes 2 servings.*

APPETIZER BEEF BALLS

1	pound lean ground beef
½	cup vacuum packed wheat germ, regular
¾	cup water
⅓	cup soy sauce
1	teaspoon grated ginger root
1	small clove garlic, minced
	Sesame seeds
	Minced parsley

Mix beef with wheat germ, water, soy sauce, ginger and garlic. Form into 6 dozen bite-size balls. Place in single layer in large shallow baking pan. Bake in 500-degree oven 4 minutes or until cooked as de-

sired. Turn beef balls and sauce into serving bowl chafing dish. Sprinkle with sesame and parsley. Serve with picks. *Makes 5 to 6 dozen appetizers.*

CHEESY CORNED BEEF ROLLS

10	ounces canned corned beef
4	ounces sliced Swiss cheese
1	can (10 biscuits) refrigerated buttermilk or country-style biscuits
2	tablespoons finely chopped onion
1	egg, slightly beaten
¾	cup crushed corn flakes, optional

Heat oven to 400 degrees. Grease cookie sheet. Cut corned beef into 10 pieces, each about 3-by-1-by-½ inches. Cut cheese into 20 pieces, each about 3-by-¾ inches.

Separate dough into 10 biscuits. Press or roll each to a 5-inch oval. Place one slice of cheese and one slice of corned beef on center of each biscuit. Top corned beef with one-half teaspoon onion and another slice of cheese.

Wrap biscuit around cheese, covering completely. Seal well. Dip rolls in egg. Coat with corn flakes, if desired. Place seam-side down on prepared cookie sheet. Bake at 400 degrees 10 to 12 minutes or until golden brown. Serve warm. *Makes 10 sandwiches.*

CLAMS IDAHO

24	fresh clams
	Rock salt (or coarse grain salt)
1	envelope (3¼ ounces) dehydrated instant mashed Idaho potatoes
2	strips bacon
2	tablespoons finely chopped onion
2	tablespoons horseradish
1	tablespoon chopped parsley
¼	teaspoon hot pepper sauce

Clean and open clams. Remove from shells; drain. Reserve halves of cleansed shells. Fill bottom of shallow baking pan with rock salt; preheat in 400-degree oven.

While salt is heating, prepare mashed potatoes according to package directions. Fry bacon until well browned; chop finely. Add bacon, onion, Shorseradish, parsley and hot pepper sauce to prepared potatoes; mix well.

Arrange clam shells on hot rock salt. Place a clam in each shell. Spoon a mound of potato mixture on top of each clam. Broil about 6 inches from heat until potato is lightly browned. Garnish each shell with a fresh parsley sprig, if desired.

Makes 24 appetizers.

DILLY SALMON APPETIZER

1	can (7¾ ounces) salmon
1	envelope unflavored gelatin
¾	cup chicken broth
½	cup mayonnaise
¼	cup *each* finely minced celery and finely shredded fresh spinach leaves
2	tablespoons *each* finely chopped green onion, chopped parsley and lemon juice
1	teaspoon dry mustard
½–1	teaspoon dill weed
¼	teaspoon bottled hot pepper sauce
	Assorted crackers

Drain and flake salmon, reserving liquid. Soften gelatin in reserved salmon liquid. Stir in chicken broth; heat to dissolve gelatin completely. Stir in remaining ingredients, pour into 3-cup mold. Chill until set. Garnish with parsley and serve with crackers.   *Makes about 12 appetizer servings.*

EGG ROLLS

¾	cup vacuum packed wheat germ, regular
1	cup bean sprouts, coarsely chopped
½	cup grated carrot
½	cup green onion, cut into 1½-inch pieces
½	cup minced water chestnuts or mushrooms
3	tablespoons soy sauce
2	teaspoons sherry
1	teaspoon grated fresh ginger
12	egg roll skins
1	teaspoon cornstarch
3	tablespoons water
	Oil for frying

Combine all ingredients except egg roll skins, cornstarch and water. Wrap egg roll skins in damp paper toweling, taking out one at a time. Place ¼ cup filling on each skin, covering only half the skin. Leave a narrow border along bottom and side edges uncovered. Fold narrow edge up over filling. Fold in side edges. Roll to within ½ inch of top edge. Brush top edge with cornstarch mixed with water. Seal well. Cover with damp paper toweling. Fry a few at a time in deep hot fat (350 to 375 degrees) 2 or 3 minutes until golden. Drain. Cut each roll diagonally into 3 pieces. Serve hot.
    Makes 3 dozen appetizers.

EGG SALAD STUFFED DILLS

4	whole refrigerated dill pickles
2	hard-cooked eggs, chopped
2	tablespoons mayonnaise
1	tablespoon sweet pickle relish

Hollow out dill pickles with vegetable corer. Combine remaining ingredients. Stuff dill pickles with egg-relish mixture.   *Makes 2 servings.*

LITTLE HAM CRESCENTS

1	cup finely chopped cooked ham
1	egg, lightly beaten
1	tablespoon dairy sour cream
1	teaspoon tarragon leaves, crumbled
⅛	teaspoon ground white pepper
1	package (10 ounces) frozen patty shells, thawed
	Beaten egg yolk mixed with 1 tablespoon water

In medium bowl combine ham, egg, sour cream, tarragon and white pepper; mix well and set aside. Place patty shells one on top of the other. Press lightly to seal together. On a lightly floured board, roll out dough 1/16-inch thick, about 16 inches square; cut into 16 four-inch squares. On one corner of each square, place about 1 teaspoon of the ham mixture. Roll up like crescents; turn ends in slightly. If desired, brush tops with a beaten egg yolk mixed with water. Place on jelly-roll pan. Bake in a preheated moderate oven (375 degrees) until golden, about 15 to 20 minutes. Serve hot.
    Makes 16 hors d'oeuvres.

POTATO-CHEESE APPETIZER BALLS

½	package (12 ounces) frozen shredded hash browns
1	cup sifted all-purpose flour
⅓	cup uncooked cornmeal
½	teaspoon baking powder
½	teaspoon salt
½	teaspoon onion powder
½	cup butter or margarine
1	tablespoon prepared mustard
1	cup grated Swiss cheese

Thaw and separate 1 block frozen potatoes (measures one and one-half cups). Grease a baking sheet. Preheat oven to 375 degrees. Sift together flour with cornmeal, baking powder, salt and onion powder. Melt one-quarter cup butter. Add potatoes with mustard and cook for 5 minutes stirring frequently until potatoes are soft. Cream remaining one-quarter butter and the Swiss cheese with potato mixture until smooth. Gather dough into a ball. Divide into 24 small balls, about 1-inch diameter. Arrange on greased baking sheet. Bake in preheated oven for 15 minutes, until golden. Serve warm or cold. *Makes 24.*

ROCK LOBSTER APPETIZER SALAD

2	cups well-drained chopped sauerkraut
2	tablespoons chopped chives
¼	cup minced parsley
½	cup shredded carrots
½	cup prepared oil and vinegar salad dressing
6	frozen South African rock lobster tails (3 ounces each)
	Thinly sliced cucumbers

In a bowl, mix sauerkraut, chives, parsley, carrots and dressing. Chill. Drop frozen rock lobster into boiling salted water. When water reboils, boil for 3 minutes. Drain and drench with cold water. With scissors remove underside membrane. Pull out meat in one piece and cut into ½-inch-thick crosswise slices. Serve salad with rock lobster slices. Garnish salad with cucumber slices.

Makes 8 to 10 servings.

ROCK LOBSTER BALLS

4	frozen South African rock lobster tails (3 ounces each)
1	cup water
½	cup butter or margarine
1	cup all-purpose flour
1	teaspoon salt
¼	teaspoon crumbled thyme and dill weed
4	eggs

Drop frozen rock lobster into boiling salted water. When water reboils, cook for 3 minutes. Drain and drench with cold water.

With scissors, remove underside membrane and pull out meat. Chop rock lobster finely and set aside. In saucepan combine water and butter and bring to a boil. Boil until butter melts. Stir in flour all at once until a large ball is formed. Remove from heat and stir in salt and herbs. Cool 5 minutes.

Beat in eggs, one at a time, beating until smooth after each addition. Stir in chopped rock lobster meat. Drop mixture in mounds the size of walnuts onto ungreased cookie sheets. Bake in a preheated 400-degree oven for 20 to 25 minutes or until puffs

are brown. Remove from heat and press the tip of a knife into each puff to allow steam to escape. Replace in oven for 5 minutes to dry. Serve warm or cold. *Makes 48 balls.*

SAUCY SAUSAGE ROLLS

2	cans (10 biscuits each) refrigerated buttermilk or country-style biscuits
6	tablespoons butter or margarine, melted
⅓	cup grated Parmesan cheese
1	pound mild Italian sausage (in casing), cut into 4 equal pieces
¾	cup water
2	tablespoons butter or margarine, softened
¼	cup chopped green pepper
¼	cup chopped onion
1	can (8 ounces) pizza sauce

Heat oven to 350 degrees. Separate each can of dough into 10 biscuits. Place 5 biscuits on edge and lightly press together. Shape ends to form a loaf. Repeat with remaining biscuits to form four rolls.

Dip rolls in melted butter. Then in cheese. Place on ungreased cookie sheet. Bake at 350 degrees for 17 to 22 minutes or until golden brown. Cool slightly.

While rolls are baking, place sausage and water in 10-inch fry pan. Cover and simmer about 10 minutes. Uncover. Drain and fry sausage 4 to 5 minutes on each side or until browned.

Slice rolls in half lengthwise. Spread with softened butter. Place 1 piece of sausage on each roll. Drain all but 2 tablespoons of drippings. Saute green pepper and onion in drippings until tender. Add pizza sauce. Heat to boiling.

Spoon about ¼ cup of the sauce over sausage on each roll. Serve warm. *Makes 4 sandwiches.*

If desired, sausage can be cut in half lengthwise before placing in roll.

HAM FINGERS

1	cup ground cooked ham
¼	cup sweet pickle relish
¼	cup mayonnaise
2	tablespoons minced green onion
2	tablespoons chopped parsley
¼	teaspoon dry mustard
12	slices cheese bread or white bread

Combine all ingredients except bread in bowl. Blend well.

Spread on 6 slices of bread. Top with remaining slices. Cut into finger sandwiches or triangles.

Makes 6 whole sandwiches or 24 triangles.

ITSY-BITSY TUNA BISCUITS

2	packages (10 ounces) refrigerated biscuits
1	can (6½ or 7 ounces) tuna in vegetable oil
1	cup (8 ounces) creamed cottage cheese
2	tablespoons milk
½	cup chopped unpared apple
½	cup chopped walnuts
¼	cup raisins (optional)
⅛	teaspoon cinnamon
⅛	teaspoon nutmeg

Cut biscuits in quarters. Place on ungreased baking sheet. Bake according to package directions for 5 to 7 minutes or until golden brown.

Place cottage cheese and milk in container of electric blender. Cover and process until smooth.

In medium bowl, flake tuna. Stir in cottage-cheese mixture, apple, walnuts, raisins, cinnamon and nutmeg.

Slit biscuits and fill with tuna mixture.

Makes 80 biscuits.

Note: Recipe may be halved if desired.

HOT CRAB APPETIZER RING

	Festive Crab Spread (recipe follows)
1	large round (11-inch) crisp rye cracker bread (knacker brod) or 2 7-inch-square rye crackers
¾	cup mashed ripe avocado seasoned to taste with salt, pepper, and lemon juice
⅓	cup sliced green onions with tops
1-2	medium tomatoes, thinly sliced, seeded and cut in half
¼	cup sliced pimiento-stuffed green olives
	Grated Parmesan cheese

Spread about 1¼ cups of Festive Crab Spread evenly on cracker bread. Spread avocado mixture in ring over crab to within 1½ inches of edges.

Layer remaining crab mixture over center of avocado ring and spread to form smaller ring. Sprinkle with onions.

Arrange tomato slices in ring over crab spread. Sprinkle with olives and reserved crab slices. Sprinkle with Parmesan cheese.

Place on baking sheet. Broil 5 to 6 inches from heat for about 2 to 4 minutes or until cheese melts.   *Makes about 16 appetizer servings.*

Note: Use crisply baked pizza or pie crust if rye cracker is unavailable.

FESTIVE CRAB SPREAD

6-8	ounces Alaska Snow crab, frozen or canned
1	package (8 ounces) cream cheese, softened
1	tablespoon mayonnaise
1	tablespoon chili sauce
3	tablespoons sliced green onions with tops
½	teaspoon dry mustard
⅛	teaspoon garlic salt
1	teaspoon lemon juice
	Dash hot pepper sauce

Thaw crab if frozen. Drain and slice. Reserve a few pieces for garnish, if desired.

In medium bowl, cream the cheese with mayonnaise and chili sauce. Blend in onions, mustard, garlic salt, lemon juice and hot pepper sauce. Fold in sliced crab.

Cover and chill at least 1 hour to blend flavors. Use for Crab Appetizer Ring or serve as spread with crisp rye crackers.   *Makes 1¾ cups.*

DOUBLE-NUT CHEESE BALL

2	cups (½ pound) shredded Cheddar cheese
1	package (8 ounces) cream cheese, at room temperature
6	tablespoons coconut rum liqueur
⅓	cup raisins
¼	cup finely chopped toasted almonds
⅓	cup sliced toasted almonds

In small bowl combine Cheddar cheese, cream cheese, liqueur, raisins and chopped almonds; mix well. Place on waxed paper; shape into a ball. Chill 2 to 3 hours or until firm.

Roll in sliced almonds. Serve with thinly sliced French bread or crackers.

Makes 1 ball about 4 inches in diameter.

MUSHROOM DIPPERS

Rinse, pat dry and trim stems from 1 pound medium-sized fresh mushrooms. Arrange in any desired fashion on a plate or in a bowl. Garnish with cherry tomatoes and green pepper "sticks" if desired. Serve with Garlic and Spicy Dips.

GARLIC DIP

1	cup mayonnaise
1	clove garlic, minced
1	teaspoon prepared mustard
⅛	teaspoon ground black pepper

Combine all ingredients; mix well. Chill. Spoon into a small serving bowl. *Makes 1 cup.*

SPICY DIP

1	cup chili sauce
2	teaspoons onion powder
2	teaspoons Worcestershire sauce
2	teaspoons horseradish

Combine all ingredients; mix well. Chill. Spoon into a small serving bowl. *Makes 1 cup.*

GREEN GODDESS PEAR DIP

1	cup dairy sour cream
½	cup mayonnaise
2	tablespoons finely chopped parsley
2	teaspoons finely chopped green onion
1	tablespoon chopped anchovies
2	teaspoons lime juice
¼	teaspoon garlic powder
6	fresh Bartlett pears, unpeeled

Blend sour cream and mayonnaise together. Add parsley, green onion, anchovies, lime juice and garlic powder. Mix well, cover and refrigerate several hours or overnight. When ready to serve, pile dip mixture in serving bowl. Halve and core pears. Cut fruit into small wedges. Arrange on serving board around bowl of dip. *Makes 8 servings.*

Note: You can also use this mixture as a dressing for a fresh pear salad.

Makes about one and one-half cups.

MEXICALI DIP

1	can (11½ ounces) condensed bean with bacon soup
1	package (3 ounces) cream cheese (softened)
2	tablespoons finely chopped onion
2	tablespoons tomatoes with green chilies

In a bowl, gradually blend soup into cream cheese; add onion and tomatoes. Chill. Serve with tortilla or potato chips. *Makes about 1½ cups.*

MUSHROOM "CAVIAR" DIP

½	pound fresh mushrooms or 1 can (6 to 8 ounces) mushroom stems and pieces
3	tablespoons butter or margarine
¾	cup finely chopped onion
1½	teaspoons paprika
1	tablespoon lemon juice
¼	teaspoon salt
1/16	teaspoon ground black pepper
½	cup dairy sour cream
¼	cup chopped dill
1	tablespoon chopped chives

Rinse, pat dry and finely chop fresh mushrooms (makes about 2¼ cups) or drain canned mushrooms and chop finely. In a large skillet, melt butter. Add onion and saute 2 minutes. Stir in paprika and cook 1 minute. Add mushrooms and saute 3 to 4 minutes. Add lemon juice, salt and black pepper. Stir in sour cream and dill. Cook only to heat through. Turn into a serving dish. Serve warm, sprinkled with chives, as a dip with crackers or black bread. *Makes about 1¾ cups.*

TUNA-MUSHROOM DIPPING SAUCE

1	can (6½ or 7 ounces) tuna in vegetable oil
¼	cup chopped onion
2	tablespoons lemon juice
1	can (6 or 8 ounces) chopped mushrooms, drained
½	teaspoon salt
¼	teaspoon pepper
1	cup sour cream

Continued

Drain excess oil from tuna into saucepan. Add onion, cook until onion is tender. Add lemon juice, mushrooms, salt and pepper; cook 2 minutes. Spoon mixture into electric blender container; add tuna and sour cream. Cover and process at high speed until smooth. Turn into saucepan and heat or chill. Serve with thin slices of French bread. This may be frozen and reheated.   *Makes 1¾ cups.*

YOGURT AND TUNA-MUSHROOM DIPPING SAUCE

1   can (6½ or 7 ounces) tuna in vegetable oil
¼   cup chopped onion
1   can (6 or 8 ounces) chopped mushrooms, drained

½   teaspoon salt
¼   teaspoon pepper
2   tablespoons flour
1   container (8 ounces) plain yogurt, divided
2   tablespoons water

Drain excess oil from tuna into saucepan. Add onion and cook until tender. Add mushrooms, salt and pepper; cook 1 minute. Blend in flour and cook 2 minutes. Stir in ½ cup yogurt. Spoon this mixture into container of electric blender; add tuna and water. Cover and process at high speed until smooth. Turn into saucepan and stir in remaining ½ cup yogurt; heat. The dip may also be chilled and served cold. Serve with thin slices of French bread. This may be frozen and reheated.   *Makes 1¾ cups.*

Breads & Baked Goods

One of my fondest memories is being coaxed awake by the scent of yeast biscuits being baked by my grandmother on a Sunday morning. Other mornings the mingled aromas might be that of bacon frying and "regular" biscuits, just out of the oven, ready at the table. There would be slathers of homemade butter, fresh apple butter, and sorghum molasses.

Few of us take the time anymore to sit down to what someone once called "a proper English breakfast." However, baking is back. Or was it ever completely abandoned? Young homemakers of both sexes are trotting out an "I-made-it-myself" look along with a variety of homemade breads and biscuits. This may result from the back-to-nature, natural health foods wave. Whatever the reason, the eating is good.

Baking is often a family project, I've discovered. Men enjoy making bread, especially doing the kneading on yeast doughs. Perhaps it allows them to work off stress and is a creative outlet. An artist I know takes a more simple approach. He's quite proud of his coffee-can bread that takes little work.

BREADS

AROMATIC BROWN BREAD

2	cups whole-wheat flour
1	cup cornmeal
2	teaspoons baking soda
1	teaspoon salt
2½	cups buttermilk
½	cup molasses
1½	tablespoons Angostura aromatic bitters
1	cup golden raisins

Combine dry ingredients in large bowl. Add remaining ingredients, stirring well.

Spoon batter into greased 2-pound coffee can. (Or use 2 1-pound coffee cans and steam for 2½ hours.)

Cover can with foil and tie securely with string.

Place can on rack in Dutch oven. Add enough hot water to cover lower half of can. Bring water to boil.

Cover Dutch oven. Steam on medium heat for 4 hours.

Remove can from water. Remove foil from top of can. Let stand 10 minutes. Turn bread out onto rack.   *Makes 1 2-pound loaf or 2 1-pound loaves.*

BANANA BROWN BREAD

2	cups unsifted whole-wheat flour
1	cup unsifted yellow cornmeal
¾	teaspoon salt
1	teaspoon baking soda
1	cup mashed ripe bananas (3 medium bananas)
1	cup buttermilk
¾	cup unsulphured molasses
¾	cup raisins

In a large bowl, mix together flour, cornmeal, salt and baking soda. Stir in bananas and remaining ingredients. Turn into 3 greased and floured 1-pound cans.

Bake in 350-degree oven 45 minutes, or until cake tester inserted in center of breads comes out clean. Cool 10 minutes, turn out of cans, slice and serve warm with butter.

Loaves may be frozen. Thaw and heat in 350-degree oven, wrapped in foil, for 20 minutes.
Makes 3 loaves.

BANANA-CURRANT BREAD

⅓	cup soft butter or margarine
⅔	cup packed dark brown sugar
1	teaspoon vanilla
2	eggs
1¾	cups unsifted all-purpose flour
1	teaspoon baking powder
½	teaspoon salt
1	tablespoon lemon juice
1	cup mashed ripe bananas (3 medium bananas)
1	cup currants

In large mixing bowl cream butter and sugar. Beat in vanilla. Beat in eggs, one at a time. In medium bowl mix together flour, baking powder and salt, blend into batter alternately with bananas and lemon juice. Stir in currants. Turn into two greased and floured one-pound coffee cans. Bake in 350-degree oven one hour, or until cake tester inserted in center of bread comes out clean. Cool 10 minutes, remove from cans and cool completely.   *Makes 2 loaves.*

BANANA-NUT BREAD

1½	cups sifted regular all-purpose flour
2	teaspoons baking powder
½	teaspoon baking soda
½	teaspoon salt
¼	cup soft shortening
½	cup sugar
1	egg
1	teaspoon vanilla flavoring
1½	cups mashed fully ripe bananas
1	cup bran cereal
½	cup coarsely chopped nuts

Sift together flour, baking powder, soda and salt. Set aside. Measure shortening and sugar into large mixing bowl. Beat until light and fluffy. Add egg and vanilla. Beat well. Mix in bananas, bran cereal and nuts. Add sifted dry ingredients, mixing only until combined. Spread batter evenly in greased 9×5×3-inch loaf pan. Bake in 350-degree oven about 50 minutes or until wooden pick inserted near center comes out clean. Let cool 10 minutes before removing from pan. Cool completely on wire rack before slicing.   *Makes 1 loaf.*

Note: Use bananas which have very brown flecked skins.

BRAIDED CRACKED-WHEAT RING

1½	cups milk
3	tablespoons sugar
2	teaspoons salt
3	tablespoons margarine
½	cup warm water (105-115 degrees F.)
1	package active dry yeast
1	cup cracked-wheat or whole-wheat flour
4¾ to 5¾	cups unsifted flour
	Melted margarine
	Coarse salt

Scald milk. Stir in sugar, 2 teaspoons salt and margarine. Cool to lukewarm. Measure warm water into large warm bowl. Sprinkle in active dry yeast; stir until dissolved. Add lukewarm milk mixture, cracked wheat and 3 cups flour. Beat until smooth. Stir in enough additional flour to form a soft dough. Turn out onto lightly floured board. Knead until smooth and elastic, about 8 to 10 minutes. Place in greased bowl, turning to grease top. Cover; let rise in warm place, free from draft, until doubled in bulk, about 1 hour.

Punch dough down. On lightly floured board divide dough in half. Divide each half into 3 equal pieces. Shape each piece into a 24-inch long rope. On a greased baking sheet, braid 3 ropes together bringing braid around to form a ring. Pinch corresponding ends together. Repeat with remaining dough. Brush with melted margarine and sprinkle with coarse salt. Cover. Let rise in warm place, free from draft, until doubled in bulk, about 1 hour.

Bake at 375-degrees about 35 minutes, or until done. Remove from baking sheets and cool on wire racks. *Makes 2 braided rings.*

BRUNCH BRAID

3½ to 4	cups sifted all-purpose flour
1	cup enriched cornmeal
1	teaspoon cinnamon
1	package dry active yeast
1¼	cups milk
½	cup sugar
¼	cup butter or margarine
1	teaspoon salt
2	eggs
1	teaspoon grated lemon peel
⅓ to ½	cup apricot filling

CINNAMON GLAZE:

1	cup sifted confectioners' sugar
½	teaspoon cinnamon
1½	teaspoons butter or margarine
2	tablespoons boiling water
½	teaspoon vanilla

In large mixer bowl combine 2 cups of the flour, cornmeal, cinnamon and yeast. In saucepan heat milk, sugar, butter and salt just until warm (115 to 120 degrees), stirring constantly to melt butter. Add to the dry mixture in mixing bowl. Add eggs and grated lemon peel. Beat at low speed with electric mixer for one-half minute, scraping sides of bowl. Beat 3 minutes at high speed.

By hand, stir in enough of the remaining flour to make a moderately stiff dough. Turn out onto lightly floured board or canvas and knead till smooth and elastic, about 10 minutes. Shape into a ball. Place in lightly greased bowl, turning once to grease top of dough. Cover; let rise in warm place until double in size, about 2 hours. Punch down. Cover; let rest 10 minutes. Divide dough into thirds. On lightly floured board or canvas roll each piece to form a 16×6-inch rectangle. Spread each piece with 2 to 3 tablespoons of apricot filling. Starting with long end, roll up jelly roll fashion. Seal ends and edge. Place three rolls on greased cookie sheet. Pinch top end of each roll together. Braid rolls. Seal bottom ends. Bake in preheated 350-degree oven 30 to 35 minutes. Remove from oven. Cool slightly on wire rack. Glaze while still warm.

FOR GLAZE: Combine all ingredients; mix until well combined and of a smooth consistency.

Makes 1 braid.

CARROT-BANANA BREAD

½	cup butter or margarine
1	cup brown sugar
2	eggs
1	cup mashed banana (3 medium-size)
2	cups all-purpose flour
1	teaspoon baking soda
½	teaspoon baking powder
½	teaspoon cinnamon
¼	teaspoon salt
1	cup grated carrot
½	cup chopped nuts

In large bowl, cream butter with sugar until light and fluffy. Beat in eggs. Mash bananas in small bowl. Mix flour, soda, baking powder, cinnamon and salt. Blend in flour mixture alternately with bananas. Combine with egg-butter-sugar mixture. Then stir in carrots and nuts. Turn into greased 9-by-5-by-3-inch loaf pan. Bake in 350-degree oven 50 to 60 minutes or until cake tester inserted in center comes out clean. Cool 10 minutes, turn out of pan and cool completely. *Makes 1 loaf.*

CHAPATI
(Pan-Fried Indian Bread)

2   cups unsalted whole-wheat flour
½   teaspoon salt
2   tablespoons peanut oil
¾   cup water
      Peanut oil

Combine flour, salt, 2 tablespoons peanut oil and enough water to make a workable dough. On lightly floured board knead dough until smooth, about 5 minutes. Cover with plastic wrap; let stand 1 hour.

Break off about 2 tablespoons dough. Roll to a 6-inch round on a lightly floured board. Flip gently back and forth several times between palms of hands.

Cook in an unoiled, hot, small skillet or crepe pan until lightly browned, about 30 seconds. Flip bread over; cook 15 seconds. Flip over again; cook until evenly puffed and cooked through, pressing dough down often with heavy cloth.

Remove from pan; brush lightly with peanut oil. Repeat with remaining dough. Serve immediately.   *Makes 18.*

CHERRY-BANANA BREAD

1¾   cups unsifted all-purpose flour
½   cup sugar
1   teaspoon double-acting baking powder
½   teaspoon salt
¼   teaspoon baking soda
½   cup shortening
1   cup mashed bananas (2 or 3 medium)
2   eggs, beaten
½   cup red maraschino cherries, finely
      chopped
¼   teaspoon grated lemon peel

In medium bowl, mix flour, sugar, baking powder, salt and baking soda. Cut in shortening until mixture resembles coarse crumbs. Add bananas, eggs, cherries and lemon peel; stir just until blended. (Mixture will be lumpy.) Spoon batter into greased 9×5×3-inch loaf pan. Bake in 350-degree oven 50 minutes or until toothpick inserted in center comes out clean. Cool on rack 15 minutes. Remove from pan and cool thoroughly before slicing.
                              Makes one 9-inch loaf.

COLONIAL OLIVE-CORN BREAD

1   cup flour
1   cup yellow cornmeal
2   tablespoons sugar
2   teaspoons baking powder
½   teaspoon salt
1   egg, slightly beaten
1   cup canned cream-style corn
¾   cup milk
2   tablespoons salad oil
½   cup stuffed green Spanish olives

In medium bowl, stir together flour, cornmeal, sugar, baking powder and salt until well mixed. Combine egg, corn, milk and oil. Stir into dry ingredients just until moistened.

Spread half of batter in greased and floured 9-by-5-inch loaf pan. Arrange olives on top of batter. Drop remaining batter by spoonfuls over olives to completely cover. Bake in 400-degree oven about 40 minutes or until done.

Remove from oven. Let stand 10 minutes. Loosen sides and turn out onto wire rack. Serve warm with butter.   *Makes 1 loaf.*

CORN BREAD

1   cup milk
1   egg
¼   cup vegetable oil
1   cup enriched cornmeal
1   cup all-purpose flour
1   tablespoon baking powder
½   teaspoon salt

Add milk, egg and oil to combined dry ingredients. Beat until smooth, about 1 minute. Bake in greased 8-inch square baking pan in preheated 425-degree oven 20 to 25 minutes.
          Makes 8-inch-square pan of corn bread.

OLIVE SPOON BREAD

2   cups milk
¾   cup enriched yellow cornmeal
2   tablespoons butter or margarine
½   cup sliced pimiento-stuffed olives
1   cup grated Muenster or Monterey Jack
      cheese (about 4 ounces)
1   tablespoon double-acting baking
      powder
1   tablespoon sugar
1   teaspoon salt
3   eggs
      Soft butter or sour cream

In large saucepan, heat milk with cornmeal to boiling, stirring constantly. Add 2 tablespoons butter and olives. Cook over low heat 10 minutes, stirring occasionally. Remove from heat and stir in cheese. Cool 10 minutes.

Combine baking powder, sugar and salt. Beat eggs until light and fluffy. Beat in sugar mixture and fold into cornmeal mixture. Quickly pour into greased one and one-half quart round or oval deep casserole. Bake in 300-degree oven, on center rack, 1 hour and 5 minutes or until top springs back when lightly touched with finger. Serve immediately, with soft butter or sour cream.   *Makes 6 servings.*

WIENER CORN BREAD

1	one-pound package wieners, split lengthwise
	CORN BREAD:
2	tablespoons chopped onion
2	tablespoons chopped green pepper
¼	cup butter or margarine
1	cup sifted all-purpose flour
1	cup enriched cornmeal
¼	cup granulated sugar
4	teaspoons baking powder
½	teaspoon salt
2	eggs
1	cup milk
	SAUCE:
1	one-pound can pork and beans with tomato sauce
⅓	cup ketchup
½	teaspoon dry mustard
2	tablespoons firmly packed brown sugar

Heat oven to hot 425 degrees. Grease an 11 × 7-inch pyrex baking dish. Open wieners along cut edge. With cut side facing up, place wieners in bottom of baking dish so that they lay flat. In saucepan, saute onion and green pepper in 1 tablespoon of the butter until tender, about 5 minutes. In mixing bowl, sift together flour, cornmeal, sugar, baking powder and salt. Melt remaining butter in saucepan containing sauteed vegetables. Remove pan from heat and add sifted dry ingredients. Stir in eggs and milk; mix until combined. Pour over wieners, spreading to cover completely. Bake in preheated 425-degree oven 25 to 30 minutes.
Makes 6 servings.

For sauce, combine all ingredients. Simmer over medium heat about 5 minutes. Cut corn bread into 6 pieces. Spoon sauce over each piece.

CRANBERRY BRAIDS

3	cups cranberries
1	cup sugar
1	cup light corn syrup
1	teaspoon ground cinnamon
¼	cup corn starch
¼	cup water
1	cup chopped walnuts
2	pounds frozen bread dough, thawed

In 2-quart saucepan, stir together cranberries, sugar, corn syrup and cinnamon. Stirring occasionally, bring to boil over medium heat. Reduce heat and simmer 10 minutes or until skins pop. Stir together corn starch and water until smooth. Stir into cranberry mixture. Stirring constantly, bring to boil over medium heat and boil 1 minute. Stir in nuts. Cover; refrigerate until cool.

Divide 1 pound dough in half. Divide each half in 3 portions. Roll out a portion to form 12-by-4-inch rectangle. Spread with 3 tablespoons cranberry mixture. Roll and seal edges. Place on greased baking sheet. Repeat with 2 more portions. Braid 3 strips together; seal ends. Following same procedure, make 3 more braids with remaining dough. Let braids rise in warm place 45 minutes or until double. Bake in 350-degree oven 25 to 30 minutes or until golden brown. Remove immediately from baking sheets. Cool on wire rack.   *Makes 4 braids.*

CRANBERRY SWEET POTATO BREAD

⅓	cup soft butter or margarine
2½	cups mashed sweet potatoes
⅓	cup sugar
1	teaspoon salt
¾	cup lukewarm milk
2	eggs
1	envelope active dry yeast
¼	cup lukewarm water
3½–4	cups unsifted all-purpose flour
½	cup cranberry orange sauce
½	cup finely chopped nuts
	GLAZE:
1½	cups confectioners' sugar
¼	cup cranberry orange sauce

In bowl, mix butter, potatoes, sugar, salt, milk and eggs. Dissolve yeast in water and then stir into potato mixture. Stir in flour and beat until well blended. Brush top of dough lightly with oil, cover and let rise until double in bulk in a warm place, about 1 to 1½ hours. Turn dough out on a floured surface and knead until a smooth ball. Roll out dough to a 10-by-14-inch oblong. Spread sauce and nuts on dough. Roll up dough, starting at the 14-inch side, like a jelly roll. Place dough seam side down with ends joining in a ring into a greased bundt pan. Let rise in a warm place until double in bulk, about 40 to 45 minutes. Bake in a preheated 350-degree oven for 1 hour and 15 minutes or until loaf sounds hollow when thumped. Unmold.

FOR GLAZE: Mix sugar with enough sauce to make a thick mixture. Spoon glaze over hot bread and allow to drip over sides. Cool thoroughly before cutting into slices.   *Makes 1 ring bread.*

GOLDEN PUMPKIN BREAD

1	can (16 ounces) pumpkin
1½	cups granulated sugar
1	cup firmly packed brown sugar
4	eggs
½	cup vegetable oil
3½	cups all-purpose flour
1	cup enriched cornmeal
2	teaspoons soda
2	teaspoons salt
2	teaspoons pumpkin pie spice
1	teaspoon baking powder
1	cup dairy sour cream
½	cup water
¾	cup raisins
½	cup chopped pecans

Beat together pumpkin, sugars, eggs and oil. Add combined dry ingredients to pumpkin mixture alternately with sour cream and water, mixing well after each addition. Stir in raisins and pecans. Pour into two well-greased 9×5-inch loaf pans. Bake in preheated 350-degree oven about 1 hour and 10 minutes. Cool 10 minutes; remove from pan.
Makes two 9×5-inch loaves.
VARIATION: Substitute one 10-inch tube pan for two 9×5-inch loaf pans; bake in preheated 350-degree oven 1 hour and 25 minutes.

HEARTY HOT CROSS LOAF

2	packages active dry yeast or 2 cakes compressed yeast
½	cup warm water
¾	cup scalded milk
⅓	cup butter or margarine
⅓	cup sugar
2	teaspoons salt
3½–4	cups all-purpose flour
1	cup quick or old-fashioned oats, uncooked
1	cup raisins or currants
1	egg, beaten
1	egg white, slightly beaten
	Confectioners' sugar frosting

Dissolve yeast in warm water. (Use lukewarm water for compressed yeast.) Pour scalded milk over butter, sugar and salt, stirring until butter melts. Cool to lukewarm. Stir in 1 cup flour, oats, raisins, dissolved yeast and 1 egg. Stir in enough additional flour to make soft dough.

Turn dough out onto lightly floured surface. Knead 8 to 10 minutes or until smooth and elastic. Shape dough to form ball. Place in greased bowl, turning once to coat surface of dough. Cover. Let rise in warm place about 1 hour and 15 minutes. Punch dough down. Cover. Let rest 10 minutes.

Divide dough in half. Shape to form 2 round loaves, about 6 inches in diameter. Place on greased cookie sheet; brush with egg white. Let rise uncovered in warm place about 1 hour or until nearly double in size. Bake in preheated 375-degree oven 20 to 25 minutes or until golden brown.

Remove from cookie sheet. While warm, make a cross on top of each loaf with thick confectioners' sugar frosting. Slice to serve.
Makes 2 round bread loaves.

HONEY-RAISIN OATMEAL BREAD

2	packages active dry or 2 cakes compressed yeast
½	cup warm water
2	cups warm milk
¼	cup honey
⅓	cup shortening, soft
2	teaspoons salt
5½–6	cups all-purpose flour
2½	cups quick or old fashioned oats, uncooked
1	cup raisins
	Vegetable oil

Dissolve yeast in warm water (use lukewarm water for compressed yeast). Pour milk over honey, shortening and salt. Stir in 2 cups flour. Add dissolved yeast, oats and raisins. Stir in enough additional flour to make soft dough.

Turn out onto lightly floured surface. Knead until smooth and elastic, about 10 minutes. Shape dough into ball. Place in greased large bowl, turning once to coat surface of dough. Cover. Let rise in warm place until double in size, about 1 to 1½ hours. Punch dough down. Cover; let rest 10 minutes.

Divide dough in half. Roll each into 16×9-inch loaf pan. Brush lightly with oil. Cover. Let rise in warm place until nearly double in size, about 1 hour. Bake in preheated 375-degree oven about 35 to 40 minutes. Remove from pans. Brush with butter or margarine if desired. Cool.   *Makes 2 loaves.*

IDAHO POTATO BREAD

¾	cup milk
½	cup butter or margarine
¼	teaspoon salt
½	cup sugar
⅔	cup instant mashed Idaho potato flakes
¼	cup warm water (105 to 115 degrees)
1	package active dry yeast
2	eggs
3½–4	cups flour

In small saucepan, combine milk, butter, salt and sugar. Heat until butter is melted. Remove from heat. Stir in potato flakes; cool to lukewarm. In large bowl, sprinkle yeast over warm water. Stir until dissolved. Add potato mixture and eggs; beat until smooth. Beat in enough flour to make a soft sticky dough. Turn out onto lightly floured board and knead until smooth and elastic (10 to 15 minutes), adding more flour when necessary to prevent dough from sticking to board. Shape into smooth ball, place in lightly greased clean bowl. Turn to grease top of dough. Cover and let rise in a warm place, free from drafts, until double in bulk, about 1½ hours. Punch dough down and turn onto board; knead for a few minutes. Divide dough in half, cover and let rest 10 minutes. Shape into loaves and place in two greased 9×5×3-inch loaf pans. Cover and let rise in warm place until double, about 45 minutes. Bake in 375-degree oven 30 to 35 minutes or until tops are golden brown and loaves sound hollow when tapped. Remove from pans and place on wire racks to cool. *Makes 2 loaves.*

IRISH BROWN BREAD

1	cup vacuum packed wheat germ, regular
1	cup flour
1	cup whole-wheat flour
½	cup sugar
1	teaspoon soda
2	teaspoons baking powder
1	teaspoon salt
½	cup butter
1	cup buttermilk

Combine wheat germ with both flours and remaining dry ingredients. Cut or rub in butter. Add buttermilk, mixing lightly with fork. Knead on floured surface one-half minute. Turn into greased 9-by-5-by-3½-inch loaf pan. Bake in 425-degree oven one hour, or until center of bread tests done.
Makes 1 loaf.

MINI MOLASSES-BANANA BREAD

⅔	cup sifted all-purpose flour
¾	teaspoon baking powder
¼	teaspoon baking soda
¼	teaspoon salt
2	tablespoons shortening
2	tablespoons sugar
1	egg yolk
2	tablespoons light molasses
½	cup mashed ripe banana

Onto waxed paper, sift together flour, baking powder, baking soda and salt. In medium bowl, cream shortening and sugar. Add egg yolk and beat well. Add molasses and mix thoroughly. Add mashed banana alternately with flour mixture, mixing just until blended after each addition. Pour batter into a well-greased 20-ounce can with a circle of waxed paper in the bottom. Bake in a preheated 350-degree oven for 45 to 50 minutes. Cool 5 minutes. Remove from can. Cool completely. *Makes 1 loaf.*

NATURE'S OWN DINNER LOAVES

3¾–4¼	cups unsifted white flour
½	cup yellow cornmeal
½	cup unsifted whole-wheat flour
⅓	cup unsifted rye flour
¾	cup milk
¼	cup sugar
4	teaspoons salt
¼	cup margarine
1½	cups warm water (105–115 degrees F.)
2	packages active dry yeast
1	cup wheat germ
	Yellow cornmeal
1	egg white, slightly beaten
1	tablespoon water

Combine 2 cups white flour, ½ cup cornmeal, whole-wheat flour and rye flour.

Scald milk; stir in sugar, salt and margarine. Cool to lukewarm. Measure warm water into large warm bowl. Sprinkle in active dry yeast, stir until dissolved. Add lukewarm milk mixture and flour mixture; beat until smooth. Add wheat germ and enough additional white flour to make a stiff dough. Turn out onto lightly floured board; knead until smooth and elastic, about 8 to 10 minutes. Place dough in greased bowl, turning dough to grease top. Cover; let rise in warm place, free from draft, until doubled in bulk, about 1¼ hours.

Punch dough down and turn out onto lightly floured board. Divide into 4 equal pieces. Shape each piece into a smooth round ball and place on greased baking sheets that have been sprinkled with cornmeal. Cover; let rise in a warm place, free from draft until doubled in bulk, about 1¼ hours.

Bake at 400-degrees for 10 minutes. Combine egg white and 1 tablespoon water. Remove bread from oven and brush tops of loaves with egg white mixture. Return to oven and bake an additional 5 minutes or until done. Remove from baking sheets and cool on wire racks.   *Makes 4 small round loaves.*

OATMEAL-MOLASSES BREAD

2½	cups unsifted all-purpose flour
½	cup old-fashioned rolled oats
1	teaspoon salt
1	package active dry yeast
½	cup water
½	cup milk
¼	cup dark molasses
2	tablespoons shortening

In large bowl of electric mixer, combine three-quarters cup of the flour, oats, salt and yeast. Heat water, milk, molasses and shortening until very warm (120 to 130 degrees). Gradually add to dry ingredients. At medium speed of electric mixer, beat 2 minutes. Add one-half cup flour and beat at high speed 2 minutes. Stir in enough of the remaining flour to make a soft dough.

On lightly floured board, knead dough until smooth and elastic, about 8 to 10 minutes. Place dough in greased bowl, turning dough over to grease top. Cover. Let rise in warm place until doubled in bulk, about 45 minutes. Punch dough down. Shape and place dough in a 9×5×4-inch greased loaf pan. Cover. Let rise in warm place until doubled in bulk, about 30 minutes. Bake in a preheated 375-degree oven for 45 minutes or until done. Remove from pan; cool on rack.

Makes 1 loaf.

O'FLYNN'S WHEAT GERM SODA BREAD

2	cups vacuum packed wheat germ, regular
2	cups flour
3	teaspoons baking powder
½	teaspoon soda
1	teaspoon salt
1	cup raisins, optional
1	tablespoon caraway seeds
¼	cup cooking oil
1¾	cups buttermilk

Combine wheat germ, flour, baking powder, soda, salt, raisins and caraway seeds, mixing well. Add

oil and buttermilk. Mix to moisten dry ingredients. Dough will be sticky. Divide dough in half and dump in two mounds on lightly greased baking sheet. Flour hands and gently shape into 2 (7-inch) loaves keeping rough surface texture. Make crosswise cut in top of each loaf with floured knife. Bake in 375-degree oven 40 to 45 minutes.

Makes 2 loaves.

Note: Dough may be baked in two greased 8-inch layer pans.

PANTRY PEAR BREAD

1⅔	cup finely chopped pear (about 2 pears)
1	cup firmly packed brown sugar
3	eggs
⅔	cup milk
½	cup vegetable oil
½	cup chopped walnuts
2½	cups all-purpose flour
1	cup quick or old-fashioned oats, uncooked
5	teaspoons baking powder
1	teaspoon ginger
1	teaspoon cinnamon
1	teaspoon salt

Grease bottom only of 9-by-5-inch loaf pan. Add combined pear, sugar, eggs, milk, oil and nuts to combined remaining ingredients, mixing just until dry ingredients are moistened. Pour into prepared pan. Bake at 350 degrees, about 1 hour and 10 to 15 minutes, or until wooden toothpick inserted in center comes out clean. Cool 10 minutes; remove from pan. Cool completely on wire rack.   *Makes 1 loaf.*

PEAR-CHEESE BREAD

½	cup butter or margarine, softened
⅔	cup sugar
2	eggs
2	cups flour
1½	teaspoons baking powder
½	teaspoon baking soda
1	teaspoon salt
1	cup peeled, coarsely grated fresh Anjou pears
1	tablespoon lemon juice
½	cup shredded sharp Cheddar cheese

Cream butter or margarine with sugar. Add eggs one at a time, beating after each addition.

Combine flour, baking powder, soda and salt. Add half of dry ingredients to creamed mixture, stirring until moistened. Repeat with remaining dry ingredients.

Combine grated pears and lemon juice. Gently stir into batter along with cheese, mixing only until completely blended.

Turn into greased 9-by-5-inch loaf pan. Bake at 350 degrees for 50 to 55 minutes or until toothpick inserted into center comes out clean.

Cool pan on wire rack 10 minutes. Remove bread from pan and continue cooling on rack. Wrap in plastic wrap or foil to store. *Makes 1 loaf.*

POTATO-CHEESE LOAF

1¼	cups milk
1¾	cups (5 ounces) shredded Cheddar cheese
1	teaspoon salt
1	tablespoon sugar
1	tablespoon butter or margarine
½	cup instant mashed Idaho potato flakes
¼	cup warm water (105 to 115 degrees)
1	package active dry yeast
1	egg
2½–3	cups flour

In small saucepan combine milk, cheese, salt, sugar and butter. Heat, stirring often, until cheese is melted. Remove from heat. Stir in potato flakes; cool to lukewarm. In large bowl sprinkle yeast over warm water. Stir until dissolved. Add potato-cheese mixture and egg; beat until smooth. Beat in enough flour to make soft, sticky dough (about 2½ cups). Turn out onto lightly floured board and knead until smooth and elastic, adding more flour when necessary to prevent dough from sticking to board. Shape into smooth ball. Place in lightly greased clean bowl. Turn to grease top of dough. Cover and let rise in a warm place, free from drafts, until double in bulk, about 1½ hours. Punch dough down and turn onto board; knead for a few minutes. Shape dough into loaf and place in greased 9×5×3-inch loaf pan. Cover and let rise in warm place until double, about 45 minutes. Bake in 375-degree oven 35 to 40 minutes or until top is golden brown and loaf sounds hollow when tapped. Remove from pan and place on wire rack to cool. *Makes 1 loaf.*

PRUNE-WHEAT GERM BREAD

1½	cups all-purpose flour
⅔	cup sugar
½	cup toasted wheat germ
1¼	teaspoons apple pie spice
1	teaspoon baking soda
¼	teaspoon salt
½	cup butter or margarine, softened
2	eggs
½	cup dairy sour cream
1	cup diced pitted prunes
½	cup chopped walnuts

Preheat oven to 375 degrees. In a large bowl, combine flour, sugar, wheat germ, apple pie spice, soda and salt. Add butter. With a pastry blender or two knives used scissor-fashion, cut in butter until mixture resembles coarse crumbs.

In a small bowl, lightly beat eggs; stir in sour cream. Blend into flour mixture along with prunes and nuts. Stir just until mixed. Spoon into a greased 9-inch loaf pan. Bake until a cake tester inserted in center comes out clean, about 50 minutes. Cool in pan on a rack for 10 minutes. Remove cake from pan and cool. Serve warm or cooled with butter or cream cheese, if desired. *Makes 1 loaf.*

PRUNE-WHEAT MUFFIN BREAD

¾	cup sun-sweetened pitted prunes
3	strips bacon
	Oil (about 2 tablespoons)
1	cup sifted all-purpose flour
4½	teaspoons baking powder
1	teaspoon salt
1	cup whole-wheat flour
⅓	cup brown sugar, packed
1	large egg, beaten
1	cup milk
1	cup shredded sharp Cheddar cheese

Snip prunes into small pieces. Cook bacon until crisp. Drain well, reserving fat; crumble bacon. Add oil to bacon fat to measure one-fourth cup and set aside. Resift flour with baking powder and salt. Stir in whole-wheat flour and brown sugar. Add egg, milk, and bacon fat mixture. Stir just until all of flour is moistened. Fold in bacon, prunes and cheese. Turn into greased 9-inch-square baking pan. Bake at 375 degrees for about 25 minutes, until nicely browned. Cut into squares or rectangles to serve. *Makes 12 rectangles about 2 by 2¾ inches.*

PULL-APART LOAVES

5½–6½	cups unsifted flour
3	tablespoons sugar
2	teaspoons salt
1	package active dry yeast
1½	cups water
½	cup milk
3	tablespoons margarine
	Melted margarine

Continued

In large bowl thoroughly mix 2 cups flour, sugar, salt, and undissolved active dry yeast. Combine water, milk and 3 tablespoons margarine in a saucepan. Heat over low heat until liquids are very warm (120–130 degrees). Margarine does not need to melt. Gradually add to dry ingredients and beat 2 minutes at medium speed of electric mixer, scraping bowl occasionally. Add ¾ cup more flour. Beat at high speed 2 minutes, scraping bowl occasionally. Stir in enough additional flour to make a stiff dough. Turn out onto lightly floured board. Knead until smooth and elastic, about 8 to 10 minutes. Place in greased bowl, turning to grease top. Cover. Let rise in warm place free from draft, until doubled in bulk, about 1 hour.

Punch dough down; divide in half. Cover. Let rest on board 15 minutes. Roll one half to a 12 × 8-inch rectangle. Brush with melted margarine. Cut into 4 equal strips, 8 inches long. Stack strips. Cut into 4 equal pieces, 2 inches wide. Place on edge in greased 8½ × 4½ × 2½-inch loaf pan so that layers form one long row down length of pan. Repeat with remaining dough. Cover; let rise in warm place, free from draft, until doubled in bulk, about 1 hour. Bake at 400 degrees about 30 minutes, or until done. Remove from pans and cool on wire racks. Serve warm or cold.   *Makes 2 loaves.*

PUMPKIN BREAD

2	cups unsifted whole-wheat flour
2	cups unsifted all-purpose flour
2	teaspoons salt
1	envelope active dry yeast
1	cup lukewarm water
1	tablespoon sugar
1	cup cooked mashed pumpkin
2	teaspoons Angostura aromatic bitters
	Grated rind of 1 orange

Sieve flours with salt into a large bowl. Dissolve yeast in lukewarm water. Add this mixture and remaining ingredients to flour. Mix to a soft dough, adding more water if necessary. Turn dough out onto a heavily floured surface and knead for 5 minutes or until smooth and elastic. Let rise covered in a greased bowl until double in bulk, about one to one and one-half hours. Knead dough again a few times and pat out to a 9-inch square. Roll up dough lightly into a 9-inch roll. Place roll, seam-side down, into a greased 9 × 5 × 3-inch loaf pan. Let rise until double in bulk, about 30 minutes. Bake in a preheated 350-degree oven for 30 to 35 minutes or until loaf sounds hollow when thumped. Cool thoroughly on a rack before cutting into slices. Serve. Spread with butter, cream cheese, honey or other favorite spread.   *Makes 1 loaf.*

QUICKEST RAISIN LOAF

1	loaf raisin bread, sliced
½	cup soft butter
	TOPPINGS:
¼	cup honey
1	tablespoon grated orange peel
1½	tablespoons sugar
1	teaspoon ground cinnamon
1½	tablespoons sugar
1	teaspoon instant powdered coffee
	MAPLE ICING:
1	cup powdered sugar
2	tablespoons milk
¼	teaspoon maple flavoring

Spread bread slices with soft butter.

Mix honey with orange peel. Spread on ⅓ of slices.

Mix 1½ tablespoons sugar with cinnamon. Spread on next ⅓ of slices.

Mix 1½ tablespoons sugar with coffee. Spread on last ⅓.

Place in loaf pan. Cover with aluminum foil. Bake at 425 degrees for 10 minutes. Remove foil. Toast for 10 more minutes.

Meanwhile, prepare maple icing by beating powdered sugar, milk and maple flavoring until smooth.

While loaf is still warm, drizzle icing over top.
                        Makes 1 loaf.

SPICED BRAN BREAD

1	cup wheat bran cereal
1	cup milk
1¼	cups whole-wheat flour
1	tablespoon lemon peel
2	teaspoons ground cinnamon
1	teaspoon baking powder
⅛	teaspoon ground nutmeg
1	cup sugar
1	cup dark raisins
1	cup chopped walnuts or pecans
2	eggs, lightly beaten
¼	cup butter or margarine, melted

In a large bowl, combine bran with milk. Let stand for 30 minutes. Preheat oven to 375 degrees. Meanwhile, combine flour, lemon peel, cinnamon, baking powder and nutmeg. Set aside.

Into bran mixture stir sugar, raisins, nuts, eggs and melted butter. Gradually spoon in flour mixture, stirring just until blended. Pour into a greased 8- or 9-inch loaf pan. Spread smooth. Bake until a cake tester inserted in center comes out clean, about 50 to 60 minutes. Cool in pan on a rack for 10 minutes. Remove cake from pan and cool. Serve warm or cooled with butter or cream cheese, if desired. *Makes 1 loaf.*

SPICY NUT BREAD

3	cups sifted all-purpose flour
1	teaspoon baking powder
1	teaspoon salt
1	teaspoon baking soda
¾	teaspoon nutmeg
¾	teaspoon ginger
½	teaspoon cinnamon
2	large eggs
1	cup firmly packed light brown sugar
1½	cups melted butter, cooled
½	cup dark molasses
1	cup chopped walnuts
1¼	cups milk
1	teaspoon vinegar

Sift together the first 7 ingredients; set aside.

In large mixing bowl, beat eggs until light and fluffy. Gradually beat in brown sugar until mixture begins to thicken. Stir in melted butter, molasses and nuts. Combine milk and vinegar; stir. Add flour mixture alternately with milk, mixing only enough to blend ingredients. Pour into two well-greased, lightly floured bread pans, about 7⅜ × 3⅝ × 2¼ inches each. Bake in a preheated 350-degree oven for 1 hour or until edges are lightly browned. Cool in pans on rack for 10 minutes. Turn out and cool completely. For easier slicing, wrap in plastic wrap or foil; store overnight. *Makes 2 loaves.*

SUPER WHEAT GERM ZUCCHINI BREAD

1¼	cups vacuum packed regular wheat germ
3	cups flour
3	teaspoons baking powder
1	teaspoon salt
2	teaspoons cinnamon
1	cup chopped nuts
2	eggs
1¾	cups sugar
2	teaspoons pure vanilla extract
⅔	cup cooking oil
3	cups grated zucchini (about 3 medium)

Mix together wheat germ, flour, baking powder, salt, cinnamon and nuts. Beat eggs until light colored and fluffy. Beat in sugar, vanilla and oil. Stir in zucchini. Gradually stir in wheat germ mixture. Turn into 2 greased and floured 8½ × 4½ × 2½-inch loaf pans. Bake in 350-degree oven 1 hour or until a toothpick inserted into center comes out clean. If using glass pans bake at 325 degrees. Cool 5 to 10 minutes. Remove from oven and cool on rack. *Makes 2 loaves.*

TANGERINE POCKET BREAD

3½–3¾	cups flour
1	package active dry yeast
1	tablespoon fresh grated tangerine peel
1	teaspoon salt
½	teaspoon sugar
1⅓	cups very warm water (120 to 130 degrees)
1	tablespoon salad oil
	Sesame seeds

In large bowl, combine one and one-half cups flour, yeast, tangerine peel, salt and sugar. With electric mixer at low speed, gradually add warm water and oil. Increase speed to medium; beat 3 minutes. With wooden spoon, gradually stir in remaining flour (about 2 cups) to make a soft dough. Place dough on lightly floured board. Knead until smooth and elastic, about 5 minutes, adding more flour as needed. Place in greased bowl, turning to coat all sides. Cover. Let rise in warm place (80 to 85 degrees) until doubled, about 1 hour. Punch down dough. Place on lightly floured board, roll each ball of dough into a 7-inch circle. Place 2 to 3 circles on each cookie sheet. Sprinkle tops with additional sesame seed; press into dough. Cover. Let rise until doubled, about 45 minutes. Bake at 475 degrees for 8 to 9 minutes until puffed and just lightly browned. Cool on racks 5 minutes; place in plastic bags to keep pliable. To serve, cut each "loaf" of bread in half to form two "pockets." Fill as desired. *Makes 8 loaves pocket bread.*

To reheat: Wrap pocket bread in foil. Bake at 350 degrees for 10 minutes or until hot.

WALNUT RAISIN BREAD

2¼	cups sifted all-purpose flour
3	teaspoons baking powder
1	teaspoon salt
⅓	cup butter or margarine, softened
¾	cup granulated sugar
1	large egg

Continued

2 teaspoons grated orange peel
¾ cup milk
⅓ cup orange juice
1 cup chopped walnuts
½ cup seedless raisins

Resift flour with baking powder and salt. Cream butter with sugar, egg and orange peel. Blend in flour mixture alternately with milk and orange juice. Fold walnuts and raisins into the batter. Turn into 3 greased and lightly floured (20-ounce) cans,* filling about half full. Let stand 10 minutes. Place in oven vertically and bake below center of oven at 350 degrees about 50 minutes, until pick inserted in center comes out clean. Remove from oven and let stand 10 minutes, then turn breads out onto wire rack to cool. *Makes 3 small loaves.*

*Entire amount of batter may be baked in 1 loaf pan (9-by-5-by-2¾ inches), if preferred. Bake 60 to 70 minutes, until loaf tests done.

WHEAT GERM POCKET BREAD

2 packages active dry yeast
1¼ cups warm water (105 to 115 degrees)
1 tablespoon sugar
½ cup vacuum-packed wheat germ, regular
1½ teaspoon salt
Cooking oil
2½–3 cups flour
Sesame seeds (optional)

In large bowl, mix yeast with water until dissolved. Stir in sugar. Let stand 5 minutes.

Add wheat germ, salt and 1½ teaspoons oil. Beat in enough flour with wooden spoon to make soft dough that leaves sides of bowl. Turn out onto lightly floured surface.

Knead about 5 minutes until smooth and elastic. Cut into 10 equal pieces. Shape each portion into smooth ball. Flatten slightly, then roll into 5½- to 6-inch rounds. Sprinkle with additional wheat germ and sesame seeds before rolling if desired.

Place rounds on greased and floured baking sheet. Brush lightly with oil. Do not cover. Let rise in warm, draft-free place until puffy, 1 to 1½ hours.

Bake in 475-degree oven 5 to 7 minutes or until bottoms are golden. Remove from baking sheets and cool on rack. If rounds don't open completely, cut open with tip of sharp knife. *Makes 10 rounds.*

BISCUITS, MUFFINS & ROLLS

BREAKFAST BISCUIT BARS

2 cups all-purpose flour
1 cup firmly packed brown sugar
2 teaspoons baking powder
⅓ teaspoon salt
⅔ cup butter or margarine
2½ cups quick or old-fashioned oats, uncooked
1½ cups (6 ounces) shredded sharp Cheddar cheese
6 crisply cooked bacon slices, crumbled
½ cup raisins
1½ cups milk

Combine flour, sugar, baking powder and salt. Cut in butter until mixture resembles coarse crumbs. Stir in oats, cheese, bacon and raisins. Add milk. Mix just until dry ingredients are moistened. Spread into greased 15.5 × 10.5-inch jelly roll pan. Bake in preheated 350-degree oven 35 to 40 minutes. Cool, cut into bars. May be frozen and reheated. *Makes 15.5 × 10.5-inch pan of bars.*

NUTTY APPLE BREAKFAST TURNOVERS

1 can (10 biscuits) refrigerated buttermilk or country-style biscuits
1 package (3 ounces) cream cheese, softened
1 tablespoon milk
2 tablespoons sugar
¾ teaspoon cinnamon
1 medium apple, pared and coarsely chopped (about 1 cup)
⅓ cup chopped peanuts
⅓ cup raisins
Powdered sugar

Heat oven to 400 degrees. Grease cookie sheet. Mix cream cheese, milk, sugar and cinnamon; stir in apple, peanuts and raisins.

Separate dough into 10 biscuits. Pat or roll each biscuit into a 4-inch circle. Place about 1½ tablespoons of the apple mixture in the center of each biscuit. Fold dough in half; press edges with fork to seal. Place on prepared cookie sheet.

Bake at 400 degrees for 11 to 13 minutes or until golden brown. Sprinkle with powdered sugar and serve warm. *Makes 10 turnovers.*

SAVORY BISCUITS

1¾ cups unsifted all-purpose flour
3 teaspoons double-acting baking powder
¾ teaspoon salt
⅓ cup shortening
¼ cup grated carrot
1 tablespoon chopped parsley
½ teaspoon grated onion (optional)
¾ cup (approximately) milk

Mix flour with baking powder and salt. Cut in shortening. Add carrot, parsley and onion; then add milk and stir with fork until soft dough is formed. Place dough on lightly floured board and knead 20 times. Pat or roll lightly until dough is ½-inch thick; cut with floured 2-inch biscuit cutter. Bake on ungreased baking sheet at 450 degrees for 10 to 12 minutes. *Makes about 16 biscuits.*

PUMPKIN BUNS

3 cups all-purpose flour
¼ teaspoon salt
1 envelope active dry yeast
½ cup lukewarm water
1 cup cooked mashed pumpkin
1 egg
2 tablespoons butter or margarine
1 teaspoon Angostura aromatic bitters
1 teaspoon grated lemon rind
½ teaspoon apple pie spice
¼ cup sugar
⅓ cup currants or chopped raisins
Confectioners' sugar and milk for glaze

Sieve flour and salt into a bowl. Dissolve yeast in lukewarm water. Add to flour with all remaining ingredients. Beat until well blended. Cover dough and let rest for 15 minutes. Knead on a floured surface a few times or until a smooth ball. With floured fingers, shape pieces of dough into egg-size buns. Place on a greased cookie sheet or into a muffin pan and let rise in a warm place until double in bulk, about 45 minutes. Bake in a preheated 400-degree oven for 15 minutes or until lightly browned. Serve as is or glaze while still warm with confectioners' sugar and milk, mixed to the consistency of heavy cream. *Makes 24 buns.*

WILLIAMSBURG BUNS

1 cup milk
½ cup sugar
¼ cup sherry (or cider)
¼ cup margarine
1 teaspoon salt
1 package active dry yeast
¼ cup warm water (105 to 115 degrees)
5 cups flour (approximately)
1 teaspoon nutmeg
1 teaspoon mace
2 eggs, well beaten
Melted margarine

Grease 36 (2½ × 1¼-inch) muffin cups. Scald milk; remove from heat and stir in sugar, sherry, margarine and salt. Cool to lukewarm. Sprinkle yeast in warm water and stir to dissolve. Stir 1 cup of the flour, nutmeg and mace into lukewarm milk mixture. Stir in yeast. Add eggs; beat until smooth. Stir in remaining flour, a little at a time, until dough can be easily handled.

Turn dough onto lightly floured surface. Knead until smooth and elastic. Place in oiled bowl smooth side down, then turn over dough so smooth side is up. Cover. Let rise in warm place until doubled, about 90 minutes. Punch down.

Divide into 3 balls. Divide each ball into 12 equal parts. Shape into balls and place in muffin pans. Let rise again until doubled in bulk, about 45 minutes. Brush balls with melted margarine. Bake in 350-degree oven 20 to 25 minutes or until golden brown. *Makes 36 buns.*

CARROT CORN MUFFINS

1 cup shredded raw carrots (2 large)
1 cup yellow cornmeal
1 cup milk
2 eggs, slightly beaten
2 tablespoons salad oil
1 cup unsifted all-purpose flour
2½ teaspoons baking powder
1 teaspoon salt

In medium bowl combine carrots and cornmeal. Heat milk to boiling and add to bowl. Let mixture cool to room temperature. Add eggs and oil. Mix together flour, baking powder and salt. Blend into carrot mixture. Fill greased muffin cups three-fourths full, and bake in 400-degree oven for 20 minutes. *Makes 12 muffins.*

BRAN MUFFINS

1½ cups all-purpose flour
¼ cup sugar
1 tablespoon double-acting baking powder
¼ teaspoon salt
1 cup wheat bran cereal

Continued

1   cup milk
1   egg
½   cup red maraschino cherries, chopped
¼   cup shortening

Grease 12 two and one-half-inch muffin pan cups. Stir together flour, sugar, baking powder and salt; set aside. In medium bowl, combine cereal, milk and egg. Let stand 1 minute to soften cereal. Into cereal mixture, add cherries and shortening and beat well. Stir in dry ingredients just until combined. Spoon batter into muffin pans. Bake in 400-degree oven for 25 minutes or until toothpick inserted in center comes out clean. *Makes 12 muffins.*

NECTARINE BRAN MUFFINS

1   cup all-bran cereal
½   cup orange juice
1   cup sifted all-purpose flour
¼   cup granulated sugar
2½   teaspoons baking powder
½   teaspoon salt
¼   cup toasted sunflower seeds (optional)
1   egg
¼   cup vegetable oil
1   cup chopped fresh nectarines

Preheat oven to 400 degrees. In a small bowl, combine bran and orange juice. Let stand several minutes for bran to absorb juice. Sift together flour, sugar, baking powder and salt. Stir sunflower seeds into flour mixture.

With a fork, stir egg and oil into bran until well mixed. Add bran mixture and chopped nectarines to dry ingredients. Stir only until dry ingredients are moistened. (Batter will be thick and lumpy.) Spoon batter into 12 2½-inch greased muffin cups. Bake at 400 degrees for 25 minutes, or until browned. Remove from pan and serve hot.

Makes 12 muffins.

ORANGE BRAN MUFFINS

1½   cups shreds of wheat bran cereal
½   cup milk
½   cup orange juice
1   egg
⅓   cup soft shortening
2   teaspoons grated orange rind
1⅓   cups unsifted all-purpose flour
½   cup sugar
2½   teaspoons baking powder
⅛   teaspoon baking soda
1   teaspoon salt

In large bowl combine shreds of wheat bran cereal, milk and orange juice. Let stand 2 minutes. Add egg, shortening and orange rind. Beat well. In small bowl mix together flour, sugar, baking powder, baking soda and salt. Add to cereal mixture, stirring only until combined. Batter will be thick. Fill greased 2½-inch muffin cups ¾ full. Bake in 400-degree oven 30 minutes or until cake tester inserted in center comes out clean. Serve warm.

Makes 12 muffins.

TEA MUFFINS

1½   cups unsifted all-purpose flour
¼   cup sugar
1   tablespoon baking powder
¼   teaspoon salt
1   teaspoon grated lemon rind
⅓   cup soft sunflower oil margarine
¾   cup skimmed milk
4   teaspoons lemon juice
1   egg white, stiffly beaten
     Sunflower seeds (optional)

In a large bowl, mix flour, sugar, baking powder and salt. Stir in lemon rind. Add margarine and break up with a fork. Add milk and lemon juice. Stir only until dry ingredients are moistened. Fold in egg white.

Brush 2-inch muffin cups with margarine. Spoon batter into cups, filling ⅔ full. Top with a sprinkling of sunflower seeds. Bake in a 425-degree oven for 20 minutes. Serve warm.   *Makes 15 to 20 muffins.*

SWEET POTATO ROLLS

2   cakes compressed or 2 packages dry yeast
½   cup lukewarm water
1   cup milk, scalded
¼   cup sugar
2   teaspoons salt
1   teaspoon cinnamon
1   teaspoon nutmeg
⅓   cup butter or margarine
1   cup mashed cooked or canned sweet potatoes or yams
5–5½ cups sifted all-purpose flour
1½   cups quick or old-fashioned oats, uncooked
     Melted or liquid shortening

Soften yeast in lukewarm water. (Use warm water for dry yeast.) Pour scalded milk over sugar, salt, cinnamon, nutmeg and butter in a large bowl. Add mashed sweet potatoes; beat until well blended. Stir in 1 cup flour and softened yeast. Add oats. Stir in enough additional flour to make a soft dough.

Turn out onto lightly floured board or canvas. Knead until smooth and elastic, 8 to 10 minutes. Place in greased large bowl, turning to grease top. Cover; let rise in warm place until double in size, about 1 hour.

Punch dough down. Divide dough in half. Divide each half into 16 equal pieces. Shape each piece into a smooth ball. Place 16 rolls in each of 2 greased 9-inch-square baking pans. Brush with melted or liquid shortening. Cover and let rise in warm place until nearly double in size, 25 to 30 minutes. Bake in preheated moderate oven 20 to 25 minutes.

Makes 32 rolls.

COFFEECAKES, SWEET ROLLS & PANCAKES

ALMOND COFFEE RING

1	cup milk
¼	cup vegetable oil
¼	cup brown sugar (packed)
½	teaspoon salt
¼	teaspoon mace
1	package active dry yeast
¼	cup warm water (105 to 115 degrees)
2	eggs, beaten with fork
2½	cups unsifted whole-wheat flour
⅓	cup sifted soy flour *or* whole-wheat flour
½	cup toasted sliced natural almonds

In saucepan, scald milk. Stir in oil, brown sugar, salt and mace. Cool slightly. Sprinkle yeast over warm water in large mixing bowl; stir until dissolved.

Blend in milk mixture and eggs. Stir in flours and mix until blended; stir in almonds. You will have a very soft dough with no kneading required. Cover bowl and let rise in warm place (about 90 degrees) for 1 to 1½ hours or until dough is doubled in bulk.

Stir dough down and spoon into a well-greased and floured 2-quart Kugelhopf or other mold. Cover and let rise again in warm place until doubled in size (about 45 minutes). Bake at 375 degrees for 25 to 30 minutes or until top is a dark golden brown.

Invert from mold onto rack; cool. Sprinkle with powdered sugar if you like. To reheat, wrap in foil and place in moderate oven until warm. Serve cool or warm with butter and honey.   *Makes 16 slices.*

CHRISTMAS STOLLEN

BREAD:

2	packages active dry yeast
½	cup warm water
¾	cup milk, scalded
⅔	cup butter or margarine
½	cup sugar
1	teaspoon salt
4¼–4½	cups all-purpose flour
1	cup enriched cornmeal
2	eggs
1	cup chopped blanched almonds
½	cup diced mixed candied fruit
½	cup golden raisins
1	tablespoon grated lemon peel
2	teaspoons butter or margarine, softened

GLAZE:

2	cups confectioners' sugar
¼	cup lemon juice

Dissolve yeast in warm water. Pour milk over butter, sugar and salt in large bowl; cool to lukewarm. Stir in dissolved yeast, 1 cup flour, cornmeal and eggs. Add nuts, candied fruit, raisins and lemon peel. Stir in enough additional flour to make soft dough. Knead on lightly floured surface 8 to 10 minutes or until smooth and elastic. Divide dough into quarters; roll out each quarter to form 9-by-7-inch oval. Fold in half lengthwise to within 1 inch of opposite side. Place on lightly greased cookie sheets; spread each loaf with ½ teaspoon butter.* Let rise in warm place about 1½ hours or until double in size. Bake at 350 degrees for 20 to 25 minutes or until light golden brown. Remove from cookie sheet; cool on wire cooling rack.

For glaze, combine all ingredients, mixing well; spoon over warm loaves. Decorate with candied cherries, if desired.   *Makes 4 loaves.*

*Note: At this point, dough can be covered with plastic wrap and refrigerated up to 24 hours. When ready to let rise, remove from refrigerator. Let rise in warm place about 2 hours or until double in size. Proceed as recipe directs.

FIG BUTTERFLY COFFEECAKE

3¼–3¾	cups unsifted flour
2	tablespoons sugar
½	teaspoon salt
1	package active dry yeast
⅓	cup milk
¼	cup water
¼	cup margarine
2	eggs
	Fig Filling (follows)

Continued

In a large bowl, combine ¾ cup flour, sugar, salt and active dry yeast.

Combine milk, water and margarine in saucepan. Heat over low heat until liquids are very warm (120 to 130 degrees F.). Margarine does not need to melt. Gradually add to dry ingredients and beat 2 minutes at medium speed of electric mixer, scraping bowl occasionally. Add eggs and ¼ cup flour. Beat at high speed 2 minutes, scraping bowl occasionally. Stir in enough additional flour to make a stiff dough. Turn out onto lightly floured board; knead until smooth and elastic, about 5 to 6 minutes. Place in greased bowl, turning to grease top. Cover; let rise in a warm place, free from draft, until doubled in bulk, about 1 hour.

Punch dough down; turn out onto lightly floured board. Roll out to an 18-by-12-inch rectangle. Spread fig filling (recipe below) over rectangle to within 1 inch of edges. Starting from long side, roll up like a jelly roll; pinch seam to seal. Place roll on a large greased baking sheet, seam side down. Cut roll in half lengthwise, starting at ends, leaving 2-inch uncut section in center. Turn cut sections filling side up. Placing roll in a vertical position, coil top 2 cut sections down in opposite directions, bringing ends to meet uncut center section. Coil bottom 2 sections up, bringing ends to meet uncut center section. Cover. Let rise in a warm place, free from draft, until doubled in bulk, about 1 hour.

Bake at 325-degrees for 35 minutes, or until done. Remove from baking sheet and cool on wire rack. Decorate with confectioners' sugar frosting if desired. *Makes 1 butterfly.*

FIG FILLING: In saucepan, combine 1 cup chopped dried figs, ¼ cup firmly-packed brown sugar, ⅔ cup water and 1 tablespoon lemon juice. Bring to a boil over medium heat, stirring. Continue cooking until mixture is thick enough to spread. Remove from heat; stir in ½ cup chopped pecans.

ORANGE 'N' HONEY GLAZED COFFEECAKE

2	cans (10 biscuits each) refrigerated buttermilk or country-style biscuits
½	cup sugar
⅓	cup chopped pecans
¼	cup butter or margarine, melted
	GLAZE:
¼	cup honey
¼	cup frozen orange juice concentrate
1	tablespoon flour
1	teaspoon cinnamon

Heat oven to 375 degrees. Grease 9-inch-square pan. Separate each can of dough into 10 biscuits.

Combine sugar and pecans. Dip biscuits in melted butter, then in sugar mixture. Arrange biscuits in prepared pan in 4 rows, overlapping biscuits slightly.

Combine glaze ingredients in saucepan. Mix well. Cook over medium heat, stirring constantly, until bubbly. Spoon glaze over biscuits.

Bake at 375 degrees for 20 minutes. Cover biscuits with aluminum foil. Bake 5 to 10 minutes more or until biscuits are golden brown and no longer doughy in center. Let stand in pan 5 minutes before turning out on serving plate. Serve warm.
Makes 9-inch coffeecake.

RAISIN-CHEESE FILLED COFFEECAKE

	Raisin-Cheese Filling (recipe follows)
2	packages active dry yeast
½	cup warm water (110 to 115 degrees)
1	cup milk
¼	cup butter or margarine
½	cup sugar
1	teaspoon salt
1	teaspoon ground cardamom
2	eggs, beaten
5½–6	cups flour
¾	cup apricot preserves
8	candied cherries, halved
½	cup slivered almonds

Prepare Raisin-Cheese Filling (recipe follows). Refrigerate until cake is assembled.

Dissolve yeast in warm water.

Scald milk. Stir in butter, sugar, salt and cardamom. Cool to lukewarm.

Stir in yeast and eggs. Mix in 4½ cups flour. Beat thoroughly.

Turn onto board and knead in enough of remaining flour to make smooth, satiny dough (about 10 minutes).

Place in greased bowl. Cover and let rise in warm place until doubled, about 1½ hours. Punch down.

On lightly floured board, roll and stretch into 22-by-12-inch rectangle.

Spread with chilled Raisin-Cheese Filling to within 1 inch of long edges. Roll from long side as for jelly roll. Pinch edges to seal.

Carefully fit into deep 10-inch tube pan, sealing ends together. Cover and let rise in warm place until doubled, about 2 to 2½ hours.

Bake at 350 degrees for 60 to 70 minutes until golden brown. Cool in pan 15 minutes before turning out on rack to cool completely.

Melt apricot preserves over low heat, stirring constantly. Strain and cool to lukewarm.

Place cooled cake on serving plate and cover with preserves. Decorate with candied cherries and slivered almonds. *Makes 12 to 16 servings.*

RAISIN-CHEESE FILLING:

1½	cups raisins
2	tablespoons lemon juice
1	package (8 ounces) cream cheese, softened
1	egg
1	egg yolk
¼	cup sugar
	Grated peel of 1 lemon
½	cup chopped walnuts

Toss together raisins and lemon juice.

Beat cream cheese, egg and egg yolk at medium speed with electric mixer until well blended, about 3 minutes. Add sugar. Mix well.

Stir in raisin mixture, lemon peel and walnuts. Refrigerate.

DEEP DARK CHOCOLATE TEA BREAD

2	cups sifted flour
1	tablespoon baking powder
⅓	cup cocoa
½	teaspoon salt
¾	cup sugar
1	egg, slightly beaten
1	cup milk
3	tablespoons melted shortening
⅓	cup semi-sweet chocolate pieces

Combine dry ingredients and sift into large bowl. Beat together egg, milk and shortening. Add to first mixture and stir only until dry ingredients are moistened. Fold in semi-sweet chocolate pieces. Pour into greased 9-by-5-by-3-inch loaf pan. Bake in 350-degree oven 1 hour.   *Makes 1 loaf.*

CHOCOLATE-WALNUT CAKE BREAD

¼	cup butter or margarine
1	square (1 ounce) unsweetened chocolate
1	cup sugar
2¾	cups sifted all-purpose flour
1½	teaspoons salt
1	teaspoon baking powder
1	teaspoon baking soda
½	teaspoon cinnamon
1	large egg, beaten
1¼	cups milk
1	cup coarsely chopped walnuts
1	cup chopped, pitted, sun-sweetened prunes

Melt butter and chocolate together over hot water. Stir in sugar. Set aside to cool.

Resift flour with salt, baking powder, soda and cinnamon. Blend egg into cooled chocolate mixture. Add flour mixture alternately with milk, mixing well.

Set aside 2 tablespoons walnuts. Stir remaining walnuts and prunes into batter and turn into greased and floured 9-inch tube pan. Sprinkle with reserved walnuts.

Bake below oven center at 350 degrees for 55 to 65 minutes, until pick inserted in center comes out clean. Let stand in pan about 15 minutes, then turn out onto wire rack to cool.   *Makes 1 large loaf.*

FRENCH APPLE CAKE

TOPPING:

3	cups sliced pared cooking apples
1	tablespoon flour
⅔	cup sugar
½	teaspoon cinnamon
3	tablespoons fresh lemon juice
2	tablespoons butter or margarine, melted

BATTER:

1	cup sifted all-purpose flour
½	cup sugar
1	teaspoon baking powder
¼	teaspoon salt
2	eggs
¼	cup milk
1	tablespoon butter or margarine, melted

To prepare topping, arrange apples in greased 8-inch-square baking pan.

Mix flour, sugar and cinnamon. Sprinkle over apples. Drizzle with lemon juice and butter.

For batter, sift flour, sugar, baking powder and salt into bowl.

Beat together eggs, milk and butter. Add to dry ingredients. Mix until moistened. Turn into pan over apples.

Bake in 425-degree oven for 30 minutes. Invert on plate and serve warm.   *Makes 8 to 12 servings.*

FRESH APPLE TEA BREAD

½	cup butter or margarine
1	cup sugar
2	eggs
½	teaspoon grated fresh lemon rind
2	cups sifted all-purpose flour
2	teaspoons baking powder
½	teaspoon baking soda
¼	teaspoon salt

Continued

1	teaspoon cinnamon
¼	teaspoon nutmeg
¼	teaspoon cloves
1½	cups finely chopped pared cooking apples
½	cup chopped nuts
¼	cup milk
1	teaspoon vanilla

Cream butter with sugar in large bowl. Beat in eggs. Add lemon rind.

Sift together flour, baking powder, baking soda, salt, cinnamon, nutmeg and cloves.

Add ½ cup of dry ingredients to apples and nuts in small bowl. Stir to coat apples.

Blend remaining dry ingredients into creamed mixture alternately with milk and vanilla. Stir in coated apples and nuts.

Turn into greased 9-by-5-by-3-inch loaf pan. Bake in 350-degree oven for 1 hour or until cake tester inserted in center comes out clean.

Cool on wire rack for 5 minutes. Then turn out of pan onto rack and cool thoroughly.   *Makes 1 loaf.*

FRESH PLUM COFFEE RING

2½–3	cups flour
1	package active dry yeast
¼	cup sugar
1	teaspoon salt
¼	cup butter, softened to room temperature
¾	cup hot water
1	egg
	Vegetable oil
	Plum Sauce (recipe follows)
	Streusel Topping (recipe follows)
1–2	tablespoons lemon juice
1	cup powdered sugar

Combine 1 cup flour with yeast, sugar and salt in a mixing bowl. Add butter and water. Beat with an electric mixer 2 minutes. Add egg and additional cup flour. Beat at high speed for 1 minute. With a wooden spoon, work in enough of the remaining flour to make a soft dough. Turn out on a floured board and knead 8 to 10 minutes or until dough is smooth and elastic. Let rest 20 minutes. Punch down. Roll dough into a rope. Starting in the center of a cookie sheet, make continuous rings, working outward from the center. Brush dough with oil and cover with plastic wrap. Refrierate for 2 to 24 hours. Preheat oven to 400 degrees. Remove dough from refrigerator and let rise for 10 minutes. Spread Plum Sauce between coils on coffeecake and sprinkle with Streusel Topping. Bake 35 to 40 minutes or until coffeecake is golden. For glaze, blend together lemon juice and powdered sugar. Drizzle over **warm coffeecake.**   *Makes one 12-inch coffeecake.*

PLUM SAUCE:

4	fresh plums, sliced
¾	cup orange juice
¼	cup sugar
2	tablespoons cornstarch

Combine orange juice, sugar and cornstarch in a saucepan. Blend thoroughly, then add plums. Cook over low heat until mixture is thick and clear, about 5 minutes. Remove from heat and cool.

STREUSEL TOPPING:

3	tablespoons butter, softened to room temperature
½	cup sugar
¼	teaspoon cinnamon
⅔	cup flour

Cream butter with sugar and cinnamon until light and fluffy. Work in flour, gradually, until mixture is crumbly.

GLAZED TEA LOAF

¼	cup butter, softened
¾	cup sugar
2	eggs
1	teaspoon grated orange rind
¼	teaspoon almond extract
½	cup chopped raw cranberries
¾	cup chopped mixed candied fruits and peels
½	cup chopped walnuts
2	cups unsifted all-purpose flour
2½	teaspoons baking powder
¾	teaspoon salt
¾	cup milk
	Orange Glaze (recipe follows)

Cream butter and sugar together. Add eggs, rind and almond extract. Beat well.

In a small bowl, combine cranberries, candied fruits and nuts. Toss with ¼ cup of the flour and set aside.

Mix together remaining flour, baking powder and salt. Add to creamed mixture alternately with milk, beating well after each addition. Stir in fruits.

Turn into greased 9-by-5-by-3-inch loaf pan. Bake in a preheated 350-degree oven about 60 minutes. Let cool in pan 15 minutes. Remove from pan. Cool before glazing.   *Makes 1 loaf.*

ORANGE GLAZE:

1¼	cups confectioners' sugar
2	tablespoons undiluted orange juice concentrate
1	teaspoon lemon juice

Mix ingredients until smooth. Spoon over top of loaf and drizzle down sides.

CRUNCH-A-BUNS

TOPPING:
½   cup butter or margarine
½   cup firmly packed brown sugar
¾   cup 100 per cent natural cereal
BUNS:
1   package active dry yeast
¼   cup warm water
¼   cup milk, scalded, cooled
¼   cup sugar
¼   cup shortening
1   egg
½   teaspoon salt
2¼–2½ cups all-purpose flour
FILLING:
2   tablespoons butter or margarine, softened
¾   cup 100 per cent natural cereal
¼   cup firmly packed brown sugar
1   teaspoon cinnamon

For topping, melt butter in 13×9-inch baking pan. Sprinkle brown sugar evenly over melted butter; top with cereal.

For buns, dissolve yeast in warm water. Combine milk, sugar, shortening, dissolved yeast, egg, salt and one and one-fourth cups flour. Mix well. Stir in enough additional flour to make soft dough. Turn out onto lightly floured surface. Knead about 5 to 7 minutes or until smooth and elastic. Shape dough to form ball. Place in greased bowl, turning once to coat surface of dough. Cover. Let rise in warm place about 1 hour or until double in size. Punch down dough; roll out to 15×10-inch rectangle.

For filling, spread dough with butter. Sprinkle with combined cereal, brown sugar and cinnamon. Roll up beginning at wide end; press together seam to seal. Cut dough into 15 one-inch-thick slices. Lay slices, cut side down, in 3 rows over topping. Cover. Let rise in warm place about 45 minutes or until double in size.

Bake in preheated moderate oven (375 degrees) about 25 minutes or until golden brown. Immediately invert onto serving tray; serve warm.   *Makes 13×9-inch pan of buns.*

KANSAS COFFEECAKE

SWEET DOUGH:
1   package active dry yeast
¼   cup warm water
¾   cup lukewarm buttermilk or skimmed milk
⅓   cup sunflower oil margarine
¼   cup sugar
½   teaspoon salt

¼   teaspoon baking soda
2½ cups unsifted all-purpose flour, divided
2   tablespoons sunflower oil margarine, melted
RAISIN-NUT FILLING:
⅓   cup chopped walnuts
⅓   cup raisins
2   tablespoons sugar
1   teaspoon cinnamon

In large mixing bowl, dissolve yeast in warm water. Add buttermilk or skimmed milk, margarine, sugar, salt, baking soda and 1 cup flour. Beat on low speed of electric mixer for 2 minutes.

Stir in remaining 1½ cups flour by hand to make a soft dough. Place in a clean bowl brushed with additional margarine, turning once to coat on all sides. Cover. Let rise in a warm place until double in bulk, about 1¼ hours.

While dough is rising, prepare raisin-nut filling. Mix all ingredients together.

Punch down dough. Roll out to a 20-by-16-inch rectangle on lightly floured surface. Brush with the 2 tablespoons melted margarine. Sprinkle filling over dough. Roll up from long side, as for a jelly roll. Cut into 10 1-inch slices.

Arrange cut side up in single layer in greased 9-inch tube pan. Repeat with second half of dough and remaining margarine and nut mixture. Make a second layer of slices in pan, placing second slices over spaces between first slices. Let rise in warm place until doubled.

Bake in 350-degree oven for 35 to 40 minutes. Separate rolls with fork to serve.   *Makes 20 rolls.*

FRESH APPLE DOUGHNUTS

5   cups all-purpose flour
4   teaspoons baking powder
1   teaspoon baking soda
2   teaspoons salt
1   teaspoon nutmeg
1   teaspoon cinnamon
¼   teaspoon mace
¼   cup shortening
1   cup sugar
3   eggs
1   teaspoon vanilla
1   cup grated raw apples
½   cup buttermilk
    Vegetable oil

Mix and sift first seven ingredients. Cream shortening. Add sugar and eggs. Beat until smooth. Add vanilla, apples and buttermilk; mix well. Add flour mixture 1 cup at a time, beating until smooth after each addition. Chill dough at least two hours.

Continued

Turn out on well floured board. Roll out dough to a thickness of one-half inch, using additional flour for handling dough if necessary. Cut with floured 2 and one-half inch doughnut cutter. Heat vegetable oil (2 inches deep) to 375 degrees. Gently drop doughnuts in hot fat, 3 or 4 at a time. Fry 1 minute on each side. Drain on paper toweling.

Makes 2 to 2½ dozen doughnuts.

DOUBLE-DELIGHT PEACH PANCAKES

1½	cups milk
3	eggs
6	tablespoons melted butter or margarine
3	cups sifted flour
2	tablespoons baking powder
¼	cup sugar
1	teaspoon salt
3	fresh peaches, peeled and diced
	Peach Sauce (recipe follows)

Combine milk, eggs and butter. Mix flour, baking powder, sugar and salt. Stir liquid ingredients into flour mixture until blended. Fold diced peaches into pancake batter. Prepare Peach Sauce; keep warm. Pour batter by ⅓ cupfuls onto hot greased griddle. Cook until pancakes are golden underneath. Turn and brown on other side. Serve pancakes with Peach Sauce.   *Makes 6 servings.*

	PEACH SAUCE:
2	tablespoons butter or margarine
2	tablespoons flour
¼	cup sugar
1	tablespoon cornstarch
3	cups orange juice
3	fresh peaches, peeled and sliced
¼	cup finely chopped maraschino cherries (optional)

Melt butter and stir in flour. Mix sugar and cornstarch and add to butter and flour mixture, stirring until blended. Gradually add orange juice. Cook, stirring constantly over low heat, until sauce bubbles and thickens. Fold in peach slices and cherries. Reheat and simmer 5 minutes.

PRINCE CHARLIE'S PANCAKES

	BATTER:
1	cup flour
2	eggs, beaten
1	cup milk
	Pinch of salt
8	teaspoons butter, for frying pancakes
	SAUCE:
2	large oranges
1	large lemon
¼	cup butter
1	cup sugar
¼	cup Drambuie
2	bananas, sliced
1	pint vanilla ice cream (optional)

Measure flour into a bowl. Make a well in the center of flour. Add eggs and mix, gradually adding milk and salt. Beat until smooth. Set aside for at least 2 hours.

Melt 1 teaspoon butter in an 8-inch frying pan. When hot, pour in ¼ cup of batter, swirling to spread evenly. Cook until top of pancake is dry. Turn and brown other side. Turn out on dish towel, and fold in quarters. Proceed with remainder of batter. This can be done ahead of time.

Grate the rinds of the oranges and lemon. Squeeze out the juice and reserve. Melt the butter in a large frying pan, add sugar and citrus juice. Bring to a boil, stir in rind and simmer 3 to 4 minutes. Remove from heat and add Drambuie.

Wrap the pancakes in foil and warm in a 300-degree oven for 10 minutes. Warm sauce, add folded pancakes and sliced bananas. Spoon sauce over all, turning pancakes once. Or serve with a scoop of vanilla ice cream, if desired, and pour sauce over all.   *Makes 8 servings.*

Soups & Stews

Soups and stews know no season. A friend once admitted that a meal wasn't a meal without a cup of soup. When he was a little boy, he recalls, his mother always set the table with a soup tureen in the middle, the ladle a welcoming flag of pleasing tastes to come. Another friend recalls she felt deprived because her mother insisted upon serving the family homemade concoctions such as hearty beef barley soup, while the large neighbor family of seven kids feasted on peanut butter and jelly sandwiches.

More and more, friends and couples get together for a soup supper, with fresh breads and special desserts, a congenial, yet less expensive, way of entertaining.

Soups and stews have a nostalgic, warming glow about them, whether they are served hot or cold. And, there is nothing more satisfying on a cold day than having a pot of soup bubbling on the stove! Those who live alone or those cooking for two have discovered the trick of enjoying homemade soup when the whim strikes by portioning soup into plastic containers, labeling them, and storing them in the freezer.

HOT SOUPS

BEAN-MUSHROOM SOUP

1   can (11¼ ounces) condensed bean with bacon soup
1   can (10¾ ounces) condensed cream of mushroom soup
2   soup cans water
3   tablespoons grated Parmesan cheese
2   tablespoons ketchup

In large saucepan, combine soups. Gradually stir in remaining ingredients. Heat, stirring occasionally.   *Makes about 5½ cups or 4 servings.*

BEEF BROTH TODDY

6   cans (10½ ounces each) condensed beef broth
3   soup cans apple cider
1½   cups light rum (optional)
1   teaspoon ground cinnamon
      Generous dash ground cloves
      Orange slices, cut in quarters

In saucepan, combine all ingredients except orange slices. Bring to boil. Reduce heat. Simmer 5 minutes. Serve with orange slices.
    Makes about 13½ cups.

CHILI TOMATO SOUP

1   can (10¾ ounces) condensed tomato soup
1   soup can water
¼   teaspoon chili powder

In saucepan, combine ingredients; simmer a few minutes to blend flavors. Stir occasionally.
    Makes about 2½ cups, 3 servings.

CORN CHOWDER

4   ears fresh corn
3   tablespoons bacon fat, butter or margarine
¾   cup diced onion
½   cup diced green pepper
¼   cup flour
1   quart milk
2   chicken bouillon cubes
¾   teaspoon salt
¼   teaspoon oregano leaves, crumbled
⅛   teaspoon ground black pepper
½   teaspoon Worcestershire sauce

Remove husks and silks from corn. Cut kernels off cobs (makes about 2½ cups). Set aside. In a large saucepan heat bacon fat, butter or margarine. Add onions and green pepper; saute for five minutes. Stir in flour; cook and stir for 2 minutes. Stir in milk and bouillon cubes. Cook and stir until thickened, about 5 minutes. Add reserved corn kernels, salt, oregano, black pepper and Worcestershire sauce. Cover and simmer for 10 minutes, stirring occasionally.   *Makes about 6 cups.*

CREAM OF PEANUT SOUP

¼   cup butter
1   cup thinly sliced celery
1   medium onion, chopped fine
2   tablespoons flour
2   quarts chicken stock or broth
1   cup creamy peanut butter
1   cup light cream

Melt butter in large saucepan over low heat and add celery and onion. Cook until tender but not browned. Add flour and stir until mixture is smooth. Gradually add chicken broth and bring to a boil. Blend in peanut butter and simmer about 15 minutes. Stir in cream just before serving. Season to taste with salt and pepper.   *Makes 8 servings.*

CREAM OF TURKEY AND MUSHROOM SOUP

3   tablespoons butter or margarine
¼   cup finely chopped onion
1   pound mushrooms, sliced
⅓   cup flour
4   cups turkey broth
1½   cups half-and-half
½   cup dry white wine
1   teaspoon salt
2   teaspoon Tabasco pepper sauce

2½   cups diced cooked turkey
¼   teaspoon dried leaf tarragon
    Chopped parsley

In large kettle, melt butter over medium heat. Add onion. Cook until tender.

Add mushrooms. Cook 10 minutes.

Blend in flour. Stir in turkey broth, half-and-half and white wine. Stir over medium heat until mixture thickens and comes to boil.

Add remaining ingredients. Simmer uncovered for 20 minutes. Garnish with chopped parsley.

Makes 4 to 6 servings.

DANISH PEA SOUP

1   pound dried split green or yellow peas
6   smoked ham hocks
1   cup chopped celery leaves
1   large onion, chopped, or 2 leeks, trimmed and chopped
1   teaspoon crumbled thyme
2   tablespoons Angostura aromatic bitters
3   quarts water
3   potatoes, cooked and diced
    Salt and pepper

In a large saucepan combine all ingredients except potatoes and salt and pepper. Simmer, covered, stirring occasionally until ham hocks are tender, about one to one and one-half hours. Add potatoes and season to taste with salt and pepper. Serve with thick slices of buttered dark bread. If any soup is left and is reheated, add a little water to thin soup to the desired consistency. *Makes 6 to 8 servings.*

NAVY BEAN SOUP

1   pound (2 cups) dry, edible navy beans
6   cups water
1   pound ham hocks
2   cups water
1   bay leaf
4   peppercorns
3   whole cloves
1   cup coarsely, chopped fresh spinach
½   cup chopped onion
⅔   cup mashed potato flakes
1   can (28 ounces) whole tomatoes
2   cloves garlic, minced
1   teaspoon basil
1   teaspoon oregano
1   teaspoon salt
½   teaspoon pepper

Place navy beans in a large soup pot with 6 cups water. Bring to a boil. Boil 2 minutes; remove from heat. Allow to stand 1 hour.

Add ham hocks, 2 cups water and bouquet garni made from bay leaf, peppercorns and cloves.

Simmer over medium heat 1 to 1½ hours or until beans are tender. Stir in spinach, onion, potato flakes, tomatoes, garlic, basil, oregano, salt and pepper. Continue to simmer 20 to 30 minutes. Remove ham hock and bouquet garni.

Trim meat from ham hocks, dice and return to soup. *Makes 3½ quarts.*

ORANGE CONSOMME

2   cups orange juice
2   cups tomato juice
1   cup beef bouillon
½   teaspoon sugar
2   whole cloves

Combine all ingredients in a saucepan. Heat. Serve in small soup cups; garnish with orange slices.

Makes 5 cups.

ORIENTAL ONION SOUP

2   large sweet Spanish onions
3   tablespoons butter
4   cups chicken broth or 3 cans (10½ ounces each)
2   teaspoons soy sauce
½   teaspoon salt
2   eggs, beaten slightly
    Mushroom slices, for garnish

Thin slice onions to equal 4 cups. Lightly saute in butter until onions are just tender. Add chicken broth, soy sauce and salt. Heat to boiling. Pour in eggs in thin stream, stirring to form shreds. Serve, garnished with slices of mushroom, if desired.

Makes 4 to 6 servings.

PICNIC SOUP

½   cup chopped green pepper
1   medium clove garlic, minced
⅛   teaspoon thyme
2   tablespoons butter or margarine
2   cans (10½ ounces each) condensed minestrone soup
2   soup cans water
1   cup sliced fresh mushrooms

Continued

In saucepan, cook green pepper, garlic and thyme in butter until green pepper is tender. Add remaining ingredients. Heat, stirring occasionally.

Makes about 5½ cups or 4 servings.

POTATO VEGETABLE SOUP

1	tablespoon butter or margarine
¾	cup thinly sliced celery
2	cans (13¾ ounces *each*) chicken broth
2	tomatoes, peeled, seeded and chopped *or*
1	can (8 ounces) tomatoes
¼	cup chopped parsley
¾	teaspoon dried leaf marjoram
½	teaspoon salt
⅛	teaspoon pepper
4	cups frozen Idaho hash brown potatoes
1½	cups cooked vegetables (green beans, carrots, limas, peas)

In a large saucepan, melt butter. Add celery and cook 5 minutes over medium heat, until tender. Add chicken broth, tomatoes, parsley, marjoram, salt and pepper. Cover and simmer over medium heat 20 minutes. Add potatoes and vegetables. Cover and cook 10 minutes longer.

Makes 8 servings.

SAVORY SOUP

4	cups water
2	cans (10¾ ounces each) condensed chicken broth
2	cups chopped cooked chicken
1	cup carrot slices
1	cup celery slices
1	cup coarsely chopped onion
½	cup regular barley
1	clove garlic, minced
1	teaspoon curry powder
1	teaspoon salt
2	medium apples, chopped (about 2 cups)

Combine all ingredients except apples in 4-quart Dutch oven. Cover. Simmer about 45 minutes.

Add apple. Simmer about 15 minutes or until barley is tender.

Serve with cheese and crackers, if desired.

Makes about 8 one-cup servings.

Note: To substitute quick barley for regular barley, add ¾ cup quick barley with apples. Proceed as recipe directs.

SO-CALLED CHICKEN SOUP

1	can (16 ounces) pork and beans in tomato sauce
1	can (10½ ounces) condensed vegetarian vegetable soup
1	can (about 8 ounces) whole kernel golden corn, undrained
½	soup can water
⅛	teaspoon onion salt
1	can (5 ounces) chunk white chicken

In large saucepan, combine all ingredients except chicken. Heat; stir occasionally. Add chicken; heat.

Makes about 5 cups, 3 to 4 servings.

SPICY HONEY CUP

3	cans (10½ ounces each) condensed consomme
3	soup cans water
½	cup honey
½	cup lemon juice
¼	teaspoon ground allspice
	Lemon slices

In large saucepan, combine all ingredients except lemon slices. Bring to boil. Reduce heat. Simmer 5 minutes. Garnish with lemon slices.

Makes about 9 cups.

STORM SOUP

4	cups chicken broth
⅔	cup dried green split peas
1	medium onion, chopped
2	cups chopped baked or broiled ham
½	teaspoon salt
¼	teaspoon freshly ground pepper
3	medium potatoes, diced
3	medium-size carrots, sliced

In a heavy kettle combine chicken broth, peas, onion, ham, salt and pepper. Place over high heat and bring to a boil. Cover and simmer over low heat for 1 hour, stirring occasionally. Add potatoes and carrots and continue to simmer for 20 minutes or until the carrots and potatoes are soft.

Makes 6 servings.

TURKISH SPINACH AND DILL SOUP

1	can (10¾ ounces each) condensed chicken broth
1	soup can water

2 teaspoons instant chopped onion
2 teaspoons parsley flakes
2 teaspoons dill weed
1/16 teaspoon ground white pepper
1 package (10 ounces) frozen chopped spinach
1½ tablespoons butter or margarine
1½ tablespoons flour
2 egg yolks
1 tablespoon lemon juice

In a large saucepot bring broth, water, onion, parsley flakes, dill weed and white pepper to boiling point. Add spinach. Simmer, covered, for 5 minutes. In a small saucepan melt butter. Add flour, cook and stir for one minute. Blend in about one-half cup of the soup mixture. Then return all to large saucepot. Cook and stir until mixture boils and thickens, about 3 minutes. Combine egg yolks with lemon juice; blend with a little of the soup mixture. Return all to saucepot; heat but do not boil. Serve hot. *Makes about 1 quart, 4 servings.*

HEARTY SOUPS & STEWS

BARBADOS STEW

1 pound pork or lamb shoulder, cut in 1-inch cubes
¼ cup flour
1¾ teaspoons salt, divided
¼ teaspoon pepper
2 tablespoons butter or margarine
1 onion, sliced
½ cup chopped celery with leaves
½ cup chopped green pepper
1 canned green chili, seeded and chopped (about 1 teaspoon)
1 clove garlic, minced
½ cup water
1 cucumber, pared, seeded and diced
2 tomatoes, peeled and diced
2 bananas

Mix flour, 1 teaspoon salt and pepper. Coat pork cubes with flour mixture. Melt butter in Dutch oven or kettle. Add meat and brown on all sides. Remove.
Add onion, celery, green pepper, chili and garlic. Cook over low heat until tender. Stir in water and remaining ¾ teaspoon salt. Return meat to pan.

Cover and simmer 1 hour or until meat is tender. Stir in cucumber and tomatoes. Simmer, covered, for 10 minutes.
Peel bananas. Slice and add to meat. Heat.
Makes 4 servings.

BAY AREA CIOPPINO

¼ cup olive or salad oil
1 cup chopped onion
4 cloves garlic, minced
1 stalk celery, chopped
1 cup chopped green pepper
½ cup chopped parsley
1 can (1 pound) Italian-style tomatoes, chopped
1 can (15 ounces) tomato sauce
1 teaspoon salt
½ teaspoon dried leaf basil
½ teaspoon dried coriander
½ teaspoon Tabasco pepper sauce
2 cups dry vermouth (or dry white wine)
1 pound boned, firm white fish (halibut, cod or bass steaks or fillets, cut in chunks)
½ pound fresh or frozen shrimp, shelled and deveined
½ pound fresh or frozen scallops
1 can (6½ ounces) crab meat (optional)
1 can (10 ounces) whole clams, drained (optional)

Heat oil in a large saucepan. Add onion, garlic, celery, green pepper, parsley. Cook until tender, stirring occasionally. Add tomatoes, tomato sauce, salt, basil, coriander and pepper sauce. Simmer, covered, for about two hours, stirring occasionally. Add wine. Cook uncovered over medium heat, for 10 minutes. Add fish, shrimp and scallops. Cover and simmer gently until fish and seafood are cooked, about 15 minutes. Add crabmeat and drain clams; simmer 5 minutes longer. Serve in soup bowls or individual casseroles accompanied by thick slices of crusty bread, lemon wedges and extra pepper sauce on the side for those who enjoy a more robust cioppino. *Makes 4 to 6 servings.*

BERMUDA FISH CHOWDER

3 pounds rockfish or sea bass
2 pounds fish fillets
1 teaspoon salt
1½ teaspoons dried leaf thyme
½ teaspoon ground cloves
1 bay leaf
¼ cup butter or margarine

Continued

2   onions, chopped
6   ribs celery, chopped
1   green pepper, chopped
1   can (28 ounces) tomatoes
1   can (8 ounces) tomato sauce
2   tablespoons chopped parsley
¾   teaspoon Worcestershire sauce
¼   teaspoon Tabasco pepper sauce
¼   teaspoon curry powder
     Lemon wedges
     Dark rum
     Sherry

Remove heads and tails of rockfish. Discard tails. Place heads, fish bodies and fillets in large kettle. Add water to cover, salt, thyme, cloves and bay leaf. Cover and simmer 15 minutes. Strain, reserving stock. Discard heads. Remove skin and bone from fish and flake the fish. In large kettle, melt butter, add onions, celery, and green pepper; cook until tender. Add tomatoes, tomato sauce, parsley, Worcestershire, pepper sauce and curry. Simmer uncovered for 15 minutes. Add reserved fish stock and flaked fish. Simmer 15 minutes. Serve in heated soup bowls, adding a squeeze of lemon juice, a dash or two each of rum and sherry, and additional pepper sauce to each serving.

Makes 8 to 10 two-cup servings.

CHICKEN SUPPER SOUP

2   cans (10¾ ounces each) condensed chicken broth
2   half breasts of chicken (about 6 ounces each)
1   cup diced raw potato
1   cup julienne-cut carrot
½   cup chopped onion
1   small clove fresh garlic, minced
1   teaspoon salt
½   bay leaf
2   medium-size fresh Bartlett pears
1   large tomato
2   cups water
1   cup whole-kernel corn (fresh, frozen or canned)
1   cup sliced zucchini
½   cup chopped celery
1   tablespoon wine vinegar
¼   teaspoon white pepper
¹⁄₁₆   teaspoon nutmeg
2   thin slices lemon
     Parmesan cheese

Combine chicken broth, chicken, potato, carrot, onion, garlic, salt and bay leaf in 4-quart kettle. Bring to boil. Cover and cook over low heat 15 minutes or until chicken is tender.

Remove chicken and cool sufficiently to handle. Remove skin and bones; shred meat. Return meat to soup kettle.

Pare, core and dice pears to measure 2 cups. Peel, seed and dice tomato. Add pears, tomato, water and all remaining ingredients except Parmesan cheese to soup kettle.

Bring to boil. Cook 5 minutes or until vegetables are tender. Skim off and discard any surface fat.

Ladle soup into serving bowls. Sprinkle with Parmesan cheese.

Makes about 5 servings or 9½ cups.

CHILI-PORK STEW

¼   cup instant minced onion
1½   teaspoons instant minced garlic
1¼   cups water, divided
2   tablespoons oil
3   pounds boneless pork shoulder, cut in 2-inch pieces
1½   teaspoons salt
3   tablespoons flour
1   tablespoon chili powder
1   teaspoon oregano leaves, crumbled
⅛   teaspoon sugar
2   pounds potatoes, peeled and quartered
1   can (1 pound) tomatoes, broken up
½   pound chorizo or pork sausage links, sliced

Rehydrate minced onion and garlic in ¼ cup of water for 10 minutes.

Heat oil in a large, heavy sauce pot or Dutch oven. Add pork. Brown well on all sides. Remove pork and set aside.

Drain all but 2 tablespoons fat from the pot. Add rehydrated onion and garlic. Saute for 5 minutes. Return pork to the pot. Add ¾ cup of the water along with the salt. Bring to boiling. Reduce heat and simmer, covered, until pork is almost tender, about 1½ hours, stirring occasionally.

Blend flour, chili powder, oregano and sugar with remaining ¼ cup water. Stir into gravy in sauce pot. Add potatoes, tomatoes and sausage. Cover and simmer until meat and potatoes are tender, 40 to 45 minutes longer. Garnish with avocado slices, if desired.   *Makes 8 servings.*

CHINESE CHICKEN SOUP

1   broiler-fryer (about 2½ pounds), cut in 6 pieces
6   cups boiling water
½   teaspoon seasoned salt
⅛   teaspoon seasoned pepper

1   bay leaf
1   tablespoon gravy seasoning and browning sauce
¼   cup butter or margarine
1   can (3 ounces) sliced mushrooms
½   cup thinly sliced onions
1   green pepper, cut in strips
3   small carrots, cut in strips
1   cup thinly sliced celery
1   tablespoon sugar
3   small tomatoes, cut in thin wedges
¼   cup cornstarch
⅓   cup cold water
2   cups cooked rice
1   can (5 ounces) Chinese noodles

Place chicken pieces, boiling water, seasonings and gravy seasoning in kettle. Cook over moderate heat until chicken is tender, about 25 minutes. Heat butter or margarine. Drain mushroom broth into kettle with chicken. Add mushrooms, onion, pepper, carrots and celery to hot fat. Saute lightly for 2 minutes, but do not brown. Stir into soup with sugar. Continue cooking for 10 minutes. Stir in tomatoes. Blend cornstarch and cold water, add to soup. Cook and stir until thickened. Simmer over low heat about 10 minutes. Serve in deep soup plates with a piece of chicken and a small ball of rice in center of each. Garnish with Chinese noodles.

Makes 6 servings.

COLONIAL-STYLE VENISON STEW

4   pounds shoulder of venison, cut in stewing pieces
2   teaspoons natural meat tenderizer, seasoned or unseasoned
1   teaspoon pepper
    Flour
½   cup diced salt pork
15   small onions
3   large carrots, sliced
3   stalks celery, sliced
2   cloves
⅛   teaspoon margarine
1   cup red wine (or wine vinegar)
1   cup beef stock or canned beef bouillon
    Garnish with parsley

Thoroughly moisten all sides of meat with water, using fingers or a brush. Sprinkle with natural meat tenderizer, coating meat well on all surfaces. Use no salt. Pierce deeply with fork at about ½-inch intervals. Sprinkle with pepper and dust lightly with flour.

Meanwhile, saute diced salt pork in Dutch oven or heavy pot. Add meat and brown over low heat, turning pieces so they brown evenly. Add remaining ingredients, cover and simmer until done, about 1 hour and 15 minutes. Test for doneness.

Thicken gravy, if desired, by rolling small balls of butter or margarine in flour and stirring into gravy. More stock or bouillon may be added if desired. Remove cloves before serving or storing.

Makes 6 servings.

DANISH DUMPLING MEATBALL SOUP

MEATBALLS:
¾   pound ground beef
⅓   cup quick or old-fashioned oats, uncooked
2   tablespoons ketchup
1   egg
¾   teaspoon salt
½   teaspoon parsley flakes
SOUP:
1   tablespoon vegetable oil
6   cups water (1½ quarts)
1½   cups carrot slices
1   cup celery slices
½   cup chopped onion
2   beef bouillon cubes
1   teaspoon salt
⅛   teaspoon pepper
DUMPLINGS:
½   cup water
¼   cup butter or margarine
½   cup original pancake mix
½   teaspoon parsley flakes
1½   teaspoon garlic powder
2   eggs

For meatballs, combine all ingredients. Mix well. Shape to form about 24 1-inch balls.

For soup, brown meatballs in oil in 4½-quart Dutch oven. Drain on absorbent paper.

Drain grease from Dutch oven. Add water, vegetables and seasonings. Cover; bring to a boil. Reduce heat; simmer 15 minutes.

For dumplings, combine water and butter in small saucepan. Bring to a boil. Add pancake mix, parsley and garlic, stirring vigorously until mixture leaves sides of pan and forms a ball. Remove from heat.

Add eggs, one at a time, beating well after each addition. To make 12 dumplings, drop by rounded tablespoonfuls into simmering soup. Cook 2 minutes or until dumplings rise to surface.

Add meatballs; cover. Continue simmering about 10 minutes or until toothpick inserted in dumplings comes out clean. *Makes about six 1½-cup servings.*

GERMAN MUSHROOM BEEF STEW

1	pound fresh mushrooms or 2 cans (6 to 8 ounces each) whole mushrooms
2	tablespoons salad oil
2	pounds shoulder or stewing beef, cut into 1½-inch cubes
3	tablespoons butter or margarine
1	cup chopped onions
1½	cups water
2	cups carrots halved lengthwise and cut into 2-inch strips
2	beef bouillon cubes
3	strips (2 inches each) lemon peel
1	tablespoon lemon juice
4	whole cloves
1	bay leaf
1	teaspoon salt
¼	teaspoon ground black pepper
1	cup grated rye bread crumbs

Rinse, pat dry and halve fresh mushrooms or drain canned mushrooms; set aside. In a large heavy saucepot heat oil. Add beef; brown on all sides, about 10 minutes. Remove and set aside. In the same saucepot melt butter; add onions and reserved mushrooms; saute for 3 minutes. Return beef to saucepot with remaining ingredients except bread crumbs. Bring to boiling point; reduce heat. Cover and simmer until beef is tender, about one and one-half to 2 hours. Stir in bread crumbs. Serve with cooked noodles, if desired.

Makes 6 to 8 portions.

HEARTY IRISH STEW

1	container packaged stew mix
1½	pounds lamb stew meat, cut into 1-inch cubes
4	large potatoes, peeled and cut into ¾-inch slices
2	medium onions, sliced
6	slices bacon, diced
½	teaspoon dill weed
¼	teaspoon marjoram
	Pepper to taste
2	cups chicken broth

In a 4-quart saucepan, evenly sprinkle stew mix over meat. Pierce meat with a fork. Let stand two minutes. Add remaining ingredients; mix well. Cover and simmer, stirring occasionally, 1 hour or until lamb is tender.   *Makes 4 to 6 servings.*

HUNGARIAN STEW

1	container packaged stew mix
1½	pounds stew beef, cut into 1-inch cubes
6	medium potatoes, peeled and quartered
¾	cup beef broth
⅔	cup water
1	medium onion, sliced
¼	cup tomato paste
3	tablespoons paprika
½	teaspoon caraway seed
	Pepper, to taste
1	cup sour cream

In a 4-quart saucepan, evenly sprinkle stew mix over meat. Pierce meat with a fork; let stand 2 minutes. Add potatoes, broth, water, onion, tomato paste, paprika, caraway seed and pepper. Simmer, covered, 1 hour. Stir occasionally. Add sour cream. Heat through; do not boil.   *Makes 4 to 6 servings.*

INDIAN CURRIED STEW

1	container packaged stew mix
1	chicken (about 2½–3 pounds), cut up and skin removed
1½	cups water
¼	cup raisins
2	cloves garlic, minced
1	large onion, finely chopped
1	medium apple, peeled and finely chopped
2–3	tablespoons curry powder
¼	teaspoon ground thyme

In large skillet, evenly sprinkle stew mix on chicken; pierce deeply with a fork and let stand 2 minutes. Add remaining ingredients, mix well and bring to a boil. Cover and simmer, stirring occasionally, 30–40 minutes or until chicken is tender. Serve over rice; sprinkle with coconut.   *Makes 4 servings.*

MACARONI FISH STEW

1	cup thinly sliced celery
⅓	cup thinly sliced onion
¼	cup butter or margarine
1	package (1 pound) frozen haddock or sole fillets, partially thawed, cut in cubes
2	teaspoons salt
1	small clove garlic, crushed
1	bay leaf

1 can (16 ounces) cut green beans, undrained
1 can (16 ounces) sliced carrots, undrained
2 cups uncooked elbow macaroni (8 ounces)
2 cups milk

Cook celery and onion in butter until crisp-tender. Add fish, salt, garlic and bay leaf. Drain bean and carrot liquids. Add enough water to vegetable liquid to measure one and one-half quarts (6 cups). Stir into fish mixture. Simmer 15 minutes; bring to boil. Gradually add uncooked macaroni. Boil 10 minutes, stirring occasionally, or until macaroni is tender. Add drained vegetables and milk; heat to serving temperature. Serve immediately.
Makes 4 to 6 servings.

MEATBALL AND BEAN SOUP

1 pound ground beef
¾ cup soft bread crumbs
3 tablespoons ketchup
1 egg, lightly beaten
1 teaspoon salt
  Worcestershire sauce
2 tablespoons oil
2 beef bouillon cubes
2 cups boiling water
1 cup carrots cut into ½-inch-thick slices
1 can (1 pound) baked beans in tomato sauce
1 package (9 ounces) frozen cut green beans
⅓ cup small noodles

In a medium bowl, lightly combine beef, bread crumbs, ketchup, egg, salt and 1 tablespoon Worcestershire sauce. Shape into about 18 meatballs. In a large skillet, heat oil until hot. Brown meatballs on all sides. Remove meatballs and set aside. In a medium saucepan, dissolve bouillon cubes in boiling water. Add carrots; simmer, covered, for 10 minutes. Add baked beans, green beans, noodles, 1 teaspoon Worcestershire sauce and reserved meatballs. Bring to the boiling point. Reduce heat and simmer, covered, for 10 minutes. Serve with hot, crisp Italian bread and a green salad, if desired.
Makes 6 portions.

NEW ENGLAND FISH CHOWDER

4 cans (10¾ ounces) condensed cream of chicken soup
2 soup cans milk
2 soup cans water

4 medium carrots, cut in 2-inch sticks (about 2 cups)
2 cups cubed potatoes
¼ cup chopped parsley
2 medium bay leaves
2 pounds fillets of white fish, cut in 1-inch pieces
1 can (about 16 ounces) stewed tomatoes
¼ cup lemon juice

In large saucepan, combine soup, milk, water, carrots, potatoes, parsley and bay leaves. Cover. Cook over low heat for 30 minutes.
Add remaining ingredients. Cook 10 minutes more or until done, occasionally stirring gently. Remove bay leaves. *Makes 6 servings.*

ORANGE MULLIGATAWNY SOUP

2 cups orange juice
2 quarts water
1 broiler-fryer chicken, whole or cut in serving pieces
1 cup chopped celery and leaves
1 cup sliced carrots
1 cup chopped onion
2 apples, pared, cored and diced, divided
2 tomatoes, peeled, diced, divided
1½ tablespoons salt
1 teaspoon curry powder
⅓ cup uncooked regular rice

In a large kettle, combine orange juice, water, chicken, celery, carrots, onion, 1 apple, 1 tomato and salt. Cover and simmer for 1 hour. Remove chicken, remove meat from bones, cut into bite-size pieces and return to broth. Add remaining apple, tomato, curry powder and rice; cover and simmer for 30 minutes. *Makes 2¾ quarts or 6 servings.*

PALM BEACH BEEF STEW

  Salad oil
3 pounds beef for stew, cut in 2-inch cubes
  Salt
  Pepper
1 can (10½ ounces) condensed beef broth
½ cup brandy (optional)
1 medium onion, sliced
  Peel of 1 orange, coarsely chopped
6 medium potatoes, peeled and quartered

Continued

2   tablespoons butter or margarine
2   large stalks celery, sliced
1   cup walnuts, coarsely chopped
3 or 4   soda crackers, crumbled

Heat enough oil in Dutch oven to cover bottom of pan. Brown meat on all sides. Season with salt and pepper. Add broth, brandy, orange peel. Cover and cook over medium-low heat 2 hours. Add potatoes and cook 30 minutes more or until tender. Meanwhile, saute celery in butter 5 minutes. Add walnuts; set aside. When meat and potatoes are done, arrange in serving bowl and keep warm. Pour juices, onion and orange peel in electric blender. Add cracker crumbs. Blend on low speed until smooth. Return to pan and bring to a boil, stirring. Pour hot sauce over meat and potatoes. Garnish with celery and walnuts.   *Makes 6 servings.*

PORK AND BRUSSELS SPROUTS RAGOUT

2½   pounds lean pork shoulder, cut in 1-inch cubes
⅓   cup flour
3   tablespoons butter
2   tablespoons shortening
1½   cups coarsely chopped onion
1   clove garlic, minced
2   teaspoons salt
½   teaspoon pepper
2   teaspoons soy sauce
1   cup beef bouillon
1   cup dry red wine (optional)
1   can (8 ounces) water chestnuts, sliced (optional)
2   packages (10 ounces each) frozen Brussels sprouts
    Chopped parsley
    Rice, noodles or boiled potatoes

Shake pork with flour in large paper bag until coated. Melt one and one-half tablespoons of the butter and all of shortening in Dutch oven or large skillet. Add pork and saute until well browned; turn meat frequently to brown evenly. Remove pork and set aside.

Add remaining one and one-half tablespoons butter to Dutch oven; add onion and garlic and saute until lightly browned. Add pork, salt, pepper, soy sauce, bouillon and wine to onion mixture. Bring mixture to a boil; reduce heat and simmer one and one-half hours.

Stir occasionally during cooking period; if necessary add water to adjust consistency. Add water chestnuts and Brussels sprouts and cook 15 minutes longer or until Brussels sprouts are tender. Serve sprinkled with parsley. Serve with rice, noodles or boiled potatoes, as desired.   *Makes 6 servings.*

QUICK BEEF STEW

1½   cups cooked cubed beef
1   cup chopped onion
1   small clove garlic, minced
2   tablespoons butter or margarine
1   can (15 ounces) beef gravy
2   large carrots, cooked and cut in 1-inch pieces
2   medium potatoes, cooked and cubed
½   teaspoon salt
    Dash black pepper

In saucepan, brown beef and cook onion with garlic in butter until tender. Add gravy, vegetables and seasonings. Heat; stir occasionally. Garnish with parsley if desired.

Makes about 5 cups, 4 to 6 servings.

BEEF BURGUNDY STEW

4   slices bacon
2½   pounds beef cubes (about 1½-inch)
1   can (15 ounces) beef gravy
1½   cups Burgundy or other dry red wine
2   large cloves garlic, minced
1   teaspoon salt
½   teaspoon thyme leaves, crushed
⅛   teaspoon pepper
1½   pounds small whole white onions (about 24)
½   pound sliced fresh mushrooms (about 2 cups)
1   cup raw regular rice
    Chopped parsley

In large heavy pan, cook bacon until crisp. Remove and crumble. Pour off all but 2 tablespoons drippings. Brown beef in drippings. Add gravy, Burgundy, garlic and seasonings. Cover. Cook over low heat 1 hour 45 minutes. Add onions and mushrooms; cook 25 minutes. Add rice. Cook 25 minutes more or until done. Stir occasionally. Stir in bacon; garnish with parsley.

Makes about 10 cups, 6 to 8 servings.

QUICK CHICKEN STEW

½   cup diagonally sliced carrots
½   cup chopped onion
¼   cup diced green pepper
2   tablespoons butter or margarine
¼   teaspoon thyme leaves, crushed
1   cup cubed cooked potatoes
1   can (10¾ ounces) condensed cream of mushroom soup
1   cup water

1   can (5 ounces) chunk white chicken
¼   teaspoon salt
½   teaspoon pepper

In saucepan, cook carrots, onion and green pepper in butter with thyme until tender. Add remaining ingredients. Heat, stirring occasionally.

Makes about 4 cups or 2 servings.

RAGOUT MISTRAL

¼   cup butter
1   cup chopped shallots or leeks
3   pounds lean chuck, cut into 1-inch cubes
     Salt and pepper
     Flour
2   cups dry French white wine
1   can (10½ ounces) condensed consomme
3   tomatoes, peeled and chopped
3   zucchini, cut into 1-inch-thick slices
1   can (15 ounces) baby whole carrots, drained
1   can (14 ounces) coeur de celeri (hearts of celery), drained
¼   cup coarsely chopped olives

Heat butter in a Dutch oven or kettle. Saute garlic and shallots until golden. Sprinkle meat with salt and pepper and roll cubes in flour. Brown meat cubes on all sides in Dutch oven. Add wine, consomme, and tomatoes. Cover and simmer gently, stirring occasionally, for 1½ hours or until meat is tender.

Add zucchini and cook 10 minutes or until zucchini are tender. Add carrots and celery, cut into halves, and olives. Reheat until bubbly.

Serve with baguette (French bread).

Makes about 6 servings.

ROCK LOBSTER FISH STEW

¼   cup oil
1   large onion, chopped
1   clove garlic, chopped
2   cups sliced celery
2   potatoes, peeled and diced
1   pound frozen South African rock lobster tails
1   package (1 pound) frozen cod fillets
3   cups chicken broth
2   cups tomato juice
1   cup dry white wine
     Juice of ½ lemon
1½   cups cooked rice
     Salt

In a kettle, heat oil and saute onion and garlic until golden, about 5 minutes. Add celery and potatoes. With sharp knife cut through shells of frozen rock lobster tails crosswise into 1-inch slices. Cut frozen cod fillets into 1-inch cubes. Add rock lobster and cod pieces to stew. Stir in chicken broth, tomato juice, wine and lemon juice. Cover and simmer for 20 minutes or until vegetables are tender. Stir in rice and season to taste with salt. Serve garnished with chopped parsley or dill, with chunks of crusty bread.

Makes 6 servings.

ROMA SAUSAGE SOUP

½   pound hot Italian sausage, cut in ½-inch pieces
2   cups coarsely chopped cabbage
½   cup chopped green pepper
1   medium clove garlic, crushed
½   teaspoon Italian seasoning, crushed
1   can (11½ ounces) condensed bean with bacon soup
1½   soup cans water
1   can (15 ounces) cheese ravioli, in tomato sauce
1   can (about 8 ounces) kidney beans, undrained
     Generous dash pepper
     Grated Parmesan cheese

In large saucepan, cook sausage until done; pour off fat. Add cabbage and green pepper and cook with garlic and Italian seasoning until just tender. Add soup; gradually stir in water. Add remaining ingredients except cheese. Heat. Stir occasionally. Serve with cheese.   *Makes about 8 cups, 6 servings.*

THREE-BEAN CHOWDER

2   cans (19 ounces each) chunky 3-bean vegetable soup
1   can (about 7 ounces) tuna, drained and flaked
1   cup quick-cooking rice, uncooked
1   can (about 8 ounces) cut green beans, drained
2   teaspoons lemon juice
¼   teaspoon hot pepper sauce

In a saucepan, combine ingredients. Bring to boil; reduce heat. Cover; simmer 10 minutes or until done. Stir occasionally.

Makes about 6 cups, 6 servings.

YELLOW PEA SOUP WITH HAM DUMPLINGS

1	pound quick-cooking dried yellow split peas, washed
4	quarts boiling water
2	bay leaves
2	pounds pork neck bones
1	large onion, chopped
2	teaspoons salt
½	teaspoon pepper
½	teaspoon dill weed
1	tablespoon gravy and browning sauce
2	leeks, chopped
	HAM DUMPLINGS:
¾	cup milk
2	cups biscuit mix
1	can (6¾ ounces) ham, shredded
2	tablespoons minced parsley

Combine the washed peas, boiling water and bay leaves in a large kettle. Bring the mixture to a boil. Reduce heat and simmer for 1 hour, stirring often. Add remaining ingredients. Cover, simmer about 40 minutes, stirring often.

To make dumplings, stir milk into mix. Stir in shredded ham and parsley. Drop by spoonfuls into center of simmering soup. Cover. Simmer 10 minutes. *Makes 6 dinner servings.*

SOUPE AU PISTOU

2	quarts chicken broth
3	medium potatoes, peeled and cut in 1-inch pieces
½	pound fresh green beans, cut up, or 1 can (16 ounces) cut green beans
3	carrots, sliced
1	medium onion, chopped
1	tablespoon salt
¼	teaspoon pepper
⅓	pound zucchini or crookneck squash, sliced, or 1 package (10 ounces) frozen zucchini sliced
1	can (16 ounces) beans, drained (kidney or navy)
4	cloves garlic, mashed
1	can (6 ounces) tomato paste
1	tablespoon dried basil
⅓	cup grated Parmesan cheese
½	cup chopped parsley
¼	cup olive oil

In large kettle, combine chicken broth, potatoes, green beans, carrots, onion, salt and pepper. Bring to a boil and simmer, covered, 10 minutes. Add squash and beans. Simmer 10 minutes more or until all vegetables are tender. Meanwhile, prepare sauce. Mix garlic, tomato paste, basil, Parmesan and parsley. Using a wire whisk, gradually beat in oil, a teaspoon at a time, until mixture resembles a thick sauce. Just before serving, stir sauce into hot soup. Warm, crusty bread is a good accompaniment. *Makes 8 to 10 servings.*

Note: It is possible to substitute 6 to 8 chicken bouillon cubes and 2 quarts water for chicken broth.

SLOOPER SOUP

4	cups chicken broth
⅔	cup dried green split peas
1	medium onion, chopped
2	cups cubed cooked ham
½	teaspoon salt
¼	teaspoon pepper
3	medium potatoes, diced
3	carrots, sliced

In a heavy kettle, combine chicken broth, peas, onion, ham, salt and pepper. Place over high heat and bring to a boil. Cover and simmer over low heat for 1 hour, stirring occasionally.

Add potatoes and carrots. Continue simmering for 20 minutes or until carrots and potatoes are soft. *Makes 6 servings.*

OLD-FASHIONED CHICKEN VEGETABLE SOUP

6	cups water
3	pounds chicken parts
2	tablespoons Worcestershire sauce
2½	teaspoons salt
1	cup diagonally sliced carrots
1	cup sliced celery
1	cup chopped onion
½	cup alphabet noodles
1	cup sliced zucchini
1	cup fresh or canned corn kernels
1	cup seeded and diced tomato

In a large sauce pot, bring water to boil. Add chicken, Worcestershire sauce and salt. Simmer, covered, for 40 minutes. Remove chicken from pot; set aside to cool for 10 minutes. Pour broth through a fine strainer. Wipe out pot and return broth to pot. (If desired, chill broth and remove fat.) Remove cooled chicken meat from the bones; cut into ½-inch pieces.

Add chicken to broth along with carrots, celery, onion and noodles. Bring to a boil. Reduce heat and simmer, covered, for 7 minutes. Add zucchini and corn; simmer, covered, for 5 minutes. Stir in tomatoes. Cook 5 minutes longer.

Makes 6 portions or 8 cups.

LAMB LENTIL SOUP

3	pounds lamb neck slices, boned
1	tablespoon butter
1	cup finely sliced leek (white part only)
½	cup chopped onion
½	cup diced carrot
½	cup diced green pepper
1½	cups (½ pound) lentils
2½	teaspoons salt
⅛	teaspoon pepper
¼	teaspoon ground thyme
¼	teaspoon oregano leaves
2	quarts cold water
1	can (8 ounces) stewed tomatoes

Brown neck slices in large skillet. Remove lamb and, using same skillet, melt 1 tablespoon butter. Saute leek, onion, carrot and green pepper until crisp-tender, about 5 minutes. Set aside.

Bring lentils, seasonings, water and tomatoes to a boil in large kettle. Add lamb. Reduce heat and simmer covered about 1 and ½ hours, stirring occasionally and adding more water as needed. Add sauteed vegetables to lentil mixture. Simmer covered about 30 minutes longer. Before serving, adjust consistency with additional water, if necessary.

Makes 2 quarts.

COUNTRY-STYLE HAM-AND-BEAN SOUP

1	cup diced cooked ham
½	teaspoon sage
2	tablespoons butter or margarine
1	can (10¾ ounces) condensed chicken gumbo soup
1	can (10¾ ounces) condensed chicken noodle soup
1½	soup cans water
1	package (10 ounces) frozen mixed vegetables
1	can (15½ ounces) kidney beans, drained

In large saucepan, brown ham with sage (rub sage in palm of hand) in butter. Add remaining ingredients. Bring to boil; reduce heat. Simmer 10 minutes or until done; stir occasionally.

Makes about 7½ cups, 4 servings.

COLD SOUPS

CHILLED CUCUMBER SOUP

1	cup condensed chicken broth
2	tablespoons lemon juice
¼	cup finely chopped onion
1	teaspoon salt
½	teaspoon dried dillweed, crushed
	Dash garlic powder
1	teaspoon grated lemon rind
1	cup sour cream
1	cup yogurt
2	medium cucumbers, peeled and chopped
	Cucumber slices
	Lemon slices

In blender, combine broth, lemon juice, onion, salt, dill, garlic and rind. Blend until smooth.

Add sour cream and yogurt. Mix until just blended.

Stir in chopped cucumber. Chill
Garnish with cucumber and lemon slices.

Makes about 4 one-cup servings.

CHILLED LEMON SOUP

3½	cups chicken broth
2	tablespoons quick-cooking tapioca
2	eggs
2	tablespoons fresh lemon juice
1	tablespoon grated fresh lemon rind
½	teaspoon salt
¹⁄₁₆	teaspoon cayenne
1	cup heavy cream

Heat chicken broth to boiling point in medium saucepan. Stir in tapioca. Cover and simmer 10 minutes. In small bowl, beat eggs with lemon juice, rind, salt and cayenne; stir in cream. Stir a little hot mixture into egg mixture. Stir warmed egg mixture into saucepan. Cook over very low heat, stirring constantly, until mixture thickens and coats a spoon. Remove from heat. Cool. Chill thoroughly. Garnish with thin lemon slices, sprinkle with paprika.

Makes about 4¼ cups.

FROSTY TOUCH OF MINT

2	cans (10¾ ounces each) condensed cream of potato soup
2	soup cans milk
½	teaspoon dried mint leaves, crushed

Continued

In saucepan, combine ingredients. Heat; stir occasionally. Pour into blender; blend until smooth, or use rotary beater. Chill 6 hours or more. Garnish with mint leaves if desired.

Makes about 5 cups, 4 servings.

GAZPACHO

2	whole pimientos
2	tablespoons olive oil or vegetable oil
1	teaspoon salt
1	small clove garlic, peeled
1½	pounds fresh ripe tomatoes, cored and quartered
2	tablespoons plain dry bread crumbs
2	tablespoons red wine vinegar
1	can (12-ounce) tomato juice
1	red pepper, seeded and quartered
1	green pepper, seeded and quartered
1	cucumber, peeled, quartered and seeded
1	bunch green onions or scallions
½	cup plain or seasoned croutons

Put pimiento, oil, salt and garlic in food processor fitted with chopping blade. Cover and process 8 to 10 seconds.

Add tomatoes, bread crumbs and vinegar. Cover and process 15 to 25 seconds longer until pureed.

Strain tomato mixture into large bowl or serving tureen. Discard seeds and tomato skins. Stir in tomato juice. Chill thoroughly before serving.

For topping, put red pepper in food processor fitted with chopping blade. Cover and process 3 to 4 seconds, stopping and starting frequently until pepper is coarsely chopped.

Repeat to chop green pepper and cucumber, keeping vegetables separate.

Fit processor with slicing disc and slice green onions. Put chopped and sliced vegetables and croutons in separate bowls.

To serve, ladle soup into individual dishes. Top with vegetables and croutons.

Makes about 4½ cups soup.

ZIPPY GAZPACHO

3	cups cocktail vegetable juice
1	green pepper, halved and seeded
1	cucumber, halved and peeled
1	small onion, coarsely chopped
1	clove garlic
1½	tablespoons Worcestershire sauce
⅛	teaspoon salt
¼	cup olive or salad oil
¼	cup wine vinegar
4	scallions or green onions
1	tomato
1	cup garlic croutons

In the jar of an electric blender, combine vegetable juice, coarsely chopped green pepper, half of the coarsely chopped cucumber, onion, garlic, Worcestershire sauce and salt. Blend until smooth. Stir in oil and vinegar. Chill well.

Meanwhile, finely dice remaining half of the cucumber. Thinly slice the scallions and dice the tomato. Pour chilled soup into chilled bowls and serve with the prepared diced vegetables, croutons and lemon wedges, if desired.   *Makes 1 quart.*

ICED PARSLEY SOUP

4	ounces parsley
1	pound potatoes
1	onion
1	ounce (2 tablespoons) butter
1½	pints chicken stock (water and stock cube will do)
½	pint milk
	Salt and freshly milled black pepper
¼	pint light cream

Thoroughly wash parsley, then remove and discard the coarser items. Chop the remainder coarsely. Scrape potatoes and cut into large dices. Peel and finely chop onion. Melt butter in a large saucepan. Add onion, cover with a lid and fry gently without browning for a few moments, until the onions are soft. Add the potatoes and chopped parsley and fry a few moments over low heat. Stir in the stock and milk. Season with salt and pepper and bring to a boil. Cover with a lid and simmer gently for one hour. Draw the pan off the heat and blend to make a puree. Set aside to cool. Stir in cream, check the seasoning, and if necessary thin down with more stock. Chill well before serving.   *Makes 6 servings.*

POTATO AND ROQUEFORT SWIRL SOUP

3	medium onions, thinly sliced
2	tablespoons butter
4	cups thinly sliced potatoes
½	cup thinly sliced celery
3	cups chicken broth
1	cup fresh chopped watercress
¼	cup fresh chopped parsley
¼	cup fresh chopped dill
½	cup water
8	ounces Roquefort cheese, crumbled
1	cup heavy cream
	Salt
	White pepper

Saute onions in butter until transparent. Add potatoes, celery and chicken broth. Simmer, covered, for 25 minutes, until vegetables are tender. Put mixture through food mill or blender.

Measure 1 cup of this pureed mixture. Combine with watercress, parsley, dill and water in saucepan. Simmer, covered, for 15 minutes. Remove from heat. Add Roquefort and put mixture through food mill.

Add ¾ cup heavy cream to potato mixture and remaining ¼ cup cream to Roquefort mixture. Season each mixture with salt and pepper to taste. Chill thoroughly.

Pour potato mixture into attractive soup tureen, then pour Roquefort mixture into center. Swirl to form contrasting abstract design. For more geometric design, move two knives, one in each hand, simultaneously in sweeping motion. Garnish with watercress, if desired.   *Makes 6 to 8 servings.*

VICHYSSOISE

4	leeks, sliced (white part only)
1	medium onion, sliced
¼	cup butter or margarine
2	pounds potatoes, pared and thinly sliced (6 medium)
1	quart chicken broth
1	tablespoon salt
2½	cups milk
2	cups half-and-half or light cream
	Chopped chives

In deep kettle lightly brown leeks and onion in butter. Add potatoes, broth and salt; boil 30 minutes or until potatoes are very tender. Puree in electric blender or rub through a fine strainer. Add half-and-half; chill thoroughly. Serve garnished with chives.   *Makes 8 to 10 servings.*

Salads & Salad Dressings

Salads are altering our eating habits. Even the so-called meat-and-potatoes guy is adding salads to his meals.

Others—from the Manhattan skyscraper window washer to the West Virginia coal miner—find salads to be pleasing, low-calorie additions to the diet.

Slimmer salads with protein items such as meats, fish, cheese, or eggs make a complete meal. And, don't you often yearn for a platter of fresh fruit, possibly with sherbet or cottage cheese, as a refreshing salad lunch?

Add hearty salads to your menus for food-loving family and friends. They won't complain about being served "just" a salad.

VEGETABLE SALADS

ATHENIAN POTATO SALAD

2	pounds new potatoes
2	tablespoons minced parsley
1	bunch celery, minced
½	cup diced black or green olives (preferably Greek)
1	tablespoon grated Parmesan cheese
¼	teaspoon dill
	Pinch leaf rosemary, crumbled
1	teaspoon salt
¼	teaspoon ground black pepper
	Juice of 1 lemon
2	tablespoons olive oil
¼	cup mayonnaise or salad dressing
8	ounces cottage cheese
⅓–½	cup milk

Boil potatoes until fork tender. Peel and slice fairly thin.

Mix together cottage cheese, mayonnaise, ⅓ cup milk, lemon juice and olive oil. Add Parmesan cheese, dill, rosemary, salt, pepper and 1 tablespoon parsley.

Add potatoes, olives and celery to dressing. Toss gently until well coated. Add additional milk if necessary.

Chill at least 2 hours to let flavor develop. Before serving, toss salad again and sprinkle with remaining 1 tablespoon parsley.   *Makes 6 to 8 servings.*

AVOCADO-TOMATO SALAD

1	teaspoon lemon juice
1	ripe avocado, peeled and diced
2	medium-sized tomatoes, peeled, seeded and cut into small pieces
2	tablespoons finely chopped onion
2	tablespoons finely chopped parsley
¼	cup peanut oil
2	tablespoons white vinegar
1	teaspoon salt
	Generous dash pepper
	Crisp salad greens

Sprinkle lemon juice over diced avocado. Add tomato, onion and parsley. Combine peanut oil, vinegar, salad and pepper in a small jar. Cover tightly and shake until well mixed. Pour over avocado mixture; toss gently. Chill thoroughly. Serve on crisp salad greens.   *Makes 5 servings.*

AVOCADO SALAD

2	avocados, peeled and sliced
2	cups spinach leaves
2	cups torn lettuce
½	red onion, sliced
3	tablespoons soy sauce
¼	cup fresh lemon juice
1	tablespoon salad oil
⅛	teaspoon dried leaf oregano
⅛	teaspoon dried leaf tarragon
1	tablespoon toasted sesame seeds

In a large bowl mix together avocado, spinach, lettuce and red onion. In smaller bowl mix together remaining ingredients, pour over avocado and toss well. Serve immediately.   *Makes 4 servings.*

CABBAGE AND CARROT SLAW

½	cup mayonnaise
1	tablespoon sugar
2	tablespoons fresh lemon juice
1	teaspoon salt
¼	teaspoon pepper
6	cups shredded cabbage
2	cups shredded pared carrots
1	cup fresh orange sections

In a large bowl blend together mayonnaise, sugar, lemon juice, salt and pepper. Add cabbage, carrots and orange sections; mix well. Cover and refrigerate several hours.   *Makes 6 servings.*

CHILLED BEAN AND PEPPER SALAD

1	can (16 ounces) pork and beans in tomato sauce
1½	cups cooked rice
¼	cup chili sauce
¼	cup diced green pepper
¼	cup chopped dill pickle
2	tablespoons finely chopped onion

In a bowl, combine all ingredients. Chill 4 hours or more. Serve on lettuce.

Makes about 3½ cups, 6 servings.

CHUCK WAGON BEAN-POTATO SALAD

1½	pounds medium-size potatoes
4	slices bacon
¼	cup chopped onion
¼	cup chopped celery
2	tablespoons chopped dill pickle
3	tablespoons vinegar
1	teaspoon dry mustard
1	teaspoon salt
½	teaspoon pepper
½	teaspoon sugar
1	can (16 ounces) pork and beans in tomato sauce

Cook potatoes with skins in boiling water until tender, about 35 minutes. Peel and slice while hot. Meanwhile, cook bacon in a skillet until crisp; remove, crumble and set aside. Pour off all but 2 tablespoons fat. Add onion, celery and pickle and saute until tender. Blend in vinegar, mustard, salt, pepper and sugar. Gently stir in beans and bacon; heat through. Turn beans into serving bowl; add hot sliced potatoes. Toss and serve immediately.
Makes 6 servings.

CREAMY COLE SLAW

8	cups green cabbage, shredded
½	cup green pepper, diced
½	cup Bermuda or Spanish onion, diced
½	cup carrots, shredded
1	small apple, grated
3	tablespoons parsley, minced
	Dressing
2	tablespoons wine vinegar
2	tablespoons lemon juice
1	tablespoon Dijon-type mustard
1	teaspoon salt
2½	teaspoons sugar
½	teaspoon celery seed
½	cup sour cream

Mix vinegar, lemon juice, mustard, salt, sugar, celery seed and sour cream together in small bowl. Pour over vegetables. Mix together. Cover and refrigerate for several hours. *Makes 6 to 8 servings.*

CRUNCHY CELERY SLAW

1	stalk celery
¼	cup oil
¼	cup pineapple juice

1½	tablespoons lemon juice
1	teaspoon poppy seed
½	teaspoon salt
⅛	teaspoon ground white pepper
½	cup grated carrots

Trim ends of celery. (Use tops for soups, stews, etc.) Separate celery into ribs. Thinly slice on the diagonal. (Makes about 6 cups.) Combine oil, pineapple juice, lemon juice, poppy seed, salt and white pepper. Pour over celery. Add carrots. Toss until well mixed. Serve on lettuce leaves, if desired.
Makes 6 to 8 servings.

EASY POTATO SALAD

3	cups water
1	package (5.5 ounces) Idaho hash brown potatoes
½	cup mayonnaise
2	tablespoons cider vinegar
1¼	teaspoons salt
1	tablespoon chopped chives
¼	teaspoon dried dill weed
1	cup chopped celery
1	medium tomato, peeled and chopped

Heat water to boil in large saucepan. Add hash brown potatoes, cover and cook 5 minutes, until tender but not soft. Immediately drain in strainer and then rinse under cold running water; drain well. In large bowl blend mayonnaise with vinegar, salt, chives and dill weed. Add drained potatoes and celery. Mix well. Cover and chill several hours. Just before serving stir in tomato. Turn into bowl lined with salad greens.   *Makes 4 to 6 servings.*

ENSALADA DE CEBOLLA ESPANA

1	large sweet Spanish onion
3	oranges
2	pounds fresh spinach
8	slices crisp cooked bacon, crumbled
2	tablespoons cider vinegar
1	tablespoon sugar
¼	teaspoon salt
¼	teaspoon dry mustard
⅓	cup salad oil

Peel and thinly slice onion. Separate into rings. Peel and slice oranges. Cut slices in halves. Wash spinach thoroughly and remove stems. Break leaves into bite-size pieces. In salad bowl, combine onion rings, oranges and spinach. Sprinkle with bacon. Combine remaining ingredients for dressing. Shake or beat well. Toss salad with dressing to coat thoroughly.   *Makes 8 servings.*

GARDEN FRESH PICNIC POTATO SALAD

1¼	pounds potatoes
2	tablespoons salad oil
1	tablespoon chopped fresh onion
1	tablespoon fresh lemon juice
1½	teaspoons salt
¼	teaspoon pepper
¼	cup chopped green pepper
1	cup chopped celery
1	cup diced cooked ham
8	hard-cooked eggs, diced
½	cup mayonnaise
	Lettuce

Cook potatoes in boiling water, covered, until tender. Peel and slice. Add salad oil, onion, lemon juice, salt and pepper. Mix well and let stand 1 or 2 hours. Add celery, green pepper, ham, eggs and mayonnaise. Mix lightly and spoon into a container with a tight lid. Refrigerate until well chilled. Pack in insulated chest to carry to picnic. Serve on lettuce.   *Makes 8 servings.*

GERMAN POTATO SALAD

1	package (16 ounces) frozen crinkle cut french fries
6	slices bacon (¼ pound)
½	cup fresh frozen chopped onions
2	tablespoons bacon drippings
1	egg, beaten
⅓	cup vinegar
⅓	cup water
⅓	cup sugar
2	teaspoons flour
¾	teaspoon dry mustard
½	teaspoon salt
1½	cups thinly sliced celery
⅓	cup thinly sliced sour pickle

Prepare french fries as package directs. Cut bacon into 1-inch pieces. Fry until crisp. Remove from pan. Saute onion in drippings until soft. Combine egg, vinegar and water. Mix together sugar, flour, mustard and salt. Stir into egg mixture. Add to skillet. Cook and stir until mixture boils and thickens. Add bacon pieces. Toss with french fries, celery and pickle. *Makes 1½ quarts (6 to 8 servings).*

GRANNY'S APPLE POTATO SALAD

| ¾ | cup mayonnaise |
| ¾ | cup sour cream |

4	ounces blue cheese, crumbled
1	teaspoon salt
½	teaspoon dill weed
⅛	teaspoon pepper
2	Granny Smith or other tart-sweet apples
2	tablespoons lemon juice
6	cups cubed cooked potatoes
3	cups cooked ham, cut in narrow strips

In large bowl, mix mayonnaise, sour cream, blue cheese, salt, dill weed and pepper. Core and chop apples. Mix with lemon juice. Add to dressing with potatoes and ham. Chill.   *Makes 6 servings.*

HOT CELERY WALDORF SALAD

2	tablespoons butter or margarine
3	cups diagonally sliced celery
½	cup finely chopped onion
1	cup diced unpeeled apple
½	cup coarsely chopped walnuts
⅓	cup dark raisins
¼	cup mayonnaise
2	teaspoons fresh lemon juice
¾	teaspoon salt
⅛	teaspoon ground black pepper

In a large skillet, melt butter. Add celery and onion. Cook over moderate heat until celery is crisp-tender, about 5 minutes. Stir in apple, walnuts and raisins. Cook and stir for 1 minute.

In a small bowl, combine mayonnaise, lemon juice, salt and black pepper. Spoon over celery mixture in skillet. Stir gently. Serve hot. If desired, sprinkle with chopped celery leaves.
  Makes 6 servings.

HOT LETTUCE SALAD

¼	pound bacon
2	tablespoons chopped fresh onion
½	teaspoon dry mustard
½	teaspoon salt
½	teaspoon sugar
2	tablespoons vinegar
3	tablespoons water
1	tablespoon fresh lemon juice
1	teaspoon flour
4	cups torn lettuce (1 small head)

Cook bacon in skillet. Remove and drain, reserving 1 tablespoon bacon fat in skillet. Crumble bacon and reserve. Add onion to skillet and cook until tender. Add remaining ingredients except lettuce; mix well. Heat until mixture comes to a boil; simmer 1 minute. Combine lettuce and crumbled bacon in large bowl, add hot dressing and toss lightly to mix well. Serve immediately.   *Makes 4 servings.*

JUGGED VEGETABLES

MARINADE:
1 cup cider or tarragon vinegar
1 cup water
1 tablespoon assorted seasonings
1 tablespoon sugar
¾ teaspoon ground ginger
1 cup salad oil

VEGETABLES:
(Select 2, 3 or more)
1 can (14 ounces) artichokes
or
1 package (10 ounces) frozen artichokes
1 pound green beans
1 medium stalk (about ½ pound) broccoli
1 pint (about 10 ounces) Brussels sprouts
1 medium head (about 1¼ pounds) cauliflower
6 large outer ribs celery
2 medium (about ¾ pound) zucchini

GARNISH:
1 bunch green onions, thinly sliced
1 jar (2 ounces) pimiento strips

Make marinade: In a large saucepan, combine vinegar, water, seasoning blend, sugar and ginger. Bring just to boiling. Stir. Reduce heat and simmer for 3 minutes. Remove from heat and cool.

Prepare selected vegetables: Drain artichokes. (If using frozen, cook as directed on package, then drain.) Cut remaining vegetables into large bite-size pieces. Cook each vegetable separately in unsalted, boiling water just until tender-crisp. Drain well. Combine drained vegetables in large, widemouth jar or a glass or ceramic bowl.

Mix cooled vinegar mixture with oil. Pour over vegetables. Chill in the refrigerator at least 6 hours or overnight. Shake or stir vegetables to distribute flavor evenly. An hour before serving, add garnish. *Makes about 6 servings.*

Note: This recipe can be doubled. If only part of the marinated vegetables are used, others may be added. If refrigerated, this recipe will keep for 5 to 7 days. For a carry-along picnic, it is not necessary to pack this salad in the cooler.

KEYSTONE POTATO SALAD

1 head cabbage (1½ to 2 pounds)
1½ cups zucchini julienne (about 3 inches long)
1½ cups carrot julienne (about 3 inches long)
1½ pounds warm cooked potatoes (4 to 5 medium), peeled and sliced ¼ inch thick
⅓ cup finely chopped onion
Bacon Dressing (recipe follows)

In a large pot simmer cabbage in boiling water 8 to 10 minutes until outer leaves are pliable. Reserve water and drain cabbage thoroughly.

Leaving core and 2 layers of outer leaves intact, cut out inside of cabbage and chop coarsely. Place outer-leaf portion on serving plate; set aside. Bring reserved water to boiling. Add zucchini; cook until crisp-tender about 1 minute. Remove to large bowl with slotted spoon. Add carrots to boiling water; cook until crisp-tender, about 4 minutes. Remove with slotted spoon and add to zucchini with potatoes, onion and chopped cabbage. Pour hot Bacon Dressing over mixture and toss gently to coat vegetables. Mound into center of outer cabbage leaves. Sprinkle with bacon reserved in dressing recipe. Serve warm. *Makes 6 to 8 servings.*

BACON DRESSING:
Cut 6 slices bacon into ½-inch pieces. Fry in skillet until almost crisp. Drain bacon and reserve. Drain all but 2 tablespoons of the drippings. Add 2 tablespoons sugar and 1 teaspoon *each* flour and salt to skillet. Cook and stir over low heat 3 minutes. Combine ½ cup water with ¼ cup vinegar. Add to skillet. Bring to boiling, stirring constantly. Remove from heat.

LAYERED FRESH SALAD

1 teaspoon salt
½ teaspoon dried leaf basil
¼ teaspoon pepper
1 clove fresh garlic, minced
3 tablespoons cider vinegar
6 tablespoons salad oil
½ cup chopped fresh parsley
4 tomatoes, peeled and sliced
2 small cucumbers, pared and sliced
1 red onion, sliced

In medium bowl combine salt, basil, pepper and garlic. Stir in vinegar, oil and parsley. Place layers of sliced tomatoes in clear container, then red onion and cucumber. Pour dressing over all. Cover and refrigerate several hours. Take to picnic in container. *Makes 6 servings.*

LETTUCE BUNDLES WITH MUSTARD SAUCE

	Water
1	head iceberg lettuce
2	cups finely chopped cooked chicken
2	tablespoons chopped fresh onion
¼	cup chopped celery
¼	pound fresh mushrooms, chopped
1	clove garlic, minced
½	teaspoon salt
⅛	teaspoon pepper
½	teaspoon dried leaf tarragon
1	egg
	Mustard Sauce (recipe follows)

Fill a large saucepan two-thirds full with water. Bring to a boil. Wash lettuce and break off 8 large leaves. Drop into boiling water and boil 1 minute. Remove carefully and lay out flat on board. In large bowl mix chicken and remaining ingredients. Place one-fourth cup filling on center of each lettuce leaf. Fold sides over filling. Place folded side down in shallow buttered baking dish. Repeat for remaining 7 bundles. Spoon Mustard Sauce over bundles. Bake in 350-degree oven 20 minutes.

Makes 4 servings, 2 bundles each.

MUSTARD SAUCE:

2	tablespoons butter or margarine
3	tablespoons Dijon-style mustard
2	tablespoons flour
¼	teaspoon salt
⅛	teaspoon cayenne pepper
1	cup chicken broth
1	cup light cream

In medium saucepan, melt butter. Blend in mustard, flour, salt, and cayenne. Remove from heat and stir in chicken broth and cream. Return to heat and cook, stirring constantly, until mixture comes to a boil and thickens.

LETTUCE CON QUESO

2	tablespoons butter or margarine
¼	cup chopped fresh onion
3	large fresh tomatoes, peeled, seeded and chopped
1	bay leaf
2	tablespoons flour
¼	cup milk
2	fresh green chilies, seeded, and chopped
1	teaspoon salt
¼	teaspoon hot pepper sauce
3	cups (¾ pound) shredded Monterey Jack or mild Cheddar cheese, divided
4	cups shredded Iceberg lettuce
	Corn bread squares

Melt butter in saucepan; add onion, tomatoes and bay leaf. Cook, stirring frequently, until onion is tender. Make a paste of the flour and milk. Add to saucepan. Simmer 10 minutes. Remove bay leaf. Add green chilies, salt, pepper sauce and 2¾ cups cheese. Stir until cheese melts. To serve, place shredded lettuce over split corn bread squares. Top with cheese mixture and remaining shredded cheese.

Makes 4 servings.

LETTUCE SLAW

½	cup sour cream
½	cup mayonnaise
1	tablespoon prepared mustard
2	tablespoons chopped fresh onion
1	tablespoon fresh lemon juice
½	teaspoon salt
⅛	teaspoon Tabasco pepper sauce
1	tablespoon dill seed
8	cups shredded iceberg lettuce (1 large head)
2	cups sliced radishes (2 bunches)

Combine sour cream, mayonnaise, mustard, onion, lemon juice, salt, pepper sauce and dill seed in small bowl or jar. Mix well. Cover and chill. To serve, combine lettuce and radishes in large bowl. Add dressing and toss to mix well.

Makes 8 servings.

LOW-CAL ICEBERG WEDGES WITH TOMATO DRESSING

1	head iceberg lettuce
½	cup tomato sauce
3	tablespoons lemon juice
2	tablespoons chopped onion
½	teaspoon salt
½	teaspoon sugar
½	teaspoon steak sauce
¼	teaspoon monosodium glutamate (optional)
¼	teaspoon caraway seed
½	cucumber, thinly sliced

Core, rinse and thoroughly drain lettuce. Chill in disposable plastic bag or crisper.

For dressing, combine all remaining ingredients except cucumber in jar. Cover and shake to blend. Chill.

Cut lettuce head into quarters. Arrange with cucumber on salad plates. Pour dressing over just before serving.   *Makes 4 servings (⅔ cup dressing) of approximately 45 calories per serving.*

MARINATED CELERY AND ITALIAN BEANS

½ cup salad oil
¼ cup white vinegar
⅓ cup minced onion
2 tablespoons sugar
1 tablespoon caraway seed
1½ teaspoons salt
  Pepper
6 cups sliced celery
1 package (9 ounces) Italian (or fresh) green beans

In a large saucepan combine oil, vinegar, onion, sugar, caraway, salt and black pepper. Bring to boiling point. Add celery, return to boiling point. Reduce heat and simmer, covered for 5 minutes. Add green beans. Cover and simmer 5 minutes longer. Cool. Refrigerate, covered, 2 to 3 hours.
Makes 6 portions.

MARINATED CUCUMBERS WITH FRESH SCALLIONS

4 large cucumbers, pared and thinly sliced
2 teaspoons salt
3 scallions, sliced, including green part
1 tablespoon chopped fresh dill
1 tablespoon chopped fresh parsley
1 lemon, thinly sliced
⅓ cup white wine or cider vinegar
1 tablespoon sugar
1 tablespoon fresh lemon juice
1 tablespoon olive or salad oil
¼–½ teaspoon pepper

Layer cucumber in a bowl or refrigerator container. Sprinkle salt between layers. Cover and refrigerate several hours. Drain, rinse with cold water, drain again. Add scallions, dill, parsley and lemon slices. Toss to mix lightly. Combine remaining ingredients and pour over cucumber mixture; toss again. Chill 1 hour or until ready to serve or pack for picnic.
Makes 6 to 8 servings.

MIXED GREEN SALAD WITH LEMON DRESSING

2½ cups iceberg lettuce, torn into bite-size pieces
2½ cups fresh spinach, torn into bite-size pieces
1 cup escarole, torn into bite-size pieces
  Lemon Dressing (recipe follows)

In a large bowl combine salad greens. Add about ⅓ cup Lemon Dressing, toss lightly.
Makes 6 servings.

LEMON DRESSING:
⅔ cup salad oil
⅓ cup fresh lemon juice
2 tablespoons chopped fresh parsley
1 clove garlic, peeled and split
1 teaspoon sugar
¾ teaspoon salt
¼ teaspoon pepper
½ teaspoon dry mustard
⅛ teaspoon paprika

In a small bowl or jar with tight-fitting lid combine all ingredients. Beat or shake until well mixed. Let stand one hour and remove garlic. Store in refrigerator.
Makes 1 cup dressing.

MOON GODDESS SALAD

3 tomatoes, sliced
1 can (8½ ounces) water chestnuts, drained and sliced
¼ cup salad oil
4½ teaspoons vinegar
1 teaspoon soy sauce
⅛ teaspoon hot pepper sauce
½ teaspoon sugar
2 teaspoons lemon juice

Arrange tomato slices in ring around edge of plate. Place water chestnuts in center. Mix remaining ingredients. Pour over tomatoes, cover and refrigerate until serving time.
Makes 6 servings.

MUSHROOM-VEGETABLE SALAD

1 pound fresh mushrooms or 2 cans (6 to 8 ounces each) sliced mushrooms
2 packages (10 ounces each) frozen mixed vegetables
1 cup bottled Italian salad dressing
⅓ cup chopped parsley
¼ teaspoon ground black pepper

Rinse, pat dry and slice fresh mushrooms (about 5 cups) or drain canned mushrooms. Place in a large bowl. Cook vegetables as label directs; drain. Cool slightly; toss with mushrooms.
  Mix salad dressing with parsley and black pepper. Pour over vegetables; toss lightly. Chill.
Makes about 1½ quarts or 8 portions.

ORIENTAL VEGETABLE SALAD

1   package (10 ounces) frozen cauliflower
1   package (9 ounces) frozen cut green beans
1   package (6 ounces) frozen pea pods with water chestnuts
1   cup thin tomato wedges
¼   cup peanut oil
2   tablespoons rice vinegar
1   tablespoon dry sherry (optional)
1   tablespoon toasted sesame seeds, crushed
2   teaspoons brown sugar
2   teaspoons soy sauce
½   teaspoon ground ginger
½   teaspoon salt

Cook cauliflower, green beans and pea pods as packages direct. Drain vegetables well and combine with tomato. In a small jar with a cover combine all remaining ingredients. Cover and shake well to mix. Pour over vegetables and mix gently. Chill thoroughly and serve.   *Makes 6 one-cup servings.*

Note: Two packages—10 ounces each—of frozen Oriental-style vegetables can be substituted for the three frozen vegetables shown above.

PAYETTE VALLEY POTATO SALAD

1   package (5.5 ounces) Idaho scalloped potatoes
3   cups water
2   tablespoons salad oil
½   cup water
1   tablespoon cider vinegar
3   tablespoons milk
¼   cup mayonnaise
1   cup chopped celery

Remove sauce packet from scalloped potatoes. Heat water to boil in large saucepan, add potatoes, cover and cook 12 to 15 minutes, until tender but not soft. Immediately drain in strainer and rinse with cold running water. Turn into large bowl. Blend sauce mix with salad oil in saucepan. Stir in water and vinegar. Cook, stirring constantly, until mixture thickens and comes to a boil. Remove from heat and stir in milk, then blend in mayonnaise. Add to potatoes in bowl, add celery and mix well. Cover and chill several hours.   *Makes 4 to 6 servings.*

PICK-UP-STICKS SALAD

6   carrots
6   celery ribs, cleaned and trimmed

4   parsnips, pared
3   apples, cored, unpared
½   head lettuce, washed, torn into bite-size pieces
    Orange Salad Dressing (recipe follows)

Cut carrots, celery, parsnips and apples into 3-inch sticks. Line individual salad plates with lettuce. Toss prepared salad sticks in Orange Salad Dressing (below); turn onto serving plates. Pour extra dressing over top.   *Makes 6 servings.*

ORANGE SALAD DRESSING:
½   cup mayonnaise
½   cup fresh orange juice
1   tablespoon sugar

Combine all ingredients in small bowl; mix well. Chill.   *Makes about 1 cup dressing.*

RATATOUILLE SALAD

1   small eggplant, peeled
1   teaspoon salt
½   cup peanut oil
2   medium zucchini, sliced ½ inch thick
1   medium green pepper, cut into strips
1   large onion, sliced and separated into rings
1   large clove garlic, minced
⅛   teaspoon pepper
5   medium tomatoes, cut into wedges
1   tablespoon chopped capers

Cut eggplant into 1-inch slices; sprinkle with salt. Place eggplant between 2 plates. Let stand about 30 minutes to drain. Heat peanut oil in large skillet. Add zucchini, green pepper, onion, garlic and pepper. Cook over medium heat about 5 minutes; stir occasionally. Cut eggplant into cubes. Add to skillet and continue cooking until vegetables are just tender. Stir in tomatoes and capers. Pour into large bowl. Chill thoroughly.   *Makes about 8 cups.*

HEARTY BROWN SALAD

SALAD LAYERS:
10   ounces fresh spinach or romaine
1½   cups cooked brown rice, cooled
1⅓   cups (about 4 ounces) alfalfa sprouts or fresh bean sprouts
1   avocado, sliced (optional)
2   tablespoons lemon juice (optional)
¾   cup shredded carrots
⅔   cup roasted, salted cashews

DRESSING:
1   cup (8 ounces) plain yogurt

2 tablespoons honey
2 teaspoons prepared yellow mustard
1¼ teaspoons assorted seasonings

To mix dressing, combine all dressing ingredients. Stir just until smooth and well blended. To assemble salad, wash spinach. Tear leaves into bite-size pieces. Discard tough stems. In salad bowl, make bottom layer with half the spinach. Layer other vegetables in bowl. Reserve a few vegetables for garnish on top. Dip avocado slices in lemon juice before adding to salad. Top salad with reserved vegetables. Pour dressing over salad just before serving. *Makes 8 servings.*

Note: The dressing and salad can be made several hours ahead. Cover and refrigerate until serving time. For carry-along picnics, pack the dressing in a cooler. Salad is crisper if packed in cooler also but this is not essential.

SLIM JANE KRAUT SALAD

2 cups sauerkraut (about 16 ounces)
3 hard-cooked eggs, sliced
⅓ cup chopped cucumber
1 cup grated sharp Cheddar cheese (about 4 ounces)
½ teaspoon salt
¼ teaspoon pepper
¼ teaspoon dried tarragon
1 teaspoon caraway seed
1 tablespoon French dressing

Drain kraut; reserve juice. Combine kraut, eggs, cucumber, cheese, salt, pepper, tarragon and caraway seed. Toss lightly. Combine kraut juice and French dressing; mix well. Add kraut juice mixture to kraut mixture; toss lightly but thoroughly. Chill one-half hour. *Makes 4 servings.*

SLIMMERS' SALAD WITH BLUE CHEESE DRESSING

1 head iceberg lettuce
¼ cup cold water
⅓ cup instant non-fat dry milk
1½ cups small-curd cottage cheese
⅓ cup (1½ ounces) crumbled blue cheese
3 tablespoons lemon juice
¾ teaspoon onion salt
¼ teaspoon garlic salt
12 slices of cored apple or 6 thick tomato slices

Core, rinse and thoroughly drain lettuce. Chill in plastic crisper or disposable plastic bag.

Combine remaining ingredients except apple or tomato in electric blender. Mix in stop-and-go fashion until blended and fairly smooth. Cover and chill.

Cut lettuce into 6 narrow wedges. Arrange with apple or tomato on salad plates.

Spoon dressing over. Sprinkle with minced parsley, if desired.

Makes 6 servings of about 130 calories each.

Note: To prepare dressing without blender, sprinkle milk powder over water and beat until soft peaks form. Add 2 tablespoons lemon juice and beat until stiff. Mix in 1 tablespoon lemon juice, cheeses and seasonings.

SPINACH SALAD

1 pound fresh spinach
2 hard-boiled eggs (diced)
2 red apples (unpeeled and diced)
1 red onion (sliced fine)
¼ pound blue cheese (crumbled)
1 cup mayonnaise
½ pint sour cream

Wash spinach and tear into bite-size pieces. Place spinach, eggs, apples and onion in large bowl.

In separate bowl, mix together cheese, mayonnaise and sour cream.

Toss salad with dressing and serve immediately. *Makes 2 large salads or 4 to 6 small servings.*

SUMMER BEAN SALAD

1 pound (2 cups) dry, edible navy beans
6 cups water
6 tablespoons olive oil
¼ cup fresh lemon juice
1 clove garlic, crushed
1 teaspoon rosemary, crushed
½ teaspoon salt
⅛ teaspoon pepper
⅓ cup chopped scallion
2 tablespoons chopped parsley
Lettuce or leaf spinach

Place navy beans in a large saucepan with 6 cups water. Bring to a boil. Boil 2 minutes; remove from heat; allow to stand 1 hour. Return to heat and simmer 1½ hours or until just tender but still firm. Drain off liquid. Combine oil, lemon juice, garlic, rosemary, salt and pepper. Pour over warm beans and mix well. Chill several hours or overnight. Just before serving, mix in scallions and parsley. Serve in a salad bowl lined with lettuce or fresh leaf spinach. *Makes 8 to 10 servings.*

SWEET AND SOUR SALAD

DRESSING:

⅓ cup sweet pickle liquid (drained from sweet mixed pickles)
¼ cup salad oil
1 tablespoon ketchup
1 teaspoon sugar
4 teaspoons soy sauce
1 teaspoon vinegar
¼ teaspoon ginger
¼ teaspoon garlic powder

SALAD:

1 bunch watercress, cut into 1-inch pieces (about 3 cups)
1 bunch green onions, cut into 1-inch pieces
2 cups bean sprouts, fresh or canned
1½ cups sweet mixed pickles
½ pound cooked roast beef, cut into julienne strips (1 cup)
Bibb lettuce leaves

FOR DRESSING: In a jar with tight-fitting lid, place all ingredients for dressing. Shake vigorously until well combined.

FOR SALAD: In large bowl, toss watercress, onion, bean sprouts, pickles and beef. Pour on dressing and toss again until well coated. Spoon onto lettuce-lined plate. Serve immediately.

Makes 4 to 6 servings.

SWITCHED SLAW

¾ cup salad oil
¼ cup wine vinegar
1 teaspoon salt
½ teaspoon dried leaf basil
¼ teaspoon dry mustard
¼–½ teaspoon Tabasco pepper sauce
1 teaspoon grated onion
4 cups shredded red cabbage
3 Granny Smith apples, cored and cubed

In large bowl, mix oil, vinegar, salt, basil, dry mustard, pepper sauce and onion. Stir in cabbage and apples. Cover and chill several hours or overnight. *Makes 6 to 8 servings.*

TOMATO MEDLEY SALAD

3 medium-sized tomatoes
1 green pepper
1 cucumber

¼ cup Herbed Italian Salad Dressing (recipe follows)
¼ cup sliced scallions or green onions

Hold tomatoes at room temperature until fully ripe. Cut into one-quarter-inch-thick slices; set aside. Slice green pepper into strips and cucumber into thin slices; set aside. On a large platter arrange tomatoes, green pepper and cucumber in strips. Spoon Herbed Italian Salad Dressing over vegetables. Let marinate for 10 minutes before serving. Sprinkle with scallions. *Makes 4 portions.*

HERBED ITALIAN SALAD DRESSING:

1 teaspoon salt
¾ teaspoon sugar
¾ teaspoon Italian seasoning
1 teaspoon minced onion
1 clove garlic, minced
¼ teaspoon grated lemon peel
¼ teaspoon coarse ground black pepper
⅔ cup olive or salad oil
¼ cup lemon juice or cider vinegar
2 tablespoons water

In a container with a tight-fitting lid combine seasoning and oil. Let stand for 10 minutes. Add vinegar and water; mix well. Lightly spoon over Tomato Medley Salad. Refrigerate remaining dressing. *Makes about 1 cup dressing.*

TOSSED ICEBERG SALAD WITH BUTTERMILK DRESSING

1 large head iceberg lettuce
2 cups pared, diced cucumber
2 cups diced tomato
½ cup buttermilk
¼ cup salad oil
3 tablespoons crumbled Danish blue cheese
1 tablespoon vinegar
1½ teaspoons seasoned salt
1 teaspoon prepared horseradish
½ teaspoon tarragon, crumbled
Dash or two black pepper

Core, rinse and thoroughly drain lettuce. Refrigerate in disposable plastic bag or plastic crisper. When ready to serve, cut lettuce crosswise into inch-thick slices, then cut into bite-size chunks to measure 2 quarts. Combine in chilled salad bowl with cucumber and tomato. Stir together all remaining ingredients, and pour over salad. Toss lightly, and serve at once. *Makes 6 to 8 servings.*

WATERCRESS-ENDIVE SALAD

6	heads Belgian endive, cut into bite-size pieces
1	bunch watercress, stems removed and torn
½	cup peanut oil
3	tablespoons white vinegar
¼	teaspoon salt
⅛	teaspoon paprika
	Dash black pepper
2	teaspoons minced onion

Combine endive and watercress in salad bowl. Set aside. Combine peanut oil, white vinegar, salt, paprika, pepper and onion in a jar with tight fitting lid. Cover tightly and shake until well mixed. Pour over salad greens and toss.   *Makes 6 servings.*

WINTER HAVEN SALAD

2	grapefruit, peeled and sectioned (2 cups sections)
2	small red onions, thinly sliced and separated into rings
1	can (1 pound) cut green beans, drained
1	can (1 pound) artichoke hearts, drained, cut in halves
⅓	cup stuffed green olives, sliced
¾	cup salad oil
⅓	cup tarragon wine vinegar
1	clove garlic, finely minced
1	teaspoon salt
¼	teaspoon pepper

Combine grapefruit sections, onions, green beans, artichoke hearts and olive slices in large bowl. In small bowl or jar combine oil, vinegar, garlic, salt and pepper; mix well. Pour dressing over salad. Cover. Refrigerate 2 hours before serving.
Makes 4 to 6 servings.

YOGURT ICEBERG SALAD

1	head iceberg lettuce
2	tomatoes
1	cucumber
1	container (8 ounces) plain yogurt
2	tablespoons finely chopped onion
½	teaspoon minced garlic
1	teaspoon seasoned salt
½	teaspoon sugar
¼	teaspoon oregano, crumbled
1/16	teaspoon white pepper
2	hard-cooked eggs

Core, rinse and thoroughly drain lettuce. Chill in plastic crisper or disposable plastic bag. Rinse and chill tomato and cucumber.

For dressing, combine yogurt with onion, garlic, salt, sugar, oregano and pepper. Chill.

When ready to serve, remove outside lettuce leaves. Cut lettuce into crosswise slices, then into bite-size chunks to measure 1 quart. Arrange lettuce leaves on chilled platter and top with lettuce chunks.

Slice tomato and cucumber. Halve eggs. Arrange over lettuce. Serve with yogurt dressing.
Makes 4 generous servings of 98 calories each using large eggs.

MEAT SALADS

BEEF AND VEGETABLE SALAD

1	head iceberg lettuce
⅔	cup corn oil
⅓	cup vinegar
4	teaspoons dried salad herbs
1	teaspoon salt
1	teaspoon tarragon
¼	teaspoon pepper
1	small cauliflower
8	ounces sliced roast beef, boiled ham· (2 packages, 4 ounces each) or another luncheon meat
½	cup chopped sweet gherkins
1	can (8¼ ounces) sliced pickled beets, drained, chilled

Core, rinse and drain lettuce; chill in disposable plastic bag or plastic crisper.

Combine oil, vinegar, salad herbs, salt, tarragon and pepper in jar; cover and shake.

Trim cauliflower and separate into flowerettes. Steam in a little boiling salted water for 5 minutes, or until tender-crisp. Drain, cover with dressing and chill 1 to 2 hours until full-flavored.

Slice lettuce head crosswise into 4 slices. (Save end pieces to put into tossed salads.) Place each lettuce slice onto luncheon plate. Drizzle each with a little marinade-dressing.

Roll roast beef slices around some of gherkins. Arrange rolled meat, cauliflower, beets and remaining gherkins on top of lettuce slices.

Serve with remaining marinade-dressing alongside.   *Makes 4 servings.*

CALICO BEEF ASPIC

1   can (10½ ounces) condensed beef broth
1   package (3 ounces) lemon-flavored gelatin
½   cup cold water
1   tablespoon grated onion
1   tablespoon vinegar
     Dash salt
     Dash pepper
1   cup diced cooked beef
⅓   cup diced red apple
2   tablespoons sliced celery

In saucepan, bring beef broth to a boil. Add gelatin; stir to dissolve. Add water, onion, vinegar, salt and pepper. Chill until slightly thickened. Fold in remaining ingredients. Pour into 3-cup mold. Chill until firm (about 4 hours).   *Makes about 2½ cups.*

CHEF'S SUMMER SUPPER SALAD

     Garlic Herb Dressing (recipe follows)
1   package (7 ounces) or 12 frozen chopped onion rings
2   quarts crisp salad greens
1½–2   cups cooked ham or chicken strips
1   cup Cheddar or Muenster cheese strips (4 ounces)

Prepare Garlic Herb Dressing. Prepare onion rings as package directs. Toss lettuce with hot onion rings, ham or chicken and cheese (reserving some of each for top of salad/garnish if desired). Serve with Garlic Herb Dressing.   *Makes 6 servings.*

GARLIC HERB DRESSING:

Combine one-half cup oil, one-third cup each garlic flavor wine vinegar and chopped tomatoes, 2 tablespoons chopped green onion, 1 teaspoon each salt and savory (crumbled) and one-eighth teaspoon cayenne in a jar. Cover tightly and shake well. Shake again before using.   *Makes about 1¼ cups.*

CREAMED SLAW WITH HAM

6   cups cabbage cut in long, thin shreds
½   cup sliced green onions
½   cup green pepper cut in 1-inch squares
½   teaspoon dried dill weed, crushed
2   tablespoons butter or margarine
1   can (10¾ ounces) condensed cream of celery soup
¼   cup water
1   cup diced cooked ham
½   cup sour cream
2   tablespoons diced pimiento

In skillet, cook cabbage, onions and green pepper with dill in butter until tender. Add remaining ingredients. Heat; stir occasionally.
    Makes about 3½ cups, 4 servings.

FIESTA SALAD OLE

1   pound ground beef
½   cup chopped onion
¾   cup quick or old-fashioned oats, uncooked
1   cup spicy sweet French dressing
1   can (6 ounces) tomato paste
¾   cup water
1   can (4 ounces) chopped green chilies
1½   teaspoons salt
5   cups shredded lettuce
2   tomatoes, chopped
1   ripe avocado, peeled and sliced
1   cup (4 ounces) shredded Monterey Jack cheese

Brown meat and onion in 10-inch skillet. Drain. Add oats, dressing, tomato paste, water, green chilies and salt to meat mixture. Bring mixture to a boil over medium heat.

Combine lettuce and tomato. For each serving, place about 1 to 1½ cups lettuce mixture on plate. Top with about ¾ cup hot meat mixture, avocado slices and cheese.   *Makes 6 servings.*

HAM SALAD WITH CHERRY DRESSING

1   cup leftover ham chunks
2   ribs celery
     Dash ground cloves
1   cup creamed cottage cheese
1   can (20 ounces) pineapple slices, drained
     Lettuce leaves
     Maraschino cherries (for garnish)
     Cherry Dressing (recipe follows)

Combine ham, celery and cloves in food processor. Process with cutting blade until chopped. Mix in cheese. (If you have no food processor, chop ham and celery. Stir together cloves and cheese, then mix into ham-celery mixture.)

Arrange 4 pineapple slices on lettuce leaves. Mound ham mixture on top of each slice. Top with maraschino cherries, if desired.

Halve remaining pineapple slices. Arrange around salads. Serve with cherry dressing.

Makes 4 servings.

CHERRY DRESSING:

Combine ½ cup mayonnaise and ¼ cup maraschino cherries.

HOT GRAPEFRUIT, HAM AND CABBAGE SALAD

2	tablespoons butter or margarine
⅓	cup chopped onion
1½	tablespoons flour
1	tablespoon sugar
1	teaspoon salt
¼	teaspoon pepper
1	tablespoon prepared mustard
1	cup grapefruit juice
2	tablespoons cider vinegar
¼	cup water
2	cups diced cooked ham
1	cup chopped walnuts
4	cups thinly shredded cabbage
2	cups grapefruit sections

In large skillet melt butter. Add onion and cook until tender. Blend in flour, sugar, salt, pepper and mustard. Stir in grapefruit juice, vinegar and water. Bring to a boil over medium heat, stirring constantly. Stir in ham, walnuts and cabbage; cook 10 minutes. Add grapefruit sections and heat.

Makes 4 servings.

HOT KRAUT-FRANKFURTER POTATO SALAD

5	medium potatoes
2	tablespoons vegetable oil
6	frankfurters, cut into thirds
⅓	cup chopped onion
2	cups well-drained sauerkraut
2	tablespoons vinegar
¼	cup beef bouillon or stock
½	teaspoon sugar
½	teaspoon salt
¼	teaspoon pepper

Cook scrubbed potatoes in boiling water to cover until just tender. Peel and slice into a large bowl while still hot.

In large skillet, heat oil. Cook frankfurters, turning frequently, about 5 minutes. Add onion and sauerkraut. Cook about 5 minutes. To the kraut mixture, add vinegar, bouillon, sugar, salt and pepper. Heat through. Add potatoes. Toss gently.

Makes 6 servings.

HUSSAR'S SALAD

2	cups diced leftover cooked veal or pork
2	green apples, peeled, cored and chopped
1	can (16 ounces) diced beets, drained
3	hard-cooked eggs, chopped
3	sweet gherkins, diced
3	pounds potatoes, cooked, peeled and diced
¼	cup oil
¼	cup cider vinegar
2	teaspoons Angostura aromatic bitters
	Salt and pepper
	Lettuce leaves
	Cucumber slices, halved tomato slices

In bowl, combine meat, apples, beets, eggs, gherkins, potatoes, oil, vinegar and bitters. When well blended, season to taste with salt and pepper. Chill.

Mound mixture on lettuce leaves and garnish with cucumber slices and halved tomato slices. Serve with crusty bread slices. *Makes 6 servings.*

PEACHY HAM-CHERRY SALAD

1½	cups leftover ham chunks
2	ribs celery
4	large canned peach halves
4	lettuce leaves
½	cup sour cream
⅛	teaspoon ground ginger
½	cup red maraschino cherries

Combine ham and celery in food processor. Process with cutting blade until chopped. (If you have no food processor, chop ham and celery.)

Place peach halves on lettuce leaves. Mound ham mixture on peaches.

Stir together sour cream and ginger. Mix in cherries. Serve this dressing with the salads.

Makes 4 servings.

PEAR-BEEF SALAD ORIENTAL

1	can (29 ounces) Bartlett pear halves or slices
1½	cups (8 ounces) cooked roast beef, in julienne strips
1	cup sliced Chinese, Napa or Savoy cabbage
1	cup torn leaf lettuce
½	cup fresh bean sprouts
3	ounces (about ½ cup) fresh or frozen Chinese pea pods, slightly cooked Dressing (recipe follows)

Drain pears, reserving 2 teaspoons syrup; if necessary, slice pears. Combine beef, cabbage, lettuce and bean sprouts. Distribute evenly over medium-sized platter. Arrange pears and pea pods over vegetable-beef mixture. To serve, drizzle dressing over salad; toss lightly. Serve at once.   *Makes 4 servings.*

DRESSING:
Combine 1 tablespoon each vegetable oil* and white wine vinegar, reserved pear syrup and 1 teaspoon soy sauce. Mix well.

*Sesame oil may be substituted for all or part of the oil.

REUBEN SALAD PLATTER

3	tablespoons butter or margarine, melted
4	slices bread, cut into strips
2	cups mayonnaise
1	can (8 ounces) tomato sauce
⅓	cup chopped sweet relish
3	cups well-drained sauerkraut (about 27 ounces) Lettuce leaves
¾	pound cooked corned beef, cut into julienne strips or 1 can (12 ounces) corned beef
¾	pound Swiss cheese slices, cut into julienne strips

For Croutons: Place butter on a jelly-roll pan and add bread strips and toss to coat well. Toast for 10 minutes or until lightly browned. Remove from oven and cool.

For Dressing: In medium bowl, combine mayonnaise, tomato sauce and sweet pickle relish until well mixed. Remove cup dressing; toss with drained kraut. Reserve remaining dressing.

For Salad: Place lettuce leaves on platter, top with kraut mixture, meat, cheese and croutons. Serve with remaining dressing.   *Makes 4 to 6 servings.*

POULTRY SALADS

BANANA CLUB SALAD

2	cups cut-up cooked chicken
2	chopped peeled tomatoes
¼	cup chopped parsley
2	ripe bananas, cut up
8	slices bacon, cooked and crumbled Salad greens Club Dressing (recipe follows)

In large bowl combine chicken, tomatoes, parsley and bananas. Add ½ Club Dressing (below). Mix well. Spoon onto a bed of salad greens and sprinkle with bacon. Serve with remaining dressing.
Makes 4 servings.

CLUB DRESSING:

½	cup mayonnaise
4	teaspoons lemon juice
1	teaspoon grated onion
½	teaspoon salt
⅛	teaspoon pepper

In medium bowl mix together all ingredients.

BANANA-TURKEY SKILLET SALAD

4	tablespoons butter or margarine, divided
1	cup diagonally sliced celery
¼	cup chopped scallions
2	cups cubed cooked turkey
1½	cups sliced bananas (3 bananas)
2	tablespoons lemon juice
2	cups shredded iceberg lettuce
1	cup chicken broth
½	teaspoon curry powder
2	tablespoons flour

Melt 2 tablespoons butter in large skillet over medium heat. Add celery and scallions. Cook just until heated through. Remove to large bowl.

Add turkey to skillet. Cook until hot. Add to celery and onions.

Melt remaining 2 tablespoons butter in skillet. Sprinkle sliced bananas with lemon juice. Heat in skillet and add to bowl. Add lettuce to skillet, cover and heat until greens are wilted, 1 to 2 minutes. Place on top of bananas in bowl.

In same skillet combine chicken broth, curry powder and flour. Cook, stirring constantly, until sauce thickens and comes to a boil. Add salad to skillet. Toss gently and serve. Or pour dressing over ingredients in bowl and mix gently.

Makes 6 servings.

CHICKEN SALAD

1	teaspoon curry powder
1	tablespoon butter or margarine
1	can (10¾ ounces) condensed cream of chicken soup
½	cup mayonnaise
¼	cup orange juice
1	tablespoon chopped chutney
4	cups cubed cooked chicken or turkey
3	cups cooked elbow macaroni
1	cup diagonally sliced celery
1	cup orange sections
1	cup chopped green pepper

In saucepan, cook curry in butter a few minutes. Stir in soup, mayonnaise, orange juice and chutney. In large bowl, combine soup mixture with remaining ingredients; chill. Serve on crisp salad greens.

Makes about 9 cups, 4 servings.

CRUNCHY TOSSED CHICKEN SALAD

2	cans (5 ounces *each*) chunk chicken
1	cup plain yogurt
1	teaspoon prepared mustard
½	teaspoon ground cumin seed
6	cups salad greens torn in bite-size pieces
1	cup alfalfa sprouts
⅓	cup sliced radishes
¼	cup pine nuts

Drain chicken, reserving broth. To make dressing, combine broth, yogurt, mustard and cumin. Toss with chicken and remaining ingredients.

Makes about 8 cups, 4 servings.

FRUITED CHICKEN SALAD WITH PEANUT CREAM DRESSING

DRESSING:

⅓	cup peanut oil
1	egg
1	cup (½ pint) light cream
½	teaspoon herb such as oregano, thyme, sage, tarragon or chervil
½	teaspoon grated orange rind
	Salt to taste

SALAD:

4	cups diced cooked chicken
2	cups diced unpeeled red apple
1	cup sliced celery
¼	cup chopped red onion
	Lettuce leaves
6	navel oranges, peeled and sliced
6	slices bacon, fried until crisp and crumbled

Combine all dressing ingredients in a blender and whirl until smooth. Chill. In a bowl mix chicken, apple, celery and onion. Toss mixture with salad dressing. Line a large platter with lettuce leaves. Pile chicken salad in a mound in center of platter. Surround salad with orange slices. Sprinkle with bacon.

Makes 6 servings.

PARADISE CHICKEN SALAD

CURRY ADD-A-CRUNCH:

2	cups quick or old-fashioned oats, uncooked
⅓	cup butter or margarine, melted
¼	cup chopped cashews
2	tablespoons shredded or flaked coconut
2	tablespoons grated Parmesan cheese
½	teaspoon curry powder
¼	teaspoon salt

CHICKEN SALAD:

1	fresh pineapple
3	cups shredded cooked chicken
¾	cup celery slices
¾	cup mayonnaise
2	tablespoons chutney

For Curry Add-A-Crunch, heat oven to 350 degrees. Combine all ingredients; mix well. Bake in ungreased 15-by-10-inch jelly roll pan at 350 degrees for 16 to 18 minutes or until light golden. Cool. Will keep in tightly covered container in refrigerator up to three months. *Makes about 2½ cups.*

For Chicken Salad, cut pineapple lengthwise through leaves into quarters. Slice out fruit, leaving shells intact to form boats; set aside. Remove core from fruit; cut fruit to make 1 cup chunks. Combine with remaining ingredients; toss lightly. Chill. To serve, mound chicken salad into pineapple boats; sprinkle each serving with 1 tablespoon Curry Add-A-Crunch; serve with additional crunch, if desired. *Makes 4 servings.*

VARIATION: Substitute lettuce leaves for fresh pineapple and 1 8¼-ounce can pineapple chunks, drained, for fresh pineapple chunks, if desired.

TURKEY AND BANANA SALAD

2	cups sliced bananas (3 bananas)
2	cups chopped cooked turkey
½	cup choped celery
2	tablespoons finely chopped onion
⅓	cup chopped pecans
½	cup mayonnaise
2	teaspoons lemon juice
¾	teaspoon salt
⅛	teaspoon pepper
1	teaspoon chopped fresh dill or ¼ teaspoon dried dill weed
	Lettuce leaves
	Cranberry sauce

Mix all ingredients except cranberry sauce and lettuce leaves in large bowl. Cover and chill. Serve on lettuce leaves and top with cranberry sauce.

Makes 4 servings.

TURKEY SOUFFLE SALAD

1	package (3 ounces) lemon or lime flavor gelatin
¼	teaspoon salt
1	cup boiling water
½	cup cold water
¼	cup mayonnaise
1	tablespoon vinegar or lemon juice
1	tablespoon grated onion
	Dash of pepper
1½	cups diced cooked turkey
⅓	cups chopped cucumber or green pepper
⅓	cup chopped celery
2	tablespoons chopped pimiento

Dissolve gelatin and salt in boiling water. Add cold water, mayonnaise, vinegar, onion and pepper. Beat until well blended. Pour into an 8-inch square pan. Freeze 15 to 20 minutes or until firm about 1 inch from edge, but soft in center. Spoon into a bowl and whip until fluffy. Fold in turkey and chopped vegetables. Pour into 4-cup mold or individual molds. Chill in refrigerator (not freezing unit) until firm, 30 to 60 minutes. Unmold. Garnish with salad greens and serve with additional mayonnaise, if desired.

Makes about 4 cups or 4 entree servings.

FISH & SEAFOOD SALADS

CHINESE BANANA AND SEAFOOD SALAD

	MUSTARD DRESSING:
2	tablespoons salad oil
1	tablespoon prepared mustard
1	tablespoon white wine or cider vinegar
1	tablespoon lemon juice
½	teaspoon salt
½	teaspoon mustard seed
¼	teaspoon pepper

Measure all ingredients into a large bowl. Stir until well blended and smooth.

	SALAD:
1	can (1 pound) bean sprouts
1	pound cooked and cleaned shrimp or 2 cans (6½ or 7 ounces each) tuna in vegetable oil
1	can (8¾ ounces) pineapple tidbits, drained
2	bananas

Drain bean sprouts, rinse in cold water, and drain again. Add to mustard dressing with shrimp and drained pineapple; mix well and chill. At serving time, peel bananas, cut into slices and mix lightly with salad. *Makes 4 servings.*

CHINESE TUNA SALAD

2	tablespoons soy sauce
1	tablespoon sherry
¼	cups salad oil
1	tablespoon red wine vinegar
¼	teaspoon salt
2	cans (6½ or 7 ounces each) tuna in vegetable oil
¼	cup sliced scallions
1	cup chopped watercress
1	cup sliced radishes
½	pound mushrooms, sliced
1	can (1 pound) bean sprouts, drained and rinsed in cold water
	Lettuce

In large bowl mix soy sauce, sherry, oil, vinegar and salt. Add tuna and scallions. Cover and chill several hours. One hour before serving, add watercress, radishes, mushrooms and bean sprouts to salad, mix well, cover and chill. Serve on a bed of lettuce.

Makes 4 servings.

CRAB NEPTUNE SALAD

2	packages (6 to 8 ounces each) frozen Alaska King crab meat
	Lettuce leaves
2	cups torn romaine lettuce
1	large tomato, sliced
1	ripe avocado, cut in eighths
1½	cups bean sprouts
	Neptune Dressing (recipe follows)

Thaw crab; separate into pieces. Line platter with lettuce leaves; mound romaine in center. Arrange all ingredients except dressing on lettuce. Serve with Neptune Dressing.   *Makes 4 servings.*

NEPTUNE DRESSING:
Combine 1 clove minced garlic, 1 tablespoon each anchovy paste and lemon juice, 2 tablespoons each tarragon wine vinegar and finely chopped chives or green onion, ⅓ cup dairy sour cream, ⅔ cup mayonnaise, 3 tablespoons finely chopped parsley, ¼ teaspoon salt and dash pepper; mix well. Garnish with chopped parsley.   *Makes 1¼ cups.*

GARDEN TUNA VINAIGRETTE

4	cups sliced pared carrots
½	cup water
1	teaspoon salt
¼	teaspoon sugar
¼	teaspoon pepper
¼	teaspoon dry mustard
½	teaspoon dried leaf basil
5	tablespoons white wine vinegar
½	cup salad oil
1	tablespoon lemon juice
1	clove garlic, minced
¼	cup chopped parsley
2	tablespoons chopped onion
2	cans (6½ or 7 ounces each) tuna in vegetable oil
2	zucchini, sliced (do not pare)

Place carrots in medium saucepan, add water. Cover and cook over medium heat 15 minutes or until crisp and tender. Drain and set aside. In large bowl combine salt, sugar, pepper, mustard and basil. Stir in vinegar, oil, lemon juice, garlic, parsley and onion. Add tuna, cooked carrots and zucchini. Cover and chill several hours. Serve with thinly sliced French bread.   *Makes 4 to 6 servings.*

HERRING COLE SLAW

1	jar (1 pound) herring party snacks in sour cream or herring tidbits in wine sauce
6	cups shredded green cabbage
4	cups shredded red cabbage
2	carrots, shredded
1	green pepper, chopped
2	apples, cored and diced
½	cup salad oil
¼	cup wine vinegar
1	teaspoon dill seed
	Salt and pepper to taste

Drain herring. Dice herring and chop onions from jar. Combine all ingredients and toss until all particles are coated. Add salt and pepper to taste. Let stand for 30 minutes at room temperature and then toss again. Serve in a large bowl lined with the large outer red and green cabbage leaves.

Makes 6 servings.

ICEBERG CRAB LOUIS

½	medium head iceberg lettuce
¼	red cabbage, shredded (about 2 cups)
2	stalks celery, sliced (about 1 cup)
1	carrot, shredded
½	onion, chopped
5-6	radishes, sliced
⅓	cup safflower mayonnaise
2½	tablespoons ketchup
½	teaspoon horseradish
¼	teaspoon salt
⅛	teaspoon dry mustard
1	cup (¼ pound) fresh King crab meat (or use 7½-ounce can, drained)

To crisp lettuce, core, rinse and drain very well. Place in disposable plastic bag or plastic crisper and chill thoroughly. Clean, cut and chill other vegetables.

For dressing, combine mayonnaise, ketchup, horseradish, salt and mustard.

Shred half lettuce head and combine with other vegetables and crab meat in salad bowl. Pour dressing over and toss for 3 to 5 minutes until everything is moist and well coated.

Makes 1 huge serving or 4 small ones.

PAPAYA CROWN SALAD

1	can (6¼ ounces) tuna, drained
½	cup finely chopped green onions
½	cup pared, finely chopped cucumber
1–2	tablespoons diced green chilies

Continued

2 tablespoons mayonnaise
Salt and pepper to taste
4 papayas
1 lemon

Combine tuna, green onions, cucumber, chilies, capers and mayonnaise in mixing bowl. Season with salt and pepper and chill for several hours. Make papaya crowns by slicing each papaya in half and removing seeds. With sliced side down cut a wedge 2 inches deep from the stem end of each half. Sprinkle each half with lemon juice and refrigerate until ready to serve. To serve, stand 2 papaya halves in a small cup and fill with tuna salad mixture. *Makes 4 servings.*

ROCK LOBSTER–GREEN NOODLE SALAD

24 ounces frozen South African rock lobster tails
1 package (8 ounces) spinach egg noodles
2 cups chicken broth
2 tablespoons lemon juice
Ground pepper
2 stalks celery cut in ½-inch pieces
1 cucumber, sliced
1 large onion, sliced
1 cup mayonnaise
1 teaspoon curry powder

Drop frozen rock lobster tails into boiling salted water. When water reboils, cook for 3 minutes. Drain immediately and drench with cold water. Cut away underside membrane, remove meat in one piece and slice into medallions. Cook and drain noodles according to package directions.

In a large bowl, combine noodles with 1½ cups hot chicken broth, lemon juice and pepper to taste. Cool. At serving time, top noodles with rock lobster medallions, celery, cucumber and onion. Mix mayonnaise with ½ cup chicken broth and curry powder until smooth. Pour over top of salad. *Makes 8 servings.*

SALMON SALAD FOR ONE

1 can (3¾ ounces) salmon
Crisp salad greens
Fresh pear wedges
Clusters of grapes
Celery sticks
2 tablespoons mayonnaise
½ teaspoon lemon juice
⅛ teaspoon dried dill weed
Parsley, for garnish

Chill and drain salmon, reserving liquid. Turn can of salmon out on salad plate lined with greens. Arrange pear wedges, grapes and celery sticks around salmon. For dressing, blend mayonnaise with reserved salmon liquid, lemon juice and dill weed. Top salad with dressing and garnish with sprig of parsley. *Makes 1 whole meal salad.*

VARIATIONS: In place of dried dill weed, use ⅛ teaspoon curry powder, ½ teaspoon prepared mustard or 1 teaspoon chopped chives.

SARDINE-ONION SALAD

1 small red onion, sliced in thin slivers
½ cup pitted black olives, sliced
1 can (4 ounces) pimientos, chopped
½ cup lemon juice
¼ cup olive oil
1 tablespoon wine vinegar
1 clove garlic, crushed
½ bay leaf, crumbled
1 tablespoon dry mustard
Dash cayenne pepper
1 teaspoon salt
Pepper to taste
1 can (3¾ ounces) Norway sardines, drained
4 cups salad greens

Combine first three ingredients in bowl.

In another bowl, combine lemon juice, oil, vinegar, garlic, bay leaf, dry mustard, cayenne pepper, salt and pepper. Mix well.

Pour over vegetable mixture. Chill 2 to 4 hours to marinate

Serve with crisp salad greens and sardines. *Makes 4 servings.*

SCANDIA SALAD

2 small tomatoes, thinly sliced
1 can (8½ ounces) small whole potatoes, drained
1 can (8¼ ounces) sliced beets, well drained
2 hard-cooked eggs, sliced
⅓ cup olive oil
3 tablespoons wine vinegar
3 tablespoons lemon juice
1 clove garlic, crushed
1 teaspoon salt
½ teaspoon sweet basil
Pepper to taste
4 cups salad greens
1 can (3¾ ounces) Norway sardines, drained

Combine first four ingredients in small bowl.

In another small bowl, combine oil, vinegar, lemon juice, garlic, salt, sweet basil and pepper. Mix thoroughly.

Pour over eggs and vegetables. Chill at least 2 hours to marinate.

Serve with salad greens. Garnish with sardines. *Makes 4 servings.*

TUNA-MACARONI SALAD

2	cups (8 ounces) elbow macaroni
	Salt
3	quarts boiling water
1	can (6½ or 7 ounces) tuna, drained
¼	cup diced cucumber
¼	cup chopped celery
¼	cup chopped parsley
2	tablespoons sliced Spanish stuffed green olives
3	tablespoons salad oil
1	tablespoon lemon juice
⅛	teaspoon pepper

Gradually add macaroni and 1 tablespoon salt to rapidly boiling water so that water continues to boil. Cook uncovered, stirring occasionally, until tender. Drain in colander. Rinse with cold water. Drain again.

Combine macaroni, tuna, cucumber, celery, parsley, olives, salad oil, lemon juice, ½ teaspoon salt and pepper. Toss well to mix thoroughly.

Refrigerate until well chilled. *Makes 4 servings.*

WALNUT-SALMON SALAD

⅔	cup toasted walnuts
1	can (1 pound) red salmon
⅔	cup sliced celery
¼	cup sweet or dill pickle, cut in strips
2	tablespoons coarsely chopped pimiento
1	tablespoon finely chopped parsley
	Crisp salad greens
	Walnut halves and lemon wedges for garnish
½	cup mayonnaise
½	teaspoon curry powder
½	teaspoon onion powder
¼	teaspoon seasoned salt
1	teaspoon lemon juice

Chopped toasted walnuts coarsely. Drain salmon; remove skin and bones and separate fish into large chunks. Gently combine chopped walnuts, salmon, celery, pickle, pimiento and parsley. Arrange salad

on bed of crisp greens. Garnish with walnut halves and lemon wedges. Combine mayonnaise with curry and onion powders, salt and lemon juice. Serve with salad. *Makes 4 servings.*

Note: Salad may be tossed gently with the dressing, if desired, instead of being served separately.

SEA SLAW

1½	pounds fresh or frozen shrimp, peeled, deveined and chopped (about 2 cups)
4	cups shredded cabbage (about ½ medium head)
¼	cup sliced green onions
¾	cup mayonnaise
¼	cup fresh lemon juice
2	teaspoons sugar
1	teaspoon seasoned salt
½	teaspoon dry mustard
¼	teaspoon Worcestershire sauce
¼	teaspoon hot pepper sauce
	Salt

Boil shrimp. Reserve a few whole shrimp for garnish and chop the remainder. Refrigerate to cool.

In a bowl, toss together cabbage, chopped shrimp and onions. Set aside. In another bowl, combine mayonnaise, lemon juice, sugar, seasoned salt, mustard, Worcestershire sauce and hot pepper sauce. Pour over shrimp mixture and toss to coat. Add salt to taste.

Chill until serving time. *Makes 4 cups.*

PASTA & RICE SALADS

BEAN-PASTA-HAM SALAD

1	cup dry navy beans
6	cups water
¼	cup vegetable oil
¼	cup wine vinegar
2	small cloves garlic, minced
½	teaspoon salt
⅛	teaspoon hot pepper sauce
1	cup julienne ham
2	cups cooked small macaroni shells
½	cup cooked peas
½	cup coarsely grated carrots
⅓	cup chopped celery
2	tablespoons finely chopped onion

Continued

Place dry navy beans in large saucepan with 6 cups water. Bring to a boil; boil 2 minutes. Remove from heat. Allow to stand covered 1 hour. Bring beans to a boil; cover; reduce heat and simmer 1 hour, or until beans are tender. Drain and reserve.

In large bowl, mix oil, vinegar, garlic, salt and pepper sauce. Add ham, macaroni, peas, carrots, celery, onions and beans, stirring to coat well. Refrigerate for 1 hour, serve at room temperature for better flavor. *Makes 4 to 6 servings.*

MACARONI GARDEN SALAD

2	cups elbow macaroni (8 ounces)
1	tablespoon salt
3	quarts boiling water
1	cup creamed cottage cheese
1	cucumber, thinly sliced
8	radishes, thinly sliced
1	cup diced celery
1	tablespoon chopped onion
1	teaspoon salt
½	teaspoon dry mustard
3	tablespoons low-calorie Italian salad dressing
1	medium head Boston lettuce

Gradually add macaroni and salt to rapidly boiling water so that water continues to boil. Cook uncovered, stirring occasionally, until tender. Drain in colander. Rinse in cold water; drain again.

Combine remaining ingredients except lettuce; toss with macaroni. Chill. Serve salad in lettuce-lined bowl. *Makes 4 servings.*

MACARONI SPRING SALAD

4	cups elbow macaroni (1 pound)
2	tablespoons salt
4	quarts boiling water
1½	cups sliced carrots
1	cup sliced radishes
2	tablespoons minced onion
1	cup thinly sliced dill or sweet pickles
	Dash pepper
½	cup bottled French dressing
	Tomato wedges, optional

Gradually add macaroni and salt to rapidly boiling water so that water continues to boil. Cook uncovered, stirring occasionally, until tender. Drain in colander. Rinse with cold water; drain again. Cool.

Combine macaroni, celery, carrots, radishes, onion and pickles. Toss well. Add pepper and dressing; toss again. Chill until serving time. Garnish with tomato wedges, if desired. *Makes 8 servings.*

MACARONI, SALAMI, AND CHEESE SALAD

2	cups elbow macaroni (8 ounces)
1	tablespoon salt
3	quarts boiling water
1	cup diced salami
1	cup cubed Cheddar cheese
1	cup thinly sliced celery
½	cup chopped green pepper (optional)
¼	cup chopped sweet pickle or pickle relish
1	cup mayonnaise
2	teaspoons prepared mustard
1	teaspoon instant minced onion
1	teaspoon salt

Gradually add macaroni and 1 tablespoon salt to rapidly boiling water so that water continues to boil. Cook uncovered, stirring occasionally, until tender. Drain in colander. Rinse with cold water; drain.

Combine macaroni, salami, cheese, celery, green pepper and pickles. Add mayonnaise, mustard, onion and 1 teaspoon salt. Toss lightly until mixed. Refrigerate in covered container. *Makes 6 to 8 servings.*

MACARONI TWO-CHEESE SALAD

2	cups elbow macaroni (8 ounces)
1	tablespoon salt
3	quarts boiling water
2	tablespoons chopped scallions or green onions
1	teaspoon salt
¼	teaspoon pepper
½	pound Swiss cheese
½	pound Cheddar cheese
¾	cup mayonnaise
¼	cup chili sauce
	Crisp lettuce

Gradually add macaroni and 1 tablespoon salt to rapidly boiling water so that water continues to boil. Cook uncovered, stirring occasionally, until tender. Drain in colander. Rinse with cold water. Drain again.

Combine macaroni, scallions, 1 teaspoon salt and pepper. Cut half of the Swiss and Cheddar cheeses in to one-half-inch cubes. Add to macaroni mixture. Blend mayonnaise with chili sauce, stir into macaroni mixture. Place lettuce leaves on salad platter. Arrange macaroni salad in center. Cut remaining Swiss and Cheddar cheeses into thin strips and arrange around salad. *Makes 6 servings.*

MACARONI-VEGETABLE PICNIC SALAD

        2   cups elbow macaroni (8 ounces)
        1   tablespoon salt
        3   quarts boiling water
        1   package (10 ounces) frozen peas
       ⅓   cup sliced radishes
       ⅓   cup sliced celery
       ⅓   cup salad oil
       ⅓   cup vinegar
       ⅓   cup water
        1   teaspoon sugar
        2   teaspoons salt
       ½   teaspoon marjoram
       ½   teaspoon chervil

Gradually add macaroni and 1 tablespoon salt to rapidly boiling water so that water continues to boil. Cook uncovered, stirring occasionally, until tender. Drain in colander. Rinse with cold water; drain. Cook peas according to package directions; drain. Combine macaroni, peas, radishes and celery. Cover and chill. Combine oil, vinegar, ⅓ cup water, sugar, 2 teaspoons salt, marjoram and chervil in 1 pint jar. Shake before serving and pour over macaroni mixture. Toss well.

MACARONI-VEGETABLE SALAD

        2   cups elbow macaroni (8 ounces)
        1   tablespoon salt
       .3   quarts boiling water
       ½   cup each: diced celery, diced green pepper
       ½   cup shredded carrot
       ¼   cup finely chopped onion
       ⅔   cup mayonnaise
        1   tablespoon lemon juice
       ½   teaspoon salt
       ¼   teaspoon each: pepper, dry mustard

Gradually add macaroni and 1 tablespoon salt to rapidly boiling water so that water continues to boil. Cook uncovered, stirring occasionally, until tender. Drain in colander. Rinse with cold water; drain again.

Combine macaroni with remaining ingredients; toss lightly and chill. For a picnic turn into chilled wide-mouth vacuum jug. At home, serve on crisp lettuce leaves, garnished with additional shredded carrot, as desired. *Makes 4 to 6 servings.*

PIQUANT MACARONI SALAD

        4   cups elbow macaroni (1 pound)
        2   tablespoons salt
        4   quarts boiling water
       ¼   cup vinegar
       ½   cup salad oil
       ½   teaspoon paprika
             Salt to taste
             Pepper to taste
       ¼   pound American cheese
        2   cups julienne ham strips
       ¾   cup chopped green pepper
       ¾   cup chopped celery
       ¼   cup sliced scallions

Gradually add macaroni and 2 tablespoons salt to rapidly boiling water so that water continues to boil. Cook uncovered, stirring occasionally, until tender. Drain in colander. Rinse with cold water; drain.

Combine vinegar, oil, paprika, salt to taste and pepper. Mix well. Add macaroni and mix lightly; cover and chill about an hour. Cut cheese into thin strips. Add ham, cheese, green pepper, celery, and scallions to macaroni mixture. Toss lightly. Chill thoroughly. *Makes 8 servings.*

SPAGHETTI SALAD ITALIANO

        8   ounces spaghetti, broken into pieces
       ½   cup diced green pepper
        1   medium onion, finely chopped
       ½   cup sliced olives
        1   cup mayonnaise
       ½   cup old-world-style spaghetti sauce
       ½   teaspoon salt
       ¼   teaspoon celery seed
             Dash pepper

Cook spaghetti *al dente* for 6 to 8 minutes; rinse in cold water and drain. Combine spaghetti and remaining ingredients and toss well. Chill.

Garnish with sliced hard-boiled egg before serving, if desired. *Makes 5 to 6 servings.*

TABOULI SALAD

       2½   cups water
        1   tablespoon butter or margarine
        1   box (6 ounces) long-grain and wild rice
        1   large tomato, diced
       ½   cup diced green pepper
       ½   cup cucumber, peeled and diced
       ½   cup sliced pitted black olives
       ½   cup minced parsley

Continued

⅓   cup olive or vegetable oil
⅓   cup lemon juice
3   tablespoons minced fresh mint or 1
     tablespoon dried mint leaves

Combine water, butter, rice and contents of seasoning packet in medium saucepan. Bring to boil.

Cover tightly and cook over low heat until all water is absorbed, about 25 minutes.

Place rice in medium bowl and cool to room temperature. Add remaining ingredients. Mix thoroughly.

Chill at least 1 hour. Mix before serving.
Makes 6 servings.

MEXICAN HOT POT PASTA-PEPPER SALAD

2   cups elbow macaroni (8 ounces)
1   tablespoon salt
3   quarts boiling water
8   pickled hot cherry peppers
     Guacamole Dressing (below)

Gradually add macaroni and salt to rapidly boiling water so that water continues to boil. Cook, uncovered, stirring occasionally, until tender. Drain in colander; rinse in cold water. Drain again and chill.

To serve, garnish with pickled hot cherry peppers. Add Guacamole Dressing and toss until macaroni is well-coated. Store any remaining dressing in covered jar in the refrigerator.   *Makes 6 servings.*

GUACAMOLE DRESSING:
1   ripe avocado, peeled and sliced
2   tablespoons lemon juice
¼   cup mayonnaise
2   tablespoons pickled hot cherry pepper
     liquid
1   large tomato, finely chopped
¼   cup finely chopped onion

Sprinkle avocado with lemon juice. Mash well with a fork. Beat in mayonnaise and pepper liquid. Stir in tomato and onion.   *Makes about 2 cups.*

FRUIT SALADS

ANTIPASTO FRUIT SALAD

1   head iceberg lettuce
½   cup salad oil
¼   cup lemon juice
1   tablespoon prepared mustard
½   teaspoon salt
½   teaspoon savory, crumbled
½   teaspoon coarse black pepper
2   tangerines
1   avocado
1   banana

Core, rinse and thoroughly drain lettuce. Chill in disposable plastic bag or plastic crisper. Combine oil, lemon juice, mustard and seasonings in jar; cover and shake well. Peel and section tangerines. Halve avocado; discard seed and skin and slice fruit into crescents. Peel and slice banana. Place fruits in groups in shallow pan; pour dressing over. Cover closely and chill about 1 hour, basting fruit occasionally. Tear enough lettuce into bite-size pieces to yield 4 cups loosely packed; chill any remainder for use another time. Turn torn lettuce into shallow bowl or platter. Spoon fruits onto lettuce in concentric circles. Pour any remaining dressing over all.
Makes about 6 servings.

BANANA-CRACKED WHEAT SALAD

2½   cups water
1   package (8 ounces) wheat pilaf mix
¼   cup lemon juice
¼   cup salad oil
2   cucumbers, pared, seeded and diced
⅓   cup sliced scallions
½   cup chopped parsley
¾   teaspoon salt, divided
¼   teaspoon pepper
2   cups plain yogurt
4   teaspoons chopped mint
4   bananas

In medium saucepan bring water to a boil. Add wheat, reduce heat, cover and simmer 15 minutes. Remove from heat. Stir in lemon juice and oil. Let stand at room temperature until cool. Stir in cucumbers, scallions, parsley, one-half teaspoon salt and pepper. Cover and chill until ready to serve. For dressing, mix yogurt, remaining one-fourth teaspoon salt and mint; chill. When ready to serve, peel bananas, cut into slices, add to salad and mix lightly. Serve with yogurt dressing.

Makes 7 cups, 6 to 8 servings.

BANANA SLAW

1	cup mayonnaise
2	tablespoons vinegar
1	tablespoon milk
2	teaspoons sugar
1	teaspoon celery salt
¼	teaspoon white pepper
8	cups finely shredded cabbage (1 medium cabbage)
½	cup chopped carrots
⅓	cup peanuts
1½	cups sliced bananas (3)

Mix mayonnaise, vinegar, milk, sugar, celery salt and pepper in a large bowl. Add cabbage, carrots and peanuts. Mix well; chill 2 hours or overnight. Add bananas just before serving.

Makes 6 to 8 servings.

New Salad Shape: To give decorative flair to salads, make fluted banana slices by turning the prongs of a fork lengthwise down a peeled banana. Slice crosswise for scallop-edged rounds, a graceful garnish.

BANANA VINAIGRETTE SALAD

6	tablespoons salad oil
2	tablespoons cider vinegar
1	teaspoon salt
½	teaspoon minced garlic
¼	teaspoon dried dill weed
⅛	teaspoon pepper
3	cups torn escarole
1	large cucumber, sliced
1½	cups halved cherry tomatoes
1	cup watercress leaves
3	bananas, peeled and cut into chunks

In a small bowl, mix oil, vinegar, salt, garlic, dill and pepper. Let stand 1 hour. In a salad bowl, combine escarole, cucumber, tomatoes, watercress and bananas. Add dressing, toss lightly and serve immediately. *Makes 6 to 8 servings.*

BARTLETT GREEN GODDESS SALAD

2	fresh Bartlett pears, chilled
	Lemon juice
1	can (15 ounces) sliced beets, chilled and drained
	Lettuce
	Green Goddess Dressing (recipe follows)

Pare, core and slice pears; brush with lemon juice. Arrange pears and beets on lettuce-lined salad plates. Serve with Green Goddess Dressing.

Makes 4 servings.

GREEN GODDESS DRESSING:
In a small bowl, combine 1 cup mayonnaise, ½ cup sour cream, ¼ cup minced parsley, 2 tablespoons *each* minced chives, wine vinegar and anchovy paste, 1 tablespoon lemon juice, 1 clove garlic, minced or pressed, and ¼ teaspoon tarragon. With a wire whisk or fork, stir ingredients until blended; cover and refrigerate for at least 2 hours.

Makes about 2 cups.

BUFFET BANANA FRUIT SALAD

1	cantaloupe
	Salad greens
4	peaches, peeled and sliced
1	bunch seedless grapes, separated into clusters
½	pound sweet cherries
3	bananas
	Cottage Cheese Lime Dressing (recipe follows)

Peel cantaloupe, cut in half and remove seeds. Cut into 6 crosswise slices. Line a platter with salad greens. Arrange cantaloupe, peaches, grapes and cherries on greens. Peel bananas, cut in diagonal slices and place on cantaloupe rings. Serve with Cottage Cheese Lime Dressing (below).

Makes 6 servings.

COTTAGE CHEESE LIME DRESSING:

1	cup cottage cheese
¼	teaspoon grated lime rind
3	tablespoons lime juice
¼	cup milk
1	teaspoon sugar
¼	teaspoon salt
1	tablespoon mayonnaise
⅛	teaspoon ginger

In blender container combine all ingredients. Cover and process at high speed until smooth or beat until smooth.

DIFFERENT BANANA SALAD

4	cups torn salad greens (spinach, chicory, escarole, lettuce)
½	cup pitted ripe olives (sliced or whole)
½	cup fresh grapefruit sections*
½	cup halved or whole cherry tomatoes
2	bananas, sliced

In large bowl combine salad greens, olives and grapefruit sections. Peel bananas, cut into slices and add with French dressing. Toss lightly to mix well and serve immediately.   *Makes 4 servings.*

*Well drained canned or chilled grapefruit sections may be used.

FRENCH DRESSING:

¼	cup salad oil
1	tablespoon lemon juice
2	teaspoons vinegar
½	teaspoon prepared mustard
½	teaspoon salt
⅛	teaspoon pepper
¼	teaspoon dried leaf basil
1	tablespoon chopped parsley

In small bowl, combine all ingredients. Stir vigorously or beat to mix well. (If desired, use ⅓ cup prepared French or Italian dressing.)

FAMILY SUPPER SALAD PLATE

2	peeled nectarines, peaches or plums, sliced
2	cups cantaloupe, honeydew or watermelon balls
1	avocado, pared and sliced
1	medium cucumber, cut in spears, or 2 cups salad greens, torn into bite-size pieces
1	tomato, cut in wedges, or 1 cup cherry tomatoes
12	whole radishes or seedless green grapes
1	small red onion, thinly sliced, or 8 scallions, trimmed
1	green pepper, seeded and cut in strips
½	pound thinly sliced cooked chicken, turkey, ham or other luncheon meat
½	pound sliced Swiss, American or Muenster cheese Creamy Curry Dressing (recipe follows)

On a large platter arrange fruits, vegetables and sliced meats and cheese. Serve with Creamy Curry Dressing, and slices of whole grain bread.
Makes 4 servings.

CREAMY CURRY DRESSING:

½	cup sour cream
½	cup mayonnaise
1	tablespoon honey
¼–½	teaspoon curry powder
⅛	teaspoon salt

In a small bowl, stir all ingredients until smooth.
Makes 1 cup dressing.

FIESTA SALAD

3	oranges, peeled and sectioned (1½ cups sections)
1	grapefruit, peeled and sectioned (1 cup sections)
1	can (1 pound) red kidney beans, drained
1	cup very thinly sliced celery
3	tablespoons chopped pimiento
2	tablespoons chopped parsley
¼	cup salad oil
3	tablespoons orange juice
2	tablespoons finely minced onion
1	teaspoon salt
½	teaspoon dried leaf oregano, crumbled
¼	teaspoon dried leaf thyme, crumbled Lettuce leaves

Combine orange and grapefruit sections, kidney beans, celery, pimiento and parsley in large bowl. In small bowl or jar, combine oil, orange juice, onion, salt, oregano and thyme. Mix well. Pour over salad. Cover. Refrigerate 2 hours. To serve, spoon into lettuce-lined bowl.   *Makes 4 to 6 servings.*

GRAPE AMBROSIA

1	package (3 ounces) strawberry flavor gelatin
2	cups boiling water
1	cup sour cream*
1	cup miniature marshmallows
1	can (11 ounces) mandarin oranges, drained
2	cups grapes, stemmed, halved and seeded
¼	cup coarsely chopped walnuts
½	can (3½ ounces) toasted coconut

In mixing bowl, dissolve gelatin in boiling water. Pour into 8-inch cake pan. Chill until firm. Meanwhile, mix together remaining ingredients, except coconut. Cut chilled gelatin into cubes. Fold into mixture. Store in refrigerator until serving time. Garnish with toasted coconut.   *Makes 6 servings.*

*May substitute whipped topping mix for sour cream. Follow package directions.

ALTERNATE METHOD: When gelatin is syrupy, beat with electric mixer rotary beater until frothy. Fold in sour cream or substitute and proceed as directed above. Chill until set.

GRAPEFRUIT-HOT BEAN SALAD

2	tablespoons butter or margarine
½	cup chopped onion
1	tablespoon cornstarch
1	cup grapefruit juice
2	tablespoons cider vinegar
1	tablespoon soy sauce
¼	cup packed brown sugar
2	cups diagonally sliced celery
1	can (1 pound, 4 ounces) kidney beans, drained
1	can (1 pound, 4 ounces) chick peas, drained
1	can (1 pound) cut green beans, drained
2	cups grapefruit sections

In large skillet melt butter. Add onion and cook until tender. In medium bowl mix cornstarch and grapefruit juice, add to skillet with cider vinegar, soy sauce and brown sugar, and mix well. Bring to a boil and cook until sauce is thickened, stirring constantly. Stir in celery, drained kidney beans, chick peas and green beans. Cook over low heat 10 minutes. Add grapefruit sections and heat.
Makes 6 servings.

To section grapefruit: Cut off slice from top, then cut off peel in strips from top to bottom, cutting deep enough to remove white membrane, cut slice from bottom. Or cut off peel round and round spiral fashion. Go over fruit again, removing any remaining white membrane. Cut along side of each dividing membrane from outside to middle of core. Remove section by section over bowl to retain juice from fruit.

GRAPEFRUIT-HOT POTATO SALAD

1	pound Italian sweet sausage, cut in 1-inch slices
½	cup chopped onion
¼	cup chopped parsley
4½	teaspoons flour
4	teaspoons sugar
½	teaspoon salt
⅔	cup grapefruit juice
2	tablespoons vinegar
½	cup water
4	cups sliced, pared cooked potatoes
2	cups grapefruit sections

Brown sausage in a large skillet over medium heat. Add onion and parsley and cook until onion is tender. Blend in flour, sugar and salt. Stir in grapefruit juice, vinegar and water. Bring to a boil, stirring constantly, add potatoes and cook over low heat 15 minutes. Add grapefruit sections and heat.
Makes 4 servings.

HAWAIIAN PAPAYA SLAW

3	cups lightly packed shredded cabbage
1	cup cubed pineapple
½	cup sliced celery
¼	cup chopped green pepper
2	green onions, sliced
	Creamy Soy Dressing (recipe follows)
3	Hawaiian papayas, halved and seeded
3	tablespoons toasted sesame seeds

In large bowl, combine cabbage, pineapple, celery, pepper, onions and Creamy Soy Dressing. Toss. Chill 1 hour.

Arrange papaya halves on platter or individual serving plates. Fill with slaw. Sprinkle with sesame seeds.
Makes 6 servings.

CREAMY SOY DRESSING:
Blend together ½ cup mayonnaise, 1½ teaspoons soy sauce, 1 teaspoon Dijon-style mustard, and ¼ teaspoon garlic powder. *Makes about ½ cup.*

HIS 'N' HERS MELONS

SALAD:

1	small cantaloupe
1	small honeydew melon
½	teaspoon salad seasoning
⅓	cup rum (optional)
1	cup (about 6 ounces) ham, cut matchstick size

DRESSING:

2	medium (about ¾ pound) avocados
2	tablespoons lemon juice
3	tablespoons mayonnaise
1	teaspoon salad seasoning

GARNISH:

½	cup roasted salted almonds

Continued

MAKE SALAD: Cut cantaloupe in half, crosswise. Scoop out seeds. With melon ball cutter, make melon balls from 1 half of cantaloupe. Slightly enlarge the cavity of other half of cantaloupe to make a "bowl." Repeat this process with the honeydew melon, making melon balls from 1 half and enlarging cavity of other half.

Sprinkle inside of each "bowl" melon with one-fourth teaspoon seasoning blend. Turn upside down on paper towel to drain.

Combine melon balls with rum. Let marinate for 15 to 30 minutes.

MAKE DRESSING: Discard pits and peel avocados. Mash or chop in blender. Add lemon juice, mayonnaise and seasoning blend. Beat or blend just until smooth.

ASSEMBLE SALAD: Cut off a thin slice from bottom of each melon "bowl" so it is steady. Spoon a small amount of dressing into each melon bowl. Add a layer of melon balls, then a layer of ham. Continue until "bowls" are filled. Cover with plastic wrap. Refrigerate until serving time.

To serve, spoon Dressing over each salad. (Dressing may be reserved for dunking.) Top with almonds. Garnish with grapes.   *Makes 2 servings.*

Note: For carry-along picnics, put wrapped salads in a cooler. Keep Dressing separate, but in cooler also.

MELON BALLS ON-A-RAFT

1	head iceberg lettuce
	Creamy Cheese Spread (recipe follows)
	Fruit Dressing (recipe follows)
40	large melon balls (cantaloupe, watermelon, Crenshaw, honeydew or an assortment)
	Mint sprigs for decoration

Core, rinse and thoroughly drain lettuce. Chill in disposable plastic bag or plastic crisper. Cut lettuce head crosswise into four 1-inch rafts; cover with plastic wrap and chill. Prepare Creamy Cheese Spread and Fruit Dressing; make melon balls. When ready to serve, spread each raft with Creamy Cheese Spread. Pile 10 melon balls in each raft. Serve with Fruit Dressing. Decorate with mint sprigs.   *Makes 4 servings.*

CREAMY CHEESE SPREAD: Beat 1 (8-ounces) package cream cheese with 2 tablespoons each sugar and lime juice.
FRUIT DRESSING: Combine 1 cup orange juice, 1 tablespoon cornstarch, teaspoon dry mustard and dash of salt in small saucepan. Cook and stir over moderate heat until mixture boils and thickens slightly. Lightly beat 1 egg yolk. Stir a spoonful of

cooked mixture into yolk, then combine with remaining hot mixture. Stir over low heat a minute or two. Remove from heat and stir in 2 tablespoons each sugar and lime juice, one-half teaspoon each chopped mint (or dry mint flakes) and grated lime peel. Cool, then blend in one-half cup real mayonnaise.   *Makes about 1¾ cups dressing.*

MEXICAN SALAD NAVIDAD

	Lime Dressing (recipe follows)
1	can (20 ounces) pineapple chunks
1	can (1 pound) pickled or plain sliced beets
2	medium green apples, thinly sliced
2	medium oranges, peeled and sectioned
2	bananas, sliced
1	cup mayonnaise or salad dressing
	Romaine lettuce
½	cup roasted, diced, salted almonds
¼	cup pomegranate seeds or sunflower nuts (optional)
	Whole natural almonds

Prepare Lime Dressing (recipe follows)

Drain pineapple and beets. Lightly rinse beets with cold water and pat dry.

Combine pineapple, beets, apple slices, orange sections and bananas.

Blend ½ cup Lime Dressing with mayonnaise. Set aside. Pour remaining dressing over fruits. Chill.

Just before serving, line serving bowl with romaine lettuce. Toss fruits and diced almonds together. Arrange in bowl.

Sprinkle with pomegranate seeds or sunflower nuts, if desired. Decorate with a few whole natural almonds. Pass reserved dressing.

   Makes 8 servings or about 2 quarts of salad.

LIME DRESSING:
Combine ½ cup salad oil, ⅓ cup lime juice, 2 tablespoons brown sugar and ¾ teaspoon salt in small jar. Cover tightly. Shake well to blend.

   Makes 1 cup dressing.

NECTARINES AND BROCCOLI IN TOMATO VINAIGRETTE

1	large bunch broccoli (or 1 pound zucchini, sliced)
4	small (or 2 large) fresh nectarines, sliced (about 2 cups)
1	small onion, thinly sliced

½   can (10¾ ounces) condensed tomato
    soup (or 1 7¼-ounce can low-sodium
    tomato soup)
½   cup wine vinegar
⅓   cup vegetable oil
2   tablespoons sugar
½   teaspoon prepared mustard

Cut broccoli into small spears.

Drop into 1 inch of boiling salted water in sauce-pan. Return water to boil. Gently boil until tender-crisp, about 3 minutes. Drain and cool.

Place broccoli, nectarines and onion in shallow baking dish or salad bowl.

Mix soup with vinegar, oil, sugar and mustard. Pour over vegetables and fruit.

Refrigerate several hours or overnight, spooning dressing over occasionally.   *Makes 4 to 6 servings.*

NECTARINE VEGETABLE SALAD

    Pesto Dressing (recipe follows)
1   cup sliced carrots
1   cup zucchini sticks
2   medium-size tomatoes
2   large fresh nectarines
    Crisp lettuce

Prepare and chill Pesto Dressing. Cook carrots and zucchini just until tender-crisp. Drain and chill. Cut tomatoes into wedges. Halve and cut nectarines in thick slices. Line salad plates with crisp lettuce. Arrange vegetables and nectarines on lettuce. Serve with Pesto Dressing.   *Makes 4 servings.*

BASIC PESTO (Italian basil and garlic sauce): 2 pounded garlic cloves, 1 cup (2 ounces) chopped fresh basil, ½ cup (2 ounces) grated Parmesan cheese and 2 ounces pounded pignoli. Beat in mortar and thicken gradually with 4 tablespoons olive oil. Will have consistency of creamed butter.

PESTO DRESSING: Blend 1 cup mayonnaise with ½ cup dairy sour cream. Stir in 2 teaspoons prepared pesto and 1 teaspoon lemon juice.
    Makes about 1½ cups.

PAPAYA MEXICORN SALAD

1   package (10 ounces) frozen corn
½   cup sliced Bermuda onion
⅓   cup chopped green pepper
10   cherry tomatoes, halved
     Salt and pepper to taste
     Marinade (recipe follows)
4   papayas

Prepare corn according to package directions. Remove from heat, rinse with cold water and drain thoroughly. In a mixing bowl combine corn, onion, green pepper and cherry tomatoes. Toss lightly with salt and pepper. Combine marinade with vegetable salad and chill for several hours. To serve: make papaya crowns by slicing each papaya lengthwise in half and removing seeds. With sliced side down, cut a wedge two inches deep from the stem end of each half. Sprinkle each half with lemon juice and refrigerate until serving time. To assemble crowns place 2 papaya halves in a small cup and fill with marinated vegetables.

    MARINADE:
¼   cup olive oil or vegetable oil
3   tablespoons red wine vinegar
1   clove garlic crushed
¼   teaspoon salt
    Dash cayenne pepper

Combine ingredients and blend well.
    Makes 4 servings.

PAPAYA SALAD WITH SEED DRESSING

½   cup white wine vinegar
1   green onion, chopped
½   cup sugar
1½   teaspoons salt
½   teaspoon dry mustard
½   cup vegetable oil
     Seeds from ½ papaya
1   box cherry tomatoes
2   cups fresh or canned pineapple
     chunks
2   papayas, quartered
2   bananas, sliced
2   cans (8 ounces each) mandarin
     orange sections, drained
1   avocado, cut in eighths

Pour vinegar into electric blender or use rotary beater. Add onion, sugar, salt and mustard. Cover; blend 30 seconds at high speed. Slowly add oil, with blender on low speed. Add papaya seeds and blend until they resemble coarse pepper. Pour into pint jar or covered container. Refrigerate.
    Makes 1½ cups.

TO SERVE: Arrange fruits in a large serving dish, surrounded with papaya quarters. Drizzle dressing over all. Serve with coconut-coated ball of cream cheese or ice cream if desired.
    Makes 8 dessert servings or 4 luncheon servings.

PEACH SUPPER SALAD

2	large fresh peaches, peeled and halved
2	teaspoons lemon juice
	Romaine lettuce
1	cup cooked chicken, diced
2	green onions, sliced
¼	cup Curry Dressing (recipe follows)
2	medium tomatoes, peeled and chopped
2	hard-cooked eggs, chopped
2	slices crisply cooked bacon, crumbled
½	avocado, diced

Prepare peaches. Sprinkle with lemon juice. Set aside.

Line large individual salad bowls with broken romaine leaves.

Mix chicken and onion with enough dressing to moisten.

Arrange peach halves in center of lettuce. Top with mound of chicken salad. Arrange remaining ingredients around peaches.

Serve cold. Pass extra Curry Dressing.

Makes 2 servings.

CURRY DRESSING:

1	cup sour cream or mayonnaise
¼	cup milk
½	teaspoon curry
¼	teaspoon salt
2	teaspoons wine vinegar

Blend sour cream and milk. Stir in remaining ingredients. *Makes ½ cup dressing.*

PEAR LUNCHEON SALADS

1	can (29 ounces) Bartlett pear halves
2	cups diced cooked chicken
¾	cup chopped celery
½	cup shredded coconut
½	cup golden raisins
¼	cup slivered almonds
	Creamy Pear Dressing (recipe follows)
	Paprika
	Parsley

Chill and drain pears, reserving 2 tablespoons syrup for dressing. Cut pear halves in two, lengthwise. Place four pear quarters upright in individual salad dishes. Combine chicken, celery, coconut, raisins and almonds. Add Creamy Pear Dressing and toss lightly. Spoon salad mixture in center of pear quarters. Sprinkle with paprika and garnish with parsley. *Makes 4 salads.*

CREAMY PEAR DRESSING:

1	cup dairy sour cream
2	tablespoons reserved pear syrup
2	tablespoons orange juice
1	teaspoon grated orange peel
1	teaspoon dry mustard
1	teaspoon salt

Combine all ingredients and chill well.

Makes about 1 cup dressing.

PEAR-MUSHROOM SALAD

	Mushroom Dressing (recipe follows)
2	fresh Bartlett pears
	Small crisp lettuce leaves
1	quart shredded iceberg lettuce
12	small triangles Cheddar or other cheese

Prepare mushroom dressing. When ready to serve, halve and core pears. Line each of 4 salad bowls with small lettuce leaves and measure 1 cup shredded lettuce into each bowl. Place 1 pear half in center of each and surround with 3 cheese triangles. Serve with mushroom dressing. *Makes 4 servings.*

MUSHROOM DRESSING:

Combine ½ cup oil, ¼ cup red wine vinegar, 1 tablespoon prepared mustard, 1 teaspoon onion salt, ½ teaspoon each tarragon (finely crumbled) and granulated sugar and ⅛ teaspoon pepper.

Shake or beat until well mixed. Add 1 cup sliced fresh mushrooms. Cover and chill an hour or so before serving. *Makes about 1⅓ cups of dressing.*

PEAR SUNDAE SALAD

½	cup plain yogurt
2	tablespoons sugar
2	teaspoons lime juice
½	teaspoon grated lime peel
½	teaspoon salt
⅛	teaspoon ground cardamom
½	cup whipping cream
4	fresh Bartlett pears
2–3	cups shredded iceberg lettuce
	Raspberry sherbet (optional)

Blend yogurt with sugar, lime juice and peel, salt and cardamom. Beat cream to soft peaks and fold into yogurt mixture. Halve, core and cut pears into bite-size chunks. Toss with lettuce and pile into large sundae glasses, compotes or spoon onto salad plates. Spoon on yogurt dressing and top each serving with a small ball of raspberry sherbet, if desired. *Makes 4 to 6 servings.*

PEARS AND TOMATOES VINAIGRETTE

½ cup olive oil
⅔ cup red wine vinegar
1 clove garlic, mashed
1 tablespoon granulated sugar
½ teaspoon seasoned salt
2 teaspoons minced fresh basil (*or* ½ teaspoon dried basil)
¼ cup coarsely chopped green onion
1 tablespoon chopped parsley
3 fresh Bartlett pears
3 medium-size tomatoes

Combine oil, vinegar, garlic, sugar, salt and basil. Beat or blend well. Cover and let stand an hour to blend flavors. Add onion and parsley. Halve and core pears. Cut fruit into lengthwise slices. Slice tomatoes. Arrange tomatoes and pears in serving bowl. Pour on dressing. Cover and chill until ready to serve.   *Makes 5 or 6 servings.*

PEARS WITH HOT MUSHROOM DRESSING

4 strips bacon
1 cup sliced fresh mushrooms
2 tablespoons chopped onion
  Pinch thyme
1½ teaspoons cornstarch
½ cup water
½ teaspoon prepared mustard
1½ teaspoons sugar
¼ teaspoon salt
2 tablespoons cider vinegar
1 tablespoon chopped parsley
1 tablespoon chopped pimiento
4 fresh Bartlett pears
  Iceberg lettuce leaves

Cut bacon in 1-inch pieces and fry until crisp. Remove bacon and drain on paper toweling. Drain and measure fat. Return 2 tablespoons drippings to skillet. Add mushrooms, onion and thyme. Saute just until onion is soft. Mix cornstarch with water. Add to skillet, along with mustard, sugar and salt. Bring to a boil, stirring. Add vinegar, parsley, pimiento and crisp bacon. Halve and core pears. Arrange 2 halves for each serving on lettuce leaves. Spoon on hot dressing.   *Makes 4 servings.*

PLUM SUMMERY SALAD

4 fresh plums, cut into slices
1 cup seedless grapes

1 cup sliced strawberries
1 cup cubed cantaloupe
  Juice of 1 lemon
½ cup fresh orange juice
¼ cup white wine (optional)
¼ teaspoon tarragon, crushed
1 banana, peeled and sliced

Combine first four ingredients in a bowl and toss lightly with lemon juice. Combine orange juice, wine and tarragon and pour over fruit. Allow to marinate for 2 or 3 hours. Just before serving add banana. Serve over cottage cheese, yogurt or as fruit chef's salad with cold cuts.   *Makes 4 servings.*

TROPICAL WALNUT SALAD

1 can (10 ounces) mandarin orange sections
1 can (8 ounces) pineapple chunks in juice (reserve juice)
½ cup sliced celery
½ cup chopped toasted walnuts
1 can (7 ounces) solid pack tuna, drained
¾ cup mayonnaise
1 tablespoon lemon juice
1½ teaspoons pineapple juice
¾ teaspoon prepared mustard
  Small lettuce leaves
1 quart shredded lettuce

Drain orange sections and pineapple chunks, saving pineapple juice. Combine fruits with celery, walnuts and tuna, broken into large chunks. Mix together mayonnaise, lemon juice, 1½ teaspoons reserved pineapple juice and mustard. Line 4 individual serving bowls with small lettuce leaves. Turn 1 cup shredded lettuce into each serving bowl and top with fruit-tuna mixture. Serve with dressing.
Makes 4 servings.

24-HOUR SALAD

4 fresh Bartlett pears
2 quarts (shredded) lettuce
½ cup sliced green onions
1 pint creamed, small curd cottage cheese
1 package (10 ounces) frozen peas, thawed
1 tablespoon finely chopped fresh mint
2 cups mayonnaise
2 teaspoons granulated sugar
2 teaspoons seasoned salt
½ cup shredded Cheddar cheese
½ pound cooked bacon, crumbled

Continued

Halve and core pears. Cut into wedges then cross-wise slices. Spread lettuce in shallow glass baking pan (13.5×8.25 inches). Sprinkle onion over lettuce. Dot cottage cheese over onions. Add peas in even layer; sprinkle with mint. Top with pears; frost with mayonnaise. Sprinkle with mixture of sugar and seasoned salt, then shredded cheese. Cover and refrigerate 24 hours. Garnish with crumbled bacon. *Makes 8 to 10 servings.*

WILTED CITRUS SALAD

10	ounces raw spinach, washed and drained
3	oranges, peeled and sliced
1	bunch scallions, sliced
1	bunch radishes, sliced
¼	cup salad oil
2	tablespoons vinegar
2	tablespoons orange juice
¼	teaspoon Tabasco pepper sauce
¼	teaspoon salt (optional)
¼	teaspoon dry mustard

Coarsely tear spinach into large salad bowl. Add sliced oranges, scallions and radishes. Heat salad oil, vinegar, orange juice, pepper sauce, salt and mustard. Pour warm salad dressing over salad and toss. Serve immediately. *Makes 6 to 8 servings.*

MOLDED SALADS

APPLENUTBERRY SALAD

2	envelopes unflavored gelatin
½	cup cold water
½	cup sugar
2¼	cups cranberry juice cocktail, divided
¼	cup lemon juice
½	cup chopped pecans
2	cups chopped pared apples
½	cup thinly sliced celery

Sprinkle gelatin over water in medium saucepan. Place over low heat and stir until gelatin dissolves, 3 to 5 minutes. Remove from heat.

Add sugar and stir until dissolved. Add cranberry juice cocktail and lemon juice. Chill, stirring occasionally, until mixture is slightly thicker than unbeaten egg white.

Fold in pecans, apples and celery. Turn into a 5-cup mold. Chill until set. Unmold and garnish with salad greens. *Makes 6 servings.*

BARBECUE SALAD

1	package (3 ounces) lemon, orange or orange-pineapple flavor gelatin
½	teaspoon salt
1	cup boiling water
1	can (8 ounces) tomato sauce
1½	tablespoons vinegar
	Dash of pepper

Dissolve gelatin and salt in boiling water. Blend in remaining ingredients. Pour into a 3-cup mold, individual molds, or a serving bowl. Chill until Sfirm, about 4 hours. Unmold. Serve with crisp salad greens and mayonnaise, if desired. *Makes about 2 cups or 4 servings.*

Note: For extra flavor, add small amount of one or more of the following seasonings to the gelatin mixture before chilling: onion juice, seasoned salt, celery salt, cayenne, Worcestershire sauce, Tabasco sauce or prepared horseradish.

BARBECUE VEGETABLE SALAD: Prepare Barbecue Salad as directed, adding 1 teaspoon onion juice and other seasonings as desired. Chill until thickened. Then fold in 1 cup drained cooked mixed garden vegetables or 1 cup mixed raw vegetables (radishes, carrots, celery, cucumber, cabbage, green pepper). Spoon into a 3-cup mold or individual molds and chill until firm. *Makes about 3 cups or 6 servings.*

CHERRY CHEESE MOLDS

1	can (16 ounces) dark sweet cherries
1	package (3 ounces) black cherry or cherry flavor gelatin
1	cup boiling water
1	package (3 ounces) cream cheese
¼	cup chopped pecans (optional)
¼	cup sliced stuffed olives

Drain cherries, measuring syrup. Add water to syrup to make 1 cup. Chop cherries and set aside. Dissolve gelatin in boiling water. Add measured liquid. Chill until slightly thickened. Meanwhile, form cheese into small balls. Fold into gelatin with cherries, pecans and olives. Spoon into individual molds. Chill until firm, about 3 hours. Unmold. Serve with crisp greens, if desired. *Makes 3½ cups or 7 servings.*

CHERRY SALAD RING

1	package (3 ounces) black cherry gelatin dessert
1	cup hot water
1	cup juice from cherries
½	cup mayonnaise
4½	ounces non-dairy whipped topping
1	can (16 ounces) dark sweet pitted cherries, drained
½	cup chopped walnuts
½	teaspoon grated orange rind

Dissolve gelatin in hot water. Add juice. Refrigerate until syrupy. Fold in mayonnaise and whipped topping. Fold in remaining ingredients and spoon into Jel-A-Ring mold. Refrigerate until firm.

Serves 10 to 12.

CHICKEN AND CRANBERRY MOLDED SALAD

CRANBERRY LAYER:

1	envelope (1 tablespoon) unflavored gelatin
½	cup water
1	can (16 ounces) whole berry cranberry sauce
1	can (8½ ounces) crushed pineapple in unsweetened juice
1	tablespoon lemon juice

In a small saucepan, sprinkle gelatin over water. Let stand 5 minutes; heat over low heat until completely dissolved. Stir in cranberry sauce, pineapple and lemon juice. Pour into a lightly oiled 1½-quart mold. Chill about 1 hour until set but still sticky to the touch. (Do not use fresh or frozen pineapple.)

CHICKEN LAYER:

1	cup chicken broth
1	envelope (1 tablespoon) unflavored gelatin
1	cup mayonnaise
1	tablespoon lemon juice
¼	teaspoon salt
1½	cups diced cooked chicken
½	cup diced celery
½	cup diced green peper
⅓	cup chopped parsley

In a small saucepan, sprinkle gelatin over chicken broth. Let stand 5 minutes; heat over low heat until completely dissolved. Stir into mayonnaise, beating constantly with a wire wisk. Stir in lemon juice, salt, chicken, celery, pepper and parsley. Chill until

slightly thickened and pour over jellied cranberry layer. Chill at least 6 hours before unmolding and serving on a bed of crisp lettuce surrounded with fresh orange segments. *Makes 4 to 6 servings.*

CHICKEN AND PINEAPPLE SALAD

1	can (13¼ ounces) pineapple tidbits
1	package (3 ounces) lemon flavor gelatin
½	teaspoon salt
1	cup boiling water
1	cup diced cooked chicken or turkey*
⅓	cup finely chopped celery
12–16	strips pimiento

Drain pineapple, measuring syrup. Add water to syrup to make 1 cup. Dissolve gelatin and salt in boiling water. Add measured liquid. Chill until thickened. Fold in chicken, celery and pineapple. Place pimiento strips in form of a cross in individual molds. Spoon gelatin mixture carefully into molds. Chill until firm, about 3 hours. Unmold. Serve with crisp salad greens and mayonnaise, if desired.

Makes about 3½ cups or 6 to 7 servings.

CHICKEN SALAD CROWN

2	envelopes unflavored gelatin
2	cups cocktail vegetable juice
1	tablespoon lemon juice
¼	teaspoon onion powder
½	cup cooked small peas
2	cups water
¼	cup low calorie creamy cucumber dressing
2	cans (5 ounces *each*) chunk thigh chicken
¼	cup shredded zucchini squash

In a saucepan, sprinkle gelatin over cocktail vegetable juice to soften. Place over low heat, stirring until gelatin is dissolved. Remove from heat; add lemon juice and onion powder. Chill until slightly thickened; fold in peas. Pour into 7-cup mold. Chill until slightly firm.

Meanwhile, sprinkle remaining gelatin over water to soften. Place over low heat, stirring until gelatin is dissolved. Add dressing. Chill until slightly thickened. Fold in chicken and zucchini. Pour onto cocktail vegetable juice layer. Chill 4 hours or until firm. Unmold on salad greens.

Makes about 6½ cups, 6 servings.

CREAMY CRANBERRY RELISH MOLD

2   envelopes unflavored gelatin
1   cup cold water
1   (3-ounce) package cream cheese, softened and cut into chunks
2   cups frozen whipped topping, thawed
1   (14-ounce) jar cranberry-orange relish
1   (8¼-ounce) can crushed pineapple, drained
½   cup chopped almonds

In small saucepan, sprinkle unflavored gelatin over water. Let stand until gelatin is moistened.

Place over low heat. Stir constantly until gelatin dissolves, about 5 minutes.

In large bowl, thoroughly blend cheese and topping. Fold in relish, pineapple and almonds. Then fold in gelatin.

Turn into 5-cup mold. Chill until firm.

Unmold and garnish, if desired, with salad greens.   *Makes 8 to 10 servings.*

DEEP SEA SALAD OF NORWAY

1   envelope unflavored gelatin
¼   cup lime or lemon juice
2   cups tomato juice
½   teaspoon *each* salt and dill weed
⅛   teaspoon cayenne pepper
2   carrots, cut in 1-inch julienne
½   cup *each* sliced celery and green onions
2   cans (3¾ ounces *each*) Norway sardines in oil, drained
    Lettuce leaves

In small bowl, soften gelatin in lime juice; set aside. In 1-quart saucepan, bring tomato juice to boil. Remove from heat. Add gelatin mixture; stir until gelatin is dissolved. Stir in salt, dill and cayenne. Chill until mixture is the consistency of unbeaten egg whites. Fold in vegetable pieces.

Arrange 1 can of the sardines on bottom of 4-cup mold. Spoon half of the gelatin mixture over sardines. Layer remaining sardines, topping with remaining gelatin mixture. Chill until firm, about 2 hours. Unmold onto lettuce-lined serving plate. Garnish with watercress sprigs and carrot curls, if desired. Cut in slices to serve.

Makes about 6 servings.

FRESH CHERRY PARFAIT SALAD

2   cups fresh sweet cherries
¾   cup water
1   package (3 ounces) lemon-flavor gelatin
1   pint pineapple sherbet
¼   cup chopped walnuts
    Whole fresh sweet cherries for garnish
    Mint sprigs or salad greens

Pit and slice cherries. Bring water to boil. Add gelatin and stir to dissolve. Add sherbet, by spoonfuls, stirring until well blended and partially set. Fold cherries into gelatin along with walnuts. Pour into 1-quart mold. Chill until firm. Unmold and garnish with whole cherries and mint sprigs or greens.   *Makes 5 to 6 servings.*

Note: Well drained canned sweet cherries or frozen cherries may be used when fresh cherries are not available.

GINGER PEACH SALAD

1   package (3 ounces) lemon or lime flavor gelatin
1   cup boiling water
1   bottle (7 ounces) ginger ale
1   cup drained diced sweetened fresh peaches
¼   cup chopped nuts
¼   cup chopped celery

Dissolve gelatin in boiling water. Add ginger ale and chill until thickened. Fold in peaches, nuts and celery. Spoon into individual molds or serving bowl. Chill until firm, about 3 hours. Unmold. Serve with crisp greens and mayonnaise or sour cream, if desired. *Makes about 3 cups or 6 servings.*

Note: Well-drained frozen peaches or canned sweet peaches may be used when fresh peaches are not available.

GRAPEFRUIT AND CELERY SALAD

1	package (3 ounces) lemon or orange-pineapple flavor gelatin
¼	teaspoon salt
1¼	cups boiling water
½	cup grapefruit juice
1	tablespoon lemon juice
¼	cup mayonnaise
1	cup diced drained grapefruit sections
1	cup diced celery

Dissolve gelatin and salt in boiling water. Add grapefruit juice and lemon juice. Blend in mayonnaise. Chill until slightly thickened. Fold in grapefruit and celery. Pour into a 4-cup ring mold. Chill until firm, at least 3 hours. Unmold. Serve with crisp lettuce and mayonnaise, if desired. Or, serve with cooked shrimp or cold sliced ham or chicken. *Makes about 4 cups or 8 servings or 4 entree servings.*

JELLIED WALDORF SALAD

1	package unflavored gelatin
2	cups apple juice
1	cup mint jelly
2	cups chopped peeled apples
1	cup chopped celery
1	cup slivered blanched almonds

Soak gelatin in a cup of apple juice; then place over low heat and stir until dissolved. Add mint jelly and stir until it is melted. Remove from heat and stir in remaining apple juice. Chill until slightly thickened. Fold in apples, celery and almonds. Spoon into molds and chill until firm. Unmold and use as garnish for meat platter or salad accompaniment. As a variation use one cup apple jelly instead of mint jelly. *Makes 4 to 6 servings.*

JEWELED LIME SALAD

2	envelopes unflavored gelatin
½	cup cold water
1½	cups boiling water
1	package (14 ounces) unsweetened lemon-lime flavor soft drink mix
1	can (14 ounces) sweetened condensed milk (NOT evaporated milk)
¼	cup reconstituted lime juice
1	container (8 ounces) plain yogurt
1	can fruit (29 ounces) cocktail, drained Lettuce leaves

In large bowl, sprinkle gelatin over cold water; let stand 1 minute. Add boiling water and stir until gelatin is dissolved. Add soft drink mix; mix well. Stir in sweetened condensed milk, lime juice and yogurt; mix well. Fold in fruit cocktail. Pour into 8-cup mold. Chill 4 hours or until set. Unmold onto lettuce leaves. Garnish as desired. Refrigerate leftovers. *Makes 12 servings.*

LAYERED CRANBERRY CHEESE MOLD

1	package (3 ounces) cream cheese
⅓	cup real mayonnaise
¾	cup milk
2	tablespoons confectioners' sugar
1	teaspoon vanilla
3	envelopes unflavored gelatin
½	cup water
¼	cup sugar
3½	cups cranberry juice
1	cup chopped cranberries
½	cup chopped pecans (optional)

In small bowl, with mixer at medium speed, beat cream cheese, mayonnaise and milk until smooth. Stir in confectioners' sugar and vanilla.

In small saucepan, sprinkle gelatin over cold water. Stir constantly over low heat until gelatin is dissolved.

Stir 2 tablespoons of dissolved gelatin into mayonnaise mixture. Add sugar to remaining gelatin in saucepan; stir until dissolved, heating if necessary.

In large bowl, stir sugar-gelatin mixture into cranberry juice. Pour 1 cup cranberry mixture (or enough to cover bottom) into bottom of 6-cup mold. Refrigerate until mixture mounds slightly when dropped from spoon. Spoon cheese mixture over cranberry mixture in mold; level with spatula.

When remaining cranberry mixture mounds slightly when dropped from spoon, stir in chopped cranberries and nuts. When cheese mixture is nearly firm, spoon on cranberry-nut mixture. Refrigerate 3 hours or until set.

Continued

Unmold on serving platter. If desired, garnish with frosted grapes.   *Makes 8 to 10 servings.*

Note: To unmold, quickly dip container into warm water for about 5 seconds and loosen around edges with knife. Invert serving dish on top of container and, holding both firmly together, turn right side up and shake gently. If gel does not come loose, repeat process.

MOLDED CHICKEN SALAD

1	package (3 ounces) lemon flavor gelatin
½	teaspoon salt
1	cup boiling water
½	cup cold water
	Dash of pepper
⅓	cup mayonnaise
1½	cups diced cooked chicken or turkey
½	cup finely chopped celery

Dissolve gelatin and salt in boiling water. Add cold water and pepper. Chill until slightly thickened. Blend in mayonnaise. Then fold in chicken and celery. Pour into a 4-cup mold or individual molds. Chill until firm, about 3 hours. Unmold. Serve with crisp salad greens, if desired.

Makes about 3 cups or 6 servings.

ORANGE-PINEAPPLE CREAM MOLD

2	cans (11 ounces) mandarin orange segments, drained
2	envelopes unflavored gelatin
1	cup orange juice
1	cup boiling water
1	can (14 ounces) sweetened condensed milk (NOT evaporated milk)
1	container (16 ounces) sour cream
1	can (8 ounces) crushed pineapple, drained
½	cup chopped nuts
	Lettuce leaves

Line bottom of 6-cup mold with desired amount of orange segments; set aside. In large bowl, sprinkle gelatin over orange juice; let stand 1 minute. Add water and stir until gelatin is dissolved. Add sweetened condensed milk and sour cream; mix well. Fold in pineapple, nuts and remaining orange segments. Turn into prepared mold. Chill 4 hours or until set. Unmold onto lettuce. Garnish as desired. Refrigerate leftovers.   *Makes 10 to 12 servings.*

PEACH 'N' CHEESE MOLDED SALAD

1	can (29 ounces) peach slices, drained
1	container (16 ounces) cottage cheese
1½	cups orange juice
1	package (3 ounces) peach flavor gelatin
1	can (14 ounces) sweetened condensed milk (NOT evaporated milk)
1	cup chopped walnuts

Line bottom of 6-cup mold with 8 peach slices; chop remaining peach slices and set aside. In blender container, blend cheese until smooth; set aside. In small saucepan, bring juice to a boil; remove from heat. Add gelatin; stir until dissolved. In large bowl, combine sweetened condensed milk and cheese. Stir in gelatin; mix well. Stir in chopped peaches and nuts. Turn into prepared mold. Chill 4 hours or until set. Unmold onto lettuce. Garnish as desired. Refrigerate leftovers.   *Makes 10 to 12 servings.*

PEAR WALDORF MOLD

2	fresh Bartlett pears
1	package (3 ounces) lemon flavor gelatin
½	teaspoon salt
1	cup boiling water
¾	cup cold water
½	cup halved and seeded red grapes
¼	cup chopped celery
¼	cup chopped walnuts
	Creamy Waldorf Dressing (recipe follows)
	Pear slices and grapes, for garnish

Core and dice pears, but do not peel. Dissolve lemon gelatin and salt in boiling water. Add cold water. Chill until partially set. Add pears, grapes, celery and walnuts. Pour into 4-cup mold and chill until firm. Unmold and serve with Creamy Waldorf Dressing. Garnish with pear slices and grapes.

Makes 6 servings.

CREAMY WALDORF DRESSING:

¾	cup mayonnaise
½	teaspoon grated lemon peel
1	tablespoon sugar
¼	cup heavy cream, whipped
	Chopped walnuts, for garnish

Combine mayonnaise, lemon peel and sugar. Fold in whipped cream. Serve, garnished with chopped nuts.   *Makes about 1¼ cups dressing.*

PINEAPPLE RELISH MOLD

1	envelope unflavored gelatin
¼	cup cold water
1	can (8¼ ounces) crushed pineapple in syrup
1	tablespoon sugar
¼	teaspoon salt
2	tablespoons vinegar
½	cup chopped celery
¼	cup chopped green pepper
1	pimiento, cut in small pieces

Sprinkle gelatin over cold water in small saucepan. Drain syrup from pineapple into 1-cup measure. Add water to make 1 cup and add one-fourth cup of mixture to gelatin in saucepan. Place saucepan over low heat. Stir constantly until gelatin dissolves, about 5 minutes. Remove from heat. Stir in sugar, salt, remaining syrup mixture, vinegar, and lemon juice. Chill, stirring occasionally, until mixture mounds slightly when dropped from spoon. Fold in drained crushed pineapple, celery, green pepper and pimiento. Turn into 2-cup mold or individual molds. Chill until firm. Unmold and garnish with salad greens. *Makes 4 servings.*

SINK AND SWIM SALAD

2	packages (3 ounces each) lime-flavored gelatin
2	cups boiling water
1½	cups cold water
⅓	cup Creme de Menthe or mint-flavored liqueur
3	small ripe pears, halved, peeled and cored
2½	cups seedless grapes

Dissolve gelatin in boiling water. Add cold water and Creme de Menthe. Chill until slightly thickened. Arrange pear halves in deep 9-inch round or square pan. Pour gelatin over pears and pat grapes firmly over surface. Chill until firm. Unmold. Serve with mayonnaise or sour cream, if desired. *Makes 5 or 6 servings.*

SPICED FRUIT MOLD

1	can (15¼ ounces) pineapple chunks in unsweetened pineapple juice, drained (reserve juice)
1	can (11 ounces) mandarin oranges, drained (reserve syrup)
2½	cups water

1	cinnamon stick
1	teaspoon whole cloves
¼	teaspoon ground ginger
2	envelopes unflavored gelatin
1	medium apple, diced

In a medium saucepan, combine reserved juice with enough reserved syrup to make 1 cup. Add 2 cups water, cinnamon stick, cloves and ginger. Simmer 10 minutes, then strain.

In a medium saucepan, sprinkle unflavored gelatin over remaining ½ cup water. Let stand until gelatin is moistened.

Add hot spiced liquid. Place over low heat and stir constantly until gelatin dissolves, about 2 minutes. Chill, stirring occasionally, until mixture is consistency of unbeaten egg white.

Fold in fruit. Turn into about 8 individual molds or a 5-cup mold. Chill until firm.
Makes about 8 servings.

SPICED HARVARD BEET RING

1	package (8 ounces) cream cheese, softened
2	tablespoons toasted sesame seed
1	jar (1 quart) borscht
1	tablespoon mixed pickling spice Boiling water
2	packages (3 ounces each) lemon flavored gelatin dessert Cold water

Divide cream cheese into 12 portions. Shape into balls, about 1-inch in diameter. Roll in sesame seed; set aside. Strain borscht, reserving slivered beets. Measure 2 cups of the liquid and pour into a saucepan. Add pickling spice. Bring to boil. Reduce heat and simmer 10 minutes. Strain and discard pickling spice.

Measure liquid from saucepan. Add boiling water to make 2 cups. Pour over gelatin; stir to dissolve. Add cold water to remaining borscht liquid to measure 2 cups. Stir into gelatin. Chill until consistency of unbeaten egg white. Pour a layer of gelatin in bottom; chill until set. Stir reserved beets into remaining gelatin mixture. Carefully pour into mold. Chill until firm. Unmold onto serving plate. Garnish with salad greens. Serve with sour cream if desired. *Makes 8 portions.*

Note: To toast sesame seed sprinkle seed evenly in bottom of pie pan. Bake in a preheated 350-degree oven until golden, about 5 to 7 minutes, stirring occasionally.

SPICY VEGETABLE MOLD

2	packages unflavored gelatin
1	can (24 fluid ounces) cocktail vegetable juice
½	teaspoon chili powder
⅛	teaspoon garlic powder
⅛	teaspoon ground cumin seed
	Generous dash ground cloves
1	cup cooked cut-up wax or green beans
½	cup thinly sliced celery
¼	cup chopped green pepper
2	tablespoons chopped red onion

In a saucepan, sprinkle gelatin on ½ cup vegetable juice to soften. Place over low heat, stirring until gelatin is dissolved. Remove from heat. Add remaining juice and seasonings. Chill until slightly thickened. Fold in vegetables. Spoon into 5-cup mold; chill until firm. Unmold on salad greens.
Makes about 4½ cups, 4 servings.

TANGY CHICKEN IN ASPIC

2	packages (3 ounces each) lemon-flavored gelatin
1	cup boiling water
1	can (24 fluid ounces) cocktail vegetable juice
2	tablespoons vinegar
1	teaspoon Worcestershire
2	cans (5 ounces each) chunk white chicken
½	cup chopped green pepper

In a large bowl, dissolve gelatin in boiling water. Stir in juice, vinegar and Worcestershire. Chill until slightly thickened. Fold in chicken and green pepper. Pour into 5-cup mold. Chill until firm.
Makes about 5 cups, 4 servings.

VINEYARD CHIFFON RING

2	envelopes unflavored gelatin
⅔	cup cold water
1	cup plus 3 tablespoons sugar
	Grated peel of 2 oranges
1	cup orange juice
¼	cup lemon juice
4	egg whites
	Dash salt
1	cup whipping cream
2	cups seedless grapes (about ¾ pound)
½	cup halved strawberries

In saucepan, soften gelatin in cold water. Add 1 cup of sugar, orange peel, orange juice and lemon juice.

Heat, stirring, just until sugar and gelatin dissolve. Cool.

Chill until thick but not completely set, 1 to 1½ hours.

In mixing bowl, beat egg whites and salt until foamy. Gradually add remaining 3 tablespoons sugar, beating until whites hold soft peaks.

In another bowl, beat cream to soft peaks. Stir half beaten whites into syrupy gelatin. Fold in remaining whites and whipped cream.

Pour into 6-cup ring mold, rinsed first with cold water. Chill until firm.

To serve, unmold on platter. Fill center with grapes and berries. *Makes 6 servings.*

Note: You may substitute 9-by-5-inch loaf pan for ring mold. After unmolding, arrange grape clusters and strawberries around loaf. Or slice and garnish each serving with grapes and berries.

WILD RICE CHICKEN SALAD MOLD

1	package (6 ounces) long grain and wild rice
2	cups cooked chicken, boned, diced
⅔	cup chopped green pepper
¾	cup diced celery
⅓	cup (2-ounce jar) chopped pimiento
2	hard-cooked eggs, diced
1	tablespoon (1 envelope) unflavored gelatin
1	cup chicken broth
2	teaspoons salt
1	tablespoon lemon juice
⅓	cup mayonnaise
⅓	cup creamy French dressing

Cook rice as directed on package. Combine cooked rice mixture, diced chicken, green pepper, celery, pimiento and hard-cooked eggs. Soak gelatin in chicken broth until soft. Heat and stir until gelatin is completely dissolved. Combine gelatin solution, salt, lemon juice, mayonnaise, French dressing and add to the salad ingredients. Mix well. Pour into salad mold. Chill and allow to set until firm (about 1 hour) before serving. Garnish with parsley or salad greens, tomato wedges and/or stuffed olives.
Makes 8 servings.

VEGETABLE GARDEN MOLD

2	packages unflavored gelatin
2	cups cocktail vegetable juice

1 cup ginger ale
1 tablespoon soy sauce
Generous dash garlic powder
½ cup fresh bean sprouts
½ cup thinly sliced mushrooms
¼ cup shredded carrot
¼ cup thinly sliced celery
2 tablespoons chopped chives
¼ cup sunflower seeds

In saucepan, sprinkle gelatin on ½ cup vegetable juice to soften. Place over low heat, stirring until gelatin is dissolved. Remove from heat. Add remaining juice, ginger ale, soy sauce and garlic. Chill until slightly thickened. Fold in vegetables and sunflower seeds. Spoon into 5-cup mold or individual molds; chill until firm. Unmold on salad greens; garnish with additional shredded carrot.
Makes 4½ cups, 4 servings.

ADDITIONAL SALAD DRESSINGS

GREEN DEVIL DRESSING

1 bag (10 ounces) fresh spinach or 1 package (10 ounces) frozen chopped spinach, thawed
1 cup oil
¼ cup fresh lemon juice
4 teaspoons Worcestershire sauce
1 teaspoon salt
1 teaspoon sugar

Thoroughly rinse, drain and remove stems from fresh spinach or place frozen spinach in a sieve and press out moisture. Place spinach in the jar of an electric blender (fresh spinach will need to be packed down). Add remaining ingredients. Cover and blend until smooth, 30 to 60 seconds, turning blender on and off. Use as a salad dressing or as a dip for fresh vegetables. Refrigerate remaining dressing in a covered container. *Makes 2 cups.*

PEANUT BUTTER DRESSING

½ cup plain yogurt
¼ cup super chunk peanut butter
2 tablespoons honey
1 tablespoon milk

In a small bowl, stir together yogurt, peanut butter, honey and milk until well mixed. Cover; refrigerate. Serve over fresh-fruit salad. *Makes about 1 cup.*

HERBED MUSTARD DRESSING

½ teaspoon powdered mustard
½ teaspoon warm water
½ cup cottage cheese
⅓ cup milk
3 tablespoons lemon juice
1 egg yolk
1 tablespoon sugar
1 tablespoon parsley flakes
1½ teaspoons onion powder
1 teaspoon garlic powder
1 teaspoon salt
1/16 teaspoon ground black pepper

Combine powdered mustard with warm water. Let stand 10 minutes for flavor to develop. Force cottage cheese through a sieve. Combine with mustard and remaining ingredients. Or, in jar of electric blender combine mustard with remaining ingredients; blend until smooth, about 1 minute. Chill and serve over salad greens, sliced tomatoes, chilled cooked vegetables. *Makes about 1¼ cups.*

NECTARINE SALAD DRESSING

2 tablespoons sugar
¾ teaspoon dry mustard
¼ teaspoon salt
3 tablespoons lemon juice
1 small (or ½ large) fresh nectarine, cubed

Continued

6   tablespoons vegetable oil
1   teaspoon sesame seeds, toasted
    (optional)

Combine sugar, mustard, salt, lemon juice and nectarine in electric blender. Whir until blended and smooth.

Gradually add oil while blending at low speed. Stir in sesame seeds, if desired.

Makes 1 cup dressing.

Note: To toast sesame seeds, turn into lightly oiled skillet. Stir over medium-high heat until light golden.

Light Meals, Sandwiches & One-Dish Meals

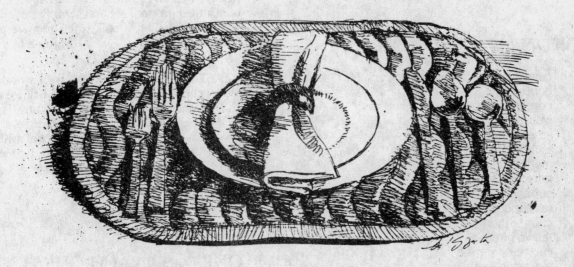

This is rush-rush time for most of us. We tend to eat on the run and insist upon dishes that take little time to prepare. Often, we consume foods at breakfast and lunch that take less than five minutes to gulp down.

Another factor in eating less at certain meal times is our feeling that we are cutting down on calories.

Taking less time to eat and consuming fewer calories are all part of our changing eating patterns. Americans tend to eat more snack-type foods and spend less time and effort on sitting down to a several-course meal.

Quiches, sandwiches of all sizes and varieties, quick-breakfast pancakes and breads, all appear on modern menus as our diet continues to change to accommodate busy lives. And let's not forget one-dish entrées, which are a very important part of today's busy life-style.

Hearty one-dish meals also come to the rescue in stretching the family dollar. They offer an inventive blend of flavors, even when the ingredients are basically leftovers. However, fondues, fish, and seafood dishes or, one of my favorites, chicken pot pie, are far from leftover fare.

LIGHT MEALS

ALMOND-SPINACH QUICHE

1½	cups firmly packed fresh spinach (4 ounces)
¼	pound fresh mushrooms, cut into wedges
1	small onion, chopped
1	tablespoon vegetable oil
1	medium tomato, diced
½	teaspoon thyme
½	cup toasted slivered almonds
2	tablespoons flour
1	cup refrigerated egg substitute (not thawed frozen)
½	cup non-fat milk
½	teaspoon salt
¼	teaspoon pepper
	Baked pie shell (9-inch)

Trim and rinse spinach and tear into small pieces. In large skillet, saute mushrooms and onion in oil. Add tomato, spinach and thyme and cook for 2 to 3 minutes, or just until spinach is limp. Stir in half the almonds and all of the flour. Turn into pie shell. In another container, mix egg substitute, milk, salt and pepper. Pour over pie. Sprinkle with remaining almonds. Bake at 350 degrees for 25 to 30 minutes or until set. *Makes 1 quiche.*

BROCCOLI-SAUSAGE QUICHE

2	packages (10 ounces each) frozen chopped broccoli
4	smoke-flavored frankfurters (6 ounces)
6	eggs
2	cups milk
1	teaspoon salt
½	teaspoon onion powder
1½	cups grated Swiss or Gruyere cheese Pastry-lined pan (recipe below) or baked pie shell
1	tablespoon butter

Cook broccoli in a small amount of boiling salted water until crisp-tender, about 5 minutes. Drain well. Slice frankfurters slightly on the diagonal. Beat eggs until blended and mix in milk, salt, onion powder, cheese and broccoli. Pour into pastry-lined pan. Arrange sausages decoratively on top. Dot with butter. Bake at 425 degrees for 15 minutes. Reduce heat to 375 degrees and bake 25 to 30 minutes longer, or until set and slightly puffed. Let cool a few minutes on a rack, then remove pan sides. Cut in wedges. *Makes 8 to 10 servings.*

PASTRY-LINED PAN: Mix together one and one-fourth cups all-purpose flour, one-half teaspoon salt and one-half cup butter until mixture is crumbly. Add one egg and mix until dough clings together in a ball. Pat into the bottom and sides of a 10-inch flan pan with removable bottom and two-inch sides (must have two-inch sides).

ONION-SPINACH QUICHE

1	pound (2 cups finely chopped) sweet Spanish onions
¼	cup butter
1	package (10 ounces) frozen chopped spinach
¾	cup grated Swiss cheese
3	eggs
1	cup milk
1	teaspoon salt
⅛	teaspoon pepper
	Dash nutmeg
1	unbaked 9-inch pie shell

Peel and chop onions. Saute slowly in butter. Cook spinach according to package directions. Drain thoroughly. Combine onion, spinach and Swiss cheese. Beat eggs. Blend in milk and seasonings. Combine with spinach mixture. Bake pie shell. Pour in egg-vegetable mixture. Bake in 375-degree oven 35 to 40 minutes, or until knife inserted in center comes out clean. *Makes 6 servings.*

CATALINA SALMON QUICHE

2	packages (3 ounces each) cream cheese, softened
½	cup dairy sour cream
2	eggs
2	tablespoons prepared yellow mustard
1	can (7¾ ounces) salmon, drained*
1	frozen 9-inch deep dish pie shell (or pastry for single crust pie)

1   package (10 ounces) frozen chopped
     broccoli, thawed and drained
¼   cup chopped pitted ripe olives
¼   cup shredded Swiss or mozzarella
     cheese

Using mixer or blender, combine cream cheese, sour cream, eggs and mustard until well blended. Break salmon into small chunks and arrange in bottom of unbaked pie shell. Top with broccoli.

Pour cream-cheese mixture over salmon and broccoli. Sprinkle with olives and cheese. Bake in 375-degree oven 40 to 45 minutes or until knife inserted in center comes out clean.

Cut in wedges and serve warm or cold.

Makes 6 servings.

*If preferred, use tuna.

CASA ITALIANO PIZZA

1½   pounds Italian sausage, sliced
2   tablespoons vegetable oil
3   small zucchini or 2 small eggplants,
     sliced
½   teaspoon garlic powder
     Pepper, to taste
2   tablespoons grated Parmesan cheese
2   tablespoons pimiento, chopped
1   round loaf of Italian bread (10 inches
     in diameter), split and toasted
1   jar (14 ounces) quick pizza sauce,
     traditional variety
1   cup shredded mozzarella cheese

Preheat oven to 425 degrees. In a large skillet, saute sausage in oil until thoroughly browned. Add zucchini, garlic powder and pepper; saute until zucchini is almost tender. Drain thoroughly.

Add Parmesan cheese and pimiento; toss. Evenly cover bread round with ½ jar of pizza sauce and meat mixture. Top with shredded cheese. Place on baking sheet and bake 13 to 15 minutes or until cheese is melted.   *Makes 8 servings.*

Note: Remaining bread may be saved or used to double recipe.

KRAUT PIZZAS

1   package (15⅜ ounces) complete pizza
     mix (includes dough, sauce, and
     grated cheese)
1   tablespoon butter or margarine
5   frankfurters (½ pound), thinly sliced

¼   cup finely chopped onion
1   medium garlic clove, crushed
2½   cups drained, loosely packed
     sauerkraut, about 1 can (16 ounces)
¼   teaspoon basil leaves
1   package (8 ounces) mozzarella
     cheese, grated
1   small green pepper, cut into 6 rings

Prepare pizza mix according to package directions. On a floured board, divide dough into six equal pieces; form each piece into a ball. Roll each ball into a 7-inch circle. Place circles on a large greased baking sheet. Fold over edge of each circle enough to form a 6-inch circle. Using folded portion form an edge, about ½-inch high, around each circle.

Melt butter in a large saucepan; add franks, onion and garlic and saute over medium heat, stirring occasionally, until onion is tender, about five minutes. Stir in canned pizza sauce, kraut and basil; heat until hot. Evenly fill pizza shells with kraut mixture and sprinkle with canned grated cheese. Sprinkle each pizza with mozzarella cheese; top with a pepper ring. Bake in a 425-degree oven for 15 to 17 minutes, or until cheese is melted and crust is lightly browned. Serve immediately.

Makes 6 servings.

SLOPPY JOE POTATO PIZZA

1   bag (32 ounces) frozen shredded
     hash browns, thawed
1   can (11 ounces) Cheddar cheese soup
1   egg
1   teaspoon salt
½   teaspoon pepper
8   ounces shredded Cheddar cheese
1   pound ground beef
2   tablespoons minced onion
1   can (15½-ounce) canned sandwich
     sauce for Sloppy Joe
2   tablespoons sliced ripe olives

To thaw potatoes quickly, place in sieve. Pour hot water over the potatoes. Drain well. In a large bowl, mix together hash browns, soup, egg, salt and pepper. Spread potato mixture over a buttered large pizza pan. Bake in a 450-degree oven for 20-25 minutes. Meanwhile, saute ground beef and onions; drain fat. Stir in canned Sloppy Joe sandwich sauce and simmer 5 minutes. Sprinkle two-thirds of the cheese over the baked potato crust. Spoon meat mixture over cheese and top with remaining cheese and olive slices. Bake 5 minutes longer.

Makes 1 pizza.

PIZZA

1	package active dry yeast
1	cup warm water (105 degrees to 115 degrees)
3–3½	cups unsifted flour
1	teaspoon sugar
1	teaspoon salt
¼	cup corn oil
	Pizza Sauce (recipe follows)
1	pound part-skim milk mozzarella cheese, shredded

In small bowl, sprinkle yeast over warm water to dissolve. In large bowl, stir together 3 cups flour, sugar and salt. Stir in yeast mixture and corn oil until dough forms. Form into ball. On lightly floured surface, knead about 3 minutes or until smooth. Place in greased bowl. Turn dough over so that top is greased. Cover with damp towel and let rise in warm place about 1 hour or until doubled. Punch dough down. Divide dough in half. On lightly floured surface roll out each half into 13-inch circle. Place each on a lightly oiled 12-inch pizza pan. Fit into pan, forming a slightly raised edge. Bake on lowest rack in 375-degree oven 20 minutes. Spread about 1½ cups Pizza Sauce on each crust. Sprinkle each with about 2 cups cheese. Bake in 425-degree oven 15 to 20 minutes longer or until cheese is melted and bubbly.

Makes two 12-inch pizzas.

Note: Pizza may be frozen whole or in slices. Wrap cooled pizza tightly in foil. Reheat, uncovered, on cookie sheet in 450-degree oven, 20-25 minutes for whole pizza or 10 to 15 minutes for slices.

PIZZA SAUCE:

¼	cup corn oil
1	cup chopped onion
2	cloves garlic, minced or pressed
2	cans (16 ounces each) tomatoes in puree
1	teaspoon dried oregano leaves
½	teaspoon dried basil leaves
½	teaspoon salt
¼	teaspoon pepper

In 5-quart saucepot or Dutch oven heat corn oil over medium heat. Add onion and garlic, stirring frequently, cook 3 to 5 minutes or until tender. Place tomatoes in blender container; cover. Blend on medium speed 5 seconds or until finely chopped. Add to onion mixture. Stir in oregano, basil, salt and pepper. Stirring occasionally, simmer 30 minutes or until thickened. *Makes about 3 cups.*

DOUBLE-CRUST PIZZA PIE

1	pound ground beef
¼	cup chopped onion
¼	cup chopped green pepper
1	jar (2½ ounces) mushrooms, drained
1	cup grated Cheddar cheese
¼	teaspoon salt
1	egg, beaten
1	cup enriched cornmeal
1½	cups sifted all-purpose flour
¾	teaspoon salt
½	cup shortening, soft
9–10	tablespoons cold water
	ITALIAN SAUCE:
1	can (15 ounces) tomato sauce
1	teaspoon Italian herbs or oregano
½	teaspoon garlic salt

Heat oven to 375 degrees. For filling, pan-fry beef, onion and green pepper until beef is browned. Pour off excess fat. Add mushrooms, cheese, salt and egg. Mix well.

For pastry, sift together cornmeal, flour and salt. Cut in shortening until mixture resembles coarse crumbs. Add water, 1 tablespoon at a time, mixing lightly only until dampened. Form into a ball. Divide dough in half with one half slightly larger than the other.

Roll out larger half to a 14-inch circle. Fit loosely into a 12-inch pizza pan or place on a cookie sheet. Spread with filling. Roll out remaining dough to a 13-inch circle and place over filling. Moisten edges of pastry and seal. Flute edges and prick top, dividing it into 6 equal wedges. (These lines will act as cutting guide when pizza is ready to serve.)

Bake in preheated 375-degree oven about 35 minutes or until lightly browned. Cut into wedges along cutting lines and serve with Italian sauce, made by heating together sauce ingredients. Garnish with sprigs of parsley.   *Makes 6 servings.*

CHEESE 'N' PEPPER SOUFFLE

2	tablespoons butter or margarine
1	medium-size green pepper, seeded and diced
1	medium-size red pepper, seeded and diced
1	recipe White Sauce Base (recipe follows)
1	cup (4 ounces) shredded Cheddar cheese
½	teaspoon dry mustard
4	egg yolks, lightly beaten
4	egg whites
¼	teaspoon cream of tartar

Prepare a 1½-quart straight-sided souffle dish with a collar. In small skillet, melt butter, saute peppers until soft; set aside. In medium saucepan, make 1 recipe White Sauce Base; add cheese and mustard. Stir over low heat until cheese is melted; remove from heat. Quickly stir white sauce into egg yolks. Add peppers; cool slightly. Beat egg whites with cream of tartar until stiff but not dry. Fold in cheese mixture. Turn into ungreased, prepared souffle dish. Bake in 350-degree oven 30 minutes or until golden brown. Serve immediately. If desired, serve with additional pepper sauce.   *Makes 4 servings.*

WHITE SAUCE BASE:

- 2 tablespoons butter or margarine
- 2 tablespoons flour
- ¼ teaspoon salt
- ½ teaspoon Tabasco pepper sauce
- 1 cup milk

Melt butter in saucepan over low heat. Blend in flour, salt and pepper sauce. Gradually stir in milk. Cook over medium heat, stirring constantly, until sauce thickens and comes to a boil. Simmer for 1 minute, continuing to stir.   *Makes about 1 cup.*

TUNA SOUFFLE

- 1 recipe White Sauce Base (recipe above)
- 2 tablespoons chopped parsley
- ¼ teaspoon celery salt
- ¼ teaspoon leaf thyme, crumbled
- 4 egg yolks, lightly beaten
- 1 can (6½ or 7 ounces) tuna in vegetable oil
- 4 egg whites
- ¼ teaspoon cream of tartar

Prepare a 1½-quart straight-sided souffle dish with a collar. In medium saucepan, prepare one recipe White Sauce Base. Add parsley, celery salt and thyme. Quickly stir white sauce into egg yolks. Add tuna; cool slightly. Beat egg whites with cream of tartar until stiff but not dry. Fold in tuna mixture. Turn into ungreased, prepared souffle dish. Bake in 375-degree oven 35 to 40 minutes or until golden brown. Serve immediately. If desired, serve with additional pepper sauce.   *Makes 4 servings.*

NECTARINE BLINTZES

- 16 Crepes (recipe follows)
- 2 packages (8 ounces) cream cheese
- ⅓ cup granulated sugar
- 2 tablespoons milk
- 1 teaspoon grated lemon peel

- 6 large fresh nectarines
  Butter for browning blintzes
  Powdered sugar
  Sour Cream Topping (optional) (recipe follows)

Prepare Crepes and set aside. Soften cheese and blend in ¼ cup of the granulated sugar, milk and lemon peel. Quarter 4 nectarines and slice crosswise. Fold into cheese mixture for filling. Use about ¼ cup filling for each blintz, placing it on center of browned side of Crepe. Fold sides over filling, then top and bottom edges, making a rectangle. Slice remaining 2 nectarines, toss with remaining granulated sugar and set aside. Brown blintzes slowly in heated skillet, using a small amount of butter and placing open sides down first, to seal folds over filling. Turn carefully and brown second side. Serve two for each person, topping with sliced nectarines and a sifting of powdered sugar. Serve with Sour Cream Topping, if desired.
Makes 8 servings.

CREPES: Combine 4 eggs, ⅔ cup each milk and water, 1 cup sifted all-purpose flour, ¼ cup melted butter or margarine and 1 teaspoon salt in a blender jar and blend smooth (or, beat with rotary beater until smooth). Let batter stand for an hour before baking. Heat a small crepe pan (about 8 inches diameter), grease lightly and add about 3 tablespoons batter. Tilt pan quickly to spread and cook over moderate heat until lightly browned on bottom and set on top. Turn out onto paper towel and repeat until all of batter is baked. Crepes may be baked in advance, if desired, and stacked when cold with waxed paper between.   *Makes 16 crepes.*
SOUR CREAM TOPPING: Stir 1 cup dairy sour cream with 1 tablespoon finely shredded lemon peel.   *Makes 1 cup topping.*

RATATOUILLE CREPES

CREPES:

- 1 cup milk
- ⅔ cup all-purpose flour
- 2 eggs
- ⅓ cup enriched cornmeal
- ⅛ teaspoon salt
  FILLING AND SAUCE:
- 2 medium-size tomatoes, chopped
- 1 cup coarsely chopped zucchini
- 1 cup coarsely chopped eggplant
- 1 medium-size green pepper, cut into ¼-inch strips
- 1 medium-size onion, thinly sliced
- 3 tablespoons vegetable oil
- 2 cans (8 ounces each) tomato sauce
- ¼ cup white wine or water
- 1 tablespoon sugar

Continued

¼   teaspoon garlic salt
¼   teaspoon basil leaves
¼   teaspoon oregano leaves

For crepes, combine all batter ingredients. Beat until smooth.

For each crepe, pour about 2 tablespoons batter into hot, lightly greased crepe pan or small skillet. Immediately tilt pan to coat bottom evenly with thin layer of batter. Cook 45 seconds or until top looks dry. Turn. Cook about 20 seconds.

Stack crepes between sheets of wax paper. Cover with plastic wrap.

In 12-inch skillet, saute vegetables for filling in oil about 15 minutes or until tender.

Combine remaining ingredients in 2-quart saucepan. Mix well. Simmer about 10 minutes, stirring occasionally.

Add ⅓ cup tomato-sauce mixture to vegetables. Mix well.

Spoon about ¼ cup vegetable mixture across center of each crepe. Roll up.

Place filled crepes in lightly greased 13-by-9-inch baking dish. Cover with aluminum foil. Bake at 375 degrees about 20 minutes.

Spoon remaining heated tomato-sauce mixture over crepes.   *Makes 10 crepes (5 servings)*

Note: Crepes may be frozen up to 3 months. Stack 5 crepes on paper plate with sheet of wax paper between each crepe. Wrap securely in foil or seal in plastic bag. Freeze. Thaw number needed overnight in refrigerator.

WHEAT GERM FRITTATA

2   cups chopped fresh spinach
1   medium chopped onion (about ½ cup)
2   cloves garlic, minced
2   tablespoons cooking oil
½   cup wheat germ, regular
½   teaspoon marjoram
¼   teaspoon basil
¼   teaspoon pepper
6   eggs
1   cup grated romano cheese
1   can (8 ounces) tomato sauce

Saute spinach, onion and garlic in oil until spinach is limp and onions tender-crisp, 4 to 5 minutes. Remove from heat.

Mix in wheat germ, marjoram, basil, pepper, eggs and ¾ cup cheese. Turn into greased 9-inch pie plate. Cover with ½ can tomato sauce.

Bake in a 350-degree oven 30 to 35 minutes or until table knife inserted in center comes out clean.

Meanwhile, heat remaining tomato sauce. Invert frittata onto serving plate. Top with hot tomato sauce and remaining ¼ cup cheese. Cut into wedges.   *Makes 4 to 6 servings.*

Note: Frittata may also be served as an appetizer. Turn mixture into 9-inch square baking pan. Top with all of the tomato sauce and sprinkle with remaining ¼ cup cheese. Bake as above. Cut into small squares.   *Makes 6 to 7 dozen appetizers.*

BANANA FOLDOVERS

1   cup pancake mix
1   cup milk
1   egg
1   tablespoon vegetable oil or melted shortening
⅛   teaspoon nutmeg
½   cup creamy peanut butter
2   medium-size bananas
     Maple-blended syrup, heated

Combine pancake mix, milk, egg, shortening and nutmeg in bowl. Stir until batter is fairly smooth. For each pancake, pour about one-third cup batter onto hot (400-degree) lightly greased griddle. Turn pancakes when tops are covered with bubbles and edges look cooked. Turn only once.

Cut each banana in half. Slice each half lengthwise through center. For each serving, spread one side of two pancakes with peanut butter. Place one banana piece on peanut butter side of pancakes; fold pancakes over banana. Serve with syrup.
    Makes 4 servings.

SHROVE TUESDAY PANCAKES

PANCAKES:
2   cups whole wheat pancake mix
⅔   cup wheat germ
2¼   cups milk
2   eggs
2   tablespoons vegetable oil

APPLE-CINNAMON SYRUP:
1   15-ounce jar applesauce
1   cup maple-blended syrup
¼   teaspoon cinnamon

For pancakes, combine mix, wheat germ, milk, eggs and oil. Stir until batter is fairly smooth. For each pancake, pour scant one-fourth cup batter onto hot (400-degree) lightly greased griddle. (If batter becomes too thick, add 1 to 2 tablespoons milk.) Turn pancakes when tops are covered with bubbles and edges look cooked. Turn only once.

For apple-cinnamon syrup, combine applesauce, yrup and cinnamon. Cook over medium heat, stir-ing occasionally, until heated. For each serving, our about one-half cup syrup over 3 pancakes. prinkle with additional wheat germ, if desired.
Makes 6 servings.

CHICKEN SALAD IN A CRUST

1	baked 8-inch Cheese Crust (recipe follows)
4	fresh nectarines
2	cups diced cooked chicken
2	tablespoons lemon juice
¼	cup sliced green onion
½	cup coarsely grated Cheddar cheese
¾	cup real mayonnaise
1	teaspoon seasoned salt
¼	teaspoon ground coriander
¹⁄₁₆	teaspoon white pepper
1½	cups shredded iceberg lettuce

Bake and cool cheese crust. Slice nectarines and combine with chicken and lemon juice and toss lightly. Add onion and cheese. Stir mayonnaise together with salt, coriander and pepper. Add to salad and mix gently. Turn lettuce into bottom of cheese crust and top with nectarine salad. Cut into pie-shaped wedges. *Makes 6 servings.*

CHEESE CRUST:
Resift 1 cup sifted flour with ¼ teaspoon *each* plain and onion salt, and dry mustard. Cut in ⅓ cup shortening to form fine particles. Stir in ⅓ cup grated Cheddar cheese. Add 4 tablespoons milk, stirring until dough holds together. Shape into ball. Roll to 12-inch circle. Fit into 8-inch cake pan with edge of dough extending about ½-inch above top of pan. Flute edge and prick pastry with fork. Place pan on cookie sheet. Bake below oven center in a 450-degree oven until crisp and golden brown, about 10 minutes.

NOODLE SQUARES WITH BEEF SAUCE

8	ounces medium egg noodles (about 4 cups)
1	tablespoon salt
3	quarts boiling water
3	eggs, beaten
1	cup dairy sour cream
½	teaspoon salt
¼	teaspoon each: paprika, garlic powder, pepper
¼	cup sliced ripe olives
½	cup butter or margarine, melted
¼	cup chopped onion
1	cup chopped celery
1	can (10½ ounces) condensed cream of mushroom soup, undiluted
1	can (10½ ounces) condensed beef consomme, undiluted
	Dash Tabasco pepper sauce
2	cups sliced cooked beef

Gradually add noodles and salt to rapidly boiling water so that water continues to boil. Cook un-covered, stirring occasionally, until tender. Drain in colander. In large mixing bowl combine noodles with eggs, sour cream, ½ teaspoon salt, paprika, garlic powder, ⅛ teaspoon of the pepper, olives and 6 tablespoons of the melted butter. Mix well. Pour mixture into greased 9-inch square pan. Place in pan of hot water. Bake in 350-degree oven 1 hour. Cut into squares and place on serving platter.

Meanwhile, saute onion and celery in remaining butter until crisp-tender. Stir in soups, pepper sauce and remaining ⅛ teaspoon pepper. Simmer 10 min-utes. Stir in beef and heat. Serve with noodle squares. *Makes 6 servings.*

CHILI

2	pounds ground beef
2	cloves garlic, minced
1	teaspoon salt
¼	teaspoon pepper
1	egg
2	tablespoons liquid brown seasoning sauce, divided
	Flour
2	tablespoons olive oil
2	tablespoons butter
1	large sweet onion, chopped
2	green peppers, coarsely chopped
½	cup parsley sprigs, chopped
2	tablespoons chili powder (use more or less to taste)
1	can (1 pound) stewed tomatoes
1	can (10½ ounces) condensed beef broth
1	quart water (or more)
1	can (1 pound) red kidney beans with liquid

Mix the first 5 ingredients and 1 tablespoon liquid brown seasoning sauce. Shape into small balls. Roll lightly in flour, brown in hot combined oil and but-ter. Stir in onion, green pepper, parsley and chili powder. Simmer 5 minutes.

Turn into a large kettle or saucepan (4 to 5 quarts).
Continued

Add tomatoes, broth, water and remaining seasoning sauce. Reduce heat and simmer about 40 minutes, stirring often. Add beans. Simmer an additional 10 minutes until heated through.
Makes 6 to 8 servings.

Note: If soup thickens too rapidly, add more water.

CRANBERRIED CHILI

2	pounds boneless chuck, cut into 1-inch cubes
1½	cups chopped onion
3	tablespoons vegetable oil
1	large green pepper, seeded and chopped
2	cans (1 pound each) whole tomatoes
1	bay leaf
1½	teaspoons salt
¼	teaspoon ground cloves
2	tablespoons chili powder
¼	teaspoon hot pepper sauce
½	teaspoon paprika
1	cup fresh cranberries

Brown meat and onion in oil in heavy skillet. Cook over medium heat until onion is tender and meat is brown. Add green pepper, tomatoes, bay leaf, salt, cloves, chili powder, hot pepper sauce and paprika. Cover; simmer for 2 hours, adding hot water if necessary to keep mixture from thickening too much. Add cranberries. Cook 10-15 minutes or until cranberries pop but still hold their shape.
Makes 6 servings.

CHILI MEXICANA

4	slices bacon
1	cup chopped onion
1	clove garlic, minced
1	pound ground beef
2	tablespoons chili powder
1	cup (8-ounce can) tomato sauce
½	cup beer
½–1	cup water
2	tablespoons chopped, canned, green chili peppers
1	teaspoon ground cumin
1	bay leaf
¼	teaspoon salt
1	can (15½ ounces) red kidney beans, drained
½	cup sliced, pitted ripe olives
1	ounce (1 square) semi-sweet chocolate
½	teaspoon Tabasco pepper sauce

In large skillet, brown bacon. Saute onion and garlic in bacon fat until soft. Add ground beef, stirring to break up meat as it browns. Add chili powder; cook, stirring, 2 minutes. Add tomato sauce, beer, ½ cup water, chili peppers, cumin, bay leaf and salt. Bring to boiling; cover. Simmer 1 hour, stirring occasionally. Add kidney beans, olives, chocolate and pepper sauce. Stir until chocolate is melted. Add ½ cup more water if chili seems dry. Cover, cook 15 minutes longer. Serve with additional pepper sauce if desired.
Makes 4 servings.

CONFETTI VEGETABLE TACOS

½	cup finely chopped onion
1½	cups finely chopped carrots
1½	cups finely chopped parsnips
1½	cups finely chopped celery
1½	cups finely chopped, unpared zucchini
½	head cabbage or lettuce, shredded
2	cups (8 ounces) shredded American cheese
1	box (5 ounces) prepared taco shells (12 shells)
	Taco Tomato Topping (recipe follows)

In large bowl, combine all ingredients except taco shells. Heat taco shells according to package directions. To serve, fill taco shells with chopped vegetables. Spoon hot Taco Tomato Topping over each.
Makes 12 tacos.

TACO TOMATO TOPPING:

2	tablespoons vegetable oil
2	teaspoons flour
3	ripe tomatoes, chopped
2	tablespoons chopped fresh parsley
1	teaspoon sugar
½	teaspoon chili powder

In saucepan, heat vegetable oil over medium heat; blend in flour. Cook 1 minute, stirring to avoid lumps. Add remaining ingredients. Cover. Cook over low heat, stirring occasionally, 10 minutes.
Makes about 2 cups sauce.

GALICIAN TUNA EMPANADA

PASTRY:

¾	cup milk
¼	cup butter or margarine
¼	cup sugar
2	teaspoons salt
¼	cup warm water (110 to 120 degrees F.)
1	package active dry yeast
2	eggs, slightly beaten

4–4½ cups sifted all-purpose flour
1 egg, slightly beaten
Tuna-Vegetable Filling or
Tuna-Almond-Olive Filling (recipes
follow)

In a saucepan, heat milk with butter, sugar and salt until butter melts. Cool to lukewarm.

Meanwhile, in a large bowl, dissolve yeast in warm water. Add cooled milk mixture along with 2 eggs. Beat in 3½ to 4 cups flour to make a soft dough.

Turn dough out onto lightly floured surface and knead in remaining flour. Knead 3 minutes or until dough is smooth. Form dough into ball. Place in a large greased bowl. Turn dough so greased side is up.

Cover and let rise in a warm place until double, about 1½ hours. Punch down dough. Turn out onto lightly floured surface. For large empanada, shape ¾ of dough into a large rectangle. Fit into ungreased 15½-by-10½-by-1-inch baking pan.

Place Tuna-Vegetable Filling or Tuna-Almond-Olive Filling down center of dough, spreading so that filling remains 2 inches from edge of dough.

Shape remaining pastry into rectangle large enough to cover filling. Place on filling. Bring edges of bottom layer of dough up and over. Pinch top and bottom edges of pastry together to seal.

Make several slashes into top layer of pastry. Brush with beaten egg. Bake in 350-degree oven for 25 to 35 minutes or until golden.

For small empanaditas, divide dough into 10 pieces. Roll 5 pieces into circles large enough to line 6-inch individual casserole dishes or individual pie pans.

Fill pastry-lined dishes with ¾-cup of tuna filling. Roll out remaining pieces of dough to cover tops of casseroles. Trim and seal edges.

Slash through top pastry and brush with beaten egg. Bake in 350-degree oven for 20 to 30 minutes or until golden.

Makes 1 large empanada or 5 small empanaditas.

TUNA-VEGETABLE FILLING:
3 tablespoons salad oil
⅓ cup diced celery
1 medium onion, chopped
2 cloves garlic, minced
1 small green pepper, chopped
2 cans (6½ or 7 ounces each) tuna in vegetable oil
½ teaspoon salt
⅛ teaspoon pepper
⅛ teaspoon ground cumin
Dash cayenne pepper
½ cup tomato sauce

Heat oil in skillet. Add celery, onion, garlic and green pepper. Cook until tender. Remove from heat.

Stir in tuna, salt, pepper, cumin and cayenne, breaking up large chunks of tuna with a fork. Stir in tomato sauce.

TUNA-ALMOND-OLIVE FILLING:
3 tablespoons salad oil
1 medium onion, chopped
2 tablespoons chopped parsley
⅓ cup slivered almonds
1 cup chopped pimiento-stuffed olives
2 cans (6½ or 7 ounces each) tuna in vegetable oil
1 can (3 ounces) mushrooms, undrained
½ teaspoon salt

Heat oil in medium skillet. Add onion, parsley and almonds. Cook until onion is tender.

Add olives. Remove from heat. Stir in tuna, mushrooms with liquid, and salt, breaking up large chunks of tuna with a fork.

MEXICAN ENCHILADAS

TORTILLAS:
¼ teaspoon Tabasco pepper sauce
1 cup milk
¾ cup cornstarch
2 eggs
⅓ cup cornmeal
½ teaspoon salt
2 tablespoons butter, melted

Add pepper sauce to milk. Add to cornstarch. Stir to smooth paste.

Beat eggs. Add cornmeal, salt and cornstarch mixture. Stir in melted butter.

Use 3 tablespoons of mixture for each tortilla. Quickly pour into lightly greased, heated 7-inch skillet. Brown on one side; turn to brown other side. *Makes 12 tortillas.*

SAUCE:
2 tablespoons olive oil
2 medium onions, chopped
1 garlic clove, minced
2 medium tomatoes, peeled and chopped
1½ cups stock or bouillon
½ teaspoon Tabasco pepper sauce
¼ teaspoon salt
2 teaspoons chili powder

Heat oil in skillet. Add onion and garlic. Cook until onion is tender but not brown.

Add tomatoes, stock and pepper sauce. Stir in salt and chili powder.

Bring to boil. Reduce heat and simmer 20 to 30 minutes or until thickened, stirring occasionally.

Makes 2½ cups.

FILLING I:

1½   cups grated American cheese
1   cup finely chopped onion

FILLING II:

1   medium avocado, peeled and diced
1   hard-cooked egg, chopped
1   cup diced cooked chicken

To make enchilada, drop tortilla quickly in heated sauce to soften. Put 2 tablespoons filling in center. Roll up and place seam side down in shallow baking dish. Pour sauce over all. Bake in 350-degree oven for 10 minutes. Sprinkle with any remaining ingredients. *Makes 6 servings.*

MEXICALI MEATBALLS

½   pound ground beef
¼   teaspoon ground cumin seed
¼   teaspoon salt
   Generous dash pepper
½   cup chopped onion
1   can (16 ounces) pork and beans in tomato sauce
1   can (12 ounces) whole kernel golden corn with sweet peppers
   Shredded lettuce
   Chopped tomato

Season beef with ⅛ teaspoon cumin, salt and pepper. Shape into 12 meatballs. In skillet, brown meatballs and cook onion until tender. Pour off fat. Add beans, corn and remaining cumin. Heat; stir occasionally. Garnish with lettuce and tomato.
Makes about 3½ cups; 3 servings.

TOMATO SUNBURSTS

4   medium-sized tomatoes
1   pound low-fat cottage cheese
½   cup diced cucumber
½   cup sliced radishes
¼   cup sliced scallions
   Salt
   Ground black pepper

Store tomatoes at room temperature until fully ripe. Remove stem ends from tomatoes. Cut each tomato part-way through into 8 wedges. Sprinkle with salt and black pepper; set aside.

In a medium bowl, combine cottage cheese, cucumber, radishes, scallions, ¼ teaspoon salt and ⅛ teaspoon black pepper. Spoon into tomato "sunbursts." Serve on a bed of lettuce with sliced cucumber and carrot sticks, if desired.   *Makes 4 servings.*

CHICKEN-STUFFED TOMATOES

2   tablespoons butter or margarine, divided
⅓   cup chopped onion
3   tablespoons chopped scallion tops
4   large tomatoes
½   teaspoon dried parsley
⅛   teaspoon dried thyme leaves
   Dash cayenne pepper
½   cup plus 3 tablespoons soft fresh bread crumbs
1   can (4¾ ounces) chunky chicken spread

Preheat oven to 350 degrees. In a skillet, melt 1 tablespoon butter or margarine over medium heat. Saute onion and scallion until tender.

Meanwhile, cut a ¼-inch thick slice off tops of each tomato. Scoop out pulp to make a shell ¼-inch thick. Chop pulp coarsely; add to onion in skillet. Stir in parsley, thyme and pepper. Simmer 10 minutes, until liquid has cooked off.

Stir in ½ cup bread crumbs and chunky chicken spread. Spoon mixture into tomato shells. In a small bowl, mix together remaining butter and bread crumbs. Sprinkle onto filled tomatoes. Bake 25 to 30 minutes. Garnish with chopped parsley.
Makes 4 servings.

DOUBLE CHEESE-STUFFED TOMATOES

6   medium-sized tomatoes
   Salt
1   pound creamed cottage cheese
½   cup shredded Cheddar cheese
1   teaspoon onion powder
⅛   teaspoon ground black pepper
2   teaspoons prepared mustard

Hold tomatoes at room temperature until fully ripe. Place tomatoes, stem side down on a board. Cut each tomato to resemble a flower, cutting into wedges almost through to the bottom. Spread wedges slightly apart. Sprinkle lightly with salt; set aside. Combine cottage and Cheddar cheeses, onion powder, one-half teaspoon salt, black pepper and mustard. Spoon into each tomato. If desired, top with sour cream and serve on a bed of lettuce.
Makes 6 portions.

SEASON'S END CORN BREAD

CORN BREAD:
1	cup enriched cornmeal
1	cup sifted all-purpose flour
2	tablespoons sugar
4	teaspoons baking powder
½	teaspoon salt
1½	cups finely chopped cooked ham
1	egg
1	cup milk
¼	cup vegetable oil

VEGETABLE SAUCE:
¼	cup chopped onion
⅓	cup butter or margarine
⅓	cup all-purpose flour
1	teaspoon salt
⅛	teaspoon pepper
1¾	cups milk
2	tablespoons grated Parmesan cheese
2	cups (8 ounces) shredded Swiss cheese
1½	cups cooked broccoli
1	cup sliced cooked carrots

For corn bread, sift together cornmeal, flour, sugar, baking powder and salt. Stir in ham. Add egg, milk and oil; mix well. Pour into greased 9-inch layer pan. Bake in preheated 425-degree oven about 30 to 35 minutes. Cool 15 minutes; remove from pan. Cut corn bread into 6 wedge-shaped pieces.

For sauce, saute onion in butter. Blend in flour, salt and pepper. Gradually add milk; cook over low heat, stirring constantly, until thickened. Stir in Parmesan cheese and Swiss cheese until Swiss cheese is melted. Add broccoli and carrots. Heat thoroughly; do not let boil.

To serve, split each corn bread wedge in half crosswise; fan out on plate. Spoon sauce over corn bread. *Makes 6 servings.*

POTATO MUFFINS

8	servings instant mashed potatoes (as indicated on package plus ½ cup additional)
	Melted butter or margarine
2½	cups creamed tuna, chicken or ham
¼	cup bread crumbs

Preheat oven to 400 degrees. Lightly butter a 12-cup muffin pan. Divide potatoes equally into muffin cups and press evenly against sides. Brush tops with butter. Bake 30 minutes until golden. Fill with creamed mixture and top with bread crumbs. *Makes 6 servings (2 per serving).*

Note: Potato muffins may be baked in advance and reheated with the filling in the oven.

FIRESIDE SUPPER RACLETTE

2	pounds small white or red potatoes
	Salt
¼	cup butter or margarine, melted
3	tablespoons lemon juice
1½	pounds Jarlsberg or Swiss cheese
2	cans (3¾ ounces each) Norway sardines, drained
	Gherkins
	Chopped green onions

Cook potatoes in boiling salted water, 15 to 20 minutes, until tender. Do not over cook. Drain. Halve potatoes, if desired. Heat butter and lemon juice. Pour over potatoes, to coat thoroughly. Keep warm. Place cheese (whole) on ovenproof serving tray. Slide tray under broiler, at least 5 inches from heat. Broil until melting begins, watching carefully. Scrape melted cheese onto plates. Surround cheese with potatoes. Serve immediately with sardines, gherkins and chopped onions. As needed, return cheese to broiler for more melting. (An electric broiler works well at the table.) *Makes 6 servings.*

SANDWICHES

BAKED BEAN SANDWICH

1	can (1 pound 6 ounces) oven-baked beans
1	tablespoon brown sugar
2	teaspoons prepared mustard
¼	cup crisp diced bacon or packaged bits
8	slices raisin bread
	Butter or margarine
	Grilled frankfurters

Mix beans with brown sugar, mustard and bacon bits. Spread raisin bread with butter and arrange 4 slices, buttered side down, in individual baking dishes or one large one. Top each slice with beans and bread, buttered side up. Bake at 400 degrees until end bread is toasted and beans are hot, about 10 minutes. *Makes 4 sandwiches.*

BLP SANDWICH

1	fresh or canned Bartlett pear
4	slices hot, buttered toast
	Lettuce leaves

Continued

6 slices crisply cooked bacon
Dijon mustard

Core and slice pear or drain canned pear. To assemble sandwiches, top 2 slices of toast with lettuce leaves, bacon and pear slices. Top with remaining toast slices. If desired, decorative wooden picks may be used to secure sandwiches. Cut each sandwich into quarters. Serve with mustard.
Makes 2 sandwiches.

BOLOGNA SANDWICH

1 package (3 ounces) cream cheese, softened
¼ cup sweet pickle relish
8 slices raisin bread
4 slices bologna
4 lettuce leaves

Mash cream cheese with relish. Blend to spreading consistency.

For each sandwich, spread 2 slices of raisin bread with about 2 tablespoons of cream cheese mixture. Between them place a slice of bologna and a lettuce leaf. Cut diagonally, wrap and chill.
Makes 4 sandwiches.

BROCCOLI-SHRIMP PITA SANDWICH

1 package (10 ounces) frozen chopped broccoli, thawed
1 can (4½ ounces) shrimp
½ cup mayonnaise
¼ cup chopped dill pickles
1 tablespoon lemon juice
1 tablespoon Dijon mustard
½ teaspoon salt
3 whole-wheat pita breads

Thaw and drain uncooked broccoli well, press out excess liquid. Drain shrimp. Mix mayonnaise, pickles, lemon juice, mustard and salt together in mixing bowl. Fold in broccoli and shrimp gently to avoid breaking shrimp. Cut pita breads in halves. Open and fill each pocket with broccoli-shrimp mixture. Serve at once. *Makes 6 half sandwiches.*

BRUNCH TOURNEDOS

1 package steak sauce flavor marinade mix
1 cup water

6 chuck top blade steaks (about 2 pounds)
1 small onion, finely chopped
4 tablespoons margarine
1½ tablespoons wine vinegar
¼ teaspoon tarragon
¼ teaspoon parsley
½ cup mayonnaise
½ cup sour cream
4 egg yolks
6 slices bread, toasted

In shallow pan, combine marinade and water. Stir well. Place meat in marinade. Pierce deeply with fork. Marinate 15 minutes, turning occasionally. Remove meat and reserve marinade.

In saucepan, combine reserved marinade and next 5 ingredients. Simmer 4 minutes. Set aside and keep warm.

Broil steaks 4 to 5 inches from heat, about 7 minutes per side.

Combine mayonnaise, sour cream and egg yolks. Stir into marinade mixture and heat through. (Do not boil.)

Place steaks over toasted bread. Top with sauce. *Makes 6 servings.*

KRAUT-EGG SALAD BUNWICHES

2 cups drained sauerkraut
6 hard-cooked eggs, shelled and chopped
½ cup Thousand Island dressing
6 hard rolls, split and buttered
6 thick slices tomato
Lettuce leaves

Combine kraut, eggs and dressing. Mix well. Arrange on bottom halves of rolls. Add tomato, lettuce and tops of rolls. Wrap in aluminum foil. Bunwiches can be carried to the office or stored in an ice cooler for picnics. *Makes 6 sandwiches.*

BEEF 'N' BEAN BURGER

1 pound ground beef
1 can (16 ounce) pork and beans
½ cup ketchup
½ cup chopped onion or 2 tablespoons instant minced onion
1 tablespoon prepared mustard
1 teaspoon salt
1 can (10 biscuits) refrigerated buttermilk or country-style biscuits
¾ cup (3 ounces) shredded Cheddar cheese

Preheat oven to 375 degrees. Brown ground beef; drain. Stir in beans, ketchup, onion, mustard and salt. Simmer while preparing dough. Separate biscuit dough into 10 biscuits. On greased cookie sheets, press each to a 4-inch circle. Spoon about ⅓ cup meat mixture over each biscuit. Sprinkle with cheese. Bake 15 to 18 minutes until golden brown. Serve immediately. (Refrigerate leftovers.)

Makes 10 sandwiches.

CHEESE 'N' NUT GOODIES

1	package (8 ounces) cream cheese, softened
¾	cup shredded Cheddar cheese
½	cup chopped walnuts
¼	cup orange marmalade
12	slices brown or nut bread

Combine cheeses in bowl. Blend well.

Blend in nuts and marmalade. Spread on 6 slices of bread. Top with remaining slices. Cut into strips.
Makes 6 sandwiches or 24 strips.

CHEESY HOT DOG TOTE

½	pound hot dogs, cubed
½	pound sharp Cheddar cheese, shredded
1	jar (2 ounces) stuffed green olives, chopped
½	cup frozen diced onions
½	cup chili sauce
1	teaspoon mustard
2	hard-cooked eggs, chopped
2	tablespoons mayonnaise
4	individual loaves of pita bread
	Heavy-duty aluminum foil

Cut hot dogs into fourths lengthwise, then slice into ¼-inch cubes. Combine with olives, hard-cooked eggs, mustard, mayonnaise, chili sauce and cheese, mixing well.

Cut pita rounds in half. Open pocket and fill with approximately ⅓ cup filling. Be generous. Wrap individually in foil and refrigerate or freeze.

TO GRILL: If frozen, allow to defrost at room temperature for about 10 minutes. When fire is ready, place foil-wrapped sandwiches on grill and heat 10 minutes. Uncover and continue heating until pita bread is crisp and filling is hot—10 to 15 minutes more, depending on desired crispness.

IN THE OVEN: Place unwrapped sandwiches in 350-degree oven for 25 minutes for crispy bread. If softer bread is preferred, reduce heating time to about 20 minutes. *Makes 8 servings.*

CUCUMBER-TUNA ROLLS

1	can (7 ounces) tuna, drained and flaked
½	cup chopped cucumber
¼	cup chopped onions
¼	cup chopped celery
½	cup mayonnaise
1	tablespoon lemon juice
¼	teaspoon dill weed
18	slices white bread or 12 finger rolls
	Lettuce leaves

In bowl, combine tuna, cucumber, onion and celery.
Blend in mayonnaise and lemon juice. Stir in dill.
Spread on rolls, placing lettuce leaves on top of filling.
Or spread on 12 slices of bread. Make double-decker sandwiches, topping with 6 remaining slices. Cut into fingers.
Makes 12 rolls or 6 sandwiches.

DANISH SURPRISE HAMBURGERS

2	medium-size onions, sliced
1	tablespoon butter
2	pounds lean ground beef
5	tomato slices, ¼-inch thick
10	slices Danish Havarti or creamy Havarti cheese, ¼-inch thick
1	tablespoon spicy mustard
	Salt and pepper

Saute onions in butter until tender, not browned. Form ground beef into 10 patties, about 4 inches wide.

Spoon sauteed onions evenly on centers of 5 patties. Place a slice of tomato and a slice of cheese on top of onions. Spread mustard on remaining 5 patties. Sprinkle with salt and pepper.

Place the mustard-spread patties on top of the patties covered with other ingredients. Pinch edges together to enclose all ingredients. It is important to seal the edges securely. Sprinkle tops with salt and pepper.

Broil on second rack in oven for about 7 minutes. (Or barbecue about 6 inches from coals.) Cook slowly so that filling cooks through. Turn carefully and broil 5 minutes more.

Just before serving, place another slice of cheese on top of burgers and cook until cheese melts.
Serve on fresh-baked bread. *Makes 5 servings.*

FRENCH TOASTED PEANUT BUTTER SANDWICH

1	loaf French or Italian bread, about 14 inches long
1	cup peanut butter
2	cups well drained sliced fruit— bananas, peaches, apricots (can use fresh, canned or frozen)
3	eggs
1	cup milk
1	tablespoon sugar
1	teaspoon vanilla
¼	cup butter or margarine
¼	cup peanut oil

Cut bread with a serrated knife into three-fourth-inch-thick diagonal slices. Spread half of the slices with peanut butter. Top peanut butter with fruit. Top with remaining bread slices. In a bowl, beat eggs with milk, sugar and vanilla. Dip sandwiches into egg mixture using slotted spoon or spatula. Heat butter and oil in a large skillet or griddle and fry sandwiches until golden brown on both sides. Serve warm. *Makes 6 servings.*

GERMAN-STYLE BURGERS

1	pound ground beef
½	cup finely shredded raw potato
½	cup finely chopped onion
2	tablespoons Worcestershire sauce
½	teaspoon salt
1	tablespoon oil

In medium-sized bowl combine all ingredients except oil. Shape meat mixture into 4 burgers, about 1-inch thick. In a large skillet, heat oil. Cook burgers over low heat until done as desired, 5 to 7 minutes on each side. Or, arrange burgers on a rack in a broiler pan. Place under a preheated hot broiler, 3 to 4 inches from heat source, until done as desired, 5 to 7 minutes on each side. *Makes 4 portions.*

HOT TURKEY SANDWICHES

1	can (10½ ounces) mushroom gravy
½	cup cranberry-orange relish
6	servings sliced cooked turkey
6	slices toast
6	pineapple rings

In saucepan, combine gravy and relish. Heat; stir occasionally. Meanwhile, arrange turkey on toast; top with pineapple. Serve with gravy mixture.
Makes 6 open-face sandwiches, 6 servings.

ICEBERG CHICKEN SANDWICH

1	head iceberg lettuce
½	cup mayonnaise
1	teaspoon prepared mustard
½	teaspoon lemon juice
1⁄16	teaspoon dried dill
8	slices rye or whole-grain bread
1	cup shredded cooked chicken
¼	cup chopped green onion
1⁄16	teaspoon salt
4	plum tomatoes

Core, rinse and thoroughly drain lettuce; refrigerate in disposable plastic bag or plastic crisper. Stir mayonnaise, mustard, lemon juice and dill together. Spread lightly on each slice bread. Shred lettuce to measure 2 cups. Combine with chicken, onion, salt and remaining mayonnaise mixture. Pile on bread. Serve open-face or put two slices together. Garnish with halved plum tomatoes.
Makes 4 salad-sandwiches.

ICEBERG SANDWICH SPECIAL

1	head iceberg lettuce
½	cup mayonnaise
½	cup chunk-style peanut butter
8	slices whole-grain bread
2	small bananas

Core, rinse and thoroughly drain lettuce; refrigerate in disposable plastic bag or plastic crisper. Shred lettuce to measure 2 cups and turn into small bowl; add ¼ cup mayonnaise and drop in peanut butter by small spoonfuls. Mix lightly. Spread remaining mayonnaise on bread slices. Cover half with sliced bananas, and half with lettuce mixture. Put together, sandwich fashion. Press lightly and cut in half. *Makes 4 salad-sandwiches.*

JOE'S SPECIAL SANDWICH

1	package (12-ounces) frozen chopped spinach, thawed
1	pound ground chuck
1	cup frozen chopped onion
1	clove garlic, minced
¾	teaspoon salt
½	teaspoon Italian herb seasoning
¼	teaspoon herb pepper seasoning
2	large eggs, beaten
1	cup shredded Cheddar cheese
4	(6-inch) pita breads, halved, or sesame hamburger buns

Drain spinach well. Press out excess liquid.

Brown meat with onion and garlic over high heat, stirring occasionally. Drain off excess fat.

Add spinach and herb seasonings. Stir over low heat until spinach is hot.

Stir in eggs and salt to taste. Sprinkle with cheese.

Continue to cook just until eggs are set, occasionally stirring gently. Remove from heat.

Gently open pita-bread halves. Fill each with about ½ cup spinach-meat mixture. Or serve on sesame hamburger buns. Serve at once.
Makes 4 servings.

Note: ½ teaspoon seasoned pepper or lemon-and-pepper seasoning may be substituted for herb pepper.

KRAUT HEROES

2	cups rinsed and well-drained sauerkraut
	Mayonnaise
½	pound sliced bacon
6	hero rolls, 7 inches long, split
10	ounces sliced liverwurst
1	medium onion, sliced
	Sweet pickle slices
	Pickles, onions

Combine kraut and ⅓ cup mayonnaise; toss lightly and chill. Fry bacon until crisp; drain on paper towels. Spread top and bottom halves of rolls with mayonnaise. On bottom halves of rolls, layer kraut mixture, bacon, liverwurst and onion. Cover with tops of rolls. Secure heroes with picks. Garnish with pickles and onions. *Makes 6 servings.*

KRAUT-TUNAWICHES

2	cups drained sauerkraut
1	can (6½ or 7 ounces) tuna, drained
½	cup mayonnaise
¼	cup diced green pepper
2	tablespoons chopped onion
2	tablespoons sweet pickle relish
¼	teaspoon celery salt
6	hamburger buns, split and buttered

Combine kraut, tuna, mayonnaise, green pepper, onion, relish and celery salt. Mix well and chill. Fill hamburger buns with kraut-tuna salad.
Makes 6 servings.

LAYERED ICEBERG SALAD-SANDWICH

1	head iceberg lettuce
2	packages (3 ounces) cream cheese
½	cup chopped ripe olives, well drained
1	tablespoon chopped pimiento
2	tablespoons diced roasted almonds
¼	cup finely chopped green pepper
	Bottled French dressing
8	thin slices whole-wheat bread
4	thin slices white bread
	Mayonnaise

Core, rinse and thoroughly drain lettuce; refrigerate in disposable plastic bag or plastic crisper. Soften cheese and beat smooth. Combine with olives, pimiento and almonds. Shred enough lettuce to measure 2 cups; toss with green pepper and French dressing. Spread each slice of bread lightly on one side with mayonnaise. Spread one slice whole-wheat bread generously with cream cheese mixture. Top with slice white bread, then shredded lettuce and place whole-wheat slice on top. Press down lightly. Cut in halves or thirds.
Makes 4 salad-sandwiches.

LONE STAR JOES

1	recipe Red Sauce Base (recipe follows)
¼	cup butter or margarine
1	medium onion, sliced
1	medium green pepper, seeded, sliced
2	cups slivered, cooked beef, chicken or ham
1	cup diced, cooked potatoes, drained
4	hamburger buns, split

Make Red Sauce Base; set aside. In large skillet, melt butter; saute onion and green pepper until soft. Add meat, potatoes and Red Sauce Base; stir until heated through. Serve over hamburger buns. *Makes 4 servings.*

	RED SAUCE BASE:
2	tablespoons salad oil
1	medium onion, chopped (½ cup)
1	can (6 ounces) tomato paste
1	cup water
1	tablespoon sugar
1	teaspoon Tabasco pepper sauce
½	teaspoon salt

Heat oil in medium saucepan; saute onion until transparent, about 5 minutes. Stir in tomato paste, water, sugar, pepper sauce and salt. Simmer 15 minutes. *Makes about 2 cups.*

MEXICALI SANDWICH

1	package (10 ounces) frozen Fordhook lima beans
	Water
½	cup frozen chopped onion
1	clove garlic, minced
1	teaspoon Tabasco sauce
½	teaspoon salt
½	cup sliced ripe olives
½	cup diced seeded tomato
¼	cup diced green pepper
½	cup dairy sour cream
3	(6-inch) pita breads
1	package (4 ounces) alfalfa sprouts
1½	cups shredded Cheddar cheese
1	package pre-fried taco shells or 6 pita breads

Combine limas with water (as package directs for cooking), onion, garlic, pepper, sauce and salt. Bring to boil, cover and cook until tender. Drain well and cool. Combine with olives, tomato, green pepper and sour cream. Serve in warm taco shells or gently open pita and fill each half with ½ cup alfalfa sprouts, ½ cup lima mixture and top with ¼ cup cheese. Serve at once.   *Makes 6 sandwiches.*

NEPTUNE POCKET SANDWICHES

2	cans (about 7 ounces each) tuna, drained, flaked
1	tablespoon fresh grated tangerine peel
3	tangerines, peeled, segmented, cut in half, peel finely chopped
½	cup mayonnaise or salad dressing
3	tablespoons finely chopped green onion
½	teaspoon salt
6	six-inch loaves pocket bread, cut in half
	Fresh spinach leaves cut in thin strips

In bowl, combine tuna, tangerine peel and segments, mayonnaise, green onion and salt. Spoon about one-fourth cup tuna mixture in pocket of each bread half; fill with spinach.   *Makes 6 sandwiches.*

NORSE SALAD SANDWICH

1	pint cottage cheese
½	teaspoon grated lemon peel
6	slices dark bread, buttered
2	medium-size red-skinned apples, thinly sliced
	Lemon juice

1	small red onion, thinly sliced
1	can (3 ounces) Norway sardines, drained
	Mustard Mayonnaise (recipe follows)

Mix cottage cheese with lemon peel. Spread ⅓ cup on each slice of bread.

Brush apple slices with lemon juice. Arrange in overlapping rows over cottage cheese. Top with onion rings and sardines.

Serve with Mustard Mayonnaise.

Makes 6 servings.

MUSTARD MAYONNAISE:
Mix ⅔ cup mayonnaise with 1 teaspoon prepared mustard and 1 tablespoon lemon juice.

ORIENTAL BURGERS

1	pound ground beef
¼	cup chopped water chestnuts
2	tablespoons thinly sliced scallion (green onion)
1	tablespoon Worcestershire sauce
¼	teaspoon salt
4	hamburger buns

In medium-sized bowl combine all ingredients. Mix gently, but thoroughly. Shape meat mixture into 4 burgers. Arrange on a rack in a broiler pan. Place under a preheated hot broiler, 3 to 4 inches from heat source, until done as desired, 5 to 7 minutes on each side. Or, place burgers in a hot skillet with a small amount of oil. Cook over high heat until done as desired, 5 to 7 minutes on each side. Serve on toasted buns garnished with sliced scallions, if desired.   *Makes 4 portions.*

PICNIC STEAKWICHES

1	beef chuck blade (2½ to 3 pounds) or 7-bone pot-roast, 1¼ inches thick (or use 1½ to 2 pounds top or bottom round steak)
	Natural meat tenderizer, seasoned or unseasoned
6	individual pita bread envelopes, slit, or 6 French rolls, hollowed out
½	medium head lettuce, shredded
2	large tomatoes, diced
1	cucumber, seeded and diced
2–3	green onions, chopped
1	medium avocado, sliced (optional)
1	cup grated Cheddar cheese
1	cup dairy sour cream

Trim excess fat from meat. Slash fat edges to prevent curling. Prepare all surfaces of meat, one side at a time, with natural meat tenderizer but use no salt.

Grill 2 inches from glowing coals a total of 15 to 20 minutes for medium rare or until desired degree of doneness, turning frequently. Slice meat diagonally across grain into thin slices. Set out meat, bread, vegetables, cheese and sour cream. Let each person fill his own sandwich with meat and accompaniments as desired. *Makes 6 servings.*

PITA KRAUT SANDWICHES

¼	cup butter or margarine
1	cup chopped onion
1	pound knockwurst, sliced diagonally
4	cups drained sauerkraut (about 32 ounces)
1½	cups sour cream
4	loaves pita bread

In a large saucepan melt butter. Add onion and knockwurst. Saute over medium heat, stirring occasionally, until onion is tender, about 5 minutes. Stir in sauerkraut and heat until hot, stirring occasionally. Stir in sour cream and heat over low heat only until sour cream is heated. Do not boil. Cut each pita bread in half. Fill halves with kraut mixture. Serve warm or cold. *Makes 4 sandwiches.*

PITA-STUFFED ROCK LOBSTER

¼	cup butter or margarine
2	large onions, finely chopped
1	teaspoon turmeric
12	ounces frozen South African rock lobster tails
1	can (4 ounces) sweet green chilies, drained and chopped
2	cups well-drained canned Italian plum tomatoes
2	tablespoons lime juice mixed with 1 tablespoon cornstarch
	Salt
6	large pita breads

Heat butter in saucepan. Saute onions for 5 minutes. Add turmeric.

Partially thaw rock lobster tails by holding under running cold water for a few minutes. With scissors, remove underside membrane and pull out meat. Dice raw meat and add to saucepan. Saute until meat becomes opaque, about 5 minutes.

Stir in chilies, tomatoes and lime-juice mixture. Stir over medium heat until sauce thickens and bubbles. Season to taste with salt.

Cut pita breads into halves. Open halves and fill with rock-lobster mixture. If desired, sprinkle filling with sliced almonds for added crunch.
Makes 6 servings.

PORK-APPLE-KRAUT SANDWICH

1⅓	cups rinsed and drained sauerkraut
2	tablespoons chopped onion
1	tablespoon chopped pimiento
8	medium-thick slices hot roast pork
4	large hard rolls, cut in half
8	unpared apple wedges
1	cup hot pork gravy

In a small bowl, mix together sauerkraut, onion and pimiento. Arrange on roll bottoms. Arrange pork slices on other roll halves. Add apple wedges for garnish. Top with gravy. Serve at once.
Makes 4 servings.

SOMBRERO BURGERS

1	pound ground beef
1	can (16 ounces) chili con carne
4	slices (1 ounce each) American cheese
¼	cup bottled chili sauce
4	hamburger buns
	Shredded lettuce

Shape ground beef into 8 thin patties. Place one tablespoon chili con carne in center of 4 patties. Top each with additional patty, making 4 chili-filled burgers.

Grill 5 inches from medium-hot charcoal coals for 8 to 10 minutes, turning once. Just before patties are done, top each burger with slice of American cheese.

Meanwhile prepare sauce by combining remaining chili con carne with bottled sauce in small saucepan. Heat over medium-hot coals until hot, stirring often. Serve burgers on buns with chili mixture and shredded lettuce. *Makes 4 servings.*

TOASTY TUNA SANDWICH-BUN

1	can (6½ or 7 ounces) tuna, in vegetable oil or water, drained and flaked
1⅓	cups chopped vegetables (zucchini, carrots, celery, parsley, etc.)*
2	tablespoons low-calorie mayonnaise
2	tablespoons low-fat yogurt
2	teaspoons lemon juice
½	teaspoon dried dill
⅛	teaspoon Tabasco pepper sauce
3	Vienna-type rolls

Continued

In a medium-size bowl, combine tuna, vegetables, mayonnaise, yogurt, lemon juice, dill, pepper sauce; mix well. Cut a thin slice off tops of rolls. Remove most of the soft centers (save for bread crumbs) and spoon tuna mixture into roll. Bake in a 350-degree oven 15 to 20 minutes or until mixture is heated through. Cover rolls with tops; serve hot. If desired, serve with additional pepper sauce.

Makes 3 servings.

*Leftover steamed or sauteed vegetables may also be used.

TUNA CHEESE MELT

1	can (6½ or 7 ounces) tuna, drained
2	tablespoons mayonnaise
1	teaspoon pickle relish
1	tablespoon butter or margarine
2	slices white or whole wheat bread
	Tomato slices
4	slices Cheddar cheese

In a large bowl, break tuna into chunks; stir in mayonnaise and relish. spread butter on one side of each slice of bread. Place bread butter-side-down on baking tray of meal-maker toaster oven. Spread tuna mixture on bread. Top with tomato slices and cheese. Place tray on rack in lower position. Bake in a 400-degree toaster oven five minutes until cheese is melted.

Makes 2 servings.

TUNA SALAD BURGERS

2	cans (7 ounces) tuna, drained, flaked
1	cup quick or old-fashioned oats, uncooked
½	cup green onion slices
½	cup mayonnaise
¼	cup dairy sour cream or sour half-and-half
2	tablespoons chopped fresh parsley or 1 teaspoon dried parsley flakes
1	teaspoon lemon juice
¼	teaspoon salt
⅛	teaspoon pepper
½	cup (2 ounces) shredded Cheddar cheese
6	hamburger buns

In medium bowl, combine all ingredients except cheese; mix well. Shape to form six 3½-inch patties. Chill for 30 minutes. Place on rack of broiler pan so patties are about 5 inches from heat. Broil for 2 to 3 minutes on each side. Sprinkle cheese evenly over patties; continue cooking for 1 minute or until cheese is melted. Serve on hamburger buns with lettuce and garnish with pickles and black olives, if desired.

Makes 6 servings.

VEGETABLE SALAD SANDWICHES

1	package (10 ounces) frozen mixed vegetables
¼	cup sour cream
½	teaspoon spicy brown mustard
¼	teaspoon salt
6	brown-and-serve rolls
2	tablespoons soft butter
	Lettuce leaves

Cook vegetables according to package directions. Place in colander; run under cold water to cool. Drain. Combine with sour cream, mustard and salt. Prepare rolls according to package directions; butter. Arrange lettuce on rolls. Place approximately two tablespoons of vegetable salad on lettuce.

Makes 6 servings.

VIKING STROGANOFF SANDWICH

1	can (3 ounces) Norwegian sardines
⅓	cup butter, softened
1	tablespoon lemon juice
8	slices dark rye bread
1	small cucumber, thinly sliced
1	small red onion, thinly sliced
½	cup dairy sour cream

Drain sardines. Reserve 8 for garnish. Mash remainder for sardine butter.

Mix mashed sardines with butter and lemon juice. Spread on slices of bread.

Arrange cucumber and onion over buttered sides of 4 bread slices; then spoon on sour cream and garnish with reserved sardines.

Serve with remaining 4 sardine-buttered bread slices.

Makes 4 servings.

ONE-DISH MEALS

MEAT

BEEF AND BEAN POT PIE

1	pound ground beef
2	cans (16 ounces each) pork and beans in tomato sauce
1	cup shredded Cheddar cheese
1	tablespoon brown sugar

1 medium green pepper, sliced
¾ cup diagonally sliced celery
½ cup sliced onion
1 prepared frozen pie crust, thawed

In a skillet, brown meat. Combine beans, cheese and sugar with meat. Spoon a layer of bean mixture in the bottom of a round 1-quart casserole. Top with a layer of green pepper, celery and onion. Continue layering with beans and vegetables. Cover casserole with pastry crust. Crimp edges and trim off any excess. (This can be used to decorate top, if desired.)

With a small sharp knife, make several vents in the top crust. Bake in a 350-degree oven for 45 minutes. Allow casserole to stand 10 minutes before serving. *Makes 6-8 servings.*

BANANA-SAUSAGE SKILLET DINNER

1 pound ground pork sausage
½ cup chopped onion
1 can (1 pound) tomatoes
1 tablespoon lemon juice
½ teaspoon salt
½ teaspoon dried leaf thyme
⅛ teaspoon pepper
6 cups shredded cabbage
3 bananas

In large skillet break up sausage and cook over moderate heat until browned. Add onion and cook until tender. Add tomatoes, lemon juice, salt, thyme and pepper; simmer uncovered for 5 minutes. Add cabbage and cook 5 minutes longer. Peel bananas, slice and add to skillet; heat.
Makes 4 to 6 servings.

BOB MERCER'S SHEPHERD PIE

1 medium onion, chopped
1 cup chopped celery
3 tablespoons butter or margarine
3 cups coarsely ground or diced cooked roast beef
1 teaspoon oregano
Salt and pepper
4 cups seasoned mashed potatoes
2 tablespoons grated Parmesan cheese
Paprika

Saute onion and celery in butter until tender. Stir in meat and oregano. Season to taste. Heat through. Pour mixture into buttered, shallow 2-quart casserole. Spoon mashed potatoes over hash. Sprinkle with cheese and paprika. Bake 350 degrees for 40 minutes. *Makes 6 servings.*

CHOP-SUEY SKILLET

1 cup green onions cut diagonally in 1-inch pieces
½ cup diagonally sliced celery
½ cup green pepper strips
Generous dash ground ginger
2 tablespoons butter or margarine
1 can (10¾ ounces) condensed golden mushroom soup
2 tablespoons dry sherry
1 cup diced cooked beef or pork
1 cup bean sprouts
1 tablespoon soy sauce
½ cup sliced radishes
Cooked rice

In skillet, cook onions, celery and green pepper with ginger in butter until *just* tender. Add soup, sherry, meat, bean sprouts and soy sauce. Heat; stir occasionally. Add radishes. Serve over rice.
Makes about 3½ cups, 4 servings.

GOLDEN CHOPS 'N' SPROUTS

1 can (10¾ ounces) condensed golden mushroom soup
1 cup cooked rice
¼ cup chopped pecans
½ teaspoon rubbed sage
¼ teaspoon celery salt
4 thick pork chops (1½ pounds)
Generous dash pepper
1 package (10 ounces) frozen Brussels sprouts
1 cup chopped canned tomatoes
1 medium onion, thickly sliced

In bowl, combine one-fourth cup soup, rice, pecans, sage and celery salt. Trim excess fat from chops. Slit each chop from outer edge toward bone making a pocket; stuff with rice mixture. Fasten with toothpicks or skewers.

In skillet, brown chops (use shortening if necessary) and pour off fat. Add remaining soup and pepper. Cover; cook over low heat 1 hour. Stir occasionally.

Add Brussels sprouts, tomatoes and onion; bring to boil. Stir to separate sprouts. Reduce heat; simmer 25 minutes more or until done.
Makes 4 servings.

GRAPEFRUIT-SAUSAGE SUPPER

1	tablespoon vegetable oil
1	pound Italian sweet sausage, cut in chunks
1	can (28 ounces) whole tomatoes, drained, reserve juice
1	clove garlic, minced
1	teaspoon salt
½	teaspoon dried leaf chervil
2	tablespoons cornstarch
1	green pepper, seeded, cut in 1-inch pieces
2	grapefruits, sectioned
	Cornbread Ring (recipe follows)

Heat oil in large skillet; brown sausage over low heat. Drain off excess fat. Add tomatoes, garlic, salt and chervil. Bring to a boil; cover and reduce heat to simmer and cook for 10 minutes.

Combine cornstarch and reserved tomato juice and add to sausage mixture. Bring to a boil, stirring. Add green pepper; reduce heat and cook 5 minutes longer. Add grapefruit sections. Heat through.

Place Cornbread Ring in center of large platter. Spoon sausage mixture into ring.

Makes 4 to 6 servings.

CORNBREAD RING:

1	cup cornmeal
1	cup all-purpose flour
2	tablespoons sugar
4	teaspoons baking powder
1	teaspoon dried leaf chervil
¾	teaspoon salt
1	cup milk
1	egg
¼	cup shortening

Combine cornmeal, flour, sugar, baking powder, chervil and salt in medium bowl. Add milk, egg and shortening. Beat until fairly smooth. Turn into well-greased 4½-cup ring mold. Bake in 425-degree oven 25 minutes.

HAM AND MUSTARD CASSEROLE

2	teaspoons powdered mustard
2	teaspoons warm water
5	tablespoons butter or margarine, divided
¼	cup all-purpose flour
2	cups milk
1	cup shredded Cheddar cheese
4	cups cooked potatoes, cut into 1-inch chunks
2	cups cooked ham cubes
2	tablespoons parsley flakes
1	teaspoon salt
1/16	teaspoon ground black pepper
1	cup soft bread crumbs

Mix mustard and warm water. Let stand for 10 minutes to allow flavor to develop. In a medium saucepan melt 4 tablespoons of the butter. Add flour. Cook and stir for 2 minutes. Stir in milk and mustard. Cook and stir until mixture boils and thickens. Boil for 1 minute. Remove from heat and add cheese; stir until cheese melts. Mix in potatoes, ham, parsley flakes, salt and black pepper. Pour into a buttered one-and-one-half-quart casserole. In a small saucepan melt remaining 1 tablespoon butter. Stir in bread crumbs. Lightly spoon around edge of casserole. Bake in preheated 350-degree oven until hot and bubbly and crumbs are golden, about 20 minutes. *Makes 6 portions.*

HAM-AND-POTATO BAKE

1	tablespoon butter or margarine
½	cup chopped onion
¼	cup chopped parsley
1	pound ground cooked ham
4	cups cubed, pared Idaho potatoes
1	teaspoon caraway seeds
½	teaspoon salt
¼	teaspoon allspice
⅛	teaspoon pepper
1	cup chicken broth
3	apples, cored and sliced crosswise

Melt butter in large skillet. Add onion and parsley. Cook until onion is tender.

Add remaining ingredients except apples. Toss to mix well.

Place layer of apples in greased 1½-quart baking dish. Spread half of potato mixture over apples. Repeat with apples and potato mixture.

Cover. Bake in 350-degree oven 1 hour or until potatoes are tender. *Makes 4 to 6 servings.*

LAYERED BEEF BAKE

1	can (10¾ ounces) condensed cream of mushroom soup
1	cup shredded Cheddar cheese
½	cup sour cream
	Generous dash pepper
4	cups thinly sliced potatoes
1	cup cubed cooked beef

Combine soup, cheese, sour cream and pepper. In 2-quart casserole, arrange alternate layers of potatoes, beef and soup mixture. Cover; bake at 375 degrees for 1 hour. Uncover; bake 15 minutes more or until done. *Makes about 6½ cups, 6 servings.*

LIVER CASSEROLE

2 cups water
1 cup milk
1 cup pearl barley or brown rice
1 large onion, chopped
1 tablespoon vegetable oil
¾ pound ground liver
¼ cup corn syrup
1 teaspoon coarse salt
½ teaspoon white pepper
1 teaspoon marjoram leaves, crushed
⅛ teaspoon ginger (optional)
⅓ cup seedless raisins
1 egg, beaten lightly
1 teaspoon oil for the casserole

Mix water with milk and bring to boil. Then add barley or rice. Heat for 10 minutes and stir so the barley won't stick. Cover and simmer until all liquid is absorbed. Let cool.

Fry chopped onion in oil until light brown. Let stand a few minutes. Then, combine barley, onion, ground liver, syrup, salt, pepper and other ingredients in a bowl, along with the beaten egg. Mix well.

Preheat oven to 350 degrees. Meanwhile, oil a larger casserole. Pour the mixture into the dish and bake in oven for about an hour or till the top turns brown. *Makes 6 to 8 servings.*

NEW ENGLAND SKILLET DINNER

2 tablespoons butter or margarine
½ cup chopped fresh onion
2 cups sliced, pared carrots
2 potatoes, cooked, peeled and cut in cubes
4 cups shredded cabbage (½ medium)
1½–2 cups corned beef, cut in strips
½ teaspoon salt
⅛ teaspoon pepper
½ teaspoon dried leaf thyme
½ cup beef broth

Melt butter in large skillet. Add onion and cook until tender, about 5 minutes.

Add carrots. Cover and cook over low heat 10 minutes.

Add remaining ingredients. Cover and cook 10 minutes until cabbage is tender. *Makes 4 servings.*

OLD-FASHIONED PORK POT PIE

1 jar (10 ounces) grape preserves
½ cup ketchup
1 tablespoon prepared mustard
1 tablespoon lemon juice
1 medium clove garlic, minced
½ teaspoon salt
¼ teaspoon pepper
1 package (1 pound, 8 ounce) frozen mixed vegetables for stew
3 cups cubed cooked pork
1 cup unsifted flour
⅓ cup margarine
½ teaspoon salt
3–4 tablespoons ice water
1 egg yolk
1 tablespoon milk

Combine grape preserves, ketchup, mustard, lemon juice, garlic, ½ teaspoon salt and the pepper. Set aside. Cook vegetables in boiling water for 5 minutes; drain. Combine pork, vegetables and sauce mixture. Spoon into a 1½-quart shallow baking dish.

Measure flour into a mixing bowl. Cut in margarine, using a pastry blender or two knives, until mixture resembles coarse meal. Stir in salt and ice water until mixture leaves sides of bowl and forms a ball. Roll out on a lightly floured board to fit top of casserole. Transfer to top of pie. Pinch to seal edges to baking dish. Cut slits in top of pastry. If desired, use scraps to decorate top of pastry. Combine egg yolk and milk. Brush top of pastry. Bake at 375 degrees for 45 minutes or until crust is golden brown. *Makes 6 servings.*

PEAR AND HAM CASSEROLES

2 Anjou, Bosc or Comice pears, diced
⅓ cup diced onion
½ cup diced celery
¼ cup diced green pepper
2 tablespoons butter
1 pound cooked ham, cut in ½-inch cubes
6 additional pear slices, for garnish
½ cup ketchup
½ cup water
2 tablespoons brown sugar
1 tablespoon vinegar
½ teaspoon Worcestershire sauce
½ teaspoon dry mustard
½ cup buttered coarse bread crumbs

Dice pears. Saute onion, celery and green pepper in butter. Combine with ham and pears and place in 6 individual buttered casseroles. Garnish with pear slices. Combine ketchup, water, brown sugar, vinegar, Worcestershire sauce and mustard. Divide evenly among casseroles. Sprinkle with buttered crumbs. Bake at 350 degrees 20 to 30 minutes. *Makes 6 servings.*

POTATO-CRESTED BEEF LOAVES

2	pounds ground beef chuck
2	eggs
1	can (8 ounces), tomato sauce
¼	cup finely chopped onion
¼	cup finely chopped green pepper
⅔	cup cracker meal
2	teaspoons salt
1	tablespoon Angostura aromatic bitters
2	cups hot seasoned mashed potatoes

Combine all ingredients except mashed potatoes. Mix until well blended.

Shape mixture into 8 individual meat loaves. Place loaves side by side on shallow baking pan. Bake in preheated 350-degree oven for 20 minutes.

Remove from oven. Spoon mashed potatoes down center of each loaf. Replace in oven and bake another 10 to 15 minutes or until potatoes are lightly browned.

Serve meat loaves with tomatoes slices, celery hearts and sweet gherkins.

Makes 8 individual loaves.

PORK AND YAM CASSEROLE

2	tablespoons vegetable oil
1½	pounds pork shoulder, cut into 1-inch cubes
1	large onion, sliced (1 cup)
1	clove garlic, crushed
⅔	cup water
⅓	cup freshly squeezed orange juice
⅓	cup soy sauce
1	tablespoon dark brown sugar
½	teaspoon ground ginger
⅛	teaspoon ground black pepper
3	medium-size yams, pared and cut in chunks
1	apple, cored and sliced
2	teaspoons chopped parsley

Heat oil in large skillet or Dutch oven. Brown pork on all sides over medium-high heat. Remove and reserve.

In same skillet, saute onion and garlic until tender. Add water, orange juice, soy sauce, brown sugar, ginger and pepper to skillet. Mix well.

Return pork to skillet. Cover. Simmer 35 to 45 minutes.

Add yams. Cook, covered, for 15 minutes.

Add apple. Cook 10 minutes longer or until yams and apple are tender. Garnish with chopped parsley.   *Makes 4 servings.*

POTATO-STUDDED MEAT LOAF

1	package (16 ounces) frozen bite-size potato nuggets
1	large egg
1½	teaspoons salt
1	teaspoon prepared mustard
1	teaspoon basil, crumbled
¼	teaspoon pepper
½	cup fresh frozen chopped onions
½	cup milk
1½	pounds lean beef
	Fresh herbs and cherry tomatoes or parsley for garnish

Preheat oven to 350 degrees. Oil a 8½ × 4½ × 2¾-inch loaf pan. Allow potato nuggets to thaw. Set aside 12 for top of loaf. Beat egg with salt, mustard, basil and pepper. Add onion, milk and beef, and mix thoroughly. In an oiled loaf pan, make a thin layer of beef mixture. Place a layer of potato nuggets on beef. Repeat using all of beef and potato nuggets, except the 12 reserved for top, and ending with a layer of beef. Loosen edges of loaf with a small spatula and invert loaf onto shallow baking pan. Bake in a preheated oven for 45 minutes. Remove from oven and arrange reserved potatoes on top, fastening with wooden picks. Return to oven and bake 15 minutes longer. Garnish with fresh herbs and cherry tomatoes or small parsley sprigs down center of loaf.   *Makes 6 servings.*

STEAK AND KIDNEY PIE

2	small veal kidneys (4 to 5 ounces), fat removed
2	pounds beef top round steak
3	tablespoons cooking oil
¾	cup chopped onion
½	pound mushrooms, sliced
3	tablespoons flour
1¼	teaspoons salt
⅛	teaspoon black pepper
¾	cup beef broth
½	cup red table wine
2	tablespoons tomato paste
1	teaspoon Worcestershire sauce
	Pastry (recipe follows)

Cut kidneys in small cubes, cover with cold water and bring to boil. Drain and cool. Cut round steak into 1½-inch cubes. Brown beef in hot oil. Remove beef. Add onion and mushrooms to skillet and brown lightly. Blend flour, salt and pepper into vegetables. Stir in broth, wine, tomato paste and Worcestershire sauce. Cook until mixture boils. Add kidney and steak cubes. Cover and simmer one and one-half to two hours until tender. Divide mixture into six shallow individual bakers. Cover each with pastry, pinching edges to sides of bakers. Cut slits in top. Bake in 425-degree oven 25 to 30 minutes or until pastry is brown. *Makes 6 servings.*

PASTRY: Combine 2 cups flour with 1 teaspoon salt. Cut in two-thirds cup shortening into flour with pastry blender. Add one-third cup cold water to make stiff dough. Divide pastry into 6 balls. Roll out balls onto floured board.

STEAK AND ROCK LOBSTER SUKIYAKI

¾	pound lean flank steak
1	pound frozen South African rock lobster tails
½	cup soy sauce
3	tablespoons sugar
¾	cup sake (rice wine) or chicken broth
1	can (8 ounces) water chestnuts, drained
1	stalk celery
6	white mushrooms
3	scallions
1	medium yellow onion, peeled
½	head Chinese cabbage or head lettuce
1	medium green pepper
1	package (6 ounces) frozen snow peas, thawed and drained
1	can (8 ounces) bamboo shoots, drained
2	tablespoons corn oil

Remove rock lobster tails from freezer. With sharp knife cut tails crosswise through hard shell into 1-inch pieces. Set aside to thaw to room temperature.

Place beef in freezer for about 30 minutes. With a sharp knife, cut the beef across the grain into slices ¼ inch thick. Then cut into ½-inch strips. Set aside. In a pitcher, stir together soy sauce, sugar and sake or chicken broth. Set aside.

Cut water chestnuts, celery, mushrooms, scallions and onion into ¼-inch slices. Cut Chinese cabbage or lettuce into ½-inch diagonal slices. Cut the green pepper in half, remove the seeds and cut into ¼-inch strips. Arrange the cut vegetables, snow peas, bamboo shoots, sliced beef and rock lobster pieces on a platter or tray.

Heat oil in an electric skillet or wok to 400 degrees. Add ⅓ of the rock lobster pieces and ⅓ of the meat to the skillet. Pour in ¼ cup of the sauce. Cook for a few minutes, stirring with a long-handled fork or fondue fork. Push the meat and lobster to the side. Add ⅓ of the vegetables in equal amounts. Pour in more sauce and cook for 7 to 8

minutes. Transfer the meat, rock lobster and vegetables to individual plates. Continue cooking the sukiyaki in batches or allow each person to select and cook his own food from the platter. If the skillet seems too hot, lower the heat or add 1 tablespoon cold water. Serve with rice. *Makes 6 servings.*

SUB GUM

¼	cup light corn syrup
3	tablespoons soy sauce
2	tablespoons dry sherry
1/16	teaspoon pepper
2	tablespoons corn oil
2	large green onions, cut in thin strips (½ cup)
1	clove garlic, minced or pressed
1	teaspoon minced ginger
¼	pound lean boneless pork, cut in thin strips
¼	pound boneless chicken, cut in thin strips
¼	pound small shrimp, peeled, deveined
¼	pound cooked ham, cut in thin strips
½	cup very thin green pepper strips
½	cup sliced bamboo shoots, cut in thin strips
½	cup water chestnuts, cut in thin strips
½	cup mung bean sprouts
1	tablespoon cornstarch mixed with
2	tablespoons water

In small bowl, stir together corn syrup, soy sauce, sherry and pepper; set aside.

In large skillet or wok, heat corn oil over medium-high heat. Add green onions, garlic and ginger; stir-fry 30 seconds. Add pork; stir-fry 3 minutes. Add chicken, shrimp and ham; stir-fry 2 minutes. Add green pepper, bamboo shoots, water chestnuts and bean sprouts; stir-fry 2 minutes. Add corn syrup mixture; cook 1 minute.

Restir cornstarch mixture; stir into pork mixture. Stirring constantly, bring to boil over medium heat and boil 1 minute. If desired, serve over rice. *Makes 4 servings.*

SWEDISH BEEF AND POTATO PIE

1	envelope (6½ ounces) instant mashed potato
2	tablespoons instant minced onion, divided
¾	teaspoon ground nutmeg, divided
2	eggs, divided
2	tablespoons mixed vegetable flakes
3	tablespoons water

1	tablespoon salad oil
1½	pounds ground lean beef
1½	tablespoons flour
1	can (8 ounces) tomato sauce
1	teaspoon salt
1	teaspoon sugar
¼	teaspoon ground black pepper

Prepare mashed potato as package directs but stir in 1 tablespoon of the minced onion and ¼ teaspoon of the nutmeg with the liquid. Cool slightly. Stir in one of the eggs. Spread all but ½ cup over the bottom and up the sides of a 9-inch pie pan. Rehydrate remaining 1 tablespoon minced onion with mixed vegetable flakes in water for 10 minutes. In a large skillet heat oil, add onion and vegetable flakes; saute for 1 minute. Add beef. Cook and stir until browned, about 5 minutes. Blend in flour. Stir in tomato sauce, salt, sugar and black pepper. Bring to boiling point. Cool slightly. Stir in remaining egg. Spoon into potato-lined pie pan. Spoon or pipe remaining potatoes through a pastry bag fitted with a star tube in any desired pattern over the top of the meat. Bake in a preheated 375-degree oven until browned, about 25 minutes. Let sit for 5 minutes before cutting. If desired, serve with green salad.

Makes 6 to 8 portions.

VERY ENGLISH SHEPHERD'S PIE

2	tablespoons beef drippings or salad oil
½	cup chopped onion
1½	pounds ground lean beef
1	can (8 ounces) tomato sauce
1	tablespoon Worcestershire sauce
2	tablespoons chopped parsley
1	teaspoon salt
2	tablespoons flour
2	tablespoons water
1	envelope instant mashed potatoes or 3 cups mashed potatoes

In a large skillet heat drippings. Add onion; saute for 1 minute. Add ground beef. Cook and stir until browned, about 5 minutes. Stir in tomato sauce, Worcestershire sauce, parsley and salt. Bring to boiling point. Blend flour with water. Blend into beef mixture. Cook and stir until mixture thickens slightly about one minute. Pour into 1- to 1½-quart casserole; set aside. Prepare mashed potatoes as label directs. Spread over beef mixture. Score top of potatoes with tines of fork. Bake in a preheated 400-degree oven until potatoes are lightly browned, about 10 minutes   *Makes 6 portions*

SWISS HAM 'N' EGGS

¼	cup butter or margarine, melted
⅛	teaspoon onion powder
1	package (10 ounces) frozen buttermilk waffles (8 jumbo-size waffles)
1	can (10¾ ounces) condensed cream of celery soup
½	cup milk
1	cup (4 ounces) shredded Swiss cheese
1	cup cubed, cooked ham
3	hard-cooked eggs, chopped
1	teaspoon dried parsley flakes
⅛	teaspoon nutmeg (optional)

Heat oven to 400 degrees. Combine butter and onion powder; mix well. Spread one side of frozen waffles with butter mixture. Cut each waffle into 2 triangles; place on ungreased cookie sheet. Bake at 400 degrees for 10 to 12 minutes or until crisp, turning waffles twice during baking.

Meanwhile, combine soup and milk in medium saucepan. Cook and stir over medium heat until well blended. Add remaining ingredients. Cook and stir over medium heat until cheese is melted and mixture is heated through. Arrange 4 waffle triangles on individual plates. Pour ham mixture over waffles to serve.   *Makes 4 servings.*

POULTRY

CHICKEN AND KRAUT SKILLET

¼	cup butter or margarine
1	large onion, sliced
1	cup green pepper strips
1	can (16 ounces) tomatoes, undrained
1	can (6 ounces) tomato paste
2	cups diced cooked chicken
2	cups drained sauerkraut (about 16 ounces)
2	tablespoons sugar
¼	teaspoon crushed oregano
¾	teaspoon salt
⅛	teaspon pepper
3	cups cooked rice

In large skillet, melt butter over low heat. Add onion and green pepper and cook 5 minutes. Add remaining ingredients except rice; mix well. Cover and cook 20 minutes. Serve chicken and kraut sauce over rice. *Makes 4 servings.*

CHICKEN-CHUTNEY PIE

1	butter-flavored ready crust pie shell
2	tablespoons sauteed onions
¾	cup chopped chicken
2	tablespoons chutney
4	ounces Monterey Jack cheese, grated (1 cup)
1	can (10¾ ounces) cream of chicken soup
¼	cup milk
2	eggs
¼	teaspoon curry powder
½	teaspoon salt
	Dash of white pepper (optional)

Layer onions, chicken, chutney and cheese in pie shell. Beat soup, milk, eggs and seasonings together; pour over chicken mixture. Bake at 400 degrees 35-40 minutes or until filling is set. Let cool lightly before cutting. *Makes 1 pie.*

CHICKEN SOUFFLE

6	slices white bread
3	cups diced cooked chicken
½	cup chopped onion
½	cup mayonnaise
½	cup chopped celery
¾	teaspoon salt
2	eggs, beaten
½	cup milk
1	can (10¾ ounces) cream of mushroom soup
1½	cups shredded sharp Cheddar cheese

Trim crust off bread. Cube 2 slices into 8-by-8-by-2-inch buttered baking dish. Combine chicken, vegetables, mayonnaise and salt. Spoon over bread. Cube remaining 4 slices of bread over top. Combine eggs with milk; pour over all. Cover and chill at least 1 hour, preferably overnight. When ready to bake, spread soup over top and bake uncovered at 325 degrees about 1 hour. Sprinkle cheese over top last 5 minutes of baking. *Makes 8-10 servings.*

CURRIED CHICKEN CASSEROLE

1½	cups water
¼	cup regular barley
½	teaspoon salt, divided
1½	cups chopped cooked chicken
1	cup chopped apple
½	cup celery slices
⅓	cup chopped walnuts
½	cup mayonnaise
1	teaspoon curry powder
½	cup dry bread cumbs
1	tablespoon butter or margarine, melted

In a small saucepan, bring water to boil. Stir in barley and ¼ teaspoon salt. Cover; simmer 50 to 60 minutes or until barley is tender. Drain. Heat oven to 350 degrees.

Combine barley, chicken, apple, celery and walnuts. Add mayonnaise, curry powder and remaining ¼ teaspoon salt to chicken mixture, mixing well. Spoon into 1-quart casserole.

Combine bread crumbs and melted butter; toss lightly. Sprinkle over chicken mixture. Bake 30 minutes or until bubbly. *Makes about 4 servings.*

Note: Substitute ⅓ cup quick barley for regular barley, if desired. Decrease water to 1 cup. Cover; simmer 10 to 12 minutes or until tender. Drain. Proceed as recipe directs.

FRUITED CHICKEN-POTATO CASSEROLE

1	tablespoon butter or margarine
1	teaspoon salt
¼	teaspoon white pepper
¼	teaspoon paprika
4	large pieces frying chicken
1	can (10¾ ounces) condensed chicken broth
1½	tablespoons cornstarch
¼	teaspoon cinnamon
⅛	teaspoon mace
1	package (16 ounces) frozen bite-size potato nuggets
1	can (8 ounces) pineapple slices, drained
2	tablespoons raisins
1	tablespoon almond slivers

Melt butter in 9 × 13 × 2-inch baking pan while heating oven to 400 degrees. Mix salt, pepper and paprika and rub over chicken pieces. Place chicken, skin side down, in butter and bake 15 minutes. Combine broth with cornstarch and spices. Turn chicken pieces and pour broth mixture over. Bake 15 minutes longer. Add frozen potatoes, drained pineapple, raisins and almonds to the pan and bake 15 minutes, or until chicken is tender. Serve at once. *Makes 4 servings.*

GRILLED CHICKEN AND CHOPS WITH KRAUT RELISH

4	cups undrained sauerkraut (about 32 ounces)
	MARINADE:
¾	cup ketchup
⅓	cup salad oil
1½	teaspoons marjoram, crushed
1	teaspoon salt
½	teaspoon garlic powder
¼	teaspoon pepper
1½–2	pounds chicken drumsticks
6–7	loin pork chops, cut 1-inch thick
	RELISH:
2	small zucchini, chopped
2	cups chopped mushrooms (about ½ pound)
1	cup chopped onion
½	cup chopped canned pimiento
⅓	cup sugar
¼	cup salad oil
¼	cup chopped parsley
½	teaspoon garlic powder
¼	teaspoon pepper
	Reserved kraut

Drain sauerkraut, reserving 1½ cups kraut liquid. Set kraut aside.

FOR MARINADE: In large shallow dish, combine kraut liquid and remaining ingredients for marinade; stir until well mixed. Add chicken and pork chops; turn to coat well. Cover and chill at least 2 hours or overnight.

FOR RELISH: In large bowl combine reserved kraut and all relish ingredients. Toss to mix well. Cover and chill at least 2 hours or overnight. For a different kraut dish, substitute the Honey-Kraut Relish recipe which follows.

TO GRILL: Remove chicken and chops from marinade. Place on grill over medium-hot coals about 5 inches from heat source. Grill, brushing frequently with marinade, about 40 to 45 minutes for chicken and 25 to 30 minutes for chops or until well done.

TO SERVE: Toss relish and serve with chicken and chops. *Makes 6 to 8 servings.*

HONEY-KRAUT RELISH:

3¼	cups drained sauerkraut
¼	cup sugar
¼	cup honey
2	tablespoons salad oil
1	teaspoon caraway seed
¼	teaspoon salt
	Dash pepper
⅓	cup finely chopped onion
3	tablespoons chopped canned pimiento

Combine all ingredients except pimiento in large saucepan. Simmer, covered, about 20 minutes. Add pimiento, toss and chill for at least 4 hours before serving. *Makes 2½ cups.*

HARVEST CHICKEN

2	pounds chicken parts
2	tablespoons shortening
1	can (10¾ ounces) condensed chicken broth
12	dried pitted prunes (about ½ cup)
2	tablespoons apricot preserves
⅛	teaspoon ground allspice
¼	cup water
3	tablespoons cornstarch
8	thin slices lemon
	Cooked rice

In skillet, brown chicken in shortening; pour off fat. Add broth, prunes, preserves and allspice. Cover. Cook over low heat 45 minutes or until tender. Stir occasionally.

Mix water and cornstarch. Gradually blend into chicken mixture. Cook, stirring, until thickened. Add lemon; heat. Serve with rice.

Makes 4 servings.

HERBED CHICKEN AND PORK CASEROLE

2	tablespoons salad oil
2	(2½ pounds each) chickens, cut into eighths
2	pounds lean boneless pork shoulder, cut into 1-inch cubes
2	chicken bouillon cubes
2	cups hot water
2	tablespoons cider vinegar
1	teaspoon salt
1	teaspoon instant minced garlic
½	teaspoon ground black pepper
½	teaspoon thyme leaves, crumbled
2	bay leaves
3	tablespoons flour
1	can (1 pound 1 ounce) whole kernel corn
1	package (9 ounces) frozen cut green beans

In a large heavy saucepot or a Dutch oven heat oil. Add chicken, a few pieces at a time. Brown well on both sides. Remove and set aside. Add pork and brown well. Add bouillon cubes, water, vinegar, salt, garlic, black pepper, thyme and bay leaves. Bring to boiling point. Reduce heat. Simmer, covered, for 30 minutes. Return chicken to pot. Simmer, covered, until pork and chicken are fork-tender, about 30 minutes. Blend flour with 3 table-spoons of the liquid from corn. Blend into liquid in saucepan along with corn kernels and green beans. Bring to boiling point, stirring constantly. Simmer, covered, for 5 minutes.

Makes 2 batches, 6 portions each.

MUSHROOM, CHEESE AND TURKEY STRATA

1	pound small fresh mushrooms or 2 cans (6 to 8 ounces each) whole mushrooms
¼	cup butter or margarine, melted
½	cup minced onion
1	small clove garlic, crushed
10	slices white bread
1	cup shredded American cheese
2	cups diced, cooked turkey or chicken
5	eggs, beaten lightly
2¾	cups milk
¾	teaspoon salt
⅛	teaspoon ground black pepper

Rinse and pat dry fresh mushrooms or drained canned mushrooms. In a medium skillet, heat butter. Add mushrooms, onion and garlic. Saute 3 min-

utes. Trim and discard crusts from bread slices. Cut each slice into a 3-inch circle; set aside. Tear remaining bread into pieces and place in a buttered 3-quart casserole. Arrange alternate layers of cheese, turkey and sauteed mushrooms in the casserole. Overlap bread circles around outer edge of the casserole. Combine eggs, milk, salt and black pepper; pour over casserole ingredients, completely moistening the bread. Bake, uncovered, in preheated 350-degree oven 1 hour and 15 minutes or until bread is lightly browned. Serve as a main dish for lunch or supper. *Makes 6 servings.*

MUSHROOM-TURKEY BAKE WITH BISCUIT TOPPING

¾	pound fresh mushrooms or 2 cans (6 to 8 ounces each) sliced mushrooms
¼	cup butter or margarine
½	cup minced onion
2	cans (10½ ounces each) condensed cream of mushroom soup
½	soup can milk
4	cups cubed cooked turkey chunks
1	package (9 ounces) frozen cut green beans
3	tablespoons dry sherry (optional) Herbed Mushroom Biscuits (recipe follows)

Preheat oven to 425 degrees. Rinse, pat dry and slice fresh mushrooms (makes about 4 cups) or drain canned mushrooms. Set aside. In a large saucepan, melt butter. Add mushrooms and onion, saute for 3 minutes. Add soup, milk, turkey, green beans and sherry. Bring to the boiling point. Reduce heat and simmer, covered, for 10 minutes. Pour into a 3-quart casserole. Drop Herbed Mushroom Biscuit dough by tablespoonful around the edge of the casserole. Bake until biscuits are golden, about 20 minutes. *Makes 6 portions.*

HERBED MUSHROOM BISCUITS:

4	ounces fresh mushrooms or 1 can (3 to 4 ounces) mushroom stems and pieces
2	tablespoons butter or margarine
2	cups buttermilk baking mix
¼	teaspoon thyme leaves, crushed
¼	cup cold milk

Rinse, pat dry and chop fresh mushrooms (makes about 1 cup) or drain canned mushrooms. In a small saucepan, melt butter. Add mushrooms; saute for 2 minutes. With a fork, lightly combine baking mix, thyme, milk and mushrooms. Drop dough by the tablespoonful around the edge of the Mushroom-Turkey Bake. Bake as directed above.

POTEE DU LENDEMAIN (TURKEY-CHEESE CASSEROLE)

1	package (8 ounces) medium noodles
	Salt
1	package (5 ounces) herb-flavored cream cheese
12	slices cooked turkey
½	cup butter
4	large onions, chopped
1	clove garlic, chopped
1	cup dry white wine
2	cups (1 pint) half-and-half
½	teaspoon crumbled tarragon
1	cup crushed French biscotte or bread crumbs (optional)

Cook noodles in boiling salted water until tender. Drain, and while they are hot pour them into a bowl and toss them with the cheese until noodles are coated with melted cheese. Pour into well-buttered 2-quart casserole. Top with turkey slices. In a skillet, heat butter and saute onion and garlic slowly until transparent but not brown. Pour onion mixture into blender and add wine. Whirl until smooth. Pour back into saucepan and stir in half-and-half and tarragon. Stir over low heat until sauce thickens, about 10 minutes. Pour evenly over turkey. If desired, sprinkle with biscotte or bread crumbs. Bake in preheated moderate oven for 35 to 40 minutes. *Makes about 6 servings.*

SAVORY CHICKEN

1	chicken breast (about 1 pound), split
¼	cup finely chopped onion
2	tablespoons butter or margarine
2	cans (7¾ ounces each) semi-condensed golden chicken and noodles soup
½	cup water
⅓	cup chopped turnip
2	tablespoons chopped parsley
1	cup biscuit mix
⅓	cup milk

In saucepan, brown chicken and cook onion in butter until tender. Add soup, water, turnip and parsley. Cover; cook over low heat 20 minutes. Stir occasionally. Meanwhile, combine biscuit mix and milk with fork. Drop by spoonfuls onto pieces of chicken. Cook uncovered 10 minutes. Cover; cook 10 minutes more. *Serves 4.*

TURKEY-CABBAGE ROLLS

4	large cabbage leaves
1	tablespoon vegetable oil
½	cup chopped fresh cabbage
¼	cup finely chopped fresh onion
¼	cup finely grated carrot
2	tablespoons finely chopped celery
½	teaspoon salt
½	teaspoon dried dill weed, divided
1	egg
¼	teaspoon hot pepper sauce
½	pound fresh ground turkey (uncooked)
¼	cup fresh bread crumbs
3	tablespoons butter or margarine
3	tablespoons flour
1	cup chicken broth
1	tablespoon freshly squeezed lemon juice
1	teaspoon grated lemon rind
2	tablespoons chopped parsley

Cook cabbage leaves 6 minutes in boiling water to cover. Drain, pat dry, set aside. Heat oil in small skillet; add chopped cabbage, onion, carrot, celery, salt and ¼ teaspoon dill. Cook until vegetables are tender. Beat egg and hot pepper sauce in medium bowl; mix in turkey, bread crumbs and cooked vegetable mixture. Place ¼ of the turkey mixture in center of each cabbage leaf. Fold sides of cabbage leaf towards center over filling, then fold and overlap ends to make a small bundle. Fasten with wooden picks. Place in a 10-by-8-by-1¾-inch baking dish.

To prepare sauce, melt butter in small saucepan. Blend in flour; gradually add chicken broth. Cook over low heat, stirring constantly, until thickened. Add lemon juice, lemon rind and remaining ¼ teaspoon dill. Pour sauce over cabbage rolls. Cover. Bake in 375-degree oven 40 minutes. Remove picks before serving. Sprinkle with parsley. *Makes 2 servings.*

TURKEY POPOVER RING

3	eggs
1	cup flour
1	cup milk
½	teaspoon salt
6	tablespoons butter or margarine, divided
½	cup diagonally sliced carrots
½	cup diagonally sliced celery
⅓	cup green onions cut in 1-inch pieces
1	medium clove garlic, minced
1	can (10½ ounces) chicken gravy
1	cup cubed cooked turkey
1	tablespoon soy sauce

To make batter, beat eggs until foamy. Add flour, milk and salt all at once. Beat until smooth. To make popover, melt 4 tablespoons butter in 1½-quart casserole at 400 degrees. (This may be done in the oven.) Remove from oven and add batter. Bake for 45 minutes or until golden and puffed.

Meanwhile, in saucepan, cook carrots, celery and onions with garlic in remaining butter until tender. Add remaining ingredients. Heat; stir occasionally. Spoon into popover. Serve immediately.

Makes 4 servings.

TURKISH CHICKEN-VEGETABLE CASSEROLE

1	medium eggplant
3	tablespoons salad oil
1	broiler-fryer chicken, cut in serving pieces
1	large onion, thinly sliced
1	package (10 ounces) frozen French-style green beans, thawed
1	package (10 ounces) frozen whole okra, thawed
2	medium zucchini, cut in quarters lengthwise, then crosswise into 2-inch pieces
4	medium potatoes, pared and quartered or sliced
2	green peppers, seeded and cut in quarters
2	large tomatoes, sliced
1	tablespoon salt
½	teaspoon Tabasco pepper sauce

Pare eggplant in lengthwise strips so that ½-inch strips of skin are left on the eggplant alternating with pared strips. Cut lengthwise in quarters, then crosswise in 2-inch pieces. Soak in salted water for 15 minutes. Drain and press between paper towels to dry.

Heat oil in large skillet. Add chicken pieces and sliced onion. Brown chicken on all sides.

Place chicken and onion in bottom of a deep 3- or 4-quart casserole. Add layers of green beans, eggplant, okra, zucchini, potatoes, peppers and tomatoes. Sprinkle with salt and Tabasco. Cover and bake in a 350-degree oven for 1½ hours, until chicken and vegetables are tender. Serve with rice if desired. *Makes 4 servings.*

VEGETABLE TURNAROUND SKILLET

2	slices bacon
1	cup zucchini squash cut in strips
¼	teaspoon oregano leaves, crushed
2	cans (10½ ounces *each*) turkey or chicken gravy
2	cups cooked small shell macaroni
1	cup cooked diagonally sliced carrots
1	cup cubed cooked chicken
1	can (about 8 ounces) whole kernel golden corn, drained

In saucepan, cook bacon until crisp; remove and crumble. Pour off all but 2 tablespoons drippings.

Cook zucchini with oregano in drippings until tender. Add remaining ingredients except bacon. Heat; stir occasionally. Garnish with bacon.

Makes about 5½ cups, 4 servings.

FISH & SEAFOOD

BUFFET TUNA AND NOODLES

⅓	cup butter or margarine
1	large clove garlic, minced
1	medium onion, finely chopped
1	large red or green pepper, chopped
2	tablespoons flour
1½	cups chicken or vegetable broth
¼	cup chopped fresh parsley
½	cup pitted black olives, sliced
1	can (6½ or 7 ounces) tuna, drained and flaked
1	package (8 ounces) spinach-egg noodles, cooked according to directions and drained

In large skillet, melt butter over medium heat; stir in garlic. Add onion and pepper; saute until tender. Blend in flour, cook 1 minute, stirring, constantly. Add chicken broth and cook, stirring, until sauce thickens. Stir in parsley, olives and tuna. Heat thoroughly. Keep warm over low heat while noodles are cooking. Place hot, drained noodles in large, heated serving dish. Spoon tuna sauce over noodles; toss gently to combine. Set out with several or all of the following: chopped walnuts, grated cheese, sieved hard-cooked eggs, cooked green peas (or cut-up, leftover cooked vegetables), minced fresh or dried herbs, crushed corn chips. *Makes 4 servings.*

FRESH CAULIFLOWER AND TUNA CASSEROLE

4	cups sliced fresh cauliflower
½	cup boiling water
1	teaspoon salt
2	tablespoons butter or margarine
2	tablespoons flour
1⅓	cups milk
⅛	teaspoon minced garlic
⅛	teaspoon thyme leaves
⅛	teaspoon pepper
1	can (6½ or 7 ounces) tuna, drained
1	tablespoon butter or margarine, melted
½	cup soft bread crumbs

Place cauliflower, water and salt in a saucepan. Bring to boiling, uncovered, and cook 5 minutes. Cover and cook 3 minutes or until partly done. Drain and set aside.

Melt 2 tablespoons butter in saucepan. Blend in flour. Remove from heat and gradually stir in milk. Stir and cook over moderate heat until of medium thickness. Remove from heat and add seasonings and tuna.

Arrange cauliflower and tuna mixture in alternate layers in a buttered 1-quart casserole. Combine 1 tablespoon melted butter and bread crumbs and sprinkle over the top. Bake in 350-degree oven 35 minutes or until golden brown.   *Makes 6 servings.*

SALMON CASSEROLE FOR TWO

1	can (7¾ ounces) salmon
1	cup diced potatoes
1	cup sliced carrots
1	cup peas, canned or frozen
1	small onion, chopped
1	tablespoon butter
1½	tablespoons flour
⅔	cup milk
¼	teaspoon salt
1	cup buttermilk biscuit mix
¼	cup milk

Cook potatoes and carrots in small amount of boiling salted water until just tender, adding peas the last few minutes, if frozen. Drain and reserve vegetable water. Saute onion in butter until tender. Add flour to onions and stir. Add one-third cup reserved vegetable water, two-thirds cup milk and salt. Cook, stirring until slightly thickened. Add vegetables. Drain and flake salmon, reserving salmon liquid. Add salmon and liquid to vegetables. Place in buttered casserole. Combine biscuit mix and one-

fourth cup milk. Pat dough to size of casserole and place over top. Make cut in top for steam to escape. Bake at 425 degrees for 15 minutes.
Makes 2 servings.

SALMON-POTATO STRATA

1	can salmon (1 pound), drained
½	cup chopped onion
½	cup chopped celery
4	eggs
2	cups milk
1½	teaspoons salt, divided
¼	teaspoon dried dill weed
⅛	teaspoon pepper
4	medium Idaho potatoes (6 cups sliced)

In large bowl, combine salmon, onion, celery, eggs, milk, ½ teaspoon salt, dill and pepper. Mix well.

Pare potatoes. Cut into thin slices.

Place half of potatoes in greased 1½-quart baking dish. Sprinkle with ½ teaspoon salt. Spread half of salmon mixture over potatoes. Repeat with remaining potatoes, salt and salmon.

Bake, uncovered, in 350-degree oven for 1 hour and 15 minutes or until potatoes are tender when pierced with fork. Remove from oven and let stand 5 minutes before serving.   *Makes 8 servings.*

SWEDISH TROUT 'N' POTATO CASSEROLE

6	small, whole dressed, fresh or frozen rainbow trout
4	cups frozen Southern-style hash brown potatoes (1 pound 2 ounces)
¼	cup chopped parsley
1	tablespoon dill weed
2	tablespoons melted butter or margarine
1	tablespoon salt
¾	cup buttermilk
1	cup whipping cream
1	jar (2 ounces) caviar (optional)
	Melted butter or margarine

Thaw trout in a plastic bag in cold water, if frozen. Remove from plastic, rinse and pat dry. Toss potatoes with parsley, dill weed, butter and salt. Put potatoes in a buttered 2-quart baking dish. Combine buttermilk and whipping cream and pour over potatoes. Bake in preheated 400-degree oven for 30 minutes. Spoon caviar evenly over potatoes. Season cavity of trout with salt and arrange on top of potatoes in baking dish. Brush fish with melted butter and bake an additional 25-30 minutes or until fish flakes easily when tested with a fork. Do not overcook. Garnish with fresh lemon slices and fresh dill weed, if desired. *Makes 6 servings.*

TUNA CLOCK WATCHER

2	cans (6½ or 7 ounces each) tuna in vegetable oil
1	cup diagonally sliced celery
½	green pepper, cut in strips
1	can (1 pound) seasoned stewed tomatoes
1	tablespoon cornstarch
½	teaspoon salt
1	teaspoon soy sauce
1	teaspoon brown sugar
1	can (13½ or 20 ounces) pineapple chunks, drained
1	package quick-cooking rice, cooked according to package directions

Drain vegetable oil from tuna into skillet. Add celery and green pepper. Cook over moderately high heat 3 minutes, stirring frequently. Drain ¼ cup of liquid from stewed tomatoes into cup; add cornstarch and blend well.

Add to skillet with tomatoes and remaining liquid, salt, soy sauce and brown sugar; mix well. Add tuna and drained pineapple. Cook, stirring constantly, until mixture thickens and comes to a boil. Serve over hot cooked rice. *Makes 4 to 6 servings.*

TUNA-CORN PUDDING

1	tablespoon butter or margarine
½	cup chopped onion
½	cup chopped green pepper
3	eggs
2	cans (6½ or 7 ounces each) tuna, drained
1	can (12 ounces) whole kernel corn, drained
1	cup milk
1	teaspoon salt
¼	teaspoon pepper
½	cup shredded Swiss cheese
1	medium tomato, sliced

In medium skillet, melt butter, add onion and green pepper and cook until tender. In 1½-quart baking dish, beat eggs; add onion mixture and rest of ingredients except cheese and tomato; mix well.

Bake in 350-degree oven 35 minutes. Sprinkle cheese over top, add tomato slices and bake 5 to 10 minutes longer, until tip of knife inserted in center comes out clean. *Makes 4 to 6 servings.*

TUNA-NOODLE-OLIVE CASSEROLE

8	ounces medium egg noodles (about 4 cups)
1	tablespoon salt
3	quarts boiling water
1	can (10¾ ounces) condensed cream of celery soup
⅔	cup milk
½	cup thinly sliced celery
¼	cup sliced stuffed green Spanish olives
1	can (6½ or 7 ounces) tuna, drained and flaked
2	tomatoes, sliced
½	cup shredded American process cheese (about 2 ounces)

Gradually add noodles and salt to rapidly boiling water so that water continues to boil. Cook uncovered, stirring, occasionally, until tender. Drain in colander.

Meanwhile, combine undiluted soup, milk, celery and olives. Add tuna and noodles. Stir to mix well. Turn into a lightly greased 2-quart casserole. Arrange tomato slices over top. Sprinkle with cheese.

Bake in 425-degree oven 20 minutes or until hot. *Makes 4 servings.*

TUNA-RICE LOAF

2	eggs
1	teaspoon salt
⅛	teaspoon pepper
¼	teaspoon celery seed
½	teaspoon curry powder
1	tablespoon lemon juice
¼	cup sweet pickle relish
⅓	cup ketchup
2	tablespoons minced onion
2	cans (6½ or 7 ounces each) tuna, drained and flaked
3	cups cooked rice
	Dill-Horseradish Sauce (recipe follows)

In large bowl, mix with fork all ingredients except tuna and rice. Blend thoroughly before stirring in tuna and rice. Turn into well buttered 8 × 4-inch loaf pan. Bake in preheated 350-degree oven until lightly browned, 50 to 60 minutes. Serve hot or cold with Dill-Horseradish Sauce. *Makes 6 to 8 servings.*

DILL HORSERADISH SAUCE: Combine 1 cup mayonnaise, 1 cup sour cream, 2 tablespoons horseradish, 1 teaspoon dill weed and 2 teaspoons lemon juice. *Makes about 2 cups.*

TUNA-VEGETABLE HEALTH PIE

1	unbaked 9-inch pastry crust
2	tablespoons sesame or sunflower seeds
3	tablespoons salad oil
1/3	cup finely chopped onion
1½	cups whole-wheat bread cubes (3 slices)
1	cup shredded unpared zucchini (2 medium)
1	cup chopped fresh tomato (2 medium)
1	cup (¼ pound) shredded American cheese
½	cup wheat germ, divided
2	eggs, slightly beaten
2	tablespoons chopped parsley
½	teaspoon dried leaf basil
2	cans (6½ or 7 ounces each) tuna, drained and flaked
2	tablespoons margarine, melted
½	cup chopped toasted almonds or peanuts

Press sesame seeds over bottom of pie shell. Bake in 400-degree oven 5 minutes. Cool. In large skillet, heat oil; saute onion until tender. Stir in bread cubes, zucchini, tomatoes, cheese, ¼ cup wheat germ, eggs, parsley, basil and flaked tuna. Mix well. Turn mixture into prepared pie shell. Combine margarine, almonds and remaining ¼ cup wheat germ; sprinkle over top of pie. Bake in 350-degree oven for 25 minutes. Let stand 10 minutes before serving. Serve with yogurt (as a topping) and accompany with pickled beets, cole slaw, grated carrots and banana muffins or bread. *Makes 6 to 8 servings.*

PASTA, RICE & GRAIN

BEEF AND MACARONI BAKE

½	cup chopped onions
1	tablespoon margarine
3	eggs, beaten
½	cup (canned) milk
1	package frozen chopped broccoli
1	can (15 ounces) beef and macaroni Dash nutmeg
¼	cup grated Parmesan cheese salt and pepper

Saute onions in margarine. Combine eggs and milk. Add onions to egg and milk mixture. Combine with remaining ingredients. Place in 8 × 8 × 2-inch baking dish. Bake in 350-degree oven for 35 minutes or until firm when knife is inserted. Serve with pickled beets and onion relish. *Makes 4 servings.*

CAMPERS' MACARONI

½	cup chopped green pepper
½	cup chopped onion
1	large clove garlic, minced
2	tablespoons salad oil
1	pound ground beef
4	cups water
4	beef bouillon cubes
⅛	teaspoon pepper
2	cups uncooked elbow macaroni (8 ounces)
½	cup sliced pimiento-stuffed olives

In a large pot, saute green pepper, onion and garlic in oil until lightly browned, stirring occasionally. Add beef. Cook and stir over high heat until meat loses its red color. Add water and bouillon cubes. Bring to a boil, stirring to dissolve cubes. Gradually mix in macaroni. Simmer, covered, 15 minutes, stirring occasionally. Add olives; cook 5 minutes longer. *Makes 4 servings.*

EASY FRANKFURTER-NOODLE CASSEROLE

6	ounces medium egg noodles (about 3 cups)
1	tablespoon salt or lemon juice
3	quarts boiling water
1	pound frankfurters
1	small onion, chopped
2	tablespoons melted butter or margarine
1	can (10¾ ounces) condensed tomato soup
¼	cup milk
1	teaspoon Worcestershire sauce
¼	cup buttered bread crumbs

Gradually add noodles and salt to rapidly boiling water so that water continues to boil. Cook uncovered, stirring occasionally, until tender. Drain in colander.

Meanwhile, brown frankfurters and onion in butter until onion is tender. Combine with noodles, soup, milk and Worcestershire sauce in 1½-quart greased casserole. Top with crumbs. Bake in a 350-degree oven 30 minutes. *Makes 4 to 6 servings.*

EASY NOODLE DINNER

1	can (11 ounces) condensed Cheddar cheese soup, undiluted
3	soup cans water
¼	teaspoon dry mustard

8   ounces fine egg noodles (about 4 cups)
1   can (12 ounces) luncheon meat, diced
1   can (1 pound) sliced carrots, drained

In large pot or skillet, combine undiluted soup, water and mustard. Bring to a boil. Gradually add noodles so that liquid continues to boil. Cover and cook slowly until noodles are tender, stirring occasionally. Stir in meat and carrots. Cook, stirring occasionally, until thoroughly heated.

Makes 4 servings.

FAMILY DINNER CASSEROLE

3   tablespoons butter or margarine
3   tablespoons flour
2   cups milk
1   package (8 ounces) pasteurized process American cheese slices, cut into strips
3   cups cooked rice
¾   cup sliced pimiento-stuffed olives
½   teaspoon sweet basil, crushed
6   hard-cooked eggs, sliced
1   bag (18 or 20 ounces) frozen broccoli cut, thawed and drained,
    or
2   packages (10 ounces each) frozen broccoli spears, thawed, drained and coarsely chopped
    Buttered bread crumbs (directions follow)
    Pimiento-stuffed olive slices for garnish

In large saucepan, melt butter; stir in flour until smooth. Gradually stir in milk and cook over medium heat, stirring constantly, until mixture thickens. Cook 1 minute. Remove from heat; add cheese and stir until cheese melts. Stir in rice, ¾ cup olives and basil. Remove from heat.

Reserve 2 or 3 egg slices for garnish. Arrange in layers, in a 12 × 8-inch baking dish, half of the rice mixture, remaining sliced eggs and broccoli; repeat layers. Sprinkle on buttered crumbs to within 1-inch of edge of dish. Cover dish with foil. Bake in a 350-degree oven for 30 minutes or until hot and bubbly. Garnish with olive slices and reserved egg slices.

Makes 4 to 6 servings.

BUTTERED BREAD CRUMBS: In small skillet, melt 2 tablespoons butter or margarine. Stir in ½ cup dry bread crumbs until well coated.

FETTUCINE WITH HAM AND RICOTTA

½   cup butter or margarine
1   large onion, chopped
1   clove garlic, chopped
2   tablespoons flour
1   cup (½ pint) light cream
1   can (14 ounces) sweetened condensed milk
    Juice of 2 lemons
    Grated rind of 1 lemon
2   containers (15 ounces each) ricotta cheese
1   jar (3 ounces) grated Parmesan cheese
2   cups finely diced smoked ham
3   packages (12 ounces each) fettucine noodles, cooked and drained

In a large saucepan, heat butter and saute onion and garlic until golden. Stir in flour. Gradually stir in cream and condensed milk. Stir over low heat until sauce thickens and bubbles. Stir in remaining ingredients except noodles. Stir until sauce is piping hot but do not boil. Season to taste with salt. Spoon noodles onto serving plates. Top with sauce. Serve with additional grated Parmesan cheese.

Makes 8 or 10 servings.

FLIP-FLOP POT PIE

¼   cup chopped onions
1   tablespoon butter or margarine
1   package (10 ounces) mixed vegetables, cooked and drained
    Dash minced garlic
1   can (15 ounces) wavy macaroni and little meatballs in tomato sauce
½   cup shredded Cheddar cheese
    Dash onion powder
2   cups biscuit mix
⅔   cup water

Saute onions in butter. Add cooked, drained vegetables, minced garlic and macaroni and meat balls. Stir. Divide mixture into four greased individual oven-proof casseroles. Add cheese and onion powder to biscuit mix. Stir water into biscuit mixture gently with fork. Spoon approximately 3 tablespoons of biscuit mixture on top of each casserole.

Bake in preheated 400-degree oven for 20 minutes. Flip out on to plates for servings or serve in baking dishes.

Makes 4 servings

LASAGNA ROLL-UPS WITH MUSHROOM SAUCE

1   can (1 pound 12 ounces) tomatoes, broken up
1   can (6 ounces) tomato paste
1   tablespoon onion powder
2   teaspoons sugar
1½   teaspoons salt, divided
2   teaspoons Italian seasoning
½   teaspoon garlic powder
¼   teaspoon ground black pepper, divided
1   can (6 to 8 ounces) sliced mushrooms
1   pound ricotta or cottage cheese
2   eggs, lightly beaten
12   lasagna noodles, cooked
4   ounces mozzarella cheese, sliced

In a large saucepan combine tomatoes, tomato paste, onion powder, sugar, Italian seasoning, one-half teaspoon of the salt, garlic powder and one-eighth teaspoon of the black pepper. Bring to boiling point. Reduce heat and simmer, uncovered, for 10 minutes. Add mushrooms; simmer, until sauce is thickened, about 10 minutes longer. Combine ricotta, eggs and remaining 1 teaspoon salt and one-eighth teaspoon black pepper. Spoon about one-fourth cup ricotta mixture onto one end of each lasagna noodle; roll-up, jelly-roll fashion. Place in a 13×9×2-inch pan. Pour mushroom sauce over all. Top with mozzarella. Bake in a preheated 400-degree until hot and cheese melts, 3 to 5 minutes.

Makes 6 portions

MACARONI-TUNA SKILLET

1   can (1 pound) whole onions
1   can (1 pint, 2 ounces) tomato juice
1   can (1 pound) stewed tomatoes
2   cups elbow macaroni (8 ounces)
1   can (6½ or 7 ounces) tuna, drained and separated into chunks
¼   cup stuffed green Spanish olives
1   teaspoon sugar

Drain liquid from onions into large skillet. Reserve onions. Stir in tomato juice and tomatoes. Bring to a boil. Gradually add macaroni so that mixture continues to boil. Cover and cook over low heat, stirring occasionally, until macaroni is tender. Mix in onions, tuna, olives and sugar.   *Makes 4 servings.*

MACARONI-TURKEY MIX

2   cups elbow macaroni (8 ounces)
1   tablespoon salt

3   quarts boiling water
1   can (10½ ounces) condensed cream of celery soup
1¼   cups milk
1½   cups grated Cheddar cheese
2   cups slivered cooked turkey

Gradually add macaroni and salt to rapidly boiling water so that water continues to boil. Cook uncovered, stirring occasionally, until tender. Drain in colander.

Meanwhile, combine soup, milk and cheese in saucepan. Stir and heat over medium heat until cheese melts. Add turkey; heat thoroughly, combine with macaroni. Sprinkle with chopped parsley, if desired.   *Makes 4 servings.*

MAIN DISH FRITTERS

2   cups all-purpose flour
2   teaspoons baking powder
1   teaspoon salt
4   egg yolks
1   cup milk
4   egg whites, stiffly beaten
2   cups diced cooked ham, chicken, turkey or sauteed cooking ground beef

Add one of the following for seasoning:

1   cup (4 ounces) shredded Cheddar cheese for ham
½   teaspoon poultry seasoning for poultry
2   tablespoons instant minced onion and ½ teaspoon oregano for beef
     Peanut oil—2 inches deep heated to 380 degrees

In a bowl, mix flour, baking powder, salt, egg yolks and milk until smooth. Fold in egg whites and cooked meat. Stir in desired seasoning. Drop mixture by heaping tablespoons into preheated peanut oil. Fry 5 to 6 minutes or until fritters are golden brown on all sides. Drain on absorbent paper. Serve topped with your favorite spicy tomato sauce or creamy mushroom sauce. Can also be served with warm maple syrup.   *Makes 24 fritters.*

MOCK LASAGNA

1   pound lean ground beef
1   tablespoon salad oil
1   large onion, chopped
2   jars (about 1 pound each) spaghetti sauce
16   ounces medium egg noodles (about 8 cups)

2	tablespoons salt
4–6	quarts boiling water
1	tablespoon butter or margarine
16	ounces creamed cottage cheese
3	slices process American cheese, cut in half diagonally

In large skillet, cook beef in oil until lightly browned, stirring frequently. Add onion and cook 2 minutes. Stir in spaghetti sauce. Simmer uncovered 5 minutes. Set aside.

Gradually add noodles and salt to rapidly boiling water so that water continues to boil. Cook uncovered, stirring occasionally, until tender. Drain in colander.

Return noodles to pot and toss with butter. Pour half the meat sauce into a 13×9-inch baking pan; cover with noodles. Pour remaining sauce in center of noodles. Spoon cottage cheese on top. Cover and bake in 375-degree oven 30 minutes. Uncover. Place American cheese slices over cottage cheese and bake, uncovered, 5 minutes. *Makes 8 servings.*

QUICK WHEAT GERM CASSEROLE

½	cup chopped onion
½	cup chopped green pepper
1	tablespoon cooking oil
2	teaspoons chili powder
1	can (15 ounces) chili with beans
1	can (7 ounces) whole-kernel corn
¾	cup pitted ripe olives, cut into wedges
⅔	cup vacuum-packed wheat germ, regular
1½	cups grated sharp Cheddar cheese

Saute onion and green pepper in oil over medium heat until tender-crisp. Add chili powder. Cook, stirring, about 30 seconds longer. Remove from heat.

Stir in chili with beans, undrained corn and ripe olives.

Turn half of mixture into 1½-quart baking dish. Sprinkle with wheat germ. Cover with remaining chili mixture. Sprinkle with cheese.

Bake in 400-degree oven for 20 minutes or until hot in center. *Makes 4 servings.*

TAVERNA WHEAT GERM AND BEEF

1	cup uncooked macaroni
½	pound lean ground beef
½	cup finely chopped onion
½	teaspoon salt
¼	teaspoon pepper
¼	teaspoon thyme leaves, crushed

2	tablespoons minced parsley
1	egg
2	egg whites
½	cup milk
1	cup vacuum-packed toasted wheat germ
½	cup grated mozzarella cheese Cheese Sauce (recipe follows)

Cook macaroni in boiling salted water until tender. Drain. Saute beef and onion until browned. Remove from heat and stir in salt, pepper, thyme, parsley, egg, egg whites, milk and macaroni. Sprinkle one-half cup wheat germ in buttered one and one-half quart baking dish. Carefully spoon in beef mixture. Sprinkle on remaining one-half cup wheat germ, then grated cheese. Spoon Cheese Sauce over top. Bake uncovered in 375-degree oven 30 to 35 minutes or until top begins to turn golden. *Makes 6 servings.*

CHEESE SAUCE: Melt 2 tablespoons butter and stir in 2 tablespoons flour. Stir in 1 cup milk. Cook, stirring, until mixture boils and thickens. Stir in one-half cup grated mozzarella cheese, one-half teaspoon salt, 2 egg yolks and pinch of nutmeg. (Servings may be topped with a tomato or mushroom sauce if desired.)

TORTELLINI BOLOGNESE SAUCE

½	cup chopped onion
2	cloves garlic, minced
3	tablespoon olive or vegetable oil
1	jar (32 ounces) old-world-style spaghetti sauce, any flavor
2	teaspoons basil
1	teaspoon oregano

In large skillet, saute onions and garlic in oil until onions are translucent. Add sauce, basil and oregano; combine well. simmer 15 minutes or until heated through.

DOUGH:

4	cups flour, sifted
3	whole eggs plus 1 egg yolk, beaten
3–6	tablespoons warm water
1	teaspoon salt

In large bowl, mix all ingredients until thoroughly blended. Turn onto floured surface and knead about 2-3 minutes or until smooth. Return to bowl. Cover with damp towel and let rest 1 hour.

FILLING:

1	package (10 ounces) frozen chopped spinach, cooked and squeezed dry
1	egg

Continued

½   cup grated Parmesan cheese
1   tablespoon butter or margarine,
     melted
⅛   teaspoon nutmeg
     Pepper, to taste

In medium bowl, combine all ingredients, set aside.

TO PREPARE TORTELLINI: Divide dough into 8 sections and roll into sheets ¹⁄₁₆-inch thick. Cut into 2-inch squares; cover with damp paper towel and keep moist. Top each square with ¼ teaspoon spinach filling; fold diagonally across to form a triangle. Press edges to seal; curve triangle around tip of your thumb to form a ring. Overlap ends and press together to seal. Repeat for remaining squares. Let dry on paper towel 15 minutes before cooking. Serve with sauce. Sprinkle with Parmesan cheese, if desired.

Makes 180 tortellini to serve 8-10. Freezes well.

WHEAT GERM AND BEEF CASEROLE

¾   cup vacuum-packed wheat germ,
     regular
½   cup soft bread crumbs
1   pound lean ground beef
½   cup chopped onion
1   can (1 pound) cream-style corn
¼   cup milk
2   teaspoons prepared mustard
1   teaspoon salt
½   teaspoon thyme leaves, crushed
½   teaspoon marjoram leaves, crushed
2   tablespoons butter
1   tablespoon minced parsley

Mix wheat germ and crumbs.

Brown beef and onion in skillet. Mix in corn, milk, mustard, salt, thyme, marjoram and half of wheat-germ mixture.

Turn into greased 1½-quart baking dish (or leave in skillet). Sprinkle with remaining wheat-germ mixture mixed with melted butter.

Bake in 375-degree oven for 20 minutes. Sprinkle with parsley.   *Makes 4 to 6 servings.*

PEACH CASSEROLES

½   pound package shell macaroni
¼   pound butter
½   tablespoons tomato paste
2   tablespoons red wine (or apple juice)
2   fresh peaches, peeled and halved
1   cup blueberries, fresh or frozen
¼   cup Swiss cheese, grated

Preheat oven to 350 degrees.

Bring large pot of salted water to boil. Add shell macaroni. Cook until just tender. Drain and rinse macaroni. Set aside.

Melt butter in small saucepan. Add tomato paste, then wine, stirring until well blended.

Toss sauce with macaroni. Spoon into 4 individual casseroles.

Place peach half in each casserole. Add blueberries. Sprinkle with grated cheese.

Bake in preheated oven for 20 minutes or until cheese melts and sauce is bubbling.

Makes 4 servings

CHICKEN-MACARONI BAKE

1   can (5 ounces) chunk white chicken
1   can (14¾ ounces) elbow macaroni and
     cheese
1   package (10 ounces) frozen mixed
     vegetables, cooked and drained
2   tablespoons mayonnaise
1   cup biscuit mix
1–2 tablespoons water
     Grated Parmesan cheese

Drain chicken, reserving broth. In 1½-quart casserole, combine chicken, macaroni, vegetables and mayonnaise. Bake at 375-degrees for 15 minutes or until hot. Stir. Meanwhile, combine reserved broth, biscuit mix and water. Drop by spoonfuls on hot chicken mixture. Sprinkle with cheese. Bake 15 minutes more or until done. Garnish with paprika if desired.   *Makes 4 servings.*

EASY MACARONI-TURKEY BAKE

2   cups elbow macaroni (8 ounces)
1   tablespoon salt
3   quarts boiling water
1½   cups cooked turkey, cut in strips
1   package (10 ounces) frozen green
     peas, cooked
1   can (10½ ounces) condensed cream
     of mushroom soup
⅓   cup milk
1   teaspoon Worcestershire sauce
1   teaspoon salt
¼   teaspoon crushed marjoram

Gradually add macaroni and 1 tablespoon salt to rapidly boiling water so that water continues to boil. Cook uncovered, stirring occasionally, until tender. Drain in colander.

Combine macaroni, turkey, peas, undiluted soup, milk, Worcestershire sauce, 1 teaspoon salt and marjoram. Turn into greased 2-quart casserole. Cover and bake in 350-degree oven 20 minutes, or until thoroughly heated.   *Makes 4 to 6 servings.*

MACARONI-TURKEY TOSS

2	cups elbow macaroni (8 ounces)
1	tablespoon salt
3	quarts boiling water
½	cup diced Cheddar cheese
2	cups diced cooked turkey
¾	cup sliced celery
3	medium oranges, pared and sectioned
½	cup mayonnaise
	Salt and pepper to taste

Gradually add macaroni and salt to rapidly boiling water so that water continues to boil. Cook uncovered, stirring occasionally, until tender. Drain in colander. Rinse with cold water; drain again.

Add remaining ingredients to macaroni; toss well and chill. Add additional mayonnaise before serving, if desired.   *Makes 6 servings.*

TURKEY-NOODLE TOSS

1	can (1 pound) cut green beans, undrained
1	can (4 ounces) sliced mushrooms, undrained
	Water
1½	cups skim milk
½	cup diced celery
¼	cup chopped onion
1	tablespoon butter or margarine
¼	cup flour
1	teaspoon salt
¼	teaspoon each pepper and marjoram leaves
2	cups diced cooked turkey
8	ounces medium egg noodles (about 4 cups)
1	tablespoon salt
3	quarts boiling water

Drain beans and mushrooms, reserving liquids; set vegetables aside. Add enough water to reserved liquid to measure one and one-half cups. Combine with milk and set aside. Saute celery and onion in butter about 3 minutes. Quickly stir in flour. Gradually stir in milk mixture, 1 teaspoon salt, pepper and marjoram. Cook, stirring constantly, until sauce boils 1 minute. Add beans, mushrooms, and turkey; heat to serving temperature.

Meanwhile, gradually add noodles and 1 tablespoon salt to rapidly boiling water so that water continues to boil. Cook uncovered, stirring occasionally, until tender. Drain in colander. Toss with turkey mixture.   *Makes 4 servings.*

EGGS & CHEESE

CURRIED EGGS

6	hard-cooked eggs
3	tablespoons mayonnaise
1	tablespoon tomato paste or ketchup
1	teaspoon salt (optional)
1	tablespoon butter or margarine
1	tablespoon curry powder

Halve eggs lengthwise. Remove yolks and put in a bowl; mash with a fork until smooth. Add mayonnaise, tomato paste or ketchup and salt. In a small saucepan, melt butter or margarine. Add curry powder. Saute until golden, about 30 seconds. Stir into egg yolk mixture. Refill cavities in egg whites with yolk mixture. Cover and chill. Serve on shredded lettuce leaves, if desired.

Makes 6 portions or 12 egg halves.

DUTCH BABY

1	cup Spanish pimiento-stuffed green olives
8	hard-cooked eggs
¼	cup butter or margarine
2	uncooked eggs
¾	cup plus 1½ cups milk
¾	cup plus 2 tablespoons all-purpose flour
½	teaspoon dry mustard
⅛	teaspoon hot pepper seasoning

Coarsely chop ⅔ cup olives; reserve whole olives for garnish. Coarsely dice 6 eggs and cut 2 eggs into wedges. Melt butter in a medium saucepan; remove from heat. Pour half of melted butter into a 9-inch pie plate and swirl to coat bottom and side; set aside.

Beat uncooked eggs with electric mixer until pale yellow and foamy. At low speed, beat in ¾ cup milk and ¾ cup flour. Pour batter into buttered pie plate. Bake in 500-degree oven 5 minutes. Reduce heat to 450 degrees and bake 10 minutes longer. Meanwhile, stir remaining 2 tablespoons flour into butter in saucepan; cook 1 minute. Gradually stir in 1½ cups milk with a wire whisk until smooth. Cook, stirring constantly, until sauce thickens. Stir in diced eggs, chopped olives, dry mustard and hot pepper seasoning. Remove from heat.

Continued

When pancake is done, carefully slide from pie plate to a serving plate. Spoon creamed eggs into center. Garnish center with wedges of eggs and whole olives. Cut into wedges to serve.

Makes 4 to 6 servings.

EGGS BENEDICT

1	quart water
1	teaspoon salt
2	teaspoons vinegar
2	teaspoons lemon juice
2	eggs
1	English muffin, cut in half and toasted
2	slices Canadian bacon
	Hollandaise Sauce (recipe follows)

Pour 1-inch or more of water into 1-quart pan. Add salt, vinegar and lemon juice. Heat to boiling.

Break eggs into saucer. One at a time, slip eggs gently from saucer into boiling water. Reduce heat so water is no longer boiling. Cover pan and let stand for about 3 minutes or until white film forms over yolks.

Remove eggs from water with skimmer or perforated ladle to drain. Slip onto toasted English muffin halves topped with sliced, broiled Canadian bacon. Serve with Hollandaise Sauce.

Makes one 2-egg serving.

HOLLANDAISE SAUCE:

2	egg yolks
1	teaspoon white wine or sherry
½	teaspoon lemon juice
¾	cup butter, melted
	Salt

Whip egg yolks with white wine or sherry and lemon juice. (Never use egg whites or you will have a runny, gooey mass.) Whip until hot over double boiler. Cool.

Whip butter slowly into egg mixture. (If mixture is cool, butter should be cool. It won't separate.)

Season and cover. Keep warm until serving time by setting next to stove; do not return it to stove.

EGGS PARMENTIER

2	cups sliced fresh mushrooms
½	cup frozen chopped onions
¼	cup butter
1	package (10 ounces) frozen peas
1½	teaspoons salt
4	cups frozen Southern-style hash browns
6	hard-cooked eggs, halved lengthwise

1	can (10¾ ounces) condensed cream of chicken soup
½	cup milk
1	tablespoon lemon juice
1	teaspoon Worcestershire sauce
¼	cup chopped pimiento
½	cup grated process Swiss cheese

Melt butter. Add mushrooms and onions and cook until onions are soft. Add peas, and saute 2 to 3 minutes longer. Stir in one-half teaspoon salt. Mix potatoes with remaining teaspoon salt and arrange in even layer in greased one and one-half quart baking dish. Spoon vegetables over potatoes and arrange halved eggs on top. Mix soup, milk, lemon juice and Worcestershire sauce together. Stir in pimiento. Spoon over all and sprinkle with cheese. Bake in 350-degree oven for about 40 minutes, until hot and bubbly, and potatoes are tender.

Makes 6 servings.

HEARTY POACHED EGGS

1	cup sliced onion
¼	teaspoon rosemary leaves, crushed
	Generous dash pepper
2	tablespoons butter or margarine
1	can (19 ounces) chunky vegetable soup
4	eggs

In an 8-inch skillet, cook onions with rosemary and pepper in butter until tender. Add soup; bring to boil. Gently slip eggs into soup mixture. Cover; cook over low heat until desired doneness.

Makes 2 servings.

POTATO FRITTATA

½	cup chopped onions
2	cloves garlic, minced
2	tablespoons butter or margarine, divided
1	can (14 ounces) artichoke hearts, drained and quartered
8	eggs
3	cups diced cooked potatoes (about 1¼ pounds)
½	cup grated Parmesan cheese, divided
2	tablespoons chopped parsley
1½	teaspoons basil
1	teaspoon salt
¼–½	teaspoon pepper
1	tablespoon vegetable oil

In a heavy, 12-inch ovenproof skillet, saute onions and garlic in 1 tablespoon of the butter 5 minutes. Add artichoke hearts; cook and stir over medium heat 2 minutes. In a large bowl, beat eggs. Mix in the artichoke mixture, potatoes, all but 2 tablespoons of the cheese, the parsley, basil, salt and pepper. Heat the remaining butter and the oil in skillet until foamy. Pour in the egg mixture. Cook over very low heat about 20 minutes until frittata is almost set. Sprinkle with the remaining cheese. Place in broiler about 4 inches below heat source. Watch closely and remove when center is just set, 2 to 3 minutes. Serve hot or chilled, cut into wedges. *Makes 8 servings.*

QUICHE A LA CANYON

4	ounces Roquefort cheese
¼	pound bacon
2	cups sour cream
2	tablespoons melted butter
1	small onion, minced
2	large fresh mushrooms, chopped
¼	teaspoon garlic salt
	Pinch of mace
	Pinch of pepper
3	eggs, well beaten
2	tablespoons white wine
1	tablespoon cornstarch
1	9-inch pie pan lined with puff paste or pie crust, unbaked

Mash Roquefort cheese. Fry bacon until crisp, drain and crumble.

Mix Roquefort and sour cream. Saute onion and mushrooms in melted butter until wilted. Stir in Roquefort mixture, garlic salt, mace and pepper.

Beat eggs with cornstarch and wine. Stir into Roquefort mixture. Pour into pie shell. Bake in a preheated 400-degree oven for 25 to 30 minutes or until firm. Serve warm. *Makes 4 to 6 servings.*

VEGETARIAN OMELET

½	cup thin carrot strips
¼	cup thin green pepper strips
½	cup thinly sliced onion
½	cup alfalfa sprouts
3–4	fresh plums
1	chicken bouillon cube
1	tablespoon water
4	French Omelets (recipe follows)
2	teaspoons oil
¼	teaspoon savory, crumbled
¼	teaspoon salt
⅛	teaspoon pepper

Measure and prepare all ingredients before starting to cook. Cut carrot and green pepper into thin strips about 1½ inches long. Cover with boiling water; boil 3 minutes, drain and set aside. Slice onion and rinse

sprouts, slice plums to measure 1½ cups. Crumble bouillon cube into 1 tablespoon water.

Make French Omelets and set on flat baking pan in warm oven (about 200 degrees) while preparing vegetarian filling. Turn oil into 9-inch skillet, add onion, carrot and green pepper strips. Stir-fry over high heat 2 minutes, until vegetables are tender-crisp. Add sliced plums, dissolved bouillon cube, savory, salt and pepper. Stir over moderate heat about 1 minute. Remove from heat, add sprouts and mix lightly. Divide mixture among the omelets and fold omelet over filling. Serve at once. *Makes 4 servings.*

FRENCH OMELETS: Beat 8 large eggs with ¾ teaspoon salt and ¼ cup cold water. For each omelet, heat 1 tablespoon butter in an 8-inch skillet and pour in ½ cup of the egg mixture. Cook over moderately low heat just until set, shaking pan, and lifting edges to allow uncooked portion to run under as edges set. Turn out onto flat baking sheet and keep warm while cooking remaining omelets. *Makes 4 omelets.*

MUSHROOM-BREAD FONDUE

1	pound medium-sized fresh mushrooms
8	tablespoons butter or margarine, divided
¾	cup chopped onions
1	loaf (6 to 8 ounces) Italian bread
2	cups (8 ounces) shredded Monterey Jack or mild Cheddar cheese
4	eggs
3	cups milk
1	tablespoon Worcestershire sauce
1	teaspoon salt

Rinse, pat dry and slice fresh mushrooms. In a large skillet melt 4 tablespoons of the butter. Add onions and all but 1 cup of the mushrooms. Saute for 3 minutes; cut Italian bread into 1-inch-thick slices. Using 2 tablespoons of the butter, spread on one side of each bread slice. Place half of the bread in a buttered 2½-quart casserole with half of the cheese. Repeat layering once more.

In a large bowl lightly beat eggs. Add milk, Worcestershire sauce and salt. Pour over bread, mushroom and cheese mixture. Bake in a preheated 350-degree oven until golden brown and a knife inserted in center comes out clean, about 45 minutes. Meanwhile, in a medium skillet melt remaining 2 tablespoons butter. Add reserved 1 cup sliced mushrooms and saute for 2 minutes. Use to garnish baked fondue. If desired, serve with tossed green salad. *Makes 6 portions.*

MUSTARD-BREAD FONDUE

2	tablespoons onion powder
1	teaspoon powdered mustard
2	tablespoons water
8	slices whole-wheat bread, crusts removed
¼	cup butter or margarine
½	pound cooked ham, cut into ½-inch chunks (1½ cups)
1½	cups shredded Cheddar cheese
4	eggs
3	cups milk
¾	teaspoon salt
⅛	teaspoon ground black pepper
¼	teaspoon paprika

Mix together onion powder, mustard and water. Let stand 10 minutes for flavor to develop.

Butter both sides of the bread slices. Cut each slice into quarters.

In a 1½-quart casserole, arrange bread, ham and cheese in alternate layers ending with layer of cheese.

In medium bowl, lightly beat eggs with onion and mustard mixture. Stir in milk, salt and black pepper. Pour over bread.

Cover and refrigerate overnight.

Sprinkle with paprika. Bake in preheated 325-degree oven until puffy and golden, about 1 hour, 20 minutes. Serve immediately. *Makes 6 portions.*

NORDIC RAREBIT

1	clove garlic
1½	cups chicken broth
1	cup dry white wine or apple cider
1	pound Swiss cheese, shredded
1	envelope instant onion soup mix Nutmeg
1	tablespoon cornstarch, dissolved in 1 tablespoon water
4	thick slices French bread, cut in large cubes
1	can (3¾ounces) Norwegian sardines, drained
2	tablespoons grated Parmesan cheese

Rub heavy saucepan with garlic clove. Heat broth and wine with garlic just to simmering point. Discard garlic. Add ½ of the Swiss cheese. Cook over low heat, stirring constantly, until cheese is melted. Gradually stir in onion soup, nutmeg and cornstarch-water mixture. Pour soup into shallow heatproof casserole that will fit under broiler.

Cover surface of hot soup with bread cubes. (You may substitute individual rolls for French bread.) Sprinkle bread with half of remaining Swiss cheese.

Arrange sardines on top. Cover sardines with remaining Swiss cheese and Parmesan. Slide casserole under broiler. Broil until cheese is bubbly and golden. Ladle into soup plates and serve at once.
Makes 4 hearty servings.

RAISIN VEGETARIAN TORTE

24	Crepes (recipe follows)
1	cup Cheddar cheese, grated
1	cup Monterey Jack cheese, grated
½	cup raisins
2	cans (4 ounces each) whole pimientos
2	green chili peppers
3	zucchini, grated and drained
½	pound mushrooms, sliced and sauteed

Toss cheeses and raisin together in a mixing bowl and set aside. Whirl pimientos and chili peppers in a blender or mix with rotary beater. Preheat oven to 350 degrees. To assemble torte, place one crepe on an ovenproof dish. Sprinkle with cheese-raisin mixture. Add another crepe and spread with pimiento-chili sauce. Top with another crepe, spreading it with zucchini; another crepe and sauteed mushrooms. Repeat until all crepes and fillings are used. Cover torte lightly with foil and bake in preheated oven for 35 to 40 minutes. Uncover the last 5 minutes to brown. Good hot or cold.
Makes 6 to 8 servings.

Note: When making ahead, assemble torte and freeze, unbaked, in tightly closed freezer bag. Baking time for frozen torte is approximately the same as above.

	CREPES:
4	eggs
½	cup flour
1	tablespoon sugar
½	teaspoon salt
2	cups milk Butter

Beat eggs well; add flour, sugar and salt and beat until smooth. Add milk gradually, beating constantly. Melt a little butter in a skillet over moderately high heat. When the butter sizzles, pour in 2 tablespoons of batter (enough for a 5-inch crepe). Cook about 1 minute on each side. Place crepes on paper towels. Do not stack without putting paper towels between crepes. Hold crepes at room temperature until ready to assemble torte.
Makes 24 crepes.

REUBEN CASSEROLE

1	can (10½ ounces) chicken gravy
6	eggs, slightly beaten
½	cup milk
9	slices rye bread, cut in 1-inch pieces (about 7 cups)
1	cup shredded Swiss cheese
1	cup diced ham
1	can (about 8 ounces) sauerkraut, rinsed and drained

In bowl, combine gravy, eggs and milk. In buttered 2-quart shallow baking dish (12-by-8-by-2 inches), arrange alternate layers of bread, cheese, ham and sauerkraut, beginning and ending with bread. Pour egg mixture over all. Cover; refrigerate 6 hours or overnight. Uncover; bake at 325 degrees for 45 minutes or until set. *Makes 6 to 8 servings.*

ROQUEFORT SOUFFLE D'AMERIQUE

6	ounces Roquefort cheese
½	cup butter
½	cup sifted flour
	Grated nutmeg
	Salt
	Cayenne
2	cups milk
8	egg yolks, beaten until light
8	egg whites

Force Roquefort cheese through sieve. Set aside.

Butter and dust with flour bottoms and sides of 6 or 7 1-cup ramekins or 3 or 4 2-cup ramekins.

Melt butter in top of double boiler over boiling water. Stir in flour until well blended. Gradually add milk. Using whisk, blend mixture until thick and smooth. Blend in cheese. Season with grated nutmeg, salt and cayenne. Remove from heat

Gradually add beaten egg yolks, stirring constantly. Cool slightly.

Beat egg whites until stiff but not dry. Pour into ramekins. Set souffles on baking sheet. Bake in preheated 400-degree oven for 35 minutes or until puffed and lightly browned. *Makes 3 to 7 servings.*

ROQUEFORT SOUFFLE PROVENCALE

4	ounces Roquefort cheese
3	tablespoons butter
½	cup plus 1 tablespoon sifted flour
1	cup scalded milk
	Grated nutmeg
	Salt
	Cayenne
6	egg yolks
6	egg whites
½	teaspoon cream of tartar

Force Roquefort cheese through sieve into bowl. Set aside.

Butter and dust with flour bottoms and sides of 4 1-cup ramekins or 2 2-cup ramekins.

Melt butter in saucepan. Stir in flour to make roux. Cook roux over low heat, stirring, for 5 minutes. Remove pan from heat.

Stir in half of cheese and blend well with roux. Add scalded milk in stream. Using whisk, blend mixture until thick and smooth. Season with nutmeg, salt and cayenne.

Let mixture cool in large bowl. Beat in egg yolks, one at time, until well blended. Stir in remaining cheese.

In another large bowl, beat egg whites together with cream of tartar until stiff but not dry. Stir ¼ of whites into cheese mixture. Gently but thoroughly fold in remaining whites.

Pour into ramekins. Set souffles on baking sheet. Bake in preheated 250-degree oven for 35 minutes or until puffed and lightly browned.

Makes 2 to 4 servings.

VEGETABLES

ASPARAGUS BRAVO CASSEROLE

1	can (10¾ ounces) condensed cream of celery soup
¼	cup mayonnaise
⅛	teaspoon salt
	Dash of pepper
3	cups chopped cooked asparagus, well drained, or use 2 packages (10 ounces each) frozen cut asparagus, thawed and well drained, or 2 cans (14½ ounces each) cut asparagus, well drained
1	cup quick or old-fashioned oats, uncooked
¼	cup grated Parmesan cheese
¼	cup butter or margarine, melted
2	teaspoons grated lemon rind

Combine soup, mayonnaise, salt and pepper in 1½-quart casserole; mix well. Stir in asparagus. Combine remaining ingredients. Sprinkle over asparagus mixture. Bake in preheated 375-degree oven about 25 minutes. *Makes 6 to 8 servings.*

BROCCOLI-CHEESE STRATA

	No-stick cooking spray
1	package (10 ounces) frozen chopped broccoli
1	medium onion, chopped
8	slices firm white bread
2½	cups milk
3	eggs
1	teaspoon salt
⅛	teaspoon pepper
1½	cups shredded Cheddar cheese (6 ounces)

Spray large skillet with no-stick cooking spray according to directions; heat over medium heat. Add broccoli and onion; cook 5 minutes, stirring often, until broccoli is crisp-tender. Remove from heat.

Spray 1½-quart shallow baking dish or 9-inch quiche pan with cooking spray. Cut each bread slice into 4 triangles. Arrange half of the triangles in the bottom of the dish to form an even layer.

Combine milk, eggs, salt and pepper in a bowl. Sprinkle 1 cup of the cheese over bread in dish; top with vegetables. Cover with remaining bread triangles and cheese. Pour milk mixture evenly over top to moisten bread.

Cover with plastic wrap; let stand 1 hour or refrigerate overnight. Uncover. Bake in 375-degree oven 45 minutes or until puffed and golden brown. Let stand 10 minutes before serving. Serve with fresh green salad, if desired.   *Makes 6 servings.*

BROCCOLI STRATA

1	package (10 ounces) frozen plain or buttermilk waffles (8 waffles)
1½	cups chopped cooked broccoli, well drained
1	cup (4 ounces) shredded Cheddar or Swiss cheese
¼	cup chopped onion
1½	cups milk
4	eggs, beaten
1	teaspoon prepared mustard
4	teaspoons grated Parmesan cheese, if desired

Heat oven to 325 degrees. Place 4 waffles onto bottom of greased 8-inch square baking dish. Sprinkle broccoli, cheese and onion evenly over waffles; top with remaining 4 waffles. Pour combined milk, eggs and mustard over waffles, moistening thoroughly. Sprinkle with Parmesan cheese. Cover; refrigerate at least 1 hour or overnight, as desired. Bake uncovered at 325 degrees about 1 hour or until knife inserted in center comes out clean. Let stand 10 minutes before serving.   *Makes 8 servings.*

VARIATION: Substitute one 10-ounce package frozen chopped broccoli, thawed, well drained, for chopped cooked broccoli.

CARROT CASSEROLE

1	cup water
⅔	cup pearl barley or brown rice
1½	cups milk, divided
4–6	sweet carrots, grated
1	teaspoon coarse salt
½	teaspoon raw sugar or honey
¼	teaspoon nutmeg
2	eggs, beaten
2	tablespoons butter, divided
2–3	tablespoons bread crumbs

Bring water to boil then add barley or rice, cover pot partially and simmer until water is absorbed. Then add a cup of milk, simmer until absorbed. Make sure the barley or rice is done but not too soft. Cool. Preheat oven to 400 degrees. Mix the carrots, honey, sugar, salt and nutmeg with the barley (or rice). Add the beaten eggs. Grease a one and one-half quart casserole dish with a tablespoon of the butter, then sprinkle the bottom with some of the bread crumbs. Pour mixture into the baking dish, sprinkle the top with balance of the bread crumbs and dot the top with the remaining butter. Bake from 30 to 40 minutes or until browned on top.

Makes 4 to 6 servings.

CARROT-HAM SHEPHERD'S PIE

	CARROT TOPPING:
2	tablespoons butter or margarine
6	cups sliced pared carrots
2	tablespoons water
¼	cup milk
1½	teaspoons salt
1	egg

	HAM FILLING:
2	pounds ground cooked ham
½	cup chopped fresh onion
¼	cup chopped fresh green pepper
1	cup chopped celery
¼	cup chopped celery leaves
2	teaspoons Worcestershire sauce
¼	teaspoon dried leaf thyme
1	tablespoon prepared mustard
¼	teaspoon Tabasco pepper sauce
1½	tablespoons flour
1¼	cups water
1	bouillon cube (chicken or beef)

To prepare carrots, melt butter in saucepan. Add carrots and water, cover and simmer 30 to 40 minutes, or until tender. Place in container of electric blender with milk and salt. Cover and process at high speed until pureed. (Or place carrots, milk and salt in large mixer bowl and beat at high speed until well mashed.) Turn into bowl and beat in egg. Set aside.

For ham filling, brown ham in large skillet over medium heat. Add onion, green pepper, celery and celery leaves. Cook, stirring occasionally, until vegetables are tender. Add remaining ingredients and cook until bouillon cube dissolves. Turn into 2-quart casserole. Top with carrot mixture. Bake in 425-degree oven 20 minutes or until top is slightly puffed and lightly browned. *Makes 8 servings.*

COPENHAGEN CASSEROLE

4	fresh zucchini squash (about 2 pounds)
5	cherry tomatoes, halved
1	cup diced cooked ham or beef
4	tablespoons butter, divided
3	tablespoons flour
2	cups half-and-half (light cream)
	Salt and pepper
1	cup shredded Danish Havarti or Samsoe cheese, loosely packed
1	egg yolk
	Dash cayenne
	Chopped parsley, for garnish

Trim zucchini. Parboil whole in salted water for 5 minutes. Drain. Cool. Slice ¼-inch thick.

Arrange zucchini, meat and cherry tomatoes in a greased shallow 7-by-12-inch baking dish. Melt 2 tablespoons butter and drizzle over casserole. Bake in a 400-degree oven for 15 minutes.

Meanwhile, melt remaining butter in a medium-size saucepan. Blend in flour to make a smooth paste. Gradually add half-and-half, stirring constantly with a wire whip. Cook over medium heat until mixture thickens. Add shredded cheese, salt and pepper to taste.

Bring just to boil. Stir a small amount of sauce into egg yolk. Then return to pan. Heat just to boiling, stirring constantly. Remove from heat. Add cayenne. Spoon over zucchini casserole. Garnish with chopped parsley to serve.

Makes 4 to 5 servings.

DOUBLE-DECK POTATO BOATS

3	large baking potatoes
1	pound ground beef
1	cup quick or old-fashioned oats, uncooked
½	cup ketchup
1	teaspoon prepared mustard
1¼	teaspoons salt
½	teaspoon dill weed
⅛	teaspoon pepper
¼	cup grated American cheese
1	teaspoon chopped chives
1	tablespoon butter or margarine

Heat oven to 375 degrees. Wash potatoes and cut in half lengthwise. From each half cut a lengthwise V-shaped wedge leaving about one quarter-inch of potato around top edge. Wrap each half in foil; wrap cut-out centers together. Place in shallow baking pan and bake in preheated 375-degree oven for 20 minutes. Meanwhile combine beef, oats, ketchup, mustard, salt, dill weed and pepper in bowl; mix well. Shape to form 6 logs about 3 and one-half inches long.

Place meat log in center of each potato; close foil over meat and continue baking 40 minutes or until potatoes are soft and meat is cooked. To serve, mash cooked potato centers. Add cheese, chives and butter; mix well. Open each potato-meat log package. Top each serving with mashed potato mixture. Return to oven a few minutes to warm topping, if desired. Remove from foil and garnish with a "cheese flag."

Note: Potatoes and meat may be prepared over grill. Baking times will vary. *Makes 6 servings.*

EGGPLANT CASSEROLE

CORN BREAD LAYER:

2½	cups crumbled corn bread (recipe follows)

EGGPLANT LAYER:

1	large eggplant, peeled
½	cup vegetable oil
1	teaspoon salt

MEAT LAYER:

1	pound ground beef
½	cup chopped onion
1	clove garlic minced
1	can (8 ounces) tomato sauce
2	tablespoons red wine or water
½	teaspoon cinnamon
¼	teaspoon salt
¼	teaspoon oregano leaves, crushed

Continued

TOPPING:

¼	cup butter or margarine
3	tablespoons all-purpose flour
½	teaspoon salt
¼	teaspoon nutmeg
1⅔	cups milk
3	eggs, beaten
1	cup ricotta cheese
½	cup grated Parmesan cheese

FOR CORN BREAD LAYER: Sprinkle 1½ cups crumbled corn bread in bottom of ungreased 11-by-7-inch baking dish.

FOR EGGPLANT LAYER: Slice eggplant ¼ inch thick; cut large slices in half. In large skillet, saute eggplant in oil for 3 to 4 minutes on each side; drain on absorbent paper. Sprinkle with salt. Pour all but 1 tablespoon oil from skillet.

FOR MEAT LAYER: In same skillet, cook meat, onion and garlic until brown; drain fat. Add tomato sauce, wine, cinnamon, salt and oregano; mix well. Set aside.

FOR TOPPING: In medium saucepan, melt butter, add flour, salt and nutmeg. Cook for 2 minutes over medium heat. Add milk; cook and stir about 1 minute or until thickened. Stir small amount of milk mixture into eggs; return to milk mixture. Add cheeses; stir until melted. Remove from heat.

TO ASSEMBLE CASSEROLE: Heat oven to 350 degrees. Layer ½ of eggplant slices over corn bread layer. Spread meat mixture over eggplant; layer with remaining 1 cup crumbled corn bread. Layer remaining eggplant slices over corn bread. Pour topping over eggplant.
Bake for 40 to 45 minutes or until golden brown. *Makes about 8 servings.*

CORN BREAD

1	cup enriched cornmeal
1	cup all-purpose flour
¼	cup sugar, if desired
1	tablespoon baking powder
½	teaspoon salt
1	cup milk
1	egg, beaten
¼	cup vegetable oil

Heat oven to 425 degrees. Grease 8-inch square baking pan. In medium bowl, combine cornmeal, flour, sugar, baking powder and salt. Add milk, egg and oil; mix just until dry ingredients are moistened. Bake in prepared pan for 20 to 25 minutes or until golden brown. Makes 8-inch-square pan of corn bread (about 6 cups crumbled).

LEBANESE OVEN DINNER

6	medium potatoes
1	can (16 ounces) tomatoes, undrained
1	eggplant, unpeeled and diced
1	medium onion, chopped
2	cloves garlic, crushed
1	teaspoon salt
¼	teaspoon pepper
1	teaspoon thyme leaves
6	shoulder lamb chops, 1-inch thick
	Orange slices for garnish
	Parsley for garnish

Preheat oven to 400 degrees. Scrub potatoes. Pierce in several places with tines of a fork. Place potatoes in small baking pan. Drain tomatoes, reserving liquid. Coarsely chop tomatoes and arrange with remaining ingredients except lamb chops in jelly-roll or large baking pan. Bake potatoes and tomato mixture 15 minutes. Remove jelly-roll pan. With large spoon or spatula, turn tomato mixture and push to one end of pan. Arrange lamb chops at other end. Return to oven and bake 30 minutes more or until meat, vegetables and potatoes are tender. To serve: Slash each potato open and fluff up flesh with a fork. Arrange with meat on a serving platter. Garnish with orange slices and parsley. Spoon vegetable mixture into serving bowl. Heat reserved tomato liquid to use as sauce. (Vegetables can be spooned over baked potatoes, if you like.
Makes 6 servings.

MUSHROOM-SPINACH STRATA

1	pound fresh mushrooms
2	tablespoons butter or margarine
1	cup chopped onions
8	slices firm-textured white bread
1	cup shredded Swiss cheese
1	package (10 ounces) frozen chopped spinach, thawed, or 2 cups cooked, chopped fresh spinach
3	eggs
2	cups milk
1	teaspoon salt
¼	teaspoon ground nutmeg
¹⁄₁₆	teaspoon ground black pepper

Grease a 10-inch quiche or pie pan (1½ quarts); set aside. Rinse, pat dry and slice mushrooms (makes about 5¾ cups).

In a large skillet, melt butter. Add mushrooms and onions; saute until tender, about 5 minutes. Set aside.

Remove crusts from bread; cut in halves diagonally. On the bottom of the prepared pan arrange 6 of the bread halves. Top with the mushrooms and onions (removing and refrigerating a few mushrooms for garnish, if desired), cheese and spinach. Arrange 8 bread halves overlapping in a circle on top of the spinach; place remaining 2 halves in center.

In a medium bowl, beat eggs; mix in milk, salt, nutmeg and black pepper. Pour over mushroom-spinach mixture. Cover and refrigerate overnight.

Preheat oven to 350 degrees. Bake, uncovered, until almost firm, about 40 minutes. Place reserved sauteed mushrooms in center; bake until a knife inserted in the center comes out clean, about 5 minutes. *Makes 6 portions.*

PEANUT BUTTER AND VEGETABLE PATTIES

¼	cup butter or margarine
½	cup chopped onion
½	cup finely chopped celery
⅓	cup peanut butter
4	Idaho potatoes, cooked, peeled and mashed or riced
1	egg, well beaten
1	cup chopped leftover vegetables (peas, green beans, squeezed dry spinach, carrots, broccoli)
1–1½	cups cornflake crumbs
	Peanut oil, ½-inch deep

In a skillet heat butter and saute onion and celery until tender, about 5 minutes. Pour into a bowl with drippings. Stir in peanut butter, potatoes, egg and vegetables. Stir until well blended. Shape mixture into 6 patties. Roll patties in crumbs until completely coated. Fry patties in shallow preheated peanut oil (about 350 degrees) until brown on one side. Turn with a pancake turner and brown on other side. Drain on absorbent paper and serve as is or topped with your favorite tomato or mushroom sauce. *Makes 6 servings.*

PEANUT-STUFFED PEPPERS

6	large green peppers
¼	cup butter or margarine
2	large onions, chopped
⅓	cup peanut butter
1	teaspoon curry powder
1	can (15½ ounces) kidney beans, drained
4	cups cooked rice (1½ cups uncooked)
1	can (11 ounces) condensed Cheddar cheese soup
2	tablespoons milk

Slice tops from green peppers and remove seeds. Drop peppers into boiling salted water and parboil for 5 minutes. Drain and cool. In a large skillet heat butter and saute onions until golden brown. Stir in peanut butter, curry powder, kidney beans and rice. Use mixture to stuff green peppers, heaping filling high. Place peppers side by side into a shallow baking pan. Add enough water to just cover bottom. Mix soup and milk and spoon mixture over tops of the peppers. Bake in a preheated 350-degree oven for 35 to 40 minutes or until piping hot. Serve with a salad of romaine leaves topped with cubes of iceberg lettuce. *Makes 6 servings.*

RATATOUILLE WITH CHEESE

2	cups sliced zucchini squash
1	cup green pepper squares
½	cup diagonally sliced green onions
1	large clove garlic, minced
½	teaspoon Italian seasoning, crushed
2	tablespoons olive oil
1	can (19 ounces) chunk vegetable soup
2	cups cherry tomatoes, cut in half
1	cup shredded American process cheese
2	tablespoons water
1	tablespoon cornstarch

In saucepan, cook zucchini, green pepper and onion with garlic and Italian seasoning in oil until *just* tender. Add soup. Cover. Cook over low heat 5 minutes. Add tomatoes and cheese. Mix water and cornstarch; gradually blend into soup mixture. Cook, stirring, until thickened and cheese melts. *Makes about 6½ cups, 6 servings.*

STUFFED EGGPLANT

1	eggplant (1 pound)
3	tablespoons chopped onion
¼	cup vegetable oil
½	pound ground beef
1	can (8 ounces) tomato sauce
¼	cup red wine
½	tablespoon chopped parsley
½	teaspoon flavor enhancer
½	teaspoon salt
⅛	teaspoon ground cinnamon
⅛	teaspoon ground pepper
⅛	teaspoon instant minced garlic
2	tablespoons grated Parmesan cheese

Preheat oven to 350 degrees. Simmer whole eggplant in a large kettle of water, covered, for 10 minutes. Drain. Cut in half lengthwise and remove pulp, leaving a shell one-half inch thick. Chop pulp into one-fourth-inch pieces.

Continued

In a skillet over medium heat, cook onion and chopped pulp in oil for 5 minutes, stirring constantly. Remove from skillet. Brown ground beef in skillet and stir in tomato sauce, wine, parsley, flavor enhancer, salt, cinnamon, pepper, nutmeg and garlic. Simmer 10 minutes. Stir eggplant mixture back into seasoned beef. Fill shells with mixture and bake 45 minutes. Sprinkle with cheese.

Makes 2 servings.

SUPER SCALLOPED POTATO DINNER

1	package (5.5 ounces) Idaho scalloped potatoes
1	cup diced cooked ham
1	cup fresh green beans, cut in 1-inch pieces (¼ pound)
2	tomatoes, peeled and sliced
1½	cups boiling water
¾	cup milk

In 2-quart casserole, lightly mix potatoes, ham, green beans and tomatoes. Sprinkle with seasoning mix. Pour water and milk over all. Bake in 375-degree oven 30 minutes, according to package directions.   *Makes 4 servings.*

TOASTED WHEAT GERM-SPINACH PIE

1	package (10 ounces) frozen chopped spinach
1	package (3 ounces) cream cheese
1½	cups half-and-half
¼	cup grated Parmesan cheese
2	eggs
½	cup wheat germ (regular)
1	teaspoon salt
½	teaspoon tarragon leaves, crushed
½	teaspoon marjoram leaves, crushed
1	onion, chopped
¼	pound mushrooms, chopped
2	tablespoons butter
	Wheat Germ Shell (recipe follows)

Thaw spinach and squeeze dry. Beat softened cream cheese, adding half-and-half gradually. Stir in Parmesan cheese, eggs, spinach, wheat germ, salt, tarragon and marjoram. Saute onion and mushrooms in butter. Add to spinach mixture. Turn into Wheat Germ Shell. Bake in 375- to 400-degree oven 35 to 40 minutes or until set in center

Makes 6 servings.

WHEAT GERM SHELL: Mix 1 cup flour, one-fourth cup toasted whet germ, one-fourth teaspoon salt and one-half teaspoon marjoram. Cut in one-fourth cup butter. Stir in 1 egg yolk and 2 to 3 tablespoons water to get crumbly mixture. Press into 9-inch pie plate. Pinch edges to form rim.

VEGETARIAN LASAGNA

	No-stick cooking spray
2	small zucchini, quartered lenghwise, then sliced (about ½ pound)
1	small onion, chopped
½	pound small mushrooms, sliced
½	teaspoon Italian seasoning
½	pound lasagne (12 pieces)
1	jar (16 ounces) meatless spaghetti sauce
1	container (16 ounces) creamy cottage cheese
½	cup freshly grated Parmesan cheese

Preheat oven to 350 degrees. Spray a large skillet with no-stick cooking spray according to directions; heat over low heat. Add zucchini, onion, mushrooms and Italian seasoning; saute until vegetables are crisp-tender, stirring often. Remove skillet from heat.

Cook lasagne as label directs. Drain; rinse with cold water; pat dry with paper towels. Spray a 12-by-8-by-2-inch baking dish with cooking spray. Put 3 to 4 tablespoons spaghetti sauce in bottom of dish. Place 4 lasagne lengthwise in dish, overlapping to fit. Spread with ½ of the cottage cheese, ⅓ of the vegetable mixture, 2 tablespoons of the Parmesan cheese, and ⅓ of the remaining sauce. Repeat, ending the last layer with noodles, vegetables, sauce, and remaining Parmesan.

Cover and bake for 20 minutes. Uncover; bake 15 minutes more or until lightly browned on top. Let lasagne stand 20 minutes before serving.

Makes 8 servings.

CHILI LIMA BEANS

1	pound dry lima beans
½	pound ham, cubed
1	large onion, chopped
1	10¾-ounce can condensed tomato soup
1	tablespoon chili powder
1	tablespoon Worcestershire sauce
2	teaspoons salt
½–1	teaspoon Tabasco sauce
1	7-ounce can whole-kernel corn, drained

TRADITIONAL WAY: Place beans in large saucepan, cover generously with water. Bring to a boil, cover, reduce heat and simmer about 1 hour, or until tender. Add remaining ingredients, plus 1 cup water. Simmer 1 hour, stirring frequently. Add water if necessary during cooking.

Makes 6 servings.

MODERN WAY: Place beans in large saucepan, cover generously with water. Bring to a boil, cover, reduce heat and simmer about 1 hour, or until tender. Drain off excess liquid; measure one cup, adding water if necessary. Place beans, liquid and remaining ingredients except corn in electric slow cooker. Cover and cook on low 8 to 10 hours. (High 4 to 5 hours.) Add corn during last hour of cooking.

Makes 6 servings.

CORN MUFFIN-BEAN BAKE

½	pound frankfurters, cut in ½-inch pieces
½	cup sliced celery
½	cup chopped onion
2	tablespoons butter or margarine
2	(16-ounce) cans pork and beans in tomato sauce
2	tablespoons ketchup
1	tablespoon brown sugar
½	teaspoon dry mustard
1	cup corn-muffin mix
1	egg
⅓	cup milk

In skillet, brown frankfurters and cook celery and onion in butter until tender.

Add pork and beans, ketchup, brown sugar and mustard. Heat, stirring occasionally.

Pour into 1½-quart shallow (10-by-6-by-2-inch) baking dish.

Meanwhile, combine muffin mix, egg and milk. Spoon around edge of dish.

Bake in medium-hot oven (400 degrees) for 25 minutes or until golden brown. *Makes 6 servings.*

FEIJOADA

1	pound dry black beans
6	cups water
1	lean ham bone (optional)
1¼	pounds boned fresh pork shoulder, cut in 1-inch pieces
¼	cup olive oil, divided
4	cloves garlic, minced
1	package (8 ounces) smoked sausage links
2	jars (1½ ounces each) dried beef

1	teaspoon salt
¼	teaspoon pepper
3	drops hot pepper sauce
	Cooked rice

Place beans in large saucepan with water; bring to a boil. Boil for 2 minutes. Remove from heat and allow to stand for 1 hour.

Add ham bone and 1 pound of pork to beans and cooking liquid; bring to boil, cover and cook over low heat about 1½ hours or until beans are fork tender.

In large frypan, heat 2 tablespoons oil. Take 1 cup of cooked beans, drain and mash; cook in oil until dry; remove and set aside. In remaining 2 tablespoons oil, saute remaining ¼ pound pork sausage and garlic until pork is done.

Add these ingredients with reserved fried bean mixture, dried beef, salt, pepper and hot sauce to bean and pork mixture in saucepan. Simmer, uncovered, 15 minutes or until meat is done and mixture is not too soupy.

Serve on large platter with rice. Garnish with chopped green onion, and orange sections, if desired. *Makes 8 servings.*

FRENCH BEAN CASSEROLE (CASSOULET)

1	duckling, 4 to 5 pounds, giblets removed
	Salt and pepper
	Liquid brown sugar
1	pound navy or pea beans
¼	cup olive oil
1	large onion, sliced
2	cloves garlic, mashed
2	tomatoes, diced
1	pound sweet Italian sausage, each link cut into halves
½	cup liquid brown sugar
1	cup dry red wine
2	tablespoons Dijon mustard
2	cans (13¾ ounces each) chicken broth (4 cups)

Thaw duck if frozen. Sprinkle duckling inside and out with salt and pepper. Brush skin with liquid brown sugar. Roast in a preheated 350-degree oven for 1½ to 2 hours or until leg can be moved up and down easily.

In a large saucepan, cover beans with plenty of water. Add 1 tablespoon salt. Cover and simmer gently for 2 to 2½ hours or until beans are tender. Drain.

Add remaining ingredients. Cover and simmer, stirring occasionally, for 1 to 1½ hours or until liquid is almost absorbed. Cut duckling into small pieces and add to beans. (Bones may be removed, if desired.)

Add ⅓ cup of duckling drippings. Continue simmering for another 30 minutes. Season to taste with salt and pepper. Serve with a salad and crusty French bread.   *Makes 6 to 8 servings.*

KIDNEY BEAN AND BISCUIT CASSEROLE

2	cans (16 ounces each) red kidney beans
1	pound ground beef
4	slices bacon
½	cup chopped onion
½	cup chopped green pepper
½	cup chopped celery
1	clove garlic, minced
1	can (8 ounces) tomato sauce
1	teaspoon chili powder
1	tablespoon prepared mustard
1	teaspoon salt
1	cup prepared biscuit mix
⅓	cup milk

In a large skillet, brown beef; remove and set aside. Add bacon and cook until crisp; remove from skillet; crumble and add to beef. Pour off all but 2 tablespoons bacon fat. Add onion, green pepper, celery and garlic to skillet and saute until tender. Drain beans, reserving 1 cup liquid (or add enough water to liquid to equal 1 cup). Combine beans, reserved liquid, beef, vegetables, tomato sauce, chili powder, mustard and salt; mix well. Spoon into a shallow 2-quart casserole. Mix biscuit mix and milk just until moistened. Spoon onto casserole, making six biscuits. Bake in a 350-degree oven for 40 minutes or until biscuits are golden brown.
Makes 6-8 servings.

MICHIGAN BEAN PICADILLO

1	cup dry black beans
3	cups water
1	cup chopped onion
3	cloves garlic, minced
½	pound beef chuck, cut into thin strips

½	cup olive oil
1	cup sliced celery
1	(28-ounce) can peeled whole tomatoes
2	cups red wine
½	cup raisins
¼	cup stuffed green olives
1½	teaspoons salt
¼	teaspoon cayenne pepper
	Cooked rice

Place beans in large saucepan with water. Bring to boil. Boil 2 minutes.

Remove from heat. Allow to stand for 1 hour.

In large frying pan or saucepan, saute onion, garlic and beef in oil until meat loses pink color.

Add beans, cooking liquid and remaining ingredients, except rice, to same pan. Cover and simmer 2 hours or until beans are fork tender.

Remove cover. Continue cooking until mixture is cooked down and not soupy.

Serve with cooked rice. Garnish with green peas and orange segments, if desired.
Makes 4 to 6 servings.

TANGY BEAN CHOPS

1	jar (22 ounces) brick-oven baked beans
1	tablespoon barbecue sauce
¼	teaspoon red pepper sauce
4	thin pork chops
½	teaspoon garlic powder
½	teaspoon salt
⅛	teaspoon pepper
1	medium onion, sliced
1	tablespoon cooking oil
1	can (8 ounces) crushed pineapple, drained
¼	cup cornflake crumbs

Combine beans, barbecue sauce and red pepper sauce. Place half of this mixture in a rectangular baking dish (6 × 9 × 2 inches). Dust the chops with a mixture of garlic powder, salt and pepper. Fry the chops and onion in the oil until browned. Add these to the dish of beans and cover with remaining beans. Put crushed pineapple on top and sprinkle crumbs over it. Bake at 375 degrees for 50 minutes.
Makes 4 servings.

Meat Dishes

There are tricks to all trades. Most good cooks through the years come up with personal touches they devise through experience and experimentation and, like foxes, often neglect to pass along the key to a recipe.

Preparing beef, lamb, pork, or ham seems pretty straightforward. However, the secret is in knowing the cut and what to do with it. If you weren't born the child of a butcher, I suggest you get some good charts of the meats in question and study them. Select the most recent, which will list the names of cuts as you find them in the meat market or supermarket meat counter.

Then, keep in mind that most of us in America tend to overcook meat unnecessarily. This removes the moisture and usually cooks out many nutrients. What it does to the flavor is another problem, but if you are accustomed to eating excessively well-done meat, you probably douse the cut with salt and a variety of sauces, so there is no flavor-escape hatch anyway. Give meat flavor a chance to reach you. You'll be surprised.

For example, for years I never ate lamb because my early experiences were of eating overcooked, tasteless meat. The same was true of liver, overcooked with an overpowering taste of iron.

Marinades are important because they tenderize lesser-quality meat cuts and leaner beef and pork. And they allow us to enjoy meat, while keeping within a food budget.

Successful marinades need the right oil and acid balance, plus proper spicing to enhance the food they bathe. If whole spices are used, heat them briefly to release their flavor. Ground spices are best used in cold marinades. Beef and lamb call for lusty spices—black pepper, bay leaf, thyme, cloves, caraway seed. Thin strips of meat need less time in a marinade than compact cuts.

Even with new dietary recommendations to the public to eat less meat and consume more complex carbohydrates (beans, fruits, and vegetables), we are a meat-eating country. Here are a variety of recipes to help you enjoy your favorite cuts and to learn to use more economical cuts to stretch the food dollar.

BEEF

AROMATIC HUNGARIAN GOULASH

2	pounds beef chuck, cut into 1-inch cubes
	Salt and pepper
⅓	cup flour
¼	cup oil
1	large onion, chopped
1	tablespoon Angostura aromatic bitters
2	cups beef broth
⅓	cup ketchup
2	teaspoons sweet paprika
½	cup sour cream
1	can (27 ounces) sauerkraut, drained
1	teaspoon caraway seeds
6	large boiled potatoes, peeled and cut into quarters

Sprinkle beef cubes lightly on all sides with salt and pepper. Roll flour and beef together until cubes are well coated. Heat oil in a large saucepan or Dutch oven and brown beef cubes on all sides.

Add onion. Saute for another 5 minutes. Stir in bitters, broth, ketchup and paprika. Cover and simmer for 1 to 1½ hours or until beef is tender.

Stir in sour cream. Correct seasoning with salt and pepper. Heat sauerkraut and caraway until piping hot. Spoon kraut onto serving platter and top with goulash. Serve with boiled potatoes.

Makes 6 servings.

BARBECUED BEEF CHUCK STEAK

1	beef chuck steak, (3 pounds) cut 1½ inches thick
½	cup chutney
3	tablespoons lemon juice
⅓	cup tomato ketchup
	Salt
	Pepper

Trim fat from edges of beef. Combine chutney, lemon juice and ketchup in blender. Whir until smooth. Pour over steak in shallow pan. Turn to coat both sides. Allow to stand one hour or longer.

Drain well. Grill steak over charcoal, sprinkling with salt and pepper to taste. Heat any remaining marinade and serve as sauce. Slice steak in diagonal strips to serve. *Makes 4 servings.*

BARBECUED MEATBALLS AND BEANS

⅓	cup finely chopped onion
3	tablespoons oil, divided
1	large egg, beaten
1	cup fine soft bread crumbs
3	tablespoons milk
1½	teaspoons salt
¼	teaspoon rosemary, crumbled
⅛	teaspoon pepper
1	pound ground lean beef
2	packages (10 ounces each) frozen Fordhook lima beans
½	cup water
1½	cups bottled barbecue sauce

Saute onion in 1 tablespoon oil. Combine with egg, bread crumbs, milk, 1 teaspoon salt, rosemary, pepper and ground beef. Mix well. Shape into 18 balls, about 1½ inches in diameter.

Brown on all sides in remaining 2 tablespoons oil. Drain and discard excess oil. Add lima beans, water and remaining ½ teaspoon salt. Bring to a boil. Cover. Turn heat to low and simmer 10 minutes.

Add barbecue sauce. Simmer, uncovered, 5 minutes. *Makes 6 servings.*

BARBECUED SHORT RIBS

1	recipe Red Sauce Base (recipe follows)
1	cup dry white wine or cider vinegar
1	beef bouillon cube
½	teaspoon chili powder
¼	teaspoon salt
6	pounds short ribs

In large saucepan, make Red Sauce Base; stir in wine, bouillon cube, chili powder and salt. Bring to boiling, reduce heat, simmer 3 to 5 minutes; cool. Brush ribs with sauce and cook over hot coals about 30 minutes; turn frequently, brushing with sauce each time. Heat any remaining sauce and serve with meat. If desired, serve with Tabasco pepper sauce. *Makes 4 servings.*

RED SAUCE BASE:
2 tablespoons salad oil
1 medium onion, chopped (½ cup)
1 can (6 ounces) tomato paste
1 cup water
1 tablespoon sugar
1 teaspoon Tabasco pepper sauce
½ teaspoon salt

Heat oil in medium saucepan; saute onion until clear, about 5 minutes. Stir in tomato paste, water, sugar, pepper sauce and salt. Simmer 15 minutes.
Makes about 2 cups.

SMOKY BEEF BARBECUE

1 recipe Red Sauce Base (recipe precedes)
⅓ cup lemon juice
⅓ cup vinegar
2 tablespoons molasses
1–2 teaspoons liquid smoke
¼ teaspoon salt
2–2½ pounds beef chuck, cut 1½-inches thick

In large saucepan, make Red Sauce Base; stir in lemon juice, vinegar, molasses, liquid smoke and salt. Bring to boiling, reduce heat and simmer 3 to 5 minutes; cool. Pour over meat in shallow glass pan. Cover, refrigerate 24 hours, turning 2 or 3 times. When ready to cook, place meat on greased grill rack; baste with marinade. Grill meat 40 minutes, turning often and basting frequently with marinade. Heat any remaining marinade and serve with meat. If desired, serve with Tabasco pepper sauce.
Makes 6 servings.

BAVARIAN BEEF BALLS AND APPLES

1½ pounds ground beef
1 cup soft bread crumbs (about 2 slices)
1½ teaspoons salt
¼ cup minced onion
1 egg
¼ cup milk
1½ cups apple juice
3 Golden Delicious or Winesap apples, pared, cored and cut into sixths
2 tablespoons flour dissolved in 2 tablespoons water

Combine ground beef, bread crumbs, salt, onion, egg and milk. Shape into one-and-one-half-inch balls. Brown in hot oil. Add apple juice. Bring to a boil. Cover and simmer 15 minutes. Add apples, continue to cook 15-20 minutes more or until apples are tender. Remove apples and meat balls to serving platter. Stir dissolved flour into liquid remaining in pan. Bring to boil, cooking until thickened. Pour over meat and apples.
Makes 5 servings.

Note: Season to taste with more salt, if necessary.

BAVARIAN BEEF STEAK

2 slices bacon, chopped
1 large onion, chopped
2 tablespoons oil
1 bottom round steak (about 1 pound), cut 2-inches thick
1 teaspoon seasoned natural meat tenderizer
¾ cup water
½ cup beef stock
⅓ cup wine vinegar
1 tablespoon sugar
¾ teaspoon fennel seed
Black pepper, to taste
1 small apple, peeled and chopped
¼ medium cabbage, sliced

In large skillet, saute bacon and onion in oil until onion is translucent; remove, drain and set aside. Moisten meat with water. Sprinkle evenly with half the amount of tenderizer and pierce deeply with fork; repeat on other side. Slice meat into ¼-inch strips. (Use no salt.) Brown thoroughly on both sides; drain fat. Combine meat, bacon, onions and remaining ingredients. Cover and simmer, stirring occasionally, 20-25 minutes or until tender.
Makes 4 servings.

BEEF HAGGERTY

1 pound potatoes
6 tablespoons butter or margarine
1 tablespoon Worcestershire sauce
1½ teaspoon salt
2 cups sliced onions
1 pound leftover sliced corned or roast beef

Cook potatoes in boiling salted water until just tender. Drain, cool slightly and peel. Slice into one-half-inch thick slices (makes about 1 quart), set aside. In a small saucepan melt butter. Stir in Worcestershire sauce and salt; set aside.
In a buttered 10×6×2-inch casserole arrange half of the potatoes. Brush with about half of the butter

mixture. Arrange onions and meat in layers over the potatoes. Top with remaining potatoes. Brush well with remaining butter mixture. Bake uncovered in a preheated 400-degree oven until hot and potatoes are golden, about 25 minutes.

Makes 4 portions.

BEEF AND MUSHROOMS ORIENTAL

1	pound fresh mushrooms or 2 cans (6 to 8 ounces each) whole mushrooms
6	tablespoons butter or margarine, divided
1½	pounds boneless beef chuck shoulder steak, 1-inch thick
½	cup sliced scallions or green onions
1	can (10½ ounces) condensed beef broth
1	cup sliced green pepper, cut in 1-inch strips
1	tablespoon cornstarch
2	tablespoons soy sauce

Rinse, pat dry and halve fresh mushrooms (makes fresh about 5 cups) or drain canned mushrooms. In a large skillet heat 4 tablespoons of the butter. Add mushrooms; saute for 3 minutes. Remove mushrooms and their liquid. Set mushrooms and skillet aside. Cut beef into strips one-quarter-inch thick. Heat remaining 2 tablespoons butter in reserved skillet. Add beef. Brown on both sides about 5 minutes. Add scallions; saute for 2 minutes. Stir in beef broth. Bring to boiling point; reduce heat, cover and simmer, 40 minutes or until beef is tender. Add green pepper and reserved mushroom mixture. Cover and simmer 5 minutes. Mix cornstarch with soy sauce. Blend into broth in skillet. Cook and stir only until thickened. If desired, serve with steamed rice. *Makes 6 portions.*

BEEF PAPRIKA

1½	pounds beef eye of round
2	tablespoons oil, divided
1½	cups chopped onion
1	medium clove garlic, minced
2	teaspoons paprika (fresh if available)
¾	teaspoon salt
¼	teaspoon white pepper
2	cups beef broth
¼	cup ketchup
1	bay leaf
1	cup dairy sour cream

Cut beef into 4 equal slices. Brown in 1 tablespoon oil in 10-inch skillet over high heat. Stack slices of

beef on one side of pan. Add onion, garlic and remaining tablespoon oil to pan. Cook, stirring 3 minutes. Add paprika and cook beef 1 minute longer. Mix in salt, pepper, broth, ketchup, bay leaf. Spread beef in single layer. Cover and heat to boiling. Simmer one and one-half hours or until beef is tender. Remove beef from pan and keep it warm. Rapidly boil sauce in skillet over high heat until it is reduced to about 1 cup. Mix in sour cream. Heat briefly but do not boil. Pour over beef.

Makes 4 servings.

BEEF RIBS TO BARBECUE

5	pounds beef ribs
	Instant unseasoned meat tenderizer
	Choice of Marinade (recipe follows)

Moisten beef ribs with water and sprinkle with tenderizer according to label directions. Prick with fork. (If using barbecue ribs omit tenderizer.) Pour marinade over ribs. Chill 8 hours or longer, turning occasionally. Drain ribs and grill 8 inches from hot coals 1 hour or until beef is tender and starts to loosen from bone. *Makes 5 or 6 servings.*

Note: Any beef ribs such as English short ribs, barbecue ribs, short ribs or boneless rib lifters may be used.

ORIENTAL MARINADE: Mix ⅓ cup each soy sauce, cider vinegar and chopped onion with 2 tablespoons brown sugar. For dark and crispy look, add ⅔ cup ketchup to remaining marinade and baste over ribs during last half hour of grilling. **Menu Suggestion:** Serve ribs with tossed salad of torn greens, pineapple chunks, green pepper rings and sliced water chestnuts.

TACO MARINADE: Mix 1 (1¼-ounce) package taco seasoning mix with ¾ cup water. **Menu Suggestion:** Serve ribs with salad of chilled marinated pinto beans and guacamole heaped onto crosswise slices of iceberg lettuce garnished with tomatoes. Pass corn chips.

BEEF STRIPS WITH FRESH VEGETABLES

1	pound boneless beef chuck
3	tablespoons soy sauce
2	tablespoons dry sherry (or wine vinegar)
1	tablespoon cornstarch
1	teaspoon sugar (optional)
1	onion, cut into thin wedges
4	tablespoons vegetable oil, divided

¼ pound mushroom caps, halved if large
1 medium green pepper, slivered
2 medium tomatoes, cut into wedges

Slice beef thinly into three-fourth × three-inch strips. Combine with soy sauce, sherry, cornstarch and sugar. Cook onion wedges in 2 tablespoons oil in large skillet, stirring, over medium heat briefly or until tinged with brown. Add mushrooms and green pepper. Cook, stirring until tender-crisp. Spread tomatoes on large plate and turn cooked vegetables from skillet over tomatoes. Add remaining 2 tablespoons oil to skillet. Add beef and cook, stirring, about 3 minutes or until done as desired. Slide all vegetables from plate into skillet. Cook 1 minute or just until heated. Serve promptly over hot cooked rice. *Makes 4 servings.*

BISTECCA ALLA FIORENTINA

1 jar (15½ ounces) old-world-style spaghetti sauce, any flavor
3 tablespoons vinegar
3 tablespoons brown sugar
1 tablespoon Worcestershire sauce
2 teaspoons prepared mustard
2 pounds round steak, 1½-inches thick, trimmed

In an 11-by-7-inch baking dish, combine first 5 ingredients listed here. Add steak and pierce deeply with fork. Cover and marinate overnight. Remove steak and set aside. In saucepan, heat remaining marinade. Basting and turning frequently, grill four to five inches from heat; about 30 minutes for medium. Serve with steak sauce. *Makes 6 servings.*

BOEUF EN DAUBE

4 pounds beef pot roast
  Salt and pepper
1 clove garlic, mashed
2 large onions, sliced
1 cup sliced celery
2 carrots, sliced
¼ cup chopped parsley
2 teaspoons salt
8 whole peppercorns
½ cup French red wine vinegar
1 cup French dry red wine (or beef broth)
1 can (10½ ounces) condensed beef broth
¼ cup butter
½ cup tomato puree
1 tablespoon cornstarch

Sprinkle roast with salt and pepper. Rub with garlic. Place into a large glass or earthenware bowl. Add onions, celery, carrots, parsley, salt, peppercorns, vinegar, wine and broth. Cover and let stand at room temperature for 2 hours.

Drain meat and reserve marinade. Heat butter in a Dutch oven. Brown beef on all sides. Add marinade and bring to a boil. Lower heat and simmer for 2 to 2½ hours or until meat is tender.

Remove roast to a platter. Skim excess fat from pan juices. Mix tomato puree with cornstarch and stir into pan juices. Stir on top of range over low heat until sauce bubbles and thickens slightly. Slice beef and top with gravy. *Makes about 6 servings.*

CANTONESE CELERY AND BEEF

1 pound boneless sirloin or other tender steak
¼ cup shortening or oil
2 cups sliced celery, cut on the diagonal
½ cup thinly sliced onion
⅓ cup soy sauce
¼ cup red wine (or apple juice)
2 tablespoons sugar
2 tablespoons water
1 tablespoon cornstarch
1 teaspoon salt

Cut meat into very thin slices. Heat shortening in large skillet. Add meat and saute until brown. Transfer meat to warm platter. Add celery and onion to skillet and saute 3 minutes. Combine remaining ingredients; stir into vegeables. Add meat and simmer 1 to 2 minutes longer.
Makes 3 to 4 portions.

CURRIED MEAT LOAVES

1½ pounds ground beef
¾ cup quick or old-fashioned oats, uncooked
½ cup chopped onion
¾ cup chopped apple
⅓ cup raisins
⅓ cup finely chopped peanuts
⅓ cup ketchup
1 egg
2½ teaspoons curry powder
1½ teaspoons cinnamon
1¼ teaspoons salt

Heat oven to 375 degrees. Combine all ingredients, mix well.

Shape to form six 4-by-2-inch loaves. Bake in large shallow baking pan at 375 degrees for 25 to 30 minutes. *Makes 6 servings.*

Microwave oven directions: Place loaves in large shallow glass baking dish. Cover with wax paper. Cook at high for 1 to 12 minutes, rotating dish ¼ turn after each 3 minutes of cooking.

DANISH BEEF LOAF

3	eggs
½	cup milk
2	teaspoons salt
¼	teaspoon black pepper
2	tablespoons finely chopped parsley
½	green pepper, finely chopped
1	cup finely chopped celery
½	cup finely chopped onion
2	teaspoons Worcestershire sauce
2½	pounds ground chuck
⅓	pound Danish cheese (Samsoe, Tybo, Havarti or Danish Blue), cut in 4 slices, each about ¼-inch thick

In a large mixing bowl, beat eggs slightly with fork. Stir in milk, salt, pepper, parsley, green pepper, celery, onion and Worcestershire sauce. Blend together.

Add ground chuck to mixture and combine all ingredients, using hands or a large mixing spoon. Divide meat in half.

On platter-like oven dish, mold half the meat loaf to form the base, about 3- to 3½-inches wide and 7- to 8-inches long. Indent the center slightly. Divide and place the cheese down the center.

Cover with remaining meat. With hands, mold and round the meat to form a loaf. Place in pre-heated 350-degree oven. Bake 45 minutes.

Makes 8 servings.

GREEK KEBABS

GREEK BARBECUE SAUCE:

2	cups bottled barbecue sauce
⅓	cup honey
2	tablespoons lemon juice
1	tablespoon dried mint leaves, crushed
2	teaspoons grated lemon peel
⅛	teaspoon garlic powder

KEBABS:

1	pound ground beef
¾	cup quick or old-fashioned oats, uncooked
½	teaspoon salt
⅛	teaspoon garlic powder
18	large pitted ripe olives
1	small zucchini, cut into ½-inch slices, blanched
1	medium onion, cut into thin wedges
1	medium tomato, cut into wedges

For Greek barbecue sauce, combine all ingredients in medium saucepan; bring to a boil. Reduce heat; simmer for 15 minutes, stirring occasionally.

For kebabs, combine meat, oats, ¼ cup of the Greek Barbecue Sauce, salt and garlic; mix well. Shape mixture around olives to form 18 meatballs. Thread meatballs alternately with zucchini and onion on six 11-inch skewers.

Place kebabs on rack of broiler pan or over ash-covered coals on outdoor grill so kebabs are 5 to 6 inches from heat. Cook about 15 minutes, turning frequently. Add tomato wedges to skewers; baste kebabs with sauce. Continue cooking about 5 minutes or until desired doneness, turning frequently and basting with sauce. Serve with any remaining sauce, if desired.

Makes 6 servings.

HARVEST PEPPER STEAK

1	medium zucchini
2	tablespoons oil, divided
1	large garlic clove, crushed
1	pound round steak, ¾- to 1-inch thick, sliced paper thin
1	cup water
¼	cup red wine
1	box (29¾ ounces) stir-fry pepper steak mix
	Soy sauce

Cut ends from zucchini. Then cut into strips 2 inches long and one-fourth inch wide; set aside.

In wok or large skillet, heat 1 tablespoon of the oil with the garlic. Add beef and stir-fry until meat loses its red color, 4 to 5 minutes. Remove to bowl. To wok or skillet, add remaining oil. Add zucchini. Stir-fry until tender-crisp, 2 to 3 minutes. Add water, wine and sauce mix from box. Bring to boiling, stirring constantly. Add drained pepper steak, vegetables and meat. Mix thoroughly and heat through. Serve with soy sauce.

Makes 4 to 5 servings.

HARVEST SWISS STEAK

1½	pounds round steak (½-inch thick)
2	tablespoons shortening
1	can (10¾ ounces) condensed cream of onion soup
1	can (16 ounces) tomatoes, drained and chopped
1	tablespoon Worcestershire sauce Generous dash pepper
¼	cup chopped sweet pickle

½ cup diagonally sliced celery
Cooked rice

Pound steak with mallet or edge of heavy saucer. Cut steak into serving-size pieces. In skillet, brown steak in shortening; pour off fat. Add soup, tomatoes, Worcestershire and pepper. Cover; cook over low heat 1 hour. Add celery; cook 30 minutes more or until done. Stir occasionally. Uncover; cook to desired consistency. Serve with rice.
Makes 6 servings, about 2½ cups gravy.

LOUISIANA YAM AND BEEF DINNER

3	pounds lean, boneless beef chuck, cut in 2-inch cubes
3	tablespoons flour
2	tablespoons salad oil
½	pound pork sausage links, cut into 1-inch pieces
	Water
6	medium yams, peeled and quartered
1	can (20 ounces) chick peas, drained
4	carrots, peeled and quartered
2	medium onions, peeled and sliced
1	cup sliced celery
	Salt and freshly ground pepper

Place beef and flour in a bag and shake until meat is coated. Heat oil in Dutch oven or large skillet. Add beef and brown well on all sides. Remove beef and set aside. Add sausage and brown over low heat for about 12 to 15 minutes. Return beef to Dutch oven. Add water to cover. Simmer, covered, for 45 minutes. Add yams and chick peas. Cook 15 minutes longer, then add remaining vegetables. Cook uncovered 12 to 15 minutes longer or until vegetables are tender. Season to taste with salt and pepper. Turn into serving dish. *Makes 6 to 8 servings.*

MARINATED FLANK STEAK

1	beef flank steak
½	cup ketchup
⅓	cup red wine vinegar
½	cup red table wine
1	tablespoon Worcestershire sauce
1	chopped small onion
¼	teaspoon garlic powder
¼	teaspoon prepared mustard
1	teaspoon salt
1	tablespoon cooking oil
1	beef bouillon cube
⅓	cup water
1	tablespoon cornstarch

Marinate beef several hours or overnight in mixture of ketchup, vinegar, wine, Worcestershire sauce, onion, garlic, mustard, salt and oil. Drain, reserving marinade. Barbecue or broil steak to rare or medium rare. Meanwhile combine marinade with bouillon cube, water and cornstarch. Heat, stirring, until sauce boils and thickens. Slice beef diagonally across the grain. Serve with sauce.
Makes 4 to 6 servings.

MINI MEAT LOAVES

1	pound ground beef
1	pound ground veal shoulder
2¾	teaspoons salt, divided
¼	teaspoon ground ginger
½	teaspoon dried leaf marjoram
¼	cup chopped onion
2	tablespoons grated orange rind
3	cups orange juice, divided
1	egg
¾	cup fresh bread crumbs
¼	cup flour
2	tablespoons orange marmalade
½	teaspoon dried leaf basil

In large mixing bowl, break up meat with fork. Sprinkle with 2 teaspoons salt, ginger, marjoram, onion and orange rind. Mix just to blend ingredients.

Beat together 1 cup orange juice and egg. Add bread crumbs. Mash. Add to meat mixture. Blend.

Divide into 6 equal portions. Shape each portion into miniature loaf or patty. Place portions on buttered shallow baking pan.

Bake in 350-degree oven 40 minutes.

Meanwhile, combine remaining 2 cups orange juice and flour in saucepan. Stir in marmalade, basil and remaining ¾ teaspoon salt. Place over medium heat, stirring constantly until mixture thickens and boils.

Brush loaves with small amount of sauce during last 10 minutes of baking. Serve 1 portion with sauce. Freeze remaining portions. *Makes 6 servings.*

TO FREEZE: Place each remaining portion with small amount of sauce into individual freezer bag or container. Seal tightly. Label. Freeze. Defrost overnight in refrigerator or several hours at room temperature. Heat slowly in covered saucepan. Do not boil.

MUSHROOM MATAMBRE

1 pound fresh mushrooms or 2 cans (6 to 8 ounces each) sliced mushrooms
¼ cup butter or margarine
2 flank steaks (2 pounds each), butterflied
2 teaspoons salt
2 teaspoons chili powder
¾ teaspoon thyme leaves, crumbled
2 garlic cloves, minced
½ pound fresh spinach or 1 package (9 ounces) frozen leaf spinach, thawed
2 cups carrot sticks
1 cup onion rings
2 tablespoons salad oil
2 beef bouillon cubes
1½ cups boiling water
2 tablespoons flour

Rinse, pat dry and slice fresh mushrooms or drain canned mushrooms. In a large skillet melt butter. Add mushrooms; saute for 5 minutes; set aside. Open steaks. Place long side of one steak over long side of second steak, overlapping by about 2-inches (shingle fashion). Pound the joined ends together to seal. Combine salt, chili powder, thyme and garlic; sprinkle on steaks. Arrange on steak a layer of spinach, carrots (place lengthwise with grain), onions and half of the mushrooms. Carefully roll the steaks, with the grain, jelly-roll fashion. Tie securely with loops of string. Coat the bottom of a large shallow roasting pan with oil. Add the meat roll. Brown in a preheated 475-degree oven for 15 minutes. Reduce oven to 350 degrees. Spoon off excess fat from pan. Cover securely with heavy-duty foil. Return to moderate oven; bake until beef is tender, about 2 hours. Remove meat to a large cutting board and let stand for 20 minutes. Meanwhile, pour pan juices into a large measuring cup; spoon off fat. Add additional water or dry red wine, if desired, to make 2 cups liquid. In a small saucepan blend flour with liquid. Cook and stir until thickened. Stir in remaining cooked mushrooms; heat until hot. Remove string from Matambre. Slice; arrange on a heated platter. Spoon some of the gravy over the meat; serve remaining gravy separately. If desired, bake ahead of time; refrigerate overnight; remove and discard congealed fat. Cover and reheat in roasting pan in moderate oven (350 degrees F.) for 1 hour. Thicken pan juices as above. *Makes 8 to 10 portions.*

MUSTARD PEARS AND BEEF PLATTER

¼ cup brown sugar, packed
¼ cup tarragon-flavor white wine vinegar
1 tablespoon prepared mustard
1/16 teaspoon dried dill
½ cup water
3–4 large California Bartlett pears
Crisp lettuce
6 slices roast beef
6 cherry tomatoes
Mustard Mayonnaise (recipe follows)

Combine sugar, vinegar, mustard and dill in 10-inch skillet. Stir together over low heat until well blended. Add water and heat to simmering.

Select firm ripe pears. Halve, pare and core pears. Place cut side down in liquid. Heat to boiling. Turn heat to low and cover. Cook about 3 minutes.

Uncover. Turn pears carefully and cook about 3 minutes longer, basting constantly. Remove from heat. Cool in syrup, then chill.

When ready to serve, arrange drained pears on lettuce. Roll up beef and arrange around pears with tomatoes. Serve with Mustard Mayonnaise.

Makes 6 servings.

MUSTARD MAYONNAISE:

Stir 2 teaspoons prepared mustard and 1 teaspoon prepared horseradish into 1 cup mayonnaise.

ORANGE POT ROAST

1 tablespoon salad oil
1 5- to 6-pound boneless rump roast
2 teaspoons salt
¼ teaspoon pepper
1 onion sliced
1 bay leaf
1 tablespoon brown sugar
½ teaspoon dried leaf thyme
1 teaspoon grated orange rind
2 cups orange juice
2 tablespoons grapefruit juice
1½ tablespoons flour

In large Dutch oven heat oil. Brown roast on all sides. Add all remaining ingredients except flour, cover and bake in 350-degree oven 3 hours, or until meat is tender. Remove meat to platter; keep warm. Stir a little of the liquid into the flour to make a smooth paste. Stir paste into liquid in pan and cook over medium heat, stirring constantly, until gravy thickens slightly. Simmer 2 minutes. Slice meat and serve with gravy. *Makes 12 servings.*

ORIENTAL GRILLED STEAK

¾ cup water
4 tablespoons margarine
¼ cup Worcestershire sauce
¼ cup soy sauce
¼ cup wine vinegar

3 tablespoons brown sugar
1½ tablespoons prepared mustard
½ teaspoon ground ginger
1 top round steak (about 2-inches thick), trimmed
1½ teaspoons unseasoned natural meat tenderizer

In saucepan, combine first 8 ingredients; simmer 10–15 minutes. Moisten meat with water. Sprinkle evenly with half the amount of tenderizer and pierce deeply with a fork; repeat on other side. (Use no salt.) Broil steak 4 to 5 inches from heat, 16–18 minutes per side for medium, basting frequently with sauce. Slice diagonally and serve with remaining sauce.   *Makes 6-8 servings.*

PADDY'S DELIGHT

1½ pounds lean ground chuck
½ cup soft bread crumbs
1 egg
3 tablespoons chopped parsley
¼ teaspoon nutmeg
  Salt and pepper
4 medium potatoes
6 carrots
6 leeks
  Juice of 1 lemon
  Bay leaf
1 small package frozen Brussels sprouts
1 small package frozen peas
6 tablespoons butter or margarine
¼ cup freeze-dried chives

Mix beef with crumbs, egg, parsley, nutmeg, salt and pepper. Form into balls. Peel and cut potatoes into large chunks and put in a soup pot with leeks and carrots. Cover with boiling water and add lemon juice, bay leaf, salt and pepper. Drop meat balls into simmering water. Cover and cook gently for 30 minutes. Add Brussels sprouts and peas; continue cooking until vegetables are tender. Ladle into bowls and top each with a spoonful of butter and some chives.   *Makes 6 servings.*

POT ROAST ALSACE-LORRAINE

3 pounds beef pot roast
2 tablespoons fat or vegetable oil
1 carrot
½ cup chopped celery
1 sliced onion
3 teaspoons salt
  Pepper to taste
¼ cup vinegar
½ cup dark or golden raisins
1 tablespoon cornstarch

Wipe meat with damp cloth and brown on all sides in hot fat. Cut carrot in small pieces and add with celery and onion to meat. Add salt, pepper, vinegar and raisins. Cover and cook until tender, one and one-half to two hours; adding a little water. Remove meat to platter and keep hot while thickening drippings for gravy. Stir cornstarch into about 2 tablespoons cold water; then into drippings. Cook, stirring, until thick and smooth.   *Makes 6 servings.*

POT ROAST ON THE GRILL

1 beef chuck roast, boneless rolled, about 4 pounds, or bone-in chuck roast, about 5 pounds
  Salt and pepper
1 clove garlic, mashed
1 teaspoon sweet basil
1 teaspoon thyme
2 large onions, chopped
1 can (1 pound) tomatoes, chopped, plus juice
2 envelopes dehydrated beef broth
½ cup dry red wine (or ⅓ cup cider, tarragon vinegar or lemon juice)
2 cups celery, cut into 1-inch pieces
12 new potatoes, partially peeled

Sprinkle beef on all sides with salt and pepper. In large bowl combine garlic, basil, thyme, onions, tomatoes, beef broth and red wine. Add beef and turn to coat well. Let stand at room temperature for 2 hours or in refrigerator overnight. Drain beef, reserving marinade. Place beef directly on grill rack 6 inches above hot coals. Sear quickly on all sides until beef is brown and crusty. Remove beef.

Place beef in a foil roasting pan and baste beef with one-half cup of the marinade. Place pan on grill rack 6 inches above medium hot coals. Cook in covered grill with cover closed. Adjust vents for proper circulation. Or, cover pan with tent of foil and cook on open grill. Grill for one and one-half hours, basting beef from time to time with pan liquid and turning beef occasionally. Add vegetables and remaining marinade. Cover again and continue cooking 1 more hour or until beef is tender. Cut beef into thick slices and spoon pan juices over meat. Add vegetables.   *Makes 6 to 8 servings.*

QUICK BRAZILIAN BEEF

¾ teaspoon salt
⅛ teaspoon pepper
1¾ pounds top round steak, 1 inch thick
  Corn oil, for frying

Continued

1   medium onion, sliced
1   can (1 pound) tomatoes
2   tablespoons chopped parsley
2   bay leaves
½   teaspoon cumin (optional)
1   tablespoon water

Mix together flour, cornstarch, salt and pepper. Coat meat with mixture. Reserve remaining flour mixture. Pour corn oil into large skillet to depth of ⅛ inch. Heat over medium high heat 3 to 4 minutes. Add meat and cook, turning once, about 25 minutes or until meat has crisp crust on both sides and has reached desired doneness. (Meat will be slightly rare in center in 25 minutes cooking time.)

Remove meat. Drain off all but about 1 tablespoon drippings from skillet. Return meat. Add onion and saute 5 minutes or until golden brown. Stir in tomatoes, parsley, bay leaves and cumin. Blend 1 tablespoon reserved flour mixture and water. Stir into mixture in skillet. Stirring constantly, bring to boil and boil 2 minutes

Makes 4 to 6 servings beef, 2 cups gravy.

Note: If desired, gravy may be omitted and beef sliced for sandwiches or served along with salad.

ROYALE ROUND STEAK

½   pound round steak (¾-inch thick)
2   tablespoons shortening
1   can (7¾ ounces) semi-condensed tomato royale soup
½   cup finely chopped onion
2   teaspoons bottled meat sauce
¼   teaspoon pepper
     Cooked rice

Pound steak. Cut steak into serving-size pieces. In skillet, brown steaks in shortening; pour off fat. Add remaining ingredients. Cover. Cook over low heat 1 hour 30 minutes or until done. Stir occasionally. Serve with rice.   *Makes 2 to 3 servings.*

SAVORY BEEF TURNOVERS

1   can (10¼ ounces) beef gravy
1   cup finely chopped cooked beef
½   cup cooked peas
1   tablespoon finely chopped onion
1   teaspoon prepared mustard
     Dash salt
     Dash pepper
     Pastry mix for two-crust pie
2   teaspoons prepared horseradish

To make filling, in bowl, combine ¼ cup gravy, beef, peas, onion, mustard, salt and pepper.

To make turnovers, roll pastry into two 10-inch squares. Cut each into 4 small squares. Place ¼ cup mixture on each square. Fold dough over to form triangle. Seal edges by fluting or pressing with fork. Arrange turnovers on lightly greased cookie sheet. Bake at 450 degrees for 20 minutes or until lightly browned. Meanwhile, in saucepan, combine remaining gravy and horseradish. Heat; stir occasionally. Serve with turnovers.   *Makes 4 servings.*

SPICY CALIFORNIA SKILLET STEAK

1   pound round steak, sliced
1   cup chopped onion
2   tablespoons oil
4   packets seasoning-and-broth
3   fresh tomatoes, quartered or 1 can tomatoes, drained
2   cups water
½   teaspoon basil
1   tablespoon spicy brown mustard
1   cup rice
1   green pepper cut in strips
2   fresh peaches, halved, or 4 canned peach halves

Brown steak and onion lightly in oil. Stir in seasoning-and-broth, tomatoes, water, basil and mustard. Cover and simmer 15 minutes.

Strain rice. Add to skillet and cover. Continue cooking for 15 to 20 minutes or until rice is fluffy and steak is tender. Add peach halves and pepper strips for the last 10 minutes of cooking.
Makes 4 servings.

STEAK PORT ANTONIO

¼   cup dark rum
1   tablespoon chopped shallots
½   cup butter or margarine (¼ pound)
2   teaspoons fresh lime juice
½   teaspoon Tabasco pepper sauce
1   tablespoon chopped parsley
4   shell steaks or boneless rib steaks (about 6 ounces each)

In small saucepan, combine rum and shallots, bring to a boil, reduce heat, simmer 2 minutes. Stir in butter, lime juice, pepper sauce and parsley. Place shell steaks under preheated broiler 6 inches from heat, brush with rum butter. Broil 4 minutes, turn steaks, brush again and broil 4 minutes longer. Serve with additional rum butter and pepper sauce, if desired.   *Makes 4 servings.*

STUFFED FLANK STEAK CALYPSO

2	flank steaks, 1½ to 2 pounds each
¼	cup finely chopped onion
1	cup chopped green pepper
¼	cup butter
1	cup water
2	eggs
1	teaspoon salt
¼	teaspoon pepper
½	teaspoon celery salt
2	tablespoons Angostura aromatic bitters
3	cups bread crumbs
	Flour
2	cups tomato sauce with mushrooms
½	cup water

Wipe steaks. For stuffing, cook onion and green pepper in butter and 1 cup of water until tender. Beat eggs. Stir in salt, pepper, celery salt and bitters. Mix in bread crumbs and sauteed vegetables. Spread this mixture on each steak. Roll up steak and tie with a string. Sprinkle with flour and brown quickly in a small amount of fat, then place in a roasting pan. Pour tomato sauce and water into pan. Bake covered in a 350- to 375-degree oven until meat is tender, about 1 and one-half hours.

Makes 8 servings.

TANGY SAUTEED STEAK

2	large onions, sliced into ½-inch rings
2	tablespoons oil
1	eye round steak (about ¾ pound), cut 2-inches thick
½	teaspoon seasoned natural meat tenderizer
½	cup beef stock
2	tablespoons water
2	tablespoons butter or margarine
1½	tablespoons lemon juice
¾	teaspoon sugar
½	teaspoon grated lemon peel
1	bay leaf, crushed
	Black pepper, to taste

In large skillet, brown onions in oil; remove and set aside. Slice meat lengthwise into 4 (½-inch) steaks. Moisten meat with water. Sprinkle evenly with half the amount of tenderizer and pierce deeply with a fork; repeat on other side. (Use no salt.) Brown meat thoroughly on both sides. Combine meat, onions and remaining ingredients; simmer, stirring occasionally, 12-15 minutes or until tender.

Makes 2 servings.

WHEAT-GERM BEEFBALLS JARDINIERE

¾	pound lean ground beef
½	cup vacuum-packed wheat germ, regular
⅓	cup minced parsley
⅓	cup minced green onion
3	tablespoons grated Parmesan cheese
1	egg
2	tablespoons milk
¼	teaspoon salt
¼	teaspoon pepper
1	cup chopped zucchini
½	cup chopped mushrooms (or 14-ounce can mushroom stems and pieces)
½	cup chopped onion
2	tablespoons vegetable or olive oil
1	can (8 ounce) tomato sauce
1	teaspoon chili powder
1	teaspoon ground cumin

Combine beef, wheat germ, parsley, green onion, cheese, egg, milk, salt and pepper. Shape into 24 balls.

Place in shallow pan. Bake in 400-degree oven for 8 to 10 minutes.

Meanwhile, lightly saute zucchini, mushrooms and onion in oil for 3 to 5 minutes. Stir in tomato sauce, chili powder and cumin. Heat thoroughly. Add beefballs.

Serve on shredded lettuce, hot cooked spaghetti, noodles, in pita bread or in hollowed French rolls, as desired. *Makes 4 servings.*

WORCESTERED BEEF SHORT RIBS

4	pounds beef short ribs
¼	cup flour
1	teaspoon salt, divided
¼	cup oil
4	teaspoons Worcestershire sauce
½	teaspoon powdered mustard
½	teaspoon curry powder
	Yorkshire Puddings (recipe follows)

Cut ribs into portion-sized pieces. Coat with flour mixed with ½ teaspoon of the salt. Place in a lightly oiled, shallow roasting pan. Brown in a preheated 450-degree oven for 15 minutes. Reduce oven temperature to 350 degrees.

Combine oil, Worcestershire sauce, mustard, curry powder and remaining ½ teaspoon salt. Brush half of the seasoning mixture over short ribs. Bake, uncovered, in a slow oven until fork-tender, about 1½ hours, brushing once more with seasoning halfway through the cooking.

Continued

Serve with rice, Worcestered Yorkshire Puddings and tossed salad, if desired.   *Makes 4 to 6 portions.*

YORKSHIRE PUDDINGS:

2	eggs
¾	cup milk
¼	cup water
1	teaspoon Worcestershire sauce
1	cup all-purpose flour
½	teaspoon salt
1	tablespoon beef drippings or oil

Place eggs, milk, water and Worcestershire sauce in the large bowl of an electric mixer. Beat for 1 minute. With electric mixer set at low speed, gradually stir in flour and salt. Mix just until blended. Mixture may stand covered in the refrigerator for 2 or 3 hours, if desired.

Place ¼ teaspoon of beef drippings in the bottom of each of 12 2½-inch muffin pan cups. Place in a preheated 400-degree oven until oil is hot, about 2 minutes. Remove pan from oven. Fill ¼ full with the batter.

Bake in hot oven until the puddings are light and golden, about 30 minutes. Remove from pans and serve immediately.   *Makes 12 Yorkshire puddings.*

ZESTY BARBECUED STEAK

1	cup finely chopped onion
½	cup prepared horseradish
⅓	cup dark corn syrup
½	cup vinegar
¼	cup corn oil
¼	cup ketchup
2	cloves garlic, minced or pressed
1	teaspoon salt
½	teaspoon pepper
1	boneless beef chuck roast or steak, (2- to 2½-pound) cut 2 inches thick

In small bowl mix together onion, horseradish, corn syrup, vinegar, corn oil, ketchup, garlic, salt and pepper. Place steak in shallow dish. Pour marinade over steak. Cover; refrigerate several hours or overnight, turning occasionally.

Drain excess marinade from steak. Grill 6 inches from source of heat, turning as needed and basting frequently with marinade, 40 to 50 minutes or until desired doneness. Cut diagonally across grain into thin slices.   *Makes 6 servings.*

LAMB

BAKED LAMB SHANKS WITH TOMATO SAUCE

4–6	lamb shanks, about ¾ pounds each, trimmed of fat
	Olive oil
2	medium-size onions, cut into ¼-inch slices
1	teaspoon ground allspice
½	teaspoon ground nutmeg
1	teaspoon salt
½	teaspoon pepper
3	cups chopped, canned tomatoes

Preheat oven to 450 degrees. Lightly coat lamb shanks with oil. Arrange in 13-by-2-by-9-inch baking dish. Bake lamb for 30 minutes, turning once. Reduce oven temperature to 350 degrees. Remove lamb from oven. Place onion slices over lamb. Sprinkle with allspice, nutmeg, salt and pepper. Pour tomatoes evenly over all. Return lamb to oven. Bake for 2 hours, or until lamb is tender, basting frequently.   *Makes 4 to 6 servings.*

COTELETTES D'AGNEAU DIJONNAISE

6	round bone shoulder lamb chops
	Salt and pepper
2	tablespoons butter
2	tablespoons Dijon mustard
1	can (14 ounces) hearts of celery
1	cup tomato juice
½	cup French dry white wine or apple juice
¼	cup finely chopped parsley

Sprinkle chops with salt and pepper. Melt butter in a skillet. Brown chops on both sides. Spread mustard on chops. Add celery and juice in can, tomato juice and white wine. Cover and simmer 1 hour or until chops are tender. Place lamb chops on a platter and keep warm. Pour pan juices into blender. Whirl until smooth. Pour into pan again and reheat until bubbly and thick. Spoon over chops. Sprinkle with parsley. Garnish platter with scalloped orange cups filled with orange sections.   *Makes about 6 servings.*

HOT BARLEY SALAD WITH MINTED LAMB MEATBALLS

HOT BARLEY SALAD:
- ⅔ cup regular barley
- 1 teaspoon salt
- 4 cups boiling water
- ⅔ cup celery slices
- ½ cup green onion slices
- ⅓ cup maple-flavored table syrup
- 3 tablespoons white wine vinegar

- 1 cup chopped tomato
- 1 package (8 ounces) frozen pea pods

MEATBALLS:
- ¾ pound ground lamb
- ½ cup quick or old-fashioned oats, uncooked
- ⅓ cup finely chopped carrot
- ¼ cup finely chopped onion
- 1 egg
- ½ teaspoon chopped fresh mint
  or
- ¼ teaspoon dried mint leaves, crushed
- ½ teaspoon salt
- ⅛ teaspoon ground coriander

FOR BARLEY SALAD: Stir barley into salted boiling water in 4-quart Dutch oven. Reduce heat. Cover; simmer about 1 hour or until tender, stirring occasionally. In medium saucepan heat together celery, onion, syrup and vinegar. Simmer for 8 to 10 minutes or until onion and celery are tender.

FOR MEATBALLS: Heat oven to 375 degrees. Place ground lamb in large mixing bowl. Add remaining ingredients; mix well. Shape to form 16 1½-inch meatballs. Bake on rack in shallow baking pan for 12 to 15 minutes or until desired doneness.

Drain barley; return to Dutch oven. Pour syrup mixture over barley. Add meatballs, tomato and pea pods. Simmer over medium heat about 5 minutes or until heated through. *Makes 4 to 5 servings.*

Note: Substitute 1 cup quick barley for regular barley, if desired. Decrease boiling water to 3 cups. Stir barley into salted boiling water. Reduce heat. Cover; simmer for 10 to 12 minutes or until tender, stirring occasionally. Proceed as recipe directs.

LAMB CURRY

- 1 package (10 ounces) frozen patty shells
- 2 tablespoons butter or margarine
- 1 large onion, chopped
- 1 tart apple, peeled, cored and chopped
- 2 teaspoons curry powder
- ⅓ cup orange marmalade
- ¼ cup flour
- 1 cup chicken broth
- 1 cup (½ pint) light cream
- 3 cups diced leftover cooked lamb
- Salt and pepper

In saucepan, heat butter and saute onion, apple and curry powder for 5 minutes. Stir in orange marmalade and flour. Gradually stir in chicken broth and cream. Stir over low heat until sauce bubbles and thickens. Stir in lamb. Simmer for 5 minutes. Season to taste with salt and pepper. Spoon lamb in curry sauce into patty shells or onto a bed of rice. Serve with a green salad or a fruit salad.
Makes 6 servings.

LAMB 'N' ZUCCHINI SUPREME

- 1½ pounds well-trimmed lamb, cut into about 1-inch cubes
- 2 tablespoons butter or margarine
- 1 can (10¾ ounces) condensed cream of chicken soup
- ¼ cup orange juice
- 1 tablespoon chopped chutney
- 1 teaspoon curry powder
- 3 small zucchini, cut into ½-inch slices (3 cups)
- Cooked rice
- Toasted slivered almonds

In skillet, brown lamb in butter. Stir in soup, orange juice, chutney and curry. Cover. Cook over low heat 1 hour 15 minutes. Add zucchini. Cook 15 minutes more; stir occasionally. Meanwhile, combine rice and almonds; serve with stew.
Makes about 4½ cups.

LAMB YUCATAN

- 1 leg of New Zealand spring lamb, (5 to 6 pounds), frozen
- 2 cloves garlic, cut in slivers
- ½ teaspoon salt
- ¼ teaspoon pepper
- 1 can (1 pound) tomatoes, undrained
- 1 cup chicken broth
- 1 large onion, cut in quarters
- ¼ cup canned, green chili peppers
- 1 teaspoon sugar
- ¼ teaspoon ground cumin

Thaw lamb in refrigerator overnight. With tip of knife, cut small slits in meat. Insert slivers of garlic in slits; sprinkle with salt and pepper. Place lamb, fat side up, in shallow roasting pan. Cover; roast in 325-degree oven 30 minutes. In container of electric blender, combine tomatoes, chicken broth, onion, chili peppers, sugar and cumin; process until smooth. Remove lamb from oven, spoon sauce over lamb; return to oven and continue roasting uncovered 1½ to 2 hours, or until meat thermometer registers 160 degrees for medium, 170 to 180 degrees for well-done. Baste often with pan juices. Remove meat to serving platter, allow to stand 10 minutes before carving.   *Makes 6 to 8 servings.*

PIQUANT SHOULDER LAMB CHOPS

4–6	New Zealand spring lamb shoulder chops, defrosted
1	cup dry white wine
3	tablespoons wine vinegar
1	tablespoon light brown sugar
¼	teaspoon salt
1	clove garlic, minced
1	tablespoon vegetable oil
½	cup beef broth
¼	cup chili sauce
2	tablespoons finely chopped onion
1	tablespoon cornstarch
1	tablespoon water
½	cup sliced, pitted black olives
1	canned green chili, seeded, chopped

Place lamb chops in flat, shallow dish. Combine wine, vinegar, brown sugar, salt and garlic; pour over chops. Marinate 2 hours at room temperature, turning once. Drain chops and pat dry. Reserve marinade.

In large skillet, heat oil; saute chops on both sides until lightly browned. Add reserved marinade, beef broth, chili sauce and onion. Simmer, uncovered, 25 to 30 minutes or until chops are tender.

Remove chops to serving platter; keep warm. Mix cornstarch and water. Add to skillet. Cook, stirring, until sauce boils and thickens. Add olives and green chili. Spoon sauce over chops.

Makes 4 to 6 servings.

ROAST LEG OF LAMB BARCELONA

1	leg of New Zealand spring lamb, (5- to 6-pound) frozen
1	cup orange juice
½	cup sherry wine
¼	cup soy sauce
½	cup chopped onion
1	tablespoon brown sugar
½	teaspoon ginger
1	clove garlic, minced
1	tablespoon flour
¼	cup water

Trim excess fat from frozen leg of lamb, place lamb in large plastic bag. Combine orange juice, sherry, soy sauce, onion, brown sugar, ginger and garlic; mix well. Pour into plastic bag with lamb; secure top. Place bag in shallow pan; refrigerate overnight, turning bag frequently.

To roast, remove lamb from bag and place in shallow roasting pan. Reserve 1 cup marinade for gravy, use remainder to brush on lamb as it roasts. Roast lamb, uncovered, in a 325-degree oven about 2 hours or until meat thermometer registers desired degree of doneness (160 degrees medium, 170 degrees to 180 degrees for well done.)

During last hour baste often with marinade. Remove to serving platter, allow to stand 10 minutes before carving. In small saucepan, combine 1 tablespoon pan drippings and flour. Stir over low heat 2 minutes. Gradually stir in 1 cup reserved marinade and water. Cook, stirring constantly, until mixture boils and thickens; serve with lamb.

Makes 6 to 8 servings.

SHISH KEBAB AND PILAF

SHISH KEBAB:
Lamb cut for kebabs, in desired amount
Red wine
Olive oil
Crushed garlic
Salt
Black pepper
Ground oregano or cumin
Cherry tomatoes
Green pepper squares
Small white onions, partially sauteed (optional)

PILAF:

2	tablespoons butter or margarine
2	cups cracked wheat, medium grind
1	cup chopped onion
3½	cups chicken broth
1	teaspoon salt
½	teaspoon grated lemon rind
1	cup halved green grapes
2	tablespoons chopped parsley

Marinate lamb in wine, oil, garlic, salt, pepper and oregano overnight in glass container. Skewer lamb and vegetables. Place kebabs on tray; brush with marinade. Cover with clear plastic wrap and set aside temporarily. Prepare Pilaf by following method: Melt butter in a 3-quart thick saucepan.

Add cracked wheat and onion; saute lightly. Remove pan from heat; cool slightly. Add broth, salt and lemon rind. Place over heat and bring to boil. Cover and cook over low heat 25 minutes. Add grapes and parsley; mix lightly. Allow to stand in warm place 5 minutes before serving. Meanwhile, in last 10-15 minutes, broil kebabs beneath high heat or over hot coals until desired doneness. Turn pilaf into serving dish and surround with kebabs.

Makes 6 to 8 servings.

STUFFED SHOULDER OF LAMB

1	boned shoulder of lamb, (5 pounds) cut with a pocket
2	teaspoons salt, divided
½	teaspoon ground black pepper, divided
2	cups diced, peeled and cored tart green apples
2	cups plain toasted croutons
¼	cup pine nuts (optional)
2	eggs, beaten
2	tablespoons instant minced onion
2	tablespoons melted butter or margarine
2	tablespoons parsley flakes
2	tablespoons water
1	tablespoon grated lemon peel
1½	teaspoons marjoram leaves
¼	teaspoon sage leaves
2	tablespoons lemon juice

Sprinkle lamb with one and one-half teaspoons of the salt and one-fourth teaspoon of the black pepper. Set aside. In a mixing bowl combine apples, croutons, nuts, eggs, minced onion, butter, parsley, water, lemon peel, marjoram, salt and remaining one-half teaspoon salt and one-fourth teaspoon black pepper; blend well. Stuff the lamb shoulder with the mixture. Tie securely with string or skewers. Place on a rack in a shallow roasting pan. Sprinkle lemon juice over the top. Roast, uncovered, in a preheated 325-degree oven two and one-half hours or until meat thermometer registers 175 to 180 degrees. *Makes 8 to 10 portions.*

WINE-BRAISED LAMB SHANKS

1	tablespoon vegetable oil
4	lamb shanks
1½	cups thinly sliced carrots
1	cup chopped onion
1	clove garlic, minced
1	cup dry white wine
1	chicken bouillon cube
½	teaspoon salt
¼	teaspoon pepper
2	tablespoons tomato paste

In large, heavy kettle, heat oil; brown shanks on all sides. Drain off all but 2 tablespoons fat; saute carrots, onion and garlic until onion is tender.

Add wine, bouillon cube, salt and pepper, bring to boiling. Cover. Reduce heat, simmer 1½ hours.

Stir in tomato paste. Simmer 30 minutes longer or until shanks are tender. *Makes 4 servings.*

PORK & HAM

CITRUS HAM BALLS

2	eggs
½	cup orange juice
3	cups fine soft bread crumbs
2	cups ground cooked ham
1	tablespoon minced onion
¼	cup chopped parsley
½	teaspoon grated orange rind
¼	teaspoon dry mustard
½	teaspoon dried leaf sage
2	tablespoons butter or margarine
	Citrus Sauce (recipe follows)
	Hot cooked rice

Beat eggs in medium bowl. Add orange juice and bread crumbs. Mix well and let stand 5 minutes. Add ham, onion, parsley, orange rind, dry mustard and sage; mix well. Shape into 18 meatballs about 1 inch in diameter. Heat butter in skillet. Add meatballs and brown lightly on all sides. Add to Citrus Sauce. Serve with hot cooked rice.

Makes 4 to 6 servings.

CITRUS SAUCE:

3	tablespoons cornstarch
3	cups orange juice
3	tablespoons sugar
½	teaspoon minced onion
¾	teaspoon salt
½	teaspoon dry mustard
½	teaspoon dried leaf sage
¼	teaspoon ginger
1	teaspoon vinegar
¼	teaspoon pepper
1	cup raisins
2	Florida oranges, sectioned

Blend cornstarch with a small amount of the orange juice in a saucepan. Add remaining orange juice, sugar, onion, salt, dry mustard, sage, ginger, vinegar, pepper and raisins. Mix well and cook, stirring constantly, until mixture thickens and comes to a boil. Add orange sections.

Note: To section Florida oranges, cut off peel round and round, spiral fashion. Go over fruit again, removing any remaining white membrane. Cut along side of each dividing membrane from outside middle of core. Remove section by section over bowl to retain juice from fruit.

COTELETTES CALVADOS

6	center-cut pork chops, 1 inch thick
	Salt and pepper
½	cup Calvados (or hard cider)
1	clove garlic, chopped
12	canned, drained button champignons de Paris (mushrooms)
1	can (8 ounces), frozen concentrated orange juice, undiluted
2	tablespoons Dijon mustard
1	cup (½ pint) heavy cream
1	tablespoon cornstarch

Sprinkle chops with salt and pepper. Place chops in large skillet and cook over high heat until brown on both sides. Add Calvados and set aflame. Add garlic, orange juice and mustard. Cover and simmer chops until tender, about 1 hour. Place chops on platter and keep warm. Mix heavy cream and cornstarch and stir into pan juices. Stir over low heat until sauce bubbles and thickens. Add mushrooms and reheat. Replace chops in sauce and reheat until bubbly. Serve with sauteed apple slices and glazed carrots. *Makes 6 servings.*

CRANBERRY-APPLE HAM LOAF

2	pounds lean ground smoked ham
1	small onion, minced
1	apple, peeled, cored and chopped
2	cups soft-firm-type white bread crumbs (about 4 slices)
3	eggs
½	cup milk
½	teaspoon dry mustard
½	teaspoon salt
¼	teaspoon ground pepper
	Dash ground cloves
1	can (16 ounces) whole berry cranberry sauce

In a bowl, mix ham, onion, apple, crumbs, eggs, milk, mustard, salt and pepper. Beat until well blended. Stir in cloves and half of the cranberry sauce.

Pack mixture tightly in a greased 9-by-5-by-3-inch loaf pan. Bake in a preheated 350-degree oven for 1 hour. Heat remaining cranberry sauce until bubbly. Drain excess juices from pan and unmold loaf onto a platter. Spoon hot cranberry sauce over loaf. Cut into thick slices to serve. *Makes 1 loaf.*

CRISPY PORK PATTIES

1	can (10¾ ounces) condensed creamy chicken-mushroom soup or chicken giblet gravy
1½	cups finely chopped cooked pork, lamb, or chicken
⅓	cup fine dry bread crumbs
1	egg, slightly beaten
	Generous dash pepper
2	tablespoons butter or margarine
¼	cup water
1	teaspoon lemon juice
¼	teaspoon rosemary leaves, crushed

Mix *thoroughly* 2 tablespoons soup, meat, bread crumbs, egg and pepper. Shape *firmly* into 4 patties.

In skillet, brown patties in butter. Add remaining soup, water, lemon juice and rosemary. Heat; stir occasionally. *Makes 4 servings.*

CURRIED PORK WITH APPLES

½	cup sliced onion
¼	cup diagonally sliced celery
1	tablespoon curry powder
2	tablespoons butter or margarine
1	can (10¾ ounces) condensed cream of chicken soup
½	cup water
1	cup apple wedges
1	cup cooked cut green beans
1	cup cubed cooked pork
1	teaspoon lemon juice
	Cooked rice

In saucepan, cook onion and celery with curry in butter until tender. Add remaining ingredients except rice. Heat; stir occasionally. Serve over rice. Garnish with sliced green onion, toasted coconut or diced green pepper if desired.
Makes about 3 cups, 4 servings.

FINGER-LICKIN' RIBS

2	racks pork spareribs (about 6 pounds)
	Salt and pepper
1	can (10¾ ounces) condensed chicken broth, undiluted
1	jar (12 ounces) pineapple preserves
½	cup chili sauce
¼	cup cider vinegar
4	cloves garlic, minced

With a sharp knife, trim off all excess fat from spareribs. Trim carefully to remove fat as cooking fat drips on charcoal and causes flares. Sprinkle ribs on all sides with salt and pepper. Place ribs in a shallow pan. Mix remaining ingredients and pour over ribs. Let stand at room temperature 2 hours or refrigerate overnight.

Drain ribs well, reserving marinade. Place ribs on grill rack 8 inches above moderately hot coals. Grill one to one and one-half hours depending on thickness of ribs. Turn ribs. Brush with marinade every 10 minutes. Place ribs on a serving platter and spoon remaining marinade over ribs. Cut into individual ribs to serve. *Makes 6 servings.*

FRUITED LOIN OF PORK

1	cup (about) dried apricots
½	cup dry sherry
1	center-cut pork loin, (3- to 5-pounds), with backbone cracked
½	cup dark corn syrup
1	tablespoon grated orange rind
¼	cup orange juice
½	teaspoon soy sauce

In small saucepan, stir together apricots and sherry. Cover and cook over medium heat, stirring occasionally, until apricots are plumped and liquid is absorbed.

Cut deep slits between each pork chop. Insert 3 or 4 apricots in each slit.

Place pork in roasting pan. (Do not add water or cover.) Roast in 325-degree oven for 2 to 3½ hours or until internal temperature reaches 185 degrees. (Allow about 40 minutes per pound.)

Meanwhile, stir together corn syrup, orange rind, orange juice and soy sauce in small saucepan. Bring to boil. Reduce heat and simmer 3 minutes. Brush pork with sauce frequently during last 30 minutes of roasting time. *Makes 6 to 10 servings.*

GORGEOUS PORK CHOPS

6	pork chops, trimmed
2	tablespoons butter, divided
	Dash salt
	Dash cayenne pepper
6	medium-size mushrooms, sliced
1	package (12 ounces) frozen spinach, thawed, or 1 bunch fresh spinach
1	recipe Easy 1-1-1 Cheese Sauce (recipe follows)

In large skillet, saute pork chops in 1 tablespoon butter over medium heat until browned on both sides and no longer pink inside. Sprinkle with salt and cayenne pepper. Remove to ovenproof dish. Set aside, reserving pan drippings.

Saute sliced mushrooms until tender in pan drippings. Remove from skillet. Melt remaining butter

in skillet. Saute spinach to heat through. Sprinkle with salt to taste. Arrange spinach on top of pork chops. Then cover with foil and place in a 250-degree oven while making cheese sauce.

Add sauteed mushrooms to sauce. Pour over hot pork chops and spinach. Serve with crisp French bread, rice or buttered noodles. *Makes 6 servings.*

EASY 1-1-1 CHEESE SAUCE:

In a small saucepan, bring 1 cup half-and-half to a slow boil over medium heat. Lightly toss 1 tablespoon of flour into 1 cup shredded Danish Havarti or creamy Havarti cheese. Add to half-and-half. Cook, stirring, until sauce is smooth. Add a dash of cayenne pepper and a dash of salt.

GOURMET CHOPS

5	smoked pork chops (about 2 pounds)
½	cup thinly sliced onion
¼	cup red table wine or apple juice
¼	cup water
1	tablespoon soy sauce
1	tablespoon honey
2	teaspoons cornstarch
¼	teaspoon dry mustard
¼	teaspoon rosemary, crumbled
3	large fresh California Bartlett pears

Trim excess fat from chops. Arrange chops in a shallow 2½- or 3-quart baking dish. Top each with onion slices. Mix wine, water, soy sauce, honey, cornstarch, mustard and rosemary in a small saucepan. Cook, stirring, until mixture boils and thickens. Spoon 1 tablespoon sauce over each pork chop. Bake uncovered at 350 degrees for 30 to 40 minutes until almost tender.

Meanwhile, core and quarter pears. Arrange pears around chops. Drizzle with remaining sauce mixture. Return to oven and bake 5 to 10 minutes longer, or until pears are tender. *Makes 5 servings.*

JAMBALAYA A LA GRILLE

¼	cup butter or margarine
1	large onion, chopped
1	clove garlic, chopped
1	green pepper, chopped
1	smoked ham steak, about 1 to 1½ pounds, cut into 1-inch cubes
1	cup converted rice
2	cans (1 pound each) stewed tomatoes
1	cup water
1	package (10 ounces) frozen peas
	Salt and pepper
	Toasted Bread Poles (recipe follows)

Continued

Place in a large skillet on grill 8 inches above medium hot coals. Heat butter and saute onion, garlic and green pepper until wilted, about 5 minutes. Add ham and rice and stir for 10 minutes. Stir in tomatoes and water. Cover tightly and simmer for 20 to 25 minutes or until rice is tender and liquid is absorbed. Stir occasionally during cooking to prevent sticking. Add peas and season to taste with salt and pepper. Cook until peas are heated through. Serve with Toasted Bread Poles.

TOASTED BREAD POLES:

Cut an unsliced loaf of bread into halves lengthwise. Cut each half into 3 pieces. Melt ½ cup butter or margarine and stir in 2 tablespoons minced chives. Roll long pieces of bread in butter mixture or use a brush to cover bread with butter. Place bread on grill above medium hot coals and cook about 3 to 4 minutes on each side. Turn bread poles on all four sides until all pieces are brown and crusty.

KRAUT 'N' KEBABS

1	can (15¼ ounces) pineapple chunks
3	tablespoons flour
3	tablespoons packed light brown sugar
3	tablespoons soy sauce
¼	teaspoon salt
1	pound pork cubes for kebabs
	Thick slices of bacon (about 9 slices)
4	cups drained sauerkraut (about 32 ounces)
2	tablespoons sugar

Drain pineapple chunks, reserving ½ cup syrup. In large bowl combine flour, brown sugar, soy sauce and salt. Mix well. Add pork cubes and drained pineapple chunks, coating thoroughly with sauce. Cover. Chill for 1 hour, turning pork and pineapple occasionally. Cut bacon, crosswise, into pieces to fit around pork. Thread marinated pork cubes and pineapple chunks onto four 9-inch skewers. Place on rack in broiler pan. Broil, or grill over charcoal, turning frequently, until pork is cooked, about 20 to 25 minutes. During last 5 minutes, brush with marinade. In large saucepan, heat sauerkraut, ½ cup reserved pineapple syrup and sugar until hot. Serve kebabs on hot sauerkraut.   *Makes 4 servings.*

MUSTARD HAM AND EGGS WITH BROILED BANANAS

3	tablespoons butter or margarine, divided
¼	cup finely chopped onion
2	tablespoons flour
1¼	cups milk
¼	cup prepared mustard
¼	teaspoon salt
⅛	teaspoon pepper
2	cups cubed cooked ham
4	hard-cooked eggs, sliced
4	firm bananas

In medium saucepan melt 2 tablespoons butter, add onion and cook until tender. Blend in flour. Stir in milk and mustard. Cook, stirring constantly, until mixture thickens and comes to a boil. Stir in salt, pepper, ham and sliced eggs. Peel bananas and cut in half lengthwise. Place on baking sheet and brush with remaining 1 tablespoon butter, melted. Broil 6 inches from heat for 2 to 3 minutes, just until tender. To serve, spoon sauce over broiled bananas.
Makes 4 servings.

ORANGE SPARERIBS SARASOTA

4–5	pounds spareribs, cut in serving pieces
1	can (6 ounces) frozen concentrated orange juice thawed, undiluted
¾	cup ketchup
2	tablespoons molasses
1	teaspoon Worcestershire sauce
½	teaspoon Tabasco pepper sauce
2	teaspoons salt
4	teaspoons grated onion

Place spareribs in large kettle; cover with water and bring to a boil. Reduce heat and simmer, covered, for 30 minutes. Drain and refrigerate until ready to grill. Mix undiluted orange concentrate with remaining ingredients. Place spareribs on grill set 6 to 8 inches from heat. Cook 15 minutes; turn and brush with orange sauce. Cook 15 to 30 minutes longer, turning and brushing frequently with sauce. If desired, garnish with halved orange slices.
Makes 4 to 6 servings.

ORIENTAL PORK WITH NECTARINES

1	pound lean pork loin
2	medium fresh nectarines, sliced
1	green pepper, cut into 1-inch cubes
1	small onion cut into 1-inch cubes
1	large clove garlic, minced
2	beef bouillon cubes
2	tablespoons plum jam
2	tablespoons red wine vinegar
⅓	cup water

2 teaspoons cornstarch
1 teaspoon chili powder
1 teaspoon grated fresh ginger root
 (optional)
2 tablespoons vegetable oil, divided
 Hot cooked rice

Cut pork into 2-by-½-inch strips. Cut nectarines and vegetables as directed. Mash bouillon cubes with jam in a small bowl. Mix in vinegar, water, cornstarch, chili powder and ginger. Heat 1 tablespoon oil in skillet until hot. Add half the pork and cook over high heat, turning occasionally with spatula, until browned, about 2 minutes. Lift pork with spatula from pan onto plate. Repeat with the other half of the pork. Heat remaining 1 tablespoon oil in skillet. Add green pepper, onion and garlic. Stir-fry over high heat for 3 or 4 minutes or until tender-crisp. Return pork to pan. Add cornstarch mixture and nectarines. Cook, stirring, over high heat until sauce is thickened and mixture is hot. Serve over rice. *Makes 4 servings.*

PAPAYA PORK

3 pounds pork loin roast
1 cup papaya pulp (1 large ripe papaya)
½ cup pineapple juice
½ cup honey
1 ripe papaya, peeled, seeded and sliced
2 bananas, peeled and sliced
1 cup pineapple chunks
4 oranges, peeled and sliced
¼ cup melted butter or margarine
⅓ cup firmly packed brown sugar

Roast pork in 400-degree oven for 25 minutes, basting with mixture of papaya pulp, pineapple juice and honey.

Reduce heat to 300 degrees. Arrange sliced papaya, bananas, pineapple and oranges in separate baking pan. Drizzle wih butter and sprinkle with brown sugar. Bake fruit and pork 45 to 60 minutes until pork is well done or registers 185 degrees on meat thermometer.

Serve slices of pork with the baked fruit.
Makes 4 servings.

PEAR-HAM-YAM BAKE

1 (16 ounces), can Bartlett pears
2 cups diced cooked ham
2 cups diced cooked yams or sweet potatoes

1 cup herb-seasoned croutons
½ cup diced celery
¼ cup finely chopped onion
1 cup dairy sour cream
¼ teaspoon salt
⅛ teaspoon pepper
2 tablespoons melted butter
¼ cup brown sugar
2 tablespoons soft butter
1 teaspoon grated orange peel

Drain pears, reserving one-half cup syrup. Combine ham, yams, croutons, celery, onion, sour cream, reserved pear syrup, salt, pepper and melted butter. Place in buttered casserole. Bake in a 375-degree oven 20 minutes. Arrange pear halves, cut side up, on top. Combine brown sugar, soft butter and orange peel. Sprinkle over pears. Place under broiler to glaze pears. *Makes 4 to 6 servings.*

POLYNESIAN KRAUT KEBABS

6 cups undrained sauerkraut (about 48 ounces)
1 can (20 ounces) pineapple chunks in pineapple juice, undrained
 Brown sugar
½ cup ketchup
2 tablespoons soy sauce
1 pound frankfurters, cut into 1-inch pieces
2 medium green peppers cut into chunks
2 tablespoons salad oil
1 cup chopped green onion
 Parsley for garnish

Drain kraut, reserving 2 tablespoons kraut liquid; set aside. Drain pineapple chunks, reserving the juice.

Make sauce. In small saucepan, measure 3 tablespoons brown sugar and 2 tablespoons reserved pineapple juice. Stir in 2 tablespoons kraut liquid, ketchup and soy sauce. Heat to boiling, stirring constantly. Reduce heat and simmer 10 minutes.

Assemble kebabs. While sauce is simmering, prepare 12 kebabs. Alternately thread pineapple chunks, franks and green pepper chunks on 12 10-inch skewers. Place on rack of broiler pan. Brush kebabs with sauce and broil 5 minutes, brushing occasionally with additional sauce. Turn kebabs, brush with additional sauce and broil 5 more minutes or until franks are heated through.

Prepare kraut mixture. While kebabs are broiling, heat salad oil in large skillet. Add onion and drained kraut. Cook, stirring constantly, until onion is tender. Stir in ½ cup brown sugar and ½ pineapple juice. Continue cooking until hot.

Continued

To serve, spoon hot kraut mixture onto large serving platter arrange kebabs on top. Garnish kraut mixture with parsley.

Makes 6 servings, 2 kebabs each.

PORC ST. HUBERT

6	pork chops, 1½ inches thick
	Salt and pepper
¼	cup olive or peanut oil
¼	cup Dijon mustard
¼	cup red wine vinegar
¼	cup butter
4	shallots, chopped
1	cup water and 2 chicken bouillon cubes
¼	cup minced parsley
2	tablespoons flour
1	jar (3 ounces) currant preserves

Sprinkle chops on both sides with salt and pepper. In bowl, mix oil, mustard and vinegar. Brush chops heavily with mustard mixture on both sides. Let stand for 2 hours or in the refrigerator overnight. Drain chops.

In large skillet, heat butter and saute shallots for 5 minutes. Add chops and brown on both sides. Add water and bouillon cubes. Stir in any remaining mustard marinade.

Cook chops uncovered for 45 to 50 minutes or until tender. Turn chops occasionally to permit even cooking. Remove chops and place on serving platter. Keep warm. Stir in parsley. Whisk in flour and currant preserves. Stir over low heat until sauce thickens and bubbles. Spoon hot sauce over pork chops. Serve garnished with French flageolets (baby lima beans) and parsley sprigs.   *Makes 6 servings.*

PORK CHOP-POTATO BAKE

6	pork chops, cut ¼ inch thick
2	teaspoons salt, divided
2	tablespoons oil
1	cup chopped onions
1	medium green pepper, diced (about 1 cup)
1	can (15 ounces), tomato sauce
1	tablespoon Worcestershire sauce
4	medium potatoes, sliced and peeled (about 6 cups)

Sprinkle both sides of pork chops with 1 teaspoon salt.

In large skillet, heat oil until hot. Add chops. Brown on both sides. Remove and set aside.

Add onions and green pepper. Saute 5 minutes.

Stir in tomato sauce, Worcestershire sauce and remaining 1 teaspoon salt. Bring to boil. Reduce heat and simmer, uncovered, for 2 minutes.

Arrange potatoes in bottom of greased 13-by-9-by-2-inch casserole. Pour half of sauce over potatoes. Top with chops. Pour remaining sauce over chops.

Cover and bake in preheated 350-degree oven for 50 minutes. Uncover and continue baking until chops are cooked and potatoes are tender, about 25 minutes longer.

Serve with salad and French bread, if desired.

Makes 6 portions.

PORK LOIN ROULADE WITH SAVORY STUFFING

1½	cups water
½	cup butter or margarine
1	package (6 ounces) stuffing mix for pork
½	cup chopped canned water chestnuts
1	boned (5 to 6 pounds) center-cut pork loin roast
½	cup dry white wine or apple juice
½	cup dark corn syrup
½	teaspoon thyme leaves, crumbled
½	teaspoon rosemary leaves, crumbled
1	teaspoon salt

Heat water, butter or margarine and seasoning packet from stuffing mix to boiling. Cover. Simmer 5 minutes. Remove from heat.

Stir in water chestnuts and bread crumbs from stuffing mix with fork just until crumbs are moistened. Cool to room temperature (or make ahead and refrigerate).

Place pork on cutting board with fat side down. With sharp knife, cut ¾ way through center of loin muscle, staying parallel to fat, to split in half. Do not cut all the way through. Open pork and fill with some of stuffing mixture. Wrap leftover stuffing in foil to bake on rear of grill area during last 30 minutes of roasting pork.

Tie loin securely with string crosswise at 1½-inch intervals. Place on grill over drip pan 6 to 8 inches above medium coals. Insert meat thermometer into center of meat. Cover grill. Roast 1½ hours, adding more briquettes to each side of drip pan at end of 1 hour as manufacturer directs.

Meanwhile, combine remaining ingredients. Uncover grill. Brush roulade with wine glaze occasionally. Grill 15 to 30 minutes more or until meat thermometer reaches 170 degrees.

Place roulade on warm platter. Let stand 15 minutes for easier slicing. Remove strings and slice pork.

If gravy is desired, remove drip pan from coals or use bulb baster to remove drippings. Pour drippings into 2-cup measure or bowl. Spoon fat from drippings. If necessary, add chicken broth or water to make 1½ cups liquid.

In saucepan, combine any leftover glaze with 1 tablespoon cornstarch. Stir in drippings. Cook until bubbly. Serve gravy with pork.

Makes 8 to 10 servings.

SOUVLAKI

1	pound ground pork
1	pound ground beef
2	tablespoons lemon juice
1	teaspoon dried leaf oregano
⅛	teaspoon Tabasco pepper sauce
1	teaspoon salt
1	tablespoon minced onion
1	clove garlic, crushed
	Marinade (recipe follows)

Combine all ingredients. Mix thoroughly.

Form into ball. Brush with marinade. Let stand for 30 minutes before cooking.

Bake in 400-degree oven for 2 hours, brushing frequently with marinade. Remove from oven and brush with marinade again before serving.

To serve, slice thinly. *Makes 8 servings.*

Note: Ground lamb or veal may also be used.

	MARINADE:
¼	cup lemon juice
3	tablespoons olive oil
½	teaspoon salt
6	bay leaves
½	teaspoon dried leaf oregano
1	small clove garlic, crushed
⅛	teaspoon Tabasco pepper sauce

Beat lemon juice into oil. Add remaining ingredients and combine.

SPARE RIBS WITH PLUM SAUCE

1	can (1 pound 15 ounces) whole purple plums, pitted
¼	cup reserved plum syrup
½	cup light corn syrup
2	thin slices onion
2	tablespoons white vinegar
½	teaspoon salt
3	pounds spare ribs, cut in serving pieces

Drain plums, reserving one-fourth cup syrup. Mix in blender the plums, reserved plum syrup, corn syrup, onion, vinegar and salt. Brush about 1 cup of mixture over ribs and bake in 350-degree oven one and one-half hours, turning and basting occasionally, with remaining sauce. *Makes 4 servings.*

STUFFED PORK CHOPS

	STUFFED CHOPS:
6	pork rib chops, cut 1 to 1¼ inches thick
	Salt and pepper
1½	cups 100 percent natural cereal with raisins and dates
1	cup chopped apple
½	cup chicken broth, divided
¼	cup chopped green onion
¼	cup butter or margarine, melted
½	teaspoon sage
¼	teaspoon salt

	GRAVY:
2	tablespoons all-purpose flour
1	cup milk

Heat oven to 350 degrees. For stuffed chops, slice into fat side of chop parallel to surface and rib bone to make pocket for stuffing. Brown meat in large skillet; season with salt and pepper.

Combine cereal, apple, ¼ cup chicken broth, green onion, butter, sage and salt, mixing well. Spoon about ⅓ cup stuffing into each chop pocket; secure cut sides of pocket together with wooden picks, if necessary.

Place chops in 13-by-9-inch baking pan. Add remaining ¼ cup chicken broth. Cover. Bake at 350 degrees about 1 hour or until meat is tender. Place meat on warm platter; keep warm while preparing gravy. Reserve 2 tablespoons pan drippings (fat and juices).

For gravy, blend together reserved pan drippings and flour in small saucepan. Cook over medium heat, stirring constantly, until mixture is smooth and bubbly. Gradually add milk. Continue cooking stirring constantly, until mixture comes to a boil.

Continue cooking and stirring for 1 minute while mixture thickens. Serve gravy over stuffed chops.

Makes 6 servings.

SWEET-AND-SOUR PORK

1	tablespoon plus ⅓ cup cornstarch
2	tablespoons soy sauce
1	tablespoon dry sherry
⅛	teaspoon pepper
1	egg yolk, well beaten

Continued

1   pound boneless pork, cut in 1-inch cubes
1   quart (about) corn oil
    Sweet and Sour Sauce (recipe follows)

In medium bowl, stir together 1 tablespoon cornstarch, soy sauce, sherry and pepper until smooth. Stir in egg yolk. Add pork; toss to coat well. Let stand 30 minutes. Pour corn oil into heavy 3-quart saucepan or deep fryer, filling no more than ⅓ full. Heat over medium-high heat to 375 degrees. Sprinkle pork with ⅓ cup cornstarch; toss to coat well. Fry, a few pieces at a time, 3 to 4 minutes or until pork is golden. Drain on paper towels. Prepare Sweet and Sour Sauce. Before serving, reheat corn oil to 375 degrees. Fry pork, a few pieces at a time, about 1 minute or more until very crisp. Drain on paper towels. Serve immediately with Sweet and Sour Sauce.   *Makes 4 to 6 servings.*

SWEET AND SOUR SAUCE:

1   can (8 ounces) pineapple chunks in own juice
¼   cup firmly packed brown sugar
2   tablespoons cornstarch
1   teaspoon salt
½   cup ketchup
⅓   cup cider vinegar
3   tablespoons water
3   tablespoons corn oil
2   green peppers, cut in 1-inch squares
2   tomatoes, cut in 1-inch cubes

Drain pineapple; reserve juice. In small bowl, stir together sugar, cornstarch and salt. Gradually stir in reserved juice, ketchup, vinegar and water until smooth. In large skillet or wok, heat corn oil over medium-high heat. Add green peppers and tomatoes. Stirring constantly, cook 1 minute or until tender-crisp. Add cornstarch mixture. Stirring constantly, bring to boil over medium heat and boil 1 minute. Stir in pineapple. Serve over pork.
Makes about 3 cups.

ZIPPY HAM TURNOVERS

1   cup (8 ounces) finely chopped, cooked ham
2   tablespoons cream
2   teaspoons instant minced onion
4   teaspoon prepared mustard
     Pepper to taste
1   can (10 biscuits) refrigerated buttermilk or country-style biscuits
1   can (10¾ ounces) condensed cream of celery soup
⅓   cup milk or cream

Preheat oven to 425 degrees. Combine first five ingredients. Separate biscuit dough into 10 biscuits. Press two biscuits together. Then press or roll each to a 7-inch circle. Spoon about 3 tablespoons of ham mixture onto center of each biscuit. Fold enough dough in half over filling. Press edges with fork to seal. Prick tops. Bake on ungreased cookie sheet 8 to 12 minutes until golden brown. While turnovers are baking, combine soup and milk: heat until smooth. Serve over hot turnovers. (Refrigerate leftovers.)
Makes 5 turnovers.

VARIETY MEATS, SAUSAGES & FRANKFURTERS

CHILI-STYLE FRANKS

1   cup sliced frankfurters
1   tablespoon butter or margarine
2   cans (about 7¾ ounces each) semi-condensed old-fashioned bean soup
2   tablespoons ketchup
½   teaspoon prepared mustard
½   teaspoon chili powder

In saucepan, brown frankfurters in butter. Stir in remaining ingredients. Heat; stir occasionally. Serve over rice or biscuits. *Makes about 2 cups, 2 servings.*

FRANK ROLL

Trim crusts from 8 slices bread (can be rye, white or both). Slightly flatten each with rolling pin and cut in 3 one-inch strips. Cut franks crosswise in thirds. Spread 8 strips of bread with mustard, 8 with cream cheese and 8 with softened blue cheese. Roll each frankfurter section in bread and secure with toothpick. Brush with melted butter and bake in 400-degree oven for about 5 minutes. Serve at once.

FRANKS WELLINGTON

1   pound ground beef
1   egg slightly beaten
½   cup bread crumbs
8   ounce can tomato sauce
¼   cup grated sharp cheese
½   teaspoon black pepper
½   teaspoon salt
1   teaspoon basil
1   teaspoon parsley
1   pound frankfurters

Combine ground beef, egg, bread crumbs, tomato sauce, grated cheese and seasonings and mix well. Mixture should be fairly stiff. Enclose each frankfurter in the ground beef mixture to form a blanket about one-fourth inch thick. Dust each Wellington with flour and saute in fry pan in melted butter or margarine until browned on all sides, about 10 to 15 minutes. Remove to baking dish. Bake covered in 350-degree oven 30 minutes. Uncover and continue baking 20 minutes or until done. Remove from oven. Top each with whole cranberry sauce and broil about two minutes.

ITALIAN LIVER AND ONIONS

2   medium sweet Spanish onions
3   tablespoons oil
1   pound beef or calves' liver
2   tablespoons flour
1   can (4 ounces) button mushrooms
½   cup dry white wine

1   tablespoon lemon juice
¾   teaspoon salt
¼   teaspoon pepper
¼   teaspoon thyme or marjoram
2   tablespoons minced parsley
      Hot buttered spaghetti
      Grated Parmesan cheese

Peel and thinly slice onions. Separate into rings. (Should measure about 4 cups.) Saute onion in oil 2 to 3 minutes.

Cut liver in ¼-by-1½-inch strips. Toss in flour. Add liver to onions. Saute until liver is browned.

Add undrained mushrooms, wine, lemon juice and seasonings. Bring to boil, stirring constantly. Cover and simmer 3 to 5 minutes or until liver is done.

Sprinkle with parsley. Serve with hot buttered spaghetti and Parmesan cheese.

Makes 4 or 5 servings.

KRAUT-SAUSAGE

1   pound sausage meat
1   medium onion, sliced
2   large red apples, cored
2   cups undrained sauerkraut (about 16 ounces)
1   teaspoon dry mustard

Shape sausage meat into 4 patties. In large skillet, cook over low heat until browned on both sides. Drain on paper towel. Reserve drippings. In sausage drippings, cook onion about 5 minutes. Drain. Chop one apple and slice the other apple. Combine chopped apple, undrained kraut, mustard and onion; mix well. Spoon into shallow baking dish. Top with apple slices and sausage patties. Bake in 350-degree oven for 30 minutes. *Makes 4 servings.*

LIVER AND ONIONS ROYALE

1   pound beef liver
5   bacon slices
⅓   cup flour
1   teaspoon paprika
½   teaspoon thyme
1   teaspoon salt
⅛   teaspoon pepper
1   can (1 pound) whole onions

Cut liver into thin strips, removing veins and membranes. Fry bacon until crisp. Crumble and set aside. Coat liver with flour mixed with seasonings. Cook quickly (4 to 5 minutes a side) in 3 tablespoons

Continued

bacon drippings over medium heat, turning once. Push beef liver to one side and add drained onions. Heat thoroughly. Sprinkle with crumbled bacon.

Makes 4 servings.

ROASTED POTATOES AND SAUSAGE

6	large baking potatoes, peeled
1	pound bulk sausage meat
3	tablespoons minced onions
1	tablespoon Angostura aromatic bitters
⅓	cup dry bread crumbs
	Salt and pepper
5	slices bacon

With an apple corer, hollow potatoes lengthwise. In a bowl, mix sausage, onion, aromatic bitters and crumbs until well blended. Use mixture to stuff hole in potatoes. If any sausage mixture remains, shape into 1 inch balls and set aside. Sprinkle potatoes with salt and pepper and place side by side in a well greased shallow baking pan. Cover with foil and bake in a preheated 350 degree oven for 50 minutes or until tender. Remove cover and place bacon slices over potatoes so top of potato is covered. Add sausage balls and bake for another 15 to 20 minutes or until bacon is brown and crisp. Serve potatoes with sausage balls.

Makes 6 servings.

ROUND DOGS WITH CARAWAY KRAUT

2	cups undrained sauerkraut (about 16 ounces)
1	teaspoon caraway seed
3	tablespoons bottled French dressing
½	teaspoon seasoned salt
2	tablespoons butter or margarine
8	frankfurters
8	frankfurter buns, split and toasted

In bowl, combine undrained kraut, caraway seed, French dressing and salt; mix well. Chill. Cut 10 deep slits in each frankfurter without cutting all the way through. In skillet, melt butter or margarine. Add frankfurters and cook until browned on all sides. Arrange kraut mixture on bottoms of buns. Top with frankfurters and tops of buns.

Makes 8 servings.

SAUSAGE FRANK JAMBALAYA

1	pound hot sausage, cooked and sliced in 1-inch pieces
1	pound frankfurters, sliced in 1-inch pieces
1	pound cooked ham, cut in half inch cubes
1	diced green pepper
1	large onion, chopped
1	clove garlic
2	cups raw rice
1	can (30 ounces) tomatoes
2	cups chicken broth
1	tablespoon basil
1	tablespoon parsley
1	pinch red pepper
1	pinch sugar

Saute garlic in one tablespoon oil. Add onions and green pepper. Combine, sausage and ham, in skillet and heat. Stir in rice, add tomatoes, broth, salt, basil, parsley, red pepper and pinch sugar. Cover, bring to boil and cook about 30 minutes until rice is tender and liquid absorbed. Add franks during last 10 minutes.

Makes 12 servings.

SMOKED BEEF TONGUE AND VEGETABLES

1	smoked beef tongue (2¼ pounds)
	Water
1	large bay leaf
½	teaspoon peppercorns
4	whole cloves
1	can (10¾ ounces) condensed golden mushroom soup
½	soup can water
2	tablespoons brown sugar
2	tablespoons frozen orange juice concentrate
1	package (10 ounces) frozen Brussels sprouts
1½	cups diagonally sliced carrots (about ¼ pound)

In large heavy pan, cover tongue with water. Add bay leaf, peppercorns and cloves. Bring to boil. Cover; reduce heat. Simmer two and one-half hours; drain. Rinse, skin and slice tongue. Meanwhile, in large heavy pan, blend soup, one-half soup can water, sugar and orange juice concentrate. Add sprouts, carrots and tongue. Cover; cook over low heat 20 minutes or until vegetables are tender. Stir occasionally.

Makes 6 to 8 servings.

Poultry Dishes

Chicken is a popular dish with most families. It is higher in protein and lower in calories than many other meats. But even before these nutritional facts were known, chicken was a favorite in most regions of the United States because of its flavor. Once upon a time, people with farms always raised a few chickens for their own table. Some still do, but most poultry eaten in the United States is commercially raised.

Because of its economy, chicken is prepared in many ways—baked, sautéed, broiled, stewed, or grilled—with fried chicken leading the list in popularity. Even Napoleon had his favorite chicken dish: Chicken Marengo, or poulet sauté, prepared by his chef to celebrate defeat of the Austrians in the north Italian village of Marengo, June 14, 1800.

Chicken recipes being served today reflect the international interest in foods with influences from the Orient, Polynesia, South America, and Africa.

However, chicken is not the only bird enjoyed these days. Turkey, once thought of as a holiday treat, is now available in parts, making it a realistic item for a daily menu. It also now appears in ground form, à la ground beef, to use as patties or for turkey loaves.

Americans also enjoy game birds such as Cornish hens, pheasant, and duck, and most of these also are available in specialty meat shops and some super-markets.

The range in preparation and flavor of poultry and game birds in this country adds to our eating variety. Here are recipes that stress the many tasty ways to use these nutritious birds.

CHICKEN

ARTICHOKE MINTED CHICKEN

1	chicken, quartered, about 3 pounds
⅓	cup imported olive oil
1	clove garlic, chopped
1	onion, chopped
1	package (9 ounces) frozen artichoke hearts
2	tomatoes, cored and chopped
1	jar (4 ounces) pimiento, drained and diced
1	tablespoon chopped fresh mint leaves or 1 teaspoon dried mint leaves
¼	teaspoon oregano
1	can (13¾ ounces) chicken broth
⅓	cup dry white wine (or apple juice)
2	tablespoons flour

Sprinkle chicken with salt and pepper. Heat oil in a large skillet and brown chicken pieces on all sides. Remove chicken pieces and set aside. Saute garlic and onion in drippings for 2 to 3 minutes or until lightly browned. Drain excess fatty drippings. Add chicken pieces, artichoke hearts, tomatoes, pimiento, mint, oregano and chicken broth. Cover and simmer gently for 45 to 50 minutes or until chicken is tender. Remove chicken pieces to a platter. In a bowl, mix wine and flour. Stir mixture into pan juices. Stir over low heat until sauce bubbles and thickens. Simmer for 5 minutes, stirring constantly. Spoon sauce over the chicken. Serve garnished with parsley.   *Makes 4 servings.*

BAKED CRANBERRY CHICKEN BREASTS

6	chicken breast halves
	Salt and pepper
¼	cup butter or margarine
1	cup chopped celery
1	onion, chopped
1	package (8 ounces) corn bread stuffing mix
½	cup cranberry-orange relish

1	cup chicken broth
1	can (6 ounces) frozen concentrated orange juice, undiluted

Sprinkle chicken breasts with salt and pepper. In a skillet, heat butter and brown chicken breasts on both sides. Remove from skillet.

Add celery and onion to skillet, sauteing for 5 minutes. Stir in stuffing mix, relish and chicken broth. Spread mixture evenly in a foil-lined 9-by-13-inch baking pan.

Place chicken breasts on top of stuffing. Pour orange juice evenly over chicken breasts. Cover and bake in a preheated 350-degree oven for 40 minutes or until chicken breasts are tender.

Makes 6 servings.

Note: This recipe may be prepared with 6 one-inch pork chops. Prepare as above but bake for 1 hour.

BANANA-AND-CHICKEN BARBECUE

1	broiler-fryer chicken (2 to 2½ pounds), cut in serving pieces
½	cup ketchup
2	tablespoons cider vinegar
1	tablespoon prepared mustard
2	tablespoons salad oil
2	tablespoons minced onion
3	medium bananas

Place chicken skin side up in shallow 2-quart baking pan. Mix ketchup, vinegar, mustard, oil and onion. Spoon ¾ of sauce over chicken.

Bake in preheated meal-maker toaster oven at 350 degrees for 1 hour or until chicken is tender. Remove from toaster oven.

Peel bananas and cut into chunks. Add to chicken. Brush bananas with remaining sauce and return to toaster oven. Bake 10 minutes. Serve immediately.   *Makes 4 servings.*

BARBECUED CHICKEN

5	pounds chicken parts
	Salt
1	can (6 ounces) frozen orange juice concentrate, defrosted
¼	cup Worcestershire sauce

Sprinkle chicken lightly with salt. Arrange on a rack over slow burning charcoal. Broil for 30 minutes, turning once.

Or, if desired, place on rack under a preheated 375-degree broiler and broil for 30 minutes, turning once.

Meanwhile, combine orange concentrate with Worcestershire sauce; blend well. Baste chicken every 5 minutes, turning often until chicken is tender, about 15 minutes.

Leftover sauce may be refrigerated in a covered container. Use on spareribs, hamburgers or ham steaks. *Makes 8 portions.*

BARBECUE RIBS AND CHICKEN

3	pounds whole chicken, cut in quarters
3	pounds pork spareribs, cut into rib sections
	Salt and pepper
1	can (16 ounces) whole berry cranberry sauce
1	cup ketchup
½	cup vegetable oil
1	small onion, minced
	Juice of 1 lemon and 1 orange

Trim excess fat from chicken and ribs. Sprinkle chicken and ribs with salt and pepper. Place on grill 8 inches above gray coals and grill for 15 minutes each side. In a saucepan, mix together remaining ingredients and heat on grill.

Brush ribs and chicken with cranberry mixture every 5 minutes and grill ribs and chicken another 10 minutes on each side. Heat any remaining sauce; spoon over each serving. Serve with fresh sweet potatoes baked in the coals or yams and grilled wedges of fresh pineapple. To cut costs, use more chicken pieces and fewer ribs.   *Makes 6 servings.*

CANTONESE PINEAPPLE CHICKEN

3	whole or 6 half chicken breasts (about 1¾ pounds), skinned and boned (or use 2½ to 3 pounds chicken thighs)
1	package 15-minute chicken marinade
1	can (1 pound 4 ounces) pineapple chunks
2	tablespoons ketchup
2	tablespoons vinegar
2	tablespoons brown sugar
1	large onion, cut in thin wedges
1	green pepper, cut in ¼-inch wedges or slices
2	tablespoons cooking oil
1	large tomato, cut in thin wedges

Cut chicken into two-by-one-quarter-inch strips. In shallow pan, thoroughly blend 15-minute chicken marinade, liquid drained from pineapple, ketchup, vinegar and sugar. Place chicken in marinade and turn to coat evenly with marinade. Saute onion and green pepper in hot oil in skillet (10- to 12-inch), stirring until vegetables are crisp-tender. Add chicken and marinade. Cook, stirring, over medium-high heat about 5 to 7 minutes, until chicken turns white and cooks through. Add pineapple chunks and heat few minutes more. Stir in tomatoes. Serve over hot cooked rice.

Makes 4 to 5 servings.

Note: BONING WHOLE CHICKEN BREASTS: Use a sharp knife with a 6-inch blade. The thinner and sharper the blade, the better for boning.

(1) Place chicken breast, skin side down, on cutting board. With knife, cut just through white gristle at neck end of breast bone (dark bone at center of breast). Bend chicken breast back and press flat with hands to expose breast bone; loosen bone by running tip of index finger around both sides; remove in one or two pieces.

(2) Insert tip of knife under long rib bone and cut free from meat. Lifting bone away from breast, cut meat from rib cage, cutting around outer edge of breast up to shoulder joint and then through joint. (This removes entire rib cage.)

(3) Working from ends of wishbone, scrape flesh away from each piece of bone.

(4) Slip knife underneath white tendons on either side of breast and loosen and pull out. Remove skin. (Bones and skin may be used for stock.)

CHICKEN AND DUMPLINGS, WEST INDIAN STYLE

6	slices bacon, chopped
1	onion, chopped
1	stewing chicken, about 5 to 6 pounds, cut up
	Salt and pepper
2	cans (10¾ ounces each) chicken broth, undiluted
	Water
1	tablespoon Angostura aromatic bitters
3	white turnips, peeled and diced
18	small white onions, peeled
6	medium potatoes, peeled and cut into 1-inch cubes
1	cup (1 pint) light cream or half-and-half
½	cup flour

Continued

DUMPLINGS:
- 4   eggs
- 1   teaspoon salt
- ½   cup milk
- 2   cups unsifted all-purpose flour (about)

In a kettle, fry bacon and onion until crisp. Add chicken pieces, which have been sprinkled with salt and pepper, and brown pieces on all sides. Add chicken broth and water to cover. Cover kettle and simmer gently for one to one and one-half hours or until chicken is tender. Add bitters and vegetables. Stir to blend and simmer covered for another 20 to 25 minutes or until vegetables are tender. In a bowl, mix cream and flour. Pour mixture into chicken kettle and stir over low heat until sauce bubbles and thickens. Season to taste with salt and pepper.

While chicken is cooking, in a bowl, beat eggs, salt and milk until well blended. Stir in flour until batter is the consistency of muffin batter. Drop mixture by heaping tablespoons into boiling salted water. Cover and simmer for 20 minutes. Serve chicken with vegetables and gravy and dumplings, garnish with finely chopped parsley.

Makes 6 servings.

CHICKEN AND EGGPLANT CASSEROLE

- 3   tablespoons shortening
- 1   frying chicken (about 3 pounds), cut up
- 1   cup chopped onion
- 1   clove garlic, minced
- ¼   cup dry white or red wine or wine vinegar
- 1   tablespoon gravy seasoning and browning sauce, divided
- Seasoned pepper
- 1   can (1 pound) stewed tomatoes
- 1   chicken bouillon cube
- 1   tablespoon cornstarch
- 1   large eggplant
- Seasoned flour
- Salad oil

Heat shortening in heavy skillet. Fry chicken pieces until browned on all sides. Add onion, garlic and wine mixed with 2 teaspoons gravy seasoning and browning sauce. Sprinkle with a little seasoned pepper. Cover. Simmer 35 to 40 minutes until chicken is tender. Arrange chicken in single layer in shallow casserole. Heat tomatoes, crushed bouillon cube and remaining gravy seasoning in skillet used for cooking chicken. Be sure to dissolve all the brown bits left in skillet. Thicken with 1 tablespoon cornstarch dissolved in one-half cup water. Pour about half the sauce over chicken. Peel and slice

eggplant. Dip slices in seasoned flour, brown in hot oil. Arrange eggplant around chicken, cover with remaining sauce. Bake in a 375-degree oven for 25 minutes.   *Makes 4 to 6 servings.*

CHICKEN AND ROCK LOBSTER COSTA BRAVA

- 1   pound frozen South African rock lobster tails
- 4   whole chicken breasts, split
- Salt and pepper
- ¼   cup butter or margarine, melted
- 2   tablespoons dry sherry
- ½   pound mushrooms, sliced
- ¼   cup flour
- 1½   cups chicken broth
- 2   tablespoons tomato paste
- 2   tablespoons chopped chives
- 3   tomatoes, each cut into 6 wedges

Parboil frozen South African rock lobster tails by dropping into boiling salted water. When water reboils, drain immediately and drench with cold water. With scissors, remove underside membrane and pull meat out in one piece. Cut each tail into one-half-inch-thick crosswise slices.

Sprinkle chicken breasts on all sides with salt and pepper. Brush chicken with melted butter or margarine. Place in a large skillet. Sprinkle sherry over chicken. Cover skillet tightly and poach chicken in its own juices for 30 to 35 minutes or until chicken is cooked. Remove pieces of chicken to a platter and keep warm. Add mushrooms to pan juices and simmer for 5 minutes.

In a bowl mix flour and chicken broth until smooth. Stir this mixture into mushrooms. Stir in tomato paste and chives. Stir over low heat until sauce bubbles and thickens. Add rock lobster to sauce, along with tomato wedges. Simmer 2 minutes until rock lobster meat is opaque and heated through, seasoning sauce to taste with salt and pepper. Pour sauce over chicken breasts. Serve hot, with rice pilaf. *Makes 8 servings.*

CHICKEN BREASTS WITH WINE

1	whole broiler-fryer chicken breast, halved
½	teaspoon salt
⅛	teaspoon pepper
2	tablespoons butter or margarine
¼	cup dry white wine or apple juice
1	chicken bouillon cube
1	can (2 ounces) whole button mushrooms, drained
½	cup half-and-half
2	tablespoons flour

Sprinkle chicken with salt and pepper. Heat butter or margarine in frypan. Add chicken and brown on both sides. Add wine and bouillon cube. Mash bouillon cube to dissolve. Simmer uncovered for 30 minutes or until tender.

Remove chicken breasts from pan. Skim excess fat from pan juices. Add mushrooms to frypan. Mix flour with half-and-half. Stir into pan juices. Heat over low heat until sauce bubbles and thickens. Spoon sauce over chicken breasts. *Makes 2 servings.*

CHICKEN CALIFORNIA STYLE

1	broiler-fryer chicken, cut in serving pieces
½	cup flour
1½	teaspoons salt, divided
1	teaspoon curry powder
¼	cup butter or shortening
¾	cup chicken broth
¾	cup dry sherry
1	package (9 ounces) frozen artichoke hearts
2	tomatoes, cut in wedges
1	onion, sliced
½	green pepper, sliced

Coat chicken pieces with mixture of flour, 1 teaspoon salt and curry powder. Melt butter in skillet; add chicken and brown on both sides, turning once. Add chicken broth and sherry. Cover. Simmer 25 to 30 minutes, until chicken is almost tender.

Push chicken to side. Add artichoke hearts, tomatoes, onion and green pepper. Sprinkle vegetables with remaining one-half teaspoon salt. Cover. Cook just until artichokes are tender, 5 to 10 minutes. *Makes 4 servings.*

CHICKEN CAPONATA STYLE

1	medium green pepper, cut in 1-inch squares
2	cups cubed eggplant
½	teaspoon basil leaves, crushed
2	tablespoons butter or margarine
1	can (10½ ounces) chicken gravy
1	cup cooked chicken, cut in strips
½	cup drained, cut up canned tomatoes
	Cooked noodles

In a saucepan, cook green pepper and eggplant with basil in butter until tender. Add remaining ingredients except noodles. Heat; stir occasionally. Serve over cooked noodles.

Makes about 3 cups, 4 servings.

CHICKEN ENCHILADAS

CREPES:

1	cup milk
¾	cup enriched corn meal
½	cup all-purpose flour
2	eggs
¼	teaspoon salt

FILLING AND TOPPING:

3	tablespoons butter or margarine
3	tablespoons all-purpose flour
1	can(10¾ ounces) condensed chicken broth
1	tablespoon instant minced onion
1	tablespoon dried parsley flakes
1	tablespoon lemon juice
2	teaspoons chili powder
2	cups chopped cooked chicken
1	16-ounce can refried beans
1	10-ounce can enchilada sauce

FOR CREPES: In medium bowl, combine all ingredients, mixing until batter is fairly smooth. Let stand 10 minutes; stir. Heat 6- to 7-inch crepe pan or skillet over medium-high heat. Grease lightly. For each crepe, pour about 2 tablespoons batter into a hot, prepared pan. Immediately tilt pan to coat bottom evenly with thin layer of batter. Cook 45 seconds or until top looks dry. Turn; cook about 20 seconds. Stack crepes between sheets of wax paper. *Makes 12 crepes.*

Continued

FOR FILLING AND TOPPING: In medium saucepan, melt butter; blend in flour. Add chicken broth, onion, parsley, lemon juice and chili powder. Bring to a boil; cook 1 minute, stirring constantly, or until thickened. Add chicken and beans; mix well.

Heat oven to 350 degrees. Spoon about ⅓ cup chicken mixture across center of each crepe; roll up. Arrange filled crepes in ungreased 13-by-9-inch baking dish. Spoon enchilada sauce over crepes; cover with foil. Bake about 25 minutes or until heated through. Serve with sour cream and pepperoncinis or chili peppers. Garnish with chopped tomato, avocado or ripe olive slices, if desired.

Makes 12 enchiladas.

CHICKEN LEGS DIJONNAISE

	Juice of 1 lemon
½	teaspoon tarragon leaves
1	teaspoon Dijon mustard
4	tablespoons soft butter
6	chicken legs
	Salt

Mix together first four ingredients and let sit at room temperature for half an hour to allow flavors to blend. With fingers, carefully lift up skin from chicken legs to make space for mustard-butter mixture. Allow one teaspoon of mixture for filling second joint area and one teaspoon for drumstick area. Place filling between skin and meat and then press down skin to spread filling evenly in area. Salt chicken legs and broil, 6 to 8 inches from source of heat, turning twice until completely cooked.

Makes about 6 servings.

CHICKEN TACOS

2½	cups diced cooked chicken
2	tablespoons vegetable oil
1	medium-sized onion, chopped
½	medium-sized green pepper, chopped
1	teaspoon salt
	Pepper to taste
1½	teaspoons chili powder
1	can (8 ounces) tomato sauce
1	jar (8 ounces) mild taco sauce, divided
12	taco shells, heated
1	cup shredded lettuce
1	tomato, chopped
1	cup shredded Cheddar cheese

Heat oil in a large frypan. Add onion and green pepper; cook until tender. Add chicken, salt, pepper, chili powder, tomato sauce and one-half jar taco sauce. Cook uncovered over low heat for 15 minutes, stirring occasionally. Spoon hot mixture into taco shells. Drizzle remaining taco sauce over chicken mixture. Top with shredded lettuce, chopped tomato and cheese.

Makes 12 tacos or 6 servings.

CHICKEN TANGERINE

1	chicken breast
	Teriyaki sauce
	Olive oil
	Juice of ½ lemon
1	teaspoon honey
	Tangerine sections

Slice chicken in strips. Marinate 15 minutes in teriyaki sauce.

Saute 5 minutes in hot olive oil. Add lemon juice and honey, being certain oil is very hot.

Add tangerine sections. Serve over rice.

Makes 1 serving.

CHIMICHANGAS

2	pounds cooked chicken, shredded
½	cup chopped onion
2	medium cloves garlic, minced
3	tablespoons salad oil
1	can (24 fluid ounces) cocktail vegetable juice
1	teaspoon salt
1	teaspoon ground cumin seed
¼	teaspoon pepper
12	flour tortillas (10 inch)
	Salsa Cruda (recipe follows)

To make filling, in skillet, brown chicken and cook onion with garlic in oil until tender. Add cocktail vegetable juice and seasonings. Bring to boil; reduce heat. Cook over low heat 15 minutes or until liquid is absorbed. Stir occasionally. To make chimichangas, spoon about ½ cup filling in center of each tortilla. Fold left and right sides over filling. Turn over; fold open ends under. In skillet, cook chimichangas seam-side down in ½-inch deep fat at 375 degrees until golden brown. Turn; cook until top side is golden brown. Drain on absorbent towels. Serve with Salsa Cruda.

Makes 12 chimichangas, 12 servings.

	SALSA CRUDA:
2	medium tomatoes, chopped
2	canned pickled jalapeno chilies, minced
1	small onion, grated
1	teaspoon finely chopped coriander leaves or Chinese parsley
1½	teaspoons salt

In small bowl, combine all ingredients.

Makes about 2 cups.

CHINESE CHICKEN AND CELERY

3	whole chicken breasts, skinned, boned and split
3	teaspoons cornstarch, divided
¼	teaspoon ground black pepper
7	teaspoons soy sauce, divided
5	tablespoons oil, divided
6	cups thinly sliced celery
1	cup thinly sliced carrots
1	cup sliced scallions (green onions)
1	chicken bouillon cube
½	cup boiling water
1	can (1 pound) bean sprouts, undrained
½	teaspoon ground ginger

Cut chicken breasts into 1-inch chunks. Place in medium bowl. Sprinkle with 1 teaspoon cornstarch, black pepper and 1 teaspoon soy sauce. Toss to coat chicken completely.

In very large skillet or wok, heat 3 tablespoons oil until hot. Add chicken a few pieces at a time. Brown on all sides. Remove and set aside.

Add remaining 2 tablespoons oil. Heat until hot. Add celery, carrots and scallions. Saute for 5 minutes.

Dissolve bouillon cube in boiling water. Add to skillet along with bean sprouts. Cook and stir, scraping drippings from bottom of skillet, for 1 minute.

Blend 2 tablespoons plus 2 teaspoons cornstarch with 2 tablespoons soy sauce and ½ teaspoon ginger.

Stir in a little of hot liquid from skillet. Then blend into skillet. Cook and stir until mixture boils and thickens.

Return chicken to skillet. Simmer, covered, for 5 minutes. Do not overcook. Serve immediately with cooked rice, if desired. *Makes 6 servings.*

CINNAMON-APRICOT CHICKEN

2	chickens (2½ pounds each), cut into eighths
1	teaspoon salt
¼	teaspoon ground black pepper
1	jar (12 ounces) apricot preserves
¼	cup mayonnaise
3	tablespoons instant minced onion
2	tablespoons ketchup
1	teaspoon ground cinnamon

Sprinkle chickens with salt and black pepper. Place on a rack in a shallow open roasting pan. Bake in a preheated 450-degree oven for 20 minutes. Remove rack. Reduce oven temperature to 325. Combine preserves, mayonnaise, minced onion, ketchup and cinnamon. Spoon over chickens in pan. Cover and bake for 25 minutes. Uncover, spoon some of the sauce over chicken. Return to oven and bake uncovered, until golden brown, 10 to 15 minutes longer. *Makes 8 portions.*

CITRUS CHICKEN ORIENTAL

3	whole broiler-fryer chicken breasts, boned, skinned, and cut into 2-inch pieces
¾	teaspoon salt (optional)
¼	teaspoon ground ginger
2	tablespoons vegetable oil
1	small garlic clove, minced
1	can (8¼ ounces) pineapple chunks, undrained
1	cup orange juice, divided
1	envelope instant chicken bouillon
2	tablespoons wine vinegar
⅓	cup sliced celery
1	small green pepper, cut into ¼-inch strips
1	small onion, sliced
1	small tomato, cut in wedges
2	tablespoons soy sauce
1	tablespoon sugar
3	tablespoons flour

Sprinkle chicken with salt and ginger. Heat oil in large skillet, over medium heat; add chicken and garlic and cook 5 minutes. Add liquid from canned pineapple, ¾ cup orange juice, bouillon and vinegar. Cover; simmer 10 minutes. Add celery, green pepper and onion. Cover, cook 5 minutes longer. Add tomato wedges and pineapple chunks. In small bowl, blend together soy sauce, sugar, flour and remaining ¼ cup orange juice. Add to skillet and cook, stirring constantly, until mixture thickens and comes to boiling; cook 1 minute longer. Serve over hot cooked rice, if desired. *Makes 4 servings.*

COUNTRY-STYLE CHICKEN

1	can (about 2 ounces) sliced mushrooms, drained
1	cup diagonally sliced celery
½	cup diagonally sliced carrot
4	tablespoons butter or margarine
1	cup chicken broth
2	tablespoons cornstarch
1	tablespoon soy sauce
½	cup sliced radishes
	Generous dash pepper
1	cup (5 ounces) boned chicken or turkey, cut up
	Cooked rice

Continued

In saucepan, brown mushrooms and cook celery and carrot in butter until just tender. Stir in remaining ingredients except chicken and rice. Cook, stirring, until thickened. Add chicken; heat. Serve over rice.   *Makes 3 cups, 2 servings.*

CURRIED OVEN-BAKED "FRIED" CHICKEN

½   cup dry bread crumbs
2   teaspoons curry powder
2   teaspoons onion powder
¾   teaspoon salt
¼   teaspoon garlic powder
1/16   teaspoon ground red pepper
1   chicken (2½ pounds), cut into eighths
    Milk

Combine bread crumbs, curry powder, onion powder, salt, garlic powder and red pepper. Mix well. Dip chicken in milk and roll in crumb mixture. Place in buttered baking pan. Bake in a preheated 375-degree oven until chicken is done, 45 to 50 minutes.   *Makes 4 portions.*

EASY CHICKEN-SPAGHETTI CACCIATORE

1   chicken (2 pounds), cut up, skin removed
2   tablespoons butter or margarine
½   cup chopped onions
½   teaspoon salt
1   jar (16 ounces) spaghetti sauce with ground beef
1   cup water
¾   cup sliced carrots
1   cup rotini or elbow macaroni
3   tablespoons chopped parsley

In a 10-inch skillet, saute chicken in butter until golden. Add onions and continue cooking for 5 minutes.

Drain off excess fat. Add salt, spaghetti sauce and water. Cover. Simmer for 10 minutes. Add carrots and macaroni. Cover. Continue simmering for 25 minutes.

Garnish with chopped parsley.
                Makes 4 to 6 servings.

EVERGLADES CHICKEN AND CELERY CASSEROLE

4   tablespoons salad oil
1   chicken (2½ to 3 pounds), cut into 8 pieces
1   cup regular cooking rice, uncooked
½   cup chopped onion
1   clove garlic, finely minced
2   cups water
3   chicken bouillon cubes
2   teaspoons paprika
¾   teaspoon salt
⅛   teaspoon ground black pepper
1   stalk celery
1   tablespoon basil leaves

In a Dutch oven or heavy saucepan heat oil. Add chicken and brown well. Remove chicken; set aside. Add rice, onion and garlic. Saute for 5 minutes, stirring constantly. Add water, bouillon cubes, paprika, salt and black pepper. Bring to the boiling point. Return chicken to Dutch oven. Cover and simmer for 15 minutes. Meanwhile, trim celery, removing sufficient leaves to make one-third cup chopped. Cut celery into 1-inch pieces (makes about 6 cups). Add celery to Dutch oven. Cover and simmer for 15 minutes. Add celery leaves and basil. Continue simmering until chicken and rice are tender, about 7 minutes.   *Makes 4 portions.*

FAVORITE CHICKEN

2   chicken legs (about 1 pound)
1   tablespoon shortening
1   can (7½ ounces) semi-condensed cream of mushroom with wine soup

In small skillet, brown chicken in shortening; pour off fat. Stir in soup. Cover; cook over low heat 45 minutes or until done. Stir occasionally.
                Makes 2 servings.

GOLDEN BAKED CHICKEN

1   broiler-fryer chicken, cut in serving pieces
1   can (8¾ ounces) crushed pineapple, drained
¼   cup honey
2   tablespoons lemon juice
2   tablespoons prepared yellow mustard
3   tablespoons sesame seeds
1   teaspoon salt

Place chicken skin side down in a foil-lined baking pan. Mix together remaining ingredients. Spread half of mixture over chicken. Bake in a 375-degree oven for 30 minutes.

Turn chicken. Spread with remaining sauce. Return to oven. Bake 30 minutes more or until chicken is tender. *Makes 4 servings.*

GRILLED CHICKEN BREASTS STUFFED WITH SHRIMP

1	cup chopped fresh mushrooms
1	red and 1 green pepper, chopped
2	tablespoons butter or margarine
½	pound small shrimp, cooked, shelled and deveined
2	cups herb stuffing mix
¾	cup cranberry juice cocktail
1	egg, well beaten
8	whole boned chicken breasts Salt and pepper
1	cup prepared Italian oil and vinegar salad dressing
½	cup jellied cranberry sauce

In a skillet, saute red and green peppers and mushrooms in butter 5 minutes. Chop shrimp and add to mushroom mixture. Stir in stuffing mix, cranberry juice cocktail and egg. Sprinkle chicken with salt and pepper and stuff with mixture. Secure chicken breasts with skewers.

Place on grill 8 inches above gray coals and grill for 10 minutes on each side. In a bowl, beat salad dressing with cranberry sauce until smooth. Brush mixture over chicken breasts every 5 minutes while grilling breasts another 15 minutes on each side. Serve with foil-wrapped grilled whole baked apples or pears and ears of baked corn in their husks.

Makes 8 servings.

KENNET SQUARE BAKED CHICKEN AND VEGETABLES

1	pound fresh mushrooms or 2 (6- to 8-ounce) cans sliced mushrooms
1	chicken (2½ pounds), cut into eighths
1	chicken bouillon cube
¾	cup boiling water
1	cup carrots, cut into 1-inch chunks
½	pound green beans, cut into 1-inch lengths, or 1 package (8 ounces) frozen cut green beans, thawed
1½	teaspoons basil leaves, crumbled
1¼	teaspoons salt
⅛	teaspoon ground black pepper
2	tablespoons flour
2	tablespoons cold water

Rinse, pat dry and halve fresh mushrooms. Or drain canned mushrooms. Set aside.

Arrange chicken on rack in 13-by-9-by-2-inch baking pan. Bake in preheated 450-degree oven until browned, about 20 minutes.

Remove chicken from rack. Pour off any chicken fat from pan.

Dissolve bouillon cube in boiling water. Stir into baking pan with carrots, green beans, basil, salt, pepper and reserved mushrooms.

Add chicken, spooning some of sauce over chicken. Cover and bake in preheated 350-degree oven until chicken and vegetables are fork tender, about 1 hour.

In medium saucepan, combine flour with cold water. Blend in liquid from baking pan. Cook and stir until mixture boils and thickens.

Pour over chicken and vegetables. Serve with cooked rice, if desired. *Makes 4 portions.*

LEMON-MUSHROOM CHICKEN

1	pound fresh mushrooms
⅓	cup coarsely chopped onion
¾	cup butter or margarine, divided
½	teaspoon salt
⅛	teaspoon ground black pepper
3	whole chicken breasts, boned, skinned and halved (8 ounces)
⅓	cup lemon juice
2½	cups soft bread crumbs
1½	teaspoons dill weed, crushed
1	egg, lightly beaten
¼	cup white wine

Continued

Rinse and pat dry mushrooms. Slice ¼ pound of the mushrooms (to make about 1½ cups); finely chop remaining mushrooms (about 3 cups). Place chopped mushrooms and onion in a clean cloth. Twist cloth tightly to extract as much moisture as possible. (Use the liquid in soups, stews, etc.)

In a large skillet, melt ¼ cup of the butter. Add mushroom and onion mixture, salt and black pepper; saute until tender and most of the liquid has evaporated, about 7 minutes, stirring frequently. Remove with a slotted spoon; set aside to cool.

Add sliced mushrooms to skillet; saute until golden, about 5 minutes. Set aside.

Preheat oven to 375 degrees. Flatten each chicken breast between pieces of waxed paper. Dip each breast in lemon juice. Place 1 rounded tablespoon of the reserved mushroom mixture in center; roll from the short side, tucking in sides. Repeat.

Combine bread crumbs with dill. Dip each chicken piece in egg and coat with bread crumb mixture. Place in a shallow baking pan.

Combine wine with remaining ½ cup butter, melted; pour over chicken. Bake, uncovered, for 30 minutes, basting frequently with pan drippings.

Heat reserved sauteed mushrooms until hot; spoon over chicken. *Makes 6 portions.*

LEMON-PEARED CHICKEN SUPREME

1	chicken fryer (2½ to 3 pounds), cut up
½	lemon
	Salt, as needed
¼	cup butter or margarine
½	teaspoon grated lemon peel
¼	cup sherry (or chicken stock or water)
1	Bosc pear, cored and sliced
1	or 2 teaspoons flour
¼	to ⅓ cup water
	Paprika, if desired

Rub chicken with lemon, squeezing juice onto chicken; sprinkle with salt to taste. Let stand 15 minutes. In skillet, brown chicken well in butter or margarine. Drain excess fat; pour sherry over chicken. Simmer, covered, 30 to 40 minutes or until chicken is tender; turn once during simmering. Add pear, simmer, covered, 5 to 10 minutes or until pear is cooked but firm. Remove chicken and pear to warm serving platter. Blend flour into drippings; cook until thickened. Add water to desired consistency. Spoon sauce over chicken and pear; sprinkle with paprika, if desired. *Makes 3 or 4 servings.*

MARASCHINO CHERRY CHICKEN DINNER

1	jar (4 ounces) red maraschino cherries
2	tablespoons butter or margarine
1	chicken breast (about 7 ounces), split
1½	cups water
3	chicken bouillon cubes
¼	teaspoon thyme, crushed
¼	cup orange juice
¼	teaspoon grated orange peel
1	tablespoon flour
1	cup hot cooked wide egg noodles
	Parsley for garnish

Drain cherries reserving 3 tablespoons maraschino cherry syrup. Cut cherries into quarters. Set aside. In a medium skillet, melt butter. Add chicken; brown well on both sides. Add water, bouillon cubes and thyme. Heat to boiling. Stir to dissolve bouillon cubes. Reduce heat to low; cover and simmer 45 minutes, or until chicken is tender, turning occasionally.

Remove chicken to serving platter; keep warm. Skim off any excess fat from broth mixture. Add orange juice and orange peel to broth mixture in skillet. Stir reserved cherry syrup into flour until smooth; add to mixture in skillet. Heat, stirring constantly, until thickened. Stir in cherries.

To serve, arrange noodles around chicken. Garnish with parsley. Spoon some of cherry sauce over noodles and chicken. Pass remaining sauce. *Makes 2 servings.*

MEXICAN PARTY CHICKEN

3	cups diced cooked chicken
1	can (4 ounces) chopped green chili peppers
1	can (10 ounces) mild enchilada sauce
1	can (10¾ ounces) condensed cream of mushroom soup
1	package (9¼ ounces) corn chips, coarsely crushed
1	medium sized onion (½ cup), chopped
1	cup (4 ounces) pasteurized process cheese spread, shredded

Mix chicken, chili peppers, enchilada sauce and soup in saucepan. Heat slowly, stirring often, until bubbly. Place ⅓ of corn chips in bottom of greased baking dish. Top with half of the chicken mixture. Top with half of the chopped onion and half of the cheese. Layer ⅓ of the corn chips, remaining chicken, onion and cheese. Top with remaining corn chips. Bake in 375-degree oven for 35 to 40 minutes or until heated through and cheese bubbles. *Makes 6 servings.*

NEAPOLITAN CHICKEN

1	small onion, finely chopped
1	tablespoon butter or margarine
1	jar (15½ ounces) old-world-style spaghetti sauce, traditional style
¼	cup firmly packed brown sugar
¼	cup lemon juice
2	tablespoons vinegar
1	tablespoon Worcestershire sauce
1	teaspoon prepared mustard
½	teaspoon salt
2	chickens (about 2½ pounds *each*), cut up

In saucepan, saute onion in butter until translucent. Add next 7 ingredients; simmer 30 minutes, stirring occasionally.

Grill chicken 4 to 5 inches from heat about 40 to 45 minutes, turning and basting occasionally with sauce.   *Makes 6 to 8 servings.*

NECTARINE-CHICKEN TOSTADAS

4	tortillas (6 inches diameter)
	Oil
¼	cup chopped green onion
1	tablespoon butter
1	(8-ounce) can tomato sauce
2	tablespoons chopped canned green chili
½	teaspoon chili powder
½	teaspoon garlic salt
1½	cups shredded cooked chicken
2	fresh nectarines
3	cups shredded crisp lettuce
¾	cup shredded Cheddar or Jack cheese

Fry each tortilla separately in hot oil (about ¼-inch deep) a few seconds on each side until crisp and golden. Remove to paper towels to drain. Saute onion in butter a minute. Add tomato sauce, green chili, chili powder and garlic salt. Simmer 10 to 15 minutes. Add chicken strips. Halve, remove pit and cut nectarines into slices. Place each tortilla on a serving plate. Spoon on chicken mixture. Top with lettuce, sliced nectarines and cheese.

Makes 4 servings.

ORANGEY-RICH CHICKEN

1	package (32 ounces) frozen fried chicken pieces
1	can (6 ounces) frozen Florida orange juice concentrate
¾	cup currant jelly

½	cup chili sauce
¼	cup frozen chopped green pepper
2	tablespoons frozen lemon juice, thawed
1	teaspoon salt

Arrange chicken pieces in shallow baking pan. Heat according to package instructions. Combine all remaining ingredients in saucepan. Simmer 10 minutes, stirring occasionally, until jelly melts and sauce is heated. Spoon over cooked chicken and bake 5 minutes longer. Serve hot, with rice or noodles.

Makes 6 servings.

PARMESAN CHICKEN BAKE

6	medium baking potatoes (about 2 pounds)
2	tablespoons butter or margarine
1	can (10¾ ounces) condensed cream of chicken soup
½	cup grated Parmesan cheese
2	tablespoons chopped parsley
1	cup cubed cooked chicken

Bake potatoes until done. Cut potatoes in half lengthwise; scoop out insides, leaving a thin shell. With electric mixer, mash potatoes with butter. Gradually add soup, cheese and parsley; beat until light and fluffy. Fold in chicken. Spoon into shells; sprinkle with additional Parmesan cheese. Arrange potatoes in 3-quart shallow baking dish (13-by-9-by-2-inch). Bake at 450 degrees for 15 minutes or until hot.   *Makes 3 to 4 servings.*

POLYNESIAN CHICKEN WITH BISCUITS

2	tablespoons butter or margarine
⅓	cup flour
1	teaspoon salt
¼	teaspoon pepper
2½–3	pounds frying chicken, cut up
1	can (13¼ ounces) pineapple chunks, drained (reserve ¼ cup syrup)
½	cup celery (cut in 1-inch diagonal slices)
1	small green pepper, sliced into rings
1	small onion, sliced and separated into rings
⅓	cup sliced stuffed green olives
1	can (10¾ ounces) condensed tomato soup
¼	cup plus 2 tablespoons chili sauce
¼	cup reserved pineapple syrup
1	can (10 biscuits) refrigerated buttermilk or country-style biscuits
2	tablespoons chili sauce

Continued

In oven, melt butter in 13×9-inch pan while preheating to 400 degrees. In a paper bag, combine flour, salt and pepper. Add 2 or 3 chicken pieces at a time. Shake to coat. Place chicken, skin side down, in butter. Bake 2 minutes; turn chicken. Top chicken with pineapple, celery, green pepper, onion and olives. Combine soup, ¼ cup chili sauce and reserved pineapple syrup. Pour over chicken. Cover pan with foil. Bake 30 to 35 minutes until tender. Move chicken to center of pan. Separate biscuit dough into 10 biscuits. Arrange around chicken. Brush biscuits with 2 tablespoons chili sauce. Bake 10 to 20 minutes until biscuits are golden brown. Serve immediately. (Refrigerate leftovers.)

Makes 4 to 6 servings.

POULET A LA NORMANDE

6	chicken breast halves
	Salt and pepper
	Flour
½	cup butter, divided
¼	cup olive oil
4	shallots, chopped
1	carrot, chopped
⅓	cup Calvados
1	cup French dry white wine
1	cup (½ pint) heavy cream
2	tablespoons flour
1	can (10 ounces) marrons au naturel (chestnuts) drained
3	Granny Smith or other crisp, tart apples, peeled, cored and cut into wedges

Sprinkle chicken on all sides with salt and pepper. Roll chicken in flour, shaking off excess.

In large skillet, heat oil and ¼ cup butter. Brown chicken on all sides. Remove chicken. Saute shallots, celery and carrot in drippings. Stir in Calvados and white wine.

Add chicken. Cover and simmer gently for 40 to 45 minutes or until chicken is tender. Remove chicken and place on platter.

In bowl, mix heavy cream and 2 tablespoons flour. Stir cream mixture into pan juices. Stir over low heat until sauce thickens and bubbles. Add chestnuts and simmer 5 minutes. Pour sauce over chicken.

Heat the remaining ¼ cup butter in skillet. Saute the apple wedges until they are translucent and tender but still hold their shape. Place apples on platter with chicken.   *Makes 6 servings.*

QUICK SWEET-AND-SOUR CHICKEN

1	medium green pepper, cut in strips
1	medium clove garlic, minced
⅛	teaspoon ground ginger
2	tablespoons salad oil
1	can (about 8 ounces) chunk pineapple in pure pineapple juice, undrained
2	tablespoons brown sugar
½	cup water
3	tablespoons vinegar
1	tablespoon soy sauce
4	teaspoons cornstarch
2	cans (5 ounces each) chunk white chicken
½	cup sliced radishes
	Chinese noodles

In skillet, cook green pepper with garlic and ginger in oil until tender. Add pineapple and brown sugar. Mix water, vinegar, soy and cornstarch. Gradually blend into pineapple mixture. Cook, stirring, until thickened. Add chicken and radishes; heat. Serve over Chinese noodles.

Makes about 3½ cups, 4 servings.

ROAST CHICKEN WITH VEGETABLES

1	frying chicken (about 2 pounds)
	Salt and pepper
½	cup margarine, softened
	Paprika
1½	pounds small round potatoes (8 to 9), peeled and halved, or 1¼ pounds potatoes (4 medium) peeled and quartered
2	carrots, peeled and halved lengthwise
1	onion, quartered
3	tablespoons lemon juice
¼	cup chopped parsley
1	teaspoon capers (optional)
¼	teaspoon garlic salt
⅛	teaspoon pepper

If chicken is frozen, thaw and remove giblets from cavity. Season cavity with salt and pepper. Rub skin with 1 tablespoon of the margarine. Sprinkle lightly with paprika.

Place in a roasting pan with potatoes, carrots and onion. Roast in a preheated 350-degree oven for 1 to 1½ hours, basting every 20 minutes with special basting sauce made by melting remaining margarine with remaining ingredients.

When vegetables are tender, arrange with chicken and juices on warmed platter.

Makes 4 servings.

SAME CHICKEN WITH PIQUANT CURRY SAUCE

½	cup flour
2	tablespoons sesame seeds
½	teaspoon salt
⅛	teaspoon pepper
1	frying chicken, (2½ pounds) cut in serving pieces
1	egg, beaten
2	tablespoons salad oil
1	can (10½ ounces) condensed cream of chicken soup
⅓	cup milk
1¼	teaspoons curry powder
½	cup coarsely chopped sweet mixed pickles

Combine flour, sesame seeds, salt and pepper. Mix well.

Dip chicken in egg. Coat with flour mixture. Cook in oil until lightly browned on all sides.

Combine remaining ingredients. Mix well. Pour over chicken.

Cover and cook over low heat until chicken is tender, about 30 minutes. Serve with hot rice and assorted condiments, as desired. *Makes 4 servings.*

SESAME FRIED CHICKEN

4	whole chicken breasts, skinned, boned, halved
1	egg, slightly beaten
1	teaspoon sugar
1	teaspoon flavor enhancer
½	teaspoon salt
¼	teaspoon pepper
¼	teaspoon baking powder
½	cup flour
1	cup sesame seeds
1	quart (about) corn oil

In a bowl, stir together egg, sugar, flavor enhancer, salt, pepper, baking powder, and 1 tablespoon of the flour until smooth. Dip chicken in mixture. Place on waxed paper. Sprinkle both sides of chicken with sesame seeds. Coat with remaining flour. Pour corn oil into heavy, sturdy flat-bottomed 3-quart saucepan or deep fryer, filling utensil no more than one-third full. Heat over medium heat to 375 degrees. Carefully add chicken a few pieces at a time. Fry about 5 minutes or until chicken is golden brown. Drain on paper towels. *Makes 8 servings.*

SHANGHAI RICE WITH CHICKEN

2	cups cooked rice
¼	cup julienne carrot sticks (1 inch)
2	tablespoons salad oil
2	eggs, slightly beaten
½	cup diagonally sliced green onions
2	cans (5 ounces each chunk thigh chicken)
2	tablespoons soy sauce
½	tablespoon sugar

In skillet, brown rice and cook carrot in oil until tender. Add eggs and green onions. Cook until eggs are set, stirring often. Add remaining ingredients. Heat; stir occasionally.

Makes about 3½ cups, 4 servings.

SPICY ORANGE CHICKEN

2	whole chicken breasts, boned, skinned, cubed into 1-inch pieces
1	teaspoon cornstarch
1	cup yellow onion, cubed into 1-inch pieces
4	scallions, cut into 2-inch lengths
5	chili peppers, minced or to taste (optional)
2	teaspoons ginger, minced
¼	cup fresh orange zest, cut into 2-inch strips
¾	teaspoon Szechuan chili paste with garlic
1	tablespoon hoisin sauce
2	tablespoons dark soy sauce
2	tablespoons orange juice
¾	teaspoon granulated sugar
1	teaspoon distilled white vinegar
1	teaspoon sesame oil
3	tablespoons pure peanut oil (for frying)

Prepare all of the ingredients. Combine chicken and cornstarch and mix well. Refrigerate for 30 minutes.

Combine onions and scallions. Combine peppers and ginger. Combine chili paste with garlic, hoisin sauce, soy sauce, orange juice and sugar.

Add peanut oil to wok and heat until hot. Add peppers and ginger and stir-fry for 10 seconds. Add chicken and stir-fry until it loses its pink appearance. Add onions and scallions and stir-fry for 15 seconds.

Add orange zest and stir-fry for 30 seconds. Add vinegar and stir-fry for 15 seconds. Add sesame oil and mix well. Serve with rice. *Makes 4 servings.*

STEWED CHICKEN

1	broiler-fryer chicken (about 3½ pounds), cut in parts
3	cups water
1	small onion, quartered
3	sprigs parsley
2	pieces celery (about 3 inches each) with leaves
1	bay leaf
3	peppercorns
1	teaspoon salt
3	tablespoons butter or margarine
3	tablespoons flour

Place chicken in large pot. Add water, onion, parsley, celery, bay leaf, peppercorns and salt. Bring water to boiling. Cover tightly and reduce heat. Simmer 1 hour or until fork can be inserted into chicken with ease.

Remove chicken from broth. Strain broth, cool slightly and skim fat from surface. In a saucepan, melt butter or margarine. Stir in flour. Heat until mixture bubbles. Remove from heat.

Gradually stir in 3 cups of chicken broth. Cook, stirring constantly, until mixture thickens. Arrange homemade noodles on a platter, top with chicken parts, pour gravy over all.   *Makes 4 servings.*

SUSIE'S HERBED FRIED CHICKEN

2	chickens (2½ to 3 pounds each), cut into eighths
1	cup all-purpose flour
½	cup dry bread crumbs
1	tablespoon onion powder
2	teaspoons paprika
2	teaspoons salt
1½	teaspoons poultry seasoning
¼	teaspoon ground black pepper
	Oil

Dredge chicken pieces in flour mixed with bread crumbs, onion powder, paprika, salt, poultry seasoning and black pepper. Fry, a few pieces at a time, in deep oil preheated to 400 degrees until golden and tender, about 20 minutes. Or, if desired, pour oil to depth of 1-inch in a large skillet. Heat until hot. Add chicken to skillet, being careful not to overcrowd. Brown slowly on both sides. Return all browned chicken to skillet. Cover and cook slowly, turning once, until chicken is tender, about 30 minutes. Remove cover last 5 minutes of cooking for a crispy crust.   *Makes 8 to 10 portions.*

SWEET-AND-SOUR CHICKEN

2	chicken drumsticks with thighs
	or
	2 chicken breasts, split
1	tablespoon flour
¼	teaspoon salt
	Dash pepper
1½	tablespoons salad oil
1½	cups cooked rice
¼	cup sliced onion
¼	cup diced green pepper
1	cup canned chicken broth
1	tablespoon light molasses
1½	teaspoons cider vinegar
1	tablespoon soy sauce
	Dash pepper
¼	teaspoon garlic powder
½	cup pineapple chunks and 2 tablespoons liquid from can
1½	teaspoons cornstarch

Wash and pat chicken dry. Combine flour, salt and pepper. Coat chicken. In hot salad oil, saute chicken until browned. Remove pieces to a 1½-quart casserole along with the rice. Pour off all but ½ tablespoon drippings and saute onion and green pepper until tender-crisp. Add chicken broth, molasses, vinegar, soy sauce, pepper and garlic powder; mix well. Add drained pineapple and heat until mixture simmers. Dissolve cornstarch in pineapple juice or syrup. Stir into sauce mixture and simmer until sauce thickens. Pour over chicken and rice. Cover and bake in a preheated 350-degree oven for 45 minutes.

Makes 2 servings with some left for second meal.

WALNUT CHICKEN

¼	cup soy sauce
¼	cup dry sherry
2	teaspoons sugar
1	teaspoon salt
½	teaspoon ground ginger
2	whole chicken breasts, boned, skinned and cut in 1-inch cubes
5	tablespoons cornstarch
1	egg, slightly beaten
⅓	cup corn oil
1	cup walnut halves
⅓	cup chopped green onion
1	clove garlic, crushed
2	cups chicken bouillon or stock
1	can (8½ ounces) bamboo shoots, drained
1	can (5 ounces) water chestnuts, drained and sliced
2	tablespoons water
1	cup diagonally sliced celery
	Hot cooked rice

Mix together soy sauce, sherry, sugar, salt and ginger. Marinate chicken in soy sauce mixture 2 to 3 hours at room temperature or overnight in refrigerator. Drain and reserve marinade. Dip chicken in 4 tablespoons (one-fourth cup) of the cornstarch, then in egg; drain. Heat corn oil in large skillet over medium heat. Add walnuts and cook 2 to 3 minutes or until toasted; remove from skillet. Add chicken and saute about 5 minutes. Stir in green onion and garlic. Saute 2 to 3 minutes longer. Add marinade, bouillon, bamboo shoots and water chestnuts. Simmer covered 15 minutes. Mix remaining 1 tablespoon cornstarch with water. Stir into chicken mixture. Bring to boil, stirring constantly, and boil 1 minute. Add walnuts and celery; heat about 5 minutes. Serve over rice. *Makes 6 servings.*

WINE-SAUCED CHICKEN AND GRAPES

3	tablespoons butter or margarine
2	whole chicken breasts, halved, skinned and boned
1½	cups green grapes, seeded if necessary
¾	cup dry white wine
⅓	cup sherry
2	tablespoons cornstarch
¾	cup chicken broth
3	tablespoons chopped parsley
½	teaspoon salt
⅛	teaspoon *each* pepper and dried tarragon, crushed

Melt butter in large skillet. Cut chicken into ½-by-¼-by-2-inch strips. Saute in butter until chicken turns opaque. Add grapes and wines; simmer, uncovered, 5 minutes or until grapes are heated through. Stir occasionally. Transfer chicken and grapes to chafing dish. Dissolve cornstarch in chicken broth; add to pan juices with parsley and seasonings. Cook and stir until thickened and clear. Pour over chicken and grapes.

Makes 4 to 6 servings.

VARIATION: Substitute 1 cup leftover cooked turkey strips for the chicken.

TURKEY

CURRY-BARBECUED TURKEY THIGHS

3	tablespoons butter or margarine
1	clove garlic, crushed
1	large onion, finely chopped
3	tablespoons flour
1	tablespoon curry powder
	Salt to taste
⅛	teaspoon ground cinnamon
1	can (13¾ ounces)
1	cup applesauce
2	tablespoons brown sugar
4	small turkey hindquarters or thighs with drumsticks, about 1 to 1½ pounds each
	Vegetable oil

Continued

Prepare grill for barbecuing.

Melt butter or margarine in medium saucepan. Add garlic and onion. Saute until tender.

Stir in flour, curry, 1 teaspoon salt and cinnamon. Cook 1 minute, stirring constantly.

Stir in broth, applesauce and brown sugar. Heat to boiling. Simmer on low heat 5 minutes, stirring occasionally.

Rinse turkey. If whole bird, cut at joints to separate drumsticks from thighs. Brush with oil. Sprinkle with salt.

Place on grill, 6 to 8 inches above medium-hot coals. Grill 45 minutes, turning occasionally. Brush with curry sauce. Continue grilling, turning and brushing occasionally until turkey is fork-tender, about 15 minutes more.

Heat remaining curry sauce and serve separately.   *Makes 8 servings.*

DEVILED TURKEY CASSEROLE

1	onion, chopped
4	tablespoons butter
6	tablespoons flour
1	tablespoon mustard
2	teaspoons salt
2½	cups milk
1	cup celery, sliced
3	cups cooked turkey, diced
1	cup ripe olives, sliced
1	jar (2 ounces) pimiento, chopped
½	cup raisins
½	cup Bacardi dark rum (optional)
1	cup seasoned bread crumbs

In saucepan, saute onion in butter until golden. Blend in flour, mustard and salt. Add milk. Cook, stirring, until mixture thickens.

Add celery, turkey, olives, pimiento and raisins. Heat thoroughly. Add rum, if desired.

Spoon into large baking dish or casserole. Top with bread crumbs. Bake in preheated 350-degree oven for 30 minutes.   *Makes 8 to 10 servings.*

HICKORY-SMOKED TURKEY HALVES

1	small turkey (about 4 to 9 pounds), frozen and thawed, or fresh
	Melted butter
	Salt and pepper
	Hickory flakes

Remove giblets and rinse turkey off with cold water; pat dry. Cut turkey in half. Brush bone side of turkey halves with butter and sprinkle with salt and pepper. Place bone side down on grill about 5 to 6 inches from medium coals and grill for 40 to 50 minutes or until meat browns nicely. After about 15 minutes of cooking, spoon about ¼ cup of hickory flakes over coals. Lower cover or lid of grill and continue cooking 25 to 35 minutes. Brush skin side of turkey halves with melted butter and sprinkle with salt and pepper. Turn turkey halves. Sprinkle about another ¼ cup of hickory flakes over coals. Cover grill and continue cooking another 40 to 50 minutes or until turkey is cooked. To test for doneness, the drumstick should move easily and the breast meat will be fork-tender.

Note: If you are using a grill without a cover, turkey will still have a hickory-smoked flavor but it will be more subtle.

MUSHROOM-TURKEY BAKE

1	package (8 ounces) broad noodles
6	tablespoons butter or margarine, divided
1	pound fresh mushrooms or 2 cans (6 to 8 ounces each) sliced mushrooms
1	cup finely chopped onion
¼	cup finely chopped green pepper
4	cups diced cooked turkey
2	tablespoons diced pimiento
1	teaspoon poultry seasoning
1	teaspoon salt
⅛	teaspoon ground black pepper
1	cup grated Cheddar cheese
2	cups medium white sauce
½	cup water or milk
1	cup soft bread crumbs

Cook noodles in unsalted boiling water until almost tender; drain. Add 2 tablespoons of the butter; toss and set aside. Rinse, pat dry and slice fresh mushrooms, or drain canned mushrooms. In a large skillet, heat 2 tablespoons of the butter. Add mushrooms, onion and green pepper; saute 5 minutes. Add turkey, pimiento, poultry seasoning, salt and black pepper. In a 3-quart casserole, place ⅓ of the noodles; top with half of the mushroom-turkey mixture. Sprinkle with ½ cup of the cheese. Repeat, ending with noodles. Mix white sauce with water. Pour over all. Melt remaining 2 tablespoons butter; stir in bread crumbs. Sprinkle over the top. Cover and bake in a preheated 350-degree oven 30 minutes. Remove cover and raise oven temperature to 450 degrees. Bake 10 to 15 minutes longer or until crumbs are golden.   *Makes 8 to 10 portions.*

SCALLOPED TURKEY ALMONDINE

3–4	cups leftover turkey stuffing (or make sausage-almond stuffing or other favorite stuffing with 2 or 3 cups stuffing mix)
2–3	cups leftover turkey, cut into strips or pieces (or cooked turkey giblets, cut into pieces)
2–3	cups leftover gravy (or Turkey Broth Cream Sauce—recipe follows)
1	cup stuffing mix
¼	cup slivered almonds

Crumble stuffing or break into pieces. Arrange in large, flat, lightly oiled casserole.

Spread turkey over stuffing.

Heat gravy just until warm. Spoon over turkey and stuffing. Sprinkle with dry stuffing mix and then with almonds.

Bake at 350 degrees for 25 to 30 minutes or until bubbling hot and almonds and stuffing mix are browned. *Makes 6 to 8 servings.*

TURKEY BROTH CREAM SAUCE:

To 2 cups turkey broth (made by simmering wing tips, bones, giblets, etc.), add about ½ cup evaporated milk or rich milk.

Mix 2 tablespoons cornstarch with 2 tablespoons cold water. Stir into broth. Heat to simmering. Season to taste with seasoned salt and pepper.

Makes about 2½ cups sauce.

STIR-FRIED CELERY AND TURKEY

1	stalk (bunch) celery
2	tablespoons cornstarch
2	teaspoons sugar
1½	teaspoons ground ginger
¼	teaspoon garlic powder
¼	teaspoon salt
	Pinch ground black pepper
1½	cups chicken broth
3	tablespoons salad oil
2	cups diced cooked turkey
1	cup chopped nuts

Trim stem end from celery; remove leaves (use in soups, stews, salads, etc.). Separate stalk into ribs; slice on the diagonal into 1-inch pieces (makes about 6 cups). Mix cornstarch with sugar, ginger, garlic powder, salt and black pepper. Blend in chicken broth; set aside. In a large skillet or wok, heat oil until hot. Add celery; stir-fry until barely crisp-tender, about 7 minutes. Add turkey; stir-fry 1 minute. Stir in nuts and reserved chicken broth mixture. Cook and stir until mixture boils and thickens, about 1 minute. Serve immediately over steamed rice, if desired. *Makes 4 portions.*

TACCHINO TONNATO

1	5-pound turkey breast
3	cans (13¾ ounces each) chicken broth
2	cups dry white wine (or chicken broth)
2	cups water
2	onions, quartered
2	carrots, pared and cut in quarters
2	ribs celery with leaves, cut in chunks
2	bay leaves
6	sprigs parsley
2	whole cloves
¼	teaspoon Tabasco pepper sauce
	Tomato Sauce (recipe follows)

In large kettle, place turkey breast and add remaining ingredients. Cover and simmer 1 hour and 40 minutes, or until turkey is tender. Remove from heat and cool in refrigerator in stock.

When cold, remove turkey from stock and cut into slices. Reserve one-third cup stock and prepare Tonnato Sauce. Spread a little sauce over bottom of a 13-by-9-by-2-inch baking dish. Arrange turkey slices over sauce and cover with remaining sauce. Cover and refrigerate overnight.

To serve, let stand at room temperature 30 minutes. Arrange on platter and garnish with lemon slices, sliced pitted black olives, sliced scallions and watercress. Serve with marinated tomatoes and Italian bread. *Makes 6 to 8 servings.*

TONNATO SAUCE:

2	egg yolks
½	teaspoon salt
3	tablespoons lemon juice
½	teaspoon Tabasco pepper sauce
¾	cup olive oil
⅓	cup reserved turkey stock (or chicken broth)
1	can (6½ or 7 ounces) tuna, drained and flaked
6	anchovy fillets, rinsed and chopped (optional)
¼	cup heavy cream
2	tablespoons capers, rinsed and drained

Place egg yolks, salt, lemon juice and pepper sauce in container of blender. Turn motor to "combine." With motor running, slowly drip in olive oil. When sauce has thickened, turn off motor.

Add turkey stock, tuna and anchovy fillets. Cover and process at high speed until smooth. (Ingredients may be processed with rotary beater.) Pour into bowl. Stir in cream and capers.

Makes about 1½ cups.

TURKEY BREAST WITH SPICY CHERRY STUFFING

1	frozen turkey breast (about 3 pounds)
4	slices day-old whole-wheat bread
2	oranges, peeled and chopped
⅔	cup whole red maraschino cherries
2	tablespoons butter or margarine
¼	cup canned chicken broth
2	tablespoons maraschino cherry syrup
¼	teaspoon cinnamon
¼	teaspoon nutmeg
1	tablespoon melted shortening

Thaw turkey according to label directions. Wipe dry with paper towels. Cut bread into small cubes. Combine bread, oranges and cherries. In a saucepan, melt butter. Add chicken broth, cherry syrup and spices. Heat until butter is melted. Pour over bread mixture. Toss well.

Separate ribs of turkey breast. Spoon stuffing into cavity. Put a double thickness of foil over stuffing and half way down sides of turkey breast. Press to seal. Invert turkey onto rack of roasting pan. Brush with shortening. Bake in 325-degree oven about 2¼ hours or until meat thermometer reaches 170 degrees. Let stand 10 to 15 minutes. Remove stuffing and carve.   *Makes 4 to 6 servings.*

TURKEY CUTLETS

1	16-ounce package fresh or frozen turkey cutlets, thawed
½	cup enriched cornmeal
¼	cup all-purpose flour
1	teaspoon salt
½	teaspoon paprika
⅛	teaspoon pepper
2	eggs, beaten
⅓	cup butter or margarine
1	10-ounce package frozen asparagus spears or 18 fresh asparagus spears, cooked and drained
6	slices Swiss cheese
¼	cup toasted almond slices

LEMON-CHIVE SAUCE:

3	tablespoons butter or margarine
3	tablespoons all-purpose flour
1½	cups chicken broth
1	teaspoon chopped chives
2	teaspoons lemon juice

Pound turkey cutlets with meat mallet or rolling pin to ⅛-inch thickness on cutting board or between 2 sheets of wax paper.

Combine cornmeal, flour, salt and spices. Dip cutlets into egg. Coat with cornmeal mixture.

In 12-inch skillet, pan-fry cutlets in hot butter over medium-high heat for 5 to 8 minutes or until golden brown on both sides, adding additional butter if necessary. Drain on absorbent paper.

Arrange cutlets in 13-by-9-inch baking dish or on ovenproof platter to form 6 equal portions. Place 3 asparagus spears over each portion. Top each portion with cheese slice.

Bake in preheated oven at 400 degrees for 6 to 8 minutes or until cheese is melted. Sprinkle with nuts. Serve immediately with Lemon-Chive Sauce.

Makes 6 servings.

LEMON-CHIVE SAUCE: Prepare while baking cutlets. Melt butter in small saucepan over medium heat until bubbly. Add flour. Continue cooking, stirring constantly, about 1 minute.

Add broth and chives, stirring constantly. Continue cooking over medium-high heat until mixture comes to full boil, stirring constantly.

Remove from heat. Stir in lemon juice. Serve over cutlets.   *Makes about 1½ cups.*

TURKEY-PEAR SWEET-AND-SOUR

¼	cup soy sauce
2	tablespoons dry sherry (or apple juice)
1	tablespoon cornstarch
1	clove garlic, minced or pressed
3	thin slices fresh ginger root, minced, *or* ¼ teaspoon ground ginger
1¼	cups turkey or chicken breast or thigh, cut into thin strips
2	fresh pears
2	tablespoons peanut oil
1	can (8 ounces) water chestnuts, sliced
2	cups bean sprouts
1	package (6 ounces) frozen pea pods, thawed
3	cups cooked rice or crispy rice noodles
¼	cup thinly sliced green onions, optional Sweet-and-Sour Sauce (recipe follows)

In a small mixing bowl, thoroughly combine soy sauce, sherry, cornstarch, garlic and ginger; add turkey and marinate for 30 minutes, stirring occasionally.

Prepare Sweet-and-Sour Sauce. Pare, core and slice pears and assemble with all remaining ingredients at cooking area.

Heat oil in heavy frying pan or wok over high heat; add turkey, reserving marinade, stir constantly and saute for about 2 minutes; add water chestnuts, bean sprouts, pea pods and pears, stirring continuously for another 2 minutes.

Add reserved marinade and Sweet-and-Sour Sauce; cook until sauce is thickened.

Serve hot over rice or crispy rice noodles. Sprinkle with green onions, if desired.

Makes 4 servings.

SWEET-AND-SOUR SAUCE:

Mix together ½ cup chicken bouillon, ¼ cup honey, ¼ cup wine vinegar and 2 tablespoons cornstarch.

TURKEY WITH ORANGE-RICE STUFFING

½	cup uncooked brown rice (2 cups cooked)
½	cup orange juice
1	pound bulk pork sausage
¾	cup chopped onion
1	teaspoon poultry seasoning
1	cup raisins
1	cup chopped walnuts
4	oranges, sectioned, drained (reserve juice)
	Salt and pepper
1	12-pound turkey
1	cup water

Cook rice according to package directions, substituting orange juice for ½ cup of the water. Break up sausage in large skillet and cook with onion until meat is done and onion is golden but not brown. Add cooked rice, poultry seasoning, raisins, walnuts and orange sections. Mix lightly. Sprinkle salt and pepper in cavities of turkey. Stuff turkey with rice mixture. Tie legs together, then to tail. Fasten wings behind back to hold neck skin. Place in roasting pan and rub outside of turkey with orange juice reserved from sections. Cover loosely with foil. Bake in 325-degree oven for 2 hours. Uncover and continue baking 1½ to 2 hours or until turkey tests done, basting occasionally with pan drippings. Remove turkey from oven; transfer to heated platter. Add water to drippings; bring to a boil. Thicken, if desired, with 2 tablespoons flour mixed with ¼ cup cold water. *Makes 8 servings.*

Note: To section oranges, cut off peel round and round, spiral fashion. Go over fruit again, removing any remaining white membrane. Cut along side of each dividing membrane from outside to middle of core. Remove section by section over bowl to retain juice from fruit.

CORNISH HEN & PHEASANT

CORNISH HENS DELUXE

3	Rock Cornish hens (1¾ pounds each)
½	cup chopped onion
½	cup chopped green pepper
¼	cup (½ stick) plus 3 tablespoons margarine
2½	cups cold cooked rice

Continued

½   cup chopped apricots
1   tablespoon sugar
½   teaspoon salt
    Generous dash celery salt
½   cup white wine
    Salt
    Pepper

In a large skillet saute onion and green pepper in ¼ cup margarine until tender, about 5 minutes. Mix in rice, apricots, sugar, salt and celery salt. Pour in wine. Heat through. Set aside to cool. Sprinkle cavities of hens with salt and pepper. Stuff cavities with cooled rice mixture. Truss birds. Dot with remaining 3 tablespoons margarine. Sprinkle with salt and pepper. Roast at 350 degrees basting occasionally until done, about 1 hour and 15 minutes. Increase oven temperature to 400 degrees for last 10 minutes of roasting.   *Makes 6 servings.*

GAME HENS WITH CALVADOS

12 French biscottes (biscuits), crumbled
¼   cup melted butter
1   can (15½ ounces) French marrons (whole chestnuts), drained and crumbled
1   cup chicken broth
1   egg
    Salt
6   Rock Cornish game hens, thawed and giblets removed
¼   cup butter
⅓   cup Calvados (or hard cider)
½   cup chicken broth
½   cup French dry white wine
4   large shallots, minced
2   carrots, diced
1   cup chopped celery
1   teaspoon herbes de Provence (or fines herbes)
2   tomatoes, cored and diced
1   can (15 ounces) coeur de celeri, (hearts of celery), drained

In bowl, mix biscottes, butter, chestnuts, chicken broth and egg. Season to taste with salt and use mixture to stuff game hens. Sew or skewer openings. Heat butter in large skillet or roasting pan and brown game hens on all sides. Add Calvados and set aflame. When flames die, add chicken broth, white wine, shallots, carrots, celery, herbs and tomatoes. Cover tightly and simmer for 1 hour or until game hens are tender. Remove lid and add coeur de celeri on serving platter. Spoon pan juices over game hens. If desired, the pan juices may be thickened with mixture of ¼ cup flour and ½ cup chicken broth.   *Makes 6 servings.*

PHEASANT WITH WILD RICE AND APPLE STUFFING

1   package (6 ounces) long-grain and wild rice mix
1¼   cups apple cider
1   slice bacon
¼   cup chopped onion
1½   cups chopped apples
½   cup chopped pecans
½   teaspoon thyme
½   teaspoon salt
¼   teaspoon pepper
1   pheasant (2½ to 3 pounds) *or substitute a roasting chicken (same weight)*
4   slices fatty bacon
3   tablespoons butter, melted

Prepare rice mix according to package directions, substituting apple cider for half the water. Set aside.

In medium fry pan, cook bacon slice until fat is rendered (melted down). Add onions and saute until transparent. Stir in apples, pecans and seasonings; cook for 2 minutes. Combine apple mixture and rice; set aside.

Remove any remaining pin feathers from the bird, rinse and pat dry inside and out with paper towels. Stuff cavity loosely with rice stuffing mixture. Close the cavity with trussing skewers or pins. Tie the legs together and tuck the wings under the body. Cover the breast and legs of the bird with bacon. Place bird in shallow, open pan; roast at 350 degrees, 25 minutes per pound, or until internal temperature on meat thermometer is 180 degrees. Place remaining stuffing in a greased covered casserole and bake in oven for last hour of cooking. Baste bird every 20 minutes with melted butter. Remove bacon last 30 minutes of cooking time to allow pheasant to brown. Serve pheasant on a bed of wild rice and garnish with spiced crab apples and orange slices.   *Makes 2 to 3 servings.*

ORANGE-GLAZED GAME HENS

2   Rock Cornish game hens, giblets removed
      Salt and pepper
2   tablespoons melted butter
¾   cup syrup from Brandied Orange-Grape Clusters (below)
2   tablespoons soy sauce
      Brandied Orange-Grape Clusters (recipe follows)

Wash hens and pat dry. Season with salt and pepper, inside and out. Tie legs together and place hens in baking dish, breast side up. Brush with melted butter. Bake in 375-degree oven 40 minutes. In small saucepan simmer syrup and soy sauce 5 minutes. Pour over hens at end of 40 minutes and continue baking 20 minutes longer, basting twice. To serve: Arrange hens on warm serving platter and surround with grape clusters and orange strips. Heat remaining glaze, strain and pour over hens. Serve at once.   *Makes 2 servings.*

Note: Recipe can be doubled or tripled.

BRANDIED ORANGE-GRAPE CLUSTERS:

4	cups sugar
2	cups water
2½	pounds grapes in small clusters
	Peel of 1 orange, cut into ¼-inch strips
1	cup brandy
¼	cup orange-flavored liqueur

Combine sugar and water in saucepan and bring to a boil. Reduce heat and simmer 5 minutes. While syrup is simmering, arrange grapes and orange peel in storage jars or a crock. Remove syrup from heat and stir in brandy and liqueur. Pour over grapes, cool and cover. Keep refrigerated.   *Makes 2 quarts.*

Fish & Seafood Dishes

"Fish dinners will make a man spring like a flea," went the line of a seventeenth-century song once dear to Sir Henry Morgan's buccaneers.

The buccaneers were on the right track, because fish and seafood protein in your diet can make you feel more energetic.

Fish is an important ingredient in a healthful diet. I remember having freshwater fish, even during the bitter winter months in the Midwest, hooked through the ice by the hardy men in the family.

We now are fortunate in all parts of the country to have access to freshwater and saltwater catches year round. Fish farming of such delicacies as trout, catfish, oysters, and even shrimp means your supermarket can offer fish or seafood every day, especially with the quick shipment of the fragile food today. As a child I remember the infrequent treat of oysters shipped in bulk all the way from the East. Now you just go "fishing" in the supermarket.

FISH

BAKED FISH WITH MUSHROOMS

½	pound fresh mushrooms or 1 can (6 to 8 ounces) sliced mushrooms
1	can (8 ounces) tomato sauce
3	tablespoons chopped onion
3	tablespoons diced green pepper
1	teaspoon lemon juice
1	teaspoon salt
½	teaspoon sugar
⅛	teaspoon ground black pepper
1½	pounds halibut steaks

Preheat oven to 350 degrees. Rinse, pat dry and slice fresh mushrooms (makes about 2½ cups) or drain canned mushrooms.

Place mushrooms in medium saucepan along with tomato sauce, onion, green pepper, lemon juice, salt, sugar and black pepper. Bring to boil, stirring constantly. Reduce heat and simmer, uncovered, for 2 minutes.

Spoon half of mushroom mixture into lightly greased 12-by-8-by-2-inch baking pan. Top with fish. Cover with remaining mushroom mixture. Bake, uncovered, until fish flakes easily when tested with fork, about 20 minutes.

Arrange fish on heated platter. Spoon mushroom sauce over fish. *Makes 4 portions.*

BAKED WHOLE FISH

1	whole, fresh, firm-fleshed fish (about 4 pounds), cleaned and scaled
1	medium zucchini, cubed
1	cup mushrooms, diced
2	onions, peeled and sliced
1	green pepper, cut in strips
1	tablespoon parsley, minced
1	teaspoon salt
¼	teaspoon pepper
	Juice of 1 lemon
2	tablespoons butter
1	tablespoon Angostura aromatic bitters
4	olives, sliced

Preheat oven to 425 degrees. Wash fish and place in well-oiled, foil-lined baking dish.

Stuff fish with cut vegetables and parsley. Secure with toothpicks.

Sprinkle fish with salt, pepper and lemon juice. Bake 35 to 40 minutes or until fish flakes when tested with fork or toothpick.

Remove fish to hot platter. Add butter and bitters to pan juices, stirring until well blended. Pour over fish and spoon on servings. Garnish with olives.
Makes 6 servings.

BARBADOS FISH ROLLS

⅔	cup bread stuffing mix
½	cup water
2	tablespoons diced, pared cucumber
3	tablespoons finely chopped green pepper
4	teaspoons grated onion
1	tablespoon chopped parsley
4	teaspoons butter or margarine, melted
1	teaspoon lemon juice
½	teaspoon salt
	Dash pepper
1	firm banana, peeled and diced
4	white fish fillets (1 pound)

SAUCE:

1	tablespoon prepared mustard
1	tablespoon Worcestershire sauce
2	tablespoons chili sauce
2	tablespoons lemon juice
2	bananas, peeled and cut in half lengthwise

For stuffing, combine in large bowl stuffing mix, water, cucumber, green pepper, onion, parsley, melted butter, 1 teaspoon lemon juice, salt and pepper. Mix well. Add diced bananas.

Divide stuffing among 4 fish fillets. Place stuffing in center of each, then roll fish around stuffing. Secure with wooden picks.

Place seam side down in shallow baking pan. Bake uncovered in preheated meal-maker toaster oven at 375 degrees for 25 minutes.

For sauce, mix in small bowl mustard, Worcestershire sauce, chili sauce and 2 tablespoons lemon juice. Add banana halves to fish fillets in baking pan. Brush fish and bananas with sauce.

Bake 10 minutes longer, until fish flakes when tested with fork. *Makes 4 servings.*

BARBECUED SALMON

1   pound fresh or frozen salmon fillets or
    steaks (4 to 6 ounces each)
3   tablespoons melted butter or
    margarine
1   tablespoon *each* lemon juice and
    white wine vinegar
¼   teaspoon grated lemon peel
¼   teaspoon *each* garlic salt and salt
    Dash hot pepper sauce

Thaw salmon, if necessary. Combine remaining ingredients; generously brush both sides of salmon with mixture. Place on oiled barbecue grill flesh-side down. Barbecue on flesh side about 2 minutes; turn salmon carefully. Brush with sauce. Make a tent of foil or use barbecue cover and place over salmon. Barbecue 8 to 10 minutes longer or until salmon flakes easily when tested with a fork; baste frequently.   *Makes 3 or 4 servings.*

BARBECUED TROUT

6   pan-dressed rainbow trout or other
    pan-dressed fish, fresh or frozen
⅔   cup soy sauce
½   cup ketchup
2   tablespoons lemon juice
2   tablespoons salad oil
1   teaspoon crushed rosemary

Thaw frozen fish. Clean, wash and dry fish. Place in single layer in shallow baking dish.

Combine remaining ingredients. Pour sauce over fish. Let stand 1 hour, turning once.

Remove fish, reserving sauce for basting. Place fish in single layer in well-greased hinged wire grills.

Cook about 4 inches from moderately hot coals for 5 to 8 minutes. Baste with sauce. Turn. Cook 5 to 8 minutes longer or until fish flakes easily when tested with fork.   *Makes 6 servings.*

BROILED FISH WITH
FRUIT 'N' LEMON SAUCE

1   tablespoon salad oil
    Grated peel of ½ fresh lemon
1   pound halibut or swordfish steaks
    (about 1-inch thick), cut in 4
    serving-size pieces
    Juice of ½ fresh lemon

1   teaspoon cornstarch
1   can (about 8 ounces) fruit cocktail
    packed in juice, undrained
1   tablespoon unsalted butter or
    margarine
    Generous dash ground cinnamon and
    nutmeg

Combine oil and lemon peel; brush fish steaks lightly with oil mixture. Place on broiler pan. Broil 4 to 5 inches from heat 5 to 7 minutes on each side or until fish flakes easily with fork. Meanwhile, to make sauce, in saucepan, gradually blend lemon juice into cornstarch. Add fruit cocktail, butter and spices. Cook over medium heat, stirring until thickened. Serve sauce over fish steaks. Garnish with lemon wedges and parsley, if desired.
    Makes 4 servings (about 1 cup sauce).

FILLETS A L'ORANGE

⅓   cup olive oil, divided
1   large onion, chopped
½   cup finely chopped celery
2   ripe tomatoes, cored and chopped
1. cup dry bread crumbs
½   cup dry sherry, divided
1½ cups orange juice
¼   cup flour mixed with remaining oil
6   flounder fillets
    Salt and pepper

In a skillet, heat one-fourth cup of the oil and saute onion and celery until soft, about 5 minutes. Stir in tomatoes and simmer until tomatoes are mushy. Stir in bread crumbs and one-fourth cup of the sherry. Cool. In a saucepan, mix remaining sherry and orange juice. Stir in flour mixture with remaining oil. Stir over low heat until sauce bubbles and thickens. Season sauce with salt and pepper, if desired. Sprinkle fillets with salt and pepper. Spread bread crumb mixture evenly on fillets. Roll up fillets like jelly rolls and place seam side down in a greased shallow baking pan. Spoon half of the sauce over fish rolls. Bake in a preheated 350-degree oven for 30 to 35 minutes or until fish flakes and becomes white. Remove fish rolls to a serving platter with a slotted pancake turner. Heat remaining sauce and spoon over fish rolls. Garnish with orange slices and sprigs of parsley.
    Makes 6 servings.

FISH FILLETS

1   pound fresh or frozen fish fillets
¼   teaspoon salt
⅛   teaspoon pepper

Continued

⅛   teaspoon dried leaf oregano or marjoram
3   tablespoons butter or margarine, melted
Paprika
1   grapefruit, sectioned

Place fillets on aluminum foil in broiler pan. Add salt, pepper and oregano to butter. Brush fish with half the mixture. Sprinkle with paprika. Place in preheated broiler about 5 inches below heat. Broil until fish is easily flaked but still moist, about 10 to 12 minutes. Three minutes before fish is cooked, place grapefruit sections on top, brush with remaining butter mixture. Continue broiling until fish is easily flaked with a fork.   *Makes 4 servings.*

FISH FILLETS WITH REMOLATA

1   pound fish fillets, fresh or frozen
½   teaspoon salt
¼   teaspoon pepper
2   tablespoons margarine, divided
¼   cup chopped parsley
1½   teaspoons grated lemon rind
1   clove garlic, minced

Place fish on foil-lined broiler pan. Sprinkle with salt and pepper and dot with 1 tablespoon margarine. Broil 6 inches from heat for 5 minutes. In small bowl cream remaining 1 tablespoon margarine with parsley, lemon rind and garlic. Spread over fish and broil 1 minute longer, until fish flakes when tested with a fork.   *Makes 4 servings.*

FISH STEAKS VALENCIA

2   cups orange juice
2   tablespoons pickling spices
½   teaspoon salt (optional)
4   slices, halibut, cod, snapper, tile fish or other fish
1   tablespoon cornstarch, optional

In a large skillet, combine orange juice, spices and salt. Heat to simmer, do not boil. Add halibut; cover and simmer about 10 minutes until fish flakes easily when tested with a fork. Remove from heat; keep warm. If desired, stir cornstarch into a little cold water and then stir into orange juice in skillet. Heat, stirring constantly, until thickened. Serve with fish.   *Makes 4 servings.*

FISH STEAKS WITH MUSHROOM-CAPER SAUCE

1   pound fresh mushrooms
6   individual fish steaks (cod, halibut, etc.)
4   tablespoons butter or margarine, divided
1½   teaspoons salt, divided
⅛   teaspoon ground white pepper
About 1 cup milk
3   tablespoons flour
1   tablespoon capers, drained

Preheat oven to 350 degrees. Rinse, pat dry and slice mushrooms (makes about 5¾ cups); set aside. Place fish in a greased 12-by-8-by-2-inch baking pan. Dot with 1 tablespoon of the butter, sprinkle with 1 teaspoon of the salt and the white pepper. Cover and bake until fish flakes easily when tested with a fork, about 30 minutes. Pour fish stock from baking pan into a 2-cup measuring cup. Add enough milk to the fish stock to make 2 cups liquid. Cover fish and keep warm.

In a large saucepan, melt remaining 3 tablespoons butter. Add sliced mushrooms; saute for 3 minutes. Add flour; cook and stir for 1 minute. Blend in fish stock mixture, capers and remaining ½ teaspoon salt. Bring to the boiling point. Cook and stir until sauce is thickened, about 1 minute. Pour over fish steaks; serve with lemon wedges, if desired.   *Makes 6 portions.*

FISH TURBANS WITH MUSHROOM-CELERY SAUCE

1   pound fresh mushrooms
6   tablespoons butter or margarine, divided
¼   cup chopped onion
1   cup diced celery
1   can (8 ounces) tomato sauce
1½   teaspoons salt, divided
¼   teaspoon ground black pepper, divided
1   pound fish fillets

Rinse, pat dry and slice mushrooms (makes about 5¾ cups). In a large skillet, melt 4 tablespoons of the butter. Add onions and celery; saute until tender, about 3 minutes. Add mushrooms; saute until golden about 5 minutes. Add tomato sauce, ½ teaspoon of the salt and ⅛ teaspoon of the black pepper. Bring to boiling point; reduce heat and simmer, uncovered, for 5 minutes.

Preheat oven to 350 degrees. Sprinkle fish with remaining 1 teaspoon salt and ⅛ teaspoon black pepper; dot with remaining 2 tablespoons butter. Roll up; secure with toothpicks if necessary. Spoon half of the tomato-mushroom sauce in bottom of a greased 10-by-6-by-2-inch baking pan. Place fish rolls on top; pour remaining sauce over fish. Cover and bake until fish flakes easily when tested with a fork, about 20 minutes. (If a thicker sauce is desired, bake uncovered for last 10 minutes). Serve with rice and bread sticks. *Makes 6 portions.*

FRIED TROUT WITH NUT BUTTER

2	pounds pan-dressed trout, fresh or frozen
	Salt and pepper
	Flour
	Shortening, salad oil or butter

NUT BUTTER:

½	cup butter
1	clove garlic, minced
¼	cup chopped parsley
¼	cup finely chopped cashews
¼	teaspoon salt

Cream butter until fluffy; blend in garlic, parsley, nuts and salt. Let stand about an hour or at room temperature before serving. Thaw fish if frozen. Clean, wash and dry fish. Season with salt and pepper. Roll trout in flour. In heavy 10-inch frypan, slowly heat enough fat to cover bottom well; put in trout. Fry at moderate heat for 4 to 5 minutes or until golden brown. Turn carefully. Fry 4 to 5 minutes longer or until fish are nicely browned and flake easily when tested with a fork. Drain on absorbent paper. To serve, put trout on warm platter; top each with some of Nut Butter; pass rest of butter. *Makes 4 servings.*

HALIBUT PEKING STYLE

1	egg white
3	teaspoons cornstarch, divided
1	pound halibut steak
½	cup corn oil
½	cup chicken broth
¼	cup dry sherry or apple juice
1	tablespoon dark corn syrup
¼	teaspoon salt

Mix egg white and 1 teaspoon of the cornstarch until blended. Thaw fish steak if frozen and dip fish steak in egg mixture, coating all sides. Heat corn oil over medium heat in large skillet. Add fish steak and sear on both sides about 2 minutes. Remove fish from skillet. Mix together broth, sherry, corn syrup, 2 teaspoons cornstarch and salt. Pour into skillet. Bring to boil over medium heat, stirring constantly, until thickened. Place fish steak in skillet

and cook about 2 minutes on each side or until fish flakes easily when tested with fork. To serve, remove fish from sauce, place on platter and pour sauce over fish. *Makes 2 to 3 servings.*

OVEN-FRIED HALIBUT

2	pounds halibut steaks
2	eggs
2	tablespoons milk
1	tablespoon lemon juice
1	teaspoon salt
1	cup cracker crumbs
¼	cup butter
½	cup sliced mushrooms (optional)
	Parsley and lemon slices, for garnish

Thaw halibut, if frozen, in the refrigerator or under cold running water. Beat eggs. Add milk, lemon juice and salt. Mix until blended. Spread crumbs in shallow pan. Dip steaks into egg mixture, then into crumbs. Shake off extra crumbs and dip into egg mixture and crumbs again. Melt butter in shallow baking pan. Arrange fish in pan, turning to coat both sides with butter. Bake at 375 degrees for 25 to 30 minutes, depending on thickness of steaks or until fish flakes easily with fork. In meantime, saute mushrooms in small amount of oil or butter to use for garnish, if desired. Serve halibut steaks on warm plates. Garnish with sauteed mushrooms, parsley and lemon slices. *Makes 6 servings.*

POMMES DE TERRE A LA MER

6	medium potatoes (about 3 pounds)
6	tablespoons butter
1½	cups hot milk
1½–2	pounds fillet of sole
	Milk or white wine (enough to cover fish for poaching)
½	to ¾ pound cooked shrimp or crabmeat
	Salt and pepper to taste
	Parmesan cheese
	Mornay Sauce (recipe follows)

Scrub potatoes and bake on oven rack without foil. Ten minutes before they are done, simmer fillet of sole in milk or white wine until tender (about 5 to 10 minutes).

When potatoes are soft, remove a lengthwise slice from top of each hot potato. Scoop out contents and mash or press through a ricer. Add salt and pepper and butter melted in hot milk. Whip until light and fluffy. Pile potato mixture lightly into shells, leaving deep hollowed centers.

Continued

Lift fillet of sole from liquid. Reserve liquid for Mornay Sauce. Divide sole into six portions and place in the hollow of each potato. Top with cooked shrimp or crabmeat.

Pour Mornay Sauce over seafood. Sprinkle top with grated Parmesan cheese. Bake at 375 degrees until lightly browned.   *Makes 6 servings.*

Note: When used as a fish course instead of a main dish, use only ½ pound fillet of sole.

MORNAY SAUCE:
3	tablespoons butter
3	tablespoons flour
1½	cups liquid from poaching plus additional milk, if needed
½	cup shredded Swiss cheese
	Salt and pepper

Over low heat, cook together butter, flour, milk or wine from poaching, adding enough milk to make 1½ cups altogether. When very hot, stir in shredded cheese, salt and pepper.   *Makes 1½ cups.*

FREEZE AHEAD: Stuffed baked potatoes can be kept in the freezer for about three months, so double-up when you prepare them. Bake one batch for immediate use; freeze the extras, unwrapped, on a cookie sheet.

When they are completely frozen, take them from the freezer and wrap in heavy-duty aluminum foil. Use enough foil for the 'drugstore' wrap method to insure complete sealing. Press foil around contours of potato to eliminate any air pockets. Date and return to freezer.

When ready to use, remove foil and bake for 30 minutes at 350 degrees. Raise temperature to 400 degrees and brown for 3 to 5 minutes.

POTUNIA CRISPIES

1	can (6½ or 7 ounces) tuna in vegetable oil
½	cup mashed potatoes
¼	cup wheat germ
1	egg, slightly beaten
2	tablespoons finely chopped onion
1	tablespoon chopped parsley
¼	teaspoon paprika
2	tablespoons butter or margarine

Drain excess liquid from tuna. Combine tuna, mashed potatoes, wheat germ, egg, onion, parsley and paprika. Mix well.

Melt butter in large skillet over medium heat. Drop tuna mixture by heaping tablespoons into skillet. Flatten slightly with spatula.

Fry until golden brown. Turn and brown other side. Repeat with rest of mixture, adding more butter to skillet if needed.

Serve with heated chili sauce or tartare sauce, if desired.   *Makes about 8 pancakes.*

RAINBOW TROUT SCANDINAVIAN

6	pan-dressed rainbow trout or other small fish, fresh or frozen
1	teaspoon salt
	Dash pepper
1	cup chopped parsley
¼	cup butter or margarine, softened
1	egg, beaten
¼	cup milk
1	teaspoon salt
¾	cup toasted dry bread crumbs
½	cup grated Swiss cheese
3	tablespoons melted fat or oil

Thaw fish if frozen. Clean, wash and dry fish. Sprinkle inside with salt and pepper. Add parsley to butter and mix thoroughly. Spread inside of each fish with apporximately 1 tablespoon parsley butter. Combine egg, milk and salt. Combine crumbs and cheese. Dip fish in egg mixture and roll in crumb mixture. Place on a well-greased cookie sheet, 12 × 15 inches. Sprinkle remaining crumb mixture over top of fish. Drizzle fat over fish. Bake in 500-degree oven for 10 to 15 minutes, or until fish flakes easily when tested with a fork.   *Serves 6.*

ROLLED FISH FILLETS WITH ORANGE TOMATO SAUCE

2	tablespoons margarine or butter
½	cup chopped onion
2	large tomatoes, peeled, seeded and chopped
½	cup orange juice
1	teaspoon salt
½	teaspoon dried leaf savory or thyme
1	pound flounder fillets, fresh or frozen

In a medium saucepan melt margarine. Add onion and cook until tender. Add tomatoes; simmer 10 minutes. Add orange juice, salt and savory. Simmer 5 minutes.

Roll flounder fillets and place in a shallow baking dish. Pour orange tomato sauce over rolls. Bake in 350-degree oven for 25 minutes, until fish flakes easily when tested with a fork. Garnish with parsley and orange slices.   *Makes 4 servings.*

SEASIDE SALMON BURGERS

SALMON BURGERS:

1	can (15½ ounces) salmon
1	cup quick oats, uncooked
2	eggs
⅓	cup chopped green pepper
⅓	cup shredded carrot
⅓	cup chopped onion
⅛	teaspoon salt
⅛	teaspoon pepper
2	tablespoons butter or margarine

MUSTARD SAUCE:

⅓	cup mayonnaise
1	teaspoon prepared mustard

For salmon burgers, drain salmon, reserving ¼ cup liquid. Combine salmon, reserved liquid and remaining ingredients except butter. Mix well. Shape to form 6 patties. Fry in butter in 10-inch skillet over medium heat 12 to 15 minutes or until golden brown.

For mustard sauce, combine mayonnaise and mustard. Mix well. Serve mustard sauce with salmon burgers. *Makes 6 servings.*

STUFFED LETTUCE SURPRISE

6	large iceberg lettuce leaves
8	small fillets of sole
	Salt and pepper
	Norwegian sardines, drained and mashed coarsely, reserving 8 whole for garnish
2	tablespoons bread crumbs
2	tablespoons each finely chopped celery, parsley and green onion
1	cup dry white wine or apple juice
1	bay leaf
1	can (10½ ounces) white sauce (or 1¼ cups homemade white sauce)
	Parsley

Parboil lettuce leaves until transparent (about 4 minutes). Drain. Season sole with salt and pepper. Mix stuffing by combining sardines, bread crumbs, and vegetables and spread a little stuffing over each fillet. Roll up stuffed sole fillets in lettuce leaves. Arrange in kettle. Add wine and bay leaf and simmer, covered, 15 minutes. Remove rolls to warm platter. Add white sauce to broth in pan. Cook and stir until smooth and hot. Season to taste. Spoon sauce over rolls. Garnish with parsley and whole sardines. Serve at once. *Makes 8 rolls.*

SWEET 'N' SOUR TROUT

6	small, whole dressed, fresh or frozen rainbow trout
2	packages (7¾ ounces each) bean threads
	Cornstarch
2	eggs, beaten
	Sesame oil

SWEET 'N' SOUR SAUCE:

1	clove garlic, crushed
1	tablespoon vegetable oil
1	can (6 ounces) pineapple juice
½	cup water
¼	cup firmly packed light brown sugar
2	tablespoons white vinegar
2	tablespoons soy sauce
2	tablespoons watermelon pickle juice
2	tablespoons chopped watermelon pickles (or 2 tablespoons sweet pickle juice and 2 tablespoons chopped sweet pickles)
2	tablespoons cornstarch
¼	cup water
¾	cup crinkle-cut carrots (3 small)
½	green pepper, cut in julienne strips
1	cup halved cherry tomatoes

Thaw trout if frozen. Wash and dry.

For sauce: In small saucepan, saute garlic in oil. Stir in pineapple juice, water, brown sugar, vinegar and soy sauce. Add watermelon pickle juice and chopped watermelon pickles. Combine cornstarch and water and stir into sauce. Place saucepan over medium heat and bring to a boil while stirring constantly. Continue to boil for 2 minutes.

In separate saucepan, cook carrots and green pepper in water until tender. Drain and add to sauce along with tomatoes. Keep sauce warm while frying trout.

To fry trout: Blend bean threads in a blender until coarsely ground. Dip trout into cornstarch to coat; then dip into beaten egg and finally into ground bean threads. (Or coat trout with cornmeal or flour.) Fry in skillet in sesame oil until golden and fish flakes easily when tested with a fork. Do not overcook.

Serve trout with sweet 'n' sour sauce and rice. *Makes 6 servings.*

SWEET 'N' SOUR FISH

12	ounces halibut, cod or perch, sliced thinly on diagonal
	Salt, to taste
2	tablespoons *each* flour and cornstarch
	Oil
⅓	cup fresh lime juice
2	tablespoons water
2	tablespoons sugar

Continued

⅛   teaspoon ground ginger
     or
¼   teaspoon fresh grated ginger
1   cup very thinly sliced red or green
    pepper
1   cup very thinly sliced julienne celery
½   cup thinly sliced onion
    Lime wedges and slices

Sprinkle fish generously with salt; let stand 5 minutes. Combine flour and cornstarch; dredge fish in mixture to coat thoroughly. Shake off excess flour.

Fry quickly in ½-inch hot oil until golden brown; drain on paper towels. Arrange on large platter.

Combine lime juice, water, sugar, 1 teaspoon salt and ginger; bring to boil. Add vegetables to lime mixture and return to boil. Remove from heat.

Spoon vegetables onto platter with fish; drizzle lime sauce over all. Garnish with lime wedges and slices. May be served hot or cold. *Makes 4 servings.*

TERIYAKI HALIBUT BAKE

4   1-inch-thick fresh or frozen thawed
      halibut steaks (2 pounds)
½   cup maple-flavored syrup
⅓   cup dry white wine
¼   cup soy sauce
2   tablespoons vegetable oil
8–10 thin fresh ginger slices
1   garlic clove, minced

Arrange fish in 11-by-7-inch baking dish. In small bowl, combine remaining ingredients; blend well. Pour mixture over fish. Cover and refrigerate about 1 hour, basting occasionally.

Heat oven to 350 degrees. Remove fish from baking dish; drain and reserve marinade. Return fish to baking dish; bake at 350 degrees for 20 to 25 minutes or until fish flakes easily with fork, basting occasionally with marinade.

Remove fish to serving platter. Garnish with sauteed mushroom slices, tomato wedges and green onion, if desired. Meanwhile, strain marinade and heat gently in small saucepan until warm. Serve as a dipping sauce with fish.
Makes 4 servings.

TUNA LOAF SURPRISE

1   can (6½ or 7 ounces) tuna, drained
    and flaked
1   egg, lightly beaten
⅓   cup fresh whole wheat bread crumbs
3   tablespoons mayonnaise
3   tablespoons shredded carrot
1   tablespoon finely chopped onion
2   hard-cooked eggs

In medium bowl combine tuna, beaten egg, bread crumbs, mayonnaise, carrot and onion; mix well. Pat half the tuna mixture around one hard-cooked egg so the egg is completely covered. Place on a well-greased baking tray of the meal-maker toaster oven. Repeat with remaining egg and tuna mixture. Place tray on rack in lower position. Bake in a 350-degree toaster oven 20 minutes. *Makes 2 servings.*

TUNA PINWHEELS WITH TARRAGON SAUCE

1   can (about 7 ounces) tuna, drained
    and flaked
1   can (10½ ounces) chicken gravy
1   teaspoon lemon juice
    Dash cayenne pepper
1   cup biscuit mix
¼   cup cold water
    Shredded processed cheese
¼   cup sliced celery
    Dash crushed tarragon leaves
1   tablespoon butter or margarine
1   tablespoon chopped parsley

In bowl, combine tuna, 2 tablespoons gravy, lemon juice and cayenne. To make pinwheels: combine biscuit mix and water; roll to form a rectangle (10 × 8 inches). Spread tuna mixture evenly on dough. Roll up starting at narrow end. Cut into 8 slices. Arrange slices in a circle on a greased cookie sheet. Bake at 450-degrees for 10 minutes; top with cheese. Bake 5 minutes more or until done.

Meanwhile, to make sauce, in saucepan, cook celery with tarragon in butter until tender. Stir in remaining gravy and parsley. Heat; stir occasionally. Serve with pinwheels.
Makes 4 servings, about 1 cup sauce.

TUNA-VEGETABLE PILAF

1	can (6½ or 7 ounces) tuna in vegetable oil or water
2	tablespoons margarine
1	cup fresh green beans, cut in 2-inch lengths
¼	cup *each* coarsely chopped onions and carrots
¼	pound mushrooms, sliced
1	cup diced fresh tomato (about 1 medium)
¼	cup minced fresh parsley
1	cup uncooked brown rice
2	tablespoons chopped walnuts

Drain tuna of excess liquid; heat margarine in large skillet. Add green beans; saute 8 minutes. Add onion, carrots and mushrooms; cook, stirring, for 5 minutes. Add tomato, parsley and tuna; heat through. Cook rice according to package directions; toss with walnuts. Spoon rice onto a serving platter. Spoon tuna mixture over rice.

Makes 2 to 3 servings.

SEAFOOD

CLAMS WITH PEARS

2	fresh Bartlett pears
1	can (6½ ounces) chopped clams
	Water
5	tablespoons dry sherry
1	tablespoon lemon juice
1	chicken bouillon cube
½	teaspoon seasoned salt
½	teaspoon basil, crumbled
½	teaspoon dill weed
½	bay leaf
1	teaspoon cornstarch
¼	cup sliced green onion
1	teaspoon chopped pimiento
2	cups hot cooked rice

Pare, core and quarter pears. Drain liquor from clams into measuring cup. Add water to measure one cup. Combine with 4 tablespoons sherry, lemon juice, crumbled bouillon cube, salt and herbs. Heat to boiling. Add pear quarters, cover and turn heat low. Poach pears just until barely tender, 2 to 3 minutes (be careful not to overcook). Remove pears with slotted spoon. Boil remaining liquid rapidly until reduced to three-fourth cup. Mix cornstarch with remaining tablespoon sherry. Combine with reduced liquid. Add clams, onion and pimiento. Cook, stirring, until mixture boils and thickens slightly. Arrange pears on hot cooked rice; spoon clam sauce over. Serve at once.

Makes 3 to 4 servings.

CRAB CORN CRUNCH

1	package frozen peas (10 ounces)
1	can King crab or 1 (7½ ounces) package frozen King crab (6 ounces)
1	can mushroom soup (10½ ounces)
½	cup milk
3	cups corn chips
½	lemon, sliced very thin

Cook peas according to package directions until almost tender; drain. Drain and slice canned crab or defrost, drain and slice frozen crab. Combine soup and milk. Add peas and crab. Spread 2 cups corn chips over bottom of one and one-half quart baking dish. Spoon half the crab mixture over chips. Layer with lemon slices. Spoon remaining crab mixture over lemon. Crush remaining cup of corn chips and sprinkle over top. Bake in 350-degree oven for 30 minutes. *Makes 4 to 6 servings.*

FESTIVE KING CRAB MOUSSE

2	(7½-ounce) cans King crab or 1 pound frozen King crab
2	envelopes unflavored gelatin
1½	cups water
1	(6-ounce) can frozen grapefruit juice concentrate

Continued

½   cup dairy sour cream
1   cup mayonnaise
1   tablespoon horseradish
1   teaspoon onion salt
½   cup chopped green pepper
2   tablespoons chopped pimiento

Drain and slice crab, saving some larger pieces for garnish. Soften gelatin in water. Heat until dissolved. Add grapefruit juice concentrate. Chill until syrupy. Fold in remaining ingredients along with crab. Pour into oiled, 5–6-cup mold. Chill until firm. Unmold. Garnish with additional crab, lemon slices, tomato wedges and parsley.

Makes 10 to 12 servings.

KING CRAB FRITTATA

½   pound frozen King crab or 1
       can (7½ ounces) King crab
1   medium zucchini
2   tablespoons olive oil
⅓   cup finely chopped onion
6   eggs
1   teaspoon salt
¼   teaspoon pepper
1   tablespoon chopped parsley
¼   teaspoon sweet basil
       Grated Parmesan cheese

Defrost, drain and slice frozen crab. Or, drain and slice canned crab. Slice zucchini and cut slices in half. Heat oil in large skillet. Add onion and saute 3 minutes. Add zucchini and saute 5 minutes longer. Add crab and heat through. Beat eggs. Season with salt and pepper. Pour eggs over crab mixture. Sprinkle with parsley and sweet basil. Cook over low heat, lifting the edges to brown the top. Serve at once, cut into wedges. Sprinkle each serving with grated Parmesan cheese.   *Makes 3 to 4 servings.*

SCANDINAVIAN BAKED EGGS WITH ROCK LOBSTER

¼   cup butter or margarine
8   ounces frozen South African rock
       lobster tails
¼   cup flour
1   cup (½ pint) light cream *and* 1 cup
       milk
¼   cup dry sherry
       Salt and pepper
4   cups well seasoned mashed potatoes
5   eggs

In a saucepan, melt butter. Partially thaw rock lobster tails by holding under running water for a few minutes. With scissors, remove underside membrane and pull out meat. Dice raw meat. Add to butter and saute for 5 minutes.

Stir in flour. Gradually stir in cream, milk and sherry. Stir over medium heat until sauce thickens and bubbles. Season to taste with salt and pepper.

Spoon mashed potatoes around the outer edge of a shallow casserole. Beat one of the eggs and brush egg over potatoes. Stir what remains of that egg into hot sauce.

Spoon rock lobster and sauce into the center of the casserole. Drop remaining 4 eggs by spoon over sauce. Sprinkle eggs with salt and pepper. Bake in a preheated 350-degree oven for 30 minutes or until eggs are set and potatoes are lightly browned. Serve sprinkled with paprika.   *Makes 4 servings.*

SESAME SHRIMP

¼   cup peanut oil, divided
3   tablespoons lemon juice
3   tablespoons soy sauce
1   tablespoon honey
¼   teaspoon ground ginger
1   large clove garlic, crushed
1   pound uncooked jumbo shrimp, shelled
       and deveined
⅓   cup toasted sesame seed

Combine 2 tablespoons peanut oil, lemon juice, soy sauce, honey, ginger and garlic. Mix well. Stir in shrimp. Cover and refrigerate two hours, stirring once or twice.

Heat remaining 2 tablespoons peanut oil in a skillet over moderate heat. Fry shrimp one and one-half to two minutes on each side, or until done. Dip each shrimp in sesame seed, lightly coating each side. Place on heated serving platter. Serve hot.

Makes 6 servings.

SHRIMP FOO YOONG

4   eggs
1   stalk celery, cut up
4   water chestnuts, halved
3   mushrooms, halved
3   scallions, cut up
¼   cup cooked shrimp
¼   cup bean sprouts
¼   teaspoon salt
       Corn oil, for frying

Put eggs into blender, then add celery, water chestnuts, mushrooms, scallions, shrimp, bean sprouts and salt. Turn on blender to high speed. Run a few seconds, turning blender off when no large pieces remain. Pour just enough corn oil into skillet to cover bottom. Heat about 2 minutes. Pour in about one-fourth cup batter. Cook, turning once, until lightly browned on both sides. Drain on absorbent paper. Continue until all batter is used, adding corn oil as needed. *Makes about 8 (5-inch) omelets.*

Pasta, Rice & Grain Dishes

Pasta and rice are basic, delicious foods and are easy to prepare.

I've always felt that there is something soothing about eating Italian, meaning a pasta dish. Historically, pasta and rice are not of Italian origin. Their roots are traced to the Orient.

Both pasta and rice go well in a myriad of dishes, hot or cold; as entrées or salads. Early in my attempts at preparing pasta or rice dishes, I committed the sin of most—that of overcooking.

Here are some tasty dishes—plain and fancy—featuring pasta and rice.

PASTA

CANNELLONI

4	eggs
1	cup milk
1	cup unsifted all-purpose flour
½	teaspoon salt
¼	cup olive oil
1	pound ground chuck
1	onion, chopped
2	packages (10 ounces each) frozen chopped spinach, thawed and squeezed dry
1	egg
½	cup tomato puree
½	teaspoon oregano
2	teaspoons Angostura aromatic bitters
½	cup fine dry bread crumbs
¼	cup melted butter or margarine
1	cup (4 ounces) shredded mozzarella cheese
½	cup grated Parmesan cheese

In a bowl, beat eggs, milk, flour and salt until smooth. Let stand for 1 hour. To prepare, spoon 2 tablespoons of mixture into a lightly-buttered 8-inch preheated small skillet or crepe pan. Rotate pan so bottom is evenly covered with dough. Brown on both sides and stack. In a skillet, heat oil and saute beef and onion until beef is brown and crumbly. Drain excess fat. Stir in spinach, egg, tomato puree, oregano, bitters and crumbs. Stir until well blended. Use mixture to fill crepes. Roll up crepes and place side by side in a single layer in a buttered shallow baking pan. Mix butter and cheeses and sprinkle mixture over crepes. Bake in a 400-degree oven for 15 to 20 minutes or until crusty brown and piping hot. *Makes 8 servings.*

CHICKEN TETRAZZINI

1	whole broiler-fryer chicken
4	cups water
1	small onion, sliced
3	celery tops
1	sprig parsley
1	teaspoon salt
¼	teaspoon pepper
1	package (10 ounces) medium egg noodles
¼	cup butter or margarine
¼	cup chopped onion
¼	cup chopped green pepper
1	can (4 ounces) sliced mushrooms, drained
1	can (10¾ ounces) condensed cream of mushroom soup
1	can (10¾ ounces) condensed cream of chicken soup
½	cup milk
½	cup sliced ripe olives
1	cup cubed pasteurized process American cheese spread
¼	cup grated Parmesan cheese
½	cup sliced almonds

Place chicken in a deep saucepan. Add water, onion, celery, parsley, salt and pepper. Bring to a boil. Cover tightly. Reduce heat and simmer about 1 hour, or until fork can be inserted with ease. Remove from heat.

Strain broth and reserve. Refrigerate chicken and broth at once. When chicken is cool, remove meat from skin and bones. Cut meat into chunks.

In a large saucepan, heat to boiling reserved chicken broth plus water to make 3 quarts. Add noodles. Cook according to package directions. Drain.

In a large frying pan, melt butter or margarine. Add onion, green pepper and mushrooms. Saute until vegetables are tender. Stir in soups, milk and olives. Heat through.

Stir in pasteurized process American cheese. Add diced chicken and drained noodles. Transfer mixture to baking dish. Sprinkle with Parmesan cheese. Bake at 375 degrees for 40 minutes, topping with almonds during last 10 minutes of baking.

Makes 8 servings.

Note: Recipe may be divided before baking into two smaller casseroles, one for immediate use and one to be frozen for use within 3 months. To use frozen casserole, remove from freezer and place in refrigerator overnight. Then bake as directed. Bake smaller casseroles only 30 minutes. Each casserole makes 4 servings.

EASY SPAGHETTI AND MEAT SAUCE

½	pound hot Italian sausage, cut in ½-inch pieces
½	pound ground beef
1	cup chopped onion
1	large clove garlic, minced
2	teaspoons Italian seasoning, crushed
2	cups vegetable juice
1	can (8 ounces) tomato sauce
1	can (about 16 ounces) tomatoes
¼	cup grated Parmesan cheese
	Cooked spaghetti

In saucepan, brown sausage and ground beef and cook onion with garlic and Italian seasoning until tender (use shortening if necessary); stir to separate meat. Add remaining ingredients except spaghetti. Bring to boil; reduce heat. Simmer 30 minutes; stir occasionally. Serve over cooked spaghetti with additional Parmesan cheese.

Makes about 5 cups, 4 servings.

HOMEMADE EGG NOODLES

2	cups sifted all-purpose flour
1½	teaspoons salt, divided
2	eggs
3	tablespoons cold water
2	quarts water

In a bowl, sift together flour and ½ teaspoon salt. Make a well in center of flour. Add eggs, one at a time, mixing slightly after each addition. Gradually add 3 tablespoons water. Mix well to make a stiff dough.

Turn dough onto lightly floured surface and knead until smooth, about 5 minutes. Shape dough into ball, cover and let rest about 5 minutes. Roll dough on lightly floured surface to ⅛-inch thickness. Turn dough over and continue rolling until paper thin.

Allow dough to partially dry, about 1 hour. Cut dough into lengthwise strips, 2½ inches wide. Stack strips. Slice crosswise into ½-inch strips. Separate noodles and allow to dry thoroughly.

Noodles can be stored in tightly covered container if not needed immediately. When ready to cook, bring 2 quarts water to boiling. Add remaining 1 teaspoon salt and noodles. Boil, uncovered, 10 minutes or until noodles are done. Rinse with hot water. Serve with stewed chicken and gravy.

Makes 6–8 servings.

KRAUT 'N' FRANK LASAGNA

4	cups well-drained sauerkraut (about 32 ounces)
1	pound frankfurters, thinly sliced
1	package (12 ounces) pasteurized American cheese slices
9	lasagna noodles (about 8 ounces)
8	tablespoons butter or margarine, divided
½	cup finely chopped onion
½	cup finely chopped parsley
1	container (16 ounces) creamed cottage cheese
1	egg
1	teaspoon caraway seed
6	tablespoons flour
1	teaspoon salt
	Dash cayenne pepper
2¾	cups milk
	Additional parsley for garnish

If garnish is desired, reserve ¼ cup kraut, 2 frankfurters (sliced) and 2 slices American cheese cut into triangles. Cut remaining cheese into strips.

Cook lasagna noodles according to package directions. Drain well and set aside.

To prepare kraut 'n' frank filling, melt 2 tablespoons butter in large skillet. Add onion and chopped parsley. Saute over medium heat, stirring constantly, until onion is tender, about 3 minutes.

Remove from heat. Stir in drained kraut, franks, cottage cheese, egg and caraway seed. Mix until ingredients are well combined. Set aside.

To prepare cheese sauce, melt remaining 6 tablespoons butter in medium saucepan. Stir in flour, salt and cayenne pepper until smooth.

Cook over medium heat, stirring constantly, until mixture is smooth and bubbly. Reduce heat to low. Gradually add milk and cook, stirring constantly, until mixture thickens and begins to boil.

Remove from heat. Add cheese strips to sauce. Stir until cheese is melted.

In ungreased 3-quart ovenproof baking dish, layer 3 noodles, ⅓ kraut 'n' frank filling and ⅓ cheese sauce. Repeat 2 times, ending with cheese sauce. Cover with foil.

Bake in 375-degree oven for 45 minutes or until center is hot and bubbly, removing foil for last 15 minutes of baking time.

If garnish is desired, arrange reserved kraut, frankfurters and cheese triangles around edges and in center of baking dish when foil is removed. For easier cutting, let stand 5 minutes after removing from oven. Decorate with parsley sprigs.

Makes 8 servings.

MACARONI AND CHEESE WITH OLIVES

1	pound elbow macaroni (4 cups)
2	tablespoons salt
4–6	quarts boiling water
½	cup butter or margarine
½	cup finely chopped onions
½	cup all-purpose flour
½	teaspoon salt
	Dash cayenne pepper
1	quart milk
3	tablespoons prepared mustard
12	ounces processed American cheese, grated (about 3 cups)
1	cup sliced pimiento-stuffed olives

Gradually add macaroni and 2 tablespoons salt to rapidly boiling water so that water continues to boil. Cook uncovered, stirring occasionally, until tender. Drain in colander.

Meanwhile, melt butter in large pot. Add onions and saute until tender, about 5 minutes. Blend in flour, half teaspoon salt and cayenne pepper. Gradually stir in milk and mustard. Cook over medium heat, stirring constantly, until thickened. Remove from heat, add cheese; stir until melted. Add olives and macaroni and mix well. Place macaroni mixture in 13 × 9-inch baking pan. Bake 25 to 30 minutes in 350-degree oven, until lightly browned and bubbly.   *Makes 12 servings.*

MARCO POLO LO MEIN

4	chicken cutlets (about ¾ pound)
1	medium red or green pepper
1½	stalks celery
1	clove garlic, minced
2	tablespoons vegetable oil
1	bunch scallions, coarsely chopped
1	cup sliced mushrooms
1	tablespoon cornstarch
2	tablespoons soy sauce
2	tablespoons water (or sherry)
¼	pound thin spaghetti, cooked and drained
½	cup old-world-style spaghetti sauce
½	teaspoon sesame oil (optional)

Slice chicken and pepper into ¼-inch strips; cut celery into ¼-inch slices.

In large skillet or wok, stir-fry chicken and garlic in oil for 5 to 7 minutes or until chicken is done. Remove chicken and set aside. Add vegetables to wok and stir-fry about 5 minutes or until almost tender.

In small bowl, dissolve cornstarch in soy sauce and water or sherry. Combine chicken and soy sauce mixture with vegetables in wok. Add spaghetti and spaghetti sauce; heat through, about 5 minutes.

Sprinkle with sesame oil and serve immediately.   *Makes about 4 servings.*

MOCK FETTUCCINE

¼	cup (½ stick) margarine
1	cup chopped onion
¼	cup chopped parsley
3	tablespoons flour
½	teaspoon salt
⅛	teaspoon white pepper
1½	cups skim milk
1	package (8 ounces) wide noodles, cooked and drained
¼	cup coarsely chopped English walnuts

Melt margarine in a skillet and saute onion until tender. Add parsley and cook about 1 minute, stirring frequently. Blend in flour, salt and pepper. Remove from heat and gradually stir in skim milk. Cook over medium heat, stirring constantly, until sauce boils.

Pour sauce over hot noodles and toss gently until thoroughly mixed.

Garnish with chopped English walnuts.

Makes 6 servings.

NOODLES ALFREDO

1	pound wide egg noodles (about 8 cups)
1½	tablespoons salt
4–6	quarts boiling water
1	cup (2 sticks) sweet butter, cut into ⅛-inch-thick slices
1	cup freshly grated Parmesan cheese

Gradually add noodles and salt to rapidly boiling water so that water continues to boil. Cook uncovered, stirring occasionally, until tender. Drain in colander.

While noodles are cooking, warm a large bowl and serving plates in a slow oven. (Butter and cheese should be ready to use.) As soon as noodles drain, place some of them into the bowl, add some butter slices and toss quickly. Add some cheese and toss again.

Continue adding noodles, butter and cheese until all noodles are completely coated. Serve at once on warm plates.   *Makes 6 to 8 servings.*

ORIENTAL HOT POT

1½	pounds flank steak or other lean beef
3	cans (13¾ fluid ounces each) beef broth diluted with 3 cans water
⅔	cup old-world-style spaghetti sauce
⅓	cup dry sherry (optional)
3	tablespoons soy sauce
1	tablespoon brown sugar
2	teaspoons finely minced fresh ginger
1	small clove garlic, pressed
2	cups (about 6 ounces) sliced mushrooms
2	cups (about 5 ounces) broccoli flowerets
1	can (8 ounces) sliced water chestnuts, drained
1	package (6 ounces) frozen Chinese snow pea pods, thawed
1	jar (4 ounces) sliced pimientos, drained
2	large scallions, thinly sliced
¼	pound thin spaghetti, cooked *al dente* and drained

Slice beef lengthwise into strips about 3 inches wide. (For easy slicing, wrap meat and freeze until firm to the touch, about 3 hours.) Slice strips crosswise into ⅛-inch-thick pieces and set aside.

To large stockpot, add broth, spaghetti sauce, sherry, soy sauce, sugar, ginger and garlic. Bring to a vigorous boil. Add vegetables and spaghetti.

Continue boiling over high heat until vegetables are almost tender, about 2 minutes. Remove vegetables and spaghetti from stock and place in a large serving bowl; cover and set aside.

Add meat to boiling stock; stir to separate slices. Boil over high heat until just cooked through, about 2 minutes. Add meat and stock to bowl with vegetables and spaghetti. *Makes 4 servings.*

PASTA DEL SOL

1	pound ground pork
½	cup chopped onion
1	clove garlic, minced
3	tablespoons flour
1½	cups orange juice
1¼	teaspoons salt, divided
½	teaspoon sugar
¼	teaspoon pepper, divided
¼	teaspoon rubbed sage
¼	teaspoon cinnamon
4	ounces lasagna noodles, cooked according to package directions
1	pound (2 cups) creamed cottage cheese
1	egg, beaten
¼	cup chopped parsley
½	teaspoon grated orange rind

In large skillet break up pork with fork. Stir over medium heat until browned. Add onion and garlic; cook until tender. Blend in flour. Stir in orange juice, 1 teaspoon salt, sugar, one-eighth teaspoon pepper, sage and cinnamon. Cook until mixture thickens and comes to a boil. Remove from heat. In medium bowl mix cottage cheese, egg, parsley, orange rind, remaining one-fourth teaspoon salt and one-eighth teaspoon pepper. Place a layer of half of lasagna noodles on bottom of 11×7-inch baking dish. Spoon half of cheese mixture over noodles, spoon half of pork mixture over cheese, then repeat with remaining lasagna noodles, cottage cheese and pork mixture. Bake uncovered in 350-degree oven 30 minutes. Garnish with orange slices.

Makes 6 servings.

PASTA PRONTO

4	ounces fettuccine
8	ounces sweet Italian sausage, casing removed
2	tablespoons butter
1	medium onion, chopped
1	clove garlic, finely minced
4	spears broccoli, cut into 2½-inch pieces
2	small zucchini, cut into 2½-inch strips
2	teaspoons salt
1	teaspoon basil
⅛	teaspoon pepper
¼	cup water
¼	cup dry vermouth
1	medium red pepper, cut in strips
4	ounces mushrooms, halved (about 1½ cups)
¼	cup sliced pitted black olives
2	tablespoons pine nuts (optional)
¼	cup heavy cream
½	cup grated Parmesan cheese

Cook fettuccine according to package directions. Drain and set aside.

In an electric wok set at 325 degrees, cook sausage until lightly browned. Remove. Cut in 1-inch pieces. Set aside.

Add butter to wok. Saute onion and garlic until wilted. Add broccoli and zucchini. Stir-fry for 1 minute. Stir in salt, basil, pepper, water and vermouth. Cover. Cook 3 minutes. Remove cover. Add red pepper and mushrooms. Continue to cook, uncovered, stirring every 30 seconds for 5 minutes or until vegetables are crisp-tender.

Add fettuccine, sausage, pitted black olives, cream, Parmesan cheese and pine nuts, if desired. Toss and heat to serving temperature.

Makes 2 servings.

SHRIMP 'N' SPAGHETTI

1	package tangy Italian-style spaghetti dinner
½	cup chopped green pepper
1	(4 ounces) can mushrooms, drained
¼	cup chopped onion
3	tablespoons margarine
1	cup (5 ounces) cooked, cleaned shrimp

Prepare spaghetti and sauce as directed on package. Saute green pepper, mushrooms and onion in margarine until tender. Add with shrimp to sauce; heat. Serve sauce over spaghetti; sprinkle with the grated Parmesan cheese.   *Makes 4 servings.*

SHRIMP-NOODLE BAKE

1	pound fresh or frozen, peeled, deveined shrimp
1	package (8 ounces) medium noodles, cooked and drained
½	pint (1 cup) dairy sour cream
1	can (10¾ ounces) condensed cream of mushroom soup
¼	cup sliced green onion (with 2 inches of green tops)
¼	cup sliced, pitted ripe olives
1	teaspoon dill weed
½	teaspoon seasoned salt
1	cup shredded Cheddar cheese, divided

Thaw shrimp if frozen. Cut shrimp in half lengthwise, if desired. Combine noodles, sour cream, soup, onion, olives, dill weed, seasoned salt, and one-half of the cheese; mix well. Fold in shrimp. Spoon into shallow 2-quart baking dish. Cover with aluminum foil, crimping it securely to edges of dish. Bake in preheated 350-degree oven for 30 minutes. Uncover. Sprinkle with remaining cheese. Return to oven about 15 minutes or until cheese melts.
Makes 6 servings.

SPAGHETTI AL TONNO

3	tablespoons olive or salad oil, divided
1	clove garlic, crushed or minced
1	cup sliced mushrooms
¼	cup diced red and green pepper
1½	cups fresh broccoli flowerets and chopped stems
1	can (6½ or 7 ounces) tuna, in vegetable oil or water, drained
¼	pound thin spaghetti
1	egg, beaten
½	cup grated Parmesan cheese, divided

In a medium skillet, heat 2 tablespoons olive oil; saute garlic, mushrooms and red pepper until tender. Add broccoli and tuna, heat through. Cook spaghetti according to package directions; drain. Immediately return spaghetti to saucepot. All at once, add egg, tuna mixture and ¼ cup Parmesan cheese; toss well. Mix in remaining 1 tablespoon olive oil. Serve immediately, topped with remaining ¼ cup Parmesan cheese.   *Makes 2 servings.*

Note: Any firm, part-skim milk cheese may be substituted for the Parmesan cheese, except Cheddar-type cheeses.

SPAGHETTI WITH FRESH TOMATO SAUCE

¼	pound bacon, diced
1	medium onion, chopped
1½	pounds tomatoes, peeled and diced
⅓	cup chicken bouillon or dry vermouth
1¼	teaspoons plus 1 tablespoon salt
½	teaspoon basil leaves
¼	teaspoon pepper
½	pound spaghetti
3	quarts boiling water
	Freshly grated Parmesan cheese

In large skillet, fry bacon 2 minutes; add onion and saute until bacon and onion are lightly browned. Mix in tomatoes, bouillon, 1¼ teaspoons salt, basil and pepper. Simmer covered 20 minutes, stirring occasionally.

Meanwhile, gradually add spaghetti and 1 tablespoon salt to rapidly boiling water so that water continues to boil. Cook uncovered, stirring occasionally, until tender. Drain in colander. Serve with tomato sauce and cheese.   *Makes 4 servings.*

SPAGHETTI WITH SPECIAL TOMATO SAUCE

½	cup salad oil
8	medium onions, sliced (about 6 cups)
4	medium green peppers, diced (about 3 cups)
2	large garlic cloves, crushed
2	cans (28 ounces each) whole tomatoes, undrained
4	teaspoons sugar
3	tablespoons salt or lemon juice
2	teaspoons oregano, crushed
1	pound spaghetti
4–6	quarts boiling water

In a Dutch oven or large saucepot, heat oil. Add onions, green pepper and garlic. Saute over medium heat, stirring constantly, until onion is soft, about 10 minutes. Stir in undrained tomatoes. Break tomatoes up into pieces with spoon. Add sugar, 2 teaspoons salt and oregano to tomato-onion mixture. Heat to boiling. Reduce heat to low. Simmer uncovered about 30 to 45 minutes or until sauce is desired consistency. Stir occasionally.

Meanwhile, bring water to a boil in second pot. Gradually add spaghetti and 2 tablespoons salt to rapidly boiling water so that water continues to boil. Cook uncovered, stirring occasionally, until tender. Drain in colander. Serve tomato-onion sauce over spaghetti.   *Makes 8 servings.*

SPAGHETTI WITH STUFFED BEEF ROLL

1	egg
1	tablespoon prepared mustard
	Salt and pepper
½	cup beef bouillon
1½	pounds ground beef
½	cup fine dry bread crumbs
4	carrots, halved and cooked
1½	cups sliced celery, cooked
½	cup chopped parsley
2	slices bacon, diced
½	cup chopped onion
1	clove garlic, crushed
1	tablespoon dark brown sugar
½	teaspoon thyme leaves
2	cans (8 ounces each) tomato sauce
1	cup water
1	pound spaghetti
2	tablespoons salt
4–6	quarts boiling water

Beat egg in large bowl with mustard, 1 teaspoon salt and ⅛ teaspoon pepper. Add bouillon, beef and bread crumbs. Mix until combined. Turn onto large sheet of waxed paper. With moistened hands pat into a 14 × 10-inch rectangle. Arrange carrots and celery over the meat; sprinkle with parsley. Roll up jelly-roll fashion, peeling off waxed paper while rolling. Place seam side down in shallow roasting pan. Seal ends of roll. Bake in 350-degree oven 1 hour. Meanwhile, prepare spaghetti sauce. Brown bacon in large saucepan over medium heat; remove with slotted spoon and set aside. Add onion and garlic and saute in drippings until lightly browned. Pour off excess fat. Stir in sugar, thyme, tomato sauce, 1 cup water and bacon. Bring sauce to a boil, reduce heat and simmer 5 minutes more. Brush some of sauce over beef roll during last 10 minutes of baking period. Keep remaining sauce hot to pour over spaghetti. During last 15 minutes of baking

time, cook spaghetti. Gradually add spaghetti and 2 tablespoons salt to rapidly boiling water so that water continues to boil. Cook uncovered, stirring occasionally, until tender. Drain in colander. Serve spaghetti with sliced beef roll and sauce.
Makes 8 servings.

Note: Allow meat to stand 5 minutes for easier slicing.

SPANISH SOFRITO AND NOODLES

8	ounces fine egg noodles (about 4 cups)
1	tablespoon salt
3	quarts boiling water
1	large onion, chopped
1	clove garlic, minced
2	tablespoons olive oil
2	medium tomatoes, peeled, seeded and coarsely chopped
½	teaspoon paprika
½	cup Spanish stuffed green olives, halved
¼	cup chopped parsley

Gradually add noodles and salt to rapidly boiling water so that water continues to boil. Cook uncovered, stirring occasionally, until tender. Drain in colander.

Meanwhile, in large skillet, saute onion and garlic in oil until golden. Add tomatoes and paprika. Cook over low heat, stirring often, for 5 minutes.

Add olives, parsley and noodles. Cook and stir until hot.   *Makes 6 servings.*

SPICY SHELLS

¼	cup chopped onion
¼	cup sliced celery
3	tablespoons butter or margarine
2	cups cubed cooked turkey
1	can (15 ounces) macaroni shells or 2 cups cooked shells
¼	cup sliced black olives
1	green pepper, sliced
½	cup shredded Cheddar cheese
¼	cup sour cream
¼	cup water

Saute celery and onion in butter until tender. Add turkey and cook for 3 more minutes. Stir in macaroni shells, olives, pepper, cheese, sour cream and water. Simmer covered, stirring occasionally, for 5 minutes. Serve garnished with chopped egg.
Makes 4 servings.

SPAGHETTI CARBONARA

1	pound spaghetti
1½	tablespoons salt
4–6	quarts boiling water
3	slices bacon, cut into julienne strips
¼	cup olive oil
2	tablespoons butter
1	cup julienne strips prosciutto or ham
¼	cup grated Parmesan cheese
2	eggs, beaten

Gradually add spaghetti and salt to rapidly boiling water so that water continues to boil. Cook uncovered, stirring occasionally, until tender. Drain in colander.

While spaghetti is cooking, cook bacon in medium-size skillet over low heat, stirring frequently, until very lightly browned. Pour off excess drippings.

Add oil and butter to skillet. When butter is melted, stir in prosciutto. Cook, stirring, about five minutes. Bacon should not brown.

Remove skillet from heat. Very quickly stir in cheese and eggs. Toss with hot spaghetti. Serve at once.   *Makes 6 to 8 servings.*

TUNA AND BOWS

½	package (4 ounces) pasta bows
1	can (6½ or 7 ounces) tuna in vegetable oil
2	tablespoons flour
1	can (8 ounces) tomatoes
1	cup milk
½	teaspoon salt
3	slices American cheese, cut into small pieces

Cook bows according to package directions; drain. Into medium saucepan, drain oil from tuna. Heat and blend in flour. Stir in tomatoes and liquid, milk and salt. Cook, stirring constantly, until mixture thickens and comes to a boil. Boil 2 minutes, breaking up tomatoes with spoon. Stir in cheese, bows and tuna. Heat. Spoon into five 5-ounce custard cups or individual dishes. Garnish with pickles, carrot or celery sticks.   *Makes 5 servings.*

Note: If prepared ahead, bake cups in 350-degree oven 15 to 20 minutes.

RICE & GRAIN

BLACK BEANS AND RICE

1	pound dry black beans
6	cups water
1	cup chopped onion
1	green pepper, chopped
1	clove garlic, minced
½	cup olive oil
2	bay leaves
2	teaspoons salt
¼	teaspoon pepper
1	lean ham bone (optional)
¼	cup wine vinegar
	Cooked rice

Place beans in large saucepan with water. Bring to a boil. Boil for 2 minutes. Remove from heat. Allow to stand for 1 hour.

In large frypan or saucepan, saute onion, green pepper and garlic in oil until tender, about 5 minutes. Add beans, cooking liquid, bay leaves, salt, pepper and ham bone to same frypan. Bring to a boil, cover and simmer for 2 hours or until beans are fork tender, adding more water if necessary. Add wine vinegar. Reheat if necessary.

Serve with cooked rice. Garnish with sliced hard-cooked egg and onion rings, if desired, or sprinkle with lime juice.   *Makes 6 to 8 servings.*

COCONUTTY PEANUT PILAF

2	tablespoons butter or margarine
1½	cups regular long-grain rice (not quick-cooking rice)
2⅔	cups water
2	chicken bouillon cubes
½	cup shelled, roasted peanuts (unsalted and unseasoned)
3	tablespoons toasted flake coconut

Melt butter or margarine in medium saucepan. Stir in rice until grains are coated.

Add water and bouillon cubes. Bring to boiling. Stir in peanuts. Cover. Cook on low heat until liquid is absorbed and rice is tender.

Fluff with fork. Transfer to ovenproof serving dish. Sprinkle with coconut.

Keep warm in oven or at side of grill until ready to serve.   *Makes 8 servings.*

CREOLE-STYLE STUFFED PEPPERS

1½	cups water
½	cup quick barley
1¼	teaspoons salt
½	cup chopped onion
1	clove garlic, minced
2	tablespoons vegetable oil
1	can (16 ounces) whole tomatoes
1	can (12 ounces) tomato paste
¼	cup white wine or apple cider
1	teaspoon sugar
½	teaspoon oregano leaves, crushed
½	teaspoon basil leaves, crushed
⅛	teaspoon pepper
4	medium green peppers
1	16-ounce package frozen shrimp, thawed, well drained, or 1 pound fresh, cooked, cut into bite-size pieces

Bring water to a boil in medium saucepan. Stir in barley and ½ teaspoon salt. Cover; simmer 10 to 12 minutes or until tender, stirring occasionally. Drain; set aside. In large saucepan, saute onion and garlic in oil. Drain tomatoes, reserving liquid; chop. Add chopped tomatoes and liquid, tomato paste, white wine, sugar, oregano, basil, pepper and remaining ¾ teaspoon salt to saucepan. Simmer, uncovered, 10 minutes.

Cut tops from peppers; remove membrane and seeds. In another large saucepan, blanch peppers 5 minutes in boiling water. Drain; cut in half vertically to form boats. Place pepper boats cut-side up in 11-by-7-inch large oval baking dish.

Heat oven to 350 degrees. Add barley and shrimp to tomato sauce mixture. Mound heaping ½ cup of mixture into each pepper. Cover with any remaining sauce. Bake, uncovered, 25 to 30 minutes or until stuffing mixture is heated through.

Makes 8 servings.

Note: Substitute ⅓ cup regular barley for quick barley, if desired. Increase boiling water to 2 cups. Simmer about 50 minutes or until tender. Drain; set aside. Proceed as recipe directs.

FISH-RICE PLATTER

¼	cup salad oil
½	cup chopped onion
1	cup brown or white rice (uncooked)
2	chicken bouillon cubes
2½	cups boiling water
1	tablespoon Worcestershire sauce
2	cups sliced carrots
½	teaspoon salt
1	cup canned chick peas, with their liquid
1	green pepper, chunked
1	pound fish fillets, cut into 1-inch pieces
½	cup roasted soy nuts or peanuts

In a large skillet, heat oil until hot. Add onion and rice; saute for 5 minutes. Dissolve bouillon cubes in water. Add to skillet along with Worcestershire sauce, carrots and salt. Mix well. Bring to the boiling point. Reduce heat and simmer, covered, 40 minutes for brown rice or 20 minutes for white. Stir in chick peas with their liquid, green pepper and fish. Cover and simmer until fish is cooked, about 10 minutes.

Serve sprinkled with nuts. *Makes 4 portions.*

GRAPEFRUIT PILAF

1	package (8 ounces) wheat pilaf mix
1	cup grapefruit juice
1½	cups water
½	cup chopped parsley
¼	teaspoon dried leaf thyme
2	cans (6½ or 7 ounces each) tuna in vegetable oil
1	package (10 ounces) frozen chopped broccoli, thawed and drained
1	cup fresh grapefruit sections

In large casserole or Dutch oven, mix together wheat pilaf mix, grapefruit juice, water, parsley and thyme. Cover and bake in 350-degree oven 30 minutes. Stir in tuna, broccoli and grapefruit sections, cover and bake 10 minutes longer. If desired, garnish with additional grapefruit sections.

Makes 4 servings.

Note: To section grapefruit, cut slice from top, then cut off peel in strips from top to bottom, cutting deep enough to remove white membrane, then cut slice from bottom. Or cut off peel round and round spiral fashion. Go over fruit again, removing any remaining white membrane. Cut along side of each dividing membrane from outside to middle of core. Remove section by section over bowl to retain juice from fruit.

LENTIL-BULGUR PILAF

½	medium onion, chopped
2	tablespoons oil
½	cup lentils
½	cup bulgur wheat
2½	cups water
1	tablespoon tomato ketchup
1	teaspoon salt
¼	teaspoon ground cinnamon
½	cup each raisins and sliced almonds
2	tablespoons chopped parsley
1	hard-cooked egg, chopped

Continued

Saute onion in oil until soft. Add lentils, bulgur, water, ketchup, salt and cinnamon. Bring to boil; cover and simmer 25 to 30 minutes. Stir in raisins and nuts. Cook, uncovered, 10 to 15 minutes or until liquid is absorbed. Garnish with parsley and egg.   *Makes 6 servings.*

MUSHROOM-WALNUT PILAF

¼	cup vermicelli, broken in 1-inch lengths
¼	cup butter
¼	cup chopped onion
1½	cups sliced fresh mushrooms
¼	teaspoon tarragon, crumbled
½	cup raw long-grain rice
1	can (10¾ ounces) condensed chicken broth
¾	cup water
½	teaspoon salt
½	cup walnut pieces

Brown vermicelli in butter over moderate heat, stirring constantly. Add onion, mushrooms and tarragon. Saute until onion becomes transparent. Stir in rice. Add broth, water and salt and heat to boiling. Turn heat low, cover and simmer 20 minutes, until rice is tender and liquid is absorbed. While rice cooks, grate walnuts, using Mouli grater (or turn ¼ cup at a time into blender jar and blend fine). Add grated walnuts to cooked rice and mix lightly with a fork. Serve at once.   *Makes about 4 cups.*

NASI GORENG

3	tablespoons instant minced onion
½	teaspoon instant minced garlic
	Water
2	tablespoons salad oil
2	tablespoons butter or margarine
2	cups uncooked regular rice
1	tablespoon curry powder
1	teaspoon ground coriander
1	can (10¾ ounces) condensed chicken broth
1	tablespoon salt
	Ground black pepper to taste
2	cups diced cooked beef
2	cups diced cooked chicken
¼	cup parsley flakes
	Egg Pancakes (recipe follows)

Rehydrate onion and garlic in 3 tablespoons water for 10 minutes; set aside. In a large skillet heat oil and butter. Add onion and garlic; saute until pale gold, about 2 minutes. Add rice, curry and coriander; saute until rice is browned, about 5 minutes.

Add broth, 3½ cups water, salt and black pepper. Bring to the boiling point. Reduce heat and simmer, cover, until rice is cooked, about 20 minutes. Stir in beef, chicken and parsley flakes. Reheat until hot. Garnish with Egg Pancakes. If desired, serve with chutney, macadamia nuts, flaked coconut, raisins and sliced cucumbers.   *Makes 8 portions.*

EGG PANCAKES:
Combine 2 eggs, 1 teaspoon flour, ¼ teaspoon salt and ground black pepper to taste. Lightly brush a crepe pan or small skillet with oil; heat until hot. Add about 2 tablespoons of the egg mixture; swirl pan so that egg spreads to completely cover bottom; cook until golden on both sides. Roll up, then cut into thin slices. Repeat until batter is used.

SPANISH RICE

1	pound ground beef
1	cup chopped onion
½	cup chopped green pepper
1	medium clove garlic, minced
1	tablespoon chili powder
4	cups cocktail vegetable juice
1	cup raw (uncooked) regular rice
1	teaspoon salt

Brown beef in skillet. Add onion, pepper, garlic and chili powder. Cook until onion and pepper are tender. (Use shortening if necessary.) Stir to separate meat.

Add remaining ingredients. Bring to boil.

Cover. Cook over low heat 20 minutes or until liquid is absorbed. Stir occasionally.
                    Makes about 6 cups or 4 servings.

VEGETARIAN PEAR RICE

1	cup raw brown rice
2	cups finely shredded cabbage
1	cup thinly sliced carrot
1	cup thinly sliced celery
½	cup chopped onion
3	tablespoons butter or margarine
1	teaspoon salt
¼	teaspoon dry mustard
¼	teaspoon dill weed
¼	teaspoon herb pepper seasoning
2	medium-size fresh Bartlett pears
2	tablespoons chopped parsley

Cook rice as package directs.

Meanwhile, prepare vegetables. Measure butter and seasonings. Pare, core and dice pears to measure 1½ cups.

When rice is cooked, saute cabbage, carrot, celery and onion in butter until tender-crisp, about 3 minutes. Stir in seasonings.

Add hot cooked rice (should measure about 3 cups). Mix lightly. Add pears and parsley.

Cover. Cook over very low heat about 5 minutes, until thoroughly heated. Serve at once.

Makes 5 cups or 4 servings.

WHEAT-GERM RICE WITH STIR-FRY BEEF

2	cups raw regular rice
½	cup vacuum packed wheat germ (regular)
1½	pounds lean boneless beef chuck steak
	Instant unseasoned meat tenderizer
	Pepper
1	clove garlic, minced
2	tablespoons oil
1	package (10 ounces) frozen cut green beans
½	pound fresh mushrooms, halved or quartered
1	can (1 pound) tomato wedges
½	cup dry sherry or consomme
2	tablespoons cornstarch
1½	teaspoons salt
1	teaspoon basil
1	teaspoon tarragon

Cook rice according to directions on package. Mix with wheat germ and pack into buttered 6-cup ring mold. Keep hot. Meanwhile, prepare beef according to directions on label of meat tenderizer. Sprinkle with pepper. Cut beef into thin strips.

Cook with garlic in oil in large skillet over high heat, tossing and stirring until browned. Add green beans and mushrooms. Cover and continue cooking, stirring often, 5 to 10 minutes or until tender. Add undrained tomato wedges. Stir in wine mixed with cornstarch, salt, basil and tarragon. Cook, stirring, until sauce comes to boil and thickens. Invert wheat-germ ring onto plate. Fill with stir-fry beef.

Makes 6 servings.

WILD RICE CHICKEN WITH WINE SAUCE

¾	cup corn flake crumbs
1	teaspoon paprika
1	teaspoon salt
1	2½ to 3-pound broiler-fryer, cut up
¼	cup butter or margarine, melted
1	package (6 ounces) long grain and wild rice
1	tablespoon butter or margarine
2¼	cups boiling water
1	can (10¾ ounces) cream of chicken soup
2	tablespoons dry white wine
½	teaspoon grated lemon rind

Combine crumbs, paprika and salt and coat chicken pieces. Place chicken, skin side up, in a shallow baking pan (15 × 10 × 1 inch). Drizzle with the melted butter. Bake at 350 degrees for about 1 hour or until chicken is tender. Meanwhile, prepare rice. Place contents of rice and seasoning packets and 1 tablespoon butter in 1-quart casserole. Add boiling water; stir and cover. Bake in oven with chicken for 40 minutes or until all liquid is absorbed. Meanwhile, prepare sauce. Combine chicken soup and wine in small saucepan. Heat through, stirring occasionally. Stir lemon rind into rice before serving. Serve sauce over chicken and rice.

Makes 6 servings.

Sauces

I once overheard a French chef destroy a colleague's reputation with "He can't make a decent sauce." A Frenchman without his rich sauces is like a fireman without his suspenders.

A good sauce *is* important. Once you learn the basics—a tomato sauce, a white sauce, and a hollandaise—you have the backbones, the mother sauces. To these you may add spices, herbs, cream, wine, cheese, meat, or seafood to serve them with pasta, vegetables, fruit, or fish.

In my opinion, however, we often overdo the use of sauces at a meal. The palate does suffer taste fatigue, an unfortunate situation when eating can be such a pleasure of the senses. Here are some sauces to enhance your meals.

GRAPE BARBECUE SAUCE

- ¾ cup soy sauce
- ¾ cup dry sherry or white grape juice
- ¼ cup olive oil
- 1 tablespoon brown sugar, firmly packed
- 2 cloves garlic, cut into tiny slivers
- 1 teaspoon grated ginger or ¼ teaspoon ground ginger
- 1 cup seedless grapes
  Grapes for garnish

Combine soy sauce, sherry (or juice) and oil in a mixing bowl. Add brown sugar, garlic and ginger, stirring to blend. Add grapes. Pour marinade over steaks in a large dish. Marinate several hours, turning steaks occasionally. Use marinade to baste while grilling or barbecuing. Garnish with small clusters of grapes. *Makes about 2½ cups.*

ORIENTAL PLUM SAUCE

- 1 medium onion, cut in wedges
- 1 tablespoon vegetable oil
- 2 tablespoons cornstarch
- ¾ cup vinegar
- ¾ cup sugar
- 2 pounds fresh plums, quartered
- ½ teaspoon salt
- ¼ teaspoon almond extract

In saucepan, cook onion in oil until soft. Mix cornstarch with vinegar and sugar. Add to onion. Cook, stirring until thickened. Add plums, salt and almond extract. Continue cooking until fruit is tender. *Makes about 2½ cups.*

Meanwhile, parboil or partially roast 5 pounds spareribs. Brush with Oriental Plum Sauce and grill over medium coals, brushing frequently with sauce. When crisp, cut into servings. Heat remaining sauce to serve with barbecued spareribs.

FRESH TOMATO BARBECUE SAUCE

- 4 pounds fresh tomatoes, peeled and chopped
- 1 cup chopped fresh onions

- 2 cloves garlic, minced
- 1 cup packed brown sugar
- ¼ cup butter or margarine
- 1 cup chili sauce
- ¼ cup Worcestershire sauce
- ¼ cup fresh lemon juice
- 2 teaspoons salt
- 1 teaspoon dry mustard

Combine all ingredients in large saucepan. Bring to a boil. Reduce heat and simmer, uncovered, for 1½ to 2 hours, or until thickened. Serve with meats and poultry. *Makes about 1 quart.*

SOUR CREAM-APRICOT SAUCE

- ¾ cup sour cream
- ½ cup apricot jam
- 3 tablespoons Dijon mustard

In small bowl combine sour cream, apricot jam and mustard. Serve at room temperature.
Makes about 1 cup.

SPICY BERRY DIP

- ¼ cup butter or margarine
- 1 onion, minced
- 1 can (1 pound) jellied cranberry sauce
- 1 cup chopped chutney
- 1 cup chili sauce

In a one-and one-half-quart saucepan, melt butter and cook onion until golden. Stir in remaining ingredients and simmer until hot and bubbly. Place over a warmer and spear meatballs, miniature frankfurters, shrimp, ham cubes, or crab meat chunks on fondue forks. Dip into hot mixture.
Makes 4 cups.

SWEET-AND-SOUR MUSHROOM SAUCE

- ½ pound fresh mushrooms or 1 (6 to 8 ounces) can sliced mushrooms
- 4 tablespoons butter or margarine
- ½ cup finely chopped onion
- ½ cup diced green pepper
- 2 tablespoons flour

1   can (8 ounces) tomato sauce
1   cup water
½   cup orange marmalade
1   tablespoon soy sauce
1   tablespoon cider vinegar
1   beef bouillon cube
½   teaspoon salt
⅛   teaspoon ground black pepper

Rinse, pat dry and slice fresh mushrooms. (Makes about 2¼ cups.) Or drain canned mushrooms.

Melt butter in large skillet. Add mushrooms, onion and green pepper. Saute 5 minutes.

Stir in flour. Cook and stir 2 minutes. Add tomato sauce, water, marmalade, soy sauce, vinegar, bouillon cube, salt and black pepper. Bring to boil, stirring constantly.

Reduce heat and simmer, uncovered, for 5 minutes. *Makes about 3 cups.*

CHILI SAUCE

8   pounds (4 quarts) skinned ripe tomatoes, cut in pieces
6   medium onions, chopped
6   green peppers, chopped
1   cup sugar
2   tablespoons salt
3   cups cider vinegar
4   teaspoons whole cloves
3   tablespoons whole allspice
1   tablespoon Tabasco

Combine tomatoes, onion, green pepper, sugar, salt and vinegar in deep kettle. Tie spices in cheesecloth bag; add to ingredients in kettle. Cook, uncovered 2½ to 3 hours, or until quite thick, stirring often. Remove spice bag; stir in Tabasco. Pour sauce at once into clean, hot sterilized jars; seal.

Makes 4 to 5 pints.

HERBED TOMATO SAUCE

1   (16-ounce) can tomatoes
2   tablespoons fresh basil or mint or 1 teaspoon dried basil or mint
1   garlic clove, crushed
½   cup olive or salad oil
¼   cup red wine vinegar
½   teaspoon salt
¼   teaspoon pepper

Drain tomatoes thoroughly. (Use juice in soups or vegetable dishes.) Chop or mash tomatoes. Put into a pint jar or plastic container that can be shaken.

Put fresh basil or mint, garlic, oil and vinegar into blender. Blend to mix thoroughly. Combine with tomatoes, salt and pepper. Refrigerate until serving time. Shake well before serving.

Makes about 1⅔ cups.

SWEET HOT MUSTARD

½   cup dry mustard
½   cup vinegar
¾   cup sugar
3   eggs, beaten slightly
½   teaspoon salt
⅛   teaspoon crushed red pepper

Combine mustard and vinegar. Let stand for 2 hours.

Put sugar, eggs, salt and red pepper in top of double boiler. Cook over simmering water about 5 to 8 minutes, stirring constantly, until mixture thickens. *Makes about 1⅔ cups.*

GARLIC MAYO

2   egg yolks
1   tablespoon vinegar
1   teaspoon sugar
½   teaspoon salt
¼   teaspoon pepper
1   cup salad oil
2–4   garlic cloves, crushed
2   tablespoons horseradish

In a blender or small mixer bowl, combine egg yolks, vinegar, sugar, salt and pepper. With blender or mixer running, begin adding oil drop by drop. As mixture thickens, oil may be poured in a slow stream. After all oil is added, beat in garlic and horseradish. *Makes about 1⅓ cups.*

RED CLAM SAUCE FOR LINGUINI

¼   cup butter or margarine
2   cloves garlic, minced
½   cup finely chopped onion
½   cup chopped celery
1   teaspoon salt
¼   teaspoon Tabasco pepper sacue
½   teaspoon dried leaf basil
¼   teaspoon dried leaf oregano
¼   teaspoon dried leaf thyme
1   can (1 pound, 12 ounces) tomatoes
2   cans (10½ ounces each) minced clams, drained with liquid reserved
⅓   cup chopped parsley
1   package (1 pound) linguini

In a large saucepan melt butter. Add garlic, onion and celery. Cook over medium heat 5 minutes, until onion and celery are tender. Add salt, pepper sauce, basil, oregano, thyme and tomatoes. Simmer uncovered for 30 minutes. Add clam liquid and simmer 30 minutes longer, until sauce is thickened. Stir in clams and parsley. Heat thoroughly. Cook linguini according to package directions. Drain. Serve clam sauce over hot linguini.

Makes 6 cups sauce; 6 servings.

WHITE CLAM SAUCE FOR LINGUINI

¼	cup butter or margarine
1	tablespoon grated onion
1	clove garlic, minced
2	tablespoons flour
2	cans (10½ ounces each) minced clams, drained with liquid reserved
¼	cup dry white wine
⅓	cup chopped parsley
½	teaspoon dried leaf marjoram
½	teaspoon salt
¼	teaspoon Tabasco pepper sauce
1	package (1 pound) linguini

In a medium saucepan melt butter. Add onion and garlic and cook over medium heat for 3 minutes. Sprinkle with flour and blend well. Add clam liquid, wine, parsley, marjoram, salt and Tabasco pepper sauce. Simmer, uncovered, 10 minutes. Stir in clams and heat thoroughly. Cook linguini according to package directions; drain. Serve clam sauce over hot linguini.

Makes 4 servings.

BLUE CHEESE SAUCE FOR VEGETABLES

¼	cup butter or margarine
¼	cup flour
1	cup milk
1	cup (½ pint) sour cream
⅓	cup firmly packed Danish blue cheese
1	teaspoon yellow mustard
1	teaspoon Worcestershire sauce
1	can (6 ounces) sliced mushrooms, drained (optional)
	Salt

Melt butter and stir in flour. Gradually stir in milk, sour cream and cheese. Cook over low heat while stirring until sauce bubbles and thickens. Stir in mustard, Worcestershire sauce and mushrooms, if desired, and remove from heat. Season to taste with salt. Serve hot or cold. *Makes about 2 cups.*

SAVORY ORANGE SAUCE

1	teaspoon curry powder
1	tablespoon butter or margarine
1	can (10¾ ounces) condensed cream of chicken soup
¼	cup orange juice
1	tablespoon chopped chutney

In saucepan, cook curry in butter a few minutes. Add soup, orange juice and chutney. Heat; stir occasionally. Serve over cooked cauliflower.

Makes about 1½ cups.

FRESH TOMATO SAUCE PIQUANT

6	slices bacon, cut into 1-inch pieces
¼	teaspoon red pepper flakes
6	large, ripe tomatoes, peeled, seeded, coarsely chopped
½	teaspoon dried leaf basil
½	teaspoon salt
½	teaspoon sugar (optional)

In large skillet, over medium heat, cook bacon until lightly browned. Pour off all but 2 tablespoons bacon fat. Tie pepper flakes in small piece of cheesecloth and add to skillet. Add tomatoes. Bring to a boil. Stir in basil, salt and sugar. Remove pepper flakes; discard. Reduce heat and simmer 25 to 35 minutes or until sauce thickens. Serve over baked potato, eggplant, zucchini or any fresh vegetable. *Makes 1 quart sauce.*

LEMON CREAM SAUCE

2	tablespoons butter or margarine
2	tablespoons flour
1	cup milk
¼	teaspoon salt
1	tablespoon fresh lemon juice

In small saucepan melt butter. Blend in flour. Gradually stir in milk. Add salt. Bring to a boil, stirring constantly. Reduce heat and simmer 2 minutes. Add lemon juice. *Makes 1 cup.*

LEMON-ORANGE CURD

4	eggs, well beaten
2	cups sugar
¼	cup fresh-squeezed lemon juice
¼	cup fresh-squeezed orange juice
1	tablespoon grated lemon peel
1	tablespoon grated orange peel
¼	pound butter or margarine

Place all ingredients in top of double boiler over hot (not boiling) water. Stir constantly until butter is melted and ingredients are combined.

Cook until thickened, stirring frequently, about 15 minutes. (Be sure water in bottom of double boiler does not boil.) Refrigerate.   *Makes about 3 cups.*

For use over pound cake, as a spread for bread, in fruit parfaits, or to fill tart shells.

OLD FAVORITE

1 cup dairy sour cream
¼ cup brown sugar

Put sour cream in serving bowl. Sprinkle brown sugar on top. Serve with fresh fruit.   *Makes 1 cup.*

CHUTNEY-YOGURT SAUCE

1 cup plain yogurt
¼ cup chutney

Put yogurt in serving bowl. Spoon chutney on top. Use as dip for fresh fruit.   *Makes 1¼ cups.*

LOW-CALORIE CREME

1 cup creamed cottage cheese
2 tablespoons milk
1 tablespoon sugar

½ teaspoon vanilla
½ teaspoon grated lemon rind

Put all ingredients into blender container. Whirl smooth. Pour into serving bowl. Wonderful with grapes or other fruit.   *Makes about 1 cup.*

RASPBERRY APPLESAUCE

½ cup raspberry jam
½ cup applesauce

Blend jam and applesauce. Pour into serving bowl.   *Makes 1 cup.*

SAVORY BLUEBERRY SAUCE

1 cup water
2 cups sugar
2 slices fresh ginger root, about ⅛ inch thick
4 canned pear halves, diced
4 cups fresh blueberries, rinsed and drained
Grated rind of 1 lemon

In saucepan combine water, sugar and ginger. Boil 5 minutes. Add pears and blueberries. Cook 10 minutes or until blueberries are soft. Stir in lemon rind. Spoon into sterilized jars. Seal and cool. Can be stored in refrigerator, 8 weeks; in freezer in freezer containers for 6 months. Use as sauce for ice cream, puddings, desserts, or pancakes.   *Makes about 3 pints.*

Preserves & Relishes

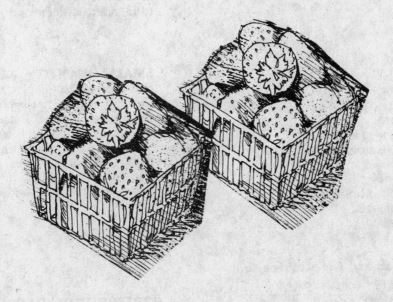

Space is at a premium in most homes—especially in apartments. Yet, a shelf or two devoted to home-canned jams, jellies, preserves, or relishes yields satisfaction far outweighing the space taken up.

When the yearning strikes, you merely reach for a jar of apple-pear jam, for example, to go with toasted muffins or freshly baked biscuits or bread.

Making small batches—four to eight jars at a time—using different fresh fruits or vegetables as they are at the height of their season gives variety to your year-round sampling. Prices also should be lower when you can as the seasons change.

Jams, jellies, and their cousins make good gifts for holidays and for shut-ins and are just right for church or club bazaars.

PRESERVES

APPLE-PEAR JAM

2	pounds apples
2	pounds pears
	Juice of 1 lemon
1	tablespoon grated lemon rind
1	package (1¾ ounces) powdered pectin
6	cups sugar
1	teaspoon cinnamon
½	teaspoon ground cloves
¼	teaspoon nutmeg
¼	teaspoon allspice

Prepare home canning jars and lids according to manufacturer's instructions.

Peel, core and finely chop apples and pears. Measure 3 cups of each fruit into large (6- to 8-quart) saucepot. Add lemon juice, rind and pectin.

Bring to a full, rolling boil over high heat. Add sugar and spices and return to a full boil. Boil hard 1 minute, stirring constantly.

Remove from heat. Skim and stir alternately for 5 minutes. Carefully ladle into hot jars, leaving ¼-inch head space. Adjust caps.

Process 10 minutes in boiling-water-bath canner.   *Makes about five 12-ounce jars.*

BANANA JAM

12	cups sliced bananas (about 20 medium)
6	cups sugar
1½	cups orange juice
¾	cup lemon juice
3	strips orange peel
6	strips lemon peel
2	cinnamon sticks
6	whole cloves

Combine sliced bananas and remaining ingredients in large kettle. Stir over moderate heat until sugar dissolves. Boil rapidly for 10 minutes, reduce heat and simmer, stirring constantly, until thickened, about 15 to 20 minutes. When jam is thick, remove from heat and ladle immediately into sterilized jelly or canning jars. Fill to within one eighth inch of top.

Screw cap on evenly and tightly. Invert for a few seconds and stand jars upright to cool. If jam is to be stored for a long time, place jars on a rack in a large kettle and cover with boiling water. Boil for 10 to 15 minutes. Remove from water and cool.

Makes about 5 pints.

SMALL QUANTITY BANANA JAM: Combine one and one half cups sliced bananas, three quarters cup sugar, 3 tablespoons orange juice, 5 teaspoons lemon juice, 1 small cinnamon stick and 1 whole clove in 2-quart saucepan. Stir over moderate heat until sugar dissolves. Boil rapidly 5 minutes, reduce heat and simmer, stirring constantly, until thickened, about 10 minutes. Pour into small jars or other container, cool, and store in refrigerator.

Makes about 1½ cups.

BLUEBERRY RHUBARB JAM

3	cups rhubarb, cut into 1-inch pieces
3	cups fresh blueberries, rinsed and drained
5	cups sugar
2	packages (3 ounces each) raspberry jello
	Juice from ½ lemon

Mix rhubarb and blueberries (frozen blueberries may be used) with sugar and lemon juice and let stand in refrigerator overnight. Following day bring mixture to a boil over low heat and cook for 12 minutes. Remove from heat and stir in jello. Chill before serving. Ladle into sterilized jelly glasses and pour a ¼-inch-deep layer of melted paraffin over tops.   *Makes about 10 glasses.*

CHERRY PINEAPPLE PEAR JAM

8	ripe pears
1	can (20 ounces) crushed pineapple in heavy syrup, undrained
3	cups sugar
1	teaspoon grated lemon peel
¼	cup lemon juice
¼	teaspoon ground nutmeg
⅛	teaspoon salt
2	jars (8 ounces each) red maraschino cherries, drained and halved

Wash, pare, core and dice the pears. Place pears and all other ingredients in large pot. Bring mixture to a boil over medium heat. Reduce heat and cook about 25 minutes or until thickened, stirring occasionally. Pour into hot sterilized jars and seal.

Makes about 4½ cups.

FREEZER FRUIT CUP JAM

- ¾ cup prepared strawberries (about 1 pint fully ripe strawberries)
- ¾ cup prepared pineapple (¼ fully ripe medium pineapple)
- ½ cup prepared oranges (2 medium oranges)
- ½ cup prepared pears (about ½ pound fully ripe pears)
- 4½ cups (2 pounds) sugar
- ¾ cup water
- 1 package (1¾ ounces) fruit pectin

Prepare containers. Use glass or plastic containers (one pint or less) with tight fitting lids. Wash, scald and drain. Thoroughly crush about 1 pint fully ripe strawberries; measure ¾ cup into a large bowl. Peel, core and grind a fourth of a fully ripe medium pineapple; measure ¾ cup into the bowl. Peel and section 2 medium oranges, discard membrane and seeds, and crush thoroughly; measure ½ cup into the bowl. Peel, core, and grind about ½ pound fully ripe pears; measure ½ cup into the bowl. Mix sugar into fruits; let stand 10 minutes. Mix water and powdered fruit pectin in a small pan. Bring to a boil and boil 1 minute, stirring constantly. Stir into fruits. Continue stirring for 3 minutes. (A few sugar crystals may remain). Ladle quickly into containers; cover at once with tight lids. Let stand until set (this may take up to 24 hours); then store in freezer. If jam is to be used within 2 or 3 weeks, it may be stored in refrigerator. *Makes about 5¼ cups.*

FREEZER STRAWBERRY JAM

- 1 quart fresh strawberries
- 4 cups sugar
- ¾ cup water
- 1 package (1¾ ounces) powdered fruit pectin

Crush berries completely. Measure 2 cups fruit with juices into bowl. Thoroughly mix in sugar; let stand 10 minutes. Combine water and pectin in saucepan. Bring to boil and boil 1 minute, stirring constantly. Stir pectin mixture into fruit; continue stirring 3 minutes. Ladle quickly into sterilized freezer jars or containers, allowing ½-inch head space. Cover with lids. Let stand at room temperature 24 hours. Store in freezer. If to be used in 2 or 3 weeks, store in refrigerator. *Makes 2½ pints.*

FREEZER STRAWBERRY-ORANGE JAM

- 1¾ cups prepared fruit (about 1½ pints fully ripe strawberries)
- 1 medium orange
- 4 cups (1¾ pounds) sugar
- 2 tablespoons lemon juice (1 lemon)
- ½ bottle (3 ounces) fruit pectin

Prepare containers as directed. Crush about 1½ pints fully ripe strawberries; measure 1½ cups into a large bowl or pan. Grate rind from 1 medium orange; add ½ teaspoon to strawberries. Section and chop orange, removing membrane and seeds; measure ¼ cup into the bowl. Mix sugar into the fruits; let stand 10 minutes. Mix lemon juice and fruit pectin; stir into fruit mixture. Continue stirring (about 3 minutes). (A few sugar crystals may remain.) Ladle into containers. Cover at once with tight lids. When jam is set (may take up to 24 hours), store in freezer. If jam will be used within 2 or 3 weeks, store in refrigerator. *Makes 5 cups.*

GINGER-CHERRY JAM

- 4 cups pitted fresh sweet cherries
  Juice of 1 medium orange
- 2 tablespoons grated orange peel
- 2 tablespoons chopped crystalized ginger
- 3 cups sugar

Pit and coarsely chop cherries. Combine in large saucepan with orange peel and juice, ginger and sugar. Bring to boil over medium heat. Stir constantly. Turn heat to high and cook rapidly for 10 to 15 minutes, or until liquid looks slightly thickened. Stir frequently.

Skim off foam. Ladle into sterilized hot canning jars, leaving ¼-inch head space. Seal according to manufacturer's directions.

Place jars on rack in canner. Process 10 minutes in boiling-water bath with boiling water 2 inches above jar tops.

Remove jars from canner. Cool away from drafts. Remove rings from sealed jars after 12 hours.

Makes about 3 half-pints.

HALF-CROCKED PEACH JAM

     3   pounds fresh, ripe peaches
     2   tablespoons lemon juice
     1   package (1¾ ounces) powdered fruit
           pectin
     5½   cups sugar
           Port, bourbon, brandy or rum
           (optional)
           Paraffin

Peel peaches by dropping peaches into boiling water for 30 seconds. Transfer with slotted spoon to cold water; slip off skins. Halve and remove pits. Finely chop or grind peaches to make 4 cups; add lemon juice. In a 6- to 8-quart saucepan, thoroughly mix peaches with powdered fruit pectin. Over high heat, cook and continuously stir until mixture comes to a full boil. Add sugar; bring to a full rolling boil and boil hard 1 minute, stirring constantly. Remove from heat; skim off foam with metal spoon. Stir and skim 5 minutes. Into clean, hot, sterilized crocks or jelly glasses, pour 1 tablespoon of suggested liquor. Add hot jam, leaving one half inch space at top. Cover jam immediately with one eighth inch hot paraffin. Gently tilt jar so paraffin "climbs" and seals edges all around. Store in dry cool place. *Makes 6 to 7 cups.*

Notes: A grosgrain ribbon "lifter" can be placed on jam to help lift out paraffin. Pour a thin layer of paraffin onto the jam, lay ribbon in paraffin and pour another layer of hot wax over the ribbon. Secure end to crock with tape, until paraffin sets firmly.

Jam can be poured into jelly glasses with 2-piece metal lids. Leave one eighth inch at top. Tighten lids on jars one by one and invert. When all jars are sealed, stand upright. Cool.

NECTARINE PLUM JAM

     1½   pounds nectarines
     1½   pounds plums
     2   tablespoons lemon juice
     1   package (1¾ ounces) powdered pectin
     7   cups sugar

Prepare home canning jars and lids according to manufacturer's instructions.

Peel and pit nectarines. Pit plums. Coarsely chop both fruits.

Place chopped fruit in large (6- to 8-quart) saucepot. Stir in lemon juice and pectin. Bring to a full, rolling boil over high heat, stirring frequently. Add sugar; return to a full boil. Boil hard 1 minute, stirring constantly.

Remove from heat. Skim foam. Carefully ladle into hot jars, leaving ¼-inch head space. Adjust caps.

Process 15 minutes in boiling-water-bath canner. *Makes about six 12-ounce jars.*

PEAR HONEY

     3½   pounds ripe pears (about 9 cups,
           chopped)
     6   cups sugar
           Juice of 1 lemon
     1   cup crushed canned pineapple,
           drained

Prepare home canning jars and lids according to manufacturer's instructions.

Peel and core pears and finely chop in a food processor or blender. Put the chopped pears, sugar and lemon juice in a large (6- to 8-quart) saucepot. Place over medium heat and cook until mixture thickens, stirring occasionally. Add the pineapple and cook an additional 15 minutes. Remove from heat and carefully ladle hot pear honey into hot jars, one jar at a time, leaving ¼-inch head space. Wipe jar rim clean, place lid on and screw band down evenly and firmly. Place closed jar in canner. Repeat for each jar.

Process 20 minutes in a boiling-water-bath canner. *Makes six 12-ounce jars.*

PINEAPPLE-STRAWBERRY JELLY

     3½   cups prepared juice (1 small fully ripe
           pineapple and about 3 pints fully ripe
           strawberries)
     5   cups (2¼ pounds) sugar
     1   box (1¾ ounces) powdered fruit pectin

First prepare the juice. Pare 1 small pineapple. Chop very fine or grind. Crush thoroughly, one layer at a time, about 3 pints strawberries. Place fruits in jelly cloth or bag and squeeze out juice. Measure 3½ cups into a large saucepan.

Then make the jelly. Measure sugar and set aside. Mix fruit pectin into juice in saucepan and stir until mixture comes to a hard boil. Immediately add all sugar and stir. Bring to a full rolling boil and boil hard 1 minute, stirring constantly. Remove from heat, skim off foam with metal spoon, and pour quickly into glasses. Cover at once with one eighth inch hot paraffin.

Makes about six (6-fluid-ounce) glasses.

SPICED PEACH BUTTER

2	quarts peach pulp (about 18 medium, fully ripe peaches)
4	cups sugar
1	teaspoon nutmeg
½	teaspoon ground ginger

Wash, peel and pit peaches. Cook until soft, adding only enough water to prevent sticking. Press through sieve or food mill. Place 2 quarts pulp, sugar and spices in medium (4- to 6-quart) saucepot.

Prepare home-canning jars and lids according to manufacturer's instructions.

Cook mixture until thick, about 30 minutes, stirring frequently. Pour, hot, into hot jars, leaving ¼-inch head space. Adjust caps.

Process 10 minutes in boiling-water-bath canner. *Makes about 4 pint-jars.*

SPICED PEACH JAM

4	pounds ripe peaches (about 8 cups chopped)
4	cups sugar
⅔	cup lemon juice
1	cinnamon stick
5	whole cloves
1	piece vanilla bean (about 4 inches)
¼	cup Scotch

Peel peaches by immersing in boiling water for 30 seconds. Slip knife under skin and remove all skin. Remove core and coarsely chop. In large, heavy saucepan, combine peaches, sugar and lemon juice. Place cinnamon, cloves and vanilla bean in square of cheesecloth. Tie and add to peach mixture. Bring mixture to boil over medium heat, stirring often. Simmer 45 minutes, stirring frequently, or until syrup is as thick as honey. Remove from heat and stir in Scotch. Pack into 5 half-pint sterilized jars, leaving ½-inch head space. Seal and process by placing jars on wire rack in large, heavy saucepan. Cover with boiling water to cover jar by 2 inches. Boil for 10 minutes in steady rolling boil. Remove from water and let stand at room temperature for 12 hours. Tighten jars and store until ready to use. *Makes 5 half-pints jam.*

SPICY PEACH 'N HONEY JAM

5	cups sliced peeled peaches (about 2½ pounds)
3	tablespoons sugar
2½	tablespoons honey
1	tablespoon lemon juice
¼	teaspoon ground cinnamon
⅛	teaspoon ground cloves
1	envelope unflavored gelatin
¼	cup cold water

In medium saucepan, combine peaches, sugar, honey, lemon juice, cinnamon and cloves. Heat 5 minutes, crushing peaches slightly. Bring to a boil. Boil rapidly, stirring constantly, for 1 minute.

In small bowl, sprinkle unflavored gelatin over water. Add to mixture and heat, stirring until gelatin dissolves, about 3 minutes.

Let jam stand 5 minutes, skimming off foam with spoon. Ladle into jars. Cover and cool slightly before refrigerating. *Makes about 3 cups.*

STRAWBERRY JAM

4	cups sliced strawberries (about 2 pints)
⅓	cup sugar
2	tablespoons lemon juice
1	envelope unflavored gelatin
½	cup cold water

In medium saucepan, combine strawberries, sugar and lemon juice. Heat mixture 5 minutes, crushing berries slightly. Bring to a boil. Boil rapidly, stirring constantly, for 3 minutes.

In small bowl, sprinkle unflavored gelatin over water. Add to mixture and heat, stirring until gelatin dissolves, about 3 minutes.

Let jam stand 5 minutes, skimming off foam with spoon. Ladle into jars. Cover and cool slightly before refrigerating. *Makes about 2 cups.*

STRAWBERRY RHUBARB JAM

4	cups strawberries, washed and stemmed
1	pound rhubarb (fresh or frozen)
¼	cup lemon juice
1	package (1¾ ounces) powdered pectin
5½	cups sugar

Prepare home canning jars and lids according to manufacturer's instructions.

Crush strawberries; place in a large (6- to 8-quart) saucepot. Wash rhubarb if fresh; remove and discard leaves. Finely chop rhubarb.

Measure 2 cups chopped rhubarb into saucepot with strawberries. Add lemon juice and pectin. Bring to a full, rolling boil over high heat. Add sugar; return to a full boil. Boil hard 1 minute, stirring constantly.

Continued

Remove from heat. Skim foam. Carefully ladle into hot jars, leaving ¼-inch head space. Adjust caps.

Process 10 minutes in boiling-water-bath canner.   *Makes about six 8-ounce jars.*

BLUEBERRY-CITRUS MARMALADE

2	navel oranges
2	lemons
2	green apples, peeled, cored and chopped
¾	cup water
3	cups crushed fresh blueberries
5	cups sugar
1	bottle (6 ounces) liquid fruit pectin

With a sharp knife thinly slice off colored part of orange and lemon peel. Cut peel into thin shreds and place in a large saucepan. Add apples and water. Cover and simmer 10 minutes, stirring occasionally. Slice away white membrane and seeds of oranges and lemons and chop pulp. Add fruit pulp and blueberries (frozen blueberries may be used) to saucepan. Cover and simmer 12 minutes. Stir in sugar. Bring mixture to a full rolling boil. Boil hard for 1 minute. Stir in fruit pectin. Remove from heat and skim foam. Ladle mixture into sterilized ½-pint jars. Pour ¼-inch-deep layer of melted paraffin over tops. Store in a cool, dry, dark place.

Makes fifteen ½-pint jars.

CHERRY-PEAR CONSERVE

6	ripe pears
2½	cups sugar
2	navel oranges
2	jars (8 ounces each) red maraschino cherries, drained and halved
½	cup dark seedless raisins
¼	cup lemon juice

Pare the pears and cut into small pieces. Add the sugar and allow to stand overnight. Wash oranges; remove orange peel in thin strips with vegetable parer or sharp knife. Chop orange peel until fine. Juice the oranges. Add orange peel and juice and remaining ingredients to pear mixture. Cook in large saucepan about 25 to 30 minutes or until thickened. Pour into hot sterilized jars and seal.

Makes about four 8-ounce jars.

FROZEN SWEET CHERRY TOPPING

4	cups prepared fresh sweet cherries
4	cups sugar
¼	cup lemon juice
1	cup water
1	package (1¾ ounces) powdered fruit pectin

Wash, stem, pit and halve cherries; measure 4 cups. Mix in sugar and lemon juice. Let stand 30 minutes; stir occasionally. Combine water and pectin; bring to boil and boil hard 1 minute. Pour over cherry mixture; stir about 3 minutes. Pour into clean containers; cover with tight-fitting lids. Let stand at room temperature until cool. Freeze.

Makes approximately 6 half-pints.

ORANGE-LEMON MARMALADE

1½	quarts water
3	cups thinly sliced orange peel (about 4 large oranges)
3½	cups chopped orange pulp (about 4 large oranges)
3½	cups thinly sliced lemon (about 4 large lemons)
	Sugar, about 5½ cups

Combine water, fruit and peel in a medium (4- to 6-quart) saucepot; simmer 5 minutes. Remove from heat. Cover; let stand 12 to 18 hours in a cool place. Then, cook rapidly until peel is tender, about 45 minutes.

Prepare home canning jars and lids according to manufacturer's instructions.

Measure fruit and liquid. Add 1 cup sugar for each cup fruit mixture. Bring slowly to boiling, stirring until sugar dissolves. Cook rapidly to jellying point (220 degrees F.), about 15 minutes, stirring frequently. Pour, hot, into hot jars, leaving ¼-inch head space. Adjust caps.

Process 10 minutes in boiling-water-bath canner.   *Makes about six 8-ounce jars.*

PEACH CHUTNEY

3	quarts peeled, coarsely chopped fresh peaches (18 medium)
1½	cups chopped fresh onion
3	cloves garlic, minced
2¼	cups light brown sugar, firmly packed
2¼	cups cider vinegar
6	tablespoons fresh lemon juice

1½   teaspoons salt
1½   teaspoons ground ginger
½   teaspoon ground nutmeg
⅛   teaspoon Tabasco pepper sauce

In large kettle, combine all ingredients. Cook slowly, uncovered, about 1 hour, or until mixture is thick; stir occasionally. Pour immediately into hot sterilized jars and seal. Since chutney improves on standing, allow at least one month before opening.   *Makes about 2 quarts.*

QUICK STRAWBERRY MARMALADE

2   pints strawberries, washed and stemmed
1   cup orange marmalade
2   tablespoons lemon juice

In blender, whirl berries with orange marmalade until smooth. Pour into heavy pan. Add lemon juice. Bring to boil, stirring. Then cook over medium heat 15 minutes, stirring occasionally, until mixture thickens slightly. Pour into sterilized jars and seal, or use at once.   *Makes 1 pint.*

QUICK STRAWBERRY PRESERVES

2   pints strawberries, stemmed and washed
7   cups sugar (3 pounds)
¼   cup lemon juice
3   ounces liquid pectin (½ of a 6-ounce bottle)

Measure 5 cups whole, ripe berries (a packed measurement, but without crushing). Layer in broad, heavy pan with sugar. Let stand 10 minutes. Bring slowly to boil, stirring gently to keep fruit whole. Remove from heat. Cool at room temperature 4 hours. Add lemon juice. Bring mixture to full rolling boil over high heat; boil hard 2 minutes, stirring gently. Remove from heat; at once, stir in liquid pectin. Skim off foam with metal spoon and stir for 10 minutes, to prevent floating fruit. Ladle into sterilized jars. Seal, or cover at once with hot paraffin.   *Makes 7 cups.*

Note: All preserves need to be stored about two weeks before eating to reach perfect consistency.

SPICED APPLE RINGS

7   pounds Delicious apples (about 16 medium)
    SOAKING SOLUTION:
8   cups water, 2 tablespoons salt
2   tablespoons vinegar
4   cups water
4   cups sugar
4   teaspoons red food coloring
1½ teaspoons ground cloves
1½ teaspoons ground cinnamon
1½ teaspoons ground allspice

Prepare home canning jars and lids according to manufacturer's instructions.

Wash and core apples. Slice into ¼-inch rings and place in soaking solution to prevent discoloration.

Combine water, sugar and food coloring in a large (6- to 8-quart) sauce pot. Bring to a boil and boil 5 minutes, stirring occasionally.

Remove syrup from heat and add drained apple rings. Let the apples remain in the syrup for 10 minutes. Add spices to apples and return to heat. Bring to a boil, then simmer until apple rings are just tender, about 30 minutes.

Remove from heat and let cool. Pack apple rings in hot jars, leaving ½-inch head space. Return the syrup to heat and bring to a boil. Carefully pour hot syrup over apple rings, leaving ½-inch space. Remove air bubbles with a non-metallic kitchen utensil. As each jar is filled, wipe jar rim clean, place lid on and screw band down evenly and firmly. Place closed jar in canner.

Process 10 minutes in a boiling-water-bath canner.   *Makes about 5 pints.*

SPICED PEACHES WITH RAISINS AND ALMONDS

2   cups sugar
1   cup raisins
5   to 6 cinnamon sticks
3   cups water
¼   cup light rum
½   teaspoon whole cloves
3   whole allspice berries
3   quarts peeled and pitted fresh peach halves (10 to 12 medium-size peaches)
½   cup slivered blanched almonds

In a large saucepot, combine sugar, raisins, cinnamon sticks, water and rum. Tie cloves and allspice in cheesecloth; place in saucepot. Stir mixture until sugar is dissolved.

Add peaches. Bring to a boil. Boil for 5 minutes, stirring frequently. Pack peaches and syrup into canning jars, leaving ¼-inch head space.

Cover, following manufacturer's directions. Process in boiling water bath for 15 minutes. Cool jars and check seals according to manufacturer's directions.　　　　　　　　　*Makes 5 to 6 pints.*

TOMATO CONSERVE

5	pounds tomatoes, red or yellow
2	pounds sugar
½	teaspoon salt
1	orange, thinly sliced
1	lemon, thinly sliced
1	stick (3-inch) cinnamon
1	piece whole ginger
2	cups seedless raisins
½	cup lemon juice
¼	teaspoon Tabasco

Peel tomatoes and chop. Combine with sugar, salt, sliced orange and sliced lemon. Stir over heat until sugar dissolves. Add cinnamon and ginger, bring to a boil; cook over low heat until thick, about 1 hour, stirring occasionally. Remove cinnamon and ginger. Add raisins and lemon juice and bring again to a boil. Stir in Tabasco, pour into hot pint or half-pint jars, and seal at once.　　　　　*Makes 3½ pints.*

TOMATO CONSERVE-CHUTNEY

3	pounds tomatoes
1	orange
½	lemon
1½	cups seedless raisins
2	cups liquid brown sugar
1	cup chopped walnuts

Remove stem ends from tomatoes. Dice tomatoes coarsely. Put into large, heavy saucepan or kettle.

Cut orange and lemon into thin slices. Discard seeds. Cut orange slices in quarters and lemon slices in halves. Add orange and lemon slices, raisins and liquid brown sugar to tomatoes.

Cook slowly, stirring frequently, until thick, about 3 hours. Stir in walnuts. Ladle into hot sterilized glasses. Seal. Cool, label and store.　　　　　　　　　*Makes about 5 cups.*

WINTER CONSERVE

6	oranges
5	cups water
6	cups sugar
½	cup raisins

¼	cup lemon juice
1	piece stick cinnamon
½	cup flaked or shredded coconut

Peel oranges and finely chop the peel. Place the peel in a large (6- to 8-quart) saucepot with 5 cups water. Bring to a boil and cook until peel is tender, about 20 minutes.

Remove membrane and seeds from oranges and dice the pulp. Add pulp to undrained peel. Continue cooking until mixture is reduced by half, about 20 minutes.

Prepare home canning jars and lids according to manufacturer's instructions.

Add sugar, raisins, lemon juice and cinnamon to the fruit mixture; stir until sugar is dissolved. Cook until thickened, about 30 minutes. Remove from heat and stir in coconut. Carefully ladle hot conserve into hot jars, one jar at a time, leaving ½-inch head space. Wipe jar rim clean, place lid on and screw band down evenly and firmly. Place closed jar in canner. Repeat for each jar.

Process 10 minutes in a simmering (180–185-degree) water bath canner.

Makes about seven 8-ounce jars.

RELISHES

BLUEBERRY MINCEMEAT

½	cup water
1	tablespoon lemon juice
1	beef bouillon cube
3	green apples, unpeeled, cored and finely chopped
1	pint fresh blueberries, rinsed and drained
2	medium zucchini squash, trimmed and finely chopped
2	tablespoons finely chopped orange peel
½	cup sugar
½	teaspoon cinnamon
¼	teaspoon nutmeg
2	envelopes unflavored gelatin
½	cup cold water

In a large saucepan, mix water, lemon juice, bouillon cube, apples, blueberries, squash, orange peel, spices and sugar. Cover and simmer for 20 minutes, stirring occasionally. Stir gelatin into cold water. Stir this mixture into hot mincemeat. Spoon mixture into jars, cover and cool. Store in refrigerator until needed.　　　　　　　　　*Makes about 2 pints.*

Note: Use as a relish for meats or poultry, or as a filling for pie. Two cups of the mincemeat is enough for one 8-inch double-crust pie. Bake pie as usual for mincemeat pie, serving warm or cold. This mixture cannot be frozen, since freezing would break the gelatin. Keeps two months easily in the refrigerator.

CARROT-PEPPER RELISH

8	medium carrots
8	medium onions
4	large green peppers
3	tablespoons salt
2	cups sugar
2	cups cider vinegar
½	teaspoon Tabasco

Scrape carrots. Peel onions and seed peppers. Slice vegetables and put through food grinder, using medium blade. Combine salt, sugar and vinegar, and bring to a boil. Add vegetables and continue boiling 5 minutes. Add Tabasco and pack at once into hot pint or half-pint jars. The liquid should cover the vegetables completely. Seal, cool and label. *Makes 4 pints.*

CORN RELISH

18	ears fresh corn
3	large green peppers, seeds and membranes removed, quartered
2	large sweet red peppers, seeds and membranes removed, quartered
3	stalks celery, cut into 1-inch pieces
2	medium onions, quartered
3	ounces pimiento
2	cups vinegar
1	cup sugar
1	tablespoon salt
1	tablespoon celery seed
1	tablespoon dry mustard
1	teaspoon ground turmeric

Bring water to a boil in 12-quart saucepot. Husk corn and cook in boiling water for 5 minutes; remove corn to cold water bath. Drain. Set speed control dial of food processor at high. In bowl of food processor, place chopping blade. Add six pieces of pepper. Lock cover into place. Pulse on-off until chopped. Remove cover and place chopped peppers in saucepot. Repeat with celery, onion and pimiento. Cut corn from cobs, taking care not to scrape the husks. Put corn (about 8 cups) into saucepot with vegetables. Add remaining ingredients to saucepot; mix well. Over medium heat, bring mixture to a boil, reduce heat and simmer for

30 minutes. Spoon into hot jars, leaving ½-inch head space. Adjust lids. Process in water bath for 15 minutes. *Makes 6 pints.*

CRANBERRY-MINCEMEAT RELISH

2	cups fresh or frozen-fresh cranberries, or 1 can (1 pound) whole berry cranberry sauce
1	can (1 pound, 4 ounces) crushed pineapple, undrained
1	cup prepared mincemeat
1	tablespoon rum flavoring

Combine all ingredients in a large saucepan and simmer for 10 minutes, stirring occasionally. Serve warm or chilled. Serve with roast beef, chicken, turkey, ham, pork roast, duckling, goose, game hens. *Makes about 5 cups.*

DILL-CRANBERRY RELISH

2	cups fresh cranberries
1	medium orange
3	medium dill pickles
¼	cup walnuts
6	tablespoons sugar

Thoroughly wash cranberries and orange. Slice orange and remove seeds.

Put cranberries, orange slices, pickles and walnuts through food chopper. Stir in sugar.

Chill several hours before serving. *Makes 3 cups.*

Note: Relish may be prepared in food processor. Put all ingredients into work bowl. Process until finely chopped.

END-OF-SUMMER FRESH FRUIT RELISH

9	ripe tomatoes, coarsely chopped
4	oranges, peeled, seeded, chopped
3	medium onions, chopped
3	large red peppers, diced
1½	cups cider vinegar
1	cup sugar
1	tablespoon salt
1	stick cinnamon (about 3 inches)
2	teaspoons chopped fresh ginger root, with skin
1	tablespoon pickling spice
6	pears, cored, coarsely chopped
6	peaches, cored, coarsely chopped

Continued

Place chopped tomatoes, oranges, onions and red peppers in large saucepot. Stir in vinegar, sugar, salt, cinnamon stick and ginger. Tie pickling spice in cheesecloth and add to mixture. Bring to boiling; reduce heat, simmer, uncovered, 1 hour, stirring often. Add pears and peaches. Simmer 1½ to 2 hours longer or until mixture is slightly thickened. Spoon into sterilized glass jars and seal.

Makes 12 half-pint jars.

FRESH CORN-ZUCCHINI RELISH

4	cups fresh corn cut from cob (8 ears)
1½	cups chopped onion
1	cup chopped red pepper
1	cup chopped green pepper
2	cups cider vinegar
1½	cups sugar
4	teaspoons salt
1	teaspoon celery seed
1	teaspoon turmeric
1	teaspoon mustard seed
½	teaspoon dry mustard
3	medium-size zucchini, sliced ¼ inch thick (4 cups sliced)

In large kettle, combine all ingredients except zucchini; mix well. Simmer, uncovered, 20 minutes, stirring occasionally. Add zucchini; simmer, uncovered 20 minutes longer. Relish can be kept in refrigerator for use within a short time, or can be poured hot into sterilized jars and sealed for future use.

Makes 2 quarts.

Note: To sterilize jars, place jars, lids, caps and rings in kettle of hot water so jars are submerged. Bring water to boil; boil jars, lids, caps and rings 10 minutes.

FRESH 'N' PICKLED ONION RING RELISH

1	tablespoon mixed pickling spices
⅓	cup water
⅓	cup cider vinegar
2	tablespoons sugar
¾	teaspoon salt
¼	teaspoon pepper
1	cup chopped fresh tomato
1	cup chopped fresh green pepper
2	cups sliced white onions

Tie pickling spices in cheesecloth. In medium saucepan, heat spice bag and remaining ingredients except onions to boiling.

Reduce heat to medium. Cover and cook 3 minutes.

Stir in onions. Cook another 3 minutes. Remove spice bag. Cover and refrigerate.

Makes 8 to 10 servings.

GRAPEFRUIT-CORN RELISH

4	grapefruit
2	cans (12 ounces each) whole kernel corn, drained
1	jar (9 ounces) sweet pickle relish
2	tablespoons chopped pimiento
½	cup salad oil
	Salad greens

Cut grapefruit in half. Remove core. Cut around each section, loosening fruit from membrane. Lift fruit out and reserve. Pull out remaining membrane; reserve cups. In medium bowl, mix together grapefruit sections and remaining ingredients. Chill. Spoon into grapefruit shells lined with salad greens to serve. *Makes 8 servings.*

GREEN TOMATO GARDEN RELISH

8	pounds medium-sized green tomatoes (about 24 tomatoes)
6	cups finely shredded green cabbage (about 1¼ pounds)
3	cups chopped onions (3 large onions)
1	cup diced celery
1	large green pepper, seeded and diced
1	large sweet red pepper, seeded and diced
⅔	cup salt
3	cups cider vinegar
2½	cups liquid brown sugar
2	tablespoons celery seeds
4	teaspoons mustard seeds
1	teaspoon pepper

Remove stem ends from tomatoes. Cut tomatoes into very thin slices. (You should have about 5½ quarts.)

Layer vegetables in very large bowl or kettle, sprinkling each layer with salt. Let stand 12 hours or overnight. Drain vegetables well, pressing lightly in sieve. Put vegetables into large kettle.

Bring vinegar, liquid brown sugar, celery and mustard seeds and pepper to boiling in medium-sized saucepan. Pour over vegetables. Cover. Bring to boiling. Reduce heat to low and cook, stirring frequently, 15 to 20 minutes until vegetables are tender-crisp. (Do not overcook.)

Ladle at once into hot sterilized jars. Seal. Cool, label and store. *Makes about 4 quarts.*

ITALIAN SWEET RELISH

1	medium eggplant
4	cups (8 pounds) chopped tomatoes
1½	cups chopped onion
1½	cups chopped green pepper
⅓	cup raisins
1	cup sugar
1	cup vinegar
¾	cup water
1	teaspoon Tabasco

Do not peel eggplant; chop into cubes (about 4 cups chopped). Place all ingredients in medium size pot. Bring to boil, stirring occasionally, do not boil. Simmer 10 minutes. Seal in hot sterilized jars.

Makes about 3 pints.

PICKLE-DATE CHOW-CHOW

1½	cups chopped sweet mixed pickles
1½	cups chopped dates (8-ounce package)
2	tablespoons slivered orange peel
½	cup sweet-pickle liquid
½	cup water

Combine pickles, dates and orange peel in bowl or jar.

Mix together pickle liquid and water. Pour over pickle mixture.

Cover and refrigerate at least 24 hours before serving. Stir several times to mix well.

Makes 3 cups.

RELISH AMERICANA

1½	cups cooked corn, drained
1	cucumber, chopped
1	medium green or red pepper, diced
¾	cup vinegar
¼	cup prepared mustard
¼	teaspoon Tabasco
¾	cup sugar
1½	teaspoons salt

Combine all ingredients. Chill at least 1 hour before serving. Store covered in clean 1-pint jar. This relish may be kept in refrigerator about 2 weeks.

Makes about 1 pint (6–8 servings).

SPICY NECTARINE RELISH

8–9	cups peeled and sliced ripe nectarines
1½	cups firmly packed light brown sugar
1	cup raisins

2	teaspoons mustard seed
1½	teaspoons ground cinnamon
½	teaspoon ground ginger
½	teaspoon ground cloves
¾	cup cider vinegar
½	cup chopped walnuts

In a large saucepot, combine all ingredients except walnuts. Bring to a boil. Simmer, uncovered, stirring frequently, until thick, about 45 minutes.

Add walnuts. Cook and stir for 2 minutes. Pack mixture and liquid into canning jars, leaving ¼-inch head space.

Cover, following manufacturer's directions. Process in boiling water bath for 15 minutes. Cool jars and check seal according to manufacturer's directions.

Makes 6 half-pints.

Note: Substitute 1½ tablespoons of mixed pickling spice in place of cinnamon, cloves, ginger and mustard, if desired.

SWEET PEPPER RELISH

12	medium green peppers, seeds and membranes removed, quartered
12	medium sweet red peppers, seeds and membranes removed, quartered
4	medium onions, quartered
	Boiling water
2	cups cider vinegar
1¾	cups sugar
1	tablespoon salt
1	teaspoon mustard seeds

Set speed control dial of food processor at high. In bowl of food processor, place chopping blade. Add six pieces of pepper. Lock cover into place. Pulse on-off to chop pepper. Put chopped pepper into 4-quart saucepot. Repeat with remaining peppers and onions. Add boiling water to saucepot to just cover vegetables. Let stand for 15 minutes. Drain in colander for 4 to 5 hours. Return drained vegetables to saucepot and add remaining ingredients. Bring to a boil, then reduce heat and simmer uncovered for 20 minutes. Spoon loosely into hot jars, leaving ½-inch head space. Adjust lids. Process in water bath for 20 minutes.

Makes 3 pints.

CORN AND RED PEPPERS WITH BASIL

1½–3	pounds corn per pint
½	sweet red pepper per pint
	Basil

Continued

Prepare home canning jars and lids according to manufacturer's instructions.

Cut corn from cob. Cut red peppers into strips. Pack corn loosely in hot jars, leaving 1-inch head space. Place 3 or 4 strips of red pepper in jars of corn. Add ½ teaspoon basil to each jar. Carefully cover with boiling water, leaving 1-inch head space. Remove air bubbles with a non-metallic spatula. Adjust caps.

Process 55 minutes at 10 pounds pressure in a steam pressure canner.

CRISP CUCUMBER RINGS

9	long, slender cucumbers
5	medium onions
2	cups water
½	cup salt
2	cups vinegar
1½	cups sugar
2	teaspoons mustard seed
2	teaspoons celery seed
½	teaspoon Tabasco

Wash and dry cucumbers; slice without paring. Peel onions and slice. Combine salt with water and pour over vegetables. Let stand 3 hours; then drain and discard liquid. Combine vinegar, sugar and spices; stir over heat until sugar is dissolved. Add cucumbers and onions; boil 5 minutes. Add Tabasco and pack at once into hot jars. The liquid should cover the vegetables completely. Seal, cool and label.

Makes 2 quarts plus 1 pint.

CURRIED FRUIT

1	package (11 ounces) dried mixed fruit
¼	cup water
3	tablespoons margarine
⅓	cup dark corn syrup
2	tablespoons firmly packed brown sugar
2	teaspoons curry powder

Place dried mixed fruit in top of large double boiler. Pour water over fruit. Cover; cook over boiling water about 25 minutes or until fruit is tender. In 2-quart saucepan melt margarine over medium heat. Stir in corn syrup, brown sugar and curry powder. Stirring constantly, bring to boil. Stir in fruit and return to boil, stirring to coat fruit with syrup. Serve warm as a meat accompaniment.

Makes about 1½ cups.

Note: Curried fruit may be stored in covered container in refrigerator and heated just before serving.

GARDEN PICKLES

1	pound green beans, ends removed
1	pound zucchini, cut into ¼-inch slices
½	pound carrots (about 3 medium), cut into ¼-inch slices
½	pound small pickling onions, peeled
2	large green peppers, cut into ½-inch strips
1	large red pepper, cut into 2-inch strips
3	cups cider vinegar
1	cup brown sugar
1	cup granulated sugar
2	tablespoons mustard seed
1½	tablespoons canning salt
1	teaspoon cinnamon
1	teaspoon ground ginger

Prepare home canning jars and lids according to manufacturer's instructions.

Combine vinegar, sugars, spices and salt in large (6- to 8-quart stainless steel, glass-ceramic or unchipped enamel) saucepot. Bring to a boil; add the prepared vegetables. Return mixture to a boil; then reduce heat and simmer 15 minutes. Remove from heat and carefully pack into hot jars, leaving ¼-inch head space. Remove air bubbles with a non-metallic spatula. Adjust caps.

Process 15 minutes in boiling-water-bath canner. *Makes about 5 pint jars.*

GREEN BEANS WITH LEMON RIND

1½ - 2½ pounds green beans per quart
Fresh lemon

Prepare home canning jars and lids according to manufacturer's instructions.

Wash and drain beans. Remove strings and cut or break into pieces. Cut yellow peel from lemon into narrow strips. Pack beans tightly into hot jars, leaving 1-inch head space. Place 1 or 2 pieces of lemon rind in each jar of beans. Carefully cover with boiling water, leaving 1-inch head space. Remove air bubbles with a non-metallic spatula. Adjust caps.

Process 25 minutes at 10 pounds pressure in a steam pressure cooker.

GREEN CHERRY TOMATO PICKLES

1¼	pounds small green cherry tomatoes
¾	cup light corn syrup
¾	cup cider vinegar
½	cup sugar

1 tablespoon mixed pickling spice
½ teaspoon salt
4 small cloves garlic

Wash, dry and remove stems of cherry tomatoes. Pierce each 2 or 3 times with a small skewer or wooden pick. In 2-quart saucepan, stir together corn syrup, vinegar, sugar, pickling spice and salt. Stirring constantly, bring to boil over medium heat; reduce heat. Stirring frequently, simmer 10 minutes. Immediately pack cherry tomatoes and 1 garlic clove into each clean, hot ½-pint jar. Pour boiling syrup into each jar covering tomatoes and leaving ½-inch head space. Remove air bubbles. Wipe top edge with damp towel. Seal according to jar manufacturer's directions. Process in boiling water bath 15 minutes. Cool on wire rack or folded towel.

Makes 4 half-pint jars.

GREEN TOMATO PICKLES

7 pounds green tomatoes
1 medium onion, diced
¾ cup cooking, canning and pickling salt (or non-iodized salt)
1 quart cider vinegar
1 cup water
½ cup sugar
2 teaspoons mustard seed
1 teaspoon mixed pickling spices
½ teaspoon celery seed
6 whole peppercorns

Choose tomatoes that are completely green, with no pink coloring.

Wash tomatoes. Cut into quarters. Trim off stem and blossom ends. Layer in large glass or ceramic bowl or jar, sprinkling each layer with cooking, canning and pickling salt, using about ⅔ cups.

Place onion in small glass or ceramic bowl. Add remaining cooking, canning and pickling salt. Mix well.

Cover vegetables. Let stand overnight or 8 to 10 hours. Then rinse and drain well. Pack tomatoes into sterilized pint jars, dividing onions evenly into each jar.

Tie mustard seed and other spices in cheesecloth. In 3-quart saucepan, boil vinegar, water, sugar and spice bag together for 3 minutes. Pour mixture over vegetables in jars until ¼ inch from top. Remove air bubbles. Wipe rims of jars.

Heat flat metal lids (one at a time) for 30 seconds in boiling water. Place on jar and screw on ring. Place jars on rack in simmering water. (Be sure water covers tops of jars.) Bring to boil. Cover and process for 15 minutes.

Remove to towel-covered surface to cool.

Makes 6 pints.

MUSTARD PICKLES

3 pounds cucumbers or zucchini
2 large onions
¼ cup salt
2 cups sugar
2 cups white vinegar
2 teaspoons mustard seed
1 teaspoon celery seed
1 teaspoon turmeric
½ teaspoon dry mustard

Set speed control dial of food processor at 4. In bowl of food processor, place slicing blade. Lock cover into place. Fill feed tube with cucumbers. Turn food processor on to slice cucumbers. Repeat with remaining cucumbers and onions. Turn food processor off. Put sliced vegetables into 5-quart saucepot. Sprinkle with salt and cover with cold water. Let stand for 2 hours. Drain in colander. Rinse; drain again. In 5-quart saucepot, mix remaining ingredients. Over medium heat, heat to boiling and boil for 2 minutes. Remove from heat and add drained vegetables. Let stand for 2 hours, stirring occasionally. Place saucepot with pickle slices over medium heat. Boil for 5 minutes. Pack into hot jars, leaving ½-inch head space. Adjust lids. Process in water bath for 15 minutes. *Makes 3 pints.*

PEAS WITH CURRY

1½–3 pounds peas per pint
Curry powder

Prepare home canning jars and lids according to manufacturer's instructions.

Wash, drain and shell fresh peas. Wash again. Pack loosely in hot jars, leaving 1-inch head space. Add 1 teaspoon curry powder to each jar. Carefully cover with boiling water, leaving 1-inch head space. Remove air bubbles with a non-metallic spatula. Adjust caps.

Process 40 minutes at 10 pounds pressure in a steam pressure canner.

PICKLED PEPPERS

3–4 pounds sweet bell peppers
1⅔ cups cooking, canning and pickling salt (or non-iodized salt)
5 quarts water
¼ cup sugar
1 quart white vinegar
1 cup water
2 cloves garlic, split

Continued

Wash peppers. Cut lengthwise into quarters. Remove membranes and seeds; discard. Place peppers in large glass or ceramic bowl.

In large kettle, combine cooking, canning and pickling salt and 5 quarts water. Heat until salt dissolves. Cool salt water, then pour over peppers.

Let stand overnight or for 12 to 14 hours. Drain. Rinse well. Drain again. Pack into hot sterilized pint jars.

In 3-quart saucepan, combine sugar, vinegar, 1 cup water and garlic. Simmer for 10 minutes. Remove garlic. Pour over peppers in jars, filling to ¼ inch from top. Remove air bubbles. Wipe rims of jars.

Heat flat metal lids (one at a time) for 30 seconds in boiling water. Remove and place on jars. Screw on rings.

Place jars on rack in simmering water. (Be sure water covers tops of jars.) Bring to boil. Cover and process for 15 minutes.

Remove to towel-covered surface to cool.

Makes 5 pints.

PICKLED WATERMELON RIND

¼	cups prepared watermelon rind (about 4 pounds of watermelon)
3	tablespoons salt
3	quarts water
1	cup fresh lemon juice
5	cups sugar
1	lemon, sliced
1	piece ginger root
2	sticks cinnamon
1	tablespoon ground nutmeg
1	tablespoon whole cloves
1½	teaspoons mace
2	cups vinegar

To prepare watermelon rind, cut off outer green skin and leave a very small amount of the red melon. Cut into cubes. Place in large kettle with salt, water and lemon juice. Bring to a boil over medium heat. Cover and simmer until rind is tender, about 10 minutes. Remove from heat and refrigerate overnight.

The next day, drain rind and rinse well. Place rind, sugar and remaining ingredients in kettle and bring to boiling. Reduce heat and simmer 2 hours, until syrup thickens. Ladle into hot jelly or canning jars, seal and cool. Or cool and store in refrigerator. *Makes seven 8-ounce jars.*

PICKLED ZUCCHINI SLICES

2	pounds zucchini, about 11 inches in diameter
1	medium onion, sliced lengthwise
⅓	cup cooking, canning and pickling salt (or non-iodized salt)
2	tablespoons mixed pickling spice
10	whole peppercorns
1½	cups sugar
½	teaspoon powdered alum
2	cups white vinegar
1	cup distilled water

Wash zucchini. Trim off stem and blossom ends. Cut into ¼-inch slices. Layer zucchini in glass or ceramic bowl, sprinkling each layer with cooking, canning and pickling salt, using about ¼ cup.

In small glass or ceramic bowl, mix remaining cooking, canning and pickling salt with onions. Cover each bowl of salted vegetables with waxed paper or clean towel. Let stand 2 hours. Rinse zucchini and onions. Drain well.

Tie spices in cheesecloth. In 3-quart saucepan, combine spices with sugar, alum, vinegar and distilled water. Bring to boil. Reduce heat and simmer pickling liquid for 5 minutes.

Add half the zucchini with half the onions. Cook for 2 minutes. Pack into hot, sterilized pint jars. Fill to ¼ inch from top with hot pickling liquid. Repeat cooking and packing with remaining zucchini, onions and pickling liquid.

Remove air bubbles. Wipe rims. Heat flat metal lids (one at a time) for 30 seconds in boiling water. Remove from water and immediately place lids on jars and screw on rings.

Place jars on rack in simmering water. (Be sure water covers tops of jars.) Bring to boil. Cover and process for 15 minutes.

Remove to towel-covered surface to cool.

Makes 2 pints.

Vegetables

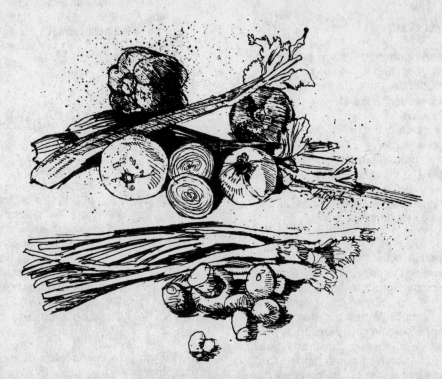

Vegetables are at their best when prepared simply. Few of us have a patch of land on which to grow our own beans, corn, and lettuce, but we *do* have a broad selection of vegetables to choose from in the supermarkets and at the fruit-and-vegetable stands that sprout like mung beans during summer months along the roadside.

Through the years I've enjoyed learning the variety of cooking methods for preparing vegetables—steaming, pureeing, grilling on the outdoor barbecue. Again, as with so many foods, preparation of vegetables is only limited by your time and imagination.

And to me there is nothing more satisfying than a potato, well-baked in its skin and not steamed in an aluminum foil "wrapper." The skin, with all its added nutrients, is a potato dessert.

BABY LIMAS IN GINGER-ORANGE SAUCE

1	cup fresh or canned orange sections, drained, reserving liquid, or 1 can (11 ounces) mandarin oranges, drained, reserving liquid
	Orange juice
2	teaspoons cornstarch
2	teaspoons sugar
¼	teaspoon ground ginger
1	package (10 ounces) frozen baby lima beans
½	cup toasted canned onion rings
	Bacon bits (optional)

Drain orange sections or mandarin oranges, reserving liquid. Add enough orange juice to drained liquid to measure 1 cup. Combine 2 tablespoons of the liquid with cornstarch, sugar and ginger. Mix until well blended. Combine with remaining orange liquid in a saucepan. Cook over medium high heat until thickened and clear, stirring constantly. Add limas and simmer for 8 minutes or until tender. Add orange sections. Stir in toasted onion rings. Serve garnished with bacon bits if desired. For a party, serve in scooped-out orange shells. Goes well with baked ham, roast turkey or pork. *Makes 4 servings.*

BAKED BEANS

1	pound dried navy (pea) beans
2	quarts water, divided
½	pound salt pork
2	teaspoons salt
1	cup chopped onion
1	cup dark corn syrup
½	cup chili sauce
1	teaspoon dry mustard
½	teaspoon pepper

Rinse and pick over beans. In large bowl, cover beans with 1 quart water. Soak 8 hours or overnight.

(Or use quick method of soaking: In 4-quart saucepan, place rinsed beans and 1 quart water. Bring to boil. Cover and boil 2 minutes. Remove from heat. Let stand 1 hour.)

Drain beans.

In 4-quart saucepan, place beans, remaining 1 quart water, salt pork and salt. Cover. Boil 1 hour. Drain, reserving bean liquid.

In 3-quart bean pot or casserole, place beans and salt pork. Stir in onion, corn syrup, chili sauce, mustard, pepper and bean liquid to cover (about 1 cup).

Cover. Bake in 325-degree oven 3 hours. Uncover and continue baking 30 minutes or until beans are browned and tender.

Makes 8 servings of ¾ cup each.

INDIAN CRANBERRY SUCCOTASH

2	packages (10 ounces each) frozen Fordhook lima beans
¼	cup butter or margarine
½	cup well seasoned chicken broth
6	slices bacon, chopped
1	onion, chopped
1½	cups fresh or frozen-fresh cranberries, rinsed and drained
½	cup chopped celery
4	slices bread, diced
¼	cup chopped parsley

Pour lima beans into a 1½-quart casserole. Dot with butter and pour broth over lima beans. In a skillet fry bacon until crisp. Add onions, cranberries and celery. Saute for 5 minutes. Stir in bread and parsley. Spoon mixture on top of limas. Bake in a preheated 350-degree oven for 40 to 45 minutes. Spoon topping in the center of serving platter. Spoon limas around topping.

Makes 6 servings.

BEANPOT

1	pound Great Northern beans
4	quarts water
1	cup sliced onion
2	large cloves garlic, unpeeled
1	pound lamb cubes, about 1-inch (or beef if preferred)
1	pound pork cubes, about 1-inch
6	pork sausage links, about 1 pound
2	tablespoons oil
1½	cups grape jelly
2	teaspoons salt
¼	teaspoon pepper
½	cup diced bacon

Pick over beans, wash and place in a large saucepot. Add water, onion and garlic. Bring to a boil. Remove from heat and let stand for 1 hour. Bring beans to boil again. Reduce heat and simmer 1 hour, until beans are tender. Add more water if necessary.

Meanwhile, in a large skillet, brown lamb, pork and sausage in oil. Set aside.

Drain beans, reserve one and one-half cups liquid. Stir grape jelly with fork until smooth. Blend in bean liquid, salt and pepper. Add bacon.

In 3-quart casserole, alternate layers of beans and cubed meat, ending with beans. Top with sausage. Place sauce over all.

Bake at 350 degrees for 30 minutes. Reduce heat to 300 degrees and bake 1 hour longer. Spoon sauce over sausage occasionally.   *Makes 8 to 10 servings.*

ITALIAN-STYLE BEANS

1	medium clove garlic, minced
¼	teaspoon oregano leaves, crushed
1	tablespoon olive oil
1	can (16 ounces) pork and beans in tomato sauce
1	cup cooked small shell macaroni
1	can (about 8 ounces) tomatoes, chopped
½	cup cooked cut green beans
2	tablespoons grated Parmesan cheese

In a saucepan, cook garlic and oregano in oil a few minutes; add remaining ingredients. Heat; stir occasionally.   *Makes about 3 cups, 6 servings.*

KIDNEY BEAN AND BISCUIT CASSEROLE

2	cans (16 ounces each) red kidney beans
1	pound ground beef
4	slices bacon
½	cup chopped onion
½	cup chopped green pepper
½	cup chopped celery
1	clove garlic, minced
1	can (8 ounces) tomato sauce
1	teaspoon chili powder
1	tablespoon prepared mustard
1	teaspoon salt
1	cup prepared biscuit mix
⅓	cup milk

In a large skillet, brown beef; remove and set aside. Add bacon and cook until crisp; remove from skillet; crumble and add to beef. Pour off all but 2 tablespoons bacon fat. Add onion, green pepper, celery and garlic to skillet and saute until tender. Drain beans reserving 1 cup liquid (or add enough water to liquid to equal 1 cup.) Combine beans, reserved liquid, beef, vegetables, tomato sauce, chili powder, mustard and salt; mix well. Spoon into a shallow 2-quart casserole. Mix biscuit mix and milk just until moistened. Spoon onto casserole making six biscuits. Bake in a 350-degree oven for 40 minutes or until biscuits are golden brown.
Makes 6-8 servings.

MEXICALI BEANS

½	pound ground beef
1	package (1¼- or 1⅛ ounces) taco seasoning mix
1	can (16 ounces) brick oven baked beans
1	package (4 ounces) taco shells (10 shells)
½	cup grated Cheddar cheese
½	cup chopped tomato
½	cup chopped green pepper
½	cup chopped black olives
½	cup chopped onion

In a large skillet saute crumbled ground beef, over high heat, stirring until brown on all sides. Add taco seasoning mix and water as directed on package, stir to mix well.

Continued

Bring to a boil, reduce heat and simmer uncovered 15-20 minutes, stirring occasionally, until liquid is reduced. Add beans and heat mixture thoroughly.

Fill warmed shells with bean mixture. Serve with remaining ingredients to use as toppings.

Makes 10 filled tacos.

MICHIGAN BEAN PICNIC LOAF

1	pound dry navy beans
6	cups water
¼	cup chopped onion
1	clove garlic, crushed
1	bay leaf
1	cup prepared herb-seasoned stuffing mix
2	eggs, beaten
1¼	cups chopped onion
2½	teaspoons salt
1	teaspoon basil
½	teaspoon powdered thyme
1½	teaspoons pepper
1	cup ketchup
½	cup chili sauce

Bring beans and 6 cups water to boil. Cook 2 minutes. Remove from heat. Let stand 1 hour.

Cook beans in same water with ¼ cup onion, garlic and bay leaf until fork tender. Drain beans. Remove garlic and bay leaf.

In large bowl, mash beans. Combine with remaining ingredients, mixing well.

Spoon into well-greased 9-by-5-inch loaf pan. Level top. Bake at 350 degrees for 1 hour. For easier serving, let loaf stand 5 minutes at room temperature after removing from oven.

Serve hot with tomato sauce, chili sauce, mustard or grated cheese. Serve cold, thinly sliced, on sandwich or salad plate. *Makes 8 servings.*

PEACHES 'N' BEANS

1	can (28 ounces) brick oven baked beans
¼	teaspoon ground cinnamon
1	can (20 ounces) sliced cling peaches, drained
¼	cup slivered almonds
¼	cup packed brown sugar

Preheat oven to 350 degrees. In a bowl, mix beans and cinnamon. Turn into a 1-quart casserole. Top with peach slices. Sprinkle with almonds and brown sugar. Bake 25 minutes. *Makes 8 servings.*

PICNIC BEAN AND SAUSAGE LOAF

1	pound pork sausage meat
2	cans (16 ounces) pork and beans in tomato sauce, mashed
2	cups prepared herb-seasoned stuffing mix
2	eggs, beaten
1	cup chopped onion
2	tablespoons prepared mustard
1½	teaspoons salt
1	teaspoon basil
½	teaspoon powdered thyme
½	cup ketchup

In medium fry pan, cook sausage until well done. Drain on paper towels. Crumble.

In large bowl, combine sausage with remaining ingredients, mixing well. Spoon into well-greased 9-by-5-inch loaf pan. Level top.

Bake at 350 degrees for 1¼ hours. For easier serving, let loaf stand 5 minutes at room temperature after removing from oven.

Serve hot with grated Cheddar cheese, tomato sauce, chili sauce or mustard. Serve cold, thinly sliced, on sandwich or salad plate.

Makes 8 servings.

Note: To serve outdoors, keep chilled in original pan until serving time. Unmold by running spatula or knife around edge of pan to loosen sides. Slice thinly and serve as suggested above.

REFRIED BEANS

1	pound dry red kidney beans
6	cups water
1	can (16 ounces) peeled whole tomatoes
1	cup chopped onion
¼	cup olive oil
1	teaspoon salt
1	teaspoon chili powder
½	teaspoon pepper
	Bean Burritos (recipe follows)

Place beans in large saucepan with water; bring to a boil. Boil for 2 minutes; remove from heat and allow to stand for 1 hour.

Cook beans about 2 hours until fork-tender; drain.

In large fry pan, saute onion in oil, until tender. Add beans and remaining ingredients. Mash the beans with a fork or in a food processor and cook over low heat; stirring frequently until beans are fairly dry. Serve on Bean Burritos. *Makes 4 cups.*

BEAN BURRITOS:

4	cups Refried Beans
12	6-inch flour tortillas
3	cups shredded Cheddar or Monterey Jack cheese
1	cup shredded lettuce
2	large tomatoes, chopped

Spoon ⅓ cup refried beans on each tortilla. Sprinkle with cheese, lettuce and tomato. Roll tortilla around filling. *Makes 6 servings of 2 burritos each.*

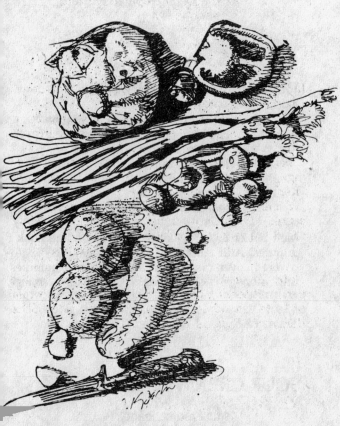

TANGY BAKED BEANS

1	pound dried baby lima beans
6	cups water
2	cups diced, peeled tart apples
½	cup chopped onions
3	tablespoons brown sugar
3	tablespoons Worcestershire sauce
3	tablespoons unsulphured molasses
2	teaspoons salt
½	pound salt pork

Wash beans; drain. Place in a large heavy saucepan. Add water. Bring to boiling point; reduce heat. Cover and simmer for 40 minutes or until skins pop. Drain beans, reserving liquid.

Place beans in a 2-quart bean pot or casserole. Combine 2 cups of the reserved liquid (add water to make 2 cups if necessary) with the apples, onions, sugar, Worcestershire sauce, molasses and salt. Stir into beans.

Score salt pork, making cuts one half inch apart and 1-inch deep. Bury in center of beans. Cover bean pot.

Bake in a preheated 325-degree oven for about 5 hours, stirring beans once or twice and adding boiling water if necessary. *Makes 6 to 8 portions.*

BRUSSELS SPROUTS IN EGG CREAM SAUCE

3	packages (10 ounces each) frozen Brussels sprouts
¼	cup butter or margarine
3	tablespoons flour
2	cups milk
1	egg, slightly beaten
¾	teaspoon salt
½	teaspoon parsley flakes
⅛	teaspoon nutmeg
1	hard-cooked egg, sliced

Cook Brussels sprouts as directed on package. Drain if necessary. Turn into serving dish and keep warm. In same saucepan, melt butter and blend in flour. Stir and cook until mixture begins to brown. Gradually add 1½ cups of milk. Cook, stirring constantly, until sauce boils 1 minute. Lower heat. Blend raw egg with remaining milk and seasonings; stir into white sauce. Cook, stirring constantly, until sauce thickens. Pour over Brussels sprouts. Garnish with hard-cooked egg. *Makes 8 servings.*

FRESH BROCCOLI WITH CHEESE SAUCE

1	bunch fresh broccoli
2	tablespoons butter or margarine
2	tablespoons flour
½	teaspoon salt
⅛	teaspoon pepper
1½	cups milk
1	cup shredded processed American cheese

Wash broccoli and remove large leaves and tough part of stalks. Separate into flowerets. Place broccoli in large saucepan with 1-inch boiling water. Cover. Cook 10 to 12 minutes, until crisp-tender. Drain.

Meanwhile, melt butter in saucepan over medium heat. Stir in flour and seasonings, blending well. Stir in milk and cook, stirring constantly, until sauce thickens and comes to boiling. Add cheese; stir until cheese melts and sauce is smooth. Serve sauce over broccoli. *Makes 6 servings.*

To prepare cabbage, remove tough outer leaves and discard. Cut head into quarters, cut out core and cut into thin shreds with a knife. Melt butter in large skillet. Add onion and cook over low heat until tender. Add cabbage and remaining ingredients, mix well, cover and cook over low heat for 5 minutes, until cabbage is crisp-tender.

Makes 4 servings.

VARIATION: Cook 1 apple, cored and cut into wedges, with the cabbage.

PUREED FRESH BROCCOLI

1	bunch fresh broccoli

Put 1¼ cups water and ½ teaspoon salt in 2-quart pot; place broccoli in steam basket. Cover pot. Simmer 15-20 minutes, until fork-tender. (Lemon juice added to water will help keep broccoli green.) Drain cooking liquid and reserve ¼ cup. Cut broccoli into 1-inch pieces. Place half of the cooked broccoli in blender container along with 2 tablespoons of cooking liquid. Cover and process until smooth. Turn into medium saucepan. Repeat with remaining broccoli and remaining 2 tablespoons liquid. Place saucepan over low heat, stir constantly until puree is hot. If desired, add 2 tablespoons butter or margarine, 2 tablespoons chopped scallions, or 3 tablespoons grated Parmesan cheese. *Makes 4 servings.*

PANNED CABBAGE

2	quarts shredded cabbage
3	tablespoons butter or margarine
½	cup chopped fresh onion
1	teaspoon caraway seeds
1½	teaspoons salt
⅛	teaspoon pepper
1	teaspoon sugar

PANNED RED CABBAGE

2	tablespoons butter or margarine
¼	cup chopped fresh onion
1	medium red cabage, shredded
1	teaspoon salt
1	teaspoon sugar
¼	teaspoon pepper
¼	teaspoon dried leaf marjoram

Melt butter in large skillet. Add onion and cook 5 minutes. Add remaining ingredients and cook, uncovered, over medium heat for 10 to 15 minutes, until cabbage is crisp-tender.   *Makes 4 servings.*

SOUR CREAM CABBAGE

1	small red cabbage
1	small green cabbage
1	tablespoon lemon juice
2	tablespoons butter or margarine
2	tablespoons flour
½	cup bouillon
2	cups sour cream
1	tablespoon vinegar
1	teaspoon salt
½	teaspoon Tabasco pepper sauce

Cut cabbage into wedges. Place in large kettle with salted water to cover. Add lemon juice. Cook until cabbage is tender but crisp, about 20 minutes.

Melt butter in saucepan. Blend in flour. Add bouillon and cook, stirring constantly, until mixture thickens and comes to a boil. Reduce heat to very low.

Add sour cream, vinegar, salt and pepper sauce. Stir until smooth and thick. Do not boil. Place cabbage in serving dish and pour sour cream sauce over all.

Makes 8 servings.

STUFFED WHOLE CABBAGE WITH CORNED BEEF

1	large cabbage
¾	teaspoon salt, divided
2	tablespoons butter or margarine
½	cup chopped fresh onion
½	cup chopped celery with leaves
¼	cup chopped fresh parsley
2	cups finely chopped cooked corned beef
2	cups diced cooked potatoes
¼	teaspoon pepper
1	teaspoon caraway seed

Remove coarse outside leaves from cabbage. Place cabbage in a large kettle with boiling salted water to cover. Cover and simmer 5 minutes. Remove from water, drain well and cool slightly. Carefully peel back 6 outside leaves. Carefully cut out center of cabbage from the top, making a hole about 3 inches wide and 2 inches deep. Sprinkle cavity with one-fourth teaspoon salt. Chop removed cabbage to make one-half cup. Set aside.

In large skillet melt butter. Add onion and cook until tender, about 5 minutes. Remove from heat. Add celery and leaves, parsley, corned beef, potatoes, remaining one-half teaspoon salt, pepper, caraway and reserved one-half cup chopped cabbage. Mix well and pack into cavity of cabbage. Reshape turned-back leaves to cover opening. Wrap cabbage in cheesecloth. Place on a rack in a large pot. Add 1 inch of boiling water. Cover and steam over moderately low heat for 30 minutes.

Makes 6 servings.

SWEET-SOUR APPLES WITH RED CABBAGE

1	medium-size head red cabbage, shredded
¼	cup corn oil margarine
4	large, slightly tart apples
1	large onion
⅓	cup brown sugar
⅓	cup cider vinegar

Melt margarine in a deep skillet or Dutch oven. Add the shredded cabbage. Toss lightly to coat with margarine. Cover and cook 10 minutes.

Core and shred (grate) apples with the peel on. Chop onion. Add both to the cabbage. Cook 10 minutes more with the cover on.

Add brown sugar and vinegar. Cook with cover off for 5 minutes or until juices are absorbed. Season with salt and pepper. *Makes 6 to 8 servings.*

SWEET-AND-SOUR MUSHROOMS AND CABBAGE

½	pound fresh mushrooms or 1 can (6 to 8 ounces) sliced mushrooms
1	small (1½ pound) green cabbage
5	tablespoons oil, divided
½	cup water
¼	cup sugar
1½	tablespoons cornstarch
¾	teaspoon salt
½	teaspoon ground ginger
¹⁄₁₆	teaspoon ground red pepper
3	tablespoons wine vinegar
1	tablespoon soy sauce

Rinse, pat dry and slice fresh mushrooms (makes about 2½ cups) or drain canned mushrooms. Core cabbage. Cut cabbage into 2-inch pieces (makes about 6 cups). In a large skillet heat 2 tablespoons of the oil. Add mushrooms; saute for 5 minutes. Remove; set aside. Heat remaining 3 tablespoons oil. Add cabbage; saute for 3 minutes. Remove; set aside. Combine remaining ingredients. Stir into skillet; cook until thickened, about 1 minute. Return mushrooms and cabbage to skillet; stir to coat with sauce; heat until hot, about 30 seconds.

Makes 8 portions.

CREAMED FRESH PARSNIPS

8	fresh parsnips
2	tablespoons butter or margarine
2	tablespoons flour
1	cup milk
2	teaspoons lemon juice
½	teaspoon sugar
¼	teaspoon salt

Place parsnips in a large saucepan with salted water to cover. Bring to a boil. Cover and simmer over low heat for 30 minutes or until tender. Drain and cool slightly. Peel and cut into 1-inch slices.

To prepare cream sauce, melt butter or margarine in a medium saucepan. Blend in flour. Stir in milk. Cook, stirring constantly, until thickened. Add lemon juice, sugar and salt. Add parsnips. Mix well. *Makes 4 servings.*

ENGLISH PARSNIP PIE

1	9-inch unbaked pastry shell
2	pounds fresh parsnips (2 cups chopped cooked parsnips)
1	teaspoon salt

Continued

2   tablespoons honey
     Pinch ginger
¼   teaspoon cinnamon
1   tablespoon fresh orange juice
2   teaspoons grated fresh orange rind
2   eggs, slightly beaten

Prick pastry shell, line with waxed paper and fill with uncooked rice or dried beans. Bake in 425-degree oven for 10 minutes, remove waxed paper and rice and bake 5 minutes longer. Remove from oven and reduce oven temperature to 375 degrees.

To prepare parsnips, place parsnips in large saucepan with water to cover. Bring to a boil, cover and simmer 30 minutes or until tender. Drain and cool slightly. Peel and chop finely. Combine in bowl with salt, honey, ginger, cinnamon, orange juice, orange rind and eggs. Mix well. Turn into prebaked pastry shell and bake in 375-degree oven for 30 minutes. Serve with meat or poultry.

Makes 8 servings.

FRIED ROSEMARY PARSNIPS

1   pound parsnips (4 to 6)
1½   teaspoons salt, divided
2   large eggs, beaten
1   cup fine dry bread crumbs
1   teaspoon dried leaf rosemary
¼   cup butter or margarine

Wash, pare, and cut parsnips into one-eighth-inch-lengthwise slices. Place parsnips in a medium saucepan with one-half inch boiling water and 1 teaspoon salt. Cover and cook for 12 minutes or until tender. Drain parsnips well and dip into beaten eggs and then into a mixture of bread crumbs, rosemary and salt. Brown on both sides in butter in a large skillet.   *Makes 6 servings.*

FRESH CARROT-POTATO PANCAKES

1   cup shredded raw carrots (2 large)
1   cup shredded pared raw potato (1 large)
⅓   cup finely chopped fresh onion
½   cup milk
½   cup unsifted all-purpose flour
2   eggs, slightly beaten
1   teaspoon salt

In medium bowl combine shredded carrots, potato and onion. Add remaining ingredients and mix well. Drop by tablespoon on hot greased griddle or

skillet. Spread to form a 3-inch circle. Cook until golden brown, about 3 minutes on each side, turning once. Top with favorite syrup.

Makes 18 pancakes.

FRESH PARSNIP PATTIES

2   cups mashed cooked parsnips
1½   teaspoons salt
¼   teaspoon pepper
1   teaspoon sugar
1   teaspoon paprika
1   teaspoon fresh lemon juice
1   egg
½   cup fine dry bread crumbs
     Flour
     Butter or bacon drippings

Combine mashed parsnips, salt, pepper, sugar, paprika, lemon juice, egg and bread crumbs. Mix well. Shape into 2½-inch patties, ½ inch thick. Dip in flour. Cook in butter or bacon drippings in skillet, turning to brown both sides. Serve hot with beef, ham, pork or lamb.   *Makes 4 to 5 servings.*

LEMON PARSNIPS

2   pounds fresh parsnips
     Water
1¾   teaspoons salt, divided
2   tablespoons butter or margarine
1   tablespoon sugar
⅛   teaspoon pepper
¼   teaspoon ginger
2   tablespoons fresh lemon juice

Pare parsnips; cut in diagonal slices. Place in medium saucepan, cover with water and add 1 teaspoon salt. Bring to a boil over medium heat and simmer 20 minutes, until crisp-tender. Drain. In large skillet, melt butter. Add parsnips, remaining three-fourth teaspoon salt, sugar, pepper, ginger and lemon juice. Cook 10 to 15 minutes, or until sugar is dissolved and parsnips are tender.

Makes 4 servings.

LEMON-GLAZED CARROTS AND GREEN GRAPES

8   carrots, scraped
4   teaspoons lemon juice
4   teaspoons butter or margarine
½   cup sugar
1⅓   cups halved and seeded green grapes
     Mint sprigs, optional

Cut carrots into slender 1-inch strips. Place in thick two and one-half-quart saucepan. Cover bottom of pan one-fourth inch deep with water. Cover tightly and steam over medium heat until nearly done, about 10 to 15 minutes. Add lemon juice, butter and sugar. Cook briefly to reduce liquid and glaze carrots with syrup. Add grapes and heat briefly. Turn carrots into serving dish and garnish with mint. Serve at once.   *Makes 4 to 5 servings.*

FRESH CARROT PUDDING

3	eggs, separated
¼	cup sugar
¼	cup orange juice
¼	teaspoon salt
1	teaspoon grated fresh orange rind
¼	teaspoon dried dill weed or 1 teaspoon snipped fresh dill
3	cups shredded raw carrots (6 large)

Beat egg yolks with sugar until light and fluffy. Gradually add orange juice. Stir in salt, orange rind, dill and carrots. Beat egg whites until stiff but not dry; fold in. Turn into a buttered 1½-quart casserole and bake in 350-degree oven for 30 minutes.
Makes 6 servings.

FRESH CARROTS AND MUSHROOMS TARRAGON

8–10	medium carrots (1 pound)
1	cup water
1	teaspoon dried leaf tarragon
½	teaspoon salt
2	tablespoons butter or margarine
¼	pound fresh mushrooms, sliced

Pare carrots and cut into ¼-inch-crosswise slices. Place in medium saucepan. Add water, tarragon and salt. Cover and cook over medium heat 20 to 30 minutes, until tender. While carrots are cooking, heat butter in a small skillet. Add mushrooms and cook until tender. If there is much water left in the pan with the carrots, drain the carrots. Add mushrooms to carrots and mix lightly.
Makes 4 to 6 servings.

FRESH RUTABAGA PUFF

3	cups mashed cooked yellow rutabaga (1 large or 2 medium)
¼	cup plus 1 tablespoon butter or margarine, divided
⅓	cup milk
⅓	cup chopped fresh onion
¾	teaspoon salt
⅛	teaspoon pepper
¼	teaspoon dried leaf tarragon
4	eggs, separated

Quarter rutabaga and place in saucepan, add lightly salted water to cover and boil 40 to 50 minutes or until tender. Drain, cool slightly and remove peel. Place rutabaga in large mixing bowl, add one-fourth cup butter and milk and beat with electric mixer on low speed until smooth. In small skillet melt remaining 1 tablespoon butter, add onion and cook until tender. Add to rutabaga with salt, pepper and tarragon. Beat in egg yolks. Beat egg whites until stiff but not dry. Fold into rutabaga mixture. Turn into a greased one and one-half-quart baking dish. Bake in 375-degree oven 50 minutes or until mixture puffs and is lightly browned.   *Makes 6 servings.*

MUSTARD-GLAZED FRESH PARSNIPS

3	pounds fresh parsnips
	Salt
¼	cup butter or margarine
¼	cup packed light brown sugar
½–1	teaspoon dry mustard

Wash parsnips. Place in a medium saucepan with salted water to cover. Bring to a boil. Cover and simmer over low heat for 20 minutes. Drain and cool slightly. Peel parsnips and cut in half.

Melt butter in a large skillet. Stir in brown sugar and mustard. Add parsnips and cook, turning frequently, until glazed and heated. *Makes 4 servings.*

ORANGE-GLAZED CARROT STICKS

8–10	medium carrots (1 pound)
2	tablespoons butter or margarine
¼	cup chopped fresh onion
⅓	cup packed light brown sugar
½	cup fresh orange juice
½	teaspoon salt

Pare carrots and cut into sticks by cutting in half lengthwise, then into lengthwise quarters and eighths. In a large skillet, cook the carrots, covered, in a small amount of water until tender. Remove carrots from skillet. Heat butter in same skillet. Add onion and cook until tender. Stir in brown sugar and orange juice; simmer 5 minutes. Add cooked carrots, sprinkle with salt, and spoon sauce over carrots until glazed and heated.

Makes 4 to 6 servings.

SWEET-SOUR CARROTS AND PEARS

1	tablespoon oil
2	cups thinly sliced carrots (about 5 small carrots)
½	teaspoon salt
1	large fresh Bartlett pear
¼	cup sliced green onion
1	tablespoon finely chopped green pepper
2	tablespoons brown sugar (packed)
2	tablespoons lemon juice
½	teaspoon cornstarch
½	teaspoon soy sauce

Heat oil in 9-inch skillet with cover. Add carrots. Sprinkle with salt.

Cover skillet. Cook over moderate heat 4 to 5 minutes, until carrots are tender-crisp.

Meanwhile, pare, core and dice pear to measure 1 cup.

Add pear, onion and green pepper to carrots. Mix lightly. Cover skillet and cook 2 minutes longer.

Combine brown sugar, lemon juice, cornstarch and soy sauce. Pour over vegetable-fruit mixture.

Cook, stirring constantly, until sauce clears, 1 to 2 minutes longer. Serve at once.   *Makes 4 half-cup servings.*

Note: If carrots are sliced thicker or if softer vegetables are preferred, add 1 tablespoon water and increase cooking time.

WINTER TURNIPS

6–8	bacon slices, reserve bacon drippings
1	medium yellow turnip, cubed
1	medium onion, sliced
¼	teaspoon Tabasco pepper sauce
½	teaspoon salt
½	teaspoon sugar

Cook bacon in skillet until crisp. Crumble and reserve. Reserve drippings.

Cook turnip in boiling salted water until tender, 25 to 30 minutes.

Heat 3 tablespoons bacon drippings in skillet. Add onion and cook until tender. Add pepper sauce.

Drain cooked turnip. Sprinkle with salt and sugar. Add onion mixture and crumbled cooked bacon. Mix well.   *Makes 4 to 6 servings.*

FRESH CAULIFLOWER WITH PARSLEY SAUCE

1	medium cauliflower
1½	teaspoons salt
	Fresh Parsley Sauce (recipe follows)

Remove outer leaves from cauliflower, leaving small tender leaves attached. Wash. Place whole head in a saucepan with 1 inch boiling water and salt. Bring to boiling without cover. Cook 5 minutes.

Cover and cook 15 minutes or until cauliflower is tender, turning head to cook uniformly. Remove from saucepan and place in a serving dish. Top with Fresh Parsley Sauce.   *Makes 6 servings.*

FRESH PARSLEY SAUCE:

1½	tablespoons butter or margarine
1½	tablespoons flour
1	cup hot chicken broth or 1 cup hot water and 1 chicken bouillon cube
½	cup light cream or undiluted evaporated milk
1½	teaspoons salt (or salt to taste)
⅛	teaspoon pepper
⅓	cup chopped fresh parsley

Melt butter in saucepan. Blend in flour. Remove from heat and stir in broth. Cook, stirring, until the mixture begins to thicken. Add light cream or evaporated milk. Cook until of medium thickness. Add seasonings and chopped parsley.   *Makes 1½ cups.*

AVERY ISLAND CELERY

¼	cup butter or margarine
1	medium onion, chopped
1	can (1 pound) tomatoes
½	teaspoon pepper sauce
1	teaspoon salt
¼	teaspoon sugar
¼	teaspoon dried leaf thyme
4	cups diagonally cut celery
1	package (10 ounces) frozen peas, thawed

Melt butter in large skillet; add onion and cook until tender. Drain tomatoes; reserve solids. Add tomato liquid, pepper sauce, salt, sugar and thyme to skillet; bring to a boil. Stir in celery and peas. Cover and cook 10 minutes or until barely tender. Add tomatoes; heat to serving temperature and turn onto serving dish.   *Makes 6 servings.*

BRAISED CELERY

6	cups celery cut in 2-inch pieces
2	tablespoons butter or margarine
⅓	cup chicken broth
½	teaspoon salt
⅛	teaspoon pepper

Combine all ingredients in a saucepan. Cover and simmer 20 to 25 minutes, just until crisp-tender. Serve at once. *Makes 4 servings.*

CELERY-CHEESE CASSEROLE

2	cups diced celery
3	cups grated Cheddar cheese
4	cups diced fresh bread cubes (5 slices)
3	eggs, lightly beaten
2	cups milk
¾	teaspoon salt
¾	teaspoon thyme leaves, crushed
¾	teaspoon powdered mustard
	Pinch ground black pepper

Cook celery in boiling salted water until almost tender, about 7 minutes. Drain and set aside to cool. In a greased 2-quart casserole, layer ⅓ each of the cheese and bread cubes and ½ of the celery; repeat twice more ending with bread cubes. In a medium bowl, mix eggs, milk, salt, thyme, mustard and black pepper. Pour over top. Let stand for 1 hour. Preheat oven to 350-degrees. Bake, uncovered in a pan of hot water until firm, about 1 hour and 15 minutes. *Makes 6 to 8 portions.*

CELERY ORLANDO

1	head (bunch) celery
3	tablespoons oil
⅓	cup chopped onion
1	clove garlic, minced
1	can (1 pound) tomatoes, broken up
½	cup diced green pepper
1	tablespoon parsley flakes
1½	teaspoons salt
½	teaspoon oregano leaves, crushed
⅛	teaspoon ground black pepper

Trim stem end of celery. Separate stalk into ribs; cut into ¼-inch-thick diagonal slices (makes about 6 cups); set aside. In a large sauce pot, heat oil until hot. Add onion and garlic; saute for 3 minutes. Add reserved celery along with remaining ingredients. Bring to the boiling point. Reduce heat and simmer, covered, until celery is crisp-tender, about 15 minutes. *Makes 6 portions.*

CELERY SAUTE

3	tablespoons butter or margarine
3	cups diagonally sliced celery
2	tablespoons chopped celery leaves
⅓	cup coarsely chopped pecans
1	teaspoon salt
⅛	teaspoon pepper

Melt butter in a skillet and add celery, celery leaves, pecans, salt and pepper. Cook, stirring constantly, 4 or 5 minutes, until celery is crisp-tender. *Makes 4 servings.*

SWEET-AND-SOUR CELERY

1	bunch celery
2	chicken bouillon cubes
1½	cups hot water
½	cup sliced onions
1½	tablespoons cornstarch
1½	tablespoons cold water
3	tablespoons orange marmalade
½	teaspoon salt
⅛	teaspoon ground black pepper
2	teaspoons lemon juice
¼	cup toasted sliced almonds

Trim tops from celery (save for soups, stews, etc.). Separate celery into ribs. Cut into 2-inch lengths (makes about 6 cups); set aside. In a large skillet combine bouillon cubes and water. Heat and stir until bouillon cubes are dissolved. Add onions and reserved celery. Bring to boiling point. Reduce heat and simmer, covered, until celery is crisp-tender, about 6 minutes. Combine cornstarch with cold water. Stir in marmalade, salt, black pepper and lemon juice. Stir into mixture in skillet. Cook and stir until mixture boils and thickens. Stir in toasted almonds. *Makes 6 portions.*

CORN BAKED IN THE HUSKS

Remove silks from corn. Replace husks and tie with string. Soak corn in water for 10 minutes. Place in a baking pan. Bake in a preheated 350-degree oven 25 to 30 minutes.

FRESH CORN AND CHEESE QUICHE

4	ears fresh corn
5	eggs
1½	cups light cream or milk

Continued

¼ cup grated Parmesan cheese
2 tablespoons finely chopped onion
2 tablespoons chopped pimiento
1 teaspoon salt
⅛ teaspoon ground black pepper
1 9-inch unbaked pie shell
6 strips crisp bacon

Remove husks and silks from corn. Cut kernels off cobs (makes about 3 cups). Set aside. Beat eggs with cream. Blend in cheese, onion, pimiento, salt and black pepper. Mix well. Stir in reserved corn. Pour into pie shell. Bake in a preheated 400-degree oven for 25 minutes. Reduce heat to 350 degrees. Arrange cooked bacon over top of quiche. Continue baking until a knife inserted near center of pie comes out clean, about 20 minutes.

Makes 6 portions.

CORN OYSTERS

1 cup fresh corn cut from cob
2 eggs, separated
¼ cup sifted all-purpose flour
½ teaspoon baking powder
1 teaspoon salt
¹⁄₁₆ teaspoon pepper
½ teaspoon grated onion
   Bacon fat or vegetable shortening

Mix corn and egg yolks in medium bowl. Mix flour with baking powder, salt and pepper; stir into corn and egg yolks. Beat egg whites until stiff and fold in. Drop from teaspoon onto a hot griddle greased with bacon fat or shortening. Cook until brown. Serve 4 corn oysters per person.

Makes 5 servings or 20 corn oysters.

Note: If bacon fat is used, cook 4 strips of bacon for sufficient fat.

FRESH CORN SAUTE

3 ears fresh corn
3 tablespoons butter or margarine
1 cup diced celery
½ cup chopped onion
¼ cup diced pimiento
½ teaspoon salt
½ teaspoon sugar
   Dash ground black pepper

Remove husk and silks from corn. Cut kernels from cobs (makes about 2 cups). Set aside. In a medium-sized skillet, melt butter. Add celery and onion; saute for 5 minutes. Add reserved corn, pimiento, salt, sugar and black pepper. Cover and simmer for 5 minutes, stirring occasionally.   *Makes 4 portions.*

LANCASTER FRESH CORN PIE

1 package (10 ounces) pie crust mix
6 ears fresh corn
3 hard-cooked eggs, sliced
2 tablespoons finely chopped onion
2 tablespoons finely chopped parsley
1 tablespoon flour
1 tablespoon sugar
1½ teaspoons salt
¼ teaspoon ground black pepper
4 tablespoons butter or margarine
¾ cup light cream or half-and-half

Prepare pie crust following package directions. Roll half of the pastry one-eighth-inch thick. Line a 9-inch pie pan with rolled pastry. Remove kernels from cob with a sharp knife (makes about three and one-half cups of kernels). Combine corn, eggs, onion and parsley; pour into pie pan. Combine flour, sugar, salt and black pepper. Sprinkle over corn mixture. Dot with butter and pour cream over all. Roll remaining pie crust one-eighth-inch thick. Place over corn mixture. Seal edges firmly. Make a gash in center of crust for steam to escape. Bake in preheated 450-degree oven for 8 minutes. Reduce heat to 350-degrees and bake until crust is browned, 50 to 60 minutes.   *Makes 6 portions.*

ARMENIAN EGGPLANT

1 pound ground lamb
½ cup chopped fresh onion
½ cup chopped celery with leaves
2 medium eggplants
2 teaspoons salt, divided
1 tablespoon fresh lemon juice
¼ teaspoon pepper
½ teaspoon cinnamon
¼ teaspoon allspice
¼ teaspoon dried leaf thyme
1 jar (3½ ounces, ½ cup) pine nuts
2 small apples, cored and diced (2 cups)

In large skillet break up lamb. Cook until browned. Add onion, celery and leaves; cook 5 minutes. Cut eggplant in half lengthwise, scoop out pulp leaving one-half inch shell. Reserve shells and sprinkle with one-half teaspoon salt. Dice eggplant, add to skillet and cook 10 minutes, stirring occasionally. Add remaining one and one-half teaspoons salt and remaining ingredients. Spoon into reserved eggplant shells. Place in baking pan and add one-half inch water to pan. Cover and bake in 350-degree oven 1 hour. Serve with plain yogurt, if desired.

Makes 4 servings.

CHILLED PICNIC RATATOUILLE

¼ cup salad or olive oil
2 cloves garlic, minced
1 onion, sliced
1 green pepper, seeded and cut in strips
3 medium unpared zucchini, cut into ¼-inch slices
1 medium eggplant, pared and cut in cubes
2 teaspoons dried leaf basil
1 teaspoon dried leaf oregano
1½ teaspoons salt
⅛ teaspoon pepper
3 tomatoes, peeled and cut in wedges

Heat oil in large skillet, add garlic, onion, green pepper and zucchini. Cook about 3 minutes or until tender, stirring frequently. Add eggplant, basil, oregano, salt and pepper. Cover and cook over medium heat 15 minutes, stirring occasionally. Add tomatoes wedges, cover and cook 5 minutes longer or just until tomatoes are heated. Refrigerate several hours or overnight. Pack in container with a tight lid to carry to picnic. *Makes 6 servings.*

Note: To remove skins from tomatoes, plunge tomatoes one at a time in saucepan of boiling water for about 30 seconds. Remove. Skins will slip off easily.

GREEN BEANS MEDITERRANEAN

1 pound fresh green beans or 2 packages (9 ounces each) frozen whole green beans
2 tomatoes, peeled and diced
1 tablespoon onion powder
1 tablespoon basil leaves, crumbled
1 teaspoon salt
½ teaspoon garlic powder
¼ teaspoon ground black pepper
2 tablespoons butter or margarine
2 slices toasted white bread, cubed

Trim ends of fresh beans. Cook fresh beans covered in 1-inch boiling salted water until tender, about 15 minutes. (Do not overcook.) Cook frozen beans as package label directs. Drain. Place beans in a serving dish. Keep warm.

In a medium saucepan, combine tomatoes, onion powder, basil, salt, garlic powder and black pepper. Bring to boiling. Reduce heat and simmer, uncovered, for 5 minutes. Stir in butter and toast. Spoon over hot beans. *Makes 6 to 8 servings.*

BARBECUED ONIONS DIABLO

1 cup ketchup
¾ cup water
¼ cup cider vinegar
1 tablespoon Worcestershire sauce
1 tablespoon sugar
1 teaspoon salt
1 teaspoon celery seed
¼ teaspoon Tabasco pepper sauce
3 cups sliced yellow onions

Combine all ingredients except onions in medium saucepan. Heat to boiling.

Reduce heat to medium. Cover and cook 4 minutes.

Stir in onions. Cook another 3 minutes. Cover and chill. *Makes 12 servings.*

SAVORY STUFFED ONIONS

6 large onions (about 1½ pounds)
6 slices bacon
1 can (10¾ ounces) condensed cream of mushroom soup

Continued

1   package (10 ounces) frozen chopped
      spinach, cooked and well drained
1   tablespoon brown sugar
1   tablespoon vinegar

Cut tops off onions. Scoop out, leaving ⅛-inch-thick shell. Chop onion centers. In skillet, cook bacon until crisp; remove and crumble. Cook chopped onion in drippings until tender. Stir in soup, spinach, brown sugar, vinegar and bacon. Fill onion shells with spinach mixture. Arrange in 2-quart shallow baking dish (12-by-8-by-2 inch); cover with foil. Bake at 375 degrees for 30 minutes or until done.   *Makes 6 servings.*

SPANISH ONION STRATA

1–2 sweet Spanish onions
8   slices white bread, cut in cubes
2   cups grated Cheddar cheese, divided
2   eggs
2   cups milk
1   tablespoon prepared mustard
1   teaspoon salt
⅛   teaspoon pepper
      Paprika

Peel and thinly slice sweet Spanish onions to measure 4 cups. Place half of bread cubes in bottom of buttered casserole. Sprinkle 1 cup grated cheese over bread and top with 2 cups onion slices. Repeat a layer of bread, cheese and onions. Beat eggs with milk, mustard, salt and pepper. Pour over onions. Sprinkle with paprika and bake at 325 degrees for 1 hour.   *Makes 6 servings.*

Note: Onion Strata may be assembled a day ahead and refrigerated until time to bake and serve. Bake 15 minutes longer if casserole is chilled.

GOLDEN APPLE-PEPPER BOATS

1   or 2 Golden Delicious apples
1   tablespoon minced onion
1   tablespoon butter or margarine
¼   cup seeded, diced tomato
¼   cup fresh or frozen, thawed peas
¼   cup grated Parmesan cheese, divided
¼   teaspoon each salt and basil leaves,
      crushed
⅛   teaspoon pepper
1   large green pepper, halved, seeded
      and parboiled

Core apples. Reserve 2 thin slices for garnish; chop remaining apples to equal ¾ cup. Saute onion in butter several minutes; stir in chopped apples, vegetables, 2 tablespoons cheese and seasonings. Spoon into green pepper halves. Bake, uncovered, at 350 degrees 20 to 25 minutes. Top with reserved apple slices; sprinkle with remaining cheese. Bake 5 minutes longer or until apples are tender.
                         Makes 2 servings.

STUFFED PEPPERS

6   large green peppers
¾   pound ground beef
¾   pound ground pork
1   onion, chopped
4   large cooked potatoes, peeled and
      diced
2   teaspoons Angostura aromatic bitters
2   cups (8 ounces) grated sharp Cheddar
      cheese
1½   cups milk
      Salt and pepper

Slice tops from peppers and remove seeds. Drop peppers into boiling water and cook for 5 minutes. Drain and cool. In a bowl, mix beef, pork, onion, potatoes, bitters, cheese and milk. Season to taste with salt and pepper. Use meat mixture to stuff peppers. Place peppers side by side in a shallow baking pan. Add water until 1 inch deep. Bake in a preheated 350-degree oven for 1 hour. Serve as is or if desired with your favorite tomato or mushroom sauce.   *Makes 6 servings.*

BAKED MUSHROOMS ON TOAST

1   pound small to medium-sized fresh
      mushrooms
10   slices (½-inch thick) Italian bread,
      toasted
½   cup dry sherry or beef bouillon
1   teaspoon salt
1½   cups heavy or light cream or
      half-and-half, divided

Rinse, pat dry and trim stem ends of mushrooms; set aside. Butter a 9- or 10-inch pie pan. Arrange toast over bottom; sprinkle with sherry. Pile mushrooms on top of toast; sprinkle with salt. (Use half teaspoon salt with bouillon). Pour 1 cup of the cream over mushrooms. Cover tightly with foil. Bake in a preheated 350-degree oven for 30 minutes. Pour remaining one-half cup cream over mushrooms. Cover and bake until mushrooms are cooked, 10 to 20 minutes longer. Serve hot.
                         Makes 6 portions.

Mix together all ingredients except mushrooms and salad greens. Place mushrooms in bowl. Add onion-celery dressing mixture and mix well. Chill at least 2 hours. Serve on salad greens.

Makes 6 to 8 servings.

TUNA-STUFFED MUSHROOMS

1	pound fresh mushrooms
1	can (6½ or 7 ounces) tuna in vegetable oil
2	teaspoons soy sauce
¼	cup chopped water chestnuts
½	teaspoon ginger

Wash mushrooms and remove stems. Place top side down on lightly greased baking sheet. In small bowl, mix remaining ingredients. Spoon into mushroom caps. Bake uncovered in a 350-degree oven 5 to 7 minutes, until hot. Serve. *Makes 8 servings.*

BALKAN POTATO BOATS

6	large potatoes
	Butter
	Parmesan cheese
1	pound ground beef
1	tablespoon anise seed
1	egg
1	clove garlic, crushed
1	small onion, minced
1	teaspoon salt
	Green peppers, onions, mushrooms

Cut a lengthwise wedge from each potato. Rub the cut edge with butter. Sprinkle surfaces with cheese. Bake at 400 degrees for about 40 minutes until almost done.

Meanwhile, mix beef with anise seed, egg, garlic, minced onion and salt. Shape into small meat balls and brown lightly in a little hot oil. String on bamboo skewers with small chunks of pepper and onion. Finish off with a mushroom half.

Set skewers on potatoes and continue baking 15 minutes, basting with melted butter.

If you like, serve with a sauce made by combining equal amounts of tomato sauce and dairy sour cream. Heat the tomato sauce until it starts to bubble, remove from heat and blend in sour cream.

POTATO PANCAKES

¾	cup dehydrated instant Idaho potato flakes

Continued

MARINATED MUSHROOMS

1	pound fresh mushrooms
6	tablespoons olive oil
¾	cup dry white wine
1½	teaspoons salt
⅛	teaspoon cayenne pepper
¼	teaspoon dried leaf oregano
¼	cup chopped fresh parsley
2	tablespoons chopped fresh onion
3	tablespoons fresh lemon juice

Slice mushrooms and place in glass or earthenware bowl. Combine remaining ingredient in saucepan and simmer 15 minutes. Remove from heat and pour over mushrooms. Cover and refrigerate several hours. *Makes about eight ½-cup servings or use as hors d'oeuvres.*

MUSHROOM SALAD

½	cup chopped fresh onion
¼	cup chopped celery
½	cup sour cream
¼	cup mayonnaise
2	tablespoons fresh lemon juice
1	tablespoon chopped fresh parsley
1	teaspoon salt
1	teaspoon horseradish
1	teaspoon prepared mustard
¼	teaspoon dried leaf oregano
⅛	teaspoon pepper
1	pound fresh mushrooms, thinly sliced
	Salad greens

```
1    egg, lightly beaten
½    cup flour
1    teaspoon baking powder
1    package (¼ ounce) dehydrated onion
     soup mix
3    tablespoons butter or margarine
```

Prepare potato flakes according to package directions; beat in 1 egg. In small bowl, combine flour, baking powder and onion soup mix. Stir into potato mixture. Melt butter in large skillet. Drop potato mixture by scant ¼ cupfuls into skillet; press lightly with spatula to flatten. Brown on both sides.

Makes about 8 pancakes.

CASCADE POTATO CASSEROLE

```
1    tablespoon butter or margarine
½    cup chopped onion
1    can (10¾ ounces) condensed cream
     of celery soup
1    package (3 ounces) cream cheese, at
     room temperature
½    teaspoon salt
¼    teaspoon pepper
4    cups frozen hash brown Idaho
     potatoes
1    cup (4 ounces) shredded sharp
     Cheddar cheese
```

Melt butter in a small skillet. Add onion and cook until tender. In a large bowl, beat undiluted soup and cream cheese together until smooth. Stir in salt, pepper, onion and potatoes. Turn into a 1½-quart casserole or baking dish. Top with shredded cheese. Bake in 350-degree oven for 1 hour.

Makes 6 servings.

CHEESY POTATO RING

```
5     cups frozen potatoes O'Brien
6     tablespoons butter or margarine
      Flour for pan coating
¹⁄₁₆  teaspoon pepper
1½    teaspoons salt
¼     cup sifted all-purpose flour
1¾    cups milk
½     teaspoon prepared mustard
1½    cups grated Cheddar cheese
4     large eggs, well beaten
3     cups hot cooked vegetables
```

Turn potatoes into colander and rinse with very hot water. Drain well and pat dry with paper towel. Butter a 5½-cup ring mold heavily, using about 2 tablespoons butter. Dust lightly with flour, shaking out excess. Set aside. Preheat oven to 350 degrees.

Melt remaining 4 tablespoons butter and blend in pepper, salt and one-fourth-cup flour. Stir in milk and cook, stirring constantly, until sauce boils thoroughly and thickens. Stir in mustard and potatoes. Add cheese and eggs, mixing well. Spoon into prepared mold. Set in pan with hot water to half the depth of mold. Bake in preheated oven for about 45 minutes, until firm on top and knife inserted in center comes out clean. Remove from hot water, and let stand 5 minutes. Loosen edges with small spatula and invert over serving plate. Fill center with hot cooked vegetables. *Makes 6 servings.*

CHILEAN CHEESE-POTATO CASSEROLE

```
6    medium-sized potatoes
1    pound creamed cottage cheese
¾    cup butter or margarine, melted
1¾   teaspoons salt
1    teaspoon oregano leaves, crumbled
¼    teaspoon ground cumin
¼    teaspoon ground black pepper
½    cup plain yogurt
1    egg, lightly beaten
```

Peel and thinly slice potatoes. Arrange a layer of potatoes in the bottom of a buttered 12 × 8 × 2-inch casserole. Combine cottage cheese, butter, salt, oregano, cumin and black pepper. Spoon some of this mixture over the potatoes. Repeat layering of potatoes and cheese mixture, ending with cheese, until all are used. Bake, uncovered, in a preheated 375-degree oven until potatoes are almost tender, about 40 minutes.

Mix together yogurt and egg. Spoon over casserole. Bake until egg mixture is lightly browned, about 20 minutes. Let stand 5 minutes before serving. *Makes 8 portions.*

IDAHO CASSEROLE TREAT

```
5    tablespoons butter or margarine,
     divided
1    package (14 ounces) frozen Idaho
     cottage fry potatoes
½    cup chopped onions
3    tablespoons flour
2    cups milk
2    cups shredded Cheddar cheese (6
     ounces)
1    tablespoon spicy prepared mustard
1    teaspoon salt
¼    teaspoon pepper
```

¼ teaspoon paprika
1 can (1 pound 4 ounces) chunk pineapple, in pineapple juice, drained
¾ pound cooked ham, cut into cubes

In large skillet, melt 2 tablespoons butter, add frozen potatoes and onion. Saute until potatoes are soft and lightly browned. In medium saucepan, melt remaining 3 tablespoons butter, blend in flour. Add milk gradually, blending well. Cook, stirring constantly, until sauce thickens. Add cheese, mustard, salt, pepper and paprika; stir until sauce is smooth. Add pineapple, ham, sauteed potatoes and onions; mix well. Turn into a buttered 2-quart casserole. Bake in 400-degree oven 15 minutes, until potatoes are lightly browned. *Makes 4 to 6 servings.*

IDAHO JOE'S BUFFET POTATOES

2 large potatoes
1 cup cooked diced ham
½ cup cooked chopped spinach
½ teaspoon nutmeg
Butter or margarine

Preheat oven to 400 degrees. Bake potatoes 1 hour until done. Split in half and remove flesh, saving skins. Mix with ham, spinach and nutmeg. Spoon mixture back into skins and serve hot with butter or margarine. *Makes 4 servings.*

IDAHO PORCUPINES

2 tablespoons butter or margarine
½ cup chopped onion
Instant mashed Idaho potatoes for 6 servings
1 teaspoon salt
½ teaspoon nutmeg
½ teaspoon pepper
1 cup (4 ounces) shredded Cheddar cheese
1 tablespoon chopped parsley
2 eggs
2 tablespoons water
1½ cups cornflakes

Melt butter in a small skillet. Add onion and cook until tender. Set aside. Prepare instant mashed potatoes according to package directions, reducing water by ½ cup. Add onion, salt, nutmeg, pepper, cheese and parsley.

Beat in 1 egg. (The mixture should be fairly dry.) Shape large spoonfuls of mixture into balls.

Beat remaining egg with water. Crush cornflakes

lightly. Coat the potato balls with egg mixture, roll in corn flakes and place on a greased baking sheet. Bake in 400-degree oven 20 to 25 minutes.
Makes 6 servings, 12 porcupines.

MINNIE'S POTATO KUGEL

4 large baking potatoes (about 2 pounds), peeled and shredded
1 large onion, grated
½ cup vegetable oil, heated
3 eggs, lightly beaten
½ cup matzoh meal
1¼ teaspoons salt
¼ teaspoon pepper sauce

In large bowl combine potatoes and onion; quickly stir in hot oil. Add eggs, matzoh meal, salt and pepper sauce; mix well. Turn into well-greased 8-by-12-inch baking dish. Bake in a 375-degree oven 1 hour, until browned. If desired, serve with additional pepper sauce. *Makes 6 to 8 servings.*

OWYHEE STUFFED POTATOES

4 Idaho potatoes
½ cup warm milk
1 cup (8 ounces) creamed cottage cheese
¼ cup finely chopped onion
2 tablespoons chopped, seeded, rinsed and drained green chilies
1 teaspoon salt
⅛ teaspoon pepper

Scrub potatoes well. Dry and prick with fork. Bake in 425-degree oven for 55 to 60 minutes, until soft. Immediately cut slice from top of each.

Carefully scoop out potato without breaking skin. Place potato in a large bowl. Mash with milk. Stir in remaining ingredients.

Pile potato mixture into shells. Bake in 350-degree oven for 25 to 30 minutes. *Makes 4 servings.*

PIZZA POTATOES

2 large potatoes
1 clove garlic, minced
Olive oil
1½ pounds Italian sausage, crumbled
3 tablespoons each chopped green pepper and pimiento
1 can (8½ ounces) peeled tomatoes, chopped
Mozzarella cheese, grated

Continued

Preheat oven to 400 degrees. Bake potatoes 1 hour until done. Cook garlic in oil. Add sausage and let brown. When potatoes are done, cut in half and remove flesh, saving jacket. Mix potato lightly with sausage, pepper, pimiento and tomato. Spoon mixture back into potato skins; top with cheese and put back in oven. Bake another 10 minutes.

Makes 4 servings.

PIZZA POTATO TOPPER

½	pound pepperoni
2	cups quartered mushrooms (about ½ pound)
2	large cloves garlic, minced
½	teaspoon Italian seasoning, crushed
2	tablespoons olive oil
2	cans (10¾ ounces each) condensed tomato soup
½	cup water
8	large baked potatoes

Split pepperoni in half lengthwise; slice. In saucepan, brown mushrooms and cook garlic and Italian seasoning in oil. Add soup, water and pepperoni. Heat; stir occasionally. Split potatoes; fluff with fork. Serve sauce over potatoes.   *Makes 8 servings.*

POTATOES ALMONDINE

1½	pounds baking or boiling potatoes
¼	cup butter or margarine
¾	cup sliced natural almonds
3	tablespoons minced green onions
½	cup sliced water chestnuts
½	teaspoon rosemary, crumbled
½	teaspoon salt
	Few dashes white pepper
¾	cup dairy sour cream
¼	cup grated Parmesan cheese
	Minced parsley
	Sliced natural almonds for garnish

Pare potatoes and cut into ½-inch cubes. Cover with water in saucepan. Bring to boil. Simmer for 5 minutes or until barely tender. Drain. Melt butter in skillet. Add almonds and onion. Stir over medium-high heat for 1 minute. Stir in potatoes, water chestnuts, rosemary, salt, pepper, sour cream and cheese. Cook over medium heat, stirring constantly with gentle folding motion, until hot through. Turn into serving dish. Sprinkle with parsley and additional almonds. Serve promptly.

Makes 4 to 6 servings.

REUBEN POTATO TOPPER

1	can (10¾ ounces) condensed creamy chicken mushroom soup
½	soup can milk
1	cup thinly sliced corned beef, torn in pieces
½	cup shredded Swiss cheese
½	cup sauerkraut
2	tablespoons sweet pickle relish
1	teaspoon prepared mustard
½	teaspoon caraway seeds
6	large baked potatoes
	Chopped parsley

In saucepan, combine all ingredients except potatoes and parsley. Heat; stir occasionally. Slit potatoes; fluff with fork. Serve sauce over potatoes. Garnish with parsley. This kitchen-tested recipe makes 5 servings.

ROASTED POTATOES

6	baking potatoes
	Cold water
¼	cup (½ stick) corn oil margarine, melted
1	teaspoon sweet basil
1	teaspoon salt
2	tablespoons dried bread crumbs
½	cup shredded low-fat Mozzarella cheese

Peel potatoes and place in cold water. Place 1 potato at a time on a wooden spoon large enough to cradle it. Slice down at ⅛-inch intervals across the potato. (The curved bowl of the spoon will prevent the knife from slicing completely through the potato.) Return potatoes to cold water.

When ready to roast, dry potatoes and place them in a greased 8-by-8-by-2-inch baking pan. Combine corn oil margarine, sweet basil and salt. Brush potatoes. Bake at 425 degrees for 35 minutes. Sprinkle with bread crumbs and cheese. Continue roasting for 10 minutes, or until done.

Makes 6 servings.

ROSEMARY POTATOES

1	pound new potatoes
¼	cup pure imported olive oil
1	clove garlic, chopped
1	teaspoon crumbled rosemary
	Salt

Cover potatoes with water and simmer until potatoes are tender. Cool and then peel. In a skillet, heat oil and saute garlic until golden. Stir in rosemary. Add potatoes and stir over medium heat until potatoes are golden brown on all sides. Season to taste with salt. *Makes 4 servings.*

SOUFFLED BAKED POTATOES

6	medium potatoes (about 3 pounds)
1	cup sour cream
½	cup butter
1	egg, lightly beaten
1	teaspoon salt
	Pepper
2	tablespoons freeze-dried or frozen chopped chives

Bake potatoes without foil, until soft. Cut thin slice lengthwise off each top. Remove contents and mash. Combine other ingredients, blend into potato and whip. Add a little cream or milk if necessary to whip until fluffy.

Pile filling lightly into potato shells. Top with grated cheese, bacon bits or slivered almonds. Bake on cookie sheet at 375 degrees until tops are lightly browned. *Makes 6 servings.*

STUFFED IDAHO POTATOES

4	Idaho potatoes
1	egg
2	tablespoons milk
2	tablespoons butter or margarine
1	tablespoon grated onion
1	teaspoon salt
⅛	teaspoon pepper

Scrub potatoes well. Dry potatoes, and prick with a fork. Bake in 425-degree oven for 55 to 60 minutes or until soft.

Cut slice off top of each potato and carefully scoop out pulp. In a large bowl, combine potato pulp, egg, milk, butter, onion, salt and pepper. Beat until smooth.

Spoon potato mixture back into potato shells. Place on a baking sheet. Bake in a 350-degree oven 30 minutes or until thoroughly heated. Serve immediately. *Makes 4 servings.*

VARIATIONS: To mashed potato mixture, add ½ cup shredded Swiss or Cheddar cheese, 2 tablespoons chopped parsley or ½ teaspoon dried dill weed.

LOW-CALORIE COTTAGE CHEESE TOPPING

1	cup (8 ounces) cottage cheese
1	tablespoon chopped parsley
¾	teaspoon chopped chives
⅛	teaspoon dried dill weed
¼	teaspoon salt
	Pepper to taste

In a small bowl, beat cottage cheese until smooth. Add parsley, chives, dill weed, salt and pepper. Mix well. *Makes 1 cup, enough topping for 4 potatoes.*

LOW-CALORIE MUSHROOM TOPPING

1	tablespoon butter or margarine
¼	cup chopped onion
¼	pound mushrooms, chopped
½	teaspoon salt
⅛	teaspoon pepper
¼	teaspoon dried leaf savory

In a skillet melt butter. Add onion and cook 3 minutes. Add mushrooms, salt, pepper and savory. Cook 5 minutes longer, stirring frequently.

Makes about 1 cup, enough topping for 4 potatoes.

VERONA-STYLE POTATO TOPPER

¼	pound mild Italian sausage casing removed
1	cup diced eggplant
½	cup sliced onion
½	teaspoon basil leaves, crushed
2	tablespoons olive oil
1	can (11 ounces) condensed tomato bisque soup
½	cup water
2	teaspoons lemon juice
4	large baked potatoes

In saucepan, cook sausage, eggplant and onion with basil in oil until done. Add soup, water and lemon juice. Heat; stir occasionally. Slit potatoes; fluff with fork. Serve sauce over potatoes. This kitchen-tested recipe makes 4 servings.

YORKSHIRE POTATO PUFF

6	medium potatoes (about 2 pounds)
¼	cup butter or margarine, melted
3	eggs, separated

Continued

1   teaspoon salt
⅛   teaspoon each pepper and nutmeg

Cook potatoes, covered, in 1 inch boiling salted water until tender, about 30 minutes. Drain, peel and rice or mash to make about 4 cups. Blend mashed potatoes with 2 tablespoons butter, the egg yolks, seasonings and cream. In large bowl with electric mixer, or rotary beater, beat egg whites until stiff. Gently fold into potato mixture. Pile into 1½-quart casserole. Drizzle remaining 2 tablespoons butter over potato mixture. Bake at 425 degrees for 15 to 20 minutes, or until puffy and golden. Serve at once.   *Makes 6 servings.*

BRAISED KALE

1   pound fresh kale
3   slices bacon, cut in 1-inch pieces
½   cup chopped fresh onion
1   small bay leaf
1   chicken bouillon cube
1   teaspoon salt

Wash kale and remove coarse stems. Drain but do not dry. Cut into 2-inch pieces. In a medium saucepan cook bacon until lightly browned. Add onion and cook until tender. Add kale, bay leaf, bouillon cube and salt. Cover and cook over medium heat for 15 minutes, or until kale is tender.

Makes 4 servings.

COOKED GREENS

To prepare greens for cooking, wash well in cold water, lifting greens out of the water and rinsing several times. Cut off root ends, tough stems and discolored leaves. Greens can be cooked in only the water that clings to the leaves during washing. Place freshly rinsed leaves in saucepan, cover and bring quickly to a boil. Reduce heat and cook gently until tender—3 to 5 minutes for kale, spinach and dandelion greens, 10 to 15 minutes for turnip greens and collards and 15 to 20 minutes for mustard greens. Older greens may require longer cooking time and additional water. When cooking older leaves place in saucepan with one-half inch water and follow directions given above. One pound raw greens when cooked will yield 3 servings.

SOUTHERN-STYLE GREENS

2   pounds greens (kale, collards, mustard greens, turnip greens)

3   tablespoons bacon drippings, butter or salad oil
1   clove garlic, mashed (optional)
2   onions, thinly sliced and separated into rings
1   teaspoon dried leaf basil
½   cup beef broth or water
1   teaspoon salt
      Pepper to taste

Wash and trim greens, cutting off stems. Drain but do not dry. Tear leaves into 2- to 3-inch pieces. Heat fat in a large skillet. Add garlic, onions and basil. Cook until onions are golden, stirring occasionally. Add greens, broth or water and salt. Cover, bring to a boil; reduce heat and cook 20 to 25 minutes until greens are tender, stirring occasionally. Season with pepper to taste.   *Makes 6 to 8 servings.*

ITALIAN GREENS

2   pounds greens
1   clove garlic, crushed
1   tablespoon olive oil
¼   teaspoon sugar
⅛   teaspoon pepper
¼   cup grated Parmesan cheese
      Raw onion rings

Mix garlic, oil, sugar and pepper in shallow pan. Add washed and trimmed greens, cover, bring to boil quickly, reduce heat and cook over low heat until tender. Turn onto serving plate and sprinkle with cheese. Top with raw onion rings.

Makes 6 servings.

FRESH LETTUCE STIR-FRY

2   tablespoons butter or margarine
¼   cup chopped fresh onion
¼   cup chopped fresh green pepper
¼   cup chopped fresh red pepper
4   cups shredded iceberg lettuce (1 small head)
¾   teaspoon salt
⅛   teaspoon pepper
½   teaspoon dried leaf basil
1   teaspoon fresh lemon juice

In large skillet melt butter. Add onion, green pepper and red pepper. Cook over low heat until crisp-tender. Stir in lettuce, salt, pepper, basil and lemon juice. Cook quickly over medium heat for 3 to 5 minutes, stirring frequently.   *Makes 4 servings.*

GERMAN-STYLE WILTED LETTUCE

6	cups lettuce torn into bite-size pieces
2	large hard-cooked eggs, diced
⅓	cup chopped Bermuda onion
4	slices bacon
1	tablespoon sugar
½	teaspoon salt
3	tablespoons cider vinegar

Wash lettuce, drain well, dry and tear into bite-size pieces. Place in a salad bowl. Sprinkle with hard-cooked egg and onion. Set aside. Cook bacon until lightly browned. Remove and drain, then crumble over lettuce. Cool fat slightly, add sugar, salt and vinegar. Heat to boiling and pour over lettuce. Toss lightly. Serve immediately. *Makes 6 servings.*

ACORN SQUASH

2	large acorn squash
½	pound bulk sausage
1	medium onion, chopped
1	small apple, pared and chopped
2	cups shredded green cabbage
¾	teaspoon salt
¼	teaspoon pepper
¼	teaspoon dried leaf thyme
1	teaspoon grated fresh orange rind

Cut acorn squash in half lengthwise and scoop out seeds and fibers. Place in baking pan, cut side down, and add one-half inch water. Bake in 400-degree oven for 20 minutes.

Meanwhile break up sausage meat in skillet and cook until browned. Drain off all but 2 tablespoons fat. Add onion, apple and cabbage; cook until tender. Add seasonings and orange rind; mix well.

Turn squash halves cut side up and fill centers with cabbage mixture. Return to baking pan and bake uncovered in 400-degree oven 30 minutes longer. *Makes 4 servings.*

ACORN SQUASH PUREE

2	medium-size acorn squash
¼	cup light cream
4	tablespoons butter
2	teaspoons bourbon, optional
1	teaspoon salt
¼	teaspoon pepper
⅛	teaspoon nutmeg

Cut squash in half and remove seeds. Place cut side down on baking sheet. Bake at 350 degrees for 45-50 minutes, or until tender. Scoop out pulp. Place pulp and remaining ingredients in blender or food processor. Blend until mixture is smooth. Reheat if necessary in double boiler. *Makes 4 servings.*

APPLE-FILLED ACORN SQUASH

3	acorn squash, about 1 pound each
⅓	cup butter or margarine
	Salt
	Pepper
3	large cooking apples, pared, cored and sliced (4 cups sliced)
½	cup golden raisins
½	cup orange marmalade

Cut squash lengthwise in half; scoop out seeds. Melt butter or margarine in saucepan. Brush some on cut surfaces of squash. Reserve remaining butter. Sprinkle squash with salt and pepper. Place cut-side down on grill 6 to 8 inches above medium coals. Grill 15 minutes.

Meanwhile, mix apples, raisins and orange marmalade with butter remaining in pan. Heat just until apples are wilted and juicy, stirring gently, about 3 minutes. Turn squash. Fill with apple mixture. Continue to grill until squash and apples are tender but firm, about 25 minutes. *Makes 6 servings.*

Note: If baked in an oven, bake cut-side down 25 minutes, turn, bake 15 to 25 minutes.

BAKED GOLDEN ACORN SQUASH

2	acorn squash
2	tablespoons butter or margarine
2	tablespoons honey
2	oranges, peeled and sectioned
½	teaspoon salt
¼	teaspoon pepper

Cut acorn squash in half lengthwise. Scoop out seeds. Place cut side down in large baking pan. Add 1 inch of water to pan. Bake in 375-degree oven 40 minutes. While squash is baking, melt butter in small saucepan; stir in honey and oranges. Turn acorn squash cavity side up. Sprinkle with salt and pepper and spoon orange mixture into cavities of squash. Bake 20 minutes longer. *Makes 4 servings.*

CRANBERRY CROWN ACORN SQUASH

3	acorn squash, halved, seeds removed
1	cup fresh or frozen fresh cranberries
½	cup sugar
¼	cup water
	Dash ground cloves
1	cup well drained crushed pineapple
6	corn muffins (store-bought or homemade), crumbled
½	cup butter or margarine, melted

Place squash halves cut side down on a buttered shallow baking pan. Bake in a preheated 350-degree oven for 35 minutes. In a saucepan, mix cranberries, sugar and water. Simmer for 5 minutes. Pour mixture into a bowl. Stir in remaining ingredients adding only one-half of the melted butter. Turn squash right side up on baking pan and fill each with cranberry mixture. Brush squash with remaining melted butter. Bake at 350 degrees for 30 minutes longer or until tops are lightly browned and squash is fork tender.   *Makes 6 servings.*

HERBED CHEESE-STUFFED SQUASH

4	medium (1½ pounds) zucchini squash
½	cup water
½	teaspoon salt, divided
2	tablespoons butter or margarine
1	tomato, peeled and diced
½	cup soft bread crumbs
½	cup cottage cheese
1	egg, beaten
1	tablespoon parsley flakes
1	tablespoon onion powder
½	teaspoon basil leaves, crumbled
¼	teaspoon garlic powder
¹⁄₁₆	teaspoon ground black pepper
½	cup grated Cheddar cheese

Cut zucchini in half lengthwise. Scoop out pulp, leaving a ¼-inch-thick shell. Chop pulp; set aside. Place shells, cut side down, in a large skillet. Add water. Bring to boiling. Cover, reduce heat and simmer until crisp-tender, about 5 minutes. Drain. Arrange shells, cut side up, in a greased 12×8×2-inch baking pan. Sprinkle with ¼ teaspoon of the salt. In the same skillet melt butter. Add reserved zucchini pulp and tomato; saute for 5 minutes. Remove from heat. Stir in bread crumbs, cottage cheese, egg, parsley flakes, onion powder, basil leaves, garlic powder, black pepper and remaining ¼ teaspoon salt. Stuff mixture into reserved shells. Cover and bake in a preheated 400-degree oven for

20 minutes. Remove cover; sprinkle with Cheddar cheese. Return to oven and bake, uncovered, until cheese is melted, about 5 minutes. Serve as an appetizer, for lunch, or as a meat accompaniment at dinner.   *Makes 4 to 8 portions.*

PEANUT-ORANGE BUTTERNUT SQUASH

2	medium-size butternut squash
⅓	cup smooth peanut butter
1	teaspoon grated orange rind
¼	cup orange juice
2	tablespoons chopped peanuts

Cut squash in half lengthwise. Place cut side down in baking pan. Add about ½-inch hot water to pan. Bake at 375 degrees for 45 minutes or until fork tender.

Remove from oven. Scoop out pulp. Place in bowl and beat with electric mixer until smooth.

Then beat in peanut butter, orange rind and juice. Pile mixture into shells. Sprinkle with peanuts. Bake 10 to 12 minutes longer or until heated through.   *Makes 4 servings.*

PEAR-STUFFED SQUASH

2	acorn squash (about 8 ounces each)
½	cup water
2	tablespoons brown sugar (packed)
1	tablespoon orange juice
½	teaspoon grated orange peel
2	small fresh Bartlett pears
½	teaspoon salt
2	tablespoons melted butter or margarine
⅛	teaspoon nutmeg

Cut squash in halves lengthwise. Remove seeds and membranes. Place cut side down in baking dish measuring 11¾-by-7½-by-1¾ inches.

Pour water around squash. Bake in 450-degree oven about 25 minutes, until squash is barely tender.

Meanwhile, stir together sugar, orange juice and peel. Set aside.

Pare, core and dice pears to measure 2 cups. Toss with orange juice mixture.

When squash is tender, remove from oven and turn cut side up. Sprinkle with salt. Fill each squash with ½ cup of pear mixture.

Brush edges of squash with butter. Drizzle remaining butter over pears. Sprinkle lightly with nutmeg. Add a little more water to dish if needed.

Cover dish with foil.

Return to oven. Bake about 30 minutes longer, until pears are tender. *Makes 4 servings.*

BACON-STUFFED YAMS

6	medium yams
2	tablespoons butter or margarine
⅛	teaspoon pepper
6	slices bacon, cooked and crumbled
1	tablespoon chopped parsley

Bake yams in 400-degree oven 35 to 40 minutes, until soft.

Cut slice from top of each yam. Scoop out insides, being careful not to break shells.

Mash pulp until fluffy with butter and pepper. Add crumbled bacon and parsley. Mix well.

Spoon into shells. Bake in 400-degree oven 15 minutes or until lightly browned. *Makes 6 servings.*

ORANGE-STUFFED YAMS

6	medium yams
3	tablespoons butter or margarine
¼	teaspoon salt
2	tablespoons brown sugar
¼	teaspoon cinnamon
½	cup diced fresh orange sections
¼	cup shredded fresh coconut
½	teaspoon grated fresh lemon rind

Bake yams in 400-degree oven 35 to 40 minutes, until soft.

Cut slice from top of each. Scoop out insides, keeping shells intact.

Mash pulp with butter. Add salt, brown sugar, cinnamon, diced orange sections, coconut and lemon rind. Mix well.

Spoon into shells. Bake in 400-degree oven 15 minutes or until lightly browned. *Makes 6 servings.*

BROILED CHEESE-TOPPED TOMATOES

3	large tomatoes
2	tablespoons lemon juice
1	teaspoon salt
⅛	teaspoon ground black pepper
3	tablespoons butter or margarine, divided
½	cup grated Cheddar cheese
½	cup soft bread crumbs
¾	teaspoon basil leaves, crumbled
6	rounds hot, buttered toast

Hold tomatoes at room temperature until fully ripe. Cut tomatoes in half. Place in shallow pan, cut side up. Dribble 1 teaspoon of the lemon juice over each half. Sprinkle halves with salt and black pepper. Dot each half with one-half teaspoon of the butter. Place under preheated broiler for 5 minutes. Melt remaining 2 tablespoons butter. Stir in cheese, bread crumbs and basil; sprinkle over tomatoes. Return to broiler. Brown lightly, about 2 minutes. Serve on toast rounds. Garnish with anchovies, if desired.

Makes 6 portions.

CHEDDAR-BAKED TOMATOES

6	medium-sized tomatoes
1	teaspoon salt, divided
1	cup grated Cheddar cheese
1	cup fresh bread crumbs
½	cup butter or margarine, melted
1½	teaspoons oregano leaves, crushed
	Dash ground red pepper

Use tomatoes held at room temperature until fully ripe. Preheat oven to 350 degrees. Core tomatoes. Cut each tomato in half crosswise. Place tomatoes, cut side up, in a greased shallow baking pan. Sprinkle with ½ teaspoon of the salt. Set aside. In a small bowl, combine cheese, bread crumbs, butter, oregano, red pepper and remaining ½ teaspoon salt. Spoon about 1 tablespoon cheese mixture on top of each tomato. Bake until hot, 10 to 12 minutes. *Makes 12 halves or 6 portions.*

GRANNY'S SKILLET SIDE DISH

2	tablespoons vegetable oil
½	cup chopped onion
¼	cup chopped green pepper
1	clove garlic, minced
½	teaspoon dried leaf basil, crumbled
¾	teaspoon salt
1	can (1 pound) whole tomatoes, undrained
3	Granny Smith or other tart apples, cored and sliced ¼-inch thick
2	tablespoons chopped parsley
¼	cup grated Parmesan cheese

In medium skillet, heat oil. Add onion, green pepper, garlic, basil and salt. Cook until onion is tender. Add tomatoes and apples. Simmer 5 to 8 minutes or until apples are tender. Sprinkle with parsley and Parmesan cheese. Serve with poultry, meat or fish. *Makes 4 to 6 servings.*

HERBED BAKED TOMATOES

6	small tomatoes
½	teaspoon salt
½	cup soft bread crumbs
1	tablespoon melted butter or margarine
2	teaspoons onion powder
1	teaspoon basil leaves, crumbled
⅛	teaspoon garlic powder
⅛	teaspoon ground red pepper

Store tomatoes at room temperature until fully ripe. Cut a thin slice from the stem end of each tomato. Place, cut side up, in a baking pan. Sprinkle cut surface of each tomato with the salt. Combine bread crumbs, butter, onion powder, basil, garlic powder and red pepper; blend well. Spoon mixture evenly on each tomato. Bake in a preheated 350-degree oven for 10 to 12 minutes.   *Makes 6 servings.*

HERBED SAUTEED TOMATOES

4	medium-sized tomatoes
3	tablespoons butter or margarine
½	cup chopped onion
1	garlic clove, minced
1	teaspoon salt
1	teaspoon basil leaves, crushed
¼	teaspoon oregano leaves, crushed
⅛	teaspoon ground black pepper

Use tomatoes held at room temperature until fully ripe. Remove stem end from each tomato; cut into 6 wedges; set aside. In large skillet, melt butter. Add onion and garlic; saute for 2 minutes. Stir in salt, basil, oregano and black pepper; stir well. Add reserved tomatoes; stir lightly over moderate heat just until tomatoes are hot, 2 to 3 minutes.
Makes 4 to 6 portions.

ITALIAN TOMATO SAUTE

4	medium tomatoes
3	tablespoons butter or margarine
1	cup diced celery
½	cup slivered onion
1	garlic clove, minced
¾	teaspoon salt
1	teaspoon oregano leaves, crushed
⅛	teaspoon ground black pepper

Hold tomatoes at room temperature until fully ripe.
Cut each tomato into 6 to 8 wedges. Set aside.
Melt butter in large skillet. Add celery, onion and garlic. Saute 5 minutes.

Stir in salt, oregano and black pepper. Cook and stir for 1 minute.
Add reserved tomatoes. Stir gently over moderate heat just until tomatoes are hot, about 3 minutes.   *Makes 6 to 8 portions.*

SAVORY STEWED FRESH TOMATOES

2	tablespoons butter or margarine
¼	cup chopped onion
½	cup diced green pepper
1	tablespoon flour
2	cups chopped fresh tomatoes
1	teaspoon salt
1	teaspoon sugar
3	slices toasted white bread, cut in ½-inch squares

In a medium saucepan melt butter. Add onion and green pepper; saute for 3 minutes. Add flour; cook and stir for 1 minute. Stir in tomatoes, salt and sugar. Cook and stir until mixture boils and thickens. Stir in half of the toast squares. Pour into a greased 1-quart casserole. Top with remaining toast squares. Bake in a preheated 375-degree oven until hot and bubbly, about 15 minutes.

Makes 4 portions.

SCALLOPED SLICED TOMATOES

4	medium-size tomatoes (held at room temperature until fully ripe)
4	tablespoons butter or margarine
1	cup diced celery
½	cup chopped onion
1	teaspoon salt
1	teaspoon sugar
1	teaspoon basil leaves, crushed
⅛	teaspoon ground black pepper
1	cup plain croutons

Preheat oven to 350 degrees. Core tomatoes. Cut into ¼-inch-thick slices.

Overlap slices in 2 rows in buttered 12-by-8-by-2-inch casserole. Set aside.

Melt butter in medium saucepan. Add celery and onion. Saute 2 minutes. Stir in salt, sugar, basil and pepper.

Spoon all but ¼ cup celery mixture over tomatoes. Toss croutons with reserved ¼ cup celery mixture. Spoon down center of casserole between tomatoes.

Cover and bake until tomatoes are cooked, about 30 minutes. *Makes 8 portions.*

SPICED SCALLOPED FRESH TOMATOES

¼	cup butter or margarine, divided
¼	cup chopped fresh onion
3	cups fresh bread cubes
3	tablespoons dark brown sugar
1	teaspoon salt
¼	plus ⅛ teaspoon ground cloves, divided
¼	teaspoon cinnamon
4	tomatoes, peeled and sliced

In large skillet melt 3 tablespoons butter, add onion and cook until tender, about 5 minutes. Add bread and toast to a light brown color. Stir in brown sugar, salt, one-fourth teaspoon cloves and cinnamon. In a greased 1-quart casserole place half of bread cube mixture, then a layer of tomatoes, repeat with remaining bread cubes and tomatoes. Dot with remaining 1 tablespoon butter and sprinkle with remaining one-eighth teaspoon cloves. Bake in 350-degree oven 30 minutes. *Makes 4 servings.*

TOMATOES FLORENTINE

8	small tomatoes (about 1½ pounds)
¼	teaspoon salt
1	package (12 ounces) frozen spinach souffle, defrosted (or substitute 1 cup cooked creamed spinach)
⅓	cup dry bread crumbs
⅓	cup shredded Swiss cheese
1	teaspoon onion powder
⅛	teaspoon ground nutmeg

Hold tomatoes at room temperature until fully ripe. Preheat oven to 350 degrees. Slice off tops of tomatoes; scoop out pulp and seeds with a teaspoon (use in soups, stews, etc.). Sprinkle inside of tomatoes with salt; turn upside down to drain for 15 minutes. In a medium bowl, combine spinach souffle, bread crumbs, cheese, onion powder and nutmeg; spoon into reserved tomato shells. Place on a baking sheet. Bake until spinach mixture is firm, about 10 minutes. *Makes 8 portions.*

TOMATOES STUFFED WITH CHICKEN LIVERS

8	medium-sized tomatoes
3	tablespoons salad oil
1½	pounds chicken livers, cut into ½-inch pieces
½	cup chopped onion
½	cup chopped parsley
¾	teaspoon salt
½	teaspoon thyme leaves
⅛	teaspoon ground black pepper
2	tablespoons dry sherry (optional)
¾	cup dry bread crumbs, divided
2	tablespoons butter or margarine

Use tomatoes held at room temperature until finally ripe. Cut a thin slice from stem end of each tomato; scoop out pulp, reserving ½ cup. Preheat oven to 350 degrees. In a large skillet, heat oil until hot. Add chicken livers, onion, parsley, salt, thyme and black pepper; saute until livers are barely pink inside, about 5 minutes. Stir in sherry and reserved tomato pulp; simmer, covered, for 5 minutes longer. Remove from heat; add ½ cup of the bread crumbs; mix well. Place tomatoes on a baking sheet or in a shallow baking pan. Fill with liver mixture. In a small saucepan, melt butter; add remaining ¼ cup bread crumbs; mix well. Sprinkle on top of each tomato. Bake, uncovered, for 20 minutes. Serve with scrambled eggs, if desired. *Makes 8 portions.*

BAKED STUFFED ZUCCHINI

4	small zucchini
3	tablespoons corn oil
¼	cup chopped onion

Continued

1 cup sliced mushrooms
¼ cup chopped green pepper
½ teaspoon dried oregano leaves
½ teaspoon salt
Dash pepper
¼ cup fine dry bread crumbs
4 tablespoons shredded Jarlsberg or Lorraine Swiss cheese

Cut a thin, lengthwise slice from each zucchini. Scoop or cut out pulp, leaving a shell about ⅛-inch thick. Coarsely chop pulp. (There should be about 1½ cups.) Place zucchini shells cut side down in a 10-by-6-by-1¾-inch baking dish. Fill with ⅛-inch hot water. Cover with foil. Bake in 425-degree oven 15 minutes or until tender.

Meanwhile, in large skillet heat corn oil over medium heat. Add onion; stirring occasionally, cook 2 to 3 minutes or until tender. Add chopped zucchini, mushrooms, green pepper, oregano, salt and pepper. Stirring occasionally, cook 10 minutes or until vegetables are tender. Stir in bread crumbs.

Drain cooked zucchini shells. Fill with mushroom mixture. Sprinkle each with 1 tablespoon of the cheese. Bake in 425-degree oven 12 to 15 minutes or until heated through. *Makes 4 servings.*

MARINATED VEGETABLE MEDLEY

MARINADE:
1 can (10¾ ounces) condensed chicken broth
½ cup vinegar
¼ cup salad oil
½ teaspoon celery seed
½ teaspoon thyme leaves, crushed
½ teaspoon salt
¼ teaspoon oregano leaves, crushed
8 peppercorns

VEGETABLES:
1 package (9 ounces) frozen cut green beans
1 package (9 ounces) frozen cut wax beans
½ cup water
2 medium tomatoes, cut in wedges
1 cup sliced onion
1 cup small fresh mushroom caps (about ¼ pound)

To make marinade, combine marinade ingredients in saucepan. Cook over low heat 10 minutes; stir occasionally.

Meanwhile, in saucepan, combine beans and water. Bring to boil; reduce heat. Cover; simmer 3 minutes. Drain.

Arrange vegetables in 3-quart shallow dish (12-by-9-by-2-inches); pour marinade over all.

Cover; refrigerate 6 hours or more. Stir occasionally. Serve with slotted spoon.

Makes 5 cups or 6 servings.

MIXED VEGETABLE CURRY

1 pound small potatoes, pared and cut in halves
1 pound fresh green beans, cut in 1-inch pieces
1 pound carrots, pared, quartered lengthwise and cut in 1-inch pieces
1 package (9 ounces) frozen peas
½ cup butter or margarine
1 tablespoon curry powder
1¼ teaspoons salt
⅛ teaspoon ground black pepper
¼ cup plain yogurt (room temperature)
1 tablespoon tomato paste

In a large covered saucepot, cook potatoes, green beans and carrots together in boiling salted water to cover, until vegetables are barely tender, about 15 minutes. Add peas; continue cooking until vegetables are just tender, about 5 minutes. Drain.

While vegetables are cooking, melt butter in a large skillet. Add curry powder, salt and black pepper. Saute until curry turns golden, about 30 seconds. Toss with vegetables. Simmer, until piping hot, about 1 minute. Remove from heat. Combine yogurt and tomato paste. Stir into vegetables. Spoon onto a serving dish.

Makes 6 to 8 portions or about 5 cups.

GARDEN VEGETABLE MEDLEY

4 quarts (1 gallon) water
2 pounds zucchini, unpared, cut into 12-inch slices
1 pound carrots, washed, pared and cut into 12-inch pieces
1 pound green beans, washed, trimmed and cut into 2-inch pieces
4 medium onions, sliced, slices cut into quarters
Butter Sauce (recipe follows)
Dried dill weed

Pour water into large kettle, bring to a boil over high heat. Place 1 pound zucchini in a cooking basket. Plunge into rapidly boiling water; when water returns to a rolling boil, cook 3 minutes, remove basket and plunge immediately into ice water for 3 minutes. Repeat procedure for remaining zucchini.

Repeat procedure for carrots and green beans, 1 pound at a time, reducing time to 2 minutes for blanching and ice water bath. Combine all vegetables in a large bowl. Pack into 8 (1 pint) freezer containers, leaving one-half-inch headspace. Add 2 tablespoons Butter Sauce to each container. Freeze. To serve, place 1 pint frozen vegetables in large saucepan, add 1 cup water. Simmer over medium heat, separating vegetables with a fork and stirring frequently until sauce is blended. Stir in one-eighth teaspoon dried dill weed. Reduce heat. Cover and simmer 3 to 5 minutes. Serve hot.

Makes 4 servings.

BUTTER SAUCE:

½ cup butter or margarine
¼ cup cornstarch
3 teaspoons flavor enhancer
1 teaspoon salt
1 teaspoon celery salt
4 packets (.19 ounces each) instant chicken flavored broth
¼ teaspoon pepper
⅛ teaspoon nutmeg

In medium saucepan, melt butter over low heat. Remove from heat, stir in remaining ingredients.

Makes 4 servings.

OTHER COMBINATIONS: Green beans, broccoli, chopped onion, mushrooms; cauliflower, carrots, green beans, onions; carrots, peas, green beans, cauliflower; corn, tomatoes, green peppers; green beans or broccoli, cauliflower, carrots, onions.
SUGGESTED SEASONINGS: Dill weed, chives, mint, parsley, oregano, thyme; almonds, walnuts; orange or lemon peel or packaged broth seasonings.

GARDEN PATCH TEMPURA

1 cup enriched cornmeal
1 cup all-purpose flour
1 teaspoon baking powder
2 teaspoons salt
1 12-ounce can (1½ cups) beer
2 eggs, beaten
2 medium-sized zucchini, sliced ¼-inch thick
2 medium-sized potatoes, cut into thin strips
2 cups cauliflower pieces
2 cups broccoli pieces
1 large sweet potato, cut into thin strips
1 cup parsley sprigs
   Vegetable oil

Combine cornmeal, flour, baking powder and salt. Add beer and eggs, mixing until well blended. Dip

vegetables into batter. Fry in deep hot oil (375 degrees) until golden brown. Drain on absorbent paper. Serve warm with soy sauce, if desired, or other favorite dips. *Makes 4 to 6 servings.*

VARIATION: Substitute 2 medium-sized carrots, cut into thin strips, for sweet potato.

HERB GRILLED VEGETABLES

½ cup butter or margarine
1 tablespoon onion powder
1 tablespoon parsley flakes
1 teaspoon basil leaves, crushed
1 teaspoon garlic powder
½ teaspoon salt
⅛ teaspoon ground black pepper
1 medium-sized eggplant, cut in ½-inch slices
2 medium zucchini, cut in half, lengthwise
2 medium tomatoes, cut in half, crosswise

In small saucepan, melt butter. Stir in onion powder, parsley flakes, basil, garlic powder, salt and black pepper; set aside. Brush both sides of vegetables with herb-butter mixture. Arrange eggplant and zucchini on a grill over hot charcoal. Grill for 5 minutes. Turn eggplant and zucchini. Place tomatoes on grill, cut side up. Grill all vegetables until done, about 5 minutes longer, brushing occasionally with remaining herb-butter mixture. If desired, all vegetables may be grilled in a hinged wire grill over hot charcoal for 10 minutes, turning and brushing occasionally with herb-butter mixture. *Makes 4 portions.*

STUFFED ZUCCHINI

12	small whole or 6 large zucchini (3 pounds)
½	pound ground beef or lamb
¼	cup regular cooking rice (uncooked)
1	can (15 ounces) tomato sauce, divided
¾	teaspoon onion powder
¾	teaspoon salt, divided
½	teaspoon basil leaves, crushed
¼	teaspoon oregano leaves, crushed
¹⁄₁₆	teaspoon ground black pepper
1	can (15 ounces) whole tomatoes, broken up
½	teaspoon garlic powder

Cut ends from zucchini. Cut large zucchini in half crosswise. Using an apple corer, scoop out pulp leaving ¼-inch-thick shell.

In a medium bowl, combine beef, rice, ¼ cup of the tomato sauce, onion powder, ½ teaspoon of the salt, basil, oregano and black pepper.

Stuff into zucchini shells until ¾ full to allow for rice to expand; set aside. In a large skillet, combine tomatoes, garlic powder and remaining ¼ teaspoon salt and tomato sauce; bring to a boil. Add reserved zucchini, spooning some of the sauce over zucchini. Reduce heat and simmer, covered, until zucchini and rice are tender, about 45 minutes, stirring occasionally. Serve hot or cold.   *Makes 6 portions.*

Desserts

Desserts are a way of life. Even a person on the strictest of diets finds a way to weave a spoonful of a favorite dessert into the restricted menu. *Someone* is eating all those rich, highly caloric parfaits, Napoleons, cream puffs, and so on that fill bakery shop windows and coffee shop displays these days.

A friend from the Orient notes that it was not their custom to end a meal, as it is done in America, with a sweet dessert. She now confesses to a sweet tooth since she has lived in the United States and enjoys her desserts.

I grew up with homemade cakes, pies, and ice cream. My favorites were the fruit pies, a very special pecan pie, and a sugar cream pie; and, at night before bedtime, ice cream . . . often homemade.

There is a special satisfaction in turning out a pie with a perfect crust or in creating a tempting dessert using simple ingredients. Here are some recipes to add to your dessert-making repertoire.

CAKES

BANANA CHIFFON CAKE

2½	cups sifted cake flour
¾	cup granulated sugar
3	teaspoons baking powder
1	teaspoon salt
½	teaspoon allspice
¾	cup packed light brown sugar
½	cup salad oil
5	egg yolks
⅓	cup cold water
1⅓	cups mashed ripe bananas (4 medium bananas)
1	teaspoon vanilla
1	cup egg whites (8 egg whites)
½	teaspoon cream of tartar

Sift flour, granulated sugar, baking powder, salt and allspice into mixing bowl. Stir in brown sugar.

Make well in center. Add oil, egg yolks, water, bananas and vanilla. Beat until smooth.

In large bowl, combine egg whites and cream of tartar. Beat until very stiff peaks form.

Pour egg-yolk batter over entire surface of beaten egg whites in steady stream. Fold in gently, just until blended. Pour batter into ungreased 10-inch tube pan.

Bake in 325-degree oven 55 minutes. Increase temperature to 350 degrees and bake 15 to 20 minutes longer or until cake tester inserted in center comes out clean.

Invert pan. Let cool thoroughly. Sprinkle with confectioners' sugar if desired.   *Makes 16 servings.*

BANANA RUM CAKE

1	package (18½ ounces) yellow cake mix
⅛	teaspoon baking soda
⅔	cup dark rum
⅔	cup water
2	eggs
1	cup mashed ripe bananas (2 to 3 medium-sized)
⅓	cup finely chopped pecans or walnuts
	Rum Frosting (recipe follows)

Preheat oven to 350 degrees. Grease and flour two 9-inch cake pans. Combine all ingredients in large bowl. Blend well, then beat at medium speed 2 to 4 minutes. Turn into prepared pans. Bake 25 to 30 minutes or until cake tests done. Cool completely. Frost with Rum Frosting.

RUM FROSTING:

⅓	cup butter or margarine, softened
3	cups confectioners' sugar
2	teaspoons vanilla
2	dark rum

Combine butter and sugar, blending thoroughly. Stir in vanilla and rum, beating until smooth.

BRANDIED PEACH POUND CAKE

1	can (29 ounces) sliced peaches, drained, reserving liquid
1	cup light corn syrup
2	tablespoons brandy
1	vanilla bean
¼	cup brandy
½	cup heavy cream, whipped
1	frozen pound cake (16½ ounces), thawed

In medium saucepan, stir together reserved peach liquid, corn syrup, 2 tablespoons brandy and the vanilla bean. Bring to full rolling boil, stirring occasionally, and boil 5 minutes. Coarsely chop peaches and add to syrup mixture. Stirring occasionally, bring to full rolling boil and boil 15 minutes. Remove from heat, stir in ¼ cup brandy. Cover and refrigerate overnight.

Next day, remove vanilla bean. Fold ½ cup cooled topping into ½ cup heavy cream. Use to fill and frost pound cake. Chill before serving, if desired. Serve remaining topping with cake or use as ice cream topping.   *Makes 2¾ cups topping.*

CALIFORNIA CAKE

4	cups sifted flour
2	tablespoons double-acting baking powder
2	teaspoons salt
¼	cup sugar
1	cup solid all-vegetable shortening
1½	cups milk

2 pints fresh California strawberries, halved
⅔ cup sugar
   Orange or lemon marmalade
1 pint dairy sour cream (or ½ pint heavy cream, flavored and whipped)

Mix flour, baking powder, salt and sugar in a large bowl. Cut in shortening with pastry blender or 2 knives until mixture resembles coarse meal. Stir in milk until blended. On floured surface, knead dough lightly about 10 times. Pat out ⅓ of dough in each of three 9-inch layer cake pans. Bake in 450-degree oven 12 minutes or until lightly browned.

Meanwhile, combine strawberries and ⅔ cup sugar. Chill 30 minutes. Stack warm biscuit layers, spreading each thinly with marmalade, then with sour cream and topping with sliced strawberries.
Makes 8 servings.

CARROT CAKE

1 pound carrots (8 to 10), trimmed and peeled
1¼ cups salad oil
1¾ cups sugar
4 eggs
2 cups all-purpose flour
2 teaspoons baking powder
2 teaspoons baking soda
2 teaspoons cinnamon
1 teaspoon salt
½ cup chopped pecans
   Pineapple Cream Cheese Frosting (recipe follows)

Grease and flour three 8-inch layer cake pans. Preheat oven to 350 degrees. Grate carrots finely. Mix oil and sugar in large bowl. Beat in eggs, one at a time. Sift together dry ingredients and add to egg mixture, blending well. Stir in grated carrots and add pecans. Turn into prepared cake pans. Bake at 350 degrees for 30 minutes or until cake is done. Cool in pans for 10 minutes, then remove cake layers and cool thoroughly before frosting. Cut each layer in half, crosswise. Spread frosting between layers and on top of cake. Garnish with pecan halves, if desired. *Makes 8 servings.*

PINEAPPLE CREAM CHEESE FROSTING:
8 ounces cream cheese, softened
¼ pound butter, softened
1 pound confectioners' sugar
1 can (8 ounces) crushed pineapple, well drained
1 teaspoon vanilla

Beat cream cheese with butter until smooth. Add confectioners' sugar, a little at a time, beating until very smooth and fluffy. Blend in vanilla and drained pineapple. Chill about ½ hour until spreading consistency.

Note: Carrot Cake freezes well, unfrosted, or frosted with Pineapple Cream Cheese Frosting.

CARROT CAKE RING

1 tablespoon vegetable shortening
¾ cup chopped pecans
1½ cups firmly packed brown sugar
¾ cup vegetable oil
4 eggs
1½ cups all-purpose flour
1 tablespoon baking powder
1 teaspoon salt
1 teaspoon allspice
1 teaspoon cinnamon
3 cups shredded carrots
¾ cup raisins
¾ cup quick or old-fashioned oats, uncooked

Heat oven to 325 degrees. Grease a 12-cup fluted tube pan with shortening; coat pan with nuts. Combine sugar and oil in large bowl. Add eggs, one at a time, beating well after each addition. Combine flour, baking powder, salt and spices; stir into egg mixture. Add carrots, raisins and oats; mix well. Pour into prepared pan; bake at 325 degrees for 55 to 60 minutes or until wooden pick inserted in center comes out clean. Cool 10 minutes. Remove from pan; cool completely on wire rack.
Makes one 12-cup fluted tube cake.

CHERRY TULIP CAKE

1 cup sifted cake flour
1½ cups sugar, divided
1¼ cups egg whites (10–12)
1 teaspoon cream of tartar
½ teaspoon salt
½ cup chopped red maraschino cherries
2 tablespoons cherry syrup
4 egg yolks, well beaten
½ teaspoon vanilla
   Cherry Icing (recipe follows)

Sift together flour and one-half cup sugar. Reserve. In large electric mixer bowl, beat egg whites until frothy, sprinkle with cream of tartar and salt and continue beating until stiff but not dry. Gradually beat in remaining sugar. Fold in flour mixture about one-fourth cup at a time. Divide mixture into 2 equal parts. Fold cherries and syrup into one part. Fold egg yolks and vanilla into other part. Put batters by spoonfuls into ungreased 10-inch tube pan alternating pink and yellow batters. Bake in 325-degree oven about 1 hour and 15 minutes. Invert pan until cake is cool. Then remove from pan. Cool completely; frost with Cherry Icing.

Makes one 10-inch cake.

CHERRY ICING: In small bowl, combine 3 cups sifted confectioners' sugar, one-fourth cup soft butter or margarine, 2 tablespoons milk, 3 tablespoons cherry syrup and dash of salt. Mix well until blended. Garnish as desired.

COCOA CREAM CAKE

⅓	cup unsweetened cocoa
⅓	cup sugar
3	tablespoons cornstarch
¼	teaspoon salt
1⅓	cups milk
3	tablespoons margarine
½	teaspoon vanilla
1	loaf (12-ounce) pound cake
¼	cup dry sherry
1	cup heavy cream
3	tablespoons confectioners' sugar

In small saucepan, stir together cocoa, sugar, cornstarch and salt. Gradually stir in milk until smooth. Stirring constantly, bring to boil over medium heat and boil 1 minute. Remove from heat. Stir in margarine and vanilla. Cover; refrigerate until chilled. Slice pound cake lengthwise into 4 layers. Brush each layer with sherry. Put bottom layer on serving plate. Spread with ⅓ of the cocoa mixture. Repeat with remaining layers and cocoa mixture, ending with cake layer. In small bowl with mixer at high speed, whip cream and confectioners' sugar. Frost cake with whipped cream. If desired, garnish with candied violets. *Makes about 8 servings.*

FRESH PEACH SHORTCAKE

3	cups sifted all-purpose flour
3¼	teaspoons baking powder
½	cup sugar
½	teaspoon salt
½	cup shortening
1	egg, well beaten
½	cup milk
1	tablespoon butter or margarine, melted
	Filling (recipe follows)

Sift together flour, baking powder, sugar and salt. Cut in shortening until mixture resembles coarse meal. Add egg and milk. Mix with a fork to form a soft dough.

On a floured board, knead dough 20 times. Divide in half. Pat one half into a greased 8-inch round layer cake pan. Spread with melted butter. Pat remaining dough over top.

Bake in 450-degree oven for 30 minutes, until golden brown. While biscuit is baking, prepare peaches for filling. Cool biscuit 5 to 10 minutes and separate biscuit layers with a fork.

	FILLING:
4	cups sliced fresh peaches
½	cup sugar, divided
2	cups heavy cream
1	teaspoon vanilla

Sprinkle peaches with ¼ cup sugar and let stand at room temperature. Whip cream with remaining ¼ cup sugar and vanilla until thick. Spread bottom layer of biscuit with half of whipped cream. Top with 2 cups sliced peaches. Add top layer and repeat. Serve immediately or chill. *Makes 8 servings.*

GOLDEN APPLE TORTE

3	cups flour
2	teaspoons baking soda
½	teaspoon salt
2	teaspoons cinnamon
1½	cups oil
1½	cups sugar
2	cups grated Golden Delicious apples
1	can (8 ounces) crushed pineapple
½	cup plus 2 tablespoons chopped walnuts
1½	teaspoons vanilla
3	eggs
	Lemon Glaze (recipe follows)

Sift together flour, soda, salt and cinnamon. Combine oil and sugar. Add half of dry ingredients, mixing well. Blend in grated apples, pineapple, one-half cup walnuts and vanilla. Add remaining dry ingredients. Add eggs, one at a time, beating well after each addition. Turn into greased 3-quart bundt pan. Bake at 350 degrees for 1 hour or until cake tests done. Cool in pan 15 minutes; turn out on wire rack. Drizzle with Lemon Glaze and sprinkle with 2 tablespoons chopped walnuts when cool.

Makes 1 Bundt cake, about 12 servings.

LEMON GLAZE: Combine 1½ cups powdered sugar, 3 tablespoons soft butter, ½ teaspoon grated lemon peel, 2 teaspoons lemon juice and 1½ tablespoons hot water. Stir until smooth.

HONEY CAKE

3¼	cups sifted all-purpose flour
2	teaspoons baking powder
1	teaspoon baking soda
1	teaspoon ground cinnamon
½	teaspoon ground ginger
½	teaspoon ground allspice
½	teaspoon salt
1	cup honey
1	can (8 ounces) frozen concentrated orange juice, thawed, undiluted
½	cup vegetable oil
⅓	cup brewed coffee
4	eggs
¾	cup sugar
1	cup chopped nuts

Grease and line two 9-by-5-by-3-inch loaf pans with waxed paper. Set aside. Sift together flour, baking powder, baking soda, cinnamon, ginger, allspice and salt. In a small bowl, combine honey, orange juice concentrate, oil and coffee. In the large bowl of an electric mixer, beat eggs; add sugar, continue beating until light and fluffy. Blend in dry ingredients alternately with orange juice mixture. Fold in nuts.

Pour batter into prepared pans. Bake in 350-degree oven 15 minutes; reduce heat to 325 degrees. Continue baking 45 minutes longer or until cake tests done when cake tester is inserted in center. Remove loaves from pans. Cool completely. Remove waxed paper before serving.

Makes two 9-inch loaves.

HONEY CAKE CHERRY ROLL

1	can (16 to 17 ounces) dark sweet cherries
3	eggs
¾	cup honey
2	tablespoons water
¾	cup flour
1	teaspoon baking powder
¼	teaspoon salt
⅛	teaspoon each cinnamon, ginger and allspice
	Powdered sugar
½	cup heavy cream
	Cherry Sauce (recipe follows)

Grease jelly roll pan (15½-by-10½-by-1-inch). Line with waxed paper and grease paper very thoroughly. Drain cherries, reserving syrup. Halve cherries and blot thoroughly with paper towel; set aside. In small mixer bowl, beat eggs until thick and lemon-colored, about 5 minutes; gradually beat in honey. On low speed, beat in water, flour, baking powder, salt and spices. Beat just until batter is smooth. Pour into prepared pan; bake at 375 degrees 12 to 15 minutes or until cake springs back when touched lightly in center.

Immediately invert cake onto clean towel liberally dusted with powdered sugar. Using spatula or table knife to help free edges, carefully remove waxed paper. While hot, and starting from narrow end, roll cake and towel together. Cool on wire rack 30 minutes.

In chilled bowl, whip cream until soft peaks form. Fold in 2 tablespoons powdered sugar. Carefully unroll cake; spread whipped cream over entire surface. Sprinkle halved cherries evenly on cream filling. Reroll without towel. Sprinkle with additional powdered sugar. Serve with cherry sauce.

Makes 8 to 10 servings.

CHERRY SAUCE: Add water to reserved cherry syrup to equal 1 cup. Gradually stir into 1 tablespoon cornstarch. Cook and stir over medium heat until thickened and clear. Stir in ¼ teaspoon almond extract. *Makes 1 cup.*

LEMON POUND CAKE

1	cup butter or margarine
2	cups sugar
5	eggs
3	cups all-purpose flour
1	teaspoon baking powder
¼	teaspoon salt
1	cup milk
2	cups 100 percent natural cereal, divided
1	teaspoon lemon extract
½	teaspoon vanilla

Beat together butter and sugar until light and fluffy. Add eggs, one at a time, beating well after each addition. Combine flour, baking powder and salt. Add to butter mixture alternately with milk, beating well after each addition. Blend in 1 cup cereal, lemon extract and vanilla.

Generously grease 10-inch tube pan. Pat remaining 1 cup cereal onto bottom of pan. Spoon batter over. Bake in preheated 325-degree oven for 1 hour and 35 minutes, or until wooden pick inserted in center comes out clean. Cool 15 minutes; remove from pan. Complete cooling on rack.

Makes one 10-inch tube cake.

MEXICAN PLUM TORTE

1	package (13¾ ounces) hot-roll mix
2	pounds fresh California plums, halved and pitted
1	cup sugar

Continued

2 tablespoons cornstarch
1 package (3 ounces) cream cheese, cubed
1 egg, lightly beaten

Prepare hot-roll mix according to package directions. Divide dough in half. On lightly floured board, roll out half; use to line 9-inch springform cake pan.

Put plums in saucepan, barely covering them with water; add sugar and simmer, stirring occasionally, about 10 minutes, until plums are tender. Drain plums, reserving liquid. Put 2 plums in blender along with cornstarch and 1 cup reserved liquid. Blend until pureed. Return to saucepan.

Cook, stirring occasionally, until sauce thickens. Arrange remaining plums in dough-lined pan. Pour plum sauce over plums. Dot with cream-cheese cubes.

Roll out remaining dough. Cut into 1-inch strips and place over plums in lattice topping, sealing edges. Brush with beaten egg.

Bake in 400-degree oven 35 minutes or until golden brown. Cool in pan. At serving time, remove pan and cut into wedges.

Makes 6 servings.

MOCHA MAYONNAISE CAKE

2 tablespoons plus 1 teaspoon instant coffee
1 cup boiling water
2 cups unsifted flour
⅓ cup unsweetened cocoa
1¼ teaspoons baking soda
¼ teaspoon baking powder
3 eggs
1⅔ cups sugar
1 teaspoon vanilla
1 cup real mayonnaise
2 tablespoons confectioners' sugar

In small bowl, stir together 2 tablespoons coffee powder and water until dissolved; cool. Grease and flour bottom of 13-by-9-by-2-inch baking pan. In medium bowl, stir together flour, cocoa, baking soda and baking powder; set aside. In large bowl with mixer at high speed, beat eggs, sugar and vanilla, occasionally scraping bowl, 3 minutes or until light and fluffy. Reduce speed to low; beat in mayonnaise. Add flour mixture in 4 additions alternately with coffee, beginning and ending with flour. Pour into prepared pan. Bake in 350-degree oven 35 to 40 minutes or until cake tester inserted in center comes out clean. Cool in pan. In small bowl, stir together confectioners' sugar and 1 teaspoon coffee powder. Sift over cake.

Makes 32 (2-by-2-inch) squares.

O'DARBY CREAM NUT ROLL

7 eggs, separated
1 cup sugar
1 teaspoon baking powder
Dash of salt
1½ cups ground almonds or pecans
2 cups heavy cream
⅓ cup Irish cream liqueur
½ teaspoon vanilla extract

Grease bottom and sides of jelly roll pan (11½-by-17½ inches). Place sheet of waxed paper in pan overlapping several inches at each end. Press paper into sides of pan. Grease paper. Beat egg yolks lightly. Beat in sugar until mixture is thick and light. Beat in baking powder and salt. Stir in nuts. Beat egg whites until stiff but not dry. Fold in yolk mixture. Spread batter in prepared pan. Bake at 350-degrees for 18 minutes or until cake springs back when lightly touched in center. Immediately invert pan onto clean kitchen towel sprinkled with confectioners' sugar. Remove waxed paper carefully. Roll up cake in towel. Cool on wire rack.

Combine heavy cream, liqueur and vanilla. Whip to stiff peaks. Unroll cake; remove towel. Spread half whipped cream mixture in cake. Reroll onto serving platter. Frost with remaining cream. Chill until ready to serve. *Makes 1 cake.*

OLD-FASHIONED BLUEBERRY CAKE

2 tablespoons plus 2 cups sugar
⅓ cup water
2 cups fresh blueberries, rinsed and drained
1 cup (2 sticks) butter
4 eggs, beaten
1 teaspoon nutmeg
1 teaspoon cinnamon
1 teaspoon ground cloves
1 teaspoon salt
3 cups all-purpose flour
1 cup seedless raisins
1 cup apricot preserves or peach jam
2 teaspoons baking soda
½ cup buttermilk
Powdered sugar

Combine 2 tablespoons sugar and ⅓ cup water. Pour over blueberries. Let stand 30 minutes. Cream butter and sugar until light and fluffy. Add eggs, spices, salt, blueberry mixture, flour, raisins and preserves. Beat at medium speed of electric mixer or by hand until well blended. Dissolve baking soda in buttermilk. Add to batter and mix well, but do not beat. Pour batter into three greased and floured 8-inch round cake pans. Bake in a preheated 350-degree oven for 25–35 minutes or until cake tester inserted in center comes out clean. Remove from pans; cool cakes on wire racks. Sprinkle powdered sugar between layers and on top of cake.

Makes one 8-inch three-layer cake.

ONE-BOWL FRUIT CAKE

2¼	cups cake flour or 2 cups all-purpose flour
1⅓	cups sugar
4	teaspoons baking powder
1	teaspoon baking soda
1½	teaspoons ground allspice
1	teaspoon ground cinnamon
½	teaspoon ground cloves
	can (10¾ ounces) condensed tomato soup
½	cup shortening
2	eggs
¼	cup water
1	cup chopped dates (tossed with flour)
1	cup chopped walnuts

Preheat oven to 350 degrees. Generously grease and lightly flour a 2½-quart bundt pan. Measure dry ingredients into large bowl. Add soup and shortening. Beat at low to medium speed for 2 minutes (300 strokes with a spoon) scraping sides and bottom of bowl constantly. Add eggs and water. Beat 2 minutes more, scraping bowl frequently. Fold in dates and walnuts. Pour into prepared pan. Bake 1 hour or until done. Cool 10 minutes; remove from pan. Sprinkle with powdered sugar.

ORANGE SPONGE CAKE

1½	cups sifted cake flour
1½	teaspoons baking powder
¼	teaspoon salt
6	eggs, separated
1	cup sugar
1	tablespoon grated orange rind
1	cup orange juice
1	teaspoon cream of tartar
1	orange, sliced
	Confectioners' sugar

Sift together flour, baking powder and salt. In a large mixing bowl, beat egg yolks until light. Gradually add sugar; beat until thick and light-colored, about 5 minutes. Stir in orange rind. Blend in dry ingredients alternately with orange juice. Beat egg

whites with cream of tartar until stiff but not dry; fold into batter.

Pour batter into ungreased 10-inch tube pan. Bake in 325-degree oven 50 to 60 minutes or until cake tester comes out clean. Invert pan over neck of bottle; let cake cool completely before removing from pan. Before serving, sprinkle with confectioners' sugar and garnish with orange slices cut in half. *Makes one 10-inch cake, about 12 servings.*

PEACHES 'N' BUTTERMILK SHORTCAKE

2	cups sifted flour
2	teaspoons baking powder
1	teaspoon salt
½	cup butter
⅔	cup buttermilk
4	fresh peaches, peeled, sliced and sugared
1	cup whipping cream, whipped and sweetened

Resift flour with baking powder and salt into mixing bowl. Cut in 6 tablespoons butter with a pastry blender until mixture resembles coarse meal. Stir in buttermilk. Shape dough into a ball. Roll out to one-half-inch thickness on a lightly floured board. Cut dough into 4-inch rounds. Bake in 450-degree oven 18 to 20 minutes. Split biscuits while warm; spread with remaining butter. Serve in individual dishes with peaches between split layers and on top. Spread whipped cream over both layers.

Makes 4 servings.

PEANUT TORTE

1	package (18½ ounces) Devil's food cake mix
3	cups ground peanuts
1⅔	cups plus ½ cup confectioners' sugar
¼	cup grated orange peel
½	cup orange juice
1	square (1 ounce) unsweetened chocolate
2	tablespoons butter
2–3	teaspoons water
½	teaspoon vanilla extract
⅓	cup coarsely chopped peanuts

Prepare cake mix according to package directions. Pour batter onto a greased and floured 15½ × 10½ × 1-inch jelly roll pan. Bake in a preheated 350-degree oven for 20–25 minutes or until cake tests done. Prepare cake filling by stirring together ground peanuts, 1⅔ cups confectioners' sugar, orange peel and juice. To assemble cake, cut cake crosswise into 3 equal pieces and remove from pan. Then split each piece of cake in half horizontally to make 6 layers. Stack and fill layers with peanut mixture. To prepare frosting, in a small saucepan melt chocolate and butter. Stir in one half cup confectioners' sugar, water and vanilla. Beat until smooth. Frost top of torte and sprinkle with chopped peanuts.   *Makes 6 servings.*

PLUM MUFFIN CAKE

TOPPING:
⅓	cup flour
½	cup chopped walnuts
1	teaspoon cinnamon
½	cup sugar
2	tablespoons soft butter or margarine

CAKE:
¼	cup crisp cookie crumbs
6	tablespoons butter or margarine, softened
¾	cup sugar
1	egg
1	tablespoon grated lemon peel
1	teaspoon vanilla
2	cups flour
2	teaspoons baking powder
½	cup milk
3	cups sliced fresh California plums (about 1½ pounds)

TOPPING: In small bowl, combine topping ingredients, blending in butter with fork or finger tips. Set aside.

CAKE: Dust well-buttered 8-inch spring form pan with cookie crumbs. Set aside. In mixing bowl, cream butter and sugar. Beat in egg, lemon peel and vanilla. Sift together flour and baking powder. Add to creamed mixture, alternately with milk. Fold in sliced plums. Spread batter in prepared pan; cover evenly with topping. Bake in 375-degree oven 60 to 70 minutes, or until toothpick inserted in middle of cake comes out clean. Cool 10 minutes before removing outer ring of pan. Serve warm.
Makes 6 servings.

Notes: Coconut cookies, vanilla wafers or ginger snaps are especially good.

A 10-inch tube pan may be substituted for the spring form pan. Decrease baking time to 45–50 minutes.

SPICED YOGURT POUND CAKE

2½	cups all-purpose flour (unsifted)
1½	teaspoons apple pie spice
½	teaspoon baking soda
¼	teaspoon salt
1	cup butter or margarine, softened
2	cups sugar
4	eggs
1	cup plain yogurt
	Spiced Yogurt Frosting (recipe follows)

Preheat oven to 350 degrees. In a medium bowl, combine flour, apple pie spice, baking soda and salt; set aside.

In the large bowl of an electric mixer, beat butter and sugar until light and fluffy. Beat in eggs, one at a time, beating well after each addition. Stir in flour mixture alternately with yogurt. Stir just until blended.

Pour into greased and floured 10-inch (12-cup) bundt or tube pan. Bake until cake tester inserted in center comes out clean, about 1 hour. Cool in pan on wire rack for 10 minutes. Remove cake from pan; cool completely.

Spoon about half of the Spiced Yogurt Frosting (below) over the cake. Serve remainder over sliced cake. Sprinkle with chopped nuts, if desired.
Makes one 10-inch tube cake.

SPICED YOGURT FROSTING:

In a small bowl, combine 1 cup plain yogurt, ½ cup firmly-packed brown sugar and ½ teaspoon apple pie spice. Stir until all of the sugar is dissolved.

SPICY PLUM CAKELETS

1	package (18½ ounces) spice cake mix
2	cups sliced fresh plums
	Cinnamon-sugar
	Whipping cream, if desired

Grease and flour bottom of 13×9×2-inch baking pan. Prepare spice cake mix according to package directions. Carefully fold plum slices into batter. Pour batter into prepared pan and bake in 350-degree oven 30 to 35 minutes. Remove from oven and sprinkle warm cake with cinnamon-sugar mixture. Cool at least 10 minutes before cutting. Serve warm or cold with whipped cream, if desired.
Makes 12 slices.

STRAWBERRY DANISH CAKE

¼	cup butter or margarine, softened
½	cup firmly packed brown sugar
1	frozen pound cake, (11½ ounces) defrosted

½ cup sherry
2 cups each milk and light cream or 4
  cups milk
1 pint fresh strawberries, sliced and
  sweetened to taste
4 eggs
2 egg yolks
¼ cup granulated sugar
  Dash salt
1 can (7 ounces) refrigerated whipped
  light cream

In mixing bowl, cream together butter and brown sugar. Spread mixture in bottom of buttered 8-inch bundt pan.

Cut cake into 1-inch cubes. Arrange over butter mixture.

Drizzle sherry over cake.

In saucepan, heat milk and light cream. (Do not boil.)

Meanwhile, in mixing bowl, lightly beat eggs, egg yolks, granulated sugar and salt. Slowly beat in hot milk. Pour mixture over cake in bundt pan.

Bake in preheated 350-degree oven 55 to 60 minutes or until knife inserted in cake comes out clean.

Cool, then chill completely in refrigerator.

To serve, unmold on serving plate. Cut slices and serve on individual dessert plates with sliced strawberries, sweetened to taste, spooned over each serving. Top with whipped light cream.

Makes 12 servings.

SWEET POTATO-PRUNE CAKE

1 can (8 ounces) sweet potatoes in
  syrup, undrained
1 cup (6 ounces) pitted prunes
1 cup water
1⅓ cups packed brown sugar
1¼ cups granulated sugar
1 cup butter or margarine, melted
2 eggs
3¾ cups flour
2 teaspoons baking soda
1½ teaspoons baking powder
1½ teaspoons salt
1½ teaspoons *each* cinnamon, ginger and
  allspice
  Powdered sugar

In blender or food processor, puree sweet potatoes, prunes and water. Set aside. In mixing bowl, blend sugars, butter and eggs. Add pureed prune mixture; mix to blend. Sift together dry ingredients; gradually stir into batter, mixing to blend. Spread butter in greased 10½-by-15½-inch jelly roll pan. Bake in 375-degree oven 30 to 35 minutes until cake tests done. Cool. Dust with powdered sugar.

Makes 12 pieces of cake.

TOASTED WHEAT GERM BUNDT CAKE

1 package (1 pound 2½ ounces) yellow
  cake mix
1 package (3¾ ounces) instant lemon
  pudding and pie filling
¼ cup vegetable oil
4 eggs
1 cup water
¼ cup frozen orange juice concentrate
1¾ cups vacuum packed toasted wheat
  germ with sugar or honey
1½ tablespoons butter

Combine cake and pudding mixes, oil, eggs, water and undiluted orange juice. Blend, then beat at medium speed with electric beater 3 minutes or use rotary beater. Stir in one and one-fourth cups wheat germ. Grease a 10-inch bundt pan or tube pan generously with butter. Coat pan with remaining one-half cup wheat germ, saving whatever wheat germ does not adhere. Carefully spoon batter into prepared pan. Top with reserved toasted wheat germ pressing lightly into batter. Bake in 350-degree oven 55 to 60 minutes or until cake tests done. Cool in pan on rack 2 or 3 minutes. Then invert cake onto rack to finish cooling. Serve plain or frosted with powdered sugar glaze. *Makes one 10-inch cake.*

CHERRY CAKE

1 can (17 ounces) pitted dark sweet
  cherries
½ cup chopped walnuts
½ cup angel flake coconut
1 teaspoon grated lemon peel
2 cups flour
1 cup sugar
1 teaspoon salt
1 teaspoon soda
1 teaspoon cinnamon
¾ cup shortening
¾ cup buttermilk
3 eggs
1½ cups powdered sugar
4–6 teaspoons lemon juice

Drain and halve cherries, reserving syrup for another use. Combine cherries with walnuts, coconut and lemon peel; set aside. In a large mixer bowl, combine flour, sugar, salt, soda, cinnamon, shortening, buttermilk and eggs. Blend at low speed until moistened; beat at medium speed 3 minutes. Pour half of the batter into a well-greased, 10-inch fluted tube pan. Spoon cherry mixture over batter. Top with remaining batter.

Continued

Bake at 350 degrees 55 to 60 minutes, until top springs back when lightly touched in center. Cool 10 minutes; remove from pan. Cool. Make glaze by combining powdered sugar and lemon juice. Drizzle over cooled cake. *Makes 12 to 16 servings.*

WALNUT CAKE

5	egg yolks
6	tablespoons sugar
¼	cup fine dry bread crumbs
1	teaspoon Angostura aromatic bitters
1	cup finely ground walnuts (use a blender)
5	egg whites, stiffly beaten

SYRUP:

1½	cups sugar
½	cup water
	Juice of ½ lemon
2	tablespoons Angostura aromatic bitters

In a bowl, beat egg yolks and sugar until thick and lemon colored. Stir in bread crumbs, bitters and walnuts. Fold in egg whites.

Pour batter into a greased and floured 8-inch fluted pan or a 9-inch square baking pan. Bake in a preheated 350-degree oven for 1 hour for the fluted pan and 50 minutes for the square pan.

Unmold cake and cool on a rack. While cake is cooling, combine syrup ingredients in a saucepan and cook over high heat until syrup boils. Boil for 2 minutes.

Place cake on a serving platter. Spoon hot syrup over cake slowly, allowing cake to absorb the syrup. Serve garnished with rosettes of sweetened whipped cream for topping and walnut halves, if desired. *Makes one 8-inch fluted or 9-inch square cake.*

WHEAT GERM-CHOCOLATE CAKE

1¼	cups flour
1	cup vacuum packed wheat germ, regular or sugar and honey
¾	teaspoon baking soda
1	cup sugar
1	cup butter
3	tablespoons cocoa
1⅓	cups buttermilk
1	egg
2	teaspoons pure vanilla extract
	Chocolate Icing (recipe follows)
	Wheat germ and walnut garnish

Mix flour with wheat germ, soda and sugar in large bowl. Heat butter, cocoa and buttermilk, stirring often, until butter melts. Combine with wheat germ mixture. Mix in egg and vanilla. Turn into two greased 8-inch round layer cake pans. Bake in 400-degree oven 20 to 25 minutes until top springs back when lightly touched in center. Cool in pans 5 minutes.

Remove from pans and finish cooling on rack. Spread tops of layers with Chocolate Icing. Stack. Sprinkle top with wheat germ and garnish with walnuts. If desired, drizzle a powdered sugar and milk glaze over sides of cake. *Makes one 8-inch cake.*

CHOCOLATE ICING:
Combine 6 tablespoons butter, 2 tablespoons cocoa and 3 tablespoons milk. Heat to boiling. Mix in 2 cups powdered sugar and ¼ cup wheat germ.

WHITE MOUNTAIN PROMISE CAKE

2½	cups sifted cake flour
3	teaspoons baking powder
¼	teaspoon salt
½	cup soft margarine
1½	cups sugar
1	teaspoon vanilla
¼	teaspoon almond extract
1	cup skimmed milk
6	egg whites
½	teaspoon cream of tartar
	White Mountain Frosting (recipe follows)

Sift together flour, baking powder and salt. In large bowl mix margarine, sugar, vanilla and almond extract. Alternately blend in flour mixture and milk. Beat egg whites with cream of tartar until stiff but not dry. Gently but thoroughly fold into cake batter. Turn into 9-inch tube pan that has been brushed with margarine and dusted with flour. Bake in 350-degree oven 1 hour and 10 minutes, until cake is golden brown and pulls away from side of pan and a cake tester inserted in cake comes out clean. Cool 15 minutes. Remove from pan and finish cooling on rack. Frost with White Mountain Frosting.
Makes 16 servings.

WHITE MOUNTAIN FROSTING:

1	cup sugar
⅓	cup water
⅛	teaspoon cream of tartar
2	egg whites
½	teaspoon vanilla

In medium saucepan mix sugar, water and cream of tartar. Place over low heat, cover and cook 3 minutes, remove cover and boil until syrup reaches 240-degree on candy thermometer. Remove from heat. In medium bowl beat egg whites until stiff, then gradually pour syrup into egg whites, beating constantly. Beat until thick enough to form peaks; beat in vanilla.

COOKIES

APPLESAUCE NUGGETS

2	cups flour
½	teaspoon cinnamon
½	teaspoon nutmeg
½	teaspoon allspice
¼	teaspoon cloves
½	cup corn-oil margarine
1	cup brown sugar, firmly packed
1	cup applesauce
1	teaspoon baking soda
1	egg, well beaten
1	package (6 ounces) butterscotch pieces
1	cup broken walnuts

Measure flour and spices onto waxed paper.

Cream margarine and sugar until light and fluffy. Add baking soda to applesauce, then add applesauce and egg to creamed shortening and sugar.

Add dry ingredients, stirring to incorporate evenly. Add butterscotch pieces and walnuts.

Drop by teaspoonfuls about 2 to 3 inches apart on greased cookie sheet. Bake at 375 degrees 12 to 15 minutes. *Makes about 4 dozen cookies.*

APRICOT WALNUT BARS

1	can (30 ounces) apricot halves
¼	cup cornstarch
1¼	cups sugar
½	cup chopped walnuts
1	cup butter or margarine, softened
2	cups unsifted all-purpose flour
1⅔	cups old-fashioned oats, uncooked
½	teaspoon double-acting baking powder
½	teaspoon baking soda
½	teaspoon salt

Drain syrup from apricots, reserving ½ cup. Drain apricots well. Chop apricots. In saucepan, combine ½ cup syrup and cornstarch until smooth. Stir in chopped apricots and ½ cup sugar. Cook over medium heat until thick and clear, stirring frequently. Cool. Stir in walnuts.

Meanwhile, beat butter and remaining sugar until creamy. Add flour, oats, baking powder, baking soda and salt and mix until coarse crumbs. Pat ⅔ of flour mixture in bottom of 9-inch square baking pan. Spread on cooled apricot mixture. sprinkle remaining flour mixture on top. Gently put into apricot mixture.

Bake in 375-degree oven for 50 minutes or until toothpick inserted in center comes out clean. Cook on wire rack. Cut into bars.
Makes about 3 dozen bars.

BRANNY COOKIES

1	cup wheat bran cereal
½	cup milk
½	cup shortening
1	teaspoon vanilla
1	cup brown sugar
2	eggs
1	cup unsifted all-purpose flour
¼	cup whole wheat flour
½	teaspoon baking soda
½	teaspoon salt
½	teaspoon cinnamon
½	cup raisins or dried currants
½	cup nuts

In small bowl, mix wheat bran cereal and milk. Let stand 1 to 2 minutes or until almost all liquid is absorbed.

In large bowl, cream shortening, vanilla and brown sugar. Beat in eggs. Stir together flour, baking soda, salt and cinnamon. Blend into creamed mixture. Stir in wheat bran cereal, raisins and nuts. Drop by level tablespoons onto greased baking sheet. Bake in 375-degree oven 10 minutes or until golden brown. Remove from baking sheet and cool on rack. *Makes 4½ to 5 dozen cookies.*

CARROT-SPICE BARS

½	cup sunflower-oil margarine
¾	cup packed brown sugar
1	teaspoon vanilla
2	cups sifted all-purpose flour
1	teaspoon baking soda
1	teaspoon baking powder
½	teaspoon salt
½	teaspoon cinnamon
¼	teaspoon cloves
1	cup mashed cooked carrots

Continued

In a large bowl, blend margarine, brown sugar and vanilla. Mix flour, baking soda, baking powder, salt, cinnamon and cloves. Stir into margarine mixture. Blend in carrots.

Turn into a greased 15-by-10-by-1-inch baking pan. Bake in a 350-degree oven 20 minutes or until cake tester inserted in center comes out clean. Cool. Cut into 2-by-1-inch bars.   *Makes 75 bars.*

CHEWY BLOND BROWNIES

½	cup butter or margarine, softened
1¼	cups firmly packed brown sugar
1⅓	cups quick or old-fashioned oats, uncooked
1⅓	cups all-purpose flour
2	eggs
½	cup semi-sweet chocolate, butterscotch or peanut butter flavored pieces
½	cup chopped nuts
2	teaspoons vanilla
¾	teaspoon salt
¾	teaspoon soda

Beat together butter and sugar until well blended. Add remaining ingredients; mix well. Spread into greased 13-by-9-inch baking pan. Bake at 350-degrees, about 25 minutes or until golden brown. Cool; cut into bars. *Makes a 13-by-9-inch pan of bars.*

COCOA ALMOND PUMPKIN SQUARES

1	cup flour
½	cup quick-cooking oatmeal
½	cup soft butter or margarine
2	cups cooked and mashed fresh pumpkin or canned pumpkin
1	can (13 ounces) evaporated milk
3	eggs
1¼	cup brown sugar
2	tablespoons cocoa
½	teaspoon salt
1	teaspoon ground cinnamon
½	teaspoon each ground ginger and cloves
½	cup chopped natural (unblanched) almonds
2	tablespoons soft butter or margarine, additional
	Whipped cream (optional)
	Chocolate decors (optional)

Make the crust by combining the flour, quick-cooking oatmeal and ½ cup butter. Mix until crumbly. Pat into 9-by-12-inch baking pan. Bake at 350 degrees for 15 minutes.

Meanwhile, make the filling by combining the pumpkin, milk, eggs, ¾ cup brown sugar, cocoa, salt and spices in mixing bowl. Beat until well blended. Pour into crust. Continue baking at 350 degrees another 25 minutes.

For the topping, combine the almonds, ½ cup brown sugar and 2 tablespoons butter. Mix well and sprinkle over filling. Bake another 20 to 25 minutes at 350 degrees until filling is set but still soft. Cool in pan.

Cut into squares and dollop with whipped cream, if you wish.   *Makes about 16 servings.*

COLLEGE BAR COOKIES

1	cup firmly packed brown sugar
¾	cup butter or margarine, melted
¼	cup molasses or honey
1	teaspoon salt
4½	cups quick or old-fashioned oats, uncooked

Line a 15-by-10-inch jelly-roll pan with foil, extending edges of foil over sides of pan. Grease.

Combine all ingredients except oats in large bowl, mixing until well blended. Add oats. Mix well.

Press firmly into prepared pan. Bake at 450 degrees for 8 to 10 minutes or until golden brown.

Cool thoroughly. Loosen edges of cookies from sides of pan. Remove from pan. Remove foil. Cut into bars.   *Makes 15-by-10-inch pan of bars.*

Note: You may substitute ½ cup wheat germ or unprocessed bran for ½ cup oats.

DATE NUT BARS

½	cup butter or margarine
1½	cups graham cracker crumbs
1	can (14 ounces) sweetened condensed milk
1	cup chopped dates
1	cup chopped nuts
1	can (3½ ounces) flaked coconut

Preheat oven to 350 degrees (325 degrees for glass dish). In 13×9-inch baking pan, melt butter. Sprinkle crumbs over butter. Pour sweetened condensed milk evenly over crumbs. Top evenly with dates, nuts and coconut; press down gently. Bake 25 to 30 minutes or until lightly browned. Cool thoroughly before cutting. Loosely cover leftovers.

Makes 24 bars.

FLORENTINES

½	cup sugar
⅓	cup whipping cream
⅓	cup honey
1½	cups sliced natural (unblanched) almonds
⅓	cup finely chopped candied orange peel
6	tablespoons flour
4	ounces semi-sweet chocolate
1	teaspoon shortening

Combine sugar, cream and honey in saucepan. Bring to boil, stirring. Then gently boil to 238 degrees (soft-ball stage). Remove from heat.

Stir in almonds, orange peel and flour. Drop by level tablespoonfuls onto foil-covered cookie sheet. Flatten cookies slightly.

Bake at 325-degrees for 10 minutes or until golden around edges and done in center. Cool thoroughly on foil, then peel off and invert on wire rack.

Melt chocolate in top of double boiler. Stir in shortening. Spread mixture over flat bottoms of cookies. *Makes 2 dozen cookies.*

FUDGE SAUCEPAN BROWNIES

3	squares (1 ounce) unsweetened chocolate
½	cup corn oil
¾	cup light corn syrup
2	eggs
1¼	cups sugar
1	cup unsifted flour
1	cup quick oats
⅔	cup chopped nuts
2	teaspoons vanilla
1¼	teaspoons salt
	Confectioners' sugar (optional)

Grease 13 × 9 × 2-inch baking pan. Melt chocolate in 2-quart saucepan over low heat. Cool to lukewarm. Stir in corn oil, corn syrup, eggs, sugar, flour, oats, nuts, vanilla and salt until well mixed. Turn into prepared pan. Bake in 350-degree oven about 35 minutes or until a slight imprint remains when top is lightly touched. Sprinkle with confectioners' sugar while still warm. Cut into 48 (1½-inch) squares.

Note: If desired, ⅔ cup margarine may be substituted for corn oil. Melt margarine with chocolate and reduce salt to 1 teaspoon.

GINGER CARROT BARS

½	cup butter or margarine
1½	cups ginger snap cookie crumbs (about 25 ginger snaps)
1	cup raisins
1	can (14 ounces) sweetened condensed milk
1½	cups finely shredded carrots
1	can (3½ ounces) flaked coconut

Preheat oven to 350 degrees (325 degrees for glass dish). In 13 × 9-inch baking pan, melt butter. Sprinkle crumbs over butter; then raisins. Pour sweetened condensed milk evenly over crumbs and raisins. Top evenly with carrots, then coconut; press down gently. Bake 25 to 30 minutes or until lightly browned. Cool thoroughly before cutting. Loosely cover leftovers. *Makes 24 bars.*

HOMEMADE FIG BARS

1	cup shortening
½	cup granulated sugar
½	cup brown sugar
2	egg yolks
3	tablespoons milk or buttermilk
1	tablespoon vanilla
2	cups sifted all-purpose flour
1	cup whole wheat flour
2	teaspoons cream of tartar
1	teaspoon soda
½	teaspoon salt
1	recipe fig filling (see below)

Beat shortening and sugars until light and fluffy. Add egg yolks, milk and vanilla, beating well.

Sift together dry ingredients and add to egg mixture. Chill dough 1 hour or longer.

Divide dough in half, keep second half refrigerated until ready to roll. Roll dough out on heavily floured board to about ⅛ inch thickness. Using a ruler as a guide, cut into strips about 4 inches long and 1½ inches wide. Place about 1 teaspoon cooled filling in center of each strip and lap sides over or roll up. Place on ungreased cookie sheet, about 1 inch apart, seam side down. Bake in moderate 350 degree oven for 15 minutes or until bottom of fig bars start to brown. *Makes about 3 dozen fig bars.*

ALTERNATE: Cookies can be cut in rounds, using a glass or 2-inch cookie cutter. Fill center of cookie with about 1 teaspoon fig filling, top with a smaller cookie, about 1½ inch round. Use a fork to seal edges.

FIG FILLING

36	California Dried Mission (or Calimyrna) figs, coarsely chopped

Continued

3   tablespoons lemon juice
¼   cup sugar
1   teaspoon grated fresh lemon peel
¼   teaspoon salt
½   cup water

Combine ingredients. Cook, stir until thick—about 5 minutes over medium heat. Cool to room temperature and use as a filling for Fig Bars. (A kitchen scissors cuts figs easily).

LIFTLINE RAISIN BARS

1   package (6 ounces) semisweet chocolate morsels (or 1 cup)
2   cups raisins
½   cup sunflower seeds
24   square graham crackers

In heavy skillet* over low heat, melt chips. Stir in raisins and sunflower seeds until evenly coated. Spoon mixture onto 12 of the graham crackers, dividing equally. Press remaining crackers gently on top of filling. Wrap sandwiches in waxed paper. Chill.   *Makes 1 dozen.*

(*Or, in top of double boiler, over simmering water.)

MOLASSES CINNAMON DROPS

2   cups sifted all-purpose flour
1   teaspoon cinnamon
¼   teaspoon ginger
¼   teaspoon cloves
¼   teaspoon baking soda
¼   teaspoon salt
½   cup butter or margarine
½   cup sugar
1   egg
¼   cup light molasses

Sift together dry ingredients; set aside.
In a mixing bowl, cream butter and sugar until light and fluffy. Beat in egg and molasses. Gradually blend in dry ingredients.
Drop by heaping measuring teaspoonsful onto ungreased cookie sheets. Bake in a preheated 375-degree oven for 10 to 12 minutes or until cookies are lightly browned around the edges. Remove to rack; cool. Store in cookie jar.

Makes about 3 dozen cookies.

NUTTY DROP COOKIES

1   cup sifted all-purpose flour
¾   teaspoon baking powder
¼   teaspoon baking soda
¼   teaspoon salt
½   teaspoon ground cinnamon
⅛   teaspoon ground allspice
⅛   teaspoon ground nutmeg
3   tablespoons butter or margarine
¼   cup sugar
1   egg
¼   cup light molasses
1   tablespoon sour milk
⅓   cup chopped walnuts or pecans
Vanilla Glaze (recipe follows)
Nuts for garnish (optional)

Onto waxed paper, sift together flour, baking powder, baking soda, salt, cinnamon, allspice and nutmeg. In medium mixing bowl, cream butter and sugar. Add egg and beat well. Add molasses and stir until blended. Add flour mixture alternately with milk, mixing just until blended. Stir in chopped walnuts. Drop batter by teaspoon onto greased cookie sheet. Bake in a preheated 400-degree oven for 8 to 9 minutes. Remove cookies and cool on wire rack. Spread about a tespoon of glaze in center of each cookie. Garnish with a piece of nut, if desired.   *Makes 2 dozen cookies.*

VANILLA GLAZE:

Heat 1 tablespoon milk and 1 tablespoon butter or margarine until butter melts. Remove from heat, add ½ teaspoon vanilla and 1 cup sifted confectioners' sugar; mix well.

OATMEAL COOKIES

¾   cup shortening
1   cup packed light brown sugar
½   cup granulated sugar
1   egg
½   teaspoon vanilla extract
1   cup red maraschino cherries, chopped
1   cup unsifted all-purpose flour
1   teaspoon salt
1   teaspoon cinnamon
½   teaspoon baking soda
½   teaspoon cloves
3   cups old-fashioned oats

In large bowl, beat shortening, sugars, egg and vanilla until light and fluffy. Stir in cherries. Combine flour, salt, cinnamon, baking soda and cloves. Stir into cherry mixture. Add oats and stir to mix well. Drop dough by rounded teaspoonfuls, 2 inches apart, on greased cookie sheets. Bake in 350-degree oven for 12 to 15 minutes or until lightly browned. Remove from cookie sheets. Cool on racks. *Makes 5½ dozen.*

OATMEAL DROPS

2	cups sifted all-purpose flour
1	cup sugar
¼	cup nonfat dry milk powder
1	teaspoon baking powder
1	teaspoon salt
¾	teaspoon cinnamon
½	teaspoon nutmeg
½	teaspoon baking soda
3	cups quick-cooking oats
1	cup dark raisins
1	cup corn oil
¼	cup light molasses
2	eggs
⅓	cup milk

In mixing bowl, sift together flour, sugar, dry milk powder, baking powder, salt, cinnamon, nutmeg and soda. Stir in oats and raisins. Add oil, molasses, eggs and milk, stirring until well blended.

Drop by rounded teaspoonsful, about 1½ inches apart, onto ungreased cookie sheets. Bake in 400-degree oven about 10 minutes or until lightly browned. Remove cookies to wire rack to cool. Store in cookie jar. *Makes about 6 dozen.*

OATMEAL-NUT COOKIES

3	cups quick oats
1	cup unsifted flour
1	teaspoon ground cinnamon
½	teaspoon baking soda
1	cup firmly packed brown sugar
¾	cup real mayonnaise
1	egg
2	teaspoons vanilla
1	cup chopped walnuts

In medium bowl, stir together oats, flour, cinnamon and baking soda. In large bowl with mixer at high speed, beat sugar, mayonnaise, egg and vanilla 2 minutes. Reduce speed to low; beat in oat mixture until well-blended. Stir in walnuts.

Drop by level tablespoonfuls 3 inches apart on greased cookie sheets. Bake in 350-degree oven 10 to 12 minutes or until lightly browned. Immediately transfer to wire rack; cool.

Makes about 4 dozen cookies.

RAISIN-BRAN COOKIES: Follow recipe for Oatmeal-Nut Cookies. Omit oats and walnuts. Use 3 cups bran cereal and 1 cup raisins.

PEANUT BLONDIES

1	cup butter or margarine
1	cup firmly packed brown sugar
½	cup granulated sugar
2	eggs
¼	cup orange juice
1¼	cups all-purpose flour
1	teaspoon baking soda
½	teaspoon salt
1½	cups quick-cooking oats
2	cups (12-ounce package) peanut butter chips, divided

Cream together butter and sugars; blend in eggs and juice. Mix together flour, soda and salt; add with oats and 1 cup chips to creamed mixture. Spread over bottom of greased 9-by-13-inch baking pan. Sprinkle remaining 1 cup chips on top.

Bake in 350-degree oven 30 minutes or until toothpick inserted in center comes out clean. Cook on rack. Cut into bars. *Makes approximately 36 bars.*

Note: This recipe may be baked in two 9-inch square pans, about 25 minutes.

PEANUT BUTTER CHIP CEREAL BARS

2	cups (12-ounce package) peanut butter chips, divided
⅓	cup honey
3	tablespoons butter or margarine
4	cups crispy rice cereal or ring-shaped toasted oat cereal
⅓	cup dry roasted sunflower seeds
⅓	cup chopped dried apricots
⅓	cup raisins

Grease a 13-by-9-inch baking pan. In a small saucepan, combine 1 cup peanut butter chips, honey and butter; stir over low heat until mixture is smooth. Remove pan from heat; set aside.

In a large bowl, combine remaining peanut butter chips, cereal, seeds and fruits. Add peanut butter mixture; mix well. Turn into prepared pan; press evenly in pan. Cool until firm. Cut into bars.

Makes 32 bars.

PEANUT BUTTER CUTOUTS

2½   cups unsifted all-purpose flour
¾   teaspoon baking soda
½   cup (1 stick) butter or margarine
1   cup peanut butter chips
⅔   cup firmly packed light brown sugar
1   egg
1   teaspoon vanilla extract

Combine flour and baking soda; set aside. Place butter and peanut butter chips in top of a double boiler and heat over hot water until melted. Transfer to mixer bowl and beat until smooth. Add sugar, egg and vanilla. Beat until very smooth. Blend in flour mixture. Chill until firm.

Roll dough out between pieces of waxed paper to ¼-inch thickness. Cut out with simple cookie cutters. Transfer with spatula to ungreased baking sheets.

Bake at 375 degrees for 6 to 8 minutes until all cookies are well browned. Cool on wire rack. Decorate as desired.   *Makes about 5 dozen cookies.*

PEANUT CHEWY BARS

1   cup butter or margarine
¾   cup firmly packed brown sugar
2   cups unsifted whole wheat flour
1   teaspoon baking powder
⅓   cup wheat germ

TOPPING:
3   eggs, well beaten
1¼   cups dark corn syrup
¼   cup flour
1½   teaspoons vanilla
1½   cups chopped oil-roasted salted
     peanuts

In bowl combine butter, brown sugar, flour, baking powder and wheat germ. Mix with the fingers until well blended and crumbly. Press crumbs evenly into a greased 15 × 10 × 1-inch baking pan. In a bowl mix eggs, corn syrup and flour until smooth and well blended. Stir in vanilla and peanuts. Pour mixture over crust in pan and spread evenly. Bake in a preheated 350-degree oven for 25 to 30 minutes or until brown and firm to the touch. Cool in pan and then cut into desired shape bars or squares.
Makes 75 bars.

PEANUT SUPERCOOKIE

1   cup butter or margarine
1   cup peanut butter
1   cup firmly packed dark brown sugar
3   eggs

1   teaspoon vanilla
1   cup wheat germ
1   package (16 ounces) any flavor
     granola
2   cups unsifted all-purpose flour
1½   teaspoons baking soda
½   teaspoon salt

In a bowl, cream butter until fluffy. Stir in peanut butter and brown sugar. Beat in eggs one at a time, beating well after each addition. Stir in vanilla, wheat germ and granola. Stir in flour, baking soda and salt. Stir until mixture forms a ball of dough.

Roll out half of the dough at a time. Roll out on a heavily floured surface to ½ inch thickness. Cut with a cookie cutter or a can into 4-inch rounds. Place on ungreased cookie sheets. Bake in a preheated 350-degree oven for 12 to 15 minutes or until golden brown.

Cool cookies on a rack and serve for breakfast with orange juice and a glass of milk for a total breakfast.   *Makes 2 dozen 4-inch cookies.*

PROMISING (OATMEAL) KISSES

⅓   cup margarine
⅓   cup plain yogurt
½   cup packed brown sugar
1   teaspoon vanilla
1½   cups sifted all-purpose flour
1   cup uncooked oats, regular or quick
¼   cup raisins
¼   teaspoon baking soda
¼   teaspoon salt

In large bowl blend margarine, yogurt, brown sugar and vanilla. In medium bowl mix rest of ingredients. Blend into margarine mixture. Form into 1-inch balls and place 1 inch apart on ungreased baking sheet. Bake in 325-degree oven 15 to 20 minutes. Remove cookies from baking sheet and cool completely.   *Makes 4½ dozen cookies.*

RAISIN WONDER COOKIES

⅓   cup vegetable oil
⅓   cup brown sugar, firmly packed
⅓   cup molasses
1   egg, lightly beaten
1   cup flour
½   teaspoon baking powder
½   teaspoon baking soda
¼   cup nonfat dry milk
1   teaspoon salt
½   teaspoon ground cinnamon
1   cup grated carrots
¾   cup raisins
½   cup quick-cooking rolled oats

Beat oil, sugar, molasses and egg together. Sift together flour, baking powder, baking soda, dry milk, salt and cinnamon. Add to oil mixture. Stir in carrots, raisins and oats and blend thoroughly.

Drop by heaping teaspoonsful onto lightly greased cookie sheet. Bake at 400 degrees about 10 minutes. Cool on rack. *Makes about 2½ dozen.*

ROLLED CHOCOLATE COOKIES

2	cups unsifted all-purpose flour
⅓	cup unsweetened cocoa
¼	teaspoon salt
½	cup (stick) butter or margarine, softened
¾	cup granulated sugar
1	egg
1	teaspoon vanilla extract
½	tablespoon grated orange peel

Combine flour, unsweetened cocoa and salt; set aside. In large bowl, cream butter with sugar until light and fluffy. Beat in egg, vanilla and orange peel. Gradually blend in flour mixture. Chill slightly for ease in handling.

Roll out between pieces of waxed paper to ¼-inch thickness. Cut with simple cookie cutters. Transfer with spatula on ungreased baking sheets. Bake at 325 degrees for 12 minutes or until firm to the touch. Decorate as desired.

Makes about 4 dozen cookies.

SLIMMA-BANANA BARS

½	cup margarine
¾	cup sugar
1	teaspoon vanilla
1½	cups sifted all-purpose flour
1	teaspoon baking powder
1	teaspoon baking soda
½	teaspoon salt
1	cup mashed ripe bananas (approximately 3 medium bananas)

In large bowl blend margarine, sugar and vanilla. In medium bowl mix flour, baking powder, baking soda and salt. Add alternately with mashed banana to margarine mixture, mixing well after each addition. Turn into lightly greased 15 × 10 × 1-inch baking pan. Bake in 350-degree oven 20 to 25 minutes or until cake tester inserted in center comes out clean. Cool completely. Cut into 2 × 1-inch bars. If desired, sprinkle lightly with confectioners' sugar. *Makes 75 bars.*

SPANISH RICE FINGERS

1	cup regular (not converted) rice
3	cups milk
¼	teaspoon saffron
	Dash salt
2	teaspoons Angostura aromatic bitters
½	cup sugar
1	egg, well beaten
1	teaspoon cinnamon
	Fat or oil 2 inches deep, heated to 360 degrees

In a saucepan, combine rice, milk, saffron, salt and bitters. Simmer stirring occasionally until rice is tender and liquid is absorbed. Stir in sugar, egg and cinnamon.

Spread mixture into an 8-by-12-inch oblong on a sheet of foil. Chill for several hours or until firm. Cut into 2-by-1-inch strips. Carefully drop strips into preheated fat and fry until brown on one side, about 5 to 6 minutes. Turn and brown on the other side about 5 to 6 minutes. Drain on absorbent paper and serve warm. *Makes about 48 pieces.*

TAKE-ALONG FRUIT BARS

¾	cup chopped pitted prunes
½	cup chopped dried apricots
⅔	cup coconut rum liqueur, divided
½	cup butter or margarine
¾	cup light brown sugar, firmly packed
2	eggs
1	teaspoon vanilla
1	cup unsifted all-purpose flour
1	teaspoon baking powder
½	teaspoon baking soda
¼	teaspoon salt
1	cup quick cooking oats
¼	cup chopped nuts
	CocoRibe Frosting (recipe follows)

Soak prunes and apricots in ⅓ cup liqueur for ½ hour. In large bowl of electric mixer cream butter and brown sugar; add eggs one at a time, beating well after each addition. Add vanilla.

Sift together flour, baking powder and baking soda; stir into creamed mixture. Add oats, nuts and fruits with liqueur. Stir just until mixed. Spread in a greased 13-by-9-by-2-inch baking pan. Bake in a 375-degree oven 25 minutes.

Remove from oven; let stand 10 minutes. Pierce cake with cake tester or three-prong fork; pour remaining ⅓ cup liqueur over cake. Cool; frost with CocoRibe Frosting. *Makes 24 bars (1-by-3 inches).*

Continued

COCORIBE FROSTING:

6	tablespoons butter or margarine
3	cups confectioners' sugar
¼	cup coconut rum liqueur

In small bowl of electric mixer cream butter; gradually add sugar and liqueur. Beat until mixture is smooth and creamy. Spread on cooled fruit bars.

WALNUT REFRIGERATOR COOKIES

1	cup walnuts
1	cup shortening (part butter)
1	cup brown sugar, packed
1	egg
1	teaspoon instant coffee
1	teaspoon vanilla
2	cups sifted all-purpose flour
½	teaspoon salt
½	teaspoon baking powder
	Browned Butter Icing (recipe follows)

Finely chop walnuts. Cream shortening, sugar and egg together until fluffy. Blend in instant coffee dissolved in vanilla. Resift flour with salt and baking powder. Stir into creamed mixture. Add walnuts and mix well. Shape dough into two rectangles, each about 5×3×1.5 inches, wrap in waxed paper and chill thoroughly (3 to 4 hours in freezer or 6 hours or overnight in refrigerator). Cut crosswise in one-eighth-inch slice, with a thin-bladed, sharp knife. Place on lightly greased baking sheets about one inch apart. Bake above oven center at 375 degrees for 8 to 10 minutes, just until edges are lightly browned.

Let stand a minute, then remove to wire racks to cool thoroughly. Store in airtight container.

To make filled cookies, spread half the cookies with Browned Butter Icing, using a scant tablespoonful for each. Top each with second cookie.
Makes 52 single cookies or 26 sandwiches.

BROWNED BUTTER ICING: Lightly brown one-fourth cup butter in a small saucepan over moderate heat. Remove from heat and blend in two and one-half cups sifted powdered sugar, 2 tablespoons milk and 1 teaspoon vanilla, beating until smooth. *Makes about 1 cup.*

VARIATION: Omit instant coffee from cookie batter. Add 2 teaspoons grated orange peel and one-fourth teaspoon cinnamon.

WALNUT THINS

⅓	cup margarine
⅓	cup vanilla yogurt
⅓	cup packed brown sugar
½	teaspoon almond extract
½	teaspoon vanilla
1½	cups whole-wheat flour
1	teaspoon baking powder
1	egg white, slightly beaten
	Walnut pieces

In large bowl blend together margarine, yogurt, brown sugar, almond extract and vanilla. In small bowl mix flour and baking powder. Blend into margarine mixture. Shape dough into ball, wrap in waxed paper and chill 2 hours or more. Roll out less than one-quarter-inch thick on lightly floured board. Cut with 2-inch cookie cutters and place on ungreased baking sheet. Brush lightly with egg white and decorate with walnut pieces if desired, or leave plain. Bake in 325-degree oven 12 to 15 minutes. *Makes 4½ dozen 2-inch cookies.*

WHOLE-WHEAT ALMOND COOKIES

¾	cup margarine or butter
1	cup brown sugar, packed
1	egg
1½	teaspoons vanilla
½	cup wheat germ
1	cup whole-wheat flour
¾	cup all-purpose flour
¾	teaspoon salt
1½	teaspoons baking powder
½	cup buttermilk
1	cup chopped prunes or dates
½	cup chopped almonds, toasted
	Sugar

Cream margarine or butter with sugar. Beat in egg and vanilla.

Mix wheat germ, flours, salt and baking powder. Blend into creamed mixture alternately with buttermilk. Stir in prunes and almonds.

Drop by level tablespoonfuls onto well-greased cookie sheets. Sprinkle cookies with sugar, if you wish. Bake at 350 degrees for 10 minutes. Cool on wire racks. *Makes 2½ dozen cookies.*

WHOLE-WHEAT COOKIES

1	cup unsifted whole-wheat flour
1½	teaspoons baking powder
½	teaspoon ground cinnamon

¾   cup corn oil
½   cup firmly packed brown sugar
2   eggs
1   teaspoon vanilla
2   cups corn flakes
½   cup coarsely chopped nuts

In a small bowl, stir together flour, baking powder and cinnamon. In a large bowl with mixer at medium speed, beat corn oil, sugar, eggs and vanilla until sugar is dissolved and batter is thick and smooth. Reduce speed to low. Add flour mixture; beat until blended. Stir in corn flakes and nuts. Drop by level tablespoonfuls 2 inches apart onto greased cookie sheets. Flatten slightly. Bake in 350-degree oven 10 to 12 minutes or until edges are browned.   *Makes about 3½ dozen.*

PIES & TARTS

PASTRY FOR 9-INCH, 2-CRUST PIE

2   cups flour
1   teaspoon salt
⅔   cup shortening
4   tablespoons ice water

Mix flour and salt. Add half the shortening and cut into the flour, using a pastry blender or two knives. When mixture looks like fine meal, add remaining shortening and cut in until particles are the size of giant peas. Add a tablespoon of water at a time, sprinkling it over the flour-shortening mixture and mixing lightly with a fork until all particles are moistened. The mixture should form a ball around the fork, cleaning the bowl. The pastry may be rolled out immediately or wrapped in moisture proof paper and refrigerated.

APPLE PIE

6–7   cups sliced, tart apples
¾   cup sugar
1–2   tablespoons flour (if apples are juicy)
¼   teaspoon salt
½   teaspoon cinnamon
2   (9-inch) pie crusts (homemade or store-bought)
2   tablespoons butter

Peel apples. Slice into one-fourth-inch slices. Measure sugar, flour, salt and cinnamon into a bowl and mix well. Toss the dry ingredients into the apples and transfer apples into pastry-lined pan. Dot with butter and cover with top crust. Seal. After the top crust has been sealed to the bottom crust the edge may be fluted or pressed with tines of a fork. Make several slits in top crust with a sharp knife to allow steam to escape. Bake at 400 degrees for 50 to 60 minutes or until juice bubbles through the slits on top of the pie.

For a shiny, dark brown crust, brush the top with a mixture of 1 egg yolk and 1 tablespoon cream. If you like a frosty appearance on the finished pie, brush the top of the pie with milk and sprinkle lightly with granulated sugar.   *Makes a 9-inch pie.*

BLUEBERRY OVEN COBBLER WITH FOAMY SAUCE

1   quart fresh or frozen blueberries, rinsed and drained
1   cup firmly packed brown sugar
1   cup flour
1   cup water
½   cup chopped walnuts
1   teaspoon each cinnamon and nutmeg
1   cup butter or margarine
1   package (10-count) refrigerator biscuits

FOAMY SAUCE:
½   cup butter or margarine
1   cup confectioners' sugar
1   egg white, unbeaten
2   tablespoons orange juice
½   cup boiling white wine or orange juice

In a 9-inch square baking pan place blueberries, sugar, flour and water. Stir to blend. Sprinkle with walnuts, spices and dot top with bits of butter. Cover and bake in a 425-degree oven for 15 minutes. Remove from oven and remove cover. Place biscuits on top of mixture. Replace in oven and bake uncovered another 15 minutes or until biscuits are puffed and brown.

While biscuits are baking, make sauce. Mix butter and sugar in a saucepan. Stir in egg white and orange juice. Stir in boiling wine. Place over low heat and stir rapidly until mixture foams. Stir for 2 minutes over low heat until sauce is thickened. Serve hot in bowl, floating a few blueberries on top. Spoon hot sauce over each serving of Blueberry Cobbler.   *Makes 8 servings.*

BRETONNE BLUEBERRY PIE

1   quart fresh blueberries, rinsed and drained
¾   cup sugar
½   cup water

Continued

2 tablespoons cornstarch dissolved in 2 tablespoons water
1 tablespoon butter or margarine
1 tablespoon Courvoisier (optional)
¼ cup slivered, toasted almonds
1 baked 9-inch pie shell
Vanilla ice cream

In saucepan, combine 1 cup blueberries, sugar and water. Bring slowly to boil. Cook 10 minutes or until berries are soft. Cool 5 minutes.

Puree in blender or food processor or rub mixture through sieve. Return to saucepan.

Add cornstarch. Cook lightly over moderate heat until mixture is thick.

Stir in butter, then Courvoisier, if desired. Cool slightly.

Add slivered almonds. Combine with remaining blueberries, reserving ½ cup berries for garnish. Mix gently but thoroughly.

Spoon into pie shell. Refrigerate several hours.

Just before serving, garnish with small scoops of ice cream (use melon baller or teaspoon) and re-served blueberries. *Makes a 9-inch pie.*

BUTTERSCOTCH PEACH PIE

Pastry for 9-inch, 2 crust pie
3 pounds fresh peaches, peeled and sliced
¼ cup firmly packed brown sugar
2 tablespoons flour
2 teaspoons lemon juice
6 tablespoons melted butter
½ teaspoon nutmeg
¼ teaspoon almond extract

On lightly floured board roll out 2 circles of pastry. Fit one in bottom of a 9-inch pie plate. Arrange peaches (there should be about 6 cups) in pie shell. In small bowl, combine remaining ingredients. Sprinkle over peaches. Top with remaining crust, crimp edges and slash top for steam to escape. Bake in 450-degree oven 15 minutes; reduce heat to 350 degrees and bake 35 to 40 minutes more, or until golden. Serve warm or cold. *Makes 6 to 8 servings.*

CRANBERRY-RAISIN PIE

1 package (11 ounces) pie crust mix
2 cups frozen-fresh cranberries or 1 can (1 pound) whole berry cranberry sauce (and omit the ½ cup honey)
2 cups raisins
½ cup honey

2 tablespoons minute tapioca
1 can (1 pound, 4 ounces) crushed pineapple, undrained

Prepare pie crust mix according to package directions. Roll out two-thirds of the crust onto a floured surface. Form into a round large enough to line the bottom and sides of an ungreased 9-inch pie pan. Allow the dough to overhang the pie pan for 1-inch. In a bowl, mix remaining ingredients until well blended. Pour mixture into lined pie pan. Roll out remaining crust on a floured surface and cut into one-half-inch strips. Arrange strips lattice-style on top of pie. Fold crust over and around edge. With fingers crimp into a fluted pattern. Bake in a pre-heated 400-degree oven for 40 to 45 minutes or until richly browned. Cool pie in pan, set on rack. Pie should be cold when cut into wedges. Serve plain or if desired top with vanilla ice cream or sweetened whipped cream. *Makes one 9-inch lattice pie.*

CRUNCHY YAM-APPLE PIE

2 large tart apples
1 tablespoon fresh lemon juice
3 medium yams (about 1 pound)
1 cup sugar
1 teaspoon grated lemon rind
1 egg
2 tablespoons light cream
1 unbaked 9-inch pastry shell

Pare apples. Grate on a coarse grater into a bowl. (Makes about 2 cups.) Stir lemon juice into apples.

Pare yams. Grate on a coarse grater into bowl with apples. (Makes about 3 cups.)

Mix in sugar and lemon rind. Beat together egg and cream. Stir into apple-yam mixture. Turn into pastry shell. Bake in a 350-degree oven for 1 hour. Cool. *Makes a 9-inch pie.*

DEEP-DISH PEACH PIE

1 9-inch pan frozen peach pie filling
Pastry for single 9-inch pie crust
Egg glaze (1 egg yolk mixed with 1 teaspoon water)
Heavy cream (optional)

Bake frozen peach pie filling in 425-degree oven for 30 minutes. Roll out pastry to 9-inch circle. Cut into 4 to 8 wedges, as desired. When pie filling has baked 30 minutes, remove from oven. Arrange wedges on pie. Brush with egg glaze. Return to oven and bake 35 to 40 minutes more, or until pastry is golden. Serve warm or cold with heavy cream, if desired. *Makes 6 to 8 servings.*

FLORIDA FRIED PIES

APPLE-ORANGE FILLING:
1 can (1 pound 4 ounces) pie sliced apples, drained
1 orange, coarsely chopped (rind included)
¾ cup sugar, divided
¼ cup butter or margarine

In medium saucepan, combine apples, chopped orange and ½ cup sugar. Bring to boiling; reduce heat, simmer 10 to 12 minutes, stirring occasionally, until orange is tender. Remove from heat; drain. Add remaining ¼ cup sugar and butter. Stir until butter is melted. Cool. Use to fill Fried Pies.

PIE DOUGH:
4 cups sifted all-purpose flour
¼ cup sugar
1 teaspoon salt
1 teaspoon baking powder
2 teaspoons grated orange rind
¾ cup shortening
¾–1 cup orange juice
Vegetable oil

Sift together flour, sugar, salt and baking powder; stir in orange rind. Cut in shortening with a pastry blender until mixture resembles coarse corn meal. Stir in enough orange juice to form a soft dough.

Divide dough into quarters. Roll out each quarter on lightly floured board to a 10-inch rectangle, ⅛-inch thick. Cut each rectangle into four 5-inch circles. Place one heaping tablespoonful Apple-Orange Filling in center of circle. Moisten edges of dough with orange juice. Fold dough over to form a semicircle. Press edges together with fork; turn pie over, press again with fork. Pie must be tightly sealed.

Pour oil into skillet to depth of 2 inches. Heat to 375 degrees on deep fat thermometer. If thermometer is not available, drop a small piece of dough into hot oil. Oil is hot enough when dough pops up. Fry pies until golden brown on one side, about 3 minutes. Turn and fry 2 minutes longer or until golden. Drain on paper towels. Sprinkle with confectioners' sugar, if desired. *Makes 16 fried pies.*

FRENCH APPLE TART

1 unbaked (9-inch) pastry shell
2 tablespoons cornstarch
1 tablespoon firmly packed light brown sugar
1½ teaspoons ground cinnamon
¼ teaspoon ground nutmeg
2 cups applesauce
1 tablespoon corn oil margarine
1 teaspoon vanilla
2 medium tart apples, peeled, thinly sliced (2 cups)
1 tablespoon lemon juice
1 tablespoon sugar

Partially bake pastry shell in 450-degree oven 8 minutes; remove. Reduce oven to 375 degrees.

In 2-quart saucepan stir together cornstarch, brown sugar, 1 teaspoon cinnamon and ⅛ teaspoon nutmeg. Gradually stir in applesauce until smooth. Add margarine.

Stirring constantly, bring to boil over medium heat and boil 1 minute. Remove from heat. Stir in vanilla. Pour applesauce mixture into tart shell.

Arrange apple slices on top to completely cover applesauce. Sprinkle with lemon juice, sugar, remaining ½ teaspoon cinnamon and ⅛ teaspoon nutmeg. Bake 35 minutes or until apples are tender. Serve warm. *Makes 8 servings.*

FRESH PEACH PICNIC PIES

1 package (11 ounces) pie crust mix or pastry for 2-crust pie
4 fresh peaches, peeled and quartered
½ cup sugar
2 tablespoons cornstarch
Dash salt
Dash nutmeg
1 tablespoon lemon juice
4 aluminum foil tart pans (5 inches in diameter)

Prepare pastry, as package directs. Divide into 4 parts. On lightly floured board, roll each part into a 7-inch circle. Ease pastry circles into tart pans. Place 4 peach quarters in each pastry-lined pan. In small bowl, combine sugar, cornstarch, salt and nutmeg. Sprinkle mixture and lemon juice onto peaches, dividing equally. Gather edges of pastry up around peaches, pinching slightly. Brush pastry with milk or beaten egg and sprinkle with sugar, if desired. Bake in 450-degree oven 15 minutes. Then reduce heat to 350 degrees and continue baking 30 minutes more. Serve warm or cold. *Makes 4 servings.*

FRESH PLUM CROQUANT

FILLING:
2 pounds fresh plums, halved and pitted (about 12 plums)
⅔ cup sugar
3 tablespoons lemon juice
3 tablespoons butter

CRUST:
½ cup flour
⅓ cup sugar
Dash salt
¼ cup butter, softened
½ cup unblanched sliced almonds (about 2¼ ounces)
1 teaspoon vanilla

For filling, gently toss plums with sugar and lemon juice in 1½-quart baking dish. Dot with butter and bake in 400-degree oven for 20 minutes.

Meanwhile, for crust, mix flour, sugar and salt in medium bowl. Cut in butter with pastry blender until mixture resembles coarse meal. Add nuts and vanilla.

Remove plums from oven. Baste with juices. Mound crumb mixture in center of plums. Return to oven and bake 15 to 20 minutes more, or until crumbs are golden. Cool slightly before serving.

Makes 6 to 8 servings.

Note: Amount of sugar may vary according to plum variety used and sweetness desired.

FROZEN BLUEBERRY PIE FILLINGS

6 pints fresh blueberries, rinsed and drained
6 cups sugar
2 cups unsifted all-purpose flour
½ teaspoon salt
¾ cup lemon juice

In large bowl mix all ingredients until well blended. Line six 8-inch pie plates with large pieces of foil. Fill pie plates with blueberry mixture. Turn foil over filling and seal.

Freeze until hard. When hard, remove filling from pie plates and stack in freezer with aluminum foil or waxed paper between layers until needed.

When ready to use, line a 9-inch pie plate with pie crust. Unwrap block of filling and place frozen block into lined pie plate. Cover with crust and seal edges as usual.

Bake as for blueberry pie, allowing 10 extra minutes in baking time.

Makes enough filling for six 9-inch pies.

FRUIT PLATTER PIE

1 cup sugar
¼ cup corn starch
1 cup water
½ teaspoon grated orange rind
¼ teaspoon grated lemon rind
1 cup orange juice
3 tablespoons lemon juice
Assorted fresh fruit, such as apple, banana, peach or pear slices, strawberry halves, seedless green grapes or blueberries
1 Platter Pie Pastry (recipe follows)
½ cup heavy cream, whipped

In 2-quart saucepan, stir together sugar and corn starch. Gradually stir in water until smooth. Stir in orange juice. Stirring constantly, bring to boil over medium heat and boil 1 minute. Remove from heat. Stir in lemon juice, orange rind and lemon rind. Turn into bowl; cover surface with waxed paper or plastic wrap. Cool to room temperature. Arrange fresh ripe fruit in season decoratively on pastry. Reserve 1 cup of the orange glaze; spoon remaining glaze over fruit. Refrigerate pie and reserved glaze until ready to serve. Just before serving, fold reserved glaze into whipped cream. Serve with pie.
Makes about 12 servings.

PLATTER PIE PASTRY:
In large bowl, stir together 2 cups minus 2 tablespoons unsifted flour and ¼ teaspoon salt. With pastry blender, or 2 knives, cut in ⅔ cup margarine until fine crumbs form. (Do not be afraid of overmixing.)

Sprinkle 3 tablespoons cold water over mixture while tossing to blend well. Press dough firmly into ball with hands. (If mixture seems crumbly, work with hands until it will hold together.) On lightly floured surface, roll out pastry to 16-inch circle. Fit loosely into 14-by-¾-inch pizza pan. If necessary, trim dough to ½-inch beyond rim of pan. Flute edge. Pierce with fork. Bake in 450-degree oven 12 minutes or until lightly browned. Cool completely on wire rack.

GLAZED APPLE TART

1 cup unsifted flour
½ teaspoon salt
½ cup (1 stick) corn oil margarine, divided
¼ cup finely chopped pecans
3–4 tablespoons ice water
6 tablespoons sugar
2 tablespoons flour
½ teaspoon ground cinnamon
Dash salt

6 cups (about 3 large) thickly sliced
pared baking apples
½ cup orange marmalade

Combine 1 cup flour and one half teaspoon salt in a bowl. Cut in one-third cup margarine until mixture resembles coarse meal. Mix in pecans. Add water and mix thoroughly. Form pastry into a ball. Roll out on a lightly floured board to a 12-inch round. Place in a 9-inch springform pan or a 9×2-inch round cake pan.

In a large bowl thoroughly combine sugar, 2 tablespoons flour, cinnamon and a dash of salt. Toss in apple slices in circles, overlapping each slice slightly. Cover pan loosely with aluminum foil. Bake at 400 degrees for 45 minutes.

Meanwhile, combine marmalade and remaining margarine in a saucepan. Heat and stir over low heat until margarine is melted. Strain.

Drizzle marmalade mixture over apples. Bake uncovered 15 minutes longer, or until apples are tender. Cool in pan on wire rack.

Makes 10 servings.

HARVEST PUMPKIN PIE

3 eggs, slightly beaten
2 tablespoons molasses
1 can (11 ounces) condensed Cheddar cheese soup
2 cups pumpkin pie filling
¼ cup light cream
1 unbaked 9-inch pie shell

Preheat oven to 450 degrees.

To make filling, combine eggs and molasses. Add soup, pumpkin and cream. Blend well.

Pour filling into pie shell. Bake 10 minutes. Reduce heat to 400 degrees. Bake 1 hour more or until knife inserted in center comes out clean.

Cool on wire rack. Serve with whipped cream.

Makes a 9-inch pie.

HEAVENLY CHOCOLATE CHIFFON PIE

1 envelope unflavored gelatin
1 cup sugar, divided
¼ teaspoon salt
½ cup unsweetened cocoa
6 eggs, separated
1 cup milk
1 teaspoon vanilla
½ teaspoon cream of tartar
1 baked 9-inch pastry shell

Mix gelatin, ¼ cup sugar, salt and cocoa in top of double boiler. Beat together egg yolks and milk; stir into gelatin mixture. Place gelatin mixture over boiling water (2-inches in the bottom of the double boiler) and cook, stirring constantly, until the gelatin dissolves and the mixture thickens slightly, about 10 minutes.

When gelatin is dissolved and custard mixture slightly thickened, remove from double boiler and stir vanilla into mixture. Chill, stirring occasionally, until the mixture mounds slightly when dropped from a spoon.

When gelatin mixture is chilled and thickened, remove from the refrigerator. Combine egg whites with cream of tartar in large bowl of an electric mixer. Beat until the egg whites begin to form soft peaks. Gradually add remaining ¾ cup sugar while continuing to beat the egg whites and beat until very stiff peaks form when the beaters are raised. Pour the thickened chocolate gelatin mixture over the egg whites and gently fold chocolate mixture through the egg whites until the two mixtures are completely blended.

Chill the chocolate chiffon filling until it will pile up and stay in high mounds without flattening out. Spoon into the pastry shell. Chill the pie until the filling is set, several hours or overnight. If you wish, garnish with whipped cream and chocolate curls to serve. *Makes one 9-inch pie, 8 servings.*

HONEYSPUN ICE CREAM PIE

CRUST:
1 cup quick or old-fashioned oats, uncooked
⅓ cup wheat germ or unprocessed bran
⅓ cup firmly packed brown sugar
¼ cup butter or margarine, melted
½ teaspoon cinnamon

FILLING:
¼ cup honey
¾ teaspoon cinnamon
¼ teaspoon nutmeg
⅛ teaspoon cloves
½ gallon vanilla ice cream, softened

For crust, combine all ingredients in bowl. Mix well. Press onto bottom and sides of 9-inch pie plate. Bake in preheated 375-degree oven about 10 minutes or until golden brown. Cool; chill. For filling, add combined honey and spices to ice cream. Mix well. Spoon into crust; freeze until firm.

Makes one 9-inch pie.

KISSIN' COUSIN PIE

Pastry for 2-crust pie or 1 package (11 ounces) pie crust mix
3 cups peeled and sliced fresh peaches (about 1 pound)
3 cups sliced fresh nectarines (about 1 pound)
½ cup sugar
3 tablespoons cornstarch
Dash salt
½ teaspoon nutmeg
½ cup dairy sour cream
Milk
Sugar

Roll out one-half of pastry. Use to line bottom of 9-inch pie plate. Alternate layers of peaches and nectarines in pastry-lined pie plate. Combine sugar, cornstarch, salt, nutmeg and sour cream, mixing well. Pour over peaches and nectarines. Roll out remaining pastry and make a lattice top. Brush pastry with milk and sprinkle with sugar. Bake in 425-degree oven for 10 minutes. Reduce heat to 350 degrees. Continue baking 45 to 50 minutes longer. Cool. *Makes 6 to 8 servings.*

LATTICE-TOP MINCE APPLE PIE

Pastry for 2-crust pie
3 cooking apples, pared and sliced
3 tablespoons flour
2 tablespoons margarine or butter
1 jar (28 ounces) ready-to-use mincemeat
1 egg yolk plus 2 teaspoons water, optional

Preheat oven to 425 degrees. Prepare pastry; line 9-inch pie plate. Toss apples with flour; arrange in pastry shell. Dot with pieces of margarine.

Top with mincemeat. Cut remaining pastry into ¾-by-11-inch strips.

Arrange in lattice design over mincemeat. Seal and trim edges; flute. For a more golden crust, brush top crust with egg yolk mixture. Bake 10 minutes. Reduce oven temperature to 375 degrees and continue baking 25 to 30 minutes or until golden brown.

Remove from oven and cool before cutting.
Makes one 9-inch pie.

LIME AVOCADO AMBROSIA PIE

1 envelope unflavored gelatin
½ cup cold water
¼ cup sugar
¼ teaspoon salt
1 can (8¼ ounces) crushed pineapple
3 tablespoons lime juice
Green food color
1 medium size ripe avocado
1 package (3 ounces) cream cheese, softened
1 cup heavy cream
½ cup flaked coconut
1 9-inch graham cracker crumb crust (store-bought or homemade)

In small saucepan, sprinkle gelatin over cold water to soften. Place over low heat and stir until gelatin is dissolved. Stir in sugar and salt. Drain pineapple liquid and lime juice into gelatin. Add few drops green food color. Chill until thickened, stirring occasionally.

Meanwhile, cut and peel avocado. In large bowl, mash avocado and mix with cream cheese. Whip cream and use same beater to thoroughly blend avocado, cream cheese, pineapple and coconut. Then beat in thickened gelatin just enough to mix thoroughly. Fold in whipped cream. Turn into crumb crust.

Chill at least 4 hours or until firm. When ready to serve, garnish with coconut and lime slices, if desired. *Makes 6 to 8 servings.*

NEVER-FAIL FRESH LEMON MERINGUE PIE

1 cup sugar, divided
⅓ cup cornstarch
½ teaspoon salt
¼ cup cold water
1¼ cups hot water
2 tablespoons butter or margarine
3 egg yolks, lightly beaten
⅓ cup fresh lemon juice
1 teaspoon grated fresh lemon rind
2 teaspoons vanilla
1 9-inch baked pastry shell

Combine one-half cup of the sugar, cornstarch, salt and cold water in the top of a double boiler. Mix well. Stir in hot water. Cook over boiling water 5 minutes or until thick, stirring constantly. Cover and continue cooking over boiling water 8 minutes or until very thick, stirring occasionally. Add butter. In large bowl mix together egg yolks and remaining one-half cup sugar. Slowly add a little of the hot mixture. Then stir into the remaining hot mixture in double boiler. Cook uncovered over simmering water (not boiling) 10 minutes or until very thick, stirring frequently. Gradually stir in lemon juice and rind. Remove from water. Cool. Add vanilla and turn into a baked pastry shell. Top with meringue. Bake in 300-degree oven 20 minutes or until lightly browned. Cool before serving. *Makes 6 servings.*

NEW ENGLAND RUM PIE

1¼	cups graham cracker crumbs
¼	cup soft butter or margarine
2	tablespoons sugar
4	packages (3 ounces each) cream cheese
½	cup sugar
2	eggs, well beaten
¼	teaspoon rum extract
1	pint fresh blueberries, rinsed and drained

TOPPING:

1	cup (½ pint) sour cream
2	tablespoons sugar
2	tablespoons sweet sherry (optional)

In a bowl mix crumbs, butter and sugar. Press mixture into the bottom and sides of an ungreased 9-inch pie plate. In a bowl beat cream cheese until fluffy. Gradually beat in sugar. Beat in eggs and rum extract. Fold in blueberries. Pour mixture into lined pie plate. Bake in a preheated 375-degree oven for 25 minutes or until filling is set. Remove from oven and cool on a rack. In a bowl mix topping ingredients and spread over pie. Garnish with additional fresh blueberries. Chill until ready to serve.

Makes one 9-inch pie.

NORTH CAROLINA YAM-PRALINE PIE

2	eggs
½	cup granulated sugar
½	cup packed light brown sugar
1	teaspoon cinnamon
½	teaspoon nutmeg
½	teaspoon ginger
¼	teaspoon salt
2	cups mashed, cooked fresh yams
¾	cup milk
1	cup light cream
1	unbaked 9-inch pastry shell
	Praline Topping (recipe follows)

Beat eggs in a mixing bowl. Beat in granulated and brown sugars, spices and salt. Blend in yams. Gradually stir in milk and cream.

Pour into unbaked pastry shell. Bake in 400-degree oven for 10 minutes. Reduce heat to 350 degrees. Bake 20 minutes more. Sprinkle Praline Topping over surface of pie. Continue baking 25 minutes longer or until knife inserted near center comes out clean.

Cool completely before serving.

Makes a 9-inch pie.

PRALINE TOPPING:
Mix ⅓ cup chopped pecans, 1 cup packed brown sugar and 3 tablespoons soft butter or margarine.

O'DARBY LIME PIE

1¼	cups graham cracker crumbs
½	cup finely chopped toasted pecans
1¼	cups sugar, divided
¼	cup (½ stick) butter, melted
5	eggs, separated
⅓	cup fresh lime juice
⅓	cup plus 2 tablespoons Irish cream liqueur
2	teaspons grated lime peel
	Dash of salt
1½	cups heavy cream
	Thin slices lime

In bowl, combine graham cracker crumbs, pecans, ¼ cup sugar and melted butter. Blend well. Press mixture evenly against sides and bottom of 9-inch pie plate. Bake at 350 degrees for 8 minutes. Cool.

In top of double boiler, beat yolks until thick and lemon colored. Gradually beat in ½ cup sugar. Stir in lime juice, ⅓ cup liqueur and lime peel. Add salt. Cook over simmering water until mixture coats back of spoon. Turn into large bowl. Cool. When yolk mixture is at room temperature, beat egg whites until foamy. Gradually beat in remaining ¼ cup sugar and beat until stiff and glossy. Fold into custard mixture. Spoon into prepared pie crust. Freeze until ready to serve. Ten minutes before serving, remove pie from freezer. Combine heavy cream, 2 tablespoons liqueur and ¼ cup sugar. Whip to soft peaks. Spread over pie. Garnish with lime slices. *Makes one 9-inch pie.*

PEACH PIE COOL

CRUST:

½	cup butter or margarine
1	cup flour
2	tablespoons powdered sugar

CUSTARD:

¼	cup light cream
2	ounces semisweet chocolate, broken
1	egg yolk

FILLING:

2	pounds fresh peaches (5 to 6 medium)

Continued

1 package unflavored gelatin
1 package (3 ounces) cream cheese, softened
¼ cup granulated sugar
1 cup whipping cream, whipped

CRUST: In small bowl, cut butter into flour and powdered sugar until crumbly. Press on bottom and 1 inch up sides of buttered 8½-inch springform pan. Prick with fork. Bake in 425-degree oven 8 to 10 minutes or until golden. Cool.

CUSTARD: In small saucepan, heat cream and chocolate until chocolate has melted. (Do not boil.) Quickly whisk in egg yolk; cook 2 minutes. Pour chocolate mixture over crust, spreading evenly. Cool.

FILLING: In small saucepan, soften gelatin in ¼ cup water; then dissolve over low heat. Set aside. Into blender, slice enough peaches, unpeeled, to measure 2 cups. Puree (there should be 1½ cups puree). Add cream cheese, sugar and dissolved gelatin; blend smooth. Pour into bowl; chill until syrupy. Fold in whipped cream; pour into crust. Chill 2 hours or overnight. To serve, garnish with additional whipped cream, peach slices and chocolate curls, if desired. *Makes 8 servings.*

RAISIN APPLE PIECUPS

4 tart cooking apples, peeled
½ cup raisins
1 cup light brown sugar
2 tablespoons cider, apple juice or water
1 cup flour
½ teaspoon salt
1 cup grated Cheddar cheese
½ cup soft butter or margarine

Preheat oven to 350 degrees. Butter 8 foil baking cups (¾-cup size). Slice apples thinly and press into baking cups, filling almost full. (Apples will shrink in cooking.) Sprinkle with raisins, half the brown sugar and a few drops of the liquid.

In small bowl, combine remaining brown sugar, flour, salt, cheese and butter to make a crumbly mixture. Spread mixture over apples. Arrange foil cups on baking sheet. Bake 40 minutes, or until apples are tender. Serve warm or cold.
Makes 8 servings.

VARIATION: Adapt to little pies using small foil pie pans and top with streusel. Or make a lattice crust, using an 11-ounce package of pie crust mix to which 2 teaspoons of cinnamon have been added. Bake as above. *Makes 4 pies.*

SPICY PEACH PIE

 Pastry for 2-crust pie
2 pounds fresh peaches, sliced (about 6 cups)
½ teaspoon cinnamon
¼ teaspoon nutmeg
⅛ teaspoon cloves
⅓ cup flour
¾ cup sugar
1 tablespoon butter

Line 9-inch pie plate with pastry. In mixing bowl, combine peaches, spices, flour and sugar; arrange in pastry-lined pie plate. Dot with butter. Cover with top pastry; seal and crimp edges; make steam vents with fork or knife. Bake in 425-degree oven 45 to 50 minutes. *Makes one 9-inch pie.*

SPICY PLUM CRUMB PIE

2 cups sliced fresh California plums, unpeeled
¾–1 cup sugar (according to tartness of plums)
3 tablespoons cornstarch
2 teaspoons cinnamon
 Dash of salt
1 unbaked 9-inch pie shell
 Butter or margarine
 Spicy Crumb Topping (recipe follows)

In mixing bowl, combine sugar, cornstarch, cinnamon and salt. Gently toss in plums. Pour mixture into unbaked pie shell. Dot with butter, sprinkle Spicy Crumb Topping over all. Bake in 400-degree oven 40 to 50 minutes. *Makes one 9-inch pie.*

SPICY CRUMB TOPPING:
1 cup crushed corn flakes
½ cup firmly packed brown sugar
½ teaspoon cinnamon
¼ teaspoon nutmeg
½ cup butter or margarine

In mixing bowl, combine corn flakes, brown sugar, cinnamon and nutmeg. Cut in butter until mixture resembles small peas. Use to top plum pie filling.

STRAWBERRY ANGEL CHIFFON PIE

1 pint fresh strawberries
¾ cup sugar
1½ envelopes unflavored gelatin

¼	cup cold water
½	cup boiling water
1	tablespoon lemon juice
½	cup heavy cream
2	egg whites
⅛	teaspoon salt
1	9-inch baked pie shell
	Whipped cream for garnish

Reserve a few strawberries for garnish.

Halve remainder of berries. Puree in electric blender with ½ cup of sugar. Or force through food mill and add sugar. Strain thoroughly to remove seeds.

Soften gelatin in cold water. Stir in boiling water until dissolved. Add with lemon juice to strawberry puree. Mix well. Chill until mixture mounds when dropped from spoon.

Whip cream. Fold into strawberry mixture.

Beat egg whites with salt until soft peaks form. Gradually add remaining sugar, beating constantly until whites are glossy and stiff. Fold into strawberry mixture. Spoon into baked pie shell. If mixture isn't stiff enough to mound, chill 10 to 15 minutes before spooning into shell.

Chill 4 hours or overnight. Garnish with reserved strawberries and additional whipped cream as desired. *Makes one 9-inch pie.*

STRAWBERRY-BANANA PIE

1	pint fresh strawberries
1	package (3 ounces) cream cheese, softened
2	tablespoons honey
½	teaspoon vanilla
½	cup heavy cream, whipped
1	9-inch baked Egg Pie Shell (recipe follows)
2	bananas
2	tablespoons lemon juice

Reserve about 4 strawberries for garnish. Slice and sweeten remainder. Blend together cream cheese, honey and vanilla. Fold in whipped cream. Spread in bottom of pie shell and chill 1 hour. Cut bananas into one-fourth-inch slices and coat with lemon juice. Reserve about 10 slices and arrange remainder in pie shell. Top with sliced strawberries. Garnish center of pie with reserved banana slices and whole or halved strawberries. *Makes one 9-inch pie.*

EGG PIE SHELL:

1⅓	cups sifted all-purpose flour
½	teaspoon salt
½	cup solid all-vegetable shortening
1	egg, slightly beaten
2	tablespoons cold water
1	teaspoon lemon juice

Combine flour and salt in bowl. Cut in shortening until uniform but coarse. Combine egg, water and lemon juice. Sprinkle over dry ingredients, tossing and stirring with fork until mixture is moist enough to hold together.

On lightly floured board, roll out pastry 1½ inches larger than inverted 9-inch pie plate. Fit into plate. Trim one-half inch beyond edge of plate, fold under to make double thickness of dough around rim and flute edge. Prick bottom and sides thoroughly with fork. Bake in 425-degree oven 10 to 15 minutes or until browned as desired. Cool on rack.
Makes one 9-inch pie shell.

STRAWBERRY ICE CREAM PIE

1	9-inch baked graham cracker pie shell
1	quart vanilla ice cream
3	cups (1½ pints) fresh strawberries, sliced
⅔	cup pineapple preserves
1	tablespoon water
2	teaspoons corn starch
¼	teaspoon vanilla

Using a number 12 scoop (or large tablespoon), fill cooled pie shell with scoops of vanilla ice cream, rounded side up. Freeze overnight or until very firm.

Combine strawberries and pineapple preserves. Chill several hours. Drain, reserving syrup in a saucepan. Slowly stir water into corn starch and mix with syrup. Cook, stirring constantly, until thickened. Stir in sliced strawberries and vanilla; cool.

Spoon some sauce over ice cream in shell and serve remaining sauce in pitcher or dish.
Makes a 9-inch pie, with 2½ cups sauce.

SWEET CHERRY BAVARIAN TORTE

1	cup pitted and halved fresh sweet cherries
1	package (3 ounces) cherry-flavored gelatin
½	cup hot water
½	cup cold water
2	egg whites
½	cup sugar
1	cup whipping cream
½	teaspoon almond extract
1	Wafer Crumb Crust (recipe follows)
	Fresh cherries and whipped cream for garnish

Continued

Halve and pit cherries. Set aside. Dissolve gelatin in hot water. Add cold water and chill until syrupy. Add 1 cup halved cherries. Beat egg whites until stiff, adding sugar gradually. In separate bowl whip cream and add almond extract. Fold egg whites and whipped cream into gelatin. Pour into baked crumb crust. Chill until set, several hours or overnight. Garnish with additional fresh cherries and whipped cream. *Makes 8 servings.*

WAFER CRUMB CRUST:
1⅓ cups vanilla wafer crumbs
⅓ cup sugar
⅓ cup melted butter

Combine wafer crumbs and sugar. Add melted butter and mix until thoroughly blended. Press on bottom and 1 inch up sides of 9-inch springform pan. Bake at 400 degrees for 8 to 10 minutes. Cool. *Makes one 9-inch shell.*

WHEAT GERM PARTY PIE

3 cups miniature marshmallows
12 vanilla caramels
⅓ cup milk
1⅓ cups vacuum-packed wheat germ, regular or sugar and honey
½ cup finely chopped pecans or walnuts
¼ cup butter, melted
2 cups whipping cream

Combine marshmallows, caramels and milk. Heat over boiling water or low heat about 10 minutes. Stir frequently until smooth and blended. Refrigerate until lukewarm. Meanwhile, combine ⅔ cup wheat germ and ¼ cup nuts with melted butter. Save ¼ cup for garnish and press remainder into bottom of an 8 or 9-inch springform pan. Whip cream. Fold into lukewarm caramel mixture. Fold in remaining ⅔ cup wheat germ and ¼ cup nuts. Turn into prepared pan. Sprinkle reserved wheat germ crust mixture on top. Chill at least 4 hours or until firm. Garnish edge with additional whipped cream if desired. *Makes 8 or more servings.*

Note: Recipe may be cut in half and assembled in 9-inch pie plate.

WHEAT GERM PUMPKIN PIE

1 envelope plain gelatin
¾ cup sugar, divided
¾ teaspoon cinnamon
½ teaspoon ginger
½ teaspoon salt

2 eggs, separated
½ cup milk
1 can (15 or 16 ounces) pumpkin
¼ cup vacuum packed regular wheat germ
½ cup whipping cream, whipped
Praline Pie Shell (recipe follows)

Combine gelatin, one-half cup sugar, cinnamon, ginger, egg yolks and milk. Cook over low heat 3 to 5 minutes or until gelatin dissolves and mixture thickens slightly. Remove from heat. Stir in pumpkin and wheat germ. Refrigerate until mixture mounds slightly when stirred. Beat egg whites until foamy. Add remaining one-fourth cup sugar gradually, beating until stiff peaks form. Fold in pumpkin mixture then whipped cream. Spoon into Praline Pie Shell. Freeze 4 hours or longer. Garnish with whipped cream and wheat germ, if desired. *Makes 6 to 8 servings.*

PRALINE PIE SHELL:
Prepare pastry for 1 crust 9-inch pie. Combine one-third cup each butter and firmly packed brown sugar in saucepan. Cook, stirring constantly, until sugar melts and mixture starts to bubble. Remove from heat. Stir in one-fourth cup each wheat germ and finely chopped pecans. Bake pie shell in 450-degree oven 5 minutes. Spread praline mixture on bottom of shell. Bake 5 minutes longer. Cool on rack.

If frozen longer than 4 hours, let stand at room temperature 10 minutes before serving.

PUDDINGS, MOUSSE & ICE CREAM

BAKED COCONUT CUSTARD

½ cup fresh coconut milk
½ cup grated fresh coconut
4 eggs
½ cup sugar
⅛ teaspoon salt
1½ cups milk

Pierce eyes of coconut and drain milk into measuring cup. Reserve. Place coconut in a 350-degree oven for 15 minutes. Remove from oven. Crack shell with hammer and remove meat. Peel brown outer rind with vegetable peeler and grate coconut meat. Beat eggs until light and lemon colored. Add sugar and salt and beat until thick. Gradually add coconut milk and stir. Pour into 6 buttered custard cups or 1-quart baking dish. Sprinkle grated coconut over top. Place in pan of water and bake in 325-degree oven 45 minutes for individual cups or one and one-fourth to one and one-half hours for large dish, until a knife inserted in center comes out clean. Serve warm or chilled. *Makes 6 servings.*

BANANA-RUM SHERBET

    ½   cup boiling water
    ¾   cup sugar
    1   package (3 ounces) lemon gelatin
    ½   cup amber rum
    3   cups milk
        Grated rind and juice of 1 lemon

Pour boiling water onto gelatin and sugar. Stir until dissolved. Continue stirring and add lemon juice, lemon rind and rum. Pour in milk, blend and freeze in a 2-quart container. When frozen, remove from freezer, beat thoroughly with a blender and refreeze.

BANANA-STRAWBERRY RIPPLE FROZEN YOGURT

    1   envelope unflavored gelatin
    ¼   cup cold water
    ½   cup sugar
    ¼   teaspoon salt
    1   cup mashed ripe bananas (3 medium)
    1   tablespoon lemon juice
    1   container (8 ounces) plain yogurt
    2   egg whites, unbeaten
    1   package frozen strawberries, thawed
        and pureed
    2   tablespoons light corn syrup

In small saucepan, mix gelatin and water. Stir over medium heat until gelatin dissolves, about 1 minute. Stir in sugar and salt.

Remove from heat. Stir in bananas and lemon juice. Stir in yogurt.

Pour into freezer tray or 9-by-5-by-3-inch loaf pan. Freeze until firm.

Turn banana mixture into large bowl. Add egg whites. Beat at high speed of electric mixer until smooth and fluffy, about 10 minutes.

In small bowl, mix strained strawberries and corn syrup.

Alternate spoonfuls of yogurt mixture with strawberries in freezer tray or loaf pan. Freeze until firm. *Makes about 5½ cups.*

BANANA RUM-RAISIN FROZEN YOGURT:

Substitute 2 tablespoons rum (or 1 teaspoon rum flavoring) for lemon juice in basic recipe. Fold in ½ cup raisins after beating banana mixture with egg whites. Return to freezer tray or loaf pan. Freeze until firm.

BANANA-TAPIOCA PUDDING

    3   tablespoons quick-cooking tapioca
    3   tablespoons sugar, divided
    1   egg, separated
    ⅛   teaspoon salt
    1½ cups milk
    1   cup mashed ripe bananas (3 medium
        bananas)
    ½   teaspoon vanilla

In a medium saucepan, mix tapioca, 2 tablespoons sugar, egg yolk, salt and milk. Let stand for 5 minutes.

Meanwhile beat egg white until foamy. Add remaining 1 tablespoon sugar and beat until stiff. Set aside.

Cook tapioca mixture over medium heat, stirring constantly, for 6 to 8 minutes. Combine mashed banana and beaten egg white. Gradually add to tapioca mixture, beating constantly to blend. Add vanilla and chill. *Makes 4 to 6 servings.*

BASIC FREEZER-TRAY YOGURT

    1   envelope unflavored gelatin
    ¼   cup cold water or orange juice
    ½   cup sugar
    ¼   teaspoon salt
    1   cup mashed ripe bananas (3 medium)
    1   tablespoon lemon juice
    1   container (8 ounces) plain yogurt
    2   egg whites, unbeaten

In small saucepan, sprinkle gelatin over water or orange juice. Place over low heat. Stir constantly until gelatin dissolves, about 3 minutes.

Stir in sugar and salt. Remove from heat. Stir in bananas and lemon juice. Stir in plain yogurt.

Pour into freezer tray or 9-by-5-by-3-inch loaf pan. Freeze until firm.

Turn mixture into large bowl. Add egg whites. Beat at high speed of electric mixer until smooth and fluffy, about 10 minutes. Return to freezer tray. Freeze until firm. *Makes about 5½ cups.*

BROWNIE ALASKA

1   jar (8 ounces) red maraschino cherries, drained and chopped
1   quart vanilla ice cream, softened
6   egg whites
⅛   teaspoon cream of tartar
¾   cup sugar
     Brownie Cake (recipe follows)

Combine cherries and ice cream; mix well. Line a one to one and one-half quart bowl with foil. Add cherry ice cream. Cover and freeze 1 day. In large bowl, beat egg whites with cream of tartar until soft peaks form. Slowly add sugar, 2 tablespoons at a time, beating constantly. Beat until stiff peaks form. Place foil on baking sheet; place cake in center. Invert bowl of ice cream onto cake. Peel off foil. Quickly cover cake and ice cream with meringue, making sure it is well sealed. Freeze 2 to 3 hours. Bake in 425-degree oven 7 minutes or until browned. Cut foil from around dessert and slice onto chilled plate. *Makes 12 servings.*

BROWNIE CAKE

¾   cup sifted all-purpose flour
½   teaspoon baking powder
¼   teaspoon salt
⅓   cup butter or margarine
2   squares (2 ounces) unsweetened chocolate
2   eggs
1   cup sugar
1   teaspoon vanilla
½   cup toasted filberts, chopped

Sift together flour, baking powder and salt. In small saucepan, melt butter and chocolate over very low heat. Beat eggs with sugar and vanilla. Gradually blend in chocolate mixture. Add sifted ingredients and mix well. Stir in filberts. Pour into greased 9-inch round layer cake pan. Bake in 350-degree oven 25 minutes or until cake tests done. Cool on rack. *Makes 9-inch layer.*

Note: Spread filberts in shallow pan and bake in 400-degree oven 10 to 15 minutes, stirring occasionally.

CHOCOLATE SOUFFLE

2   envelopes unflavored gelatin
2   cups milk
1   cup sugar, divided
¼   teaspoon salt
4   eggs, separated
1   12-ounce package or 2 six-ounce packages (2 cups) semi-sweet chocolate pieces
1   teaspoon vanilla
2   cups heavy cream, whipped

Sprinkle gelatin over milk in saucepan to soften. Add one-half cup sugar, salt and egg yolks. Mix well. Add chocolate pieces. Cook over low heat, stirring constantly, until gelatin is dissolved and chocolate melted, 6 to 8 minutes. Remove from heat. Beat with rotary beater until chocolate is blended. Stir in vanilla. Chill, stirring occasionally, until mixture mounds slightly when dropped from spoon (about 20 minutes in refrigerator). Beat egg whites until stiff but not dry. Gradually add remaining one-half cup sugar and beat until very stiff. Fold into chocolate mixture. Fold in whipped cream. Turn into 2-quart souffle dish or casserole with two-inch collar. Chill until firm. Garnish with additional whipped cream. *Makes 12 servings.*

Note: To make collar, fold foil into four thicknesses three inches wide and long enough to go around souffle dish with generous overlap. Attach to dish with sealing tape, leaving one inch of the foil around dish to make collar two inches high. Carefully remove foil collar to serve.

CITRUS TASTY PUDDING

3   oranges, peeled, sliced and quartered
2   apples, sliced (Rome Beauty preferred)
1   tablespoon sugar
¾   teaspoon nutmeg
½   teaspoon cinnamon
1   cup flour
1   cup sugar
1   teaspoon baking powder
½   teaspoon salt
¼   teaspoon orange rind
1   egg, beaten
2   tablespoons butter
½   cup orange juice

Place orange and apple slices in layers in 8 × 8 × 2-inch baking pan or a 1-quart casserole. Combine sugar, nutmeg and cinnamon. Sprinkle half of this mixture over the fruit. Blend flour, sugar, baking powder, salt, orange rind and egg until crumbly. Sprinkle over sliced fruit. Sprinkle remaining cinnamon mixture over all. Dot with butter. Pour orange juice over all. Bake in 350-degree oven 45 minutes. Serve warm or cold with whipped cream, if desired. *Makes 6 to 8 servings.*

CRUNCH-TOPPED YOGURT PUDDING

TOPPING:

2	cups quick or old-fashioned oats, uncooked
⅔	cup firmly packed brown sugar
½	cup butter or margarine, melted
⅓	cup unprocessed bran
⅓	cup wheat germ
1	teaspoon cinnamon

PUDDING:

1	8-ounce carton (1 cup) plain or vanilla yogurt
½	cup milk
1	package (3¾ ounces) vanilla-flavor instant pudding and pie filling
1	cup heavy cream, whipped

For crunch topping, combine all ingredients. Mix well. Spread into 15½-by-10½-inch jelly-roll pan.

Bake in 350-degree preheated oven about 25 minutes, stirring occasionally. Cool.

For pudding, combine yogurt, milk and pudding mix in small mixing bowl. Beat at low speed on electric mixer about 2 minutes.

Fold in whipped cream. Spoon into 4 to 6 dessert dishes. Chill.

To serve, sprinkle each serving with about 2 tablespoons crunch topping.   *Makes 4 to 6 servings.*

Note: Refrigerate remaining crunch topping in tightly covered container to serve over ice cream, yogurt, frozen yogurt or fruit, as desired.

FRESH PEACH ICE CREAM

2½	cups (2 pounds) mashed, peeled fresh peaches
1½	cups sugar, divided
1½	tablespoons fresh lemon juice
1	teaspoon vanilla
1	teaspoon almond extract
2½	tablespoons flour
⅛	teaspoon salt
3	eggs, slightly beaten
2½	cups milk
2	cups heavy cream
	Crushed ice
	Rock salt

In large bowl, mix mashed peaches with ½ cup sugar, lemon juice, vanilla and almond extract. Set aside.

In large saucepan, mix together flour, remaining 1 cup sugar and salt. Stir in eggs. Scald milk and gradually stir into egg mixture. Place over low heat and stir constantly until mixture thickens enough to coat a spoon. Remove from heat and cool.

Stir in heavy cream and prepared peach mixture. Pour into can of electric ice cream freezer. Insert dasher. Place can in freezer container. Layer crushed ice and rock salt in freezer around container according to directions for freezer. Follow manufacturer's directions for freezing ice cream.

To ripen ice cream, turn into plastic containers or bowls. Cover and freeze 2 hours. Serve with sliced peaches.   *Makes 2 quarts.*

FRESH PLUM SHERBET

1	cup buttermilk
¼	cup concentrated orange juice, undiluted
3	cups sliced fresh plums
1¼	cups sugar

Combine all ingredients in blender. Blend at highest until mixture is smooth. Pour into freezer tray and freeze as quickly as possible with refrigerator at coldest setting. When mixture is frozen ½-inch from the edges, remove from freezer, pour into mixing bowl, a little at a time, and beat until smooth. Return to tray and continue freezing until firm.

Makes 1 quart or 6 to 8 servings.

FRESH PLUM SORBET

3	cups water
3	cups sugar
3	pounds fresh plums, halved and pitted
	Lemon juice or plum brandy (optional)

In saucepan, combine water and sugar; stir until sugar dissolves. Boil until syrup spins a thread when dropped into cold water (230 to 234 degrees). Puree plums in blender and strain, or peel fruit and put through food mill. Combine pureed fruit pulp with sugar syrup (there should be 4 cups of syrup). Pour into ice cube trays and freeze 30 to 40 minutes. At serving time, pour into stemmed glasses and top with a dash of lemon juice or plum brandy.

Makes 4-6 servings.

Note: If mixture become too solid (or if you wish to store it) before serving, return to blender or beat a few minutes until sorbet is thick and foamy. Should it become too liquid, return to freezer a few minutes.

FRESH STRAWBERRY RUM TRIFLE

1	9-inch cake layer
½	cup strawberry jam
2	cups sweetened whipped cream
¼	cup light rum
2	cups boiled custard (recipe follows)
1	cup fresh strawberries, sliced

BOILED RUM CUSTARD:

4	egg yolks, beaten
2	tablespoons cornstarch
½	cup sugar
1¾	cups hot milk
¼	cup light rum
	Pinch of salt

In a saucepan, mix sugar and cornstarch. Stir in the scalded milk. Cook over medium-low heat until mixture starts to thicken, stirring constantly.

In another bowl, stir a small amount of the hot mixture into the beaten yolks. Then pour yolks into saucepan with custard. Cook over low heat, stirring until smooth and thick. Add salt and rum. Stir well. Cool.

To assemble, cut sponge cake into 1-inch cubes. Place half the cake pieces into a serving dish. Sprinkle with ¼ cup light rum. Top with strawberry jam. Spread half of the whipped cream over the layer of jam.

Add the rest of the cake pieces. Pour the custard over the cake. Top with the remaining whipped cream. Garnish with sliced strawberries. Refrigerate. *Makes 8 servings.*

FROZEN PEACH YOGURT

3	cups sliced peeled peaches
¾	cup light corn syrup
⅓	cup sugar
3	containers (8 ounces each) plain yogurt (3 cups)
1¾	cups table salt (for processing)

Place peaches, corn syrup and sugar into blender container; cover. Blend at medium speed 30 seconds or until liquefied. Add yogurt. Blend at medium speed 10 seconds or until well mixed.

Place ice bucket of electric ice-cream freezer onto motor and base assembly so drive socket engages with drive shaft. Rotate ice bucket until it drops down and seats firmly. Pour yogurt mixture into cream can. Place dasher in cream can. Place can lid over dasher shaft and snap into place. Place cream can into ice bucket so drive socket engages with drive shaft. Lock support arm into place.

With motor running pour 1 cup cold water into ice bucket. Add 1 layer of ice cubes. Sprinkle about 6 tablespoons of salt evenly over ice. Continue layering ice and salt until ice bucket is full. Sprinkle any remaining salt over ice. Pour 1 cup cold water evenly over top.

When machine makes laboring sound or motor slows, unplug. (Do not allow machine to operate more than 50 minutes.) Wipe cover carefully. Lift out dasher. Place covered can directly in freezer or spoon frozen yogurt into plastic container leaving at least ½-inch headspace; cover with tight-fitting lid and place in freezer. *Makes 1½ quarts.*

Note: Peach-corn syrup-sugar mixture may be frozen for use after fresh peach season has passed. Thaw before using.

HOT PRALINE SUNDAES

¼	cup butter or margarine
1	cup firmly packed dark brown sugar
1	cup blended maple syrup
1	can (6 ounces) pecan halves
	Vanilla ice cream

In saucepan, combine all ingredients except ice cream. Place on grill above medium hot coals. Stirring constantly, heat until sauce bubbles. Let simmer gently for 5 minutes. Scoop vanilla ice cream into serving dishes. Spoon on hot sauce. Serve at once. *Makes about 2 cups.*

Note: This sauce is also delicious when served on slices of pound cake which have been toasted.

NECTARINE-LEMON MOUSSE

⅓	cup granulated sugar
1	tablespoon cornstarch
⅛	teaspoon salt
½	cup milk
2	egg yolks, beaten
2	teaspoons grated lemon peel
¼	cup lemon juice
2	fresh nectarines
1	cup whipping cream
	Nectarine Sauce (recipe follows)

Blend sugar, cornstarch and salt in small saucepan; stir in milk. Cook, stirring, over moderate heat until mixture boils and thickens. Beat cooked mixture into egg yolks. Return to saucepan, and cook a minute longer, stirring constantly. Do not allow mixture to boil after adding egg yolks. Remove from heat. Stir in lemon peel and juice. Cool. Slice and with a fork coarsely crush nectarines. Fold into lemon mixture. Beat cream to soft peaks and fold in. Turn into loaf pan and freeze firm. Spoon into serving dishes and top with Nectarine Sauce.

Makes 6 to 8 servings.

NECTARINE SAUCE: Dice 2 fresh nectarines. Toss lightly with 1 tablespoon sugar. Cover and chill one-half hour before serving.

Makes sauce for 6 to 8 servings.

ORANGE-ALMOND BLANCMANGE

2	envelopes unflavored gelatin
1½	cups orange juice, divided
1	cup sugar
2	cups heavy cream
1	cup whole or slivered blanched almonds, groud finely

In medium saucepan, sprinkle gelatin over 1 cup orange juice. Place over low heat and stir constantly until gelatin dissolves, about 3 minutes. Remove from heat. Stir in sugar and remaining ½ cup orange juice. Cool. Stir in heavy cream and almonds. Turn into 4-cup mold and chill until firm. Unmold and garnish with orange sections and whole almonds.

Makes 8 servings.

ORANGE NESSELRODE

4	egg yolks
1	cup sugar, divided
2	cups light cream

1	can (8¾ ounces) chestnut puree or 1 cup ground almonds
¾	cup orange juice, divided
¼	cup currants
¼	cup raisins
½	cup sugar
2	cups chilled orange and grapefruit sections, well drained
¾	cup heavy cream, whipped

In small bowl, beat egg yolks until thick. Gradually add ½ cup sugar and beat until light and fluffy. Stir in light cream. Pour into saucepan. Place over low heat and stir constantly until mixture thickens. Remove from heat and stir in chestnut puree and ¼ cup orange juice. Freeze in shallow 2-quart pan until mushy.

In medium saucepan, combine remaining ½ cup orange juice, ½ cup sugar, currants and raisins. bring to a boil and boil until syrup thickens. Remove from heat and stir in chilled sections. Fold syrup mixture and whipped cream into frozen mixture. Turn into 4-cup mold. Freeze until firm.

To unmold, dip mold into hot water, loosen around edges and invert on chilled plate. Garnish, if desired, with marrons (canned chestnuts) and orange sections. *Makes 8 servings.*

ORANGE-RAISIN SAUCED SOUFFLE

1	orange
1	cup raisins
¼	cup orange liqueur, divided
3	tablespoons flour
¾	cup milk, divided
6	tablespoons sugar, divided
4	eggs, separated,
1	egg white (additional)
2	tablespoons butter
1½	teaspoons vanilla
	Dash salt

Grate orange peel. Set aside.

Juice orange. Combine with raisins in small pan. Bring to boil. Remove from heat. Add 1 tablespoon of liqueur. Cover and set aside.

Butter 2-quart souffle dish or charlotte mold. Dust with sugar. Set aside.

Put flour and ½ of milk in saucepan. Beat until smooth with wire whisk. Blend in remaining milk and all but 1 tablespoon sugar. Bring to boil over medium heat. Cool 3 minutes.

Quickly whisk in egg yolks, one at a time. Blend in butter, vanilla and remaining 3 tablespoons liqueur. Cover pan. Set aside.

In large mixing bowl, beat 5 egg whites and salt to soft peaks. Add remaining tablespoon sugar. Beat until stiff.

Continued

Stir ¼ of beaten whites into warm sauce. Gently fold in remaining whites. Pour all but about ⅔ cup of mixture into prepared pan.

Bake in preheated 375-degree oven 30 to 35 minutes or until straw inserted into side comes out clean.

Meanwhile, stir raisin mixture into remaining souffle mixture. Spoon into sauce dish. Serve souffle at once, spooning some sauce over each serving.   *Makes 4 to 6 servings.*

Note: For nicer final effect, dust top of souffle with powdered sugar 10 minutes before it is done.

PINEAPPLE-APRICOT GELATO

1	envelope unflavored gelatin
½	cup sugar
½	cup nonfat dry milk powder
1½	cups skim milk
⅓	cup unsweetened pineapple juice
⅓	cup apricot nectar
2	egg whites

In medium saucepan, mix unflavored gelatin, sugar and nonfat dry milk powder. Stir in milk. Place over low heat. Stir constantly until gelatin dissolves, about 5 minutes. Remove from heat, cool slightly and stir in juices. Pour into freezer tray and freeze until firm.

In large chilled bowl, beat gelatin mixture and egg whites at high speed until smooth and fluffy. Turn into 9×5×3-inch loaf pan. Return to freezer and freeze.   *Makes about 5½ cups.*

PINEAPPLE-LIME MOUSSE

3	packages (3 ounces each) lime gelatin
1½	cups water (1 cup boiling, ½ cup cold)
1	can (29 ounces) crushed pineapple, undrained
3	cups dairy sour cream
¼	cup light rum

Dissolve gelatin in boiling water. Then add the cold water. Add pineapple and light rum. Spoon about 3 or 4 tablespoons into a large jar, add half the sour cream and shake vigorously for a few minutes, until smooth.

Pour into a large bowl. Repeat with more gelatin and the remainder of the sour cream. Combine in a bowl. Coat an 8- or 9-cup mold well with vegetable oil. Pour in the mixture. Chill. (This recipe may be made a day in advance.)   *Makes 8 servings.*

PLUM CLAFOUTI

1	pound fresh plums (about 6)
1	large fresh peach, peeled and sliced
	Sugar to taste
1½	cups milk
4	eggs
2	teaspoons vanilla
½	cup flour
¼	cup sugar
	Powdered sugar

Preheat oven to 350 degrees. Slice and pit plums. Arrange plum and peach slices in a buttered 2-quart casserole (glass or ceramic). Sprinkle fruit with sugar, if desired. Into blender pour milk, eggs and vanilla. Blend 2 seconds. Add flour and ¼ cup sugar and blend 5 seconds on high speed. Pour batter over fruit. Bake in middle of oven 1½ hours. Cool slightly before dusting with powdered sugar, if desired. Serve warm or cool.   *Makes 8 servings.*

Note: The fruit rises to the top during baking. Dessert resembles a baked custard and will sink a little as it cools.

POTATO SPICED PUDDING

½	package (12 ounces) frozen shredded hash browns
½	cup dark brown sugar (packed)
½	cup light molasses
¼	cup soft shortening
1	large egg
¾	cup finely shredded carrot
1½	cups sifted all-purpose flour
1¼	teaspoons salt
1	teaspoon cinnamon
½	teaspoon nutmeg
¾	teaspoon baking soda
1	cup raisins, coarsely chopped
⅔	cup mixed candied fruits, chopped
⅔	cup chopped walnuts

Thaw and separate 1 block potatoes (will measure 1½ cups). Grease a 6½ cup ring mold. Set aside. Sift flour, salt, cinnamon, nutmeg and soda. Set aside. Preheat oven to 375 degrees. Cream sugar, molasses and shortening together well. Beat in egg, the potatoes and carrot (batter will appear curdled). Gradually stir flour mixture into potato mixture, blending well. Stir in raisins, candied fruits and nuts. Turn into greased ring mold, and spread level. Cover loosely with foil, crimping edges tightly against side of mold. Set in pan with 1 inch hot water. Bake in oven 1 hour 10 to 15 minutes, or until pudding tests done. Let stand 10 minutes, then turn out and cool. Wrap closely in foil to store. Reheat

before serving. Serve with Orange Mace Hard
Sauce. *Makes 8 servings.*

Note: Pudding may be steam-baked in 8 individual
molds (1-cup capacity). Bake individual puddings
50 to 55 minutes.

ORANGE MACE HARD SAUCE:
3 cups sifted powdered sugar
¾ cup soft butter
¼ cup orange juice
2 teaspoons grated orange peel
½ teaspoon mace

Mix together the sugar, butter, orange juice, orange
peel and mace. Blend until sugar is moistened and
then beat until light and fluffy. *Makes 2 cups.*

RASPBERRY MOUSSE

1 package (10 ounces) frozen raspberries
2 tablespoons gelatin
1 teaspoon lemon juice
½ teaspoon vanilla
1½ tablespoons Kirschwasser
1 egg white
Pinch salt
¼ cup sugar
1 cup cream

Thaw raspberries. Combine with gelatin, lemon
juice, vanilla, Kirschwasser and salt.
Beat egg white until it forms stiff peak.
In separate bowl, beat cream and sugar until it
peaks.
Fold cream mixture, then egg white, into raspberries. Chill. *Makes 4 to 6 servings.*

RASPBERRY-PEAR BAKED ALASKA

2–3 fresh Bartlett pears
1 quart raspberry sherbet
Meringue (recipe follows)
1 chocolate 9-inch cake layer

Pare, core and chop pears to measure 2 cups. Soften
sherbet slightly and fold in pears. Transfer sherbet
to a bowl with a diameter about 1 inch smaller than
the cake; refreeze.
Just before serving prepare meringue. Preheat
oven to 500 degrees. Place cake on a cookie sheet;
remove sherbet from freezer, loosen it from bowl
with a metal spatula or knife and invert onto cake.
Working very quickly, cover the outside of the
cake and sherbet with the meringue, making sure

there is no cake or sherbet showing. (The meringue
serves as insulation to prevent the sherbet from
melting.)
Bake at 500 degrees for 3 minutes, or until
meringue is lightly browned. Carefully transfer
baked Alaska with wide spatulas to a chilled serving
plate. Slice and serve immediately.
Makes 8 to 10 servings.

MERINGUE: In medium bowl, with mixer at high
speed, beat 3 egg whites and ⅛ teaspoon cream of
tartar until soft peaks form. Beating at high speed,
gradually sprinkle in ¼ cup granulated sugar, 1
tablespoon at a time. Continue beating until stiff
peaks form. Do *not* overbeat or whites will begin to
collapse.

RUM-CHOCOLATE ICE CREAM

¼ cup candied slivered orange peel
¼ cup amber rum
2 quarts chocolate ice cream, softened

Combine orange peel and rum. Blend into softened
chocolate ice cream. Blend and refreeze.
Makes 8 servings.

STEEPLE CREAM

½ cup corn starch
⅓ cup sugar
½ teaspoon salt
3½ cups milk
½ cup light corn syrup
1 teaspoon almond extract
1 cup ground almonds
Candied violets (optional)
Blanched almonds (optional)

In medium saucepan, stir together corn starch,
sugar and salt. Gradually add milk, stirring until
smooth. Bring to boil over medium heat, stirring
constantly. Boil 1 minute. Remove from heat, stir in
corn syrup and extract. Chill about 1 hour or until
slightly thickened. Fold in almonds. Turn into 5-cup
mold. Chill 3 hours, or until well set. Unmold.
Garnish with violets and almonds, if desired.

STRAWBERRY ALASKA NO-BAKE

2 packages (10 ounces each) frozen
sliced strawberries with sugar (slightly
thawed and chopped into small blocks)
Continued

¼ cup orange-flavored liqueur (or orange juice)
1 frozen pound cake (11½ ounces), defrosted
1 can (7 ounces) refrigerated whipped light cream

Early in the day or the day before, prepare strawberry ice. In blender, whirl berries smooth. Add liqueur or juice. Whirl again to dissolve. Pour into deer back pan (10-by-4-by-2 inches) or loaf pan (9-by-5-by-2¾ inches). Freeze until almost firm.

Cut cake into 6 slices. Arrange evenly over strawberry ice. Return to freezer for at least one hour. Then unmold strawberry ice onto serving plate by loosening along edges with knife. Touch bottom of pan in hot water for 10 seconds. (If melting occurs, place dessert in freezer for 10 minutes.)

Frost entire cake with whipped light cream. Return to freezer for an hour, or cut and serve at once. (For ease in cutting, remove from freezer 20 minutes before serving.) *Makes 8 servings.*

STRAWBERRY MOUSSE WITH RUM

1 quart fresh strawberries
¾ cup sugar
6 tablespoons light rum
2 envelopes unflavored gelatin
1 pint heavy cream, whipped
   Fresh mint leaves or shaved chocolate curls or extra whole perfect berries (optional)

Wash and hull strawberries. Mash or process in food processor or blender until crushed. Add sugar. Stir gently until sugar is dissolved.

Measure rum into small pan. Sprinkle gelatin over rum. Allow to stand a moment or two until gelatin is softened.

Place over low heat. Cook, stirring until mixture is clear and gelatin is dissolved, about 2 or 3 minutes. Cool, then combine with sweetened fruit.

Fold whipped cream into strawberry mixture. Spoon into oiled mold or decorative bowl. Refrigerate until firm, about 3 hours. (You may refrigerate up to 2 days before serving.)

To serve, unmold onto chilled platter. Decorate with berries, fresh mint leaves or shaved chocolate curls. *Makes 8 servings.*

STRAWBERRY SPRING THAW

½ cup butter or margarine, melted
¼ cup firmly packed brown sugar
1 cup flour
½ cup chopped nuts
2 egg whites
1 cup sugar
1 pint strawberries, sliced
1 tablespoon lemon juice
1 teaspoon vanilla
1 cup whipping cream, whipped

In a jelly-roll pan, stir melted butter and brown sugar. With a fork, mix in flour and nuts. Distribute over bottom of pan. Bake at 400 degrees for 15 to 20 minutes, stirring occasionally. Set aside to cool.

In a large mixing bowl, beat whites to soft peaks, gradually adding the cup of sugar. Add berries, lemon juice and vanilla. (Note that beater crushes sliced berries sufficiently.) Beat on high speed until triple in volume and stiff peaks form. Fold in whipped cream.

Spread all but ½-cup crumbs in bottom of 9-inch spring-form pan. Top with egg white mixture, then remaining crumbs. Freeze.

To serve, remove ring of pan. Transfer to serving platter. Cut in wedges. *Makes 12 servings.*

SUMMER FRUIT PUDDING

1 large loaf French bread
3 cups sliced fresh plums
1⅔ cups sugar, divided
½ teaspoon cinnamon
2 cups sliced fresh peaches

Trim crusts from bread; cut into half-inch slices. Line a one and one-half quart Charlotte mold or round bowl with bread, pressing firmly with fingers. In saucepan, cook plums with 1 cup sugar and cinnamon, stirring constantly, until plums are soft, about 10 minutes. Cook peaches with two-thirds cup sugar, stirring constantly, until peaches are soft, about 10 minutes. Layer plums and peaches in the bread-lined mold. Cover top of mold with remaining bread slices. Place flat plate and heavy weight on top. Refrigerate overnight. Unmold and serve with sweetened whipped cream, if desired. *Makes 6 servings*

TWENTY-MINUTE LEMON MOUSSE

2 envelopes gelatin
½ cup cold water
1 cup boiling water
2 cups (1 pint) lemon sherbet
1 container (9 ounces) frozen whipped topping, thawed

In a large bowl, mix unflavored gelatin with cold water. Add boiling water and stir until gelatin is completely dissolved. Gradually add sherbet; stir until completely melted. Blend in whipped topping. Spoon into dessert dishes; chill 15 minutes.

Makes 8 servings.

WATERMELON ICE CREAM

4	cups watermelon juice, divided
5	tablespoons flour
¼	teaspoon salt
3	cups sugar
5	eggs, slightly beaten
2	tablespoons fresh lemon juice
5	cups heavy cream

To prepare watermelon juice, cut watermelon in cubes and rub through strainer to remove seeds (⅓ of a medium watermelon yields about 4 cups juice). In large saucepan mix together flour, salt and sugar. Stir in eggs and 2 cups watermelon juice. Cook over low heat, stirring constantly, until mixture thickens enough to coat a metal spoon. Remove from heat. Cool. Stir in remaining 2 cups watermelon juice, lemon juice and heavy cream. Pour into can of 6-quart ice cream freezer. Insert dasher. Place can in freezer container. Layer crushed ice and rock salt in freezer around container according to directions for freezer. Follow manufacturer's directions for freezing ice cream. Ripen ice cream in freezer, or turn into plastic containers or bowl, cover and freeze 2 hours.

Makes 4 quarts.

Note: If freezer is not large enough for 4 quarts, freeze ice cream in 2 batches.

WATERMELON POPSICLES

3	cups watermelon juice
½	cup sugar
½	cup water
2	teaspoons fresh lemon juice

To prepare watermelon juice, cut watermelon into cubes and rub through a strainer to remove seeds. In small saucepan mix together sugar and water. Simmer 3 minutes. Remove from heat. Stir in watermelon juice and lemon juice. Turn into 2 ice trays. Freeze until very mushy and insert a popsicle stick in each cube. Freeze solid.

Makes about 36 small popsicles.

WHOLE PINEAPPLE WITH RUM ICE CREAM

1	large whole ripe pineapple
2	tablespoons sugar
1	quart vanilla ice cream
¼	cup dark rum

Cut off pineapple top about 2 inches down from base of green fronds. Wrap top in foil and freeze.

Cut around rind with sharp knife, being careful not to pierce shell. Remove pieces of pineapple as you progress. Continue to cut out fruit until shell is hollow. Refrigerate shell.

Chop about 1 cup of fruit. Place in small bowl. Add sugar.

Soften ice cream. When soft but not melted, add the cup of chopped, sugared pineapple.

Stir in rum. Spoon into pineapple shell. Cover with plastic wrap and place in the freezer.

Remove from freezer about 15 minutes before serving. Replace pineapple top. To serve, scoop out ice cream with large spoon.   *Makes 4 servings.*

OTHER GOODIES

APPLE BROWN BETTY

½	cup wheat germ, regular or brown sugar and honey
½	cup fresh bread crumbs (1 slice bread)
¼	teaspoon cinnamon
¼	teaspoon nutmeg
2	tablespoons butter or margarine, melted
2½	cups peeled, sliced apples (2 large)
3	tablespoons packed brown sugar
1	tablespoon lemon juice
1	teaspoon grated lemon rind
3	tablespoons hot water

Combine wheat germ, bread crumbs, cinnamon and nutmeg. Add melted butter, tossing to combine. Set aside. Combine apples, sugar, lemon juice and rind. Mix well to coat apples. Place 1 tablespoon wheat germ mixture in each of three 10-ounce custard cups. Divide apple mixture into 3 portions. Divide one portion equally into custard cups. Repeat layers of wheat germ and apples twice. Top with remaining wheat germ mixture. Add 1 tablespoon hot water to each custard cup.

Continued

Cover with foil. Bake at 350 degrees for 15 minutes. Uncover and bake 10 minutes longer. Serve warm with ice cream, whipped cream or cream if desired.   *Makes 3 servings.*

Note: Dessert may be baked in 1-quart casserole. Bake, covered, at 350 degrees for 25 minutes. Uncover and bake 15 minutes longer.

APPLE-CRANBERRY BROWN BETTY

1½	cups fresh bread crumbs
¼	cup butter or margarine, melted
3	cups sliced pared apples (about 3 large apples)
1	teaspoon grated fresh lemon rind
3	tablespoons fresh lemon juice
½	cup fresh cranberries
½	cup packed brown sugar
½	teaspoon salt
1	teaspoon cinnamon
¼	teaspoon nutmeg
	Dash cloves
⅓	cup chopped walnuts

Mix bread crumbs and butter. Line the bottom of a shallow one and one-half-quart baking dish with one-third of the bread crumb mixture. Toss apples and cranberries with lemon rind and juice. Mix brown sugar, salt and spices. Place half the apples and cranberries over the bread crumbs. Sprinkle with half the sugar mixture. Top with one-third the bread crumb mixture and half the walnuts. Add remaining apples and cranberries, sprinkle with remaining sugar mixture, bread crumbs and walnuts. Cover and bake in 350-degree oven about 30 minutes or until apples are nearly tender. Uncover and bake about 15 minutes longer. Serve warm or cooled with whipped cream or ice cream.
                    Makes 4 servings.

BABAS AU RHUM

1	package (13¾ ounces) hot roll mix
2	egg yolks
1½	cups plus 2 tablespoons sugar
2	tablespoons grated lemon peel
1	cup water
½	slice lemon
½	slice orange
1	stick cinnamon
1	whole clove
¾	cup dark rum

Pour water as directed on package into large bowl and stir in yeast from packet until dissolved. Blend in egg yolk. Add flour from package, lemon peel and 2 tablespoons sugar. Stir until well blended. Cover bowl and let rise in warm place, free from draft, until doubled in bulk (about 45 minutes).

While batter is rising, make rum syrup. Combine water, remaining 1½ cups sugar, lemon, orange, cinnamon and clove in saucepan. Simmer 5 minutes. Remove from heat and stir in rum.

Stir down dough and spoon into greased small muffin cups, about two-thirds full. Let rise again until batter reaches the top.

Bake at 350 degrees for 10 minutes or until done. Place in shallow dishes and cover with rum sauce. Baste several times. Cover and refrigerate for up to two weeks.   *Makes 2 to 3 dozen babas.*

Note: To give as gifts pack in attractive lidded jars, cover with sauce.

BAKED HAWAIIAN PAPAYA

2	papayas
	Cinnamon
	Nutmeg
4	teaspoons brown sugar
4	teaspoons butter or margarine
	Lemon or lime wedges

Cut each papaya in half lengthwise. With spoon, scoop out seeds and discard. Sprinkle each papaya half with cinnamon, nutmeg and some of brown sugar. Place a teaspoon butter in hollow of each half. Place papayas, cut sides up, in baking pan or cookie sheet. Bake at 300 degrees for 30 minutes. Serve with lemon or lime wedges.
                    Makes 4 servings.

BANANA CHEESECAKE SUPREME

1	cup graham cracker crumbs, divided
⅔	cup sugar, divided
3	tablespoons butter or margarine, melted
2	envelopes unflavored gelatin
2	eggs, separated
½	cup milk
2	teaspoons lemon juice
1	teaspoon grated lemon rind
3	cups (24 ounces) cottage cheese
5	medium bananas, divided
1	cup heavy cream, whipped
	Lemon Glaze (recipe follows)

Combine ¾ cup cracker crumbs and 2 tablespoons sugar; blend in butter. Press mixture evenly on the bottom of a 9-inch springform pan. Chill.

Mix gelatin and remaining sugar in medium saucepan. Beat together egg yolks and milk; stir into gelatin mixture. Stir over low heat, until gelatin is completely dissolved, about 5 minutes. Remove from heat, stir in lemon juice and rind. Beat cottage cheese on high speed of electric mixer until smooth, 4 to 5 minutes; gradually beat in gelatin mixture. Chill, stirring occasionally, until mixture mounds slightly when dropped from a spoon. Beat egg whites until stiff, but not dry; fold into gelatin mixture. Peel 2 bananas and dice; fold into gelatin mixture. Fold in whipped cream. Pour into prepared pan. Chill until firm, about 3 hours. Remove sides of pan. Press remaining ¼ cup crumbs around sides of cake.

Peel 3 bananas and cut into slices; dip in Lemon Glaze. Arrange slices in rings on top of cheesecake starting at outside rim of cake and working toward the center. Chill 30 minutes before serving.
Makes 12 servings.

LEMON GLAZE:
⅓ cup lemon juice
½ cup sugar
1 teaspoon cornstarch
¼ cup water

Combine lemon juice and sugar in medium saucepan, cook over low heat until sugar is dissolved. Mix cornstarch with water; stir into saucepan. Cook, stirring constantly, until mixture boils and thickens.

BELGIAN WAFFLES

4 frozen waffles
1 pint strawberries, hulled and halved
2 tablespoons confectioners' sugar
2 tablespoons orange juice
½ teaspoon grated orange rind
1 cup frozen whipped topping, thawed

Toast waffles, and cool. Place on dessert dishes. Combine strawberries, sugar, orange juice and rind, stirring until sugar dissolves. Spoon onto waffles and top with whipped topping. Serve at once.
Makes 4 servings.

BLUEBERRY-BANANA CRISP

4 cups fresh blueberries, rinsed and drained
2 ripe bananas, sliced
¼ cup cornstarch
½ cup sugar
1 cup water
½ teaspoon cardamom

½ teaspoon nutmeg
1 cup cornflake crumbs
½ cup flour
½ cup chopped walnuts
1 cup sugar
½ cup butter or margarine

In a bowl, mix blueberries, bananas, cornstarch, sugar, water and spices. Pour mixture into a 1½-quart casserole. In a bowl, mix remaining ingredients with fingers until crumbly. Sprinkle crumbs evenly over blueberries.

Bake in a preheated 350-degree oven for 40 to 45 minutes or until very brown and crisp. Serve warm topped with whipped cream or small scoops of vanilla ice cream.
Makes 8 servings.

BLUEBERRY BUCKLE

¼ cup butter or margarine
½ cup sugar
1 egg
¼ teaspoon grated fresh lemon rind
4 teaspoons fresh lemon juice
1 cup unsifted all-purpose flour
1 teaspoon baking powder
¼ teaspoon salt
¼ cup milk
2 cups (1 pint) fresh blueberries, washed
Topping (recipe follows)

In small bowl, cream butter and sugar. Beat in egg, lemon rind and lemon juice. Mix flour, baking powder and salt. Blend into creamed mixture alternately with milk. Turn into greased 9-by-9-by-2-inch baking pan. Sprinkle blueberries over batter. Then sprinkle Topping over blueberries.

Bake in 375-degree oven 60 to 65 minutes or until cake tester inserted in center comes out clean. Serve warm, plain or with whipped cream or lemon sauce.
Makes 8 servings.

TOPPING:
½ cup sugar
⅓ cup unsifted all-purpose flour
¼ teaspoon grated fresh lemon rind
¼ cup butter or margarine

In small bowl, mix sugar, flour and lemon rind. Cut in butter until mixture resembles coarse crumbs. Sprinkle over blueberries.

BLUEBERRY CRUNCH

1¾ cups graham cracker crumbs
⅓ cup butter or margarine, softened
1⅙ cups sugar, divided

Continued

4   cups fresh blueberries, washed and drained
3   tablespoons corn starch
¼   cup water or fruit juice
1   teaspoon nutmeg
½   teaspoon cinnamon
1½   tablespoons butter
4   egg whites, room temperature
½   teaspoon cream of tartar
½   teaspoon vanilla extract

Blend cracker crumbs, butter and ¼ cup sugar. Press firmly against bottom and up sides of well-greased 9-by-9-by-2 inch square pan. Bake in a 325-degree oven for 5 minutes. Cool.

Mix corn starch with water or fruit juice. Toss blueberries with ⅔ cup sugar and spices. Gently fold into corn starch mixture. Let stand for 15 minutes before putting it into crumb crust.

Whip egg whites until frothy. Add cream of tartar. Whip until egg whites are stiff but not dry. Beat in ¼ cup sugar, 1 teaspoon at a time. Do not overbeat. Beat in vanilla. Pour blueberry mixture evenly over crumb crust. Dot with small pieces of butter. Cover with topping. Bake in a 325-degree oven for 40 minutes. Cool on wire rack. Cut into squares. (Dry-pack fresh blueberries can be used in this recipe.)

Makes nine 3-inch-by-3-inch squares.

BOMBAY SCALLOPED APPLES

2   tablespoons butter or margarine
½   cup molasses
⅓   cup fresh lemon juice
½   teaspoon ginger
½   teaspoon curry powder
¼   teaspoon dry mustard
¼   teaspoon salt
5   cups sliced, pared, cored cooking apples
½   cup toasted slivered almonds

Melt butter in small saucepan. Add molasses, lemon juice, ginger, curry powder, dry mustard and salt. Mix well. Arrange apples in a shallow 2-quart baking dish. Pour molasses mixture over apples. Sprinkle with almonds. Bake, covered, in 375-degree oven 40 minutes, or until tender, basting occasionally with liquid in baking dish. Serve with chicken, pork or duck.   *Makes 6 servings.*

CHEESECAKE IN A GLASS

CHEESECAKE:
1   tablespoon lemon juice
    Thin yellow peel of ½ lemon
1   envelope unflavored gelatin
½   cup hot water
⅓   cup sugar
2   egg yolks
1   package (8 ounces) cream cheese
4   regular-sized ice cubes
1   cup dairy sour cream

PLUM SAUCE:
12   fresh ripe plums, quartered and pitted
1   cup sugar
¾   cup water

CRUST (OPTIONAL):
¼   cup Zwieback or cookie crumbs
1   teaspoon sugar

CHEESECAKE: Put lemon juice, peel, gelatin and hot water into blender container. Blend at high speed 40 seconds (or use rotary beater). Scrape down sides with spatula; blend again. Add sugar, yolks and cream cheese. Blend 10 seconds. Add ice cubes one at a time and sour cream; blend until smooth. Pour into covered refrigerator container. Chill until set.

PLUM SAUCE: Put plums, sugar and water in saucepan. Bring to a boil, stirring gently to dissolve sugar; cover and simmer 8 minutes. remove 12 plum slices with slotted spoon; reserve for garnish. Pour remaining plums and juice into blender container. Blend on high speed until smooth. Taste for sweetness, adding more sugar if desired; blend again, if necessary. Pour into pitcher and refrigerate.

CRUST: In small mixing bowl, combine Zwieback crumbs with sugar; cover and set aside.

To serve: Sprinkle crumbs into 6 tall stemmed dessert glasses. Spoon cheesecake into glasses, dividing evenly. Top each serving with reserved poached plum slices. Serve with Plum Sauce.

Makes 5 to 6 servings; makes 25 cups sauce.

CHERRIES WITH ENGLISH CREAM

2   egg yolks
2   tablespoons sugar
2   teaspoons flour
½   cup hot milk
½   teaspoon vanilla extract
½   cup heavy cream
1   tablespoon powdered sugar
1–2   tablespoons sherry (optional)

4 cups fresh sweet cherries
Whole fresh sweet cherries for
garnish, optional

Combine egg yolks, sugar and flour in top of double boiler. Place over simmering water. Gradually add hot milk and vanilla. Cook and stir until thickened and smooth, about 5 minutes.

Cool thoroughly. Stir occasionally.

Whip cream with powdered sugar until stiff. Fold whipped cream and sherry into cooled sauce.

Wash and stem cherries. Pit, if desired.

Divide cherries among 4 dessert dishes. Pour sauce over cherries just before serving. Garnish with whole cherry if desired.   *Makes 4 servings.*

CHERRY PARTY COMPOTE

2 cups fresh or frozen blueberries
2 cups fresh, frozen or canned
pineapple chunks, drained
4 cups fresh sweet cherries, stemmed
and pitted if desired
2 cups fresh apricot or peach halves
1½ cups chilled white wine
2 tablespoons orange liqueur
1 cup club soda
Mint sprigs

In large glass bowl or compote, layer blueberries, pineapple chunks, half of the cherries, apricots and remaining cherries. Combine wine and liqueur; pour over fruits. Chill thoroughly. Just before serving, pour club soda over all and garnish with mint sprigs.   *Makes 12 to 15 servings.*

CHINESE CRACKLING FRUIT

½ cup light corn syrup
¾ cup water
2 cups sugar
1 tablespoon sesame seeds
1½ pounds fresh plums, halved
1 basket strawberries
2 bananas, peeled and cut into chunks
1 pound fresh seedless grapes,
separated into small clusters
Bamboo skewers
Bowl of ice water

Combine corn syrup, water and sugar in a 2½-quart saucepan. Cook over high heat, stirring until sugar is dissolved. Boil until temperature reaches 300 degrees on a candy thermometer. Pour syrup into a chafing dish over a simmering water bath. Add sesame seeds. Adjust heat to keep syrup at a gentle

simmer. Skewer fruit onto bamboo skewers and dip into syrup. Plunge into ice water. Remove and serve at once.   *Makes 6 servings.*

CHOCOLATE FONDUE

6 ounces (6 squares) semi-sweet
chocolate
1 tablespoon instant coffee
½ teaspoon dried orange rind
¼ cup butter or margarine
1 teaspoon rum flavoring

DIPPERS:
Banana chunks, dark sweet cherries,
large marshmallows, cubes of pound
cake, mandarin orange sections,
maraschino cherries

In a 1-quart saucepan combine chocolate, coffee, orange rind and butter. Place 8 inches over low coals (on aluminum foil if desired) and stir constantly until melted and well blended. Stir in rum flavoring. Keep warm. Serve with a variety of dippers.   *Makes 6 to 8 servings.*

CREPES WITH FRUIT CUSTARD

2½ cups diced assorted soft fresh or
canned fruits
1 teaspoon pure vanilla extract
¼ teaspoon ground nutmeg
12 Crepes (recipe follows)
Low-Sugar Custard Sauce (recipe
follows)

In a small bowl combine fruit with vanilla and nutmeg. Spoon about 2 tablespoons of the fruit in center of each crepe. Fold into cylinder shape and arrange on platter. Pour custard sauce over all and serve.   *Makes 12 portions.*

CREPE BATTER:
2 eggs
⅔ cup milk
1 tablespoon salad oil
½ teaspoon pure vanilla extract
½ cup all-purpose flour
¼ teaspoon salt
¼ teaspoon ground nutmeg

In a small mixing bowl beat eggs. Add milk, oil and vanilla extract; mix well. Add flour, salt and nutmeg; beat until smooth. Lightly grease and heat a 5-inch skillet. Pour approximately 2 tablespoons crepe batter into skillet, quickly tilting pan to spread over bottom. When delicately brown, turn to brown on other side. Repeat, lightly greasing skillet each time.   *Makes approximately 12 crepes.*

LOW-SUGAR CUSTARD SAUCE:

2	tablespoons cornstarch
¼	cup sugar
⅛	teaspoon salt
2	cups milk
3	egg yolks
1	teaspoon pure vanilla extract
¼	teaspoon ground nutmeg

In a medium saucepan mix cornstarch, sugar and salt. Blend in 2 tablespoons of the milk until smooth. Stir in remaining milk. Cook and stir over moderate heat until mixture thickens. In a medium bowl mix egg yolks, vanilla extract and nutmeg with 2 tablespoons of the hot custard mixture. Blend in remaining custard. Cover surface with waxed paper and cool. Serve over fruit-filled crepes.   *Makes 2 cups.*

CREPES INDIE WITH PEACH SAUCE

1	cup milk
2	eggs
¼	teaspoon salt
⅔	cup flour
	Butter (about 3 tablespoons)
½	cup honey
1	cup water
	Cinnamon stick
3	cups sliced fresh peaches (about 1 pound)
2	tablespoons sliced almonds

Early in the day, prepare crepes as follows: Put milk, eggs, salt and flour into blender container. Whirl 30 seconds. Scrape down sides; cover and whirl 10 seconds more. Refrigerate 1 hour.

To cook crepes, heat a 7-inch crepe pan, brushed with butter, until almost smoking. Pour about 2 tablespoons batter into hot pan, tipping it to allow batter to cover bottom of pan. Cook 1 minute. turn crepe and cook ½ minute on second side. Repeat operation for remaining batter, sliding each crepe onto rack to cool before stacking. Wrap and refrigerate crepes until needed.

To serve: Put honey, water and cinnamon stick in saucepan or chafing dish. Bring to boil; reduce heat and simmer 5 minutes. Add peaches, simmer 5 minutes more or until peaches are tender. Fold crepes in quarters and place in pan. Spoon sauce over folded crepes. When heated through, serve onto individual dessert plates, spooning sauce over all. Garnish each serving with sliced almonds. If desired, top with a scoop of vanilla ice cream. Serve at once.   *Makes 6 servings, 18 crepes.*

Note: Any extra crepes can be stored in freezer for future use

DELICATE DESSERT CREPES

2	eggs
1	tablespoon sugar
1	teaspoon salt
1	cup cold water
½	cup light cream (or substitute half-and-half plus 2 tablespoons melted butter or margarine)
⅔	cup all-purpose flour

Beat eggs with hand beater, electric mixer or in an electric blender until very light and frothy. Then beat in sugar and salt. Add water and cream alternately with the flour, a small amount at a time, beating well after each addition. Let stand 1 hour. For each crepe, pour 2 tablespoons batter into hot well-buttered 5-inch skillet, or 3 tablespoons into a 6½-inch skillet, tilting pan to spread batter and turning to brown both sides. Spread with jam, fold in half, then in half again to form a triangle.

Makes about 18 five-inch or 12 6½-inch crepes.

Note: Store leftover batter in the refrigerator; beat thoroughly before using. Recipe may be halved.

To freeze crepes, stack between layers of wax paper, wrap and freeze. To reheat, brush frozen crepes with butter and place in shallow baking dish. Cover and heat at 350 degrees for 20 minutes.

EASY CARAMEL APPLES

6	medium red apples
1	package (14 ounces) light caramels
¼	cup light corn syrup
2	tablespoons water

Wash and dry apples; remove stems and insert wooden skewers or spoons into stem ends. Melt caramels in top of double boiler. Add corn syrup and water and mix until smooth. Remove pan from heat and swirl apples, one at a time, in caramel mixture. Let excess drip off, place on waxed paper and refrigerate. *Makes 6 apples.*

FRESH FRUIT REFRAIN

4	fresh nectarines
	Lemon juice
1	cup blueberries
1	cup plain yogurt
3	tablespoons maple syrup
½	teaspoon grated orange peel
	Cinnamon

Slice nectarines from pit; sprinkle with lemon juice to prevent discoloration. Arrange in rows in shallow serving dish. Sprinkle blueberries between and at ends of nectarine rows. In small bowl, combine yogurt, maple syrup and orange peel. Pour into serving dish and sprinkle with cinnamon.
Makes 5 to 6 servings.

FRESH PEACH DUMPLINGS

1	package (8 ounces) crescent rolls
¼	cup firmly packed brown sugar
1	tablespoon flour
½	teaspoon nutmeg
4	fresh peaches, peeled, halved and pits removed
8	walnut halves
	Milk
	Brown sugar or coarse sugar

Divide crescent rolls into 4 portions (2 triangles to each portion) and roll into squares. Combine brown sugar, flour and nutmeg in a mixing bowl; blend thoroughly. Roll peach halves in brown sugar mixture. Place two walnut halves in center cavity and sandwich two halves together to form whole peach. Place in center of dough squares and bring ends of dough up, pinching to seal. Brush with milk and sprinkle with sugar. Place on cookie sheet and bake in 375-degree oven 12 to 15 minutes or until golden brown. Serve warm or at room temperature.
Makes 4 servings.

FRESH STRAWBERRY FRITTERS

2	pints fresh strawberries
1	cup complete buttermilk pancake mix
⅔	cup water
	Powdered sugar
	Whipped cream (optional)

Wash whole strawberries and pat dry with paper towels. (Remove stems or leave them intact.)

Combine pancake mix with water using rotary beater. Beat just until smooth. Dip berries in batter, coating all but stem. Fry in hot oil (400 degrees) until golden, about 30 seconds. Drain.

Dust with powdered sugar. Serve at once. If desired, offer whipped cream for dipping.
Makes 6 servings.

GRANOLA APPLE BETTY

6	cups sliced, peeled apples
½	cup sugar
2	tablespoons flour
2	teaspoons lemon juice
1	teaspoon apple-pie spice
¼	teaspoon salt
2	tablespoons butter or margarine, divided
3	cups spiced granola, divided

In large bowl combine apples, sugar, flour, lemon juice, apple-pie spice and salt. Arrange half of apple mixture in buttered shallow 1½-quart casserole. Dot with 1 tablespoon butter. Sprinkle with 1½ cups of granola.

Repeat layering using remaining apple mixture, butter and granola.

Cover and bake in preheated 375-degree oven until apples are tender, about 40 minutes.

Let cool slightly. Serve with whipped cream or ice cream, if desired. *Makes 9 portions.*

HAWAIIAN FRUIT BOATS WITH MAIDEN HAIR

3	ripe papayas
1½	cups sliced sugared strawberries

Continued

3   egg yolks
1   cup dry white wine
     Juice of lemon
3   tablespoons sugar
     A good pinch of ginger

Cut papayas in half. Scoop out seeds and fill hollows with strawberries. Beat rest of ingredients in top of double boiler until light and frothy. Spoon immediately over strawberries and papaya.

Makes 6 servings.

HOT CITRUS CUP

1   32-ounce jar chilled fruit salad
1   cup chutney
1   teaspoon curry
1   teaspoon powdered ginger
1   teaspoon nutmeg
1   tablespoon wine vinegar

Preheat broiler. Drain the fruit salad (save the juice in an empty jar for a refreshing drink or another recipe) and divide it among 6 scallop shells or custard cups, or place in an 8-inch pan. Chop the chutney until it is rather fine. Scrape the chutney into a mixing bowl and stir in the curry, ginger, nutmeg and vinegar. Distribute the chutney topping over the top of the fruits and broil for about 3 minutes or until the fruit is heated through and the topping is hot and bubbly.   *Makes 6 servings.*

MOCHA CHEESECAKE ROYALE

     Nut-Crumb Shell (recipe follows)
4   large eggs, separated
¼   teaspoon salt
¼   teaspoon cream of tartar
1   cup sugar
3   (8 ounce) packages cream cheese
1   teaspoon instant coffee crystals
¼   cup brandy
1   cup dairy sour cream
     Chocolate Curls (directions follow) and
     strawberries (optional)
     Mocha Brandy Sauce (recipe follows)

Prepare Nut-Crumb Shell. Beat egg whites with salt and cream of tartar until stiff. Gradually beat in ½ cup sugar, beating to a stiff meringue; set aside. With same beater, beat cream cheese until softened. Add egg yolks, remaining ½ cup sugar, coffee crystals and brandy. Continue beating until mixture becomes thick and smooth. Fold in meringue, half at a time, and turn into the baked Nut-Crumb Shell. Bake in a 350-degree oven about 30 minutes, until mixture is barely firm in center when pan is gently shaken back and forth.

Stir sour cream until smooth and gently spread over top of cake. Return to oven, turn heat off and bake 5 minutes longer. Then open oven door and let cake cool on oven rack 1 hour. Remove from oven and cool thoroughly before cutting. Decorate with chocolate curls and fresh strawberries, if desired. Serve with Mocha Brandy Sauce.

Makes 8 to 12 servings.

NUT-CRUMB SHELL:

Finely crush zweiback to measure 1 cup crumbs (about 16 small slices). Combine with 3 tablespoons each sugar and melted butter, ⅓ finely chopped filberts (or walnuts or pecans), mixing well. Pack firmly over bottom and up sides of an 8 or 9-inch spring form pan, to make a shell 2 to 2½ inches deep. Bake in 350-degree oven 10 minutes.

MOCHA BRANDY SAUCE:

Blend together 1 tablespoon cornstarch, 1 teaspoon instant coffee crystals, ⅛ teaspoon salt and 1 cup water in a medium-size saucepan. Heat to boiling stirring.

Add ¼ cup brown sugar (packed), stirring until dissolved. remove from heat and add ¼ cup California brandy, 1 teaspoon chocolate extract and ¼ teaspoon vanilla. Cool before serving.

Makes 1⅓ cups sauce.

TO MAKE CHOCOLATE CURLS:

Use a piece of semi-sweet or milk chocolate about the width of the blade of a vegetable peeler. Hold blade of peeler firmly against chocolate and draw it toward you to form a curl. Chocolate must be at room temperature. If it tends to shatter rather than curl, warm chocolate slightly by placing palm of hand on it a few seconds.

NECTARINE DESSERT OMELET

5   large eggs, separated
     Custard Sauce (recipe follows)
¼   teaspoon salt
¼   teaspoon cream of tartar
3   tablespoons sugar
¼   cup mashed fresh nectarines
1   tablespoon amber rum (optional)
1   teaspoon lemon juice
1   tablespoon butter
     Rum-Glazed Nectarines (recipe
     follows)
     Mint (for garnish)

Separate egg, placing 3 yolks for omelet in 1 small bowl, 2 yolks for sauce in another.

Prepare Custard Sauce. Set aside to cool.

Beat all egg whites with salt and cream of tartar to stiff peaks. Beat in 2 tablespoons sugar, 1 at a time.

With same beater, beat 2 yolks with mashed nectarines, rum and lemon juice until thick and light yellow.

Melt butter in 9-inch skillet over moderate heat. Pour egg yolk mixture over egg whites and gently fold together.

Pour mixture into skillet. Sprinkle remaining 1 tablespoon sugar over top. Cook over moderate heat 2 to 3 minutes, then place in 350-degree oven. Bake 15 to 20 minutes, until well puffed and lightly browned on top.

Meanwhile, prepare rum-glazed nectarines.

When omelet is done, turn onto serving plate. Top with some of rum-glazed nectarines. Fold over. Top with remaining nectarines.

Decorate with mint sprigs, if desired. Cut into wedges and serve with custard sauce.

Makes about 4 servings.

CUSTARD SAUCE:

Mix 2 tablespoons sugar with 1 teaspoon cornstarch and dash salt in small saucepan. Stir in 1¼ cups half-and-half (thin cream).

Cook, stirring constantly, over moderate heat until mixture reaches full boil.

Beat 2 reserved egg yolks lightly. Stir hot sauce into yolks. Return to saucepan. Cook 1 minute longer over very low heat without allowing to boil, stirring constantly.

Remove from heat. Stir in 1 teaspoon vanilla.

Makes 1⅓ cups sauce.

RUM-GLAZED NECTARINES:

Melt 2 tablespoons butter in small skillet. Stir in ¼ cup sugar, 2 tablespoons amber rum, 1 teaspoon lemon juice and dash mace.

Add 2 cups sliced fresh nectarines. Simmer 3 to 4 minutes, until nicely glazed.

ORANGE FRITTERS

2	tablespoons soft butter or margarine
½	cup sugar
2	eggs
½	cup orange juice
	Grated rind of 1 orange
1	teaspoon Angostura aromatic bitters
2	cups sifted all-purpose flour
½	teaspoon salt
3	teaspoons baking powder
	Fat or oil at least 2 inches deep, heated to 360 degrees

In a bowl, cream butter and sugar until well blended. Stir in eggs. Stir in orange juice and rind. Stir in bitters, flour, salt and baking powder. Beat until smooth.

Drop mixture by heaping teaspoons into preheated fat. Fry 2 to 3 minutes or until brown, turn and brown on the other side. Drain on absorbent paper. Cool. Roll in confectioners' sugar just before serving.

Makes 24 fritters.

PARADISE FRUIT COMPOTE

4	oranges
1	papaya
1	pineapple
2½	cups halved, pitted Ribier and Tokay grapes (about ½ pound)
1	lemon, sliced and seeded
1	cup Marsala wine
1	cup water
¾	cup sugar
1	stick cinnamon
3	whole cloves

Cut 3 strips orange peel from 1 orange, using vegetable peeler; reserve. Peel oranges and cut into crosswise slices. Pare papaya, cut in half lengthwise and remove seeds. Cut into cubes. To prepare pineapple, cut off stem and crown ends. Cut off rind all around from top to bottom. Remove eyes with pointed knife. Cut into quarters lengthwise. Cut away core. Cut remaining meat into fingers about 2-inches long. Combine orange slices, papaya, pineapple, grapes, lemon slices and kiwi slices in large bowl. Combine wine, water, sugar, cinnamon stick, cloves and orange peel in saucepan. Stir over medium heat until sugar dissolves. Reduce heat and simmer 5 minutes. Remove spices and peel. Cool to lukewarm. Pour syrup over fruit in bowl; cover and refrigerate 6 hours or overnight.

Makes about 2½ quarts or 12 servings.

PATRIOTIC CHERRY CHEESECAKE

1¼	cups graham cracker crumbs
3	tablespoons softened butter or margarine
2	envelopes unflavored gelatin
¾	cup sugar
¼	teaspoon salt
2	eggs, separated
1	cup milk
1	teaspoon grated lemon peel
1	tablespoon lemon juice
3	cups creamed cottage cheese
½	cup red maraschino cherries
1½	cups blueberries
3	tablespoons sugar
	Stemmed red maraschino cherries

Continued

Thoroughly blend together crumbs and butter; press on bottom and 1 inch up sides of 9-inch spring-form pan; chill.

In small saucepan, mix gelatin, ¾ cup sugar and salt. Beat together egg yolks and milk; stir into gelatin mixture. Cook over medium heat, stirring constantly, until mixture thickens enough to coat a metal spoon. Add lemon peel and juice; cool.

Blend cheese in electric blender until smooth; stir into gelatin mixture. Chill until mixture is thick enough to mound slightly when dropped from a spoon. Beat egg whites until foamy; gradually add 3 tablespoons sugar, beating until stiff. Fold into cheese mixture.

Pour half over crust; chill about 20 minutes or until set. Sprinkle ½ cup cherries and 1 cup blueberries over filling. Pour remaining filling on top. Chill until firm, about 3 hours. Garnish with remaining blueberries and stemmed cherries.

Makes one 9-inch cake or 12 servings.

PEACHES IN AMARETTO

10	pounds peaches
	SOAKING SOLUTION:
8	cups water
1	tablespoon salt
1	tablespoon vinegar or commercial ascorbic acid mixture
3	cups water
2	cups sugar
½	cup Amaretto

Prepare home canning jars and lids according to manufacturer's instructions.

Peel peaches; cut into halves and remove pits. Place halves in soaking solution to prevent darkening. Rinse and drain. Cook a few peaches at a time in water until heated through. Drain and pack into hot jars, leaving ½-inch head space. Cook water and sugar until sugar dissolves. Carefully ladle over peaches, leaving ¾-inch head space. Add 2 tablespoons Amaretto to each quart jar, leaving ½-inch head space. Remove air bubbles with a non-metallic spatula. Adjust caps.

Process 25 minutes in boiling-water-bath canner. *Makes about 4 quart-jars.*

PEANUT BUTTER PANOCHA

3	cups firmly packed light brown sugar (1 pound)
¼	teaspoon salt
½	cup milk
1	cup crunchy peanut butter
2	teaspoons vanilla
¼	cup chopped salted peanuts

In a large saucepan combine brown sugar, salt and milk. Cook at a boil without stirring until a candy thermometer registers soft ball or 238 degrees or until a small amount of syrup dropped into cold water forms a soft ball. Remove from heat and stir in peanut butter and vanilla. Stir until mixture is well blended. Pour mixture into a buttered 8-inch square pan. Sprinkle top with peanuts. Let stand at room temperature until mixture hardens. With a sharp knife cut panocha into small squares. Wrap each square in plastic wrap and store until ready to serve. *Makes about 18 pieces.*

PEANUT BUTTER CREAM CHEESE DESSERT

1	cup graham cracker crumbs
¼	cup firmly packed brown sugar
¼	cup crunchy peanut butter
2	tablespoons melted butter or margarine
½	cup confectioners' sugar
3	tablespoons crunchy peanut butter
1	package (3 ounces) cream cheese
6	tablespoons sugar
1	cup (½ pint) heavy cream, whipped
1	can (1 pound, 4 ounces) pie-sliced apples, drained
	Ground cinnamon, ¼ teaspoon, or as desired

Combine crumbs, brown sugar, ¼ cup peanut butter and butter. Mix until crumbly. In another bowl combine confectioners' sugar and 3 tablespoons peanut butter. Mix until crumbly. Mash cream cheese and beat in sugar gradually until mixture is very soft and creamy. Fold in whipped cream. Sprinkle two-thirds of the graham crumb mixture over the bottom of a 6×10×2-inch pan. Press crumbs into place evenly. Spoon half the cheese mixture over the crumbs. Carefully spread cheese into an even layer. Place apple slice evenly over cheese. Sprinkle with cinnamon. Sprinkle two-thirds of the confectioners' sugar mixture over apples. Top with remaining cheese mixture, spreading cheese evenly over crumbs. Top with remaining graham cracker crumbs and remaining confectioners' sugar mixture. Cover pan with foil and chill 24 hours before serving. Cut into squares to serve.

Makes about 18 squares.

PEARS ANNA

3	tablespoons melted butter, divided
3	tablespoons each packed brown sugar and flour
1/8	teaspoon ground ginger
8	cups cored and thinly-sliced Bosc or other fresh pears
1	teaspoon grated orange peel

Coat a 9-inch oven-proof skillet with 1 tablespoon butter. Combine sugar, flour and ginger. Layer pear slices in pan, spoke-fashion, with stem ends toward center; sprinkle layers with sugar mixture.

Top with remaining sugar mixture, melted butter and orange peel. Cook, uncovered, over medium heat 10 minutes. Bake, uncovered, at 400 degrees for 30 minutes; baste once. *Makes 6 servings.*

PEAR CRISP

2	cans (1 pound each) pear halves, drained
1/3	cup unsifted flour
1/2	cup rolled oats
1/2	cup firmly packed light brown sugar
3/4	teaspoon ground cinnamon
1/2	teaspoon ground nutmeg
1/3	cup corn oil margarine

Arrange pears in a greased 8-inch square baking dish.

Combine flour, oats, brown sugar, cinnamon and nutmeg. Mix in margarine until mixture is crumbly. Sprinkle over pears.

Bake at 375 degrees 30 minutes, or until topping is browned. Serve warm. *Makes 6 servings.*

PEARS IN CREME DE MENTHE

7	pounds pears
	SOAKING SOLUTION:
8	cups water,
1	tablespoon salt,
1	tablespoon vinegar or commercial ascorbic acid mixture
4	cups water
1½	cups sugar
1/2	cup creme de menthe

Prepare home canning jars and lids according to manufacturer's instructions.

Peel pears, cut into halves and core. Place in soaking solution to prevent darkening. Rinse and drain. Cook the pears in water, a layer at a time, until just tender, about 5 minutes. Drain and pack pears into hot jars, leaving ¼-inch head space. Heat water and sugar to make syrup. Remove syrup from heat; stir in creme de menthe. Carefully ladle over pears, leaving ¼-inch head space. Remove air bubbles with a non-metallic spatula. Adjust caps.

Process 20 minutes in boiling-water-bath canner. *Makes about 5 pint-jars.*

PEARS WITH ALMOND CREAM

1	can (29 ounces) Bartlett pear halves
3	large egg yolks
3	tablespoons sugar
1	tablespoon flour
	Dash salt
1	cup half-and-half
1/4	cup almond liqueur
	Poached Meringues (recipe follows)
	Sliced almonds

Drain pears; set aside. Beat yolks, gradually add sugar, beating until mixture thickens and is pale yellow in color. Beat in flour and salt. Gradually add half-and-half. Cook over medium heat, stirring constantly, until custard heavily coats spoon. Do not boil. Add liqueur; remove from heat and cool quickly by placing pan in bowl of ice water. Place plastic wrap directly on surface of custard; refrigerate until chilled. To serve, place 1 Poached Meringue in each individual dessert dish. Top with pear half; spoon about ¼ cup custard over pears. Garnish with almonds. *Makes 6 servings.*

POACHED MERINGUES: Beat 2 egg whites and dash salt until soft peaks form. Gradually add ¼ cup sugar, 1 tablespoon at a time; beat well after each addition until stiff peaks form. In skillet, simmer 3 cups water or milk; drop 6 mounds of meringue on water. Cook slowly, about 5 minutes or until meringues are set; with slotted spoon or spatula remove from pan and drain of towels. *Makes 6 servings.*

PINEAPPLE IN CHABLIS

6	cups pineapple spears (about 2 medium pineapples)
2	cups Chablis
2	cups sugar
1	cup water

Prepare home canning jars and lids according to manufacturer's instructions.

Simmer pineapple in water to cover until heated through. Combine Chablis, sugar and water; simmer over medium-low heat until sugar dissolves. remove from heat. Drain and pack pineapple into hot jars, leaving ¼-inch head space.

Carefully ladle syrup over pineapple, leaving ¼-inch head space. Remove air bubbles with a non-metallic spatula. Adjust caps.

Process 15 minutes in boiling-water-bath canner.   *Makes about 4 pint-jars.*

PLUM 'N' BISCUIT BAKE

1	pound plums, pitted and sliced (about 6-8 plums)
½	cup brown sugar, firmly packed
1	package (3 ounces) cream cheese, softened
¼	cup sugar
1	egg
¼	teaspoon lemon juice
1	package (8 ounces) refrigerator biscuits

Arrange plums in 9-inch layer cake pan. Sprinkle with brown sugar. Bake in 400-degree oven for 20 minutes. Meanwhile in mixing bowl, blend cream cheese, sugar, egg and lemon juice. Remove plums from oven and reduce heat to 350 degrees. Pour cream cheese mixture over plums. Open package of dinner rolls. Arrange them in an overlapping ring over plums. Bake 30 minutes longer. Serve warm.
Makes 8 to 10 servings.

PLUM NOODLE KUGEL

6	ounces farfalla (bow knots) or medium egg noodles (about 2½ cups), uncooked
3	eggs
1	cup sugar
1	teaspoon cinnamon
3¾	cups (1½ pounds) fresh plums, quartered and pitted
1	cup applesauce
1	cup soft bread crumbs
½	cup chopped nuts
2	tablespoons melted butter

Cook noodles in boiling salted water until barely tender. Drain and rinse in cold water. Beat eggs. Add sugar and cinnamon; mix well.

Toss noodles in egg mixture; stir in plums and applesauce. Pour into buttered 2-quart casserole. Combine bread crumbs, nuts and butter; sprinkle over top.

Bake in 350-degree oven, 50 minutes, or until golden. Serve warm with heavy or whipped cream.   *Makes 6 to 8 servings.*

PUMPKIN CHEESECAKE

½	cup graham-cracker crumbs
1	teaspoon ground cinnamon
1½	cups sugar, divided
3	tablespoons flour
1½	teaspoons pumpkin-pie spice
2	packages (8 ounces) cream cheese, softened
1	cup canned pumpkin
1½	teaspoons pure vanilla extract
6	eggs, separated
⅛	teaspoon salt
½	teaspoon cream of tartar
	Whipped cream (optional)

Preheat oven to 275 degrees.

Mix graham-cracker crumbs with cinnamon. Coat bottom and sides of 9-inch well-buttered spring-form pan with crumbs. Set aside.

In large bowl of electric mixer, combine 1 cup sugar with flour and pumpkin-pie spice. Add cream cheese, pumpkin and vanilla extract. Beat until smooth.

In small bowl, beat egg yolks until light and lemon colored. Blend into cheese mixture.

Add salt to egg whites. Beat until foamy. Add cream of tartar. Beat until soft peak form. Gradually beat in remaining ½ cup sugar. Beat until stiff but not dry. Fold into cheese mixture.

Turn into prepared pan. Bake until cake is firm in center, about 1½ hours.

Turn off oven. Open door about 6 inches at top, propping it open with a cake pan. Allow cake to remain in oven until cool, about 2 hours.

Remove cake from oven. Decorate with whipped cream, if desired.   *Makes one 9-inch cake.*

QUICK PEANUT BUTTER CANDY

½	cup margarine
½	cup milk
2	cups sugar
⅔	cup super chunk peanut butter
2	cups quick oats

Mix together margarine, milk and sugar in 2-quart saucepan. Bring to boil and boil 3 minutes. Remove from heat; cool 5 minutes. Add peanut butter and mix thoroughly. Stir in oats. Drop by teaspoonfuls onto waxed paper.   *Makes 60 (1½-inch) candies.*

RAISIN BONANZA BATTER

2	cups flour
1	cup sugar
1	tablespoon cornstarch

3	tablespoons cocoa
2	teaspoons baking soda
1	teaspoon salt
1	teaspoon cinnamon
½	teaspoon each cloves and nutmeg
1½	cups raisins
¼	cup chopped walnuts
1	tablespoon grated orange peel (optional)
2	eggs
1½	cups unsweetened applesauce (15-ounce jar)
½	cup cooking oil

Sift the 9 dry ingredients into a large mixing bowl. Blend in raisins, nuts and peel. Add remaining ingredients. Then beat just until smooth. Pour into greased and floured 10-inch bundt or tube pan. Bake in preheated 350-degree oven 30 minutes. Reduce heat to 300 degrees and bake 20 to 25 minutes more, or until cake tests done. Cool in pan 10 minutes. Invert onto cake rack and cool completely. Before cutting, sprinkle with powdered sugar, if desired.   *Makes 1 large cake or 10 to 12 servings.*

BAR COOKIES:
Spread batter in greased 13-by-9-inch cake pan. Bake 20 to 25 minutes. Cool slightly before cutting.   *Makes about 3 dozen bars (approximately 2-by-3 inches).*

AGED FRUITCAKE:
Brush surface of warm cake with 2 tablespoons brandy. Wrap in cheesecloth, then in foil. Let stand at room temperature 24 hours. Store in refrigerator or freezer until needed, repeating the brandying process each week, if desired.

STEAMED PUDDING:
Wrap cake in foil. Place in steamer on rack over boiling water. Steam 20 minutes. Serve hot, with brandy sauce or hard sauce. (This is especially appropriate if part of cake becomes stale.)

RAISIN COCOA BALLS

4	ounces semi-sweet chocolate
2	tablespoons water
¼	cup butter or margarine (½ stick)
3	egg yolks
¾	cup sifted powdered sugar
1	cup raisins
	Instant hot chocolate mix

In heavy saucepan, over very low heat, melt chocolate with water.

Remove from heat and stir in butter, then egg yolks, one at a time, blending well. Stir in ¾ cup

powdered sugar, beating until mixture is smooth. Add raisins and mix well.

Chill 15 minutes. Pour chocolate mix into paper bag. Then drop chocolate candy by teaspoon into bag one at a time. Shake until coated.

Chill candies until firm. Store in refrigerator.
Makes 2 dozen.

SAUTEED BANANAS

Melt 2 tablespoons butter or margarin in large skillet. Add 4 whole bananas or 3 bananas, halved lengthwise. Cook over low heat, turning once, just until tender, 2 or 3 minutes for halves or 5 minutes for whole bananas.

For dessert, add 1 teaspoon grated lemon or lime rind and 2 teaspoons juice and 2 tablespoons sugar.

For Bananas Flambe, add 2 tablespoons cognac to dessert bananas and ignite.   *Makes 3 to 4 servings.*

SPICY FRUIT TARTS

1	cup frozen whipped topping, thawed
2	tablespoons brown sugar
⅛	teaspoon cinnamon dash of nutmeg
6	individual commercial pastry shells in aluminum foil cups
	Sliced sweetened strawberries

Combine whipped topping, brown sugar and the spices. Spoon into pastry shells and make a depression in center of each. Spoon in strawberries. Chill.   *Makes 6 servings.*

STRAWBERRIES AND POUND CAKE

4	slices (about) pound cake, cut into cubes
¼	cup orange juice
1½	cups sliced sweetened strawberries
1	container (4½ ounces) frozen whipped topping, thawed
½	teaspoon almond extract

Arrange cake cubes in a glass bowl or individual dessert dishes. Sprinkle with orange juice. Spoon strawberries over the cake cubes. Combine whipped topping and almond extract and spread over strawberries. Chill.   *Makes 6 servings.*

STRAWBERRY BISCUIT SHORTCAKE

2	pints strawberries, sliced
1	teaspoon grated orange peel
	Honey
1¾	cups unsifted all-purpose flour
2	tablespoons sugar
1	tablespoon baking powder
1	teaspoon salt
⅓	cup solid vegetable shortening
½	cup plus 2 tablespoons milk
2	tablespoons orange juice
	Butter or margarine, melted
	Honey Pour Cream (recipe follows)

Combine strawberries and one-half teaspoon grated orange peel. Sweeten to taste with honey (about one-fourth cup). Refrigerate 30 minutes. In large mixing bowl, combine remaining one-half teaspoon orange peel and dry ingredient. Cut in shortening with pastry blender or 2 knives until mixture resembles coarse crumbs. Add milk and orange juice. Mix quickly with fork until mixture forms a soft dough. Turn onto lightly floured surface and knead about 6 times. Roll or pat dough to one-half-inch thickness and cut into 3-inch biscuits. Place on ungreased baking sheet and bake in 450-degree oven 12 to 15 minutes, or until golden brown. Split hot biscuits. Brush inside with melted butter, then spoon on about 1 teaspoon honey per biscuit. Fill with sliced strawberries and replace biscuit tops. Spoon additional berries on top of shortcakes. Serve shortcakes warm with Honey Pour Cream.

Makes 8 individual shortcakes.

HONEY POUR CREAM: Combine 1 cup heavy cream with 1 tablespoon honey.

STRAWBERRY FONDUE SPECIAL

1	frozen pound cake (11½ ounces), defrosted
2	pints fresh strawberries, washed, hulled and chilled
	Bamboo skewers or fondue forks
1	package (12 ounces) semi-sweet chocolate morsels
1	package (8 ounces) cream cheese, softened
⅓	cup orange-flavored liqueur or milk
1	can (7 ounces) whipped light cream

Cut pound cake into 1-inch cubes. Thread skewers with one or two cubes of cake and a strawberry. Arrange on serving tray. In fondue pot, over hot water, melt chocolate. Stir in cream cheese until

blended; then liqueur or milk. Fill 1 quart bowl or pitcher with whipped cream.

To serve, dip skewered cake and berries into warm fondue, then into whipped cream.

Makes about 2 cups chocolate sauce, enough for 8 to 10 servings.

Note: One package (16 ounces) frozen, whole, unsweetened strawberries, partially thawed, can be substituted for fresh strawberries. Leftover chocolate sauce can be stored, covered, in refrigerator, and reheated covered. Milk chocolate can be substituted for some of the semi-sweet chocolate.

STRAWBERRY-LEMON DESSERT

1½	teaspoons grated lemon rind
1	cup frozen whipped topping, thawed
2	cups sweetened sliced strawberries

Combine grated lemon rind and whipped topping. Layer in dessert dishes with strawberries.

Makes 4 servings.

STRAWBERRY PARTY CREAM PUFFS

	CREAM PUFFS:
1	cup water
½	cup butter or margarine
1	cup packaged pancake mix
4	eggs

	STRAWBERRY FILLING:
1	package (3⅛ ounces) vanilla pudding and pie filling mix
2	cups fresh strawberry slices
2	teaspoons orange-flavored liqueur (optional)

	STRAWBERRY SAUCE:
2	tablespoons sugar (optional)
2	teaspoons orange-flavored liqueur or orange juice
1½	cups fresh strawberry slices

Heat oven to 375 degrees. For cream puffs, bring water and butter to a boil in medium saucepan; add pancake mix. Stir vigorously until mixture leaves sides of pan and forms a ball; remove from heat.

Add eggs, one at a time, beating well after each addition. Drop by rounded tablespoonfuls onto ungreased cookie sheet. Bake for 25 to 30 minutes or until golden brown; cool.

For filling, prepare pudding according to package directions. Stir in strawberries and liqueur. Chill.

For sauce, sprinkle sugar and liqueur over strawberries; let stand about 1 hour.

To assemble, slice tops off of each cream puff. Fill with pudding mixture; replace tops. Chill. Serve with strawberry sauce and whipped cream, if desired. *Makes 30 cream puffs.*

TOFFEE CRUNCH SQUARES

1¾	cups sugar
⅓	cup light corn syrup
¼	cup heavy cream
¾	cup margarine

Line 2 cookie sheets with aluminum foil. Grease foil. In heavy 2-quart saucepan, stir together sugar, corn syrup and heavy cream until well blended. Stirring constantly, bring to boil over low heat. Add margarine. Stirring occasionally, cook, until temperature on candy thermometer reaches 285 degrees or until a small amount of mixture dropped into cold water separates into threads which are hard but not brittle.

Pour onto prepared cookie sheets. Spread with greased spatula to cover entire surface. Cool a few minutes until a film forms on top. Using a sharp knife, mark surface in squares.

Begin marking candy from outside and work toward center. With wide metal spatula, press along marked lines. Do not break through the film surface. If lines do not hold, cool candy a while longer, then continue to press along marked lines, pressing the spatula deeper without breaking film. When spatula can be pressed to bottom of candy in all lines, candy is shaped. Cool. Break into squares. Store in tightly covered container. *Makes 60 candies.*

WHEAT GERM APPLE BUNDLES

1	cup flour
¼	cup vacuum-packed wheat germ, regular
2	tablespoons sugar
½	teaspoon salt
6	tablespoons butter, softened
2–3	tablespoons water
	Apple Filling (recipe follows)
	Melted butter
	Sugar for tops

Mix flour, wheat germ, sugar and salt in mixing bowl. Cut in butter until mixture is moist and crumbly. Add water gradually, tossing with fork, adding just enough to make a dough. Knead dough briefly on floured board to blend thoroughly.

Divide dough into 4 equal parts. Roll out each into 6- or 7-inch square. Trim edges with pastry wheel if desired. Spoon apple filling into center of squares. Fold in corners to meet in center. Pinch edges together.

Brush with melted butter. Sprinkle with sugar. Lift to baking sheet with wide spatula. Bake in 375-degree oven 25 minutes or until lightly browned. *Makes 4 servings.*

APPLE FILLING:

Pare, core and slice 2 to 3 cooking apples, either tart or mild. That should make about 3 cups. Toss with 1 tablespoon lemon juice. Add ¼ cup sugar, ½ teaspoon cinnamon and ¼ cup regular wheat germ. Toss to mix. Spoon onto prepared squares.

WO-JA-PI (INDIAN BLUEBERRY DESSERT)

SAUCE:
1	quart fresh blueberries, rinsed and drained
1	cup honey
¼	cup flour
1	cup water
2	tablespoons chopped fresh mint leaves

FRIED BREAD:
2	cups sifted all-purpose flour
2	teaspoons baking powder
½	teaspoon salt
2	tablespoons sugar
1	cup milk
	Deep fat or oil heated to 375 degrees

In a saucepan, combine blueberries, honey and enough water to just cover the berries. Bring berries to a boil and boil 5 minutes. In a bowl, mix flour with water until smooth. Stir mixture into hot berries. Add mint. Stir over low heat until berries thicken. Cool. In a bowl, mix flour, baking powder, salt and sugar. Stir in milk until a soft dough is formed. It may be necessary to add more milk.

Knead dough on a floured surface a few times until it is smooth dough. Roll out to one-half-inch thickness and cut with a sharp knife into 3-inch squares. Fry squares in preheated deep fat until brown, about 3 to 4 minutes. Turn and brown on other side. Drain on absorbent paper. Serve warm with blueberry sauce spooned over. *Makes 8 servings.*

Index